S0-AKQ-272

BUILD YOUR OWN LOW-COST HOME

BUILD YOUR OWN LOW-COST HOME

Complete Working Drawings and Specifications for Eleven Homes Suitable for Year-round and Vacation Use,
With Step-by-step Construction Information

by L. O. ANDERSON and HAROLD F. ZORNIG

Dover Publications, Inc.

New York

Published in Canada by General Publishing Company, Ltd., 30 Lesmill Road, Don Mills, Toronto, Ontario.

Published in the United Kingdom by Constable and Company, Ltd., 10 Orange Street, London WC 2.

Build Your Own Low-Cost Home, first published in 1972 by Dover Publications, Inc., incorporates U. S. Dept. of Agriculture Handbook No. 364, "Low Cost Wood Homes for Rural America—Construction Manual" (March, 1969) and the following working plans for individual designs published by the U. S. Dept. of Agriculture (December, 1969): Plan #1—FPL-1; Plan #2—FPL-2; Plan #3—FPL-3; Plan #4—FPL-4; Plan #5—FPL-5; Plan #6—SE-1; Plan #7—SE-2; Plan #8—SE-3; Plan #9—SE-4 (revised, March, 1971); Plan #10—SE-5 (revised, March, 1971); Plan #11—SE-6.

International Standard Book Number: 0-486-21525-3
Library of Congress Catalog Card Number: 73-188955

Manufactured in the United States of America
Dover Publications, Inc.
180 Varick Street
New York, N.Y. 10014

Introduction

For over half a century the Forest Service, U. S. Department of Agriculture, has pioneered in research to more effectively utilize wood and wood products. In an effort to help alleviate the nation's housing crisis for low-income families, the Forest Service has applied this research expertise to the design of low-cost homes.

Eleven house designs of varying style and size have been developed. These houses can be built for approximately one-half the normal construction costs. Five of the designs were developed at the Forest Products Laboratory at Madison, Wisconsin by L. O. Anderson. Six of the designs, including the tubular, duplex, and round houses, were developed at the Southeastern Forest Experiment Station in Athens, Georgia by H. F. Zornig. Some of the designs are for homes of a conventional appearance; some are for homes of a more innovative nature. None are meant to represent luxury living. They all have one aim: to obtain as much comfortable living space as possible for people of very limited means. They have all the essentials necessary to provide comfortable living for families with up to 12 children. They were intended primarily for rural America, where housing for low-income families is often well below acceptable standards, but they can be easily used for vacation homes. Improved housing for most rural families means a home that is low in cost, easily maintained, and equipped for good family living. In addition, it should be attractive. These requirements can be met using presently available equipment, skills and materials.

The basic building materials are wood and the many wood-base materials now on the market—the same basic materials used in the most expensive homes. Economies have been made through simplicity of design and elimination of frills, by specification of economical but durable wood materials, and by employing unconventional new materials, systems, and uses of wood and wood products. The fact that these homes are "low cost" does not mean that they use second-rate materials or construction methods. Strength, safety and durability have not been sacrificed to obtain reduced costs. The suggested use of preservative-treated wood for the foundation system accounts for an important part of the cost saving in these homes. This type of construction should not be considered as a temporary measure. Experience indicates that a home constructed in accordance with the principles presented in this book and properly maintained will be sound and serviceable well beyond 35 years.

The Forest Products Laboratory of the Forest Service has conducted research for many years on all phases of house construction. The construction manual on pages 147-204 presents the application of some of these findings with special references to methods and materials which will hold down costs, but insure quality. It gives step-by-step information on every phase of house construction, from the construction of the foundation or supporting units to the final painting and finishing.

This book will be particularly useful to: (a) Those who finance the building of these homes—in assurance that they are making a sound investment; (b) the contractors and skilled and unskilled laborers who will be concerned with the actual construction; and (c) the owner who will gain an understanding of how his home is constructed and how to make improvements as his situation allows. The construction manual will also be useful to those who wish to incorporate these sound techniques in low-cost houses of their own design.

The Forest Service does not build nor market these homes. But it is the hope of the Service that others will make use of the designs in helping to meet the need for low-cost housing. Plans 6-11 are reproduced here actual size. Plans 1-5 have been slightly reduced and larger working drawings can be obtained from the Superintendent of Documents, Washington, D. C., for a nominal fee.

Other References

Anderson, L. O.
   1969. Wood-frame house construction. U.S. Department of Agriculture. Agr. Hdbk. No. 73.

Federal Housing Administration
   1965. Minimum property standards for one and two living units. FHA No. 300, 315 pp.

U.S. Department of Housing and Urban Development
   1967. Manual on design for low-cost and aided self-help housing. PB—179, 385, 111 pp.

Additional materials are also available from such groups as:

National Forest Products Association
1619 Massachusetts Avenue NW.
Washington, D.C. 20036

Western Wood Products Association
Yeon Building
Portland, Oreg. 97204

Southern Pine Association
P.O. Box 52468
New Orleans, La. 70150

West Coast Lumber Inspection Bureau
P.O. Box 25406
Portland, Oreg. 97225

American Plywood Association
1119 A Street
Tacoma, Wash. 98401

Insulation Board Institute
111 West Washington Street
Chicago, Ill. 60602

American Hardboard Association
20 North Wacker Drive
Chicago, Ill. 60606

Contents

Summary of House Plans

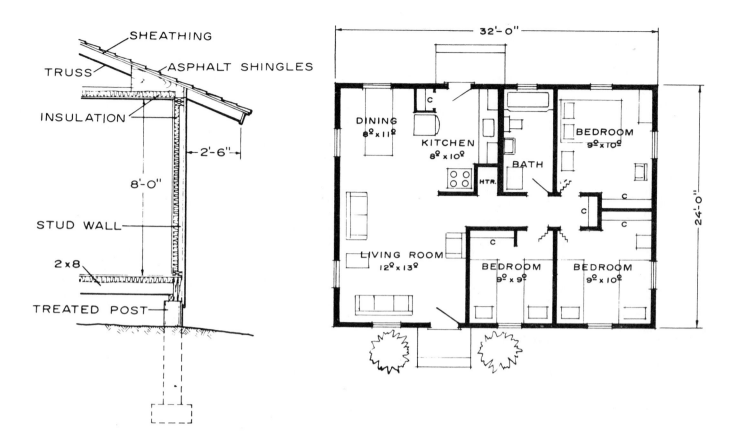

HOUSE PLAN No. 1   AREA = 768 sq. ft.

This house was developed to provide a good livable house at a cost much lower than most houses now being constructed. It is 24 by 32 feet in size and contains 768 square feet of living space. In spite of its relatively small size, this home has three bedrooms, affording desirable privacy for a family with three to five children. There is little wasted space, and the bath and kitchen are conveniently arranged. The open living-dining-kitchen area gives a feeling of spaciousness not possible when walls separate these rooms.

This crawl-space house has a treated wood post foundation which reduces the cost without reducing its performance. It can be constructed on sloping sites without costly grading and masonry work. Most of the materials used can be obtained at local lumber yards or small local mills.

A single layer of tongued-and-grooved plywood serves as a subfloor and as a base for resilient tile. Walls are conventionally framed and are covered on the exterior with a panel siding which serves as a sheathing and siding material. This exterior siding and the trim are finished with long-lasting stains which can be obtained in many contrasting colors. The interior walls and ceilings are covered with gypsum board. Two types of roof construction are offered: (a) King-post truss and (b) conventional rafter and ceiling joist framing; both roofed with asphalt shingles. The wide overhangs at the cornice

and gable ends provide a good appearance as well as excellent protection for the side walls. Insulation in the walls, floors, and ceiling reduce heating costs as well as provide a cool house during the hot summer months.

A number of additions to the original plans can be included initially or at a later date. These include: (a) front porch, (b) rear entry storage area, (c) skirt board around crawl space, (d) extra cabinets for the kitchen and bathrooms, and (e) masonry foundations and related details. Other additions include installation of bedroom doors and completion of open shelves of cabinets in the kitchen area. These changes will, of course, increase the overall cost of the house.

Several items now included in the working drawings and specifications can be altered or eliminated to decrease the cost of the house. These include: (a) substitution of a space heater for the existing forced-air system; (b) use of a paint finish on the plywood floor and use of low-cost linoleum as an alternate finish to replace the tile floor; and (c) use of less insulation in walls, floors, and ceiling. Further savings could be realized by substitution or elimination of some of the bathroom fixtures and the water heater.

Designed by L. O. Anderson
Forest Products Laboratory

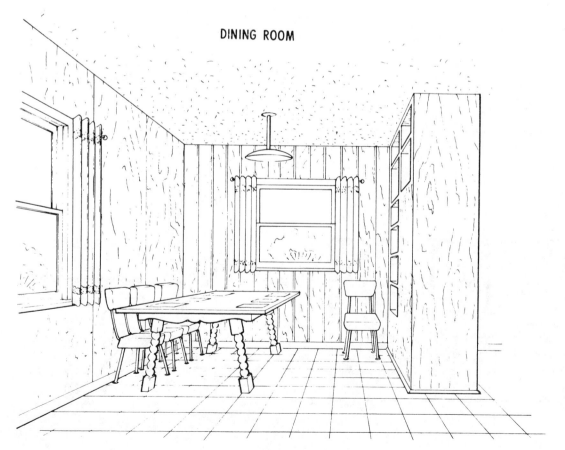

DINING ROOM

Plans for this house begin on page 15; specifications on page 21.

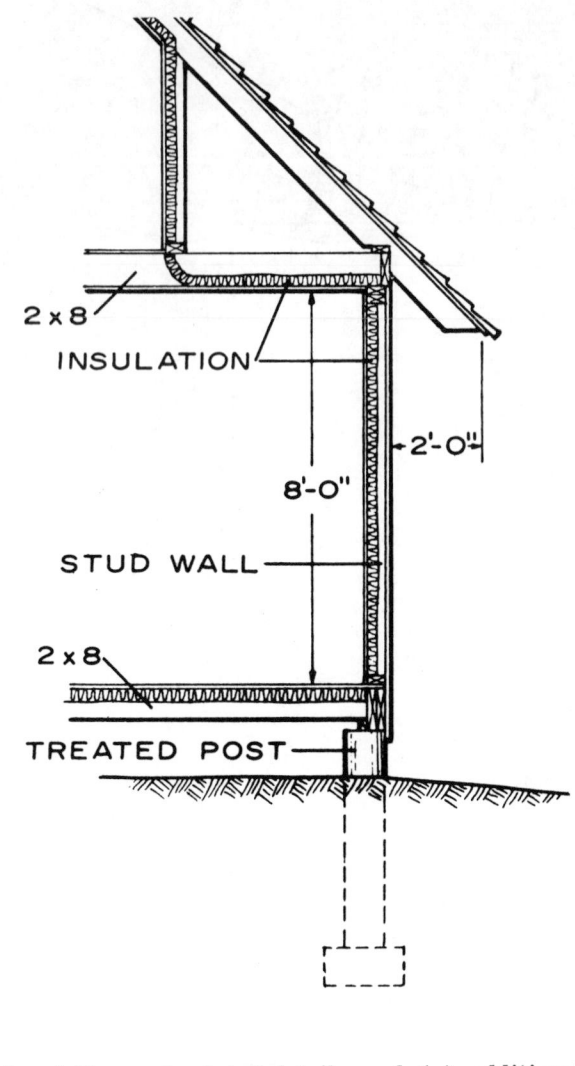

2x8

INSULATION

STUD WALL

8'-0"

2'-0"

2x8

TREATED POST

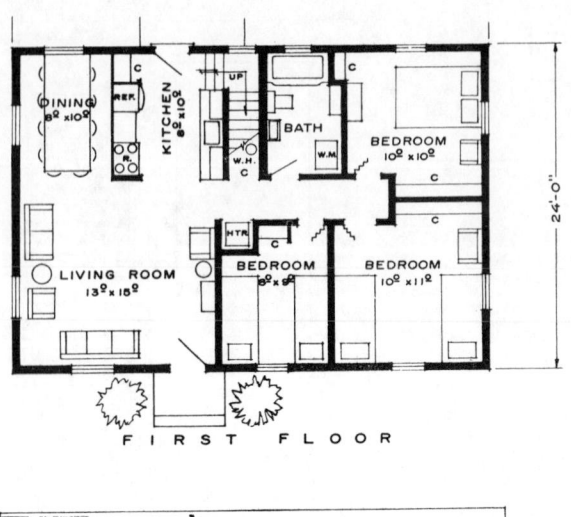

FIRST FLOOR

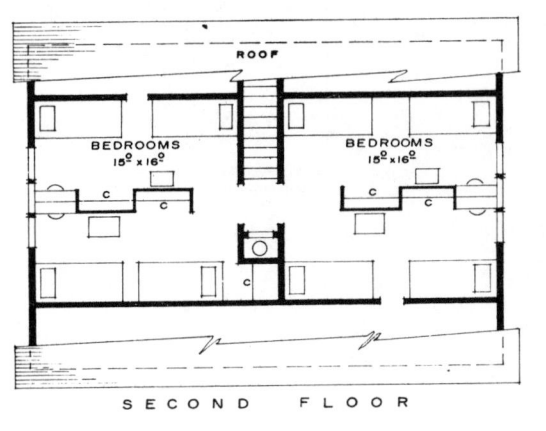

SECOND FLOOR

HOUSE PLAN No. 2   AREA = 1404 sq. ft.

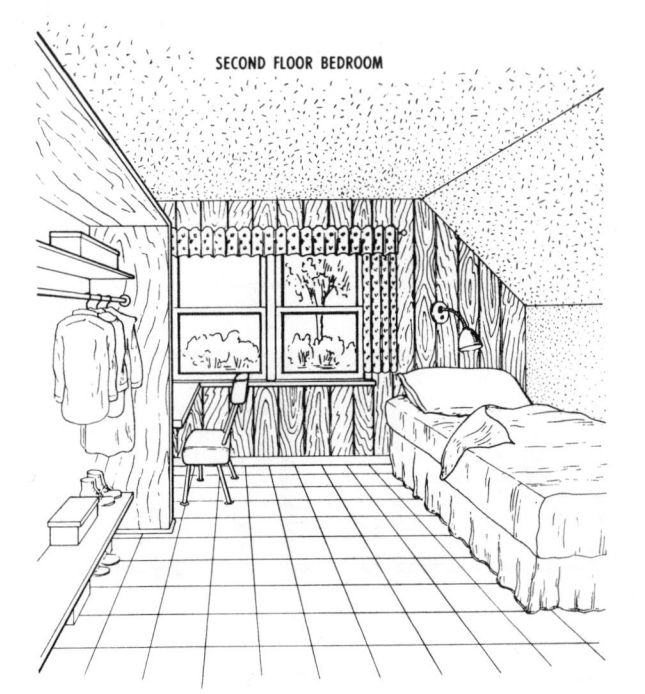

SECOND FLOOR BEDROOM

This home was developed for a large family of up to 12 children at a reasonable cost. It is 24 by 36 feet in size and is one and one-half stories. The first floor has 864 square feet, consisting of three bedrooms, a bath, and a living-dining-kitchen area. The second floor contains about 540 square feet and consists of two large dormitory-type bedrooms. Each is divided by a wardrobe-type closet which, in effect, contains space for two single beds on each side.

The design features which aid in reducing the cost and in providing maximum space for the over-all size are: (a) the treated post foundation with a crawl space and (b) the steeply sloped roof. The long-lived treated foundation posts can be installed with little or no costly grading and leveling. They serve as a rugged base for the beams and joists of the floor system. The one-half pitch (12 in 12 slope) roof with a 4-foot-high knee wall encloses two large 15- by 16-foot dormitory bedrooms. Windows are installed at the gable ends of the second floor.

A single layer of tongued-and-grooved plywood serves as a subfloor and as a base for resilient tile. Walls are conventionally framed and are covered on the exterior with a panel siding which serves both as a sheathing and siding material.

This exterior siding, the trim, and the shutters are finished with a pigmented stain which can be obtained in a variety of colors. The interior walls and ceilings are covered with gypsum board except for accent areas of prefinished plywood.

Wide overhangs at both the gable ends and the cornice provide desirable protection to the side and end walls. Floors, walls, and ceiling are insulated to reduce heat loss. The thickness of this insulation can be varied, and the amount usually depends on whether the house is located in the northern part of the United States or in a milder climate.

A number of additions to the original plans can be included initially or at a later date. These include: (a) front porch, (b) rear entry storage area, (c) skirt board around crawl space, (d) shutters, (e) extra cabinet for the bathroom, (f) masonry foundation and related details, and (g) additional second-floor bathroom. Other additions include installation of bedroom and closet doors and completion of open shelves of cabinets in the kitchen area. These changes will, of course, increase the overall cost of the house.

Several items now included in the working drawings and specifications can be altered or eliminated to decrease the cost of the house. These include: (a) substitution of a space heater for the existing forced-air system; (b) use of a paint finish on the plywood floor and the use of low-cost linoleum as an alternate finish to replace the tile floor; and (c) use of less insulation in walls, floors, and ceiling. Further savings could be realized by substitution or elimination of some of the bathroom fixtures and the water heater.

Designed by L. O. Anderson
Forest Products Laboratory

Plans for this house begin on page 29; specifications on page 35.

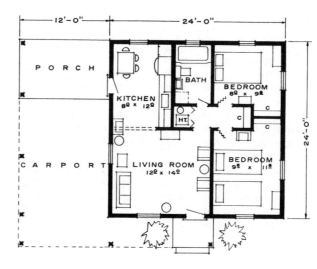

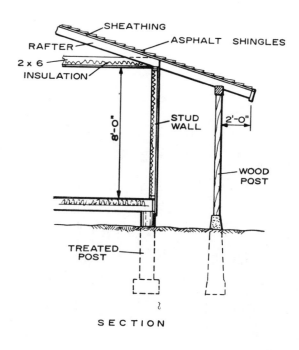

SECTION

HOUSE PLAN No. 3 AREA = 576 sq. ft.

This house plan was developed to serve a small family or senior citizens who require only one main bedroom and a spare room which can serve as a sewing room, workroom, or also as a second bedroom. The kitchen and living room are open with a drop beam between them. The main house is 24 by 24 feet in size and has 576 feet of living area. As shown in the plan, an 8- by 12-foot porch is included as well as a carport. When a minimum house is desired, the porch and the carport can be eliminated. The bathroom contains space for a small washing machine. Closet space is sufficient for a small family. More storage area can be provided by the installation of small plywood wardrobes in the bedrooms.

This crawl space house has a treated wood post foundation which reduces the cost of the house without reducing its performance. This type of house can be constructed on a sloping lot, eliminating costly grading which is normally necessary

for houses with other designs. A single layer of tongued-and-grooved plywood serves as a subfloor and as a base for resilient tile. Walls are conventionally framed and are covered on the exterior with a panel siding which serves as a sheathing and siding material. This panel siding and other exterior wood can be finished with a pigmented stain. These materials are not only easily applied, but they are long lasting and available in many colors.

The interior has a gypsum board wall and ceiling finish which is painted. In addition, the bath and part of the living room walls have prefinished plywood for a desirable contrast. The floors, walls, and ceilings are well insulated, insuring comfort both winter and summer. The small forced-air heating unit can be either the oil or the gas-fired type.

Roof construction is conventional rafter and ceiling joist framing with asphalt shingles.

A number of additions to the original plans can be included initially or at a later date. Possible

additions include: (a) use of a masonry foundation rather than the treated posts, (b) installation of bedroom doors, and (c) completion of open shelves of cabinets in the kitchen area. These changes will, of course, increase the overall cost of the house.

Several items now included in the working drawings and specifications can be altered or eliminated to decrease the cost of the house. These include: (a) elimination of the porch and/or carpart, (b) substitution of a space heater for the existing forced-air system, (c) use of a paint finish on the plywood floor and the use of low-cost linoleum as an alternate finish to replace the tile floor, and (d) use of less insulation in walls, floors, and ceiling in warmer climates. Further savings could be realized by substitution or elimination of some of the bathroom fixtures and the water heater.

Designed by L. O. Anderson
Forest Products Laboratory

KITCHEN

Plans for this house begin on page 43; specifications on page 48.

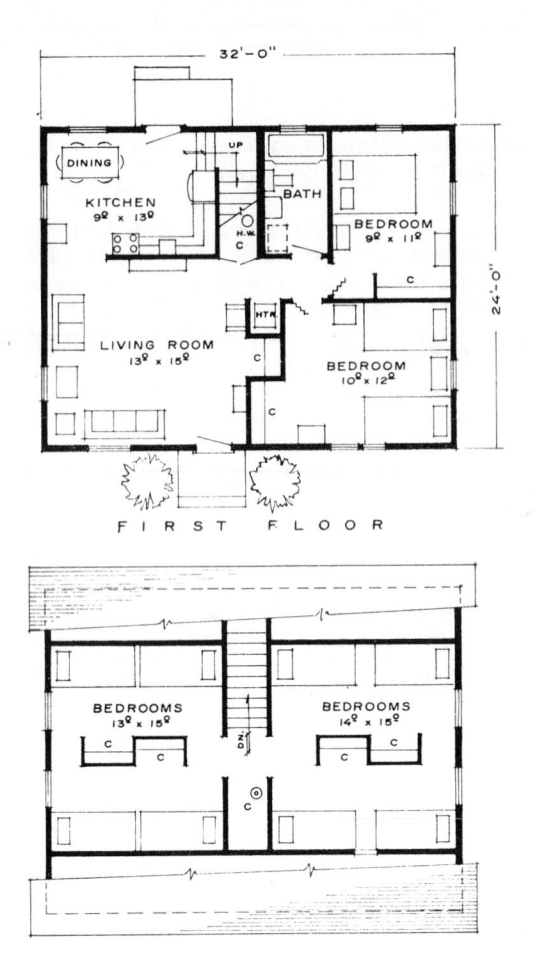

FIRST FLOOR

SECOND FLOOR

ASPHALT SHINGLES

2 x 8

INSULATION

2'-0"

8'-0"

STUD WALL

2 x 8

TREATED POST

HOUSE PLAN No. 4   AREA = 768 sq. ft. expandable to 1228 sq. ft.

This home is an expandable type. With its steeply pitched roof, there is more than adequate space on the second floor for two dormitory-type bedrooms, which can accommodate up to eight children. The working drawings also provide for an additional bath on the second floor if it is desired. The house is 24 by 32 feet in size with an area of 768 square feet on the first floor and about 460 square feet of usable space on the second. The first floor contains a moderate-size living room, a compact kitchen with a large adjoining dining area, two bedrooms and a bath. Storage space is adequate with four closets on the first floor and five on the second. The first-floor bath is arranged to accommodate a washing machine.

There are several important factors which aid in reducing the cost of this home. One is the fact that it is a crawl-space house, which eliminates the need for extensive excavation and grading. In addition, the floor framing is supported by long-lived treated wood foundation posts resting on concrete footings. A more costly masonry foundation is included in the working drawings as an alternate. Roof construction is conventional with a 12 in 12 slope to provide for second-floor bedrooms.

The use of a single covering material for the subfloor and the exterior walls also leads to reduced costs. The subfloor consists of tongued-and-grooved plywood or square-edge plywood with edge blocking and serves as a base for resilient floor covering. The panel siding, with perimeter nailing, eliminates the need for corner bracing as well as the need for sheathing. Such coverings are usually rough-textured exterior-grade plywood, which can be finished with a pigmented stain. Suitable stains are available in many colors, and contrasts can be obtained by treating the trim and shutters with a different color or shade.

Further cost reductions are obtained by eliminating much of the exterior trim as well as some of the less important interior millwork. However, these refinements can be added in the future. An adequate forced-air heating unit with relatively short heat runs is also a part of the design. Insulation is included in the floor, wall, and ceiling areas; the thickness selected depending on the location of the home. In the colder climates, the ceiling and floor insulation might be 4 inches or thicker with 2-inch thick blanket insulation in the walls.

A number of additions to the original plans can be included initially or at a later date. These include: (a) front porch, (b) rear entry storage area, (c) skirt board around crawl space, (d) masonry foundation and related details, (e) additional second-floor bathroom, (f) bedroom dormer, and (g) shutters. Other additions include installation of bedroom and closet doors and completion of open shelves of cabinets in the kitchen area. These changes will, of course, increase the overall cost of the house.

Several items now included in the working drawings and specifications can be altered or eliminated to decrease the cost of the house. These include: (a) substitution of a space heater for the existing forced-air system; (b) use of a paint finish on the plywood floor and the use of low-cost linoleum as an alternate finish to replace the tile floor; and (c) use of less insulation in walls, floors, and ceiling. Further savings can be realized by substitution or elimination of some of the bathroom fixtures and the water heater.

Designed by L. O. Anderson
Forest Products Laboratory

Plans for this house begin on page 55; specifications on page 61.

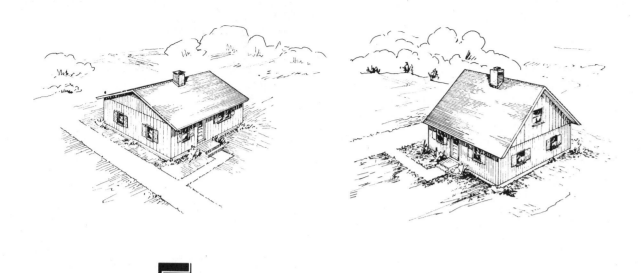

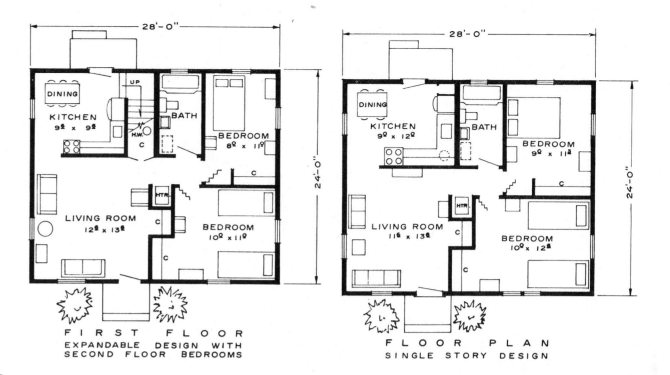

F I R S T   F L O O R
EXPANDABLE DESIGN WITH
SECOND FLOOR BEDROOMS

F L O O R   P L A N
SINGLE STORY DESIGN

HOUSE PLAN No. **5**   AREA = 672 sq. ft. expandable to 1064 sq. ft.

This low-cost home can be built with a low- or high-pitched roof providing a choice of one (Design A) or one-and-a-half (Design B) stories. It is designed to provide all the modern facilities necessary for comfortable living for a family of 4 in the one-story design or a family of up to 10 in the one-and-a-half story design. The house is 24 by 28 feet in size, with a gross area of 672 square feet on the first floor. The one-and-a-half story design has an additional 392 square feet. The second floor can be left unfinished at the same time the house is constructed, and finished at a later date when additional space is needed.

Both plans include a kitchen, bath, living room, and two bedrooms on the first floor. The second floor in Design B contains two bedrooms and an optional bath. One second-floor bedroom is 9½ by 14 feet and the other is 13 by 14 feet. The larger bedroom may be divided by the addition of a wardrobe wall, which provides two closets and also serves as a room divider. To accommodate the stairway to the second-floor bedrooms in the expandable plan, the first-floor bedrooms and the kitchen are slightly smaller than those in the one-story plan.

Both plans have a front entrance closet and a closet for each bedroom. The expandable house also has a storage area under the stairway in which the hot water heater is located. The heating unit is located in a small closet adjacent to the bath-bedroom hallway. Walls, floors, and ceiling areas are insulated. Dining space is provided in each kitchen.

There are a number of factors which aid in reducing the cost of these homes. They are designed as crawl-space houses with treated wood-posts providing a long-lived foundation which supports the wood-frame floor system and eliminates the need for extensive grading on sloping building sites. Details for an alternate masonry foundation are also included. A single layer of tongued-and-grooved plywood serves as a subfloor and as a base for resilient tile or a low-cost linoleum rug.

Walls are conventionally framed and are covered on the exterior with a panel siding which eliminates sheathing and the need for a braced wall. Exteriors are finished with long-lasting pigmented stains. Many contrasting colors are available in this type of finish. Exterior and interior trim and millwork have been reduced to a minimum, and many of these refinements can be made at any time after the house has been completed. The interior walls and ceilings are covered with gypsum board except for accent areas of prefinished plywood.

Roof construction is conventional with a 4 in 12 slope for the one-story plan, or a 12 in 12 slope to provide for second-floor bedrooms in the one-and-a-half story plan.

A number of additions to the original plans can be included initially or at a later date. These include: (a) front porch, (b) skirt board around crawl space, (c) masonry foundation and related details, (d) additional second-floor bathroom, (e) bedroom dormer, and (f) shutters. Other additions include installation of bedroom and closet doors and completion of open shelves of cabinets in the kitchen area. These changes will, of course, increase the overall cost of the house.

Several items now included in the working drawings and specifications can be altered or eliminated to decrease the cost of the house. These include: (a) substitution of a space heater for the existing forced-air system; (b) use of a paint finish on the plywood floor and the use of low-cost linoleum as an

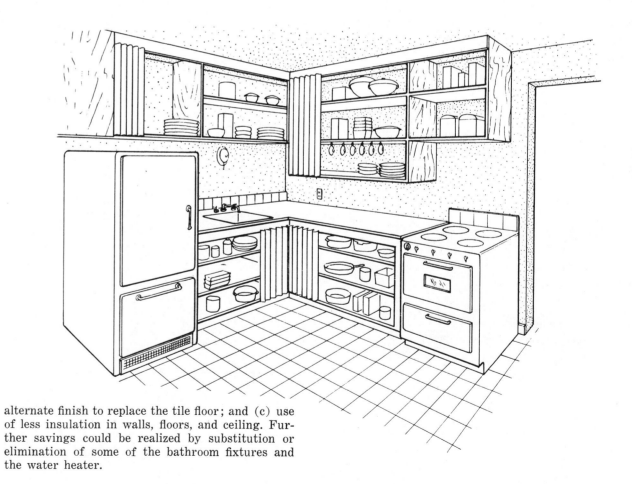

alternate finish to replace the tile floor; and (c) use of less insulation in walls, floors, and ceiling. Further savings could be realized by substitution or elimination of some of the bathroom fixtures and the water heater.

Designed by L. O. Anderson
Forest Products Laboratory

Plans for this house begin on page 69; specifications on page 75.

BUNK-BEDROOM
SHOWING CLOSET/DESK AREA

HOUSE PLAN No. **6**   AREA = 1024 sq. ft.

This home, intended for a flat site, encloses 1,024 square feet. The square plan provides much more usable space, within the same exterior walls, than a typical rectangular plan.

While essentially conventional, the design features a novel floating-wood-floor system. The space under the floor serves as a return-air plenum from a centrally located forced-air furnace. Air will flow into each room through the opening above the door, then enter a space behind the baseboard for return under the floor to the furnace. Alternate designs are available for a conventional wood floor over a crawl space and for a concrete slab floor.

The house is unique in that it incorporates a central hall in which the furnace and washer are located. Useful storage space is provided in a central attic area over the hall. The square floor plan provides maximum floor area within the exterior walls.

The removable particle board partitions can be relocated to provide many alternative room arrangements.

Large bedrooms, closets, built-in desks, and shelving in the bedrooms are bonus features. These bedrooms are really multi-purpose rooms for play, study and sleeping.

Economical, nonbearing partition walls of particle board have replaced conventional hollow-core interior walls. Being nonbearing, they can be located in various positions without affecting the structure.

Plywood combination siding and sheathing on the exterior walls can be finished with modern natural finishes and stains for durability and easy maintenance.

Designed by Harold F. Zornig
Southeastern Forest Experiment Station

Plans for this house begin on page 87; specifications on page 94.

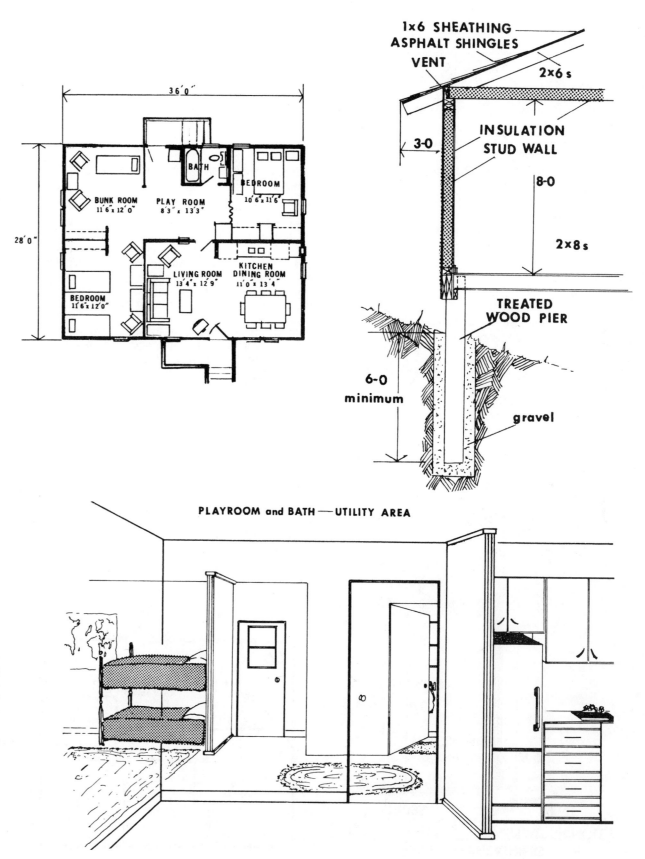

HOUSE PLAN No. **7** AREA = 1008 sq. ft.

Wood piers used for the foundation make this plan particularly suited to sloping sites. The piers are pressure treated with a clean, non-leaching preservative. A carport and storage area under the house might be considered for steeply sloping sites.

The play area is a bonus feature in a three-bedroom house of this size. Elimination of a central hall has provided more usable living space in the 1,008 square feet of floor area. The large bedrooms will also provide extra, multi-purpose space for large families.

Conventional framing, stock-sized windows and doors, and the simple rectangular plan were selected with the small contractor in mind. Rafters and joists, instead of roof trusses, help to open up the attic space for convenient storage. Plywood combination sheathing and siding on exterior walls is finished with a natural finish or stain to provide attractive, economical, easy-to-maintain exterior walls. The skirting could be placed around the foundation piers in cold climates to lower the heating bill. If this is done, the floor insulation and insulation board under the floor joists could be eliminated.

Heat is provided by a centrally located forced-air wall furnace, or by electric heaters.

Designed by Harold F. Zornig
Southeastern Forest Experiment Station

Plans for this house begin on page 97; specifications on page 101.

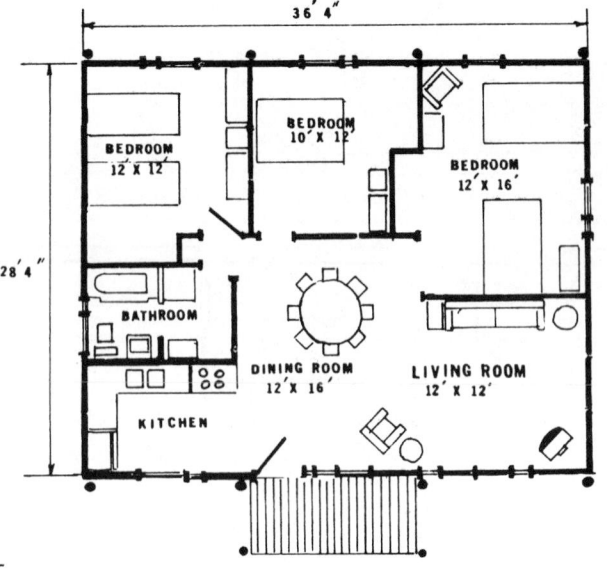

HOUSE PLAN No. **8**   AREA = 1008 sq. ft.

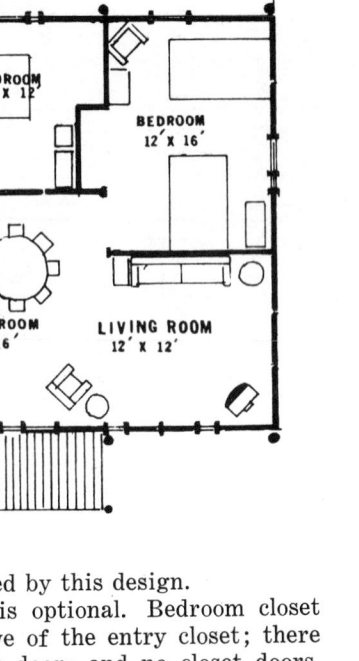

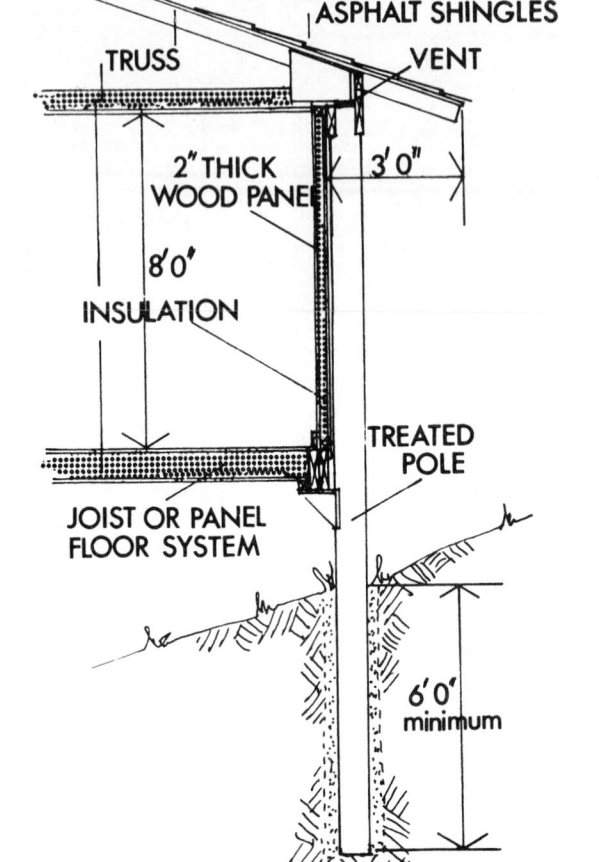

SHEATHING
ASPHALT SHINGLES
TRUSS   VENT
2" THICK
WOOD PANEL   3'0"
8'0"
INSULATION
TREATED
POLE
JOIST OR PANEL
FLOOR SYSTEM
6'0"
minimum

KITCHEN - DINING AREA
CUT OUT TO SHOW UTILITY AND BATH AREA

This attractive house was designed especially for large families wanting a low-cost three-bedroom home. The bedrooms and dining room will accommodate a large family without crowding. A utility room has been provided next to the bathroom, and the laundry tub will be useful as a second lavatory. The sizeable open space of the kitchen-dining-living area will make this house seem much larger than its 1008 square feet.

When this house is constructed on a sloping site, a carport and storage room under the house are bonus features. The furnace and hot water heater will usually be located in the storage room under the house; however, if the site is level, the furnace could be in the linen closet location, and the under-counter type of hot water heater could be installed in the kitchen.

Strong, durable pressure-treated wood poles support this house, which is particularly suitable for sloping sites.

This pole-truss structural system has several advantages over conventional foundation and framing systems. It is economical, very little site grading will be needed, and construction need not be delayed by weather or frozen ground. In addition, all walls are non-load bearing. This makes all walls easy to prefabricate and erect, and it provides design flexibility in that the interior walls can be easily moved to alternate locations.

Since all of the walls, except those around the plumbing core, are prefabricated in 4 x 8 foot panels, window and door panels have also been designed for use with the wall panels. This prefabricated panel system of construction can be used very effectively with pole-frame construction.

Southern pine flooring is used throughout the house. A single layer of tongue and groove, 1 x 4 inch strip flooring is fastened to the joists with nails and adhesive. This provides a strong, stiff, and durable floor. Inlaid linoleum protects the floor in the bath and utility area.

Plywood combination siding and sheathing, finished with a natural finish or stain, provides attractive exterior walls that are economical and easy to maintain.

A number of cost-saving features are found in this design. These features listed below make it possible to build this house for about one-half the cost of a similar-sized house of conventional design, and in much less time.

1. The pressure-treated pole foundation and structural frame is the most significant cost-saving feature. It greatly reduces the cost of the foundation, provides a low-cost carport, and makes it possible to build the house on marginal, steeply sloping land with minimum grading. It also makes possible the use of low-cost, non-bearing interior and exterior walls.

2. Two-inch non-bearing exterior and interior walls are designed for prefabrication in 4 x 8 foot prefinished panels. These are stressed-skin panels which can be prefabricated by any small contractor with ordinary carpenter tools. The walls are similar to those used in mobile homes except that the 2 x 2-inch frame pieces are not fastened together before placing the skin material. The skins glued to the frame pieces will hold them together. Since the panels are anchored with small metal angles, they are removable and can be replaced if damaged.

3. A special 4 x 8-foot window wall unit was designed for the 2-inch thick walls, which can be constructed by the contractor for less than the cost of a manufactured unit.

4. A wood baseboard electrical raceway has been designed for this house to simplify wiring installation. All horizontal wiring shall be in this raceway, whereas vertical wiring shall be concealed in the framing around door openings.

5. The design of an alternate stressed-skin prefabricated floor system has been included which would shorten erection time.

6. There is no exterior trim, and only a minimum of interior trim required by this design.

7. The entry closet is optional. Bedroom closet space is ample exclusive of the entry closet; there are only three interior doors and no closet doors. The bedroom closets might be covered with low-cost fiber glass curtains as an optional expense. One large bedroom does not have a door because it is anticipated that this bedroom would be more like a bunkroom with little privacy. The door to this bedroom should be curtained from floor to ceiling.

8. Only one exterior door has been provided. The open plan makes this design feature practical and safe.

It is recognized that this plan has fewer doors, less privacy, and some undesirable traffic patterns through living areas, but this departure from conventional design was felt justified in order that maximum usable space be provided at minimum cost.

There are many different floor plans which could be made with these construction drawings, and it is expected that modifications of the plan will be made to suit individual family preferences. Interior walls can be placed in various positions, since they carry no roof loads. Many of the basic cost-saving features described above will help to provide a low-cost house no matter what floor plan is used.

Designed by Harold F. Zornig
Southeastern Forest Experiment Station

Plans for this house begin on page 103; specifications on page 110.

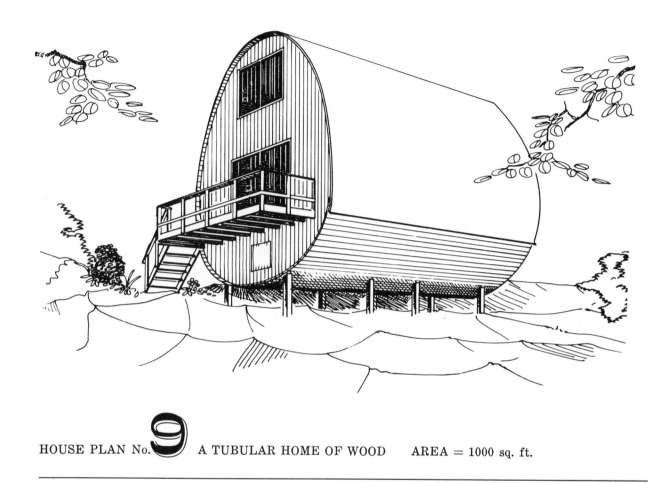

FIRST FLOOR

DINING & FAMILY ROOM
9' x 18'

WASHER

UP

KITCHEN

LIVING ROOM
9' x 18'

SECOND FLOOR

BEDROOM
10' x 14'

DN

BATH

BEDROOM
10' x 14'

HOUSE PLAN No. **9**   A TUBULAR HOME OF WOOD   AREA = 1000 sq. ft.

This unusual home offers attractive living space within its curved walls. It is primarily intended for sloping sites in rural areas. It also has particular advantages for second homes on lakeside or ocean front sites. Very little site disturbance is necessary for construction. This home provides a total of 1,000 square feet of floor area, with either two or three bedrooms on the second floor. The estimated cost of this home is about one-half the cost of equivalent conventional construction. Lumber and plywood requirements are also about half of such conventional construction.

This is an experimental design, and all structural construction features have not yet been completely evaluated. There is a good reason to believe that the general design is practical and satisfactory. In locations where heavy wind loads or other unusual conditions may exist, competent engineering assistance should be solicited. Although experimental features are not always clearly defined in the plans, experienced builders can readily identify them as being somewhat different from conventional construction. Builders should decide whether such experimental features can be modified from actual design satisfactorily and safely.

These ideas are based on previous research and development on wood utilization in various Forest Service laboratories, universities, and by industry. It is anticipated that various changes in aesthetic design, room arrangements, and similar features can be made by architects and builders.

Many economies have been incorporated into this design. These include: elimination of unnecessary hallways, trim and doors, and efforts to make one component serve more than one function, such as the use of single-layer wood floors, and combination of sheathing and siding. Opportunities to reduce labor were used wherever possible. Natural wood finishes are used widely to reduce original costs, to emphasize the attractive wood characteristics and yet provide durable finishes which can be renewed easily and inexpensively.

Foundation System

Eight preservative-treated 6x6 square posts support this home. Tretated round poles could be used instead. The posts extend up to the second floor and are bolted to the laminated ribs and the floor beams. Embedment and footing requirements will depend on local soil conditions and the height of the house above the ground.

Exterior Curved Walls

Eight egg-shaped, glue-laminated wood ribs form the curved exterior walls. The ribs are manufactured in half sections. They should be produced by an experienced laminator. A complete rib is located at the front and back faces of each pair of foundation posts. The ribs are bolted to the posts and to the ends of each floor beam.

Tongue-and-grooved 2 x 6 wood decking is nailed to the ribs around the entire circumference of the house. The decking is covered on the outside with foamed-in-place rigid polyurethane down to the

first floor level. The foam provides excellent thermal insulation and a water-tight roof covering. It is coated on the outside with a suitable, weather-resistant material recommended by the applicator. Below the first floor, conventional batt-type insulation of either fiberglass or rock wool, 3-inches thick, should be installed on the inside between the floor joists to insulate the living quarters from the crawl space below.

Exterior End Walls

Exterior ⅜-inch plywood is placed over 2x4 framing to enclose the end walls. These walls will resist racking loads and stiffen the entire structure. Interior finish is ⅜-inch gypsum board, or 1x6 wood paneling placed horizontally. Conventional insulation is placed in the walls. The frame members are installed flatwise so that they can be face nailed to the ribs and floor joists. A cantilevered deck is provided at each end of the home by extending the first-floor joists through the end walls. Joists on the

Plans for this house begin on page 113; specifications on page 123.

second floor can also be extended for an upper deck if desired.

Floor System

Single layer wood-strip flooring is placed directly on the floor joists over a ¼-inch bead of construction adhesive and nailed at each joist location. Construction adhesive will insure a stiffer floor and help to eliminate squeaking. The joists are exposed, and the lower side of the flooring on the second floor is the ceiling of the first floor.

Interior Partitions

Single-layer, self-supporting, panels of particleboard or plywood are used to partition interior spaces. Tongue-and-grooved solid wood paneling can also be used. Partitions are installed without framing except where a hollow wall is needed to enclose wiring, pipes, or ducts.

Additional Information

The Housing Research Unit of the Southeastern Forest Experiment Station is not an architectural design agency. It has developed this and other designs primarily to illustrate new and effective ways to use wood and wood products more efficiently in house construction.

A prototype of this tubular house has been built in eastern North Carolina as part of an experimental housing project in cooperation with the Forest Service and the Federal Housing Administration. Experience gained in construction of the prototype was incorporated in the plans. Various room arrangements, door and window placement, and interior details can be varied, because the interior walls are nonbearing. Other construction details must be followed closely, however, because they may affect structural strength and performance. Experienced builders can generally modify the plans and specifications satisfactorily. The tubular house is suitable for a wide range of climates.

Certain experimental features may not meet all requirements of some building codes. Prospective builders should confer with local code officials to determine the applicability of the design for the particular area in which the house is to be built.

For technical questions on this design, write to the Housing Research Unit, Forestry Sciences Laboratory, Carlton Street, Athens, Georgia 30601.

Designed by Harold F. Zornig
Southeastern Forest Experiment Station

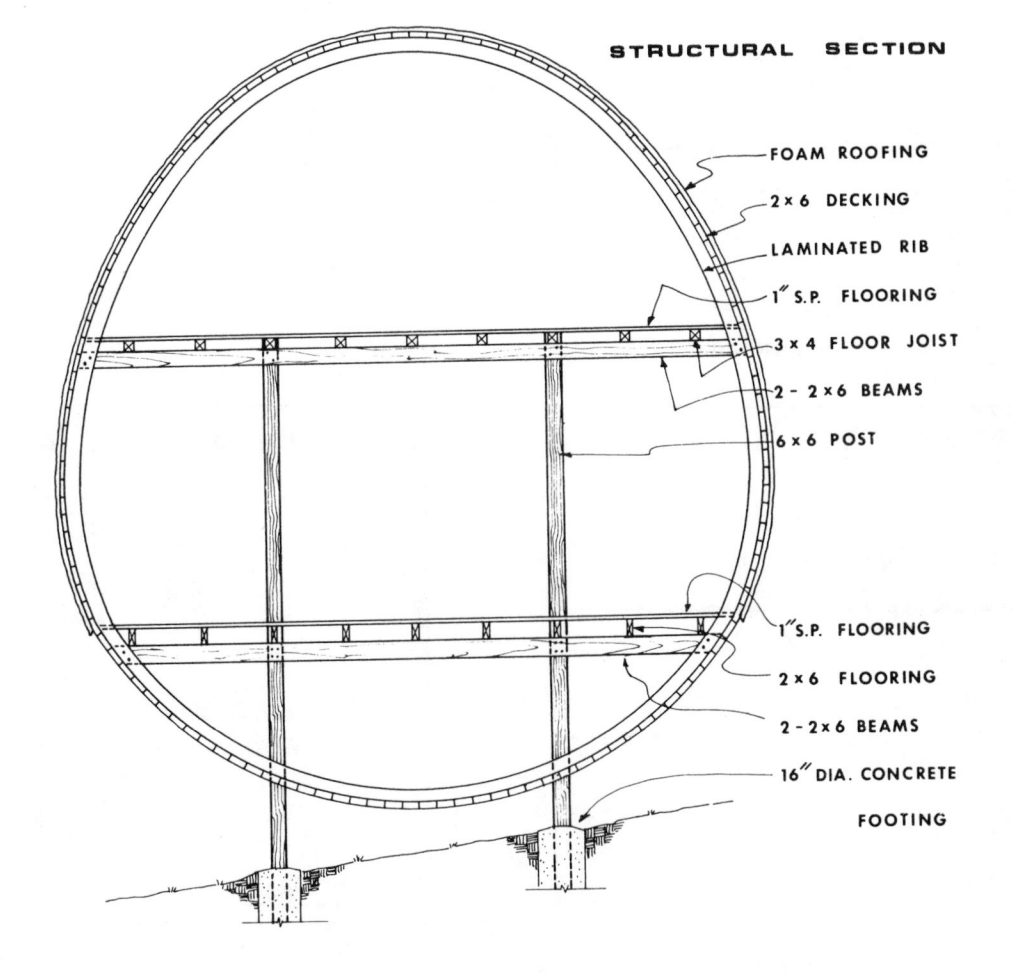

STRUCTURAL SECTION

FOAM ROOFING
2 x 6 DECKING
LAMINATED RIB
1" S.P. FLOORING
3 x 4 FLOOR JOIST
2 - 2 x 6 BEAMS
6 x 6 POST
1" S.P. FLOORING
2 x 6 FLOORING
2 - 2 x 6 BEAMS
16" DIA. CONCRETE
FOOTING

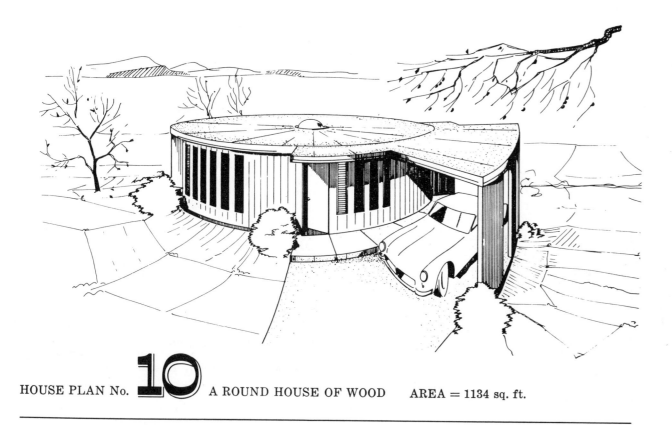

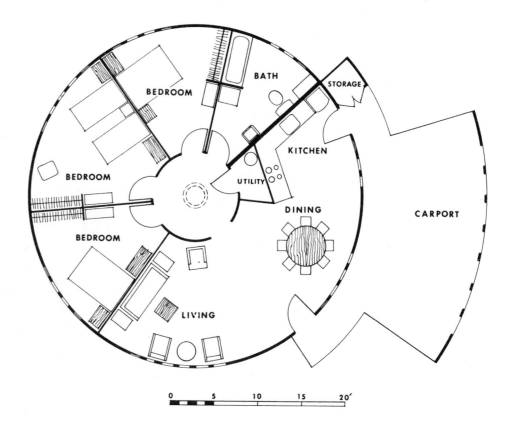

HOUSE PLAN No. 10   A ROUND HOUSE OF WOOD   AREA = 1134 sq. ft.

This unique design provides a three-bedroom home with 1,134 square feet of living area. It is designed for a flat site. A smaller version provides three bedrooms and a total of 804 square feet.

General Background

Round homes are an efficient means of providing housing space. In this design, interior walls are spaced radially from a central atrium hall. The design permits good arrangements of rooms and furniture. It includes a number of experimental features evaluated in the laboratory and in full-size prototypes built under the auspices of the Experimental Housing Program of the Federal Housing Administration.

It is estimated the round house will cost about half as much as a conventional house with an equal amount of floor space. The house should be easy to build and suitable for self-help programs.

This is an experimental design, and all structural construction features have not yet been completely evaluated. There is a good reason to believe that the general design is practical and satisfactory. Although experimental features are not always clearly defined in the plans, experienced builders can readily identify them as being somewhat different from conventional construction. Builders should decide whether such experimental features can be modified from actual design satisfactorily and safely.

Plans for this house begin on page 125; specifications on page 134.

These ideas are based on previous research and development on wood utilization in various Forest Service laboratories, universities, and by industry. It is anticipated that various changes in aesthetic design, room arrangements and similar features can be made by architects and builders.

This design is intended for a flat site and to be erected on a circular concrete slab. It features wood perimeter walls of 2-inch softwood lumber with a rough-sawn surface on one or both faces. A similar round center hall of the same construction provides entry to each room.

Many economies were incorporated into this design. These include: reduction in hallway space; elimination of much of the trim; elimination of conventional wall framing through the use of the single-layer plank wall system, and reduction in labor required. Many of the component wood parts can be pre-cut and assembled on the site. Natural wood finishes are used on the rough-sawn surfaces to reduce original costs, take advantage of the attractive wood grain and texture, and yet provide durable finishes which can be renewed easily and inexpensively.

Floor System

A circular concrete slab is placed within a low brick foundation wall. The perimeter insulation and vapor barrier are conventional. Where needed, the soil is treated or poisoned to prevent attack by ter-

mites and other insects. A preservative-treated wood member is fixed around the edge of the slab. The ends of the exterior plank walls are nailed to this member.

Partition Walls

The interior partition walls are particleboard panels located under the roof beams and fitted into slots in 2x2 members at the vertical joints. The panels can be moved to alternate locations to provide two, three, or four bedrooms. Closet shelving and sidewalls serve to stiffen the particleboard walls. The walls may be finished with conventional wall paints or with natural finishes, either pigmented or clear.

Roof System

The roof system, which is essentially flat, consists of radially placed 4x6 beams, rough sawn or finished, inserted into slots cut in the tops of the perimeter planks and those around the atrium. The beams are covered with 1x6 tongue-and-grooved lumber decking in a herringbone pattern. The lower surface of the decking and the exposed beams are finished with natural stains. The roof surface of the decking is covered with a 1-inch layer of foamed-in-place rigid polyurethane insulation (2 pounds per cubic foot). The polyurethane is then overlaid with a suitable, exterior, weather-resistant coating recommended by the foam applicator (see specification). When thus protected, the foam pro-

vides thermal insulation, a good seal against moisture, and roofing in one operation. A clear plastic dome may be placed over the atrium hall, if natural illumination is desired.

Mechanical Systems

Heating is provided either with electric baseboard units, or with a furnace located in the utility room. If a furnace is used, a heat duct carries warm air to a plenum chamber created by dropping the ceiling in the atrium hall. Openings through the plank wall carry warm air to each room. A minimum of sheet metal work is required. Electrical outlets around the exterior walls and along the interior partitions are provided in a wood baseboard-raceway system. A water heater is installed in the utility room. Some of these features are illustrated in the sketch of the atrium wall section.

Exterior Wall System

Exterior walls consist of rough-sawn 2x8 softwood planks, placed on end around the slab and joined with hardboard splines inserted in slots in the plank edges. To minimize dimensional changes in service, moisture content of the planks should be no more than 12 to 16 percent when they are installed. A fascia board is fitted around the edge of the roof. The wall of the atrium hall is of similar plank construction. Exterior wall surfaces are finished with a pigmented natural finish containing a preserva-

tive and water repellent. This attractive finish is
easy to apply and maintain and it has good durability. Interior wall surfaces are finished with
pigmented or natural stains.

Window System

Sections of two adjacent planks are omitted at appropriate locations in the exterior wall, and fixed
glass panels are fitted into the openings, framed
with a simple wood frame, and properly sealed.
Ventilation is provided by a system of vertically
sliding hardboard panels. As an alternate method,
single-hung aluminum windows are fitted into the
plank openings.

Carport

The extended roof over the carport is supported by
another plank wall, with apropriate openings. The
roofline is also extended over exterior doors by
cantilevering interior roof beams out beyond the
exterior walls.

Additional Information

The Housing Research Unit of the Southeastern
Forest Experiment Station is not an architectural
design agency. It has developed this and other designs primarily to illustrate new and effective ways
to use wood and wood products more efficiently in
house construction.

Two prototype homes of this design have been
built by a commercial contractor and are now occu-
pied in eastern North Carolina. Experience gained
in construction of these homes was incorporated in
the plans. Various room arrangements, door and
window placement, and interior details can be
varied, because the interior walls are all nonbearing. Other construction details must be followed
closely, however, because they affect structural
strength and performance. Experienced builders
can generally modify the plans and specifications
satisfactorily. Although the design was intended
primarily for warmer southern climates, some modification and insulation of the exterior walls should
make the house suitable for northern climates.

Certain experimental features may not meet all
requirements of some building codes. Prospective
builders should confer with local code officials to
determine the applicability of the design for the
particular area in which the house is to be built.

For technical questions on this design, write to
the Housing Research Unit, Forestry Sciences
Laboratory, Carlton Street, Athens, Georgia 30601.

Designed by Harold F. Zornig
Southeastern Forest Experiment Station

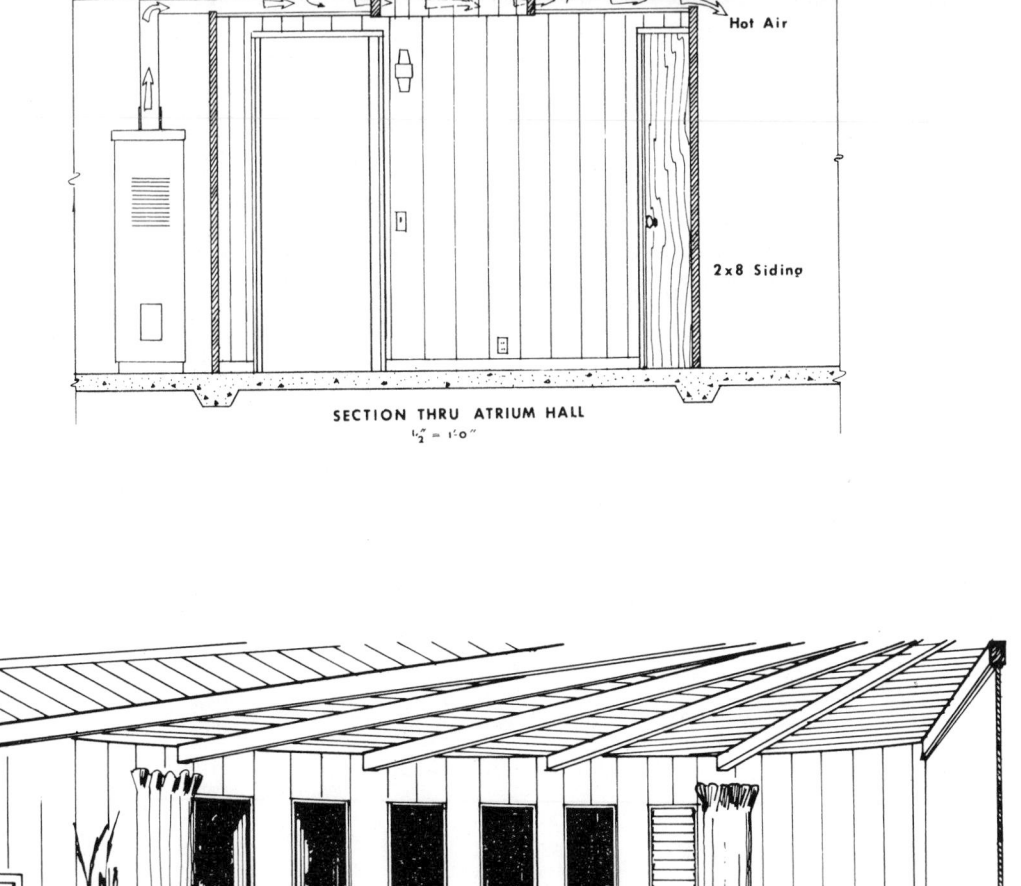

SECTION THRU ATRIUM HALL

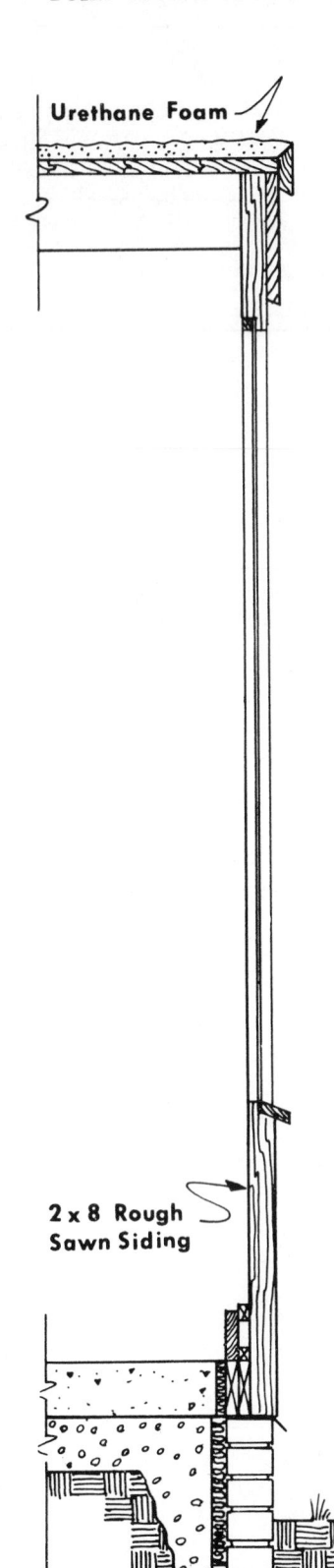

EXTERIOR WALL SECTION
1" = 1'- 0"

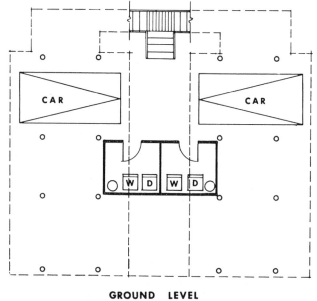

GROUND LEVEL

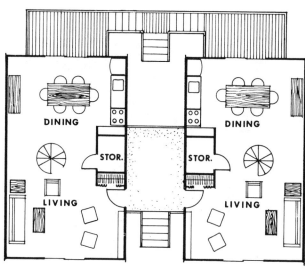

FIRST FLOOR

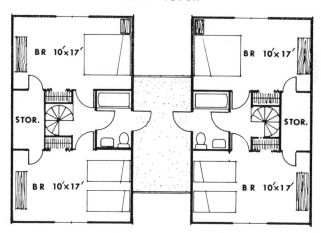

SECOND FLOOR

HOUSE PLAN No. **11** A HILLSIDE DUPLEX OF WOOD AREA = 900 sq. ft. each unit

This interesting design for a two-family home is intended particularly for sloping sites. It provides a total of 900 square feet in each of the two units, approximately half on each of two floors. The design is based on a pole-frame structure combined with wood arches that can be built in a simple shop. The compact design gives surprisingly open space, with complete privacy for each family. A pleasing wood deck is provided. One unit can be built separately for single-family homes. The simple design makes it particularly attractive for second homes to be built in isolated areas. Estimated costs are about one half that of conventional construction of the same size. Lumber and plywood requirements are about half of such conventional construction.

This is an experimental design, and all structural construction features have not yet been completely evaluated. There is a good reason to believe that the general design is practical and satisfactory. Although experimental features are not always clearly defined in the plans, experienced builders can readily identify them as being somewhat different from conventional construction. Builders should decide whether such experimental features can be modified from actual design satisfactorily and safely.

These ideas are based on previous research and development on wood utilization in various Forest Service laboratories, universities, and by industry. design, room arrangements, and similar features It is anticipated that various changes in aesthetic can be made by architects and builders. Although some of the unique and experimental features may not be approved under some existing building codes, it is believed that the designs are safe and adequate. Prospective builders should consult their local code authorities on approval, and local lending agencies on financing arrangements.

This design is for all-wood construction, but much less wood is used than for conventional residential wood-frame construction of the same floor area. Each unit has about 1,000 sq. feet of heated floor area, half on each floor, providing approximately 900 sq. feet of livable area. In addition, there is 375 sq. feet of outside wood deck and 116 sq. feet of utility room area on a lower level for the combined units.

Foundation System

Preservative-treated poles or posts are set into the ground with a minimum of soil disturbance. Posts extend to the second-floor level. Wood girders are

bolted to the posts for each floor, and a conventional wood-joist system is installed. One layer of softwood tongue-and-grooved flooring is nailed to the joists, with a bead of construction mastic adhesive applied to the top of joists for increased stiffness and to reduce floor squeaking. No subfloor is required. Joist spaces of the first floor are insulated, and the lower joist surfaces are covered with plywood or other suitable sheet material.

Roof System

The unique feature of the design is a simple Gothic-type arch, made in two sections, as illustrated on page 14. An arch consists of 1x2 lumber flanges nailed to short length of 2x4's with spacing between them. Arch sections can be assembled on a simple jig. Each section weighs only about 30 pounds. The sections are assembled on the ground, and the joist for the second floor is nailed to the arch. The sections are joined at the peak with a plywood gusset. The assembly is then raised into place and fastened to the ends of the first-floor joist.

Several roof sheathings may be used. In one prototype, erected in Athens, Georgia, ½-inch softwood plywood was used, with arches 24 inches on center. The plywood was covered with building paper and

asphalt shingles with a stapled lower tab so that shingles were tight on the reverse curvature of the lower roof sections. Alternate sheathing might be bevelled siding nailed to the arches and finished with a water-repellent pigmented stain. The latter system is easier to install without scaffolding, and the problem of bending plywood in large sheets to the slight curvature of the arches is avoided. Insulation is installed between arches, and the inner surface is covered with thin gypsum board, plywood, or lap siding to provide various interior treatments.

End Walls and Partitions

All walls are essentially nonbearing, although end walls do provide stiffening of the arch frame. End walls are 2-inch thick lumber-framed panels, erected in place, covered with plywood on the outside, and finished with natural or pigmented stains. The inner surface may be covered with plywood or other panel materials. Insulation is provided in the spaces between framing. Aluminum or wood windows are installed as desired. Sliding patio doors in each unit open to the cantilevered deck.

Plans for this house begin on page 135; specifications on page 143.

SHINGLE
3/8" PLYWOOD
1x2 RIB
2x4 BLOCK
1x2 RIB
3/8" GYPSUM BD.

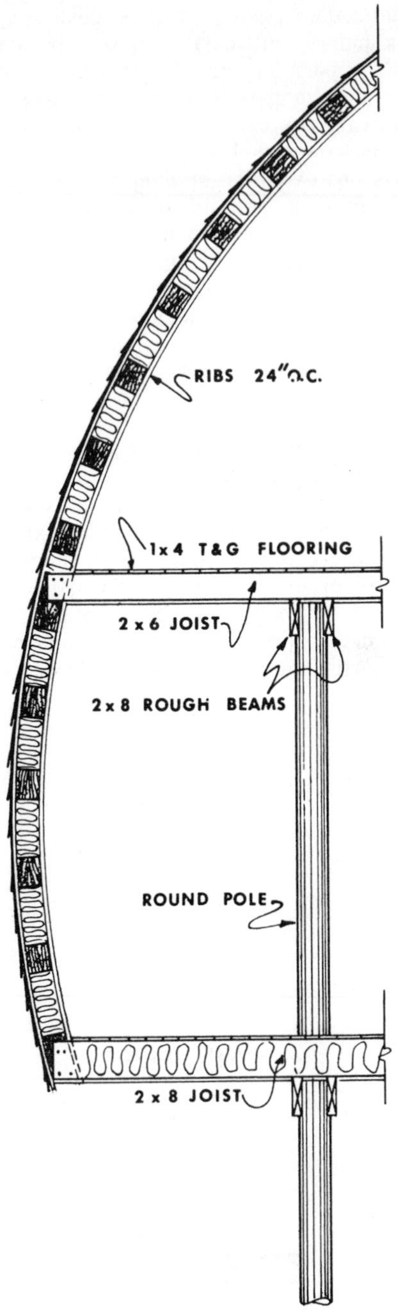

RIBS 24" O.C.

1x4 T&G FLOORING

2x6 JOIST

2x8 ROUGH BEAMS

ROUND POLE

2x8 JOIST

STRUCTURAL SECTION

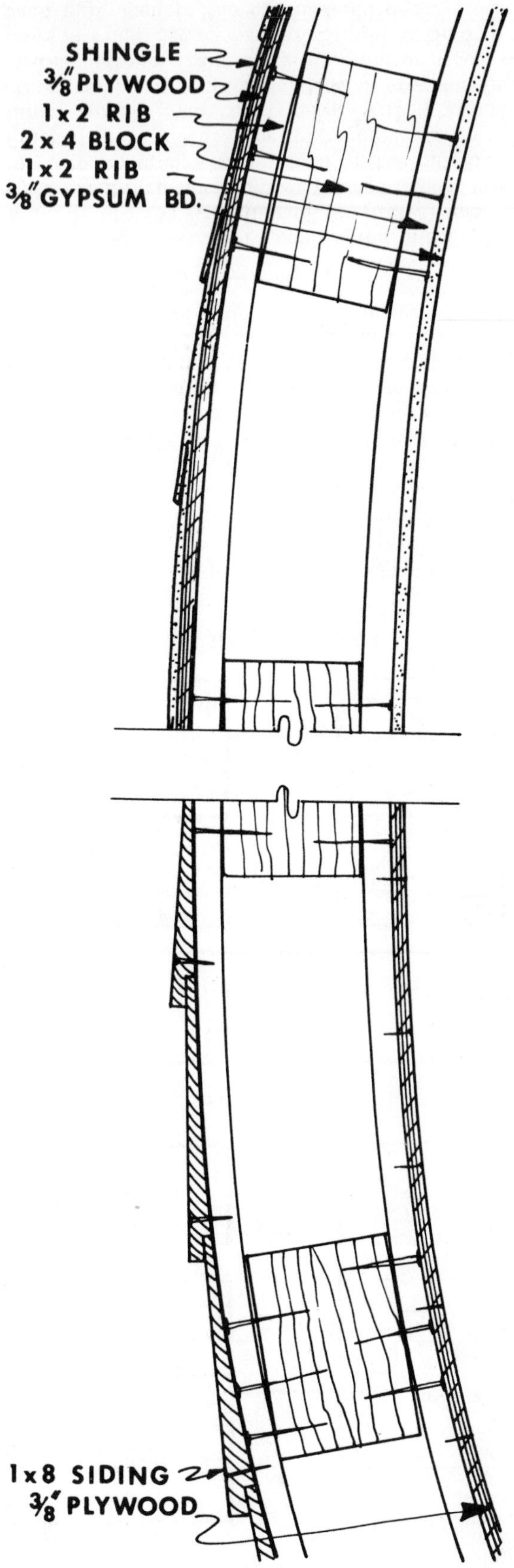

1x8 SIDING
3/8" PLYWOOD

Interior partitions may be of a single thickness of particleboard with panels fitted into slots in vertical 2x2 member at joints. The walls can also be of conventional construction.

Spiral Wood Stairs

Although the units can be provided with conventional wood stairs, a spiral stair unit was designed for easy fabrication on the site. It is estimated to cost about one-third as much as conventional metal spiral stair units. The stairway is shown in the sketch of the interior. It is constructed of spacer blocks cut from wood poles, and drilled to receive a metal rod threaded at the ends for bolts and washers. Treads are cut from 2x12 timbers, and sandwiched between the spacers with mastic adhesive. Metal pipe balusters are fastened to edges of adjacent treads, front to back, and capped with a wood plug into which a large screw eye is inserted to take a rope banister or rail. Once in place, the unit is tightened with the bolts at top and bottom. The wood can then be stained.

Utility Space and Utilities

An enclosure for utility space is provided under both sections below the first floor. This is an on-grade concrete slab, over which either a concrete block wall, or a conventional wood-frame wall of treated lumber and plywood is erected. This provides space, entered from outside, for the water heater and heating system and for washing and ironing.

Electrical wiring is installed conventionally. Horizontal runs are easy to install through openings between the block web members in the arches. Plumbing and heating is conventional, as required by local codes.

Additional Information

The Housing Research Unit of the Southeastern Forest Experiment Station is not an architectural design agency. It has developed this and other designs primarily to illustrate new and effective ways to use wood and wood products more efficiently in house construction.

A prototype of duplex unit has been built privately in Athens, Georgia. Experience gained in construction of the prototype was incorporated in the plans. Room arrangements, door and window placement, and interior details can be varied, because the interior walls are nonbearing.

For technical questions on this design, write to the Housing Research Unit, Forestry Sciences Laboratory, Carlton Street, Athens, Georgia 30601.

Designed by Harold F. Zornig
Southeastern Forest Experiment Station

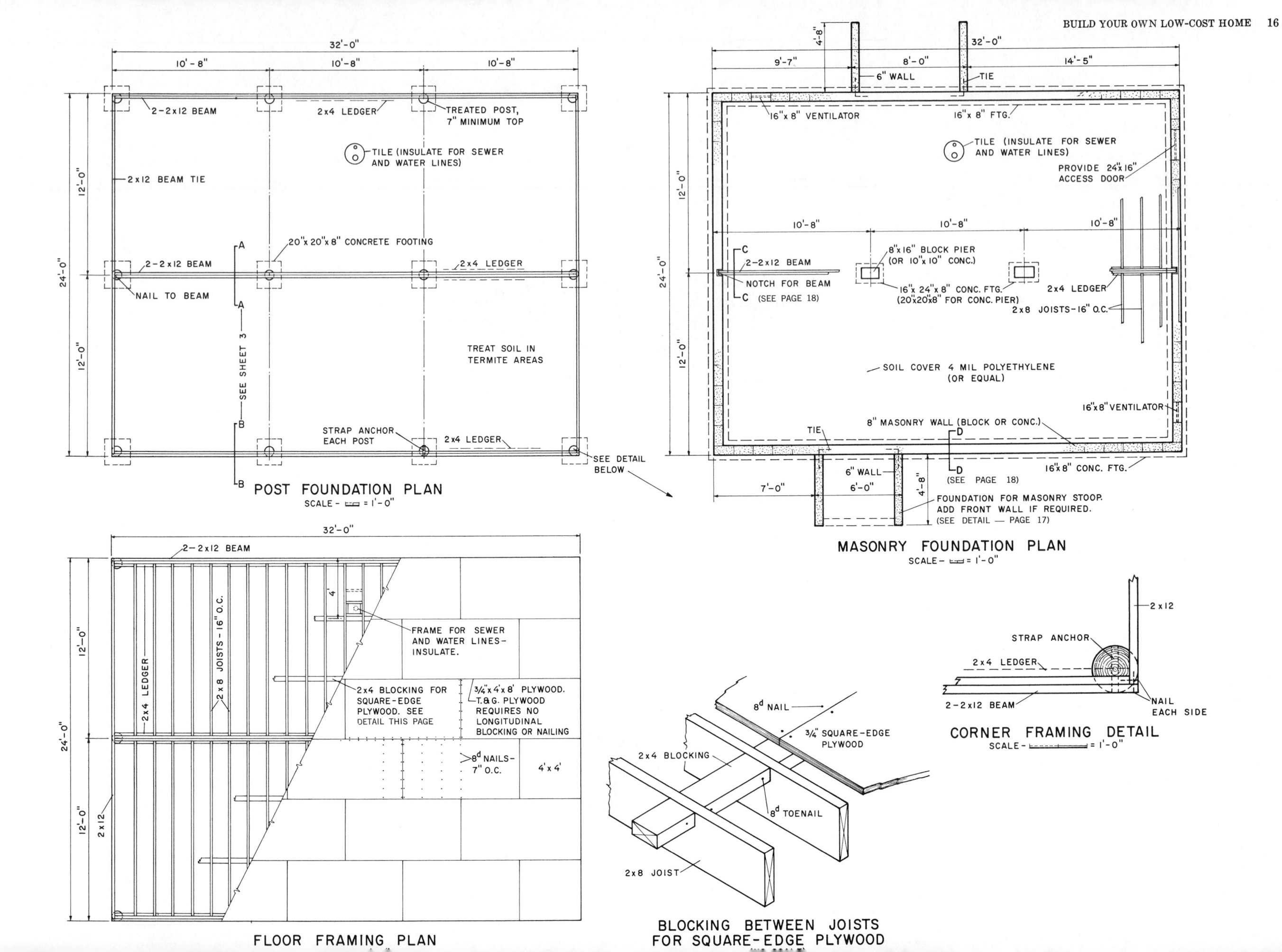

POST FOUNDATION PLAN
SCALE - ▭ = 1'-0"

32'-0"
10'-8" 10'-8" 10'-8"
12'-0"
24'-0"
12'-0"

2-2x12 BEAM
2x4 LEDGER
TREATED POST, 7" MINIMUM TOP
TILE (INSULATE FOR SEWER AND WATER LINES)
2x12 BEAM TIE
20"x 20"x 8" CONCRETE FOOTING
2-2x12 BEAM
2x4 LEDGER
NAIL TO BEAM
SEE SHEET 3
TREAT SOIL IN TERMITE AREAS
STRAP ANCHOR EACH POST
2x4 LEDGER
SEE DETAIL BELOW
A A
B B

MASONRY FOUNDATION PLAN
SCALE - ▭ = 1'-0"

4'-8"
32'-0"
9'-7" 8'-0" 14'-5"
6" WALL TIE
16"x 8" VENTILATOR
16"x 8" FTG.
TILE (INSULATE FOR SEWER AND WATER LINES)
PROVIDE 24"x16" ACCESS DOOR
12'-0"
24'-0"
12'-0"
10'-8" 10'-8" 10'-8"
2-2x12 BEAM
NOTCH FOR BEAM
C C (SEE PAGE 18)
8"x16" BLOCK PIER (OR 10"x 10" CONC.)
16"x 24"x 8" CONC. FTG. (20"x20"x8" FOR CONC. PIER)
2x4 LEDGER
2x8 JOISTS-16" O.C.
SOIL COVER 4 MIL POLYETHYLENE (OR EQUAL)
16"x8" VENTILATOR
TIE
8" MASONRY WALL (BLOCK OR CONC.)
D D (SEE PAGE 18)
16"x 8" CONC. FTG.
7'-0" 6'-0" 4'-8"
6" WALL
FOUNDATION FOR MASONRY STOOP. ADD FRONT WALL IF REQUIRED. (SEE DETAIL — PAGE 17)

FLOOR FRAMING PLAN

32'-0"
2-2x12 BEAM
12'-0"
24'-0"
12'-0"
2x4 LEDGER
2x8 JOISTS-16" O.C.
2x12
4'
FRAME FOR SEWER AND WATER LINES- INSULATE.
2x4 BLOCKING FOR SQUARE-EDGE PLYWOOD. SEE DETAIL THIS PAGE
3/4"x 4'x 8' PLYWOOD. T.& G. PLYWOOD REQUIRES NO LONGITUDINAL BLOCKING OR NAILING
8d NAILS- 7" O.C.
4'x 4'

BLOCKING BETWEEN JOISTS FOR SQUARE-EDGE PLYWOOD

8d NAIL
3/4" SQUARE-EDGE PLYWOOD
2x4 BLOCKING
8d TOENAIL
2x8 JOIST

CORNER FRAMING DETAIL
SCALE - ▭ = 1'-0"

2x12
STRAP ANCHOR
2x4 LEDGER
2-2x12 BEAM
NAIL EACH SIDE

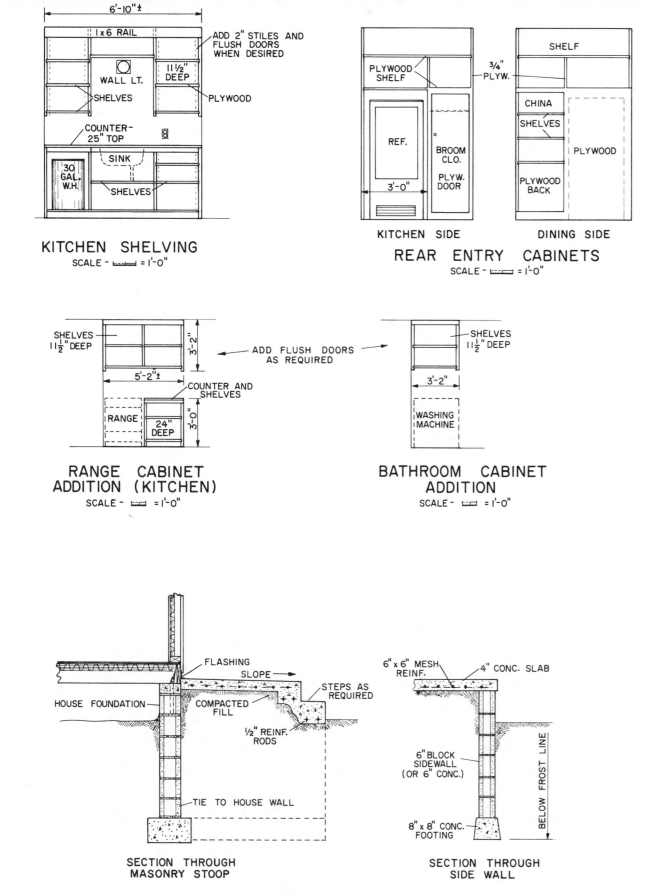

KITCHEN SHELVING
SCALE - ▭ = 1'-0"

6'-10"±
1x6 RAIL
ADD 2" STILES AND FLUSH DOORS WHEN DESIRED
WALL LT.
11½" DEEP
SHELVES
PLYWOOD
COUNTER-25" TOP
30 GAL. W.H.
SINK
SHELVES

REAR ENTRY CABINETS
SCALE - ▭ = 1'-0"

SHELF
PLYWOOD SHELF
¾" PLYW.
REF.
CHINA
SHELVES
PLYWOOD
BROOM CLO.
PLYW. DOOR
PLYWOOD BACK
3'-0"
KITCHEN SIDE
DINING SIDE

RANGE CABINET ADDITION (KITCHEN)
SCALE - ▭ = 1'-0"

SHELVES 11½" DEEP
3'-2"
5'-2"±
ADD FLUSH DOORS AS REQUIRED
COUNTER AND SHELVES
RANGE
24" DEEP
3'-0"

BATHROOM CABINET ADDITION
SCALE - ▭ = 1'-0"

SHELVES 11½" DEEP
3'-2"
WASHING MACHINE

ENTRANCE PLATFORM
(FRONT AND REAR)
SCALE - ▭ = 1'-0"

FLASHING
SLOPE
STEPS AS REQUIRED
HOUSE FOUNDATION
COMPACTED FILL
½" REINF. RODS
TIE TO HOUSE WALL
SECTION THROUGH MASONRY STOOP

6"x6" MESH REINF.
4" CONC. SLAB
6" BLOCK SIDEWALL (OR 6" CONC.)
BELOW FROST LINE
8"x8" CONC. FOOTING
SECTION THROUGH SIDE WALL

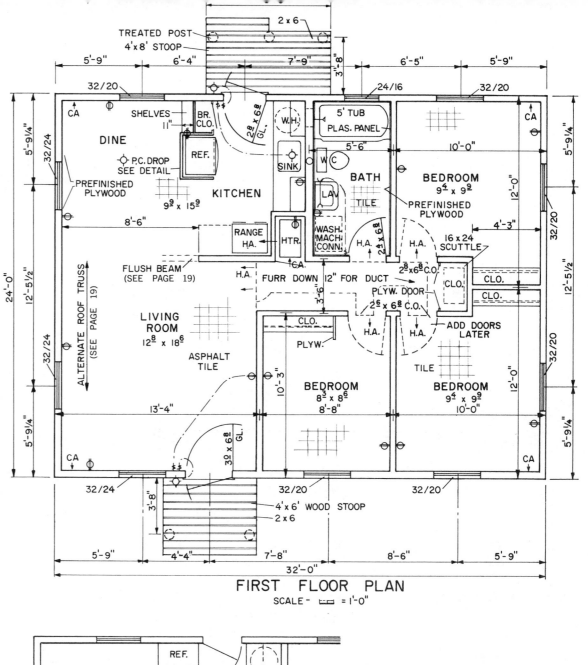

FIRST FLOOR PLAN
SCALE - ▭ = 1'-0"

TREATED POST
4'x8' STOOP
2 x 6
5'-9" 6'-4" 7'-9" 6'-5" 5'-9"
32/20 24/16 32/20
CA
SHELVES 11"
BR. CLO.
W.H.
5' TUB PLAS. PANEL
CA
DINE
P.C. DROP SEE DETAIL
REF.
SINK
W C
BATH
BEDROOM 9⁴ x 9²
TILE
PREFINISHED PLYWOOD
5'-9¼"
32/24
KITCHEN 9⁹ x 15⁹
LAV
10'-0"
4'-3"
16 x 24 SCUTTLE
32/20
8'-6"
RANGE H.A.
HTR
WASH. MACH. CONN.
H.A.
PREFINISHED PLYWOOD
FLUSH BEAM (SEE PAGE 19)
CA
H.A.
CLO.
CLO.
12'-5½"
24'-0"
ALTERNATE ROOF TRUSS (SEE PAGE 19)
H.A.
FURR DOWN 12" FOR DUCT
PLYW. DOOR
ADD DOORS LATER
LIVING ROOM 12⁸ x 18⁶
ASPHALT TILE
CLO.
PLYW.
H.A.
TILE
32/24
10'-3"
BEDROOM 8³ x 8⁶ 8'-8"
BEDROOM 9⁴ x 9² 10'-0"
5'-9¼"
12'-0"
13'-4"
32/24
5'-9"
4'-4"
7'-8"
8'-6"
5'-9"
32/20
32/20
4'x6' WOOD STOOP
2 x 6
3'-8"
32'-0"

ALTERNATE KITCHEN ARRANGEMENT
SCALE - ▭ = 1'-0"

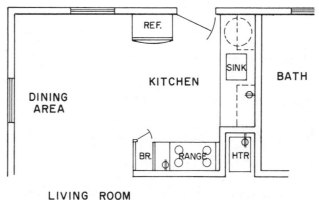

REF.
SINK
BATH
DINING AREA
KITCHEN
BR.
RANGE
HTR
LIVING ROOM

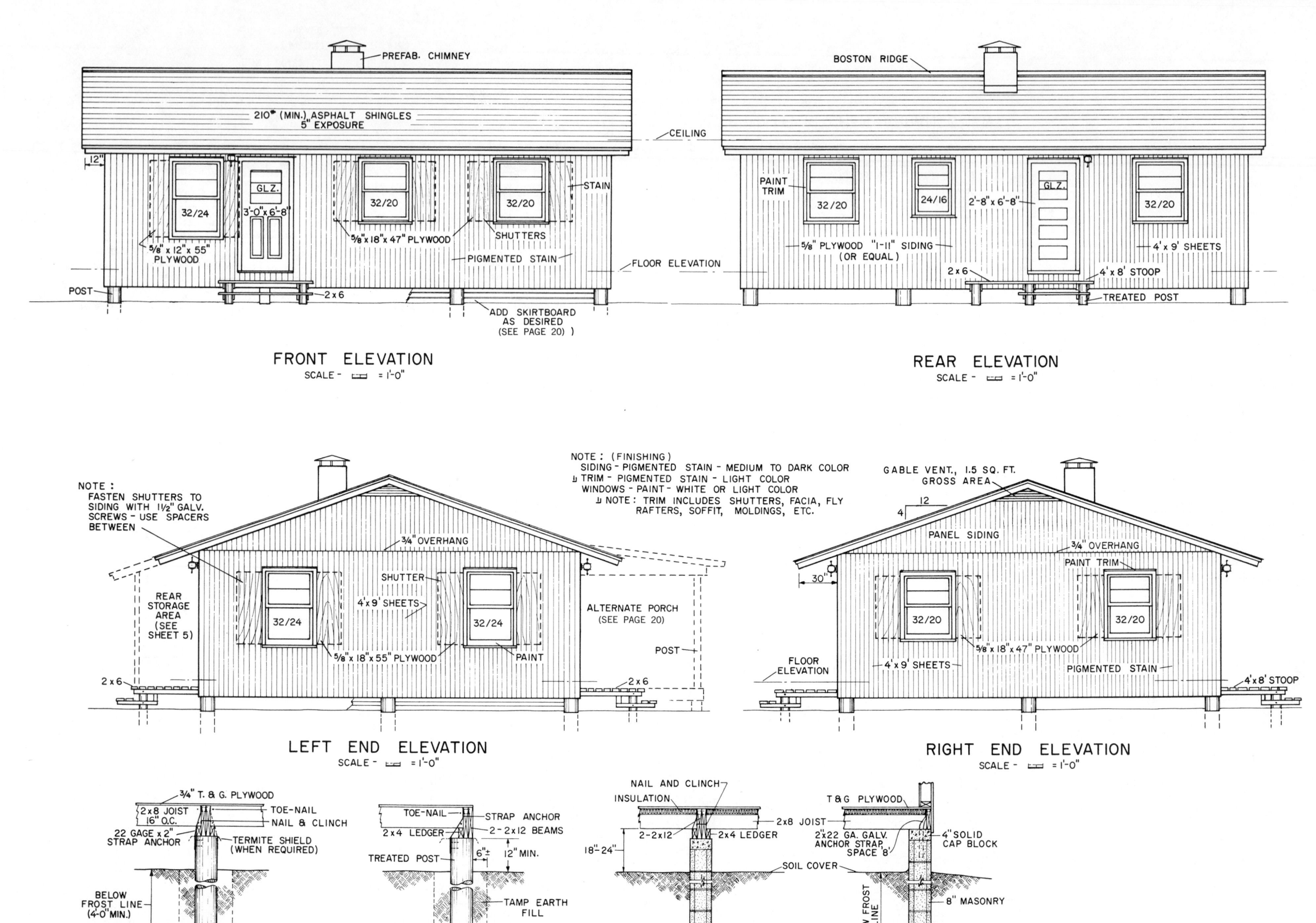

FRONT ELEVATION
SCALE - ▭ = 1'-0"

REAR ELEVATION
SCALE - ▭ = 1'-0"

PREFAB. CHIMNEY

210# (MIN.) ASPHALT SHINGLES
5" EXPOSURE

12"

GLZ.
3'-0" x 6'-8"

32/24

5/8" x 12" x 55"
PLYWOOD

POST

2 x 6

5/8" x 18" x 47" PLYWOOD

32/20   32/20

STAIN

SHUTTERS

PIGMENTED STAIN

ADD SKIRTBOARD
AS DESIRED
(SEE PAGE 20))

BOSTON RIDGE

CEILING

PAINT
TRIM

32/20   24/16

GLZ.
2'-8" x 6'-8"

32/20

5/8" PLYWOOD "1-11" SIDING
(OR EQUAL)

2 x 6

4' x 9' SHEETS

4' x 8' STOOP

TREATED POST

FLOOR ELEVATION

NOTE :
FASTEN SHUTTERS TO
SIDING WITH 1 1/2" GALV.
SCREWS - USE SPACERS
BETWEEN

NOTE : (FINISHING)
SIDING - PIGMENTED STAIN - MEDIUM TO DARK COLOR
↳ TRIM - PIGMENTED STAIN - LIGHT COLOR
WINDOWS - PAINT - WHITE OR LIGHT COLOR
↳ NOTE : TRIM INCLUDES SHUTTERS, FACIA, FLY
RAFTERS, SOFFIT, MOLDINGS, ETC.

3/4" OVERHANG

SHUTTER

REAR
STORAGE
AREA
(SEE
SHEET 5)

32/24

4' x 9' SHEETS

32/24

5/8" x 18" x 55" PLYWOOD

PAINT

ALTERNATE PORCH
(SEE PAGE 20)

POST

2 x 6   2 x 6

LEFT END ELEVATION
SCALE - ▭ = 1'-0"

GABLE VENT., 1.5 SQ. FT.
GROSS AREA

12
4

PANEL SIDING

3/4" OVERHANG

PAINT TRIM

30"

32/20   32/20

FLOOR
ELEVATION

4' x 9' SHEETS

5/8" x 18" x 47" PLYWOOD

PIGMENTED STAIN

4' x 8' STOOP

RIGHT END ELEVATION
SCALE - ▭ = 1'-0"

3/4" T. & G. PLYWOOD

2 x 8 JOIST
16" O.C.

22 GAGE x 2"
STRAP ANCHOR

TOE-NAIL

NAIL & CLINCH

TERMITE SHIELD
(WHEN REQUIRED)

BELOW
FROST LINE
(4'-0" MIN.)

8"

20" x 20" x 8" CONCRETE FOOTING

SECTION A-A, CENTER POST

TOE-NAIL

2 x 4 LEDGER

TREATED POST

STRAP ANCHOR

2 - 2 x 12 BEAMS

6" ±   12" MIN.

TAMP EARTH
FILL

SECTION B-B, EDGE POST

NAIL AND CLINCH

INSULATION

2 - 2 x 12

18"-24"

2 x 8 JOIST

2 x 4 LEDGER

SOIL COVER

16" x 24" x 8" FTG.

SECTION C-C

T & G PLYWOOD

2" x 22 GA. GALV.
ANCHOR STRAP
SPACE 8'

4" SOLID
CAP BLOCK

BELOW
FROST
LINE

8" MASONRY

16" x 8" CONC. FTG.

SECTION D-D

FOUNDATION DETAILS

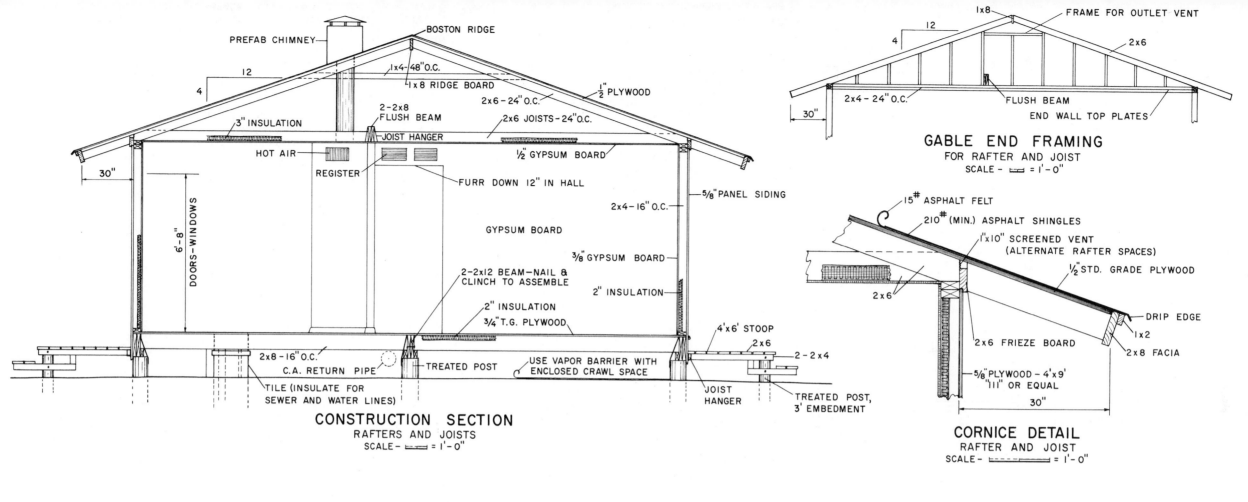

PREFAB CHIMNEY
BOSTON RIDGE
1x4-48"O.C.
1x8 RIDGE BOARD
2x6-24" O.C.
1/2" PLYWOOD
3" INSULATION
12
4
2-2x8 FLUSH BEAM
2x6 JOISTS-24" O.C.
JOIST HANGER
30"
HOT AIR
REGISTER
1/2 GYPSUM BOARD
FURR DOWN 12" IN HALL
5/8"PANEL SIDING
6'-8" DOORS-WINDOWS
GYPSUM BOARD
2x4-16" O.C.
3/8 GYPSUM BOARD
2-2x12 BEAM-NAIL & CLINCH TO ASSEMBLE
2" INSULATION
2" INSULATION
3/4" T.G. PLYWOOD
4'x6' STOOP
2x6
2x8-16" O.C.
C.A. RETURN PIPE
TREATED POST
USE VAPOR BARRIER WITH ENCLOSED CRAWL SPACE
2-2x4
TILE (INSULATE FOR SEWER AND WATER LINES)
JOIST HANGER
TREATED POST, 3' EMBEDMENT

CONSTRUCTION SECTION
RAFTERS AND JOISTS
SCALE- ⬜⬜⬜ = 1'-0"

GABLE END FRAMING
FOR RAFTER AND JOIST
SCALE- ⬜⬜ = 1'-0"

1x8
FRAME FOR OUTLET VENT
12
4
2x6
2x4-24" O.C.
FLUSH BEAM
END WALL TOP PLATES
30"

CORNICE DETAIL
RAFTER AND JOIST
SCALE- ⬜⬜⬜⬜ = 1'-0"

15# ASPHALT FELT
210# (MIN.) ASPHALT SHINGLES
1"x10" SCREENED VENT (ALTERNATE RAFTER SPACES)
1/2" STD. GRADE PLYWOOD
2x6
2x6 FRIEZE BOARD
DRIP EDGE
1x2
2x8 FACIA
5/8" PLYWOOD - 4'x9' "111" OR EQUAL
30"

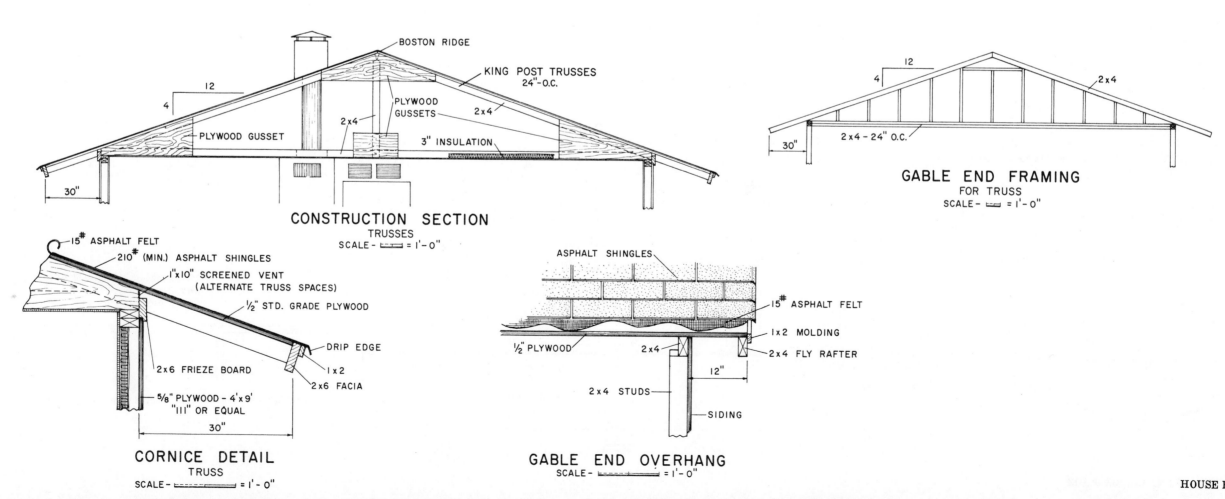

CONSTRUCTION SECTION
TRUSSES
SCALE- ⬜⬜⬜ = 1'-0"

BOSTON RIDGE
KING POST TRUSSES 24"-O.C.
PLYWOOD GUSSETS
2x4
2x4
PLYWOOD GUSSET
3" INSULATION
12
4
30"

GABLE END FRAMING
FOR TRUSS
SCALE- ⬜⬜ = 1'-0"

12
4
2x4
2x4
2x4-24" O.C.
30"

CORNICE DETAIL
TRUSS
SCALE- ⬜⬜⬜⬜ = 1'-0"

15# ASPHALT FELT
210# (MIN.) ASPHALT SHINGLES
1"x10" SCREENED VENT (ALTERNATE TRUSS SPACES)
1/2" STD. GRADE PLYWOOD
DRIP EDGE
1x2
2x6 FRIEZE BOARD
2x6 FACIA
5/8" PLYWOOD - 4'x9' "111" OR EQUAL
30"

GABLE END OVERHANG
SCALE- ⬜⬜⬜ = 1'-0"

ASPHALT SHINGLES
15# ASPHALT FELT
1x2 MOLDING
1/2" PLYWOOD
2x4
2x4 FLY RAFTER
2x4 STUDS
12"
SIDING

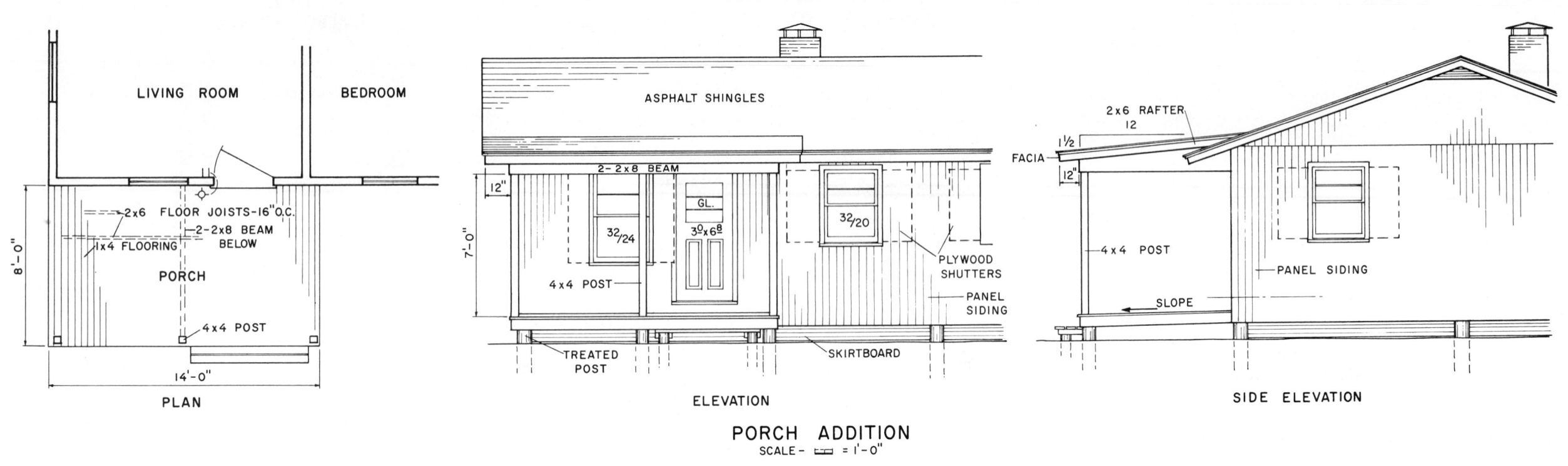

LIVING ROOM   BEDROOM

2x6 FLOOR JOISTS-16"O.C.
2-2x8 BEAM BELOW
1x4 FLOORING

8'-0"

PORCH

4x4 POST

14'-0"

PLAN

ASPHALT SHINGLES

2-2x8 BEAM

12"

GL.

7'-0"

32/24

3⁰x6⁸

32/20

4x4 POST

PLYWOOD SHUTTERS

PANEL SIDING

TREATED POST

SKIRTBOARD

ELEVATION

2x6 RAFTER
12

1½

FACIA

12"

4x4 POST

PANEL SIDING

SLOPE

SIDE ELEVATION

PORCH ADDITION
SCALE - ▭ = 1'-0"

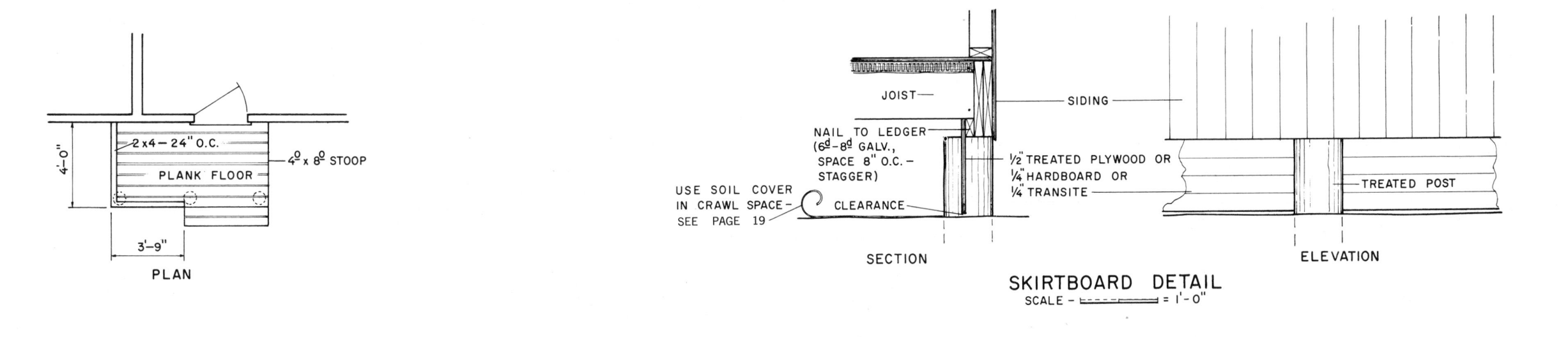

2x4-24" O.C.

PLANK FLOOR

4'-0"

4⁰ x 8⁰ STOOP

3'-9"

PLAN

JOIST

NAIL TO LEDGER
(6ᵈ-8ᵈ GALV.,
SPACE 8" O.C. -
STAGGER)

USE SOIL COVER
IN CRAWL SPACE -
SEE PAGE 19

CLEARANCE

SIDING

½" TREATED PLYWOOD OR
¼" HARDBOARD OR
¼" TRANSITE

TREATED POST

SECTION

ELEVATION

SKIRTBOARD DETAIL
SCALE - ▭ = 1'-0"

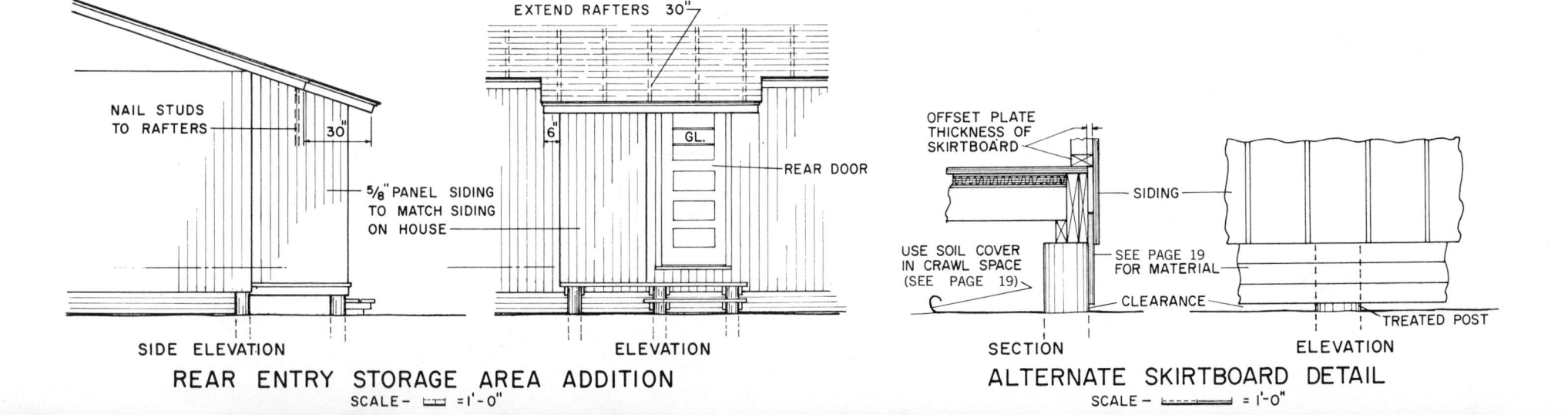

NAIL STUDS
TO RAFTERS

30"

5/8" PANEL SIDING
TO MATCH SIDING
ON HOUSE

SIDE ELEVATION

EXTEND RAFTERS 30"

6"

GL.

REAR DOOR

ELEVATION

REAR ENTRY STORAGE AREA ADDITION
SCALE - ▭ = 1'-0"

OFFSET PLATE
THICKNESS OF
SKIRTBOARD

USE SOIL COVER
IN CRAWL SPACE
(SEE PAGE 19)

SIDING

SEE PAGE 19
FOR MATERIAL

CLEARANCE

TREATED POST

SECTION

ELEVATION

ALTERNATE SKIRTBOARD DETAIL
SCALE - ▭ = 1'-0"

SPECIFICATIONS

for

A LOW-COST, THREE BEDROOM WOOD HOUSE

Plan No. 1

(One-story house, 24'-0" x 32'-0" in size, constructed over a crawl space)

All work related to construction of this house shall be done in a first-class manner. Details not included in specifications or plans shall comply with general details in the "Construction Manual" or to accepted practices for wood-frame construction.

Excavation - Grading

Sod, growing plants, shrubs, stumps, and trees shall be removed and ground smoothed in building area and 2 feet outside of building line. Excavate footings to required depth and size shown in plans. No forms are required if soil is stable. Locate excavated soil conveniently for backfilling around treated wood posts.

Concrete Work

Footings shall be poured over undisturbed soil in excavations to indicated thickness and size as shown on plan. Top surface to be level.

Mix concrete to a 1:2-1/2:3-1/2 mix. If premixed concrete is available, use 5-bag mix.

Treated Wood Posts

Pressure-treated wood posts with 7-inch minimum top diameter shall be treated to conform to Federal Specification TT-W-571.

Carpentry

General

This branch of the work comprises all rough and finish carpentry necessary to complete the house, as shown on the plans and as specified. This includes layout, cutting and fitting framing, and other carpentry items. Any phase which is necessary for the completion of the house and not specifically covered in the plans or specifications shall be included as required.

Wood Framing

Dimension material for studs to be Standard (third grade); and for floor joists and framing, ceiling joists, rafters, beams, and trusses construction (second grade) in Douglas-fir, southern pine, or equivalent, unless otherwise noted on the plans. Floor joists and studs shall be spaced 16 inches on center. Trusses or ceiling joists and rafters shall be spaced 24 inches on center. Moisture content of framing lumber not to exceed 19 percent.

Subfloor

The subfloor shall be plywood to serve as a floor alone or as a base for resilient tile and shall consist of 3/4-inch C-C plugged Exterior grade, touch-sanded, and with matched edges in Douglas-fir, southern pine, or equivalent. When matched-edge plywood is not obtainable, square-edged plywood in the same grade and thickness can be substituted but 2- by 4-inch blocking shall be used for all longitudinal joints. Toenail 2- by 4-inch blocks flatwise in each joist space.

Roof Sheathing

Roof sheathing shall be 1/2-inch Douglas-fir or southern pine plywood or equal in Standard sheathing grade or nominal 1- by 6- or 1- by 8-inch boards in No. 3 Douglas-fir, southern pine, or equivalent. Boards shall be square edge, shiplap, or dressed and matched, and laid up tight at a moisture content of not more than 15 percent. Roof sheathing shall be covered with 15-pound asphalt felt.

Insulation

All ceilings to be insulated with standard batt- or blanket-type flexible insulation with vapor barrier placed toward the inside of the building. Wall and floor insulation to consist of flexible blanket insulation. Thicknesses shall comply with the recommended thicknesses outlined in the "Construction Manual" or as otherwise required. Vapor barrier shall be placed toward the inside of the building. Vapor barrier to have a maximum perm value of 0.30.

Siding

Siding shall be 5/8-inch by 4- by 9-foot plywood panel siding in Texture 1-11 (4-in. grooves) or equal. It shall be nailed at each stud, including vertical joints, and at the top and bottom plate and floor framing with eightpenny galvanized siding nails spaced 7 to 8 inches apart. The vertical edges of the sheets shall be brush-coated with a water-repellent preservative before installing.

Exterior Millwork

(a) Exterior finish.--Exterior trim and similar materials shall be No. 2 ponderosa pine or equivalent suitable for staining.

(b) Window frames and sash.--Complete double-hung windows shall be used with upper sash cut to two horizontal lights, glazed with single-strength glass. Units to be treated with water-repellent preservative as outlined in Commercial Standard CS 190-64. Sash to be furnished fully balanced and fitted and with outside casing in place. Set in openings, plumb, and square. Screens shall be furnished, and storms when required.

(c) Exterior door frames and doors.--Exterior door frames shall have 1-3/8-inch rabbeted jambs and 1-5/8-inch oak sill or softwood sill with metal edge, all assembled. Set in openings, plumb, and square.

Exterior doors to be standard 1-3/4-inch with solid stiles and rails; panel type with glazed openings as shown on plans. Screen doors shall be furnished, or combinations when required.

(d) Screens.--Galvanized fly screen shall be used for inlet and outlet ventilators.

Interior Millwork

(a) Interior door frames and doors.--Interior door frames and cased openings shall be nominal 1-inch ponderosa pine or equal in "D" Select. Stops shall be installed only where doors are specified.

Interior doors shall be 1-3/8 inches thick, five-cross-panel style with solid stiles and rails.

(b) Interior trim.--Interior trim shall be ponderosa pine or equal in "D" Select in ranch pattern in the following sizes:

Casings	-- 11/16 by 2-1/4 inches
Stops	-- 7/16 by 1-3/8 inches or wider
Base	-- 7/16 by 2-1/4 inches
Base shoe	-- 1/2 by 3/4 inch (when required)

Note: (1) Casing to be used at bottom of windows in place of stool and apron.

(2) Base shoe used along plywood wardrobe and closets where required.

(c) Walls and ceilings.--All ceilings shall be finished with 1/2-inch gypsum board with recessed edges and with the length applied across the ceiling joists or bottom chords of the trusses. End joints shall be staggered at least 2 feet. Walls shall be finished with 3/8-inch gypsum board with recessed edges and applied vertically. Application and joint treatment shall follow the recommendations in the "Construction Manual."

Walls of tub recess shall be covered with plastic-finished hardboard panels over gypsum board. Install with mastic in accordance with manufacturer's directions. Inside corners, edges, and tub edges shall be finished with plastic moldings.

(d) Flooring.--Finish flooring throughout shall be 1/8-inch thick asphalt tile in 9- by 9-inch size, "B" quality. Combination plywood sub-floor shall be cleaned, nails driven flush, and joints sanded smooth where required. Tile shall be applied in accordance with manufacturer's recommendations. Rubber baseboard shall be furnished and installed in the bathroom, wood base in the remainder of the house.

(e) Hardware.--Furnish and install all rough and finish hardware complete as needed for perfect operation. Locks shall be furnished for all outside doors. Outside doors to be hung with three 4- by 4-inch loose-pin butt hinges and inside doors with two 3-1/2- by 3-1/2-inch loose-pin butt hinges. Bathroom five-cross-panel door shall be furnished with standard bathroom lock set. Standard screen door latches, hinges, and door closers shall be furnished and installed. Furnish and install semi-concealed cabinet hinges, pulls, and catches where required for cabinet or closet doors. All finish hardware to be finished in dull brass.

Sheet Metal Work and Roofing

Sheet Metal

Sheet metal flashing, when required for the prefabricated chimney and vent stack, shall be 28-gage galvanized iron or painted terneplate.

Termite shields, when required, shall be 28-gage galvanized iron, painted terneplate, or aluminum in equivalent thickness. (See section on "Termite Protection.")

Roofing

Roofing shall be a minimum of 210-pound square tab 12- by 36-inch asphalt shingles installed over a single underlay of 15-pound asphalt felt. A minimum of four 7/8-inch galvanized roofing nails shall be used for each 12- by 36-inch shingle strip. Any defects or leaks shall be corrected.

Electrical Work

The work shall include all materials and labor necessary to make the systems complete as shown on the plans. All work and materials shall comply with local requirements or those of the National Electrical Code. All wiring shall be concealed and carried in BX or other approved conduit to each outlet, switch, fixture, and appliance or electrical equipment such as furnace, hot water heater, and range when required; and as shown on the plan. Panel shall be 100 amp. capacity with overload cutout. Wall fixtures to consist of the following:
Two outside wall fixtures with crystal glass.
Overhead (wall) (fluorescent fixture in bath and incandescent in kitchen).

Heating

Heater and prefabricated chimney shall be installed as shown on the plans with supply ducts located in furred-down ceiling of hall. Heater shall be for LP or natural gas with a 75,000 minimum B.t.u. input or as required by design for each specific area. Cold air return at furnace base and from each corner of the house. Cold air duct shall consist of 1/8-inch transite-covered joist spaces along outside walls and connection to 10-inch-diameter galvanized ducts to heater.

Plumbing

All plumbing shall be installed in accordance with local or National plumbing codes. Hot- and cold-water connections shall be furnished to all fixtures as required. Sewer and water and gas lines (when required) shall extend to building line with water shutoff valve. Framed and insulated box shall be used to protect water and sewer lines from freezing in crawl space where required. Cover with 1/8-inch transite or equal and insulate with 3 inches of fiberglass or styrofoam when required. Use a 16- by 16-inch vitrified tile or equal below groundline.

Furnish and install the following fixtures:
One kitchen sink--21 by 15 inches, self rim, steel, white, with fixtures.
One bathtub--5 foot, cast iron, white, left-hand drain, complete with shower rod and shower head with fixtures.
One water closet--Reverse trap, white, with seat, fixtures, and shutoff valve.
One lavatory--19 by 17 inches, steel, white, and with fixtures and shutoff valve.
One hot water heater--30 gallon (minimum), gas or electric under-counter type).
Washing machine connection with hot and cold water and drain.

Painting and Finishing

Exterior

Exterior plywood panel siding, facia, shutters, and soffit areas shall be stained with pigmented stain as outlined in the "Construction Manual." Use light gray, yellow, or another light color stain for the trim and shutters and a darker stain (brown, olive, gray, etc.) for the panel siding or reverse color selection as desired by owner.

Window and door frames, window sash, screen doors, and similar millwork shall be painted a light color, or as owners request. Types of paint and procedures to comply with recommendations in "Construction Manual."

Interior

All woodwork shall be painted in semigloss. Walls and ceilings finished in latex flat as outlined in the "Construction Manual," except bathroom, which shall be finished in semigloss.

Termite Protection

Termite protection shall be provided in termite areas by means of soil treatments or termite shields or both. -- See "Construction Manual."

Concrete Blocks

Concrete blocks (used as an alternate to foundation of treated wood posts) shall comply with ASTM C-90, Grade U-II, for standard size and quality.

Concrete blocks shall be laid over concrete footings, as shown on the foundation plan. Footings shall be level and laid out to conform to the building line. Blocks shall be laid up with 3/8-inch-thick mortar joints, tooling the joints on all exposed exterior surfaces. Anchor straps, when used, shall be embedded to a depth of at least 12 inches.

BILL OF MATERIAL FOR RURAL HOME

Plan No. 1

The following material is required for construction of the rural home detailed in Plan No. 1; quality of material and treatments are given in the specifications.

Foundation

The foundation of treated posts set on concrete footings requires:

    1 cubic yard concrete
    12 treated posts, 5 feet long, with 7-inch minimum
        top diameter

Floor Framing

Floor framing consisting of floor joists supported on ledgers nailed to the anchored floor beams requires:

4 --	2 x 12's	12 feet long
12 --	2 x 12's	16 feet long
46 --	2 x 8's	12 feet long
12 --	2 x 4's	12 feet long

    36 lineal feet 22-gage x 2-inch anchor strap

Floor

Requirements of floor tile and subfloor are:

    24 -- 4- x 8-foot sheets of 3/4-inch tongued-
            and grooved plywood
    1,500 -- 9- x 9-inch asphalt tile (10 pct. waste)
            (with adhesive)

Wall and Partition Framing

Framing material for walls and partitions includes:

122 --	2 x 4's	8 feet long
69 --	2 x 4's	12 feet long
17 --	2 x 6's	12 feet long

Ceiling and Roof Framing
(Conventional Rafter and Joist)

Materials for rafters, joists, and a flush beam over the living area are:

8 --	2 x 4's	16 feet long
18 --	2 x 6's	12 feet long
12 --	2 x 6's	14 feet long
34 --	2 x 6's	16 feet long
2 --	2 x 8's	14 feet long
3 --	1 x 8's	12 feet long
14 --	Joist hangers for 2 x 6's	

Roof

Roofing and sheathing requirements are:

34 -- 4- x 8-foot sheets of 1/2-inch
plywood sheathing grade (CD)
5 -- 432-square-foot rolls of 15-pound
asphalt felt

12 squares -- 210-pound asphalt shingles

Siding

The siding requirement of rough textured 5/8-inch Texture 1-11 or equivalent is:

32 -- 4- x 9-foot sheets

Windows

All windows are double-hung and purchased treated and complete with screens, and storms when required. Quantity of each size is:

3 -- 32/24
6 -- 32/20
1 -- 24/16

Exterior Doors

Doors are glazed and frame, trim, and hardware are required for each. Screen doors shall be furnished, or combinations when required. Sizes are:

Front -- 3 feet 0 inches wide and 6 feet 8 inches high
Rear -- 2 feet 8 inches wide and 6 feet 8 inches high

Insulation

Blanket insulation with aluminum foil on one side is required for ceiling, walls, and floor.

1,700 square feet -- 2 inches thick, 16 inches wide
800 square feet -- 3 inches thick, 24 inches wide

Roof Ventilators

Requirements for ventilating the roof are:

1 pair -- Peak-type outlet vents
16 square feet -- Screen for inlet vent slots

Exterior Trim

Exterior trim including frieze board, facia, molding, and shutters requires:

6 -- 2 x 6's   12 feet long
6 -- 2 x 8's   12 feet long
11 -- 1 x 2's   12 feet long
3 -- 4- x 8-foot sheets of 5/8-inch Texture 1-11 or
equivalent, rough-textured

Interior Wall and Ceiling Finish

Gypsum board is used for all interior finish and plastic-coated hardboard is added on the wall above the bathtub. Requirements are:

50 -- 4- x 8-foot sheets of 3/8-inch gypsum board
24 -- 4- x 8-foot sheets of 1/2-inch gypsum board
3 -- 4- x 8-foot sheets of coated hardboard
3 -- 250-foot rolls of joint tape
6 -- 25-pound bags of joint compound
12 -- 4- x 8-foot sheets of 1/4-inch prefinished plywood

Interior Doors

Interior door requirements are:

1 set   -- 2-foot 4-inch x 6-foot 8-inch hollow-core
door with jambs, stops, and hardware
3 sets   -- Jambs for 2-foot 6-inch x 6-foot 8-inch doors

Interior Trim

Trim for windows, doors, and base includes:

280 feet -- 9/16- x 2-1/8-inch casing
240 feet -- 1/2- x 3-inch base

Cabinets

Material requirements for wood-frame and plywood cabinets are:

```
       6 -- 4- x 8-foot sheets of 3/4-inch plywood, interior AC
       2 -- 4- x 8-foot sheets of 3/8-inch plywood, interior AC
       3 -- 1 x 3's          12 feet long
       2 -- 1 x 4's           8 feet long
       1 -- 1 x 6            14 feet long
  2 pair -- Cabinet door hinges
       2 -- Wooden door pulls
       2 -- Friction door catches
```

Wardrobes

Wardrobes consisting of closet poles with a shelf over require:

```
       2 -- 4- x 8-foot sheets of 3/4-inch plywood, interior AA
       3 -- Closet poles, 1-5/16-inch diameter x 7 feet long
  4 pair -- Pole sockets
```

Front Stoop

The front stoop, consisting of planks laid across 2 by 4 framing supported by treated posts, has the following material requirements:

```
       2 -- Treated posts, 5 feet long with 6-inch minimum top
              diameter
       3 -- 2 x 4's          10 feet long
      10 -- 2 x 6's           8 feet long
       4 -- 1/2-inch galvanized carriage bolts, 8 inches long
```

Rear Stoop

Material requirements for the rear stoop are:

```
       2 -- Treated posts, 5 feet long, with 6-inch minimum top
              diameter
       3 -- 2 x 4's          10 feet long
      10 -- 2 x 6's           8 feet long
       4 -- 1/2-inch galvanized carriage bolts, 8 inches long
```

Nails

Nails required for all phases of construction are:

```
   50 pounds -- Eightpenny common
   27 pounds -- Sixteenpenny common
    2 pounds -- Twentypenny common
    3 pounds -- Tenpenny common, galvanized
    2 pounds -- Sixteenpenny common, galvanized
    2 pounds -- Fourpenny finish
   12 pounds -- Eightpenny finish
   15 pounds -- 3/4-inch galvanized roofing
   12 pounds -- Fourpenny cooler
    8 pounds -- Fivepenny cooler
```

Paint and Finish

Quantities required for one coat of paint inside and one coat of stain outside are:

```
   8 gallons -- Walls and ceiling
   1 gallon  -- Interior trim
   5 gallons -- Exterior siding and trim
```

Electrical

In addition to rough wiring and 100-amp. service, the following items are required:

```
   15 -- Duplex outlets
    2 -- Wall-mounted interior lights
    2 -- Wall-mounted exterior lights
    5 -- Switches
```

Heating

The heating system requires a 75,000 B.t.u. gas furnace with 7 registers, 4 cold-air returns, duct, and a prefab chimney.

Plumbing

Plumbing must be provided for the following required fixtures:

```
1 -- 5-foot bathtub
1 -- Water closet
1 -- Lavatory
1 -- Kitchen sink
1 -- 30-gallon water heater (under-counter, electric)
1 -- 16- x 16- x 24-inch vitrified tile or equal
       (at sewer and water entrance)
```

ALTERNATES

Floor (Square-Edge Plywood)

When tongued-and-grooved plywood is not available, square-edge plywood with all edges blocked can be used. Material requirements for flooring and subfloor are:

```
   24 -- 4- x 8-foot sheets of 3/4-inch plywood
   16 -- 2 x 4's        12 feet long
1,500 -- 9- x 9-inch asphalt tile (10 pct. waste)
            (with adhesive)
```

Ceiling and Roof Framing (Trussed-Rafter)

When trussed rafters are used instead of conventional rafter and joist system, materials required for constructing trusses and framing gable ends are:

```
64 -- 2 x 4's        16 feet long
15 -- 4- x 8-foot sheets of 3/8-inch standard
         grade plywood with exterior glue
```

Foundation (Concrete-Block)

The foundation of concrete blocks on poured concrete footings, plus masonry front and rear stoops, requires: (Note: Based on 4-ft. foundation depth.)

```
  6 cubic yards of concrete (footings)
504 -- 8- x 8- x 16-inch concrete blocks
 84 -- 4- x 8- x 16-inch concrete solid-cap blocks
 72 -- 8- x 6- x 16-inch concrete blocks
 24 -- 8- x 6- x 8-inch concrete blocks (stoop)
 18 sacks prepared mortar
  2 cubic yards mason's sand
 60 square feet 6- x 6-inch mesh reinforcing (stoops)
  4 -- 1/2-inch reinforcing rods, 5 feet long (step)
  4 -- 1/2-inch reinforcing rods, 7 feet long (step)
800 square feet 4-mil polyethylene film (soil cover)
  2 -- 8- x 16-inch foundation vents
  1 -- 16- x 16-inch (minimum) access door and frame
```

Floor Framing (For Concrete-Block Foundation)

```
 3 -- 2 x 12's            12 feet long
 3 -- 2 x 12's            10 feet long
 4 -- 2 x 8's             16 feet long
50 -- 2 x 8's             12 feet long
 3 -- 2 x 4's             22 feet long
45 lineal feet 22-gage x 2-inch anchor strap
```

2

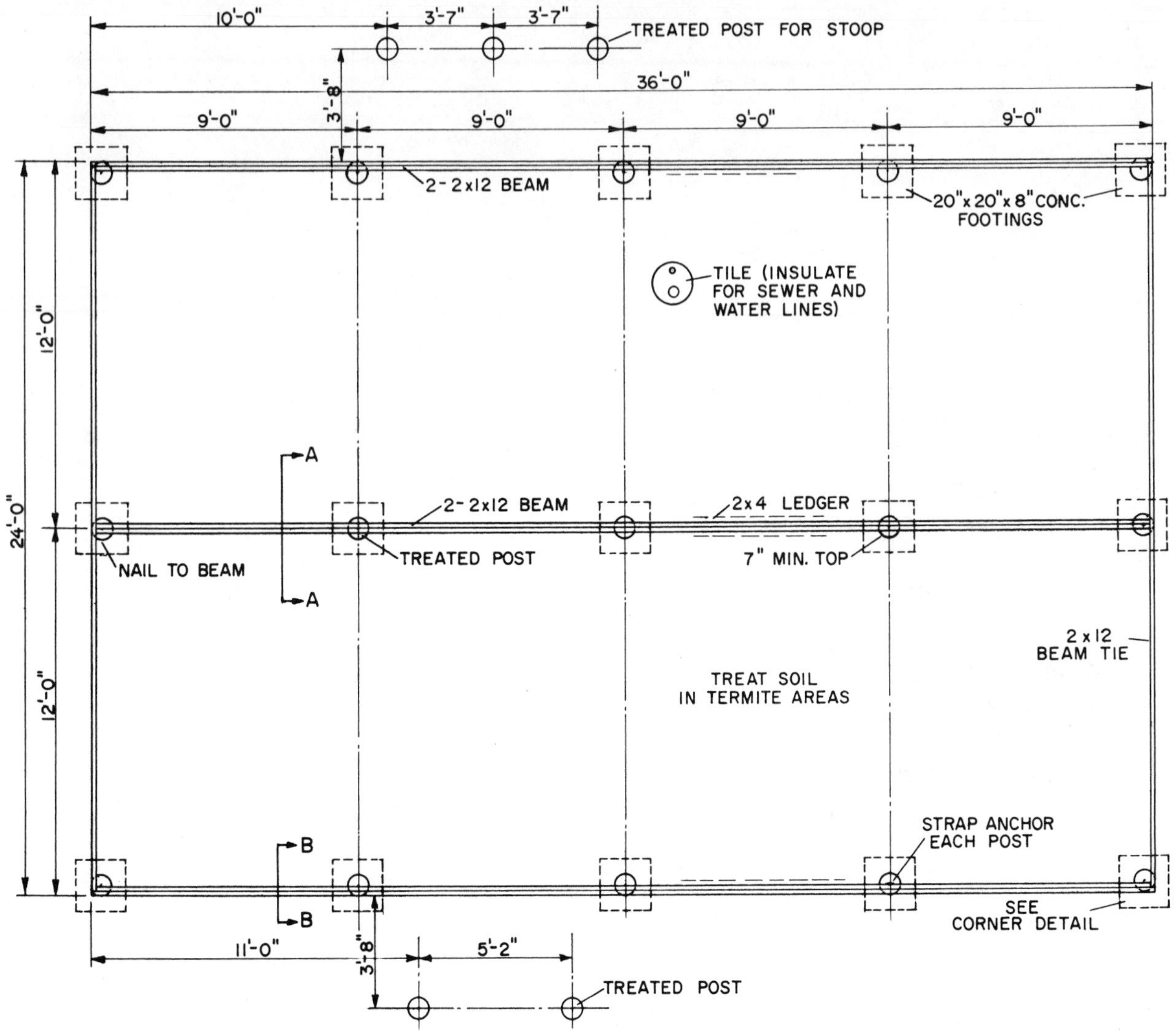

FOUNDATION PLAN

SCALE- ⊏▭⊐ =1'-0"

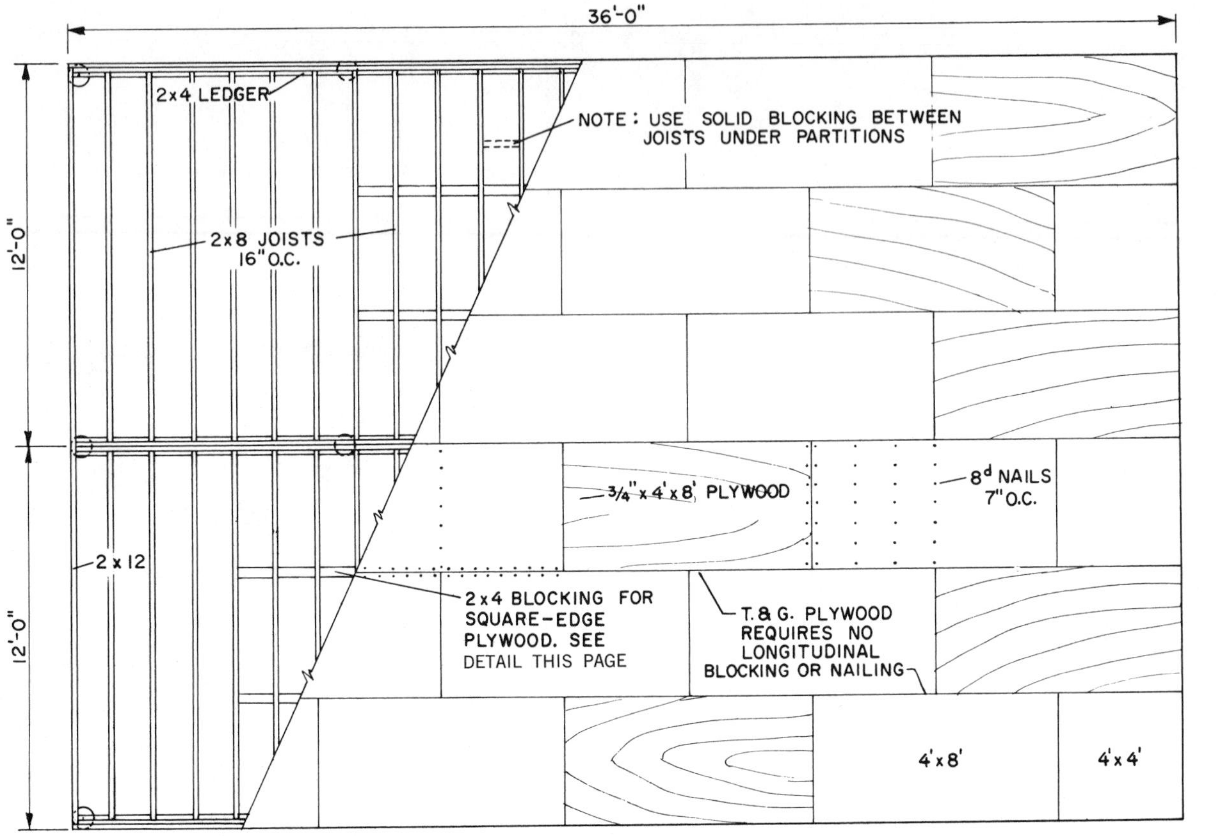

10'-0"   3'-7"   3'-7"   TREATED POST FOR STOOP

36'-0"

9'-0"   3'-8"   9'-0"   9'-0"   9'-0"

2-2x12 BEAM

20"x 20"x 8" CONC. FOOTINGS

TILE (INSULATE FOR SEWER AND WATER LINES)

12'-0"

24'-0"

2-2x12 BEAM

2x4 LEDGER

7" MIN. TOP

TREATED POST

NAIL TO BEAM

2x12 BEAM TIE

12'-0"

TREAT SOIL IN TERMITE AREAS

STRAP ANCHOR EACH POST

SEE CORNER DETAIL

11'-0"   3'-8"   5'-2"

TREATED POST

FLOOR FRAMING PLAN

SCALE- ▭ =1'-0"

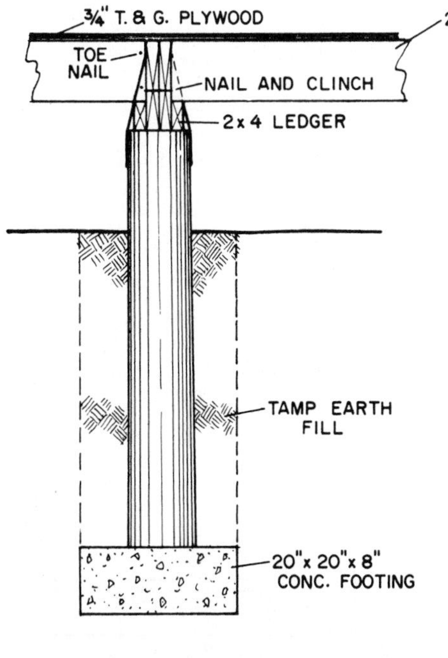

36'-0"

2x4 LEDGER

NOTE: USE SOLID BLOCKING BETWEEN JOISTS UNDER PARTITIONS

2x8 JOISTS 16" O.C.

12'-0"

¾"x 4'x 8' PLYWOOD

8ᵈ NAILS 7" O.C.

2 x 12

2x4 BLOCKING FOR SQUARE-EDGE PLYWOOD. SEE DETAIL THIS PAGE

T. & G. PLYWOOD REQUIRES NO LONGITUDINAL BLOCKING OR NAILING

12'-0"

4'x 8'   4'x 4'

SECTION A-A

¾" T. & G. PLYWOOD

TOE NAIL

NAIL AND CLINCH

2 x 4 LEDGER

TAMP EARTH FILL

20"x 20"x 8" CONC. FOOTING

SECTION B-B

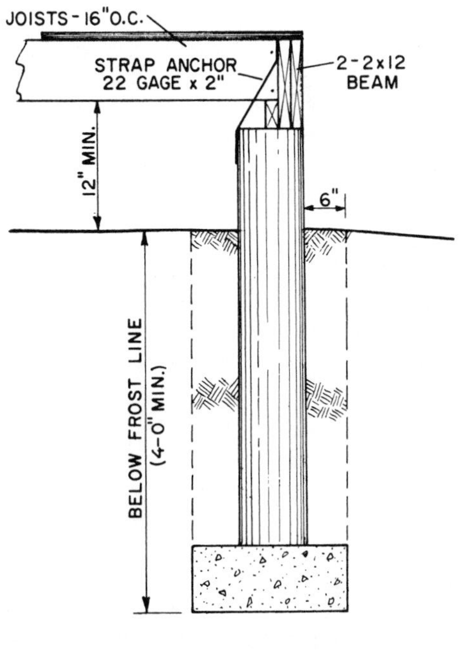

2x8 JOISTS- 16"O.C.

STRAP ANCHOR 22 GAGE x 2"

2-2x12 BEAM

12" MIN.

6"

BELOW FROST LINE (4'-0" MIN.)

SCALE- ⊏▭⊐ =1'-0"

BLOCKING BETWEEN JOISTS FOR SQUARE-EDGE PLYWOOD

(NO SCALE)

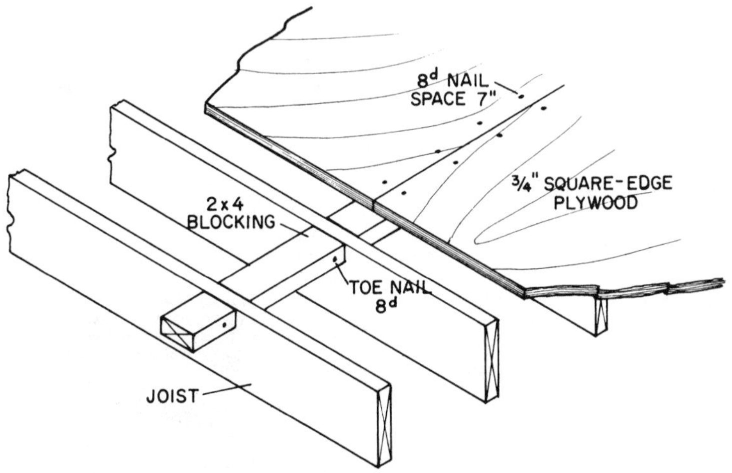

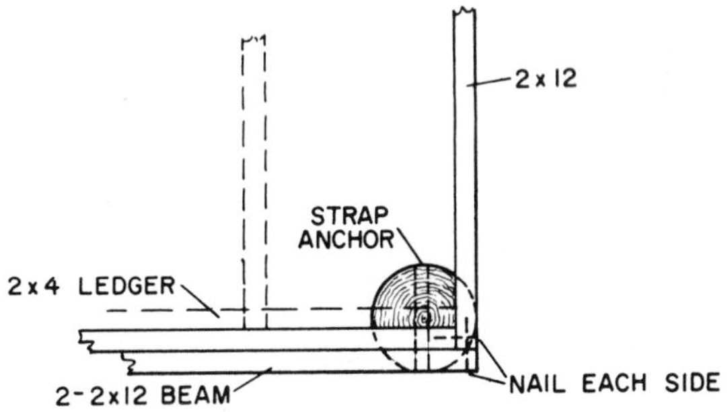

8ᵈ NAIL SPACE 7"

¾" SQUARE-EDGE PLYWOOD

2x4 BLOCKING

TOE NAIL 8ᵈ

JOIST

CORNER FRAMING DETAIL

SCALE- ⊏▭▭⊐ =1'-0"

2 x 12

STRAP ANCHOR

2 x 4 LEDGER

2-2x12 BEAM

NAIL EACH SIDE

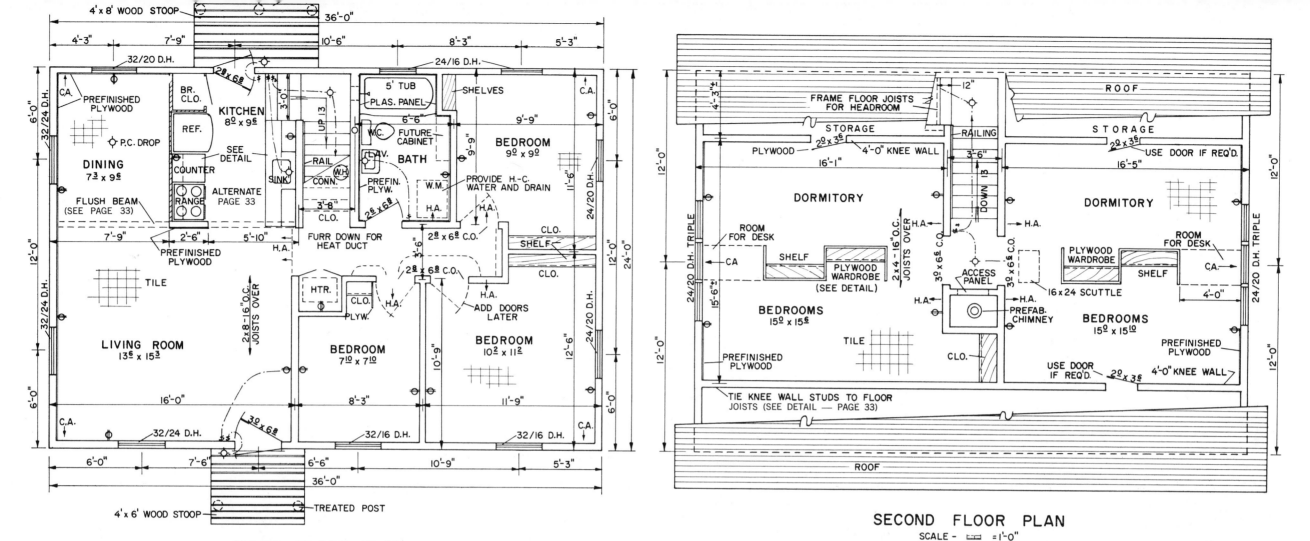

FIRST FLOOR PLAN
SCALE - = 1'-0"

SECOND FLOOR PLAN
SCALE - = 1'-0"

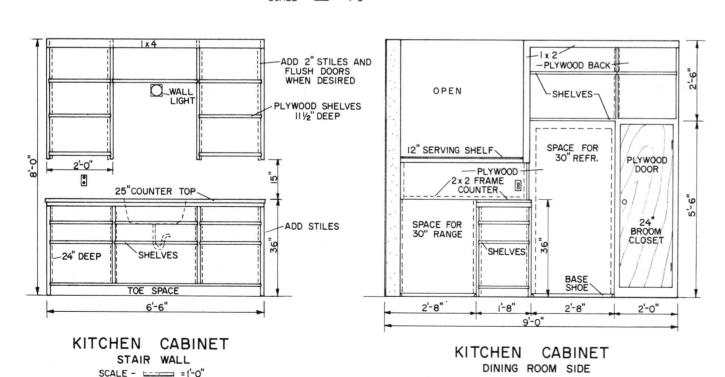

KITCHEN CABINET
STAIR WALL
SCALE - = 1'-0"

KITCHEN CABINET
DINING ROOM SIDE
SCALE - = 1'-0"

WARDROBE - SECOND FLOOR BEDROOMS
SCALE - = 1'-0"

ELEVATION

SECTION

NOTE: FOR ALTERNATE KITCHEN-DINING AREA DESIGN SEE PAGE 33

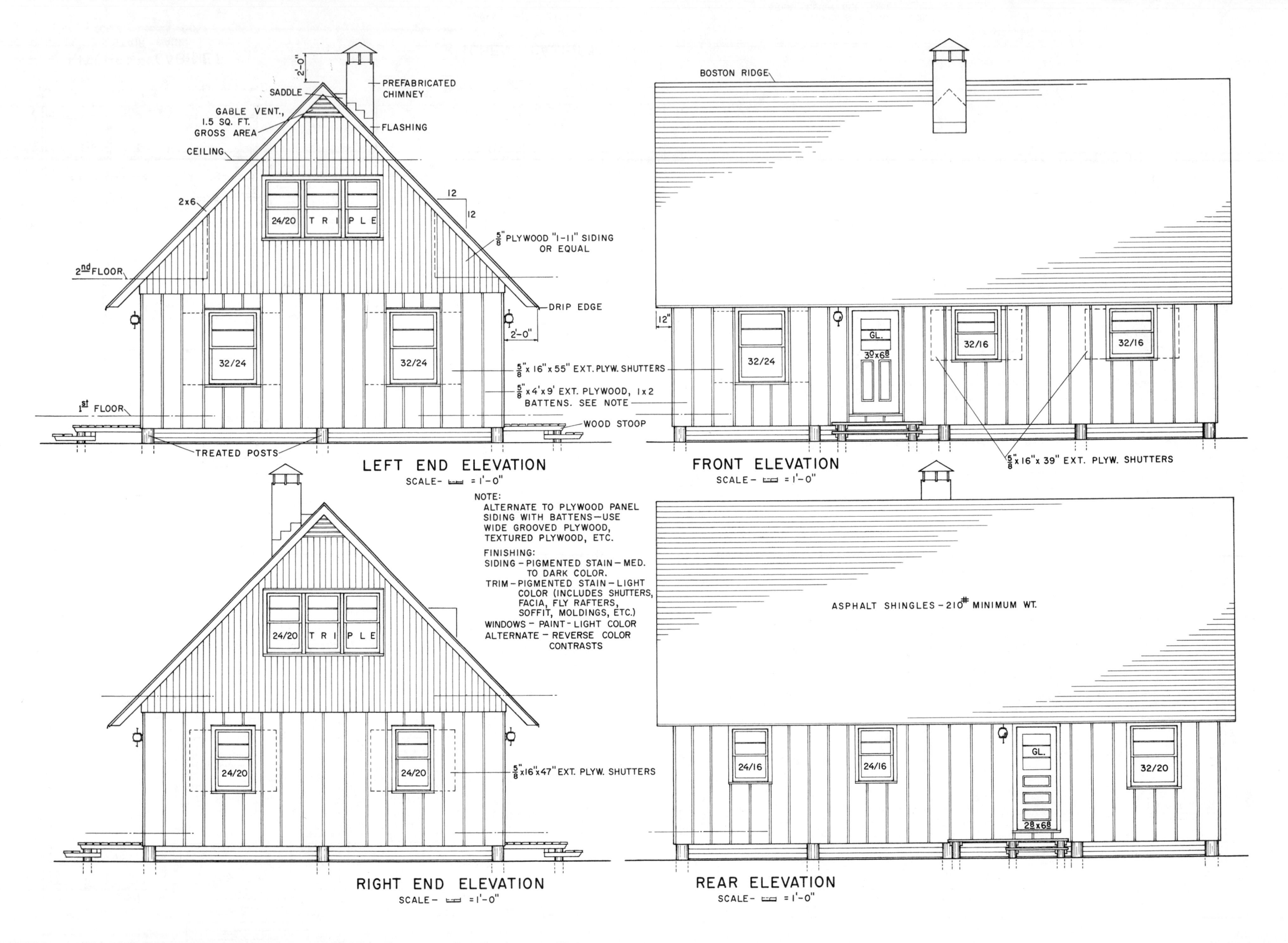

PREFABRICATED CHIMNEY

2'-0"

SADDLE

FLASHING

GABLE VENT,
1.5 SQ. FT.
GROSS AREA

CEILING

2x6

24/20 T R I P L E

5/8" PLYWOOD "I-11" SIDING OR EQUAL

2nd FLOOR

12
12

DRIP EDGE

2'-0"

32/24   32/24

5/8" x 16" x 55" EXT. PLYW. SHUTTERS

5/8" x 4' x 9' EXT. PLYWOOD, 1 x 2 BATTENS. SEE NOTE

1st FLOOR

WOOD STOOP

TREATED POSTS

LEFT END ELEVATION
SCALE- = 1'-0"

BOSTON RIDGE

12

32/24   GL. 30x68   32/16   32/16

5/8" x 16" x 39" EXT. PLYW. SHUTTERS

FRONT ELEVATION
SCALE- = 1'-0"

NOTE:
ALTERNATE TO PLYWOOD PANEL
SIDING WITH BATTENS—USE
WIDE GROOVED PLYWOOD,
TEXTURED PLYWOOD, ETC.

FINISHING:
SIDING—PIGMENTED STAIN—MED.
TO DARK COLOR.
TRIM—PIGMENTED STAIN—LIGHT
COLOR (INCLUDES SHUTTERS,
FACIA, FLY RAFTERS,
SOFFIT, MOLDINGS, ETC.)
WINDOWS—PAINT—LIGHT COLOR
ALTERNATE—REVERSE COLOR
CONTRASTS

24/20 T R I P L E

24/20   24/20

5/8" x 16" x 47" EXT. PLYW. SHUTTERS

RIGHT END ELEVATION
SCALE- = 1'-0"

ASPHALT SHINGLES—210# MINIMUM WT.

24/16   24/16   GL.   32/20
28x68

REAR ELEVATION
SCALE- = 1'-0"

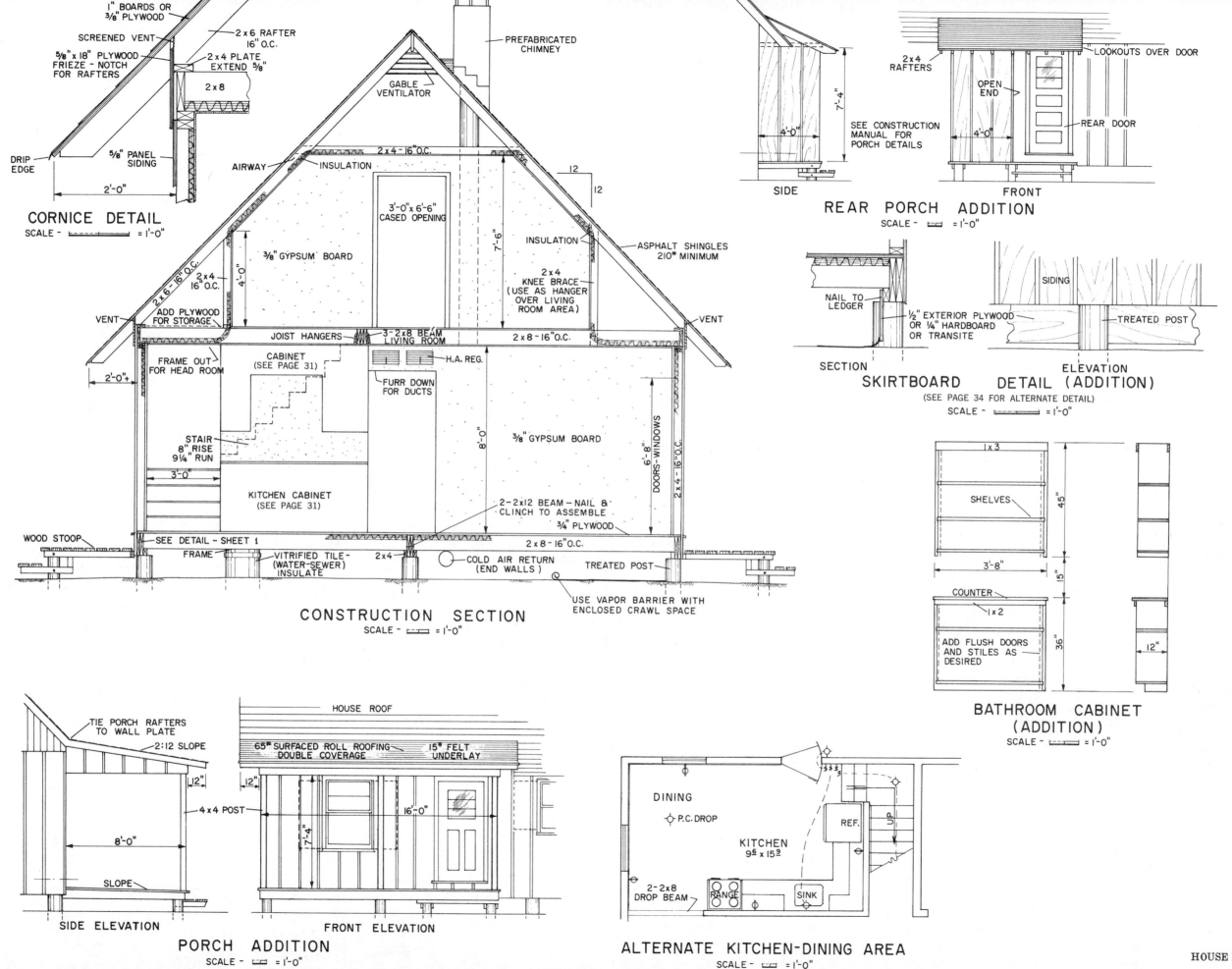

CORNICE DETAIL

CONSTRUCTION SECTION

REAR PORCH ADDITION

SKIRTBOARD DETAIL (ADDITION)

BATHROOM CABINET (ADDITION)

PORCH ADDITION

ALTERNATE KITCHEN-DINING AREA

HOUSE PLAN 2 33

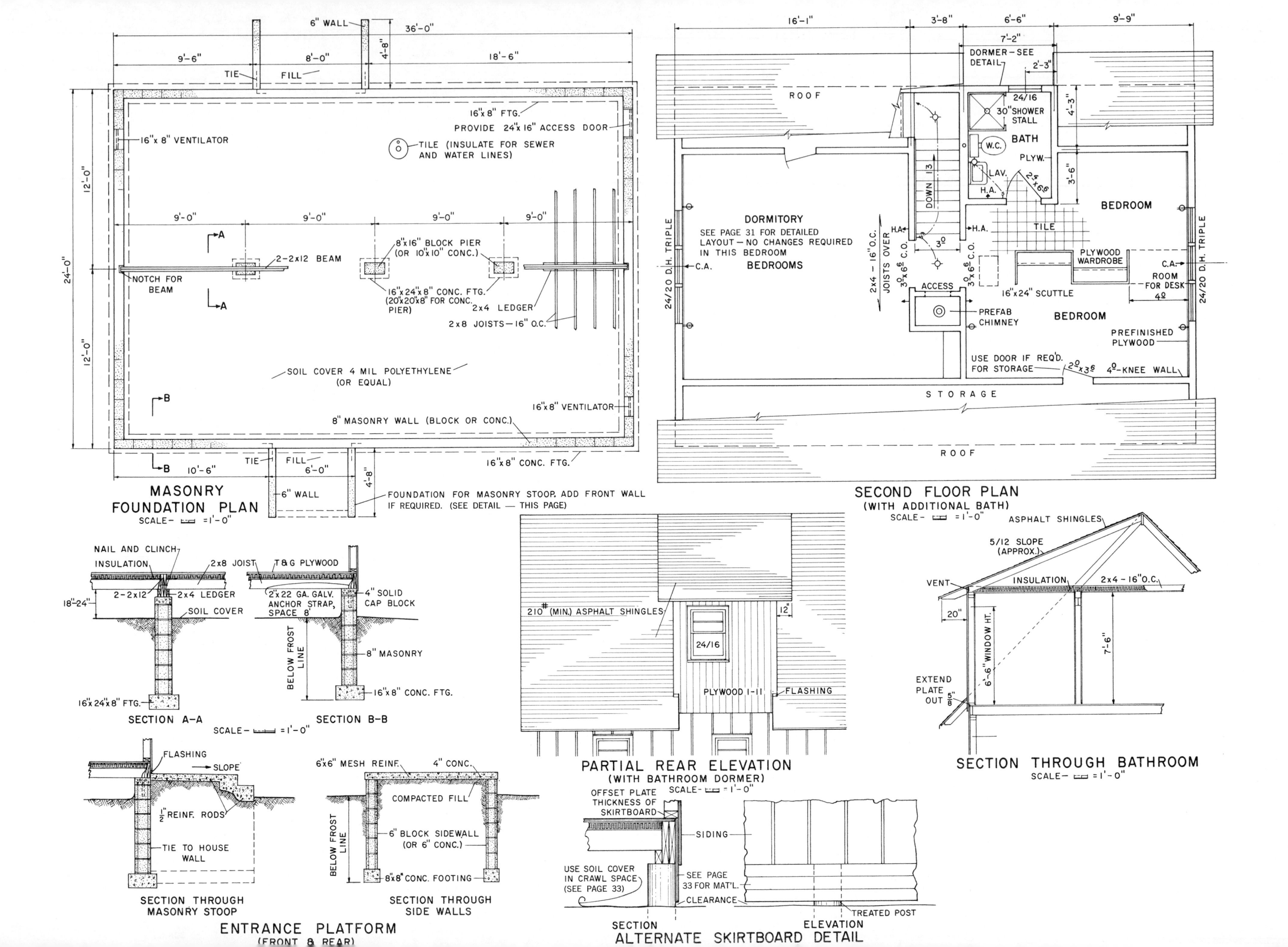

MASONRY FOUNDATION PLAN
SCALE— ▭▭ =1'-0"

6" WALL
36'-0"
9'-6" 8'-0" 18'-6"
4'-8"
TIE FILL
16"x 8" FTG.
PROVIDE 24"x 16" ACCESS DOOR
16"x 8" VENTILATOR
TILE (INSULATE FOR SEWER AND WATER LINES)
12'-0"
24'-0"
9'-0" 9'-0" 9'-0" 9'-0"
2-2x12 BEAM
NOTCH FOR BEAM
8"x16" BLOCK PIER (OR 10"x10" CONC.)
16"x24"x8" CONC. FTG. (20"x20"x8" FOR CONC. PIER)
2x4 LEDGER
2x8 JOISTS—16" O.C.
SOIL COVER 4 MIL POLYETHYLENE (OR EQUAL)
12'-0"
16"x 8" VENTILATOR
8" MASONRY WALL (BLOCK OR CONC.)
16"x 8" CONC. FTG.
10'-6"
TIE FILL
6'-0"
4'-8"
6" WALL
FOUNDATION FOR MASONRY STOOP. ADD FRONT WALL IF REQUIRED. (SEE DETAIL — THIS PAGE)

SECOND FLOOR PLAN
(WITH ADDITIONAL BATH)
SCALE— ▭▭ =1'-0"

16'-1" 3'-8" 6'-6" 9'-9"
7'-2"
DORMER—SEE DETAIL
2'-3"
ROOF
24/16
30"SHOWER STALL
4'-3"
W.C.
BATH
PLYW.
LAV.
H.A.
3'-6"
BEDROOM
DORMITORY
SEE PAGE 31 FOR DETAILED LAYOUT — NO CHANGES REQUIRED IN THIS BEDROOM
DOWN 13
2x4 – 16" O.C. JOISTS OVER
3"x6" C.O.
TILE
3"x6" C.O.
PLYWOOD WARDROBE
C.A. ROOM FOR DESK
BEDROOMS
C.A.
H.A.
ACCESS
16"x24" SCUTTLE
PREFAB CHIMNEY
BEDROOM
PREFINISHED PLYWOOD
USE DOOR IF REQ'D. FOR STORAGE
KNEE WALL
STORAGE
ROOF
24/20 D.H. TRIPLE
24/20 D.H. TRIPLE

SECTION A-A
NAIL AND CLINCH
INSULATION
2x8 JOIST
T & G PLYWOOD
2-2x12
2x4 LEDGER
18"-24"
SOIL COVER
16"x24"x8" FTG.

SECTION B-B
SCALE— ▭▭ =1'-0"
2"x 22 GA. GALV. ANCHOR STRAP, SPACE 8'
4" SOLID CAP BLOCK
BELOW FROST LINE
8" MASONRY
16"x 8" CONC. FTG.

PARTIAL REAR ELEVATION
(WITH BATHROOM DORMER)
SCALE— ▭▭ =1'-0"
210# (MIN.) ASPHALT SHINGLES
24/16
12
PLYWOOD 1-11
FLASHING

SECTION THROUGH BATHROOM
SCALE— ▭▭ =1'-0"
ASPHALT SHINGLES
5/12 SLOPE (APPROX.)
VENT
INSULATION
2x4 – 16" O.C.
20"
6'-6" WINDOW HT.
7'-6"
EXTEND PLATE OUT 5"

ENTRANCE PLATFORM
(FRONT & REAR)

SECTION THROUGH MASONRY STOOP
FLASHING
SLOPE
½" REINF. RODS
TIE TO HOUSE WALL

SECTION THROUGH SIDE WALLS
6"x6" MESH REINF.
4" CONC.
COMPACTED FILL
BELOW FROST LINE
6" BLOCK SIDEWALL (OR 6" CONC.)
8"x8" CONC. FOOTING

ALTERNATE SKIRTBOARD DETAIL
OFFSET PLATE THICKNESS OF SKIRTBOARD
SIDING
USE SOIL COVER IN CRAWL SPACE (SEE PAGE 33)
SEE PAGE 33 FOR MAT'L.
CLEARANCE
SECTION
ELEVATION
TREATED POST

SPECIFICATIONS

for

FIVE BEDROOM WOOD HOUSE

Plan No. 2

(One-and-one-half-story house, 24' -0" x 36' -0" in size, constructed over a crawl space)

All work related to construction of this house shall be done in a first-class manner. Details not included in specifications or plans shall comply with accepted practices for wood-frame construction.

Excavation - Grading

Sod, growing plants, shrubs, stumps, and trees shall be removed and ground smoothed in building area and 2 feet outside of building line. Excavate footings to required depth and size shown in plans. No forms are required if soil is stable. Locate excavated soil conveniently for backfilling around treated wood posts.

Concrete Work

Footings shall be poured over undisturbed soil in excavations to indicated thickness and size as shown on plan. Top surface to be level.

Mix concrete to a 1:2-1/2:3-1/2 mix. If premixed concrete is available, use 5-bag mix.

Treated Wood Posts

Pressure-treated wood posts with 7-inch minimum top diameter shall be treated to conform to Federal Specification TT-W-571.

Carpentry

General

This branch of the work comprises all rough and finish carpentry necessary to complete the house, as shown on the plans and as specified. This includes layout, cutting and fitting framing, and other carpentry items. Any phase which is necessary for the completion of the house and not specifically covered in the plans or specifications shall be included as required.

Wood Framing

Dimension material for studs to be Standard (third grade); and for floor joists and framing, ceiling joists, rafters, beams and trusses construction (second grade) in Douglas-fir, southern pine, or equivalent,[1] unless otherwise noted on the plans. All floor and ceiling joists, studs, and rafters shall be spaced 16 inches on center. Moisture content of framing lumber not to exceed 19 percent.

Subfloor

The subfloor shall be plywood to serve as a floor alone or as a base for resilient tile and shall consist of 3/4-inch C-C plugged Exterior grade, touch-sanded, and with matched edges in Douglas-fir, southern pine, or equivalent. When matched-edge plywood is not obtainable, square-edged plywood in the same grade and thickness can be substituted but 2- by 4-inch blocking shall be used for all longitudinal joints. Toenail 2- by 4-inch blocks flatwise in each joist space.

Roof Sheathing

Roof sheathing shall be 3/8-inch Douglas-fir or southern pine plywood or equal in Standard sheathing grade or nominal 1- by 6- or 1- by 8-inch boards in No. 3 Douglas-fir, southern pine, or equivalent. Boards shall be square edge, shiplap, or dressed and matched, and laid up tight at a moisture content of not more than 15 percent.

---

[1] See wall framing grades and span tables for allowable spans of other species (Federal Housing Administration tables) and American Lumber Standards for sizes and other information.

Insulation

Floors and walls of the first floor, walls and ceiling of the second floor, and the second floor area outside of the knee walls to be insulated with standard batt- or blanket-type flexible insulation with vapor barrier placed toward the inside of the building. Unless otherwise specified, minimum insulation thicknesses in the central and northern tiers of states shall be: Ceiling, 3 inches; wall and floor, 2 inches. Vapor barrier shall be placed toward the inside of the building. Vapor barrier to have a maximum perm value of 0.30.

Siding

Siding shall be 5/8-inch by 4-foot-wide plywood panel siding in Texture 1-11 (4-in. grooves) or equal at gable ends. Remaining walls shall be covered with 5/8-inch by 4- by 9-foot panel siding in wide-groove pattern or rough-surfaced plywood siding with 1- by 2-inch battens spaced 16 inches on center. Plywood shall be nailed to each stud, including vertical joints, and at the top and bottom with eightpenny galvanized siding nails spaced 7 to 8 inches apart. The edges of the sheets shall be brush-coated with a water-repellent preservative before installing.

Exterior Millwork

(a) Exterior finish.--Exterior trim and similar materials shall be No. 2 ponderosa pine or equivalent suitable for staining.

(b) Window frames and sash.--Complete double-hung windows shall be used with upper sash cut to two horizontal lights, glazed with single-strength glass. Units to be treated with water-repellent preservative as outlined in Commercial Standard CS 190-64. Sash to be furnished fully balanced and fitted and with outside casing in place. Set in openings, plumb, and square. Screens shall be furnished, and storms when required.

(c) Exterior door frames and doors.--Exterior door frames shall have 1-3/8-inch rabbeted jambs and 1-5/8-inch oak sill or softwood sill with metal edge, all assembled. Set in openings, plumb, and square.

Exterior doors to be standard 1-3/4-inch with solid stiles and rails; panel type with glazed openings as shown on plans. Screen doors shall be furnished, or combinations when required.

(d) Screens.--Galvanized fly screen shall be used for inlet and outlet ventilators located in the plywood frieze board, as shown on plans.

Interior Millwork

(a) Interior door frames and doors.--Interior door frames and cased openings shall be nominal 1-inch ponderosa pine or equal in "D" Select. Stops shall be installed only where doors are specified.

Interior doors shall be 1-3/8 inches thick, five-cross-panel style with solid stiles and rails.

(b) Interior trim.--Interior trim shall be ponderosa pine or equal in "D" Select in ranch pattern in the following sizes:

Casings	-- 11/16 by 2-1/4 inches
Stops	7/16 by 1-3/8 inches or wider
Base	7/16 by 2-1/4 inches
Base shoe	-- 1/2 by 3/4 inch (when required)

Note: (1) Casing to be used at bottom of windows in place of stool and apron.
(2) Base shoe used along free-standing plywood wardrobes.

(c) Walls and ceilings.--All ceilings shall be finished with 3/8-inch gypsum board with recessed edges and with the length applied across the ceiling joists. End joints shall be staggered at least 16 inches. Walls shall be finished with 3/8-inch gypsum board with recessed edges and applied vertically. Application and joint treatment shall follow accepted practices. Install prefinished plywood in wall areas shown on plans.

Walls of tub recess shall be covered with plastic-finished hardboard panels over gypsum board. Install with mastic in accordance with manufacturer's directions. Inside corners, edges, and tub edges shall be finished with plastic moldings.

(d) Flooring.--Finish flooring throughout shall be 1/8-inch-thick asphalt tile in 9- by 9-inch size, "B" quality. Combination plywood subfloor shall be cleaned, nails driven flush, and joints sanded smooth where required. Tile shall be applied in accordance with manufacturer's recommendations. Rubber baseboard shall be furnished and installed in the bathroom, wood base in the remainder of the house.

(e) Hardware.--Furnish and install all rough and finish hardware complete as needed for perfect operation. Locks shall be furnished for all outside doors. Outside doors to be hung with three 4- by 4-inch loose-pin butt hinges and inside doors with two 3-1/2- by 3-1/2-inch loose-pin butt hinges. Bathroom five-cross-panel door shall be furnished with standard bathroom lock set. Standard screen door latches, hinges, and door closers shall be furnished and installed. Furnish and install semiconcealed cabinet hinges, pulls, and catches where required for cabinet or closet doors. All finish hardware to be finished in dull brass.

Sheet Metal Work and Roofing

Sheet Metal

Sheet metal flashing, when required for the prefabricated chimney and vent stack, shall be 28-gage galvanized iron or painted terneplate.

Roofing

Roofing shall be a minimum of 210-pound square-tab 12- by 36-inch asphalt shingles. A minimum of four 7/8-inch galvanized roofing nails shall be used for each 12- by 36-inch shingle strip. Any defects or leaks shall be corrected.

Electrical Work

The work shall include all materials and labor necessary to make the systems complete as shown on the plans. All work and materials shall comply with local requirements or those of the National Electrical Code. All wiring shall be concealed and carried in BX or other approved conduit to each outlet, switch, fixture, and appliance or electrical equipment such as furnace, hot water heater, and range when required, and as shown on the plan. Panel shall be 100 amp. capacity with overload cutout. Wall fixtures to consist of the following:

Two outside wall fixtures with crystal glass.
Two overhead (wall) fixtures, for kitchen and bath.

Heating

Heater and prefabricated chimney shall be installed as shown on the plans with supply ducts located in furred-down ceiling of hall. Heater shall be for LP or natural gas with a 100,000 minimum B.t.u. input or as required by design for each specific area. Cold air return at furnace base and from each corner of the house. Cold air duct shall consist of 1/8-inch transite-covered joist spaces along outside walls and connection to 10-inch-diameter galvanized ducts to heater.

Plumbing

All plumbing shall be installed in accordance with local or National plumbing codes. Hot- and cold-water connections shall be furnished to all fixtures as required. Sewer and water and gas lines (when required) shall extend to building line with water shutoff valve. Framed and insulated box shall be used to protect water and sewer lines from freezing in crawl space where required. Cover with 1/8-inch transite or equal and insulate with 3 inches of fiberglass or styrofoam when required. Use a 16- by 16-inch vitrified tile or equal below groundline.

Furnish and install the following fixtures:
One kitchen sink--21 by 15 inches, self rim, steel, white, with fixtures.
One bathtub--5 foot, cast iron, white, left-hand drain complete with shower rod and shower head, with fixtures.
One water closet--Reverse trap, white, with seat, fixtures, and shutoff valve.
One lavatory--19 by 17 inches, steel, white, and with fixtures and shutoff valve.
One hot water heater--50-gallon (minimum), gas or electric.
Washing machine connection with hot and cold water and drain.

Painting and Finishing

Exterior

Exterior plywood panel siding, facia, shutters, and soffit areas shall be stained with pigmented stain as required. Use light gray, yellow, or another light color stain for the trim and shutters and a darker stain (brown, olive, gray, etc.) for the panel siding or a reverse color selection as desired by owner. (Optional shutters to be stained on faces and edges.)

Window and door frames, window sash, screen doors, and similar millwork shall be painted a light color, or as owners request. Types of paint and procedures to comply with recommended practices and materials.

Interior

All woodwork shall be painted in semigloss. Walls and ceilings finished in latex flat, except bathroom, which shall be finished in semigloss.

Termite Protection

Termite protection shall be provided in termite areas by means of soil treatment or termite shields or both, as required by local practices and regulations.

Concrete Blocks

Concrete blocks (used as an alternate to foundation of treated wood posts) shall comply with ASTM C-90, Grade U-II, for standard size and quality.

Concrete blocks shall be laid over concrete footings, as shown on the foundation plan. Footings shall be level and laid out to conform to the building line. Blocks shall be laid up with 3/8-inch-thick mortar joints, tooling the joints on all exposed exterior surfaces. Anchor straps, when used, shall be embedded to a depth of at least 12 inches.

BILL OF MATERIAL FOR RURAL HOME

Plan No. 2

The following material is required for construction of the rural home detailed in Plan No. 2; quality of material and treatments are given in the specifications.

Foundation

The foundation of treated posts set on concrete footings requires:

    1-1/4 cubic yards concrete
    15 treated foundation posts, 5 feet long, with 7-inch minimum
        top diameter

Floor Framing

Floor framing consisting of floor joists supported on ledgers nailed to the anchored floor beams requires:

    4 -- 2 x 12's   12 feet long
    12 -- 2 x 12's   18 feet long
    56 -- 2 x 8's   12 feet long
    12 -- 2 x 4's   12 feet long
    45 lineal feet 22-gage x 2-inch galvanized anchor strap

Floor

Requirements of floor tile and subfloor are:

    54 -- 4- x 8-foot sheets of 3/4-inch tongued-and-grooved
            plywood
    2,800 -- 9- x 9-inch asphalt tile (10 pct. waste) (with adhesive)

Wall and Partition Framing

Framing material for walls and partitions includes:

    153 -- 2 x 4's   8 feet long
    118 -- 2 x 4's   12 feet long
     16 -- 2 x 6's   12 feet long

Ceiling and Roof Framing

Materials for rafters, joists, and a flush beam over the living area are:

    28 -- 2 x 4's   10 feet long
     6 -- 2 x 4's   12 feet long
    60 -- 2 x 6's   20 feet long
    22 -- 2 x 8's   10 feet long
    10 -- 2 x 8's   12 feet long
    26 -- 2 x 8's   14 feet long
     3 -- 2 x 8's   18 feet long
     3 -- 1 x 8's   12 feet long
    24 -- Joist hangers for 2 x 8's

Roof

Roofing and sheathing requirements are:

    48 -- 4- x 8-foot sheets of 3/8-inch plywood sheathing
            grade (CD)
    15 squares -- 210-pound asphalt shingles

Siding

The following siding or equivalent alternates are required:

    32 -- 4- x 9-foot sheets 5/8-inch plywood, exterior grade
            (textured surface)
    94 -- 1 x 2 battens, 9 feet long
    10 -- 4- x 9-foot sheets rough-textured, 5/8-inch Texture
            1-11 or equal

Windows

All windows are double-hung and purchased treated and complete with screens, and storms when required. Quantity of each size is:

    3 -- 32/24
    1 -- 32/20
    2 -- 32/16
    2 -- 24/20
    2 -- 24/16
    2 -- triple units 24/20 (top window, 2 light horizontal)

Exterior Doors

Doors are 1-3/4 inches thick, glazed; and frame, trim, and hardware are required for each. Screen doors shall be furnished, or combinations when required. Sizes are:

    Front -- 3 feet 0 inches wide and 6 feet 8 inches high
    Rear -- 2 feet 8 inches wide and 6 feet 8 inches high

Insulation

Blanket insulation with aluminum foil vapor barrier on one side is required for ceiling, walls, and floor.

    2,100 square feet -- 2 inches thick, 16 inches wide
    1,300 square feet -- 3 inches thick, 16 inches wide

Roof Ventilators

Requirements for ventilating the roof are:

    1 pair -- Peak-type outlet vents
    18 square feet -- Screen for inlet vent slots

Exterior Trim

Exterior trim including frieze board requires:

    4 -- 4- x 8-foot sheets 5/8-inch plywood, exterior grade,
            textured surface

Interior Wall and Ceiling Finish

Gypsum board is used for all interior finish except two accent walls in living-dining area, second floor bedroom end walls, and bathroom, except for plastic-coated hardboard above the bathtub. Requirements are:

    86 -- 4- x 8-foot sheets of 3/8-inch gypsum board
    3 -- 4- x 8-foot sheets of coated hardboard with corner
            and edge moldings
    20 -- 4- x 8-foot sheets of 1/4-inch prefinished plywood
            paneling
    3 -- 250-foot rolls of joint tape
    6 -- 25-pound bags of joint compound

Stairs

Material required for stairs is:

    2 -- 1 x 10's   14-foot-long stringers
    2 -- 2 x 4's   10 feet long
    2 -- 2 x 12's   14 feet long
    3 -- 1 x 8's   10 feet long
    11 -- Treads 5/4 x 10 x 3 feet 0 inches
    16 board feet of 1 x 4 fir flooring (platform)

Interior Doors

Interior door requirements are:

        1 set -- 2-foot 6-inch x 6-foot 8-inch hollow-core door
                      with jambs, stops, and hardware
        3 sets -- Jambs for 2-foot, 8-inch x 6-foot 8-inch doors
        2 -- 4- x 8-foot sheets 1/2-inch plywood, interior AC

Interior Trim

Trim for windows, doors, and base includes:

        360 feet -- 9/16- x 2-1/8-inch casing
        380 feet -- 1/2- x 3-inch base

Cabinets

Material requirements for wood-frame and plywood cabinets are:

        8 -- 4- x 8-foot sheets 3/4-inch plywood, interior AC
        8 -- 4- x 8-foot sheets 3/8-inch plywood, interior AC
        4 -- 1 x 3's   12 feet long
        3 -- 1 x 4's   8 feet long
        1 -- 1 x 6   14 feet long
        2 -- 2 x 2's   12 feet long
        1 pair -- Cabinet door hinges
        1 -- Wooden door pull
        1 -- Friction door catch

Wardrobes

Wardrobes consisting of closet poles with a shelf over require:

        5 -- 4- x 8-foot sheets 3/4-inch plywood, interior AA
        4 -- 4- x 8-foot sheets 1/2-inch plywood, interior AA
        4 -- Closet poles, 1-5/16-inch diameter x 8 feet long
        2 -- 1 x 2's, 8 feet long
        7 pair -- Pole sockets for 1-5/16-inch poles

Front Stoop

The front stoop, consisting of planks laid across 2 x 4 framing supported by treated posts, has the following material requirements:

        2 -- Treated posts, 5 feet long with 6-inch minimum top
                  diameter
        3 -- 2 x 4's   8 feet long
        10 -- 2 x 6's   6 feet long
        4 -- 1/2-inch galvanized carriage bolts, 8 inches long

Rear Stoop

Material requirements for the rear stoop are:

        3 -- Treated posts, 5 feet long, with 6-inch minimum top
                  diameter
        4 -- 2 x 4's   8 feet long
        9 -- 2 x 6's   8 feet long
        6 -- 1/2-inch galvanized carriage bolts, 8 inches long

Nails

        58 pounds -- Eightpenny common
        32 pounds -- Sixteenpenny common
        3 pounds -- Twentypenny common
        4 pounds -- Tenpenny common, galvanized
        2 pounds -- Sixteenpenny common, galvanized
        3 pounds -- Fourpenny finish
        20 pounds -- Eightpenny finish
        20 pounds -- 3/4-inch galvanized roofing
        30 pounds -- Fourpenny cooler

Paint and Finish

Quantities required for one coat of paint inside and one coat of stain outside are:

        12 gallons -- Walls and ceiling (interior)
        2 gallons -- Interior trim
        7 gallons -- Exterior siding and trim (Use different body and
                      trim color, as desired)

Electrical

In addition to rough wiring and 100-amp. service, the following items are required:

        23 -- Duplex outlets
        2 -- Wall-mounted interior lights
        2 -- Wall-mounted exterior lights
        3 -- Ceiling lights
        5 -- Switches, single pole
        2 -- Switches, 3-way

Heating

The heating system requires a 100,000 B.t.u. gas furnace with 9 registers, 6 cold-air returns, duct, and a prefab chimney.

Plumbing

Plumbing must be provided for the following required fixtures:

    1 -- 5-foot bathtub
    1 -- Water closet
    1 -- Lavatory
    1 -- Kitchen sink
    1 -- 50-gallon water heater
    1 -- 16- x 16- x 24-inch vitrified tile or equal (at sewer and
         water entrance)

ALTERNATES AND OPTIONS

Floor (Square-Edge Plywood)

When tongued-and-grooved plywood is not available, square-edge plywood with all edges blocked can be used. Material requirements for flooring and subfloor are:

       54 -- 4- x 8-foot sheets 3/4-inch plywood
       24 -- 2 x 4's, 12 feet long
    2,800 -- 9- x 9-inch asphalt tile (10 pct. waste) (with adhesive)

Foundation (Concrete-Block)

The foundation of concrete blocks on poured concrete footings, plus masonry front and rear stoops, requires: (Note: Based on 4-ft. foundation depth.)

      7 cubic yards of concrete (footings)
    546 -- 8- x 8- x 16-inch concrete blocks
     91 -- 4- x 8- x 16-inch concrete solid-cap blocks
     72 -- 8- x 6- x 16-inch concrete blocks
     24 -- 8- x 6- x 8-inch concrete blocks (stoop)
     18 sacks prepared mortar
      2 cubic yards mason's sand
     60 square feet 6- x 6-inch mesh reinforcing (stoops)
      4 -- 1/2-inch reinforcing rods, 5 feet long (step)
      4 -- 1/2-inch reinforcing rods, 7 feet long (step)

900 square feet 4-mil polyethylene film (soil cover)
  2 -- 8- x 16-inch foundation vents
  1 -- 16- x 16-inch (minimum) access door and frame

Floor Framing (For Concrete-Block Foundation)

     4 -- 2 x 12's   18 feet long
    62 -- 2 x 8's   12 feet long
     4 -- 2 x 4's   4 feet long
    50 lineal feet 22-gage x 2-inch anchor strap

Second-Floor Bathroom

A second bathroom can be added in a second-floor dormer. Materials required for constructing the dormer and providing bathroom fixtures are: (Note: As a less costly addition, a lavatory could be installed in each upstairs bedroom.)

    29 -- 2 x 4's   8 feet long
    14 -- 2 x 4's   16 feet long
    12 -- 2 x 6's   8 feet long
     4 -- 4- x 8-foot sheets of rough-textured 5/8-inch Texture 1-11
     7 -- 4- x 8-foot sheets of 1/4-inch prefinished plywood
     2 -- 4- x 8-foot sheets of 3/8-inch gypsum board
    40 -- 9- x 9-inch asphalt tile (with adhesive)
     1 -- 24/16 treated double-hung window (storm and screen)
     1 set -- 2-foot 4-inch x 6-foot 6-inch hollow-core door with
              jambs, stops, and hardware
     1 -- wall-mounted interior light
     1 -- switch
     1 -- hot-air register with duct
     1 -- 30- x 30-inch shower stall
     1 -- lavatory
     1 -- water closet

Shutters (Optional)

Material required for shutters is:

    4 -- 4 x 8 sheets 5/8-inch plywood, exterior grade, textured
         surface.

3

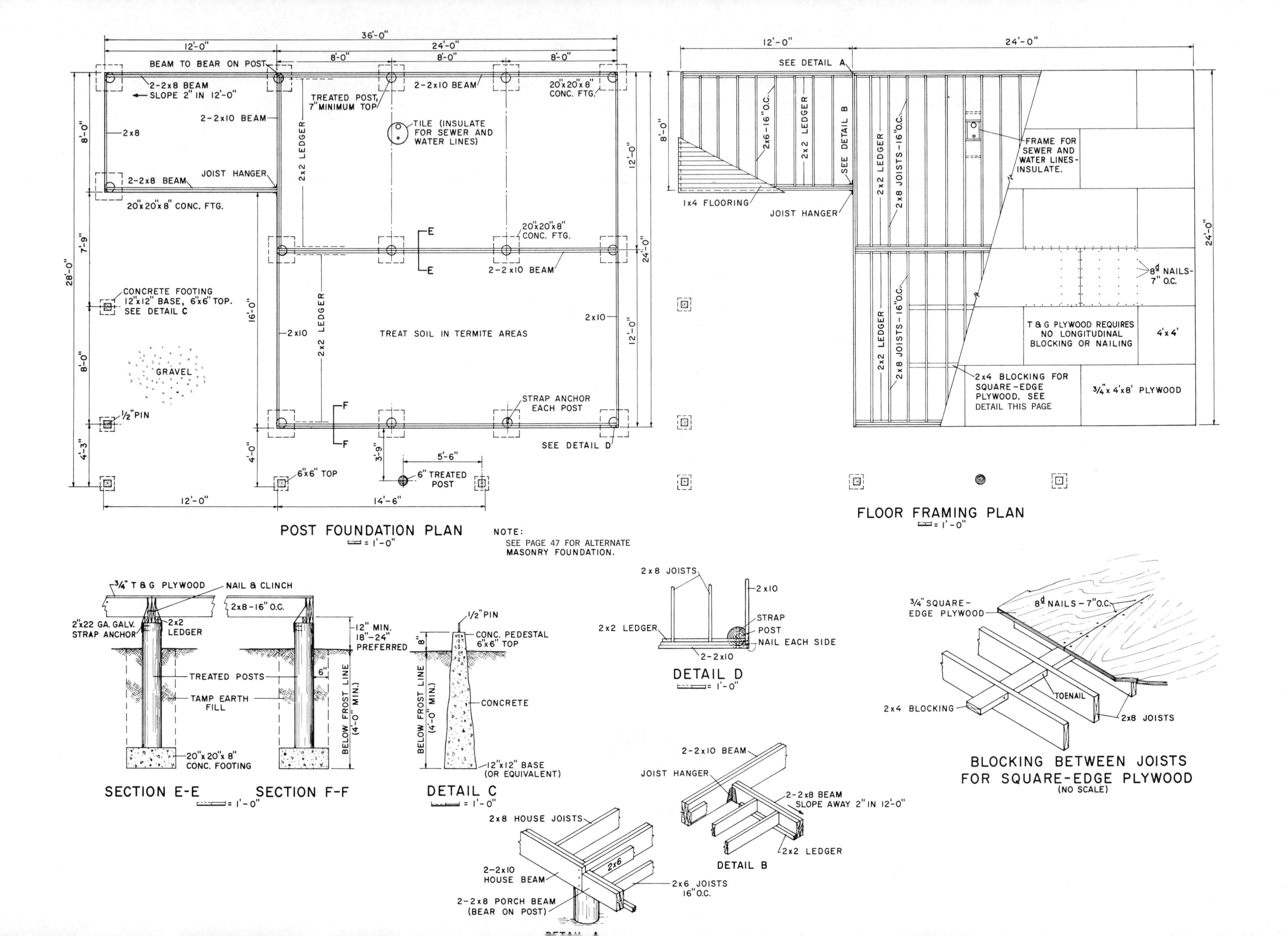

POST FOUNDATION PLAN

1/2" = 1'-0"

NOTE:
SEE PAGE 47 FOR ALTERNATE MASONRY FOUNDATION.

FLOOR FRAMING PLAN

1/2" = 1'-0"

SECTION E-E   SECTION F-F

1/2" = 1'-0"

DETAIL C

1/2" = 1'-0"

DETAIL D

1/2" = 1'-0"

BLOCKING BETWEEN JOISTS FOR SQUARE-EDGE PLYWOOD
(NO SCALE)

DETAIL B

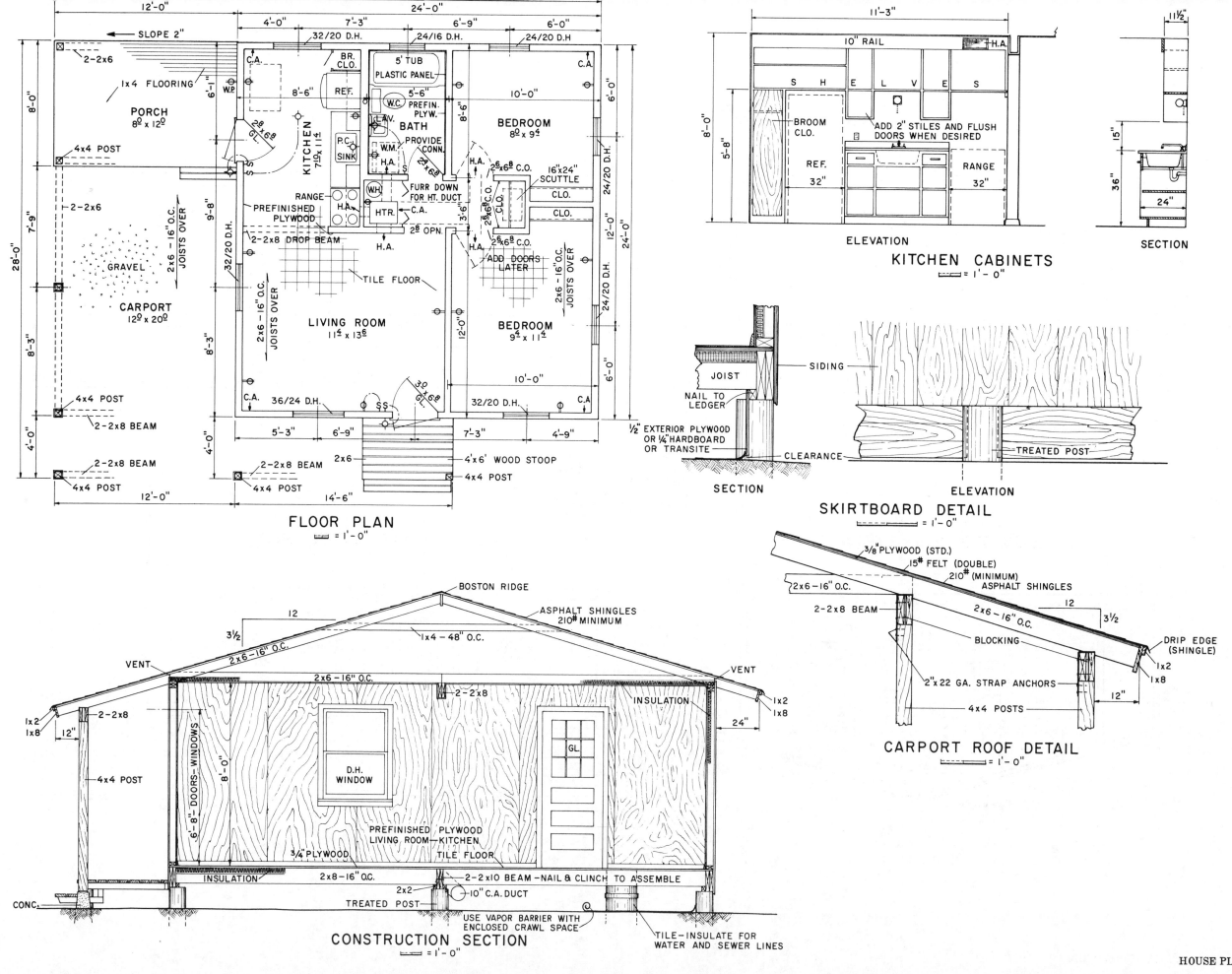

FLOOR PLAN
⌐⊐ = 1'-0"

PORCH 8⁰ x 12⁰

SLOPE 2"
2-2x6
1x4 FLOORING
4x4 POST
2-2x6
GRAVEL
CARPORT 12⁰ x 20⁰
4x4 POST
2-2x8 BEAM
2-2x8 BEAM
4x4 POST

2x6 - 16" O.C. JOISTS OVER

12'-0"
24'-0"
4'-0"
7'-3"
6'-9"
6'-0"
28'-0"
8'-0"
7'-9"
8'-3"
4'-0"

32/20 D.H.
24/16 D.H.
24/20 D.H.

BR. CLO.
C.A.
5' TUB PLASTIC PANEL
C.A.

W.P.
8'-6"
5'-6"
W.C.
PREFIN. PLYW.
10'-0"
BEDROOM 8⁰ x 9⁴

KITCHEN 7¹⁰ x 11⁴
REF.
BATH
LAV.
PROVIDE CONN.
16"x24" SCUTTLE
CLO.

P.C.
SINK
W.M.
H.A.
2⁶x6⁸ C.O.
CLO.

RANGE
WH
FURR DOWN FOR HT. DUCT
CLO.

PREFINISHED PLYWOOD
H.A.
HTR.
C.A.
2⁸ OPN.
ADD DOORS LATER
2⁶x6⁸ C.O.

2-2x8 DROP BEAM
H.A.
2⁶x6⁸ C.O.

LIVING ROOM 11⁴ x 13⁶
TILE FLOOR
BEDROOM 9⁴ x 11⁴

C.A.
36/24 D.H.
32/20 D.H.
C.A

5'-3"
6'-9"
7'-3"
4'-9"

2x6 WOOD STOOP
4'x6' WOOD STOOP
4x4 POST
2-2x8 BEAM
4x4 POST
14'-6"

KITCHEN CABINETS
⌐⊐ = 1'- 0"

11'-3"
10" RAIL
H.A.
S H E L V E S
8'-0"
5'-8"
BROOM CLO.
ADD 2" STILES AND FLUSH DOORS WHEN DESIRED
REF. 32
RANGE 32

ELEVATION

11½
15"
3.6"
24"

SECTION

SKIRTBOARD DETAIL
⌐⊐ = 1'- 0"

JOIST
SIDING
NAIL TO LEDGER
½" EXTERIOR PLYWOOD OR ¼"HARDBOARD OR TRANSITE
CLEARANCE
TREATED POST

SECTION   **ELEVATION**

CARPORT ROOF DETAIL
⌐⊐ = 1'- 0"

3/8"PLYWOOD (STD.)
15# FELT (DOUBLE)
210# (MINIMUM) ASPHALT SHINGLES
2x6-16" O.C.
2-2x8 BEAM
2x6 - 16" O.C.
12
3½
BLOCKING
DRIP EDGE (SHINGLE)
1x2
1x8
2"x 22 GA. STRAP ANCHORS
4x4 POSTS
12"

CONSTRUCTION SECTION
⌐⊐ = 1'- 0"

BOSTON RIDGE
ASPHALT SHINGLES 210#MINIMUM
1x4 - 48" O.C.
12
3½
2x6-16" O.C.
2x6-16" O.C.
2-2x8
VENT
VENT
INSULATION
24"
1x2
1x8
2-2x8
1x2
1x8
4x4 POST
12"
8'-0"
6'-8" DOORS-WINDOWS
D.H. WINDOW
GL.
PREFINISHED PLYWOOD LIVING ROOM-KITCHEN
¾"PLYWOOD
TILE FLOOR
INSULATION
2x8-16" O.C.
2x2
2-2x10 BEAM - NAIL & CLINCH TO ASSEMBLE
10" C.A. DUCT
CONC.
TREATED POST
USE VAPOR BARRIER WITH ENCLOSED CRAWL SPACE
TILE-INSULATE FOR WATER AND SEWER LINES

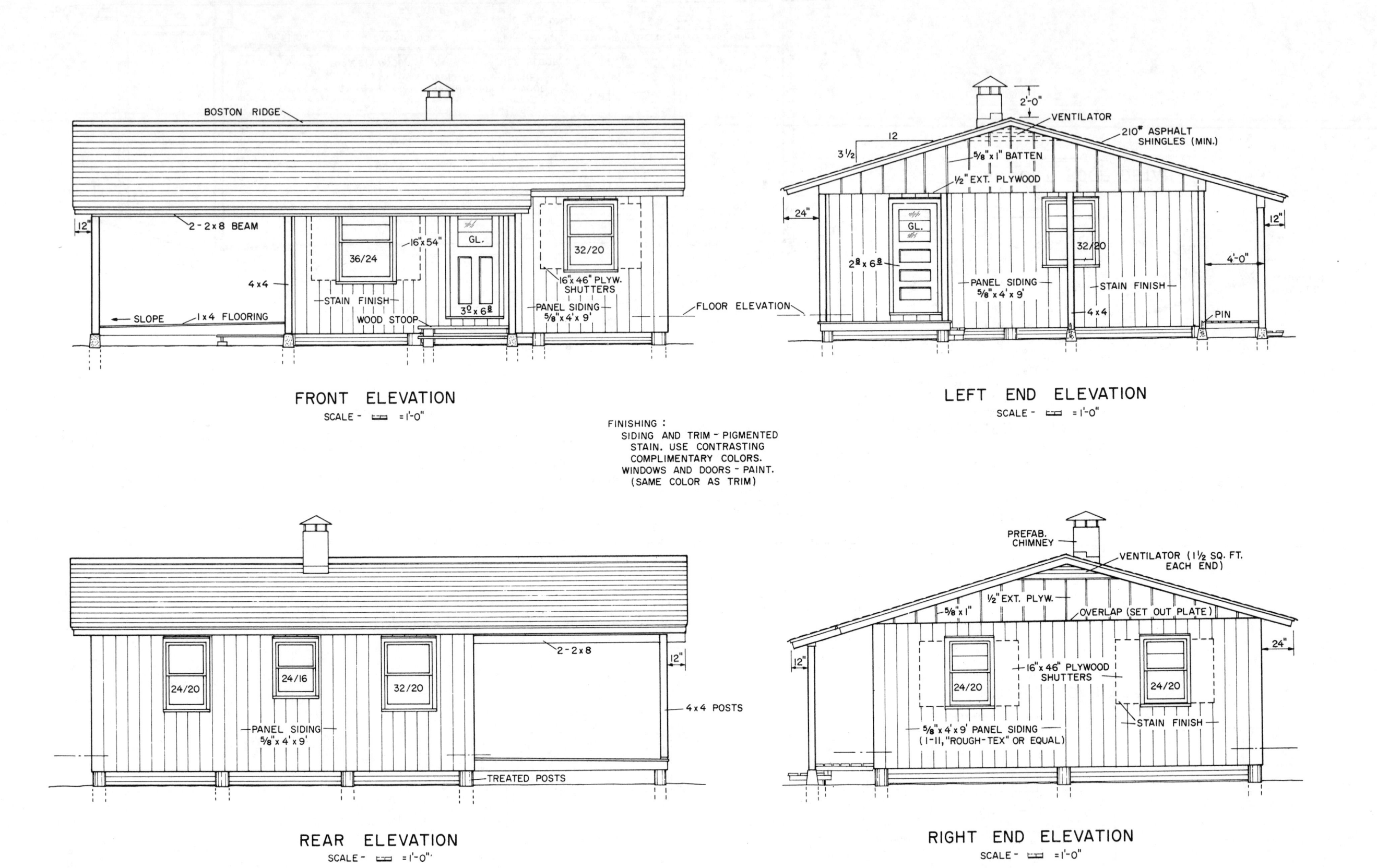

FINISHING :
SIDING AND TRIM - PIGMENTED
STAIN. USE CONTRASTING
COMPLIMENTARY COLORS.
WINDOWS AND DOORS - PAINT.
(SAME COLOR AS TRIM)

FRONT ELEVATION
SCALE - ⊏⊐ =1'-0"

LEFT END ELEVATION
SCALE - ⊏⊐ =1'-0"

REAR ELEVATION
SCALE - ⊏⊐ =1'-0"

RIGHT END ELEVATION
SCALE - ⊏⊐ =1'-0"

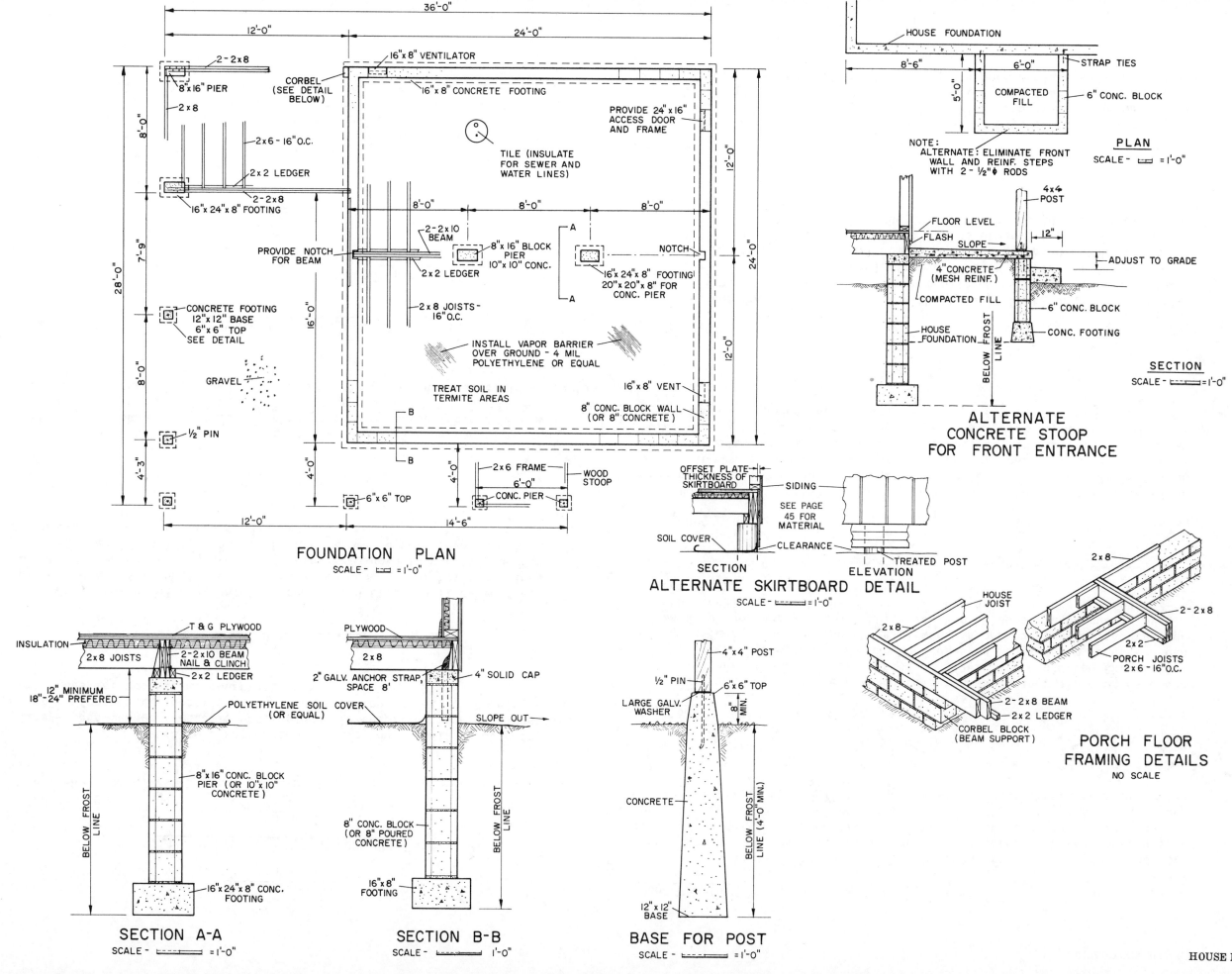

FOUNDATION PLAN
SCALE- = 1'-0"

- 36'-0"
- 12'-0"
- 24'-0"
- 2-2x8
- 8"x16" PIER
- 16"x8" VENTILATOR
- CORBEL (SEE DETAIL BELOW)
- 16"x8" CONCRETE FOOTING
- PROVIDE 24"x16" ACCESS DOOR AND FRAME
- 2x8
- 2x6-16" O.C.
- 2x2 LEDGER
- TILE (INSULATE FOR SEWER AND WATER LINES)
- 2-2x8
- 16"x24"x8" FOOTING
- 8'-0"
- 8'-0"
- 8'-0"
- 8'-0"
- A
- A
- NOTCH
- 12'-0"
- PROVIDE NOTCH FOR BEAM
- 2-2x10 BEAM
- 2x2 LEDGER
- 8"x16" BLOCK PIER 10"x10" CONC.
- 16"x24"x8" FOOTING 20"x20"x8" FOR CONC. PIER
- 24'-0"
- 7'-9"
- 28'-0"
- CONCRETE FOOTING 12"x12" BASE 6"x6" TOP SEE DETAIL
- 2x8 JOISTS-16" O.C.
- 16'-0"
- INSTALL VAPOR BARRIER OVER GROUND - 4 MIL POLYETHYLENE OR EQUAL
- 12'-0"
- GRAVEL
- ½" PIN
- TREAT SOIL IN TERMITE AREAS
- 16"x8" VENT
- 8" CONC. BLOCK WALL (OR 8" CONCRETE)
- 8'-0"
- B
- B
- 4'-3"
- 6"x6" TOP
- 4'-0"
- 4'-0"
- 2x6 FRAME
- 6'-0"
- WOOD STOOP
- CONC. PIER
- 12'-0"
- 14'-6"

HOUSE FOUNDATION
- 8'-6"
- 5'-0"
- 6'-0"
- STRAP TIES
- COMPACTED FILL
- 6" CONC. BLOCK
- NOTE: ALTERNATE: ELIMINATE FRONT WALL AND REINF. STEPS WITH 2 - ½"⌀ RODS

PLAN
SCALE- = 1'-0"

- 4x4 POST
- FLOOR LEVEL
- FLASH
- SLOPE
- 12"
- ADJUST TO GRADE
- 4" CONCRETE (MESH REINF.)
- COMPACTED FILL
- 6" CONC. BLOCK
- HOUSE FOUNDATION
- BELOW FROST LINE
- CONC. FOOTING

SECTION
SCALE- = 1'-0"

ALTERNATE CONCRETE STOOP FOR FRONT ENTRANCE

- OFFSET PLATE THICKNESS OF SKIRTBOARD
- SIDING
- SEE PAGE 45 FOR MATERIAL
- SOIL COVER
- CLEARANCE
- TREATED POST
- **SECTION**
- **ELEVATION**

ALTERNATE SKIRTBOARD DETAIL
SCALE- = 1'-0"

SECTION A-A
SCALE- = 1'-0"
- T & G PLYWOOD
- INSULATION
- 2x8 JOISTS
- 2-2x10 BEAM NAIL & CLINCH
- 2x2 LEDGER
- 12" MINIMUM 18"-24" PREFERED
- POLYETHYLENE SOIL COVER (OR EQUAL)
- 8"x16" CONC. BLOCK PIER (OR 10"x10" CONCRETE)
- BELOW FROST LINE
- 16"x24"x8" CONC. FOOTING

SECTION B-B
SCALE- = 1'-0"
- PLYWOOD
- 2x8
- 2" GALV. ANCHOR STRAP, SPACE 8'
- 4" SOLID CAP
- SLOPE OUT
- 8" CONC. BLOCK (OR 8" POURED CONCRETE)
- BELOW FROST LINE
- 16"x8" FOOTING

BASE FOR POST
SCALE- = 1'-0"
- 4"x4" POST
- ½" PIN
- 6"x6" TOP
- 8" MIN.
- LARGE GALV. WASHER
- CONCRETE
- BELOW FROST LINE (4'-0" MIN.)
- 12"x12" BASE

PORCH FLOOR FRAMING DETAILS
NO SCALE
- 2x8
- HOUSE JOIST
- 2x8
- 2-2x8
- 2x2
- PORCH JOISTS 2x6-16" O.C.
- 2-2x8 BEAM
- 2x2 LEDGER
- CORBEL BLOCK (BEAM SUPPORT)

SPECIFICATIONS
for
A LOW-COST, TWO BEDROOM WOOD HOUSE
Plan No.3

(One-story house, 24'-0" x 24'-0" in size, constructed over a crawl space)

All work related to construction of this house shall be done in a first-class manner. Details not included in specifications or plans shall comply with general details in the "Construction Manual" or to accepted practices for wood-frame construction.

Excavation - Grading

Sod, growing plants, shrubs, stumps, and trees shall be removed and ground smoothed in building area and 2 feet outside of building line. Excavate footings to required depth and size shown in plans. No forms are required if soil is stable. Locate excavated soil conveniently for backfilling around treated wood posts.

Concrete Work

Footings shall be poured over undisturbed soil in excavations to indicated thickness and size as shown on plan. Top surface to be level.

Mix concrete to a 1:2-1/2:3-1/2 mix. If premixed concrete is available, use 5-bag mix.

Treated Wood Posts

Pressure-treated wood posts with 7-inch minimum top diameter shall be treated to conform to Federal Specification TT-W-571.

Carpentry

General

This branch of the work comprises all rough and finish carpentry necessary to complete the house, as shown on the plans and as specified. This includes layout, cutting and fitting framing, and other carpentry items. Any phase which is necessary for the completion of the house and not specifically covered in the plans or specifications shall be included as required.

Wood Framing

Dimension material for studs to be Standard (third grade); and for floor joists and framing, ceiling joists, rafters, and beams construction (second grade) in Douglas-fir, southern pine, or equivalent, unless otherwise noted on the plans. Floor joists, studs, ceiling joists, and rafters shall be spaced 16 inches on center. Moisture content of framing lumber not to exceed 19 percent.

Subfloor

The subfloor shall be plywood to serve as a floor alone or as a base for resilient tile and shall consist of 3/4-inch C-C plugged Exterior grade, touch-sanded, and with matched edges in Douglas-fir, southern pine, or equivalent. When matched-edge plywood is not obtainable, square-edged plywood in the same grade and thickness can be substituted but 2- by 4-inch blocking shall be used for all longitudinal joints. Toenail 2- by 4-inch blocks flatwise in each joist space.

Roof Sheathing

Roof sheathing shall be 1/2-inch Douglas-fir or southern pine plywood or equal in Standard sheathing grade or nominal 1- by 6- or 1- by 8-inch boards in No. 3 Douglas-fir, southern pine, or equivalent. Boards shall be square edge, shiplap, or dressed and matched, and laid up tight at a moisture content of not more than 15 percent. Roof sheathing shall be covered with 15-pound asphalt felt.

Insulation

All ceilings to be insulated with standard batt- or blanket-type flexible insulation with vapor barrier placed toward the inside of the building. Wall and floor insulation to consist of flexible blanket insulation. Thicknesses shall comply with the recommended thicknesses outlined in the "Construction Manual" or as otherwise required. Vapor barrier shall be placed toward the inside of the building. Vapor barrier to have a maximum perm value of 0.30.

Siding

Siding shall be 5/8-inch by 4- by 9-foot plywood panel siding in Texture 1-11 (4-in. grooves) or equal and 1/2-inch exterior plywood with 5/8- by 1-inch battens (gables). It shall be nailed at each stud, including vertical joints, and at the top and bottom plate and floor framing with eightpenny galvanized siding nails spaced 7 to 8 inches apart. The vertical edges of the sheets shall be brush-coated with a water-repellent preservative before installing.

Exterior Millwork

(a) Exterior finish.--Exterior trim and similar materials shall be No. 2 ponderosa pine or equivalent suitable for staining.

(b) Window frames and sash.--Complete double-hung windows shall be used with upper sash cut to two horizontal lights, glazed with single-strength glass. Units to be treated with water-repellent preservative as outlined in Commercial Standard CS 190-64. Sash to be furnished fully balanced and fitted and with outside casing in place. Set in openings, plumb, and square. Screens shall be furnished, and storms when required.

(c) Exterior door frames and doors.--Exterior door frames shall have 1-3/8-inch rabbeted jambs and 1-5/8-inch oak sill or softwood sill with metal edge, all assembled. Set in openings, plumb, and square.

Exterior doors to be standard 1-3/4-inch with solid stiles and rails; panel type with glazed openings as shown on plans. Screen doors shall be furnished, or combinations when required.

(d) Screens.--Galvanized fly screen shall be used for inlet and outlet ventilators.

Interior Millwork

(a) Interior door frames and doors.--Interior door frames and cased openings shall be nominal 1-inch ponderosa pine or equal in "D" Select. Stops shall be installed only where doors are specified.

Interior doors shall be 1-3/8 inches thick, hollow-core type.

(b) Interior trim.--Interior trim shall be ponderosa pine or equal in "D" Select in ranch pattern in the following sizes:

Casings	-- 11/16 by 2-1/4 inches
Stops	-- 7/16 by 1-3/8 inches or wider
Base	-- 7/16 by 2-1/4 inches
Base shoe	-- 1/2 by 3/4 inch (when required)

Note: (1) Casing to be used at bottom of windows in place of stool and apron.
(2) Base shoe used along closets where required.

(c) Walls and ceilings.--All ceilings shall be finished with 3/8-inch gypsum board with recessed edges and with the length applied across the ceiling joists. End joints shall be staggered at least 2 feet. Walls shall be finished with 3/8-inch gypsum board with recessed edges or with 1/4-inch prefinished plywood. Both shall be applied vertically. Application and joint treatment shall follow the recommendations in the "Construction Manual."

Walls of tub recess shall be covered with plastic-finished hardboard panels over gypsum board. Install with mastic in accordance with manufacturer's directions. Inside corners, edges, and tub edges shall be finished with plastic moldings.

(d) Flooring.--Finish flooring throughout shall be 1/8-inch-thick asphalt tile in 9- by 9-inch size, "B" quality. Combination plywood sub-floor shall be cleaned, nails driven flush, and joints sanded smooth where required. Tile shall be applied in accordance with manufacturer's recommendations. Rubber baseboard shall be furnished and installed in the bathroom, wood base in the remainder of the house.

(e) Hardware.--Furnish and install all rough and finish hardware complete as needed for perfect operation. Locks shall be furnished for all outside doors. Outside doors to be hung with three 4- by 4-inch loose-pin butt hinges and inside doors with two 3-1/2- by 3-1/2-inch loose-pin butt hinges. Bathroom five-cross-panel door shall be furnished with standard bathroom lock set. Standard screen door latches, hinges, and door closers shall be furnished and installed. Furnish and install semi-concealed cabinet hinges, pulls, and catches where required for cabinet or closet doors. All finish hardware to be finished in dull brass.

Sheet Metal Work and Roofing

Sheet Metal

Sheet metal flashing, when required for the prefabricated chimney and vent stack, shall be 28-gage galvanized iron or painted terneplate.

Termite shields, when required, shall be 28-gage galvanized iron, painted terneplate, or aluminum in equivalent thickness. (See section on "Termite Protection.")

Roofing

Roofing shall be a minimum of 210-pound square tab 12- by 36-inch asphalt shingles installed over a double underlay of 15-pound asphalt felt. A minimum of four 7/8-inch galvanized roofing nails shall be used for each 12- by 36-inch shingle strip. Any defects or leaks shall be corrected.

Electrical Work

The work shall include all materials and labor necessary to make the systems complete as shown on the plans. All work and materials shall comply with local requirements or those of the National Electrical Code. All wiring shall be concealed and carried in BX or other approved conduit to each outlet, switch, fixture, and appliance or electrical equipment such as furnace, hot water heater, and range when required, and as shown on the plan. Panel shall be 100 amp. capacity with overload cutout. Fixtures to consist of the following:

Two outside wall fixtures with crystal glass.

Overhead (wall) (fluorescent fixture with outlet in bath and incandescent in kitchen).

Overhead (ceiling) (incandescent fixture in kitchen).

Heating

Heater and prefabricated chimney shall be installed as shown on the plans with supply ducts located in furred-down ceiling of hall. Heater shall be for LP or natural gas with a 75,000 minimum B.t.u. input or as required by design for each specific area. Cold air return at furnace base and from each corner of the house. Cold air duct shall consist of 1/8-inch transite-covered joist spaces along outside walls and connection to 10-inch-diameter galvanized ducts to heater.

Plumbing

All plumbing shall be installed in accordance with local or National plumbing codes. Hot- and cold-water connections shall be furnished to all fixtures as required. Sewer and water and gas lines (when required) shall extend to building line with water shutoff valve. Framed and insulated box shall be used to protect water and sewer lines from freezing in crawl space where required. Cover with 1/8-inch transite or equal and insulate with 3 inches of fiberglass or styrofoam when required. Use a 16- by 16-inch vitrified tile or equal below groundline.

Furnish and install the following fixtures:

One kitchen sink--21 by 15 inches, self rim, steel, white, with fixtures.

One bathtub--5 foot, cast iron, white, left-hand drain, complete with shower rod and shower head with fixtures.

One water closet--Reverse trap, white, with seat, fixtures, and shutoff valve.

One lavatory--19 by 17 inches, steel, white, and with fixtures and shutoff valve.

One hot water heater--30 gallon (minimum), gas or electric.

Washing machine connection with hot and cold water and drain.

Painting and Finishing

Exterior

Exterior plywood panel siding, facia, shutters, and soffit areas shall be stained with pigmented stain as outlined in the "Construction Manual." Use light gray, yellow, or another light color stain for the trim and shutters and a darker stain (brown, olive, gray, etc.) for the panel siding or reverse color selection as desired by owner.

Window and door frames, window sash, screen doors, and similar millwork shall be painted a light color, or as owners request. Types of paint and procedures to comply with recommendations in "Construction Manual."

Interior

All woodwork shall be painted in semigloss. Walls and ceilings finished in latex flat as outlined in the "Construction Manual," except bathroom, which shall be finished in semigloss.

Termite Protection

Termite protection shall be provided in termite areas by means of soil treatments or termite shields or both. --See "Construction Manual."

Concrete Blocks

Concrete blocks (used as an alternate to foundation of treated wood posts) shall comply with ASTM C-90, Grade U-II, for standard size and quality.

Concrete blocks shall be laid over concrete footings, as shown on the foundation plan. Footings shall be level and laid out to conform to the building line. Blocks shall be laid up with 3/8-inch-thick mortar joints, tooling the joints on all exposed exterior surfaces. Anchor straps, when used, shall be embedded to a depth of at least 12 inches.

BILL OF MATERIAL FOR RURAL HOME

Plan No. 3

The following material is required for construction of the rural home detailed in Plan No. 3; quality of material and treatments are given in the specifications.

Foundation

The foundation of concrete piers and treated posts set on concrete footings requires:

2 cubic yards concrete
14 treated posts, 5 feet long, with 7-inch minimum top diameter
1 treated post, 5 feet long, with 6-inch minimum top diameter
5 -- 1/2-inch pins, 16 inches long

Floor Framing

Floor framing consisting of floor joists supported on ledgers nailed to the anchored floor beams requires:

5	2 x 10's	12 feet long
9	2 x 10's	16 feet long
38	2 x 8's	12 feet long
1	2 x 8	8 feet long
9	2 x 6's	8 feet long
10	2 x 2's	12 feet long

1 joist hanger for two 2 x 8's
36 lineal feet 22-gage x 2-inch anchor strap
3 -- 4- x 8-foot sheets 1/2-inch exterior plywood

Floor

18 -- 4- x 8-foot sheets of 3/4-inch tongued-and-grooved plywood
1200 -- 9- x 9-inch asphalt tile (10 pct. waste) (with adhesive)
120 board feet 1- x 4-inch fir flooring

Wall and Partition Framing

Framing materials for walls and partitions, and posts for porch and carport, include:

120	2 x 4's	8 feet long
52	2 x 4's	12 feet long
8	2 x 6's	12 feet long
3	4 x 4's	8 feet long
4	4 x 4's	10 feet long

Ceiling and Roof Framing

Materials for rafters, joists, and a drop beam over living area are:

12	2 x 4's	12 feet long
8	1 x 4's	10 feet long
9	2 x 6's	10 feet long
17	2 x 6's	12 feet long
17	2 x 6's	14 feet long
46	2 x 6's	16 feet long
22	2 x 6's	18 feet long
3	1 x 8's	12 feet long
11	2 x 8's	12 feet long
2	2 x 8's	16 feet long

Roof

Roofing and sheathing requirements are:

37 -- 4- x 8-foot sheets of 3/8-inch plywood sheathing grade (CD)
6 -- 432-square-foot rolls of 15-pound asphalt felt
13 squares -- 210-pound asphalt shingles

Siding

The siding requirement is:

24 -- 4- x 9-foot sheets of rough-textured 5/8-inch Texture 1-11
6 -- 4- x 8-foot sheets of 1/2-inch exterior plywood
11 -- 1-inch battens 12 feet long

Windows

All windows are double-hung and purchased treated and complete with screens, and storms when required. Quantity of each size is:

Glass Size (Each Sash)	Rough Opening
1 -- 36/24	3'-6" x 4'-10"
3 -- 32/20	3'-2" x 4'-2"
3 -- 24/20	2'-6" x 4'-2"
1 -- 24/16	2'-6" x 3'-6"

Exterior Doors

Doors are glazed and frame, trim, and hardware are required for each. Size is:

Front -- 3 feet 0 inches wide and 6 feet 8 inches high
Rear -- 2 feet 8 inches wide and 6 feet 8 inches high

Insulation

Blanket insulation with aluminum foil on one side is required for ceiling, walls, and floor:

    1400 square feet -- 2 inches thick, 16 inches wide
     600 square feet -- 3 inches thick, 16 inches wide

Roof Ventilators

Requirements for ventilating the roof are:

    1 pair   -- Peak-type outlet vents
   12 square feet -- Screen for inlet vent slots

Exterior Trim

Exterior trim including facia, molding, and shutters requires:

    6 -- 1 x 8's   12 feet long
    6 -- 1 x 2's   12 feet long
    2 -- 4- x 8-foot sheets 1/2-inch exterior plywood

Interior Wall and Ceiling Finish

Gypsum board, prefinished plywood, and plastic-coated hardboard are used as interior finish. Requirements are:

    60 -- 4- x 8-foot sheets of 3/8-inch gypsum board
     6 -- 4- x 8-foot sheets prefinished plywood
     3 -- 4- x 8-foot sheets plastic-coated hardboard
     2 -- 250-foot rolls of joint tape
     4 -- 25-pound bags of joint compound

Interior Doors

Interior door requirements are:

    1 set -- 2-foot 4-inch x 6-foot 8-inch hollow-core door with
        jambs, stops, and hardware
    2 sets -- Jambs for 2-foot 6-inch x 6-foot 8-inch doors
    1 set -- 3-foot x 6-foot 8-inch folding closet door with
        jambs, stops, and hardware
    1 -- 4- x 8-foot sheet 1/2-inch plywood, interior grade AC
    4 pair -- Cabinet hinges
    4 -- Wooden door hinges
    4 -- Friction catches

Interior Trim

Trim for windows, doors, and base includes:

    270 feet -- 9/16- x 2-1/8-inch casing
    180 feet -- 1/2- x 3-inch base

Cabinets

Material requirements for wood-frame and plywood cabinets are:

    3 -- 4- x 8-foot sheets of 3/4-inch plywood, interior AC
    3 -- 4- x 8-foot sheets 3/8-inch plywood, interior AC
    1 -- 1 x 3   6 feet long
    2 -- 1 x 4's 12 feet long
    1 -- 1 x 10   12 feet long
  1 pair -- Cabinet door hinges
    1 -- Wooden door pull
    1 -- Friction door catch

Wardrobes

Wardrobes consisting of closet poles with shelf over require:

    1 -- 4- x 8-foot sheet of 3/4-inch plywood, interior AC
    1 -- Closet pole, 1-5/8-inch diameter x 7 feet long
  2 pair -- Pole sockets

Front Stoop

The front stoop, consisting of planks laid across 2 x 4 framing, has the following requirements:

     2 -- 2 x 4's 10 feet long
    10 -- 2 x 6's   6 feet long
     4 -- 1/2-inch galvanized carriage bolts, 8 inches long

Nails

Nails required for all phases of construction are:

    40 pounds -- Eightpenny common
    20 pounds -- Sixteenpenny common
     2 pounds -- Twentypenny common
     3 pounds -- Tenpenny common, galvanized
     2 pounds -- Sixteenpenny common, galvanized
     2 pounds -- Fourpenny finish
     9 pounds -- Eightpenny finish
    18 pounds -- 3/4-inch galvanized roofing
    16 pounds -- Fourpenny cooler
     1 pound -- Eightpenny flooring

Paint and Finish

Quantities required for one coat of paint inside and one coat of stain outside are:

        7 gallons -- Walls and ceiling
        1 gallon -- Interior trim
        5 gallons -- Exterior siding and trim

Electrical

In addition to rough wiring, entrance 100-amp. service, etc., the following items are required:

        1 -- Exterior outlet
       17 -- Duplex outlets-complete
        2 -- Wall-mounted interior lights with octagon boxes complete
        1 -- Ceiling light with octagon boxes complete
        2 -- Wall-mounted exterior lights with octagon boxes complete
        5 -- Switches, plates, etc.,-complete

Heating

The heating system requires a 75,000 B.t.u. gas furnace with 5 registers, 4 cold-air returns, duct, and a prefab chimney.

Plumbing

Plumbing must be provided for the following required fixtures:

        1 -- 5-foot bathtub
        1 -- Water closet
        1 -- Lavatory
        1 -- Kitchen sink
        1 -- 30-gallon water heater
        1 -- 16- x 16- x 24-inch vitrified clay tile or equal
               (at sewer and water entrance)

ALTERNATES

Floor (Square-Edge Plywood)

When tongued-and-grooved plywood is not available, square-edge plywood with all edges blocked can be used. Material requirements for flooring and subfloor are:

        18 -- 4- x 8-foot sheets of 3/4-inch plywood
        12 -- 2 x 4's   12 feet long
      1200 -- 9- x 9-inch asphalt tile (10 pct. waste) (with adhesive)
       120 board feet 1 x 4 fir flooring

Foundation (Concrete-Block)

The foundation of concrete blocks on poured concrete footings requires:

          4 cubic yards concrete
        456 -- 8- x 8- x 16-inch concrete blocks
         76 -- 4- x 8- x 16-inch concrete block caps
         16 bags prepared mortar
        1-1/2 cubic yards mason's sand
        600 square feet 4-mil polyethylene film
          2 -- 8- x 16-inch foundation vents

Floor Framing (For Concrete Block Foundation)

         4 -- 2 x 10's   12 feet long
         6 -- 2 x 10's   16 feet long
         1 -- 2 x 8   8 feet long
        38 -- 2 x 8's   12 feet long
         8 -- 2 x 6's   8 feet long
        10 -- 2 x 2's   12 feet long
         1 -- Joist hanger for two 2 x 8's
        36 lineal feet 22-gage x 2-inch anchor strap

4

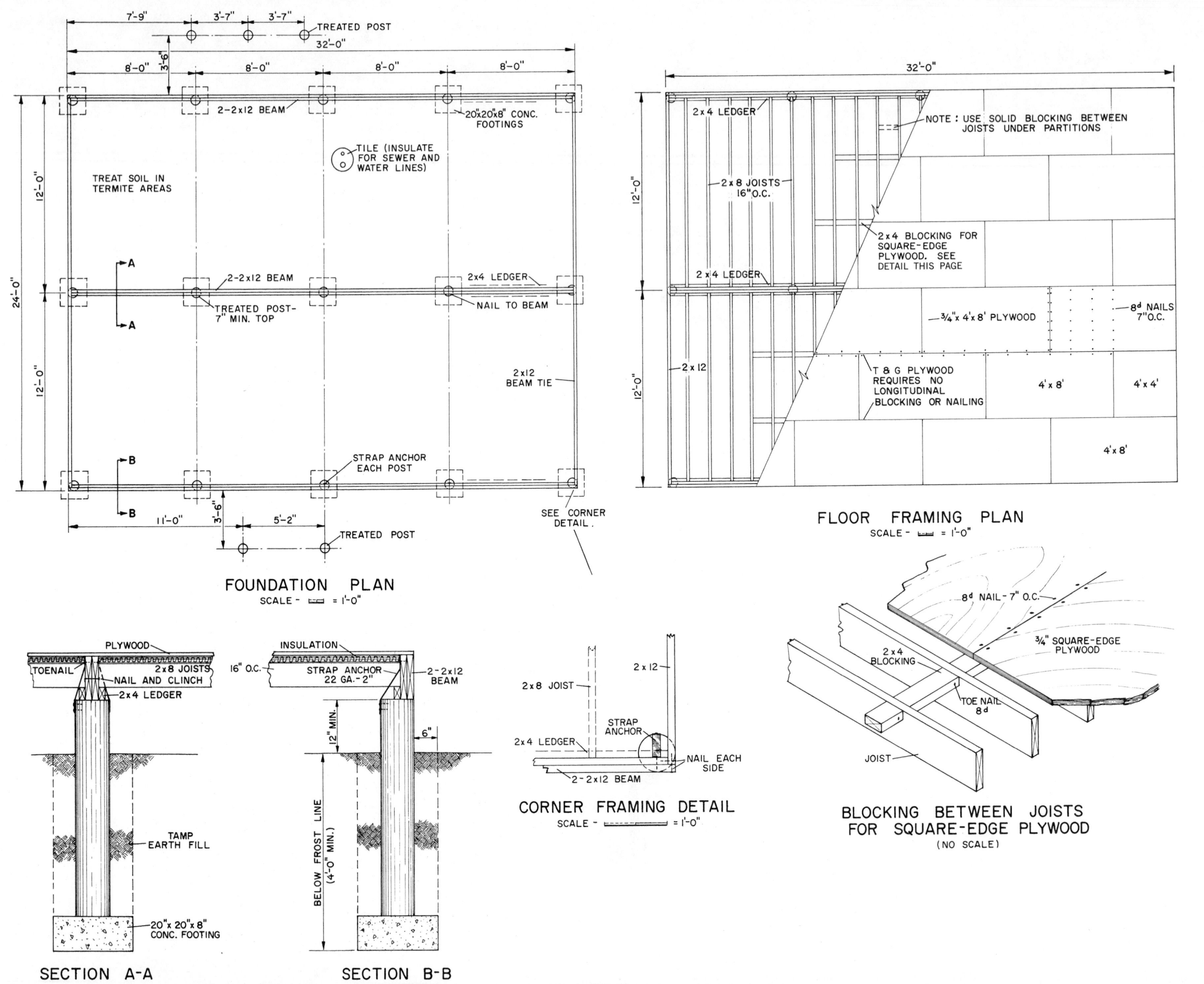

FOUNDATION PLAN
SCALE - = 1'-0"

7'-9"   3'-7"   3'-7"   TREATED POST
32'-0"
8'-0"   8'-0"   8'-0"   8'-0"
3'-6"
2-2x12 BEAM   20"x20"x8" CONC. FOOTINGS
TILE (INSULATE FOR SEWER AND WATER LINES)
TREAT SOIL IN TERMITE AREAS
12'-0"
2-2x12 BEAM   2x4 LEDGER
TREATED POST- 7" MIN. TOP   NAIL TO BEAM
24'-0"
12'-0"
2x12 BEAM TIE
STRAP ANCHOR EACH POST
SEE CORNER DETAIL.
11'-0"   3'-6"   5'-2"
TREATED POST

FLOOR FRAMING PLAN
SCALE - = 1'-0"

32'-0"
2x4 LEDGER   NOTE: USE SOLID BLOCKING BETWEEN JOISTS UNDER PARTITIONS
12'-0"
2x8 JOISTS 16" O.C.
2x4 BLOCKING FOR SQUARE-EDGE PLYWOOD. SEE DETAIL THIS PAGE
2x4 LEDGER
3/4" x 4' x 8' PLYWOOD   8d NAILS 7" O.C.
12'-0"
2x12
T & G PLYWOOD REQUIRES NO LONGITUDINAL BLOCKING OR NAILING   4' x 8'   4' x 4'
4' x 8'

SECTION A-A

PLYWOOD
TOENAIL   2x8 JOISTS
NAIL AND CLINCH
2x4 LEDGER
TAMP EARTH FILL
20" x 20" x 8" CONC. FOOTING

SECTION B-B
SCALE - = 1'-0"

INSULATION
16" O.C.   STRAP ANCHOR 22 GA.- 2"   2-2x12 BEAM
12" MIN.
BELOW FROST LINE (4'-0" MIN.)   6"

CORNER FRAMING DETAIL
SCALE - = 1'-0"

2x12
2x8 JOIST
STRAP ANCHOR
2x4 LEDGER
NAIL EACH SIDE
2-2x12 BEAM

BLOCKING BETWEEN JOISTS FOR SQUARE-EDGE PLYWOOD
(NO SCALE)

8d NAIL - 7" O.C.
3/4" SQUARE-EDGE PLYWOOD
2x4 BLOCKING
TOE NAIL 8d
JOIST

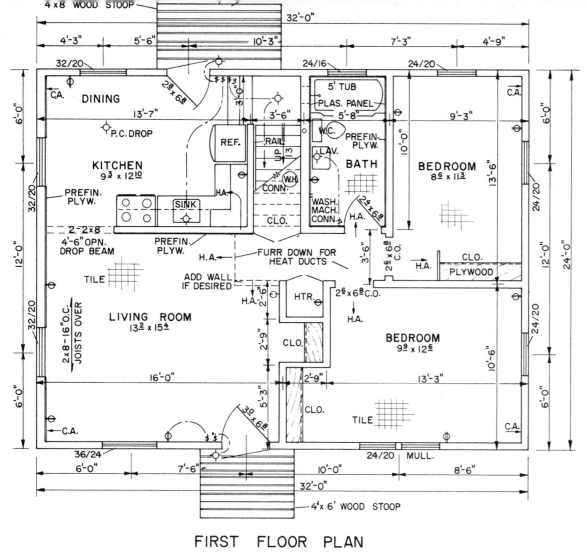

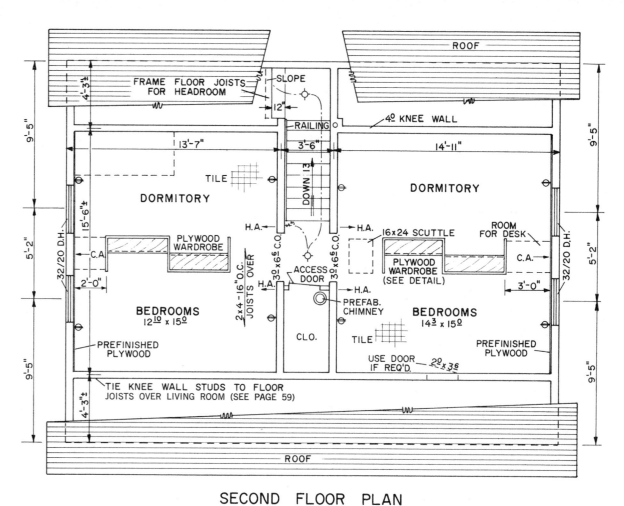

FIRST FLOOR PLAN
SCALE - = 1'-0"

SECOND FLOOR PLAN
SCALE - = 1'-0"

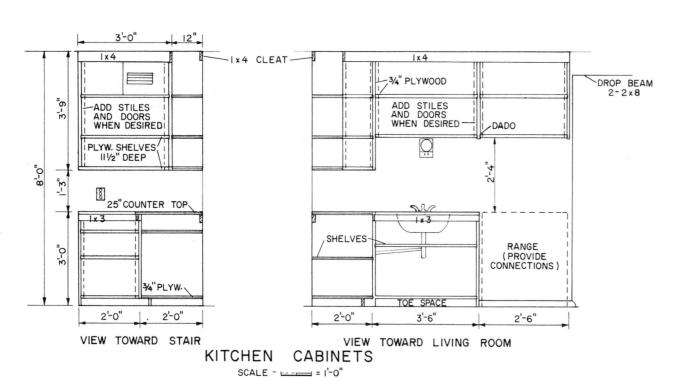

KITCHEN CABINETS
SCALE - = 1'-0"

VIEW TOWARD STAIR

VIEW TOWARD LIVING ROOM

ELEVATION

SECTION

WARDROBE - SECOND FLOOR BEDROOMS
SCALE - = 1'-0"

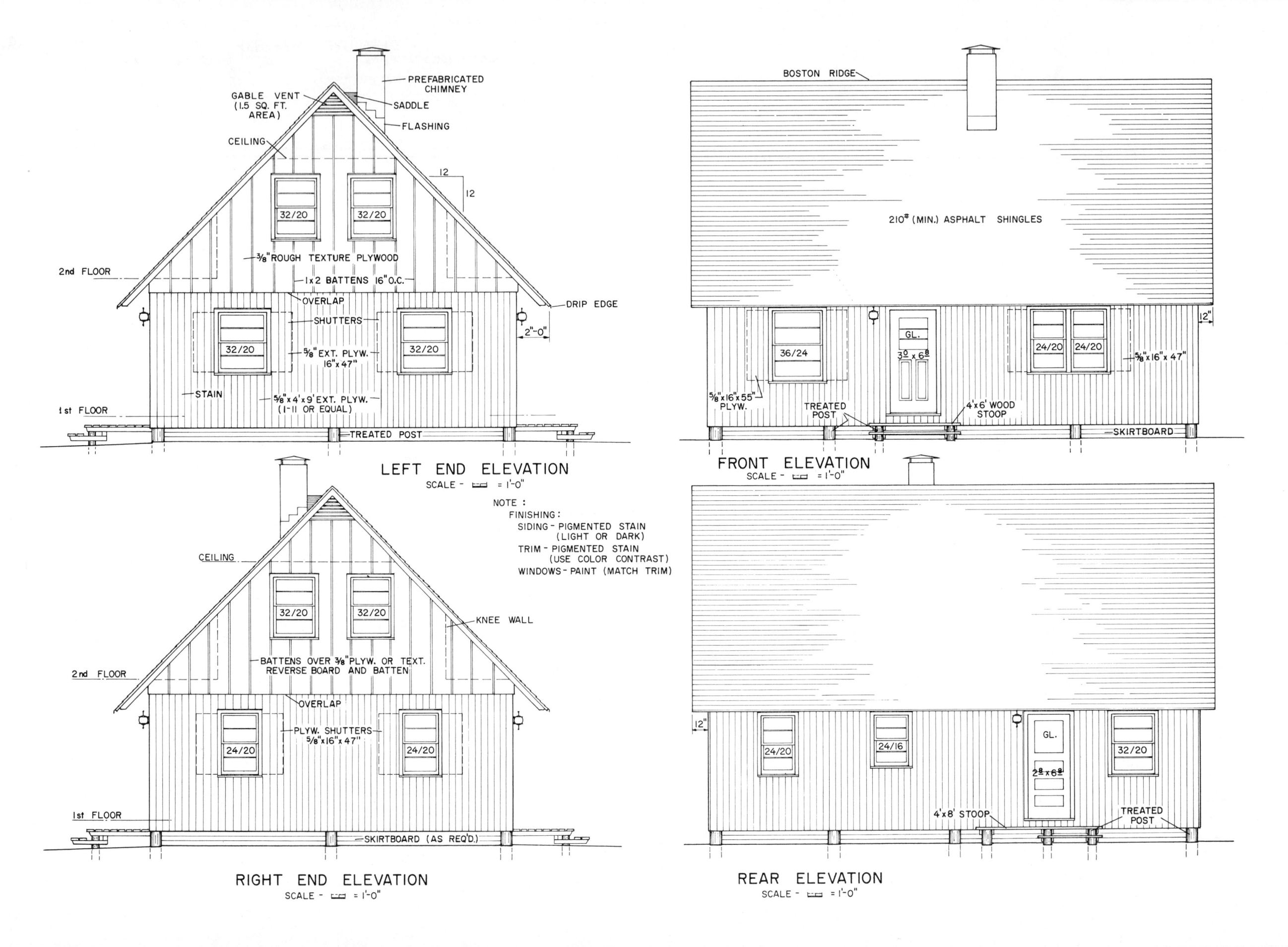

LEFT END ELEVATION
SCALE - ▱ = 1'-0"

PREFABRICATED CHIMNEY
GABLE VENT (1.5 SQ. FT. AREA)
SADDLE
FLASHING
CEILING
12
12
2nd FLOOR
3/8" ROUGH TEXTURE PLYWOOD
1x2 BATTENS 16" O.C.
OVERLAP
SHUTTERS
DRIP EDGE
2"-0"
5/8" EXT. PLYW. 16"x 47"
32/20   32/20
32/20   32/20
STAIN
5/8" x 4'x 9' EXT. PLYW. (1-11 OR EQUAL)
1st FLOOR
TREATED POST

RIGHT END ELEVATION
SCALE - ▱ = 1'-0"

CEILING
KNEE WALL
2nd FLOOR
32/20   32/20
BATTENS OVER 3/8" PLYW. OR TEXT. REVERSE BOARD AND BATTEN
OVERLAP
PLYW. SHUTTERS 5/8" x 16" x 47"
24/20   24/20
1st FLOOR
SKIRTBOARD (AS REQ'D.)

NOTE :
FINISHING :
SIDING - PIGMENTED STAIN (LIGHT OR DARK)
TRIM - PIGMENTED STAIN (USE COLOR CONTRAST)
WINDOWS - PAINT (MATCH TRIM)

FRONT ELEVATION
SCALE - ▱ = 1'-0"

BOSTON RIDGE
210# (MIN.) ASPHALT SHINGLES
12"
36/24
GL. 3⁰ x 6⁸
24/20   24/20
5/8"x16"x 47"
5/8"x16"x55" PLYW.
TREATED POST
4'x6' WOOD STOOP
SKIRTBOARD

REAR ELEVATION
SCALE - ▱ = 1'-0"

12"
24/20   24/16   GL.   32/20
2⁸ x 6⁸
4'x8' STOOP
TREATED POST

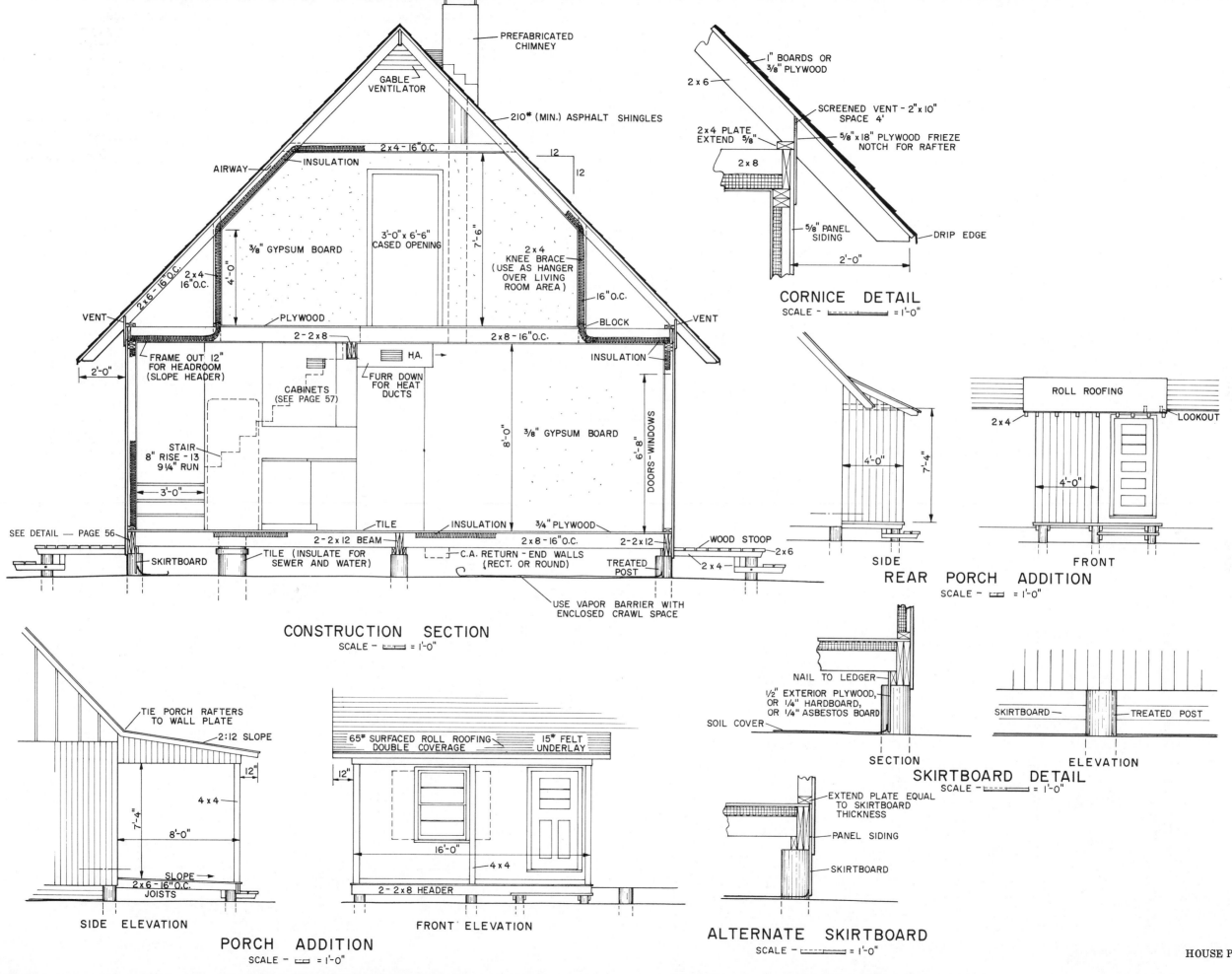

PREFABRICATED CHIMNEY

GABLE VENTILATOR

210# (MIN.) ASPHALT SHINGLES

12
12

AIRWAY
INSULATION
2 x 4 - 16" O.C.

3/8" GYPSUM BOARD

3'-0" x 6'-6" CASED OPENING

7'-6"

2 x 4 KNEE BRACE (USE AS HANGER OVER LIVING ROOM AREA)

16" O.C.

2 x 4 16" O.C.

4'-0"

2 x 6 - 16" O.C.

VENT

PLYWOOD

2 - 2 x 8

H.A.

2 x 8 - 16" O.C.

BLOCK

INSULATION

VENT

2'-0"

FRAME OUT 12" FOR HEADROOM (SLOPE HEADER)

CABINETS (SEE PAGE 57)

FURR DOWN FOR HEAT DUCTS

STAIR 8" RISE - 13 9 1/4" RUN

3/8" GYPSUM BOARD

8'-0"

6'-8" DOORS-WINDOWS

3'-0"

SEE DETAIL — PAGE 56

SKIRTBOARD

TILE (INSULATE FOR SEWER AND WATER)

2 - 2 x 12 BEAM

TILE

INSULATION

C.A. RETURN - END WALLS (RECT. OR ROUND)

3/4" PLYWOOD

2 x 8 - 16" O.C.

2 - 2 x 12

WOOD STOOP

TREATED POST

2 x 6

2 x 4

USE VAPOR BARRIER WITH ENCLOSED CRAWL SPACE

CONSTRUCTION SECTION
SCALE - ▭ = 1'-0"

CORNICE DETAIL
SCALE - ▭ = 1'-0"

1" BOARDS OR 3/8" PLYWOOD

2 x 6

SCREENED VENT - 2" x 10" SPACE 4'

2 x 4 PLATE EXTEND 5/8"

5/8" x 18" PLYWOOD FRIEZE NOTCH FOR RAFTER

2 x 8

5/8" PANEL SIDING

DRIP EDGE

2'-0"

REAR PORCH ADDITION
SCALE - ▭ = 1'-0"

SIDE

4'-0"

7'-4"

FRONT

ROLL ROOFING

2 x 4

LOOKOUT

4'-0"

PORCH ADDITION
SCALE - ▭ = 1'-0"

SIDE ELEVATION

TIE PORCH RAFTERS TO WALL PLATE

2:12 SLOPE

12"

4 x 4

7'-4"

8'-0"

SLOPE

2 x 6 - 16" O.C. JOISTS

FRONT ELEVATION

65# SURFACED ROLL ROOFING DOUBLE COVERAGE

15# FELT UNDERLAY

12"

16'-0"

4 x 4

2 - 2 x 8 HEADER

SKIRTBOARD DETAIL
SCALE - ▭ = 1'-0"

NAIL TO LEDGER

1/2" EXTERIOR PLYWOOD, OR 1/4" HARDBOARD, OR 1/4" ASBESTOS BOARD

SOIL COVER

SECTION

SKIRTBOARD

TREATED POST

ELEVATION

ALTERNATE SKIRTBOARD
SCALE - ▭ = 1'-0"

EXTEND PLATE EQUAL TO SKIRTBOARD THICKNESS

PANEL SIDING

SKIRTBOARD

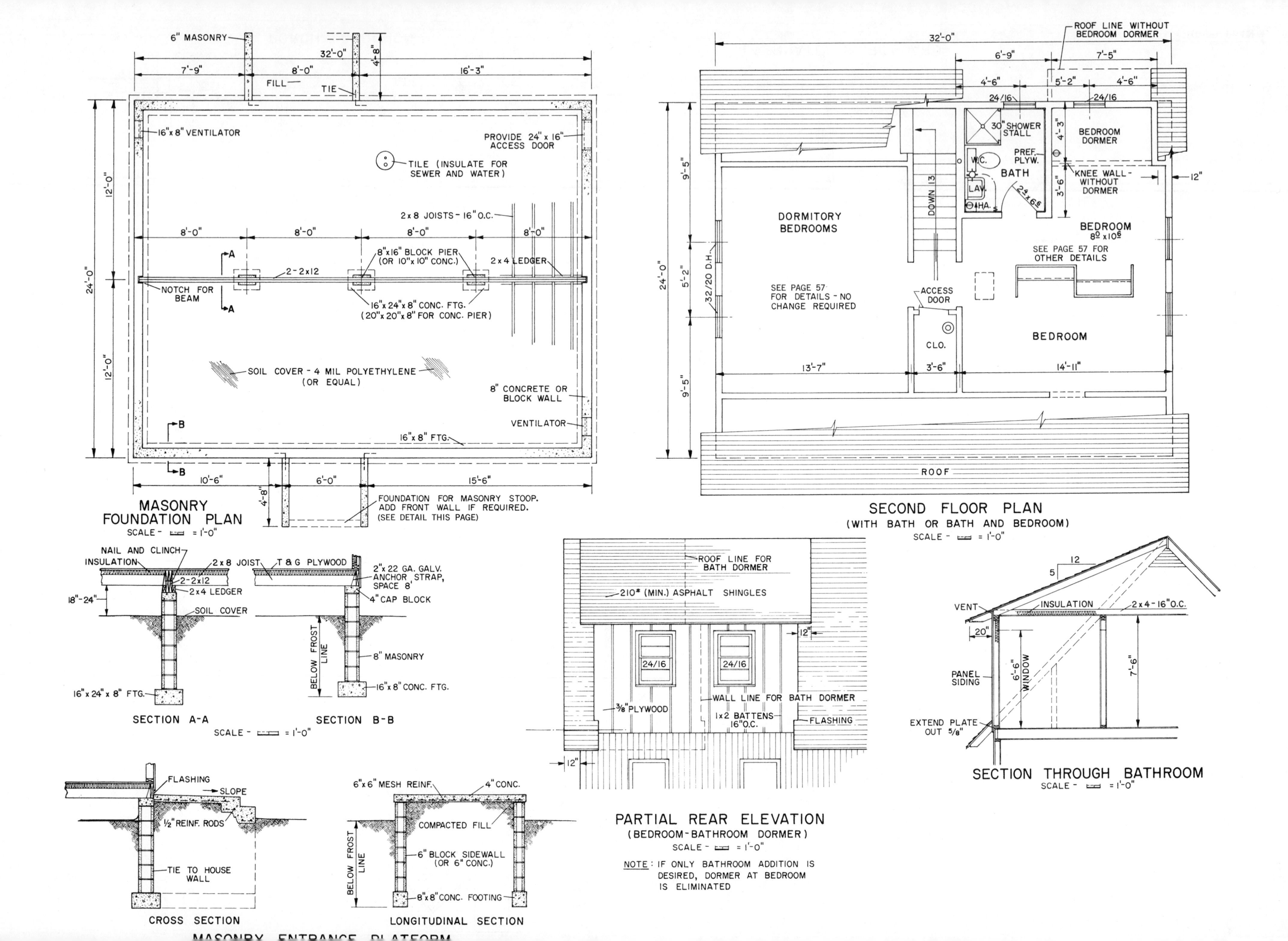

MASONRY FOUNDATION PLAN
SCALE - □ = 1'-0"

6" MASONRY
32'-0"
7'-9"
8'-0"
4'-8"
16'-3"
FILL
TIE
16" x 8" VENTILATOR
PROVIDE 24" x 16" ACCESS DOOR
TILE (INSULATE FOR SEWER AND WATER)
12'-0"
24'-0"
12'-0"
8'-0"
8'-0"
8'-0"
8'-0"
2 x 8 JOISTS - 16" O.C.
A
A
2 - 2 x 12
8" x 16" BLOCK PIER (OR 10" x 10" CONC.)
2 x 4 LEDGER
NOTCH FOR BEAM
16" x 24" x 8" CONC. FTG. (20" x 20" x 8" FOR CONC. PIER)
B
B
SOIL COVER - 4 MIL POLYETHYLENE (OR EQUAL)
8" CONCRETE OR BLOCK WALL
VENTILATOR
16" x 8" FTG.
B
B
10'-6"
6'-0"
15'-6"
4'-8"
FOUNDATION FOR MASONRY STOOP. ADD FRONT WALL IF REQUIRED. (SEE DETAIL THIS PAGE)

SECOND FLOOR PLAN
(WITH BATH OR BATH AND BEDROOM)
SCALE - □ = 1'-0"

32'-0"
6'-9"
7'-5"
ROOF LINE WITHOUT BEDROOM DORMER
4'-6"
5'-2"
4'-6"
24/16
24/16
30" SHOWER STALL
BEDROOM DORMER
9'-5"
W.C.
PREF. PLYW.
BATH
4'-3"
DOWN 13
LAV.
KNEE WALL WITHOUT DORMER
HA.
3'-6"
2'-4'-6'
12"
DORMITORY BEDROOMS
24'-0"
5'-2"
32/20 D.H.
BEDROOM 8⁰ x 10⁸
SEE PAGE 57 FOR OTHER DETAILS
SEE PAGE 57 FOR DETAILS - NO CHANGE REQUIRED
ACCESS DOOR
BEDROOM
9'-5"
CLO.
13'-7"
3'-6"
14'-11"
ROOF

SECTION A-A   **SECTION B-B**
SCALE - □ = 1'-0"

NAIL AND CLINCH
INSULATION
2 x 8 JOIST
T & G PLYWOOD
2 - 2 x 12
2 x 4 LEDGER
2" x 22 GA. GALV. ANCHOR STRAP, SPACE 8'
4" CAP BLOCK
18"-24"
SOIL COVER
BELOW FROST LINE
8" MASONRY
16" x 24" x 8" FTG.
16" x 8" CONC. FTG.

CROSS SECTION   **LONGITUDINAL SECTION**
MASONRY ENTRANCE PLATFORM

FLASHING
SLOPE
½" REINF. RODS
TIE TO HOUSE WALL
6" x 6" MESH REINF.
4" CONC.
COMPACTED FILL
BELOW FROST LINE
6" BLOCK SIDEWALL (OR 6" CONC.)
8" x 8" CONC. FOOTING

PARTIAL REAR ELEVATION
(BEDROOM-BATHROOM DORMER)
SCALE - □ = 1'-0"

ROOF LINE FOR BATH DORMER
210# (MIN.) ASPHALT SHINGLES
12"
24/16
24/16
⅜" PLYWOOD
WALL LINE FOR BATH DORMER
1 x 2 BATTENS 16" O.C.
FLASHING
12"

NOTE: IF ONLY BATHROOM ADDITION IS DESIRED, DORMER AT BEDROOM IS ELIMINATED

SECTION THROUGH BATHROOM
SCALE - □ = 1'-0"

12
5
VENT
INSULATION
2 x 4 - 16" O.C.
20"
6'-6" WINDOW
7'-6"
PANEL SIDING
EXTEND PLATE OUT ⅝"

SPECIFICATIONS

for

FOUR BEDROOM WOOD-FRAME HOUSE

Plan No. 4

(One-and-one-half-story house, 24' -0" x 32' -0" in size, constructed over a crawl space)

All work related to construction of this house shall be done in a first-class manner. Details not included in specifications or plans shall comply with accepted practices for wood-frame construction.

Excavation - Grading

Sod, growing plants, shrubs, stumps, and trees shall be removed and ground smoothed in building area and 2 feet outside of building line. Excavate footings to required depth and size shown in plans. No forms are required if soil is stable. Locate excavated soil conveniently for backfilling around treated wood posts.

Concrete Work

Footings shall be poured over undisturbed soil in excavations to indicated thickness and size as shown on plan. Top surface to be level.

Mix concrete to a 1:2-1/2:3-1/2 mix. If premixed concrete is available, use 5-bag mix.

Treated Wood Posts

Pressure-treated wood posts with 7-inch minimum top diameter shall be treated to conform to Federal Specification TT-W-571.

Carpentry

General

This branch of the work comprises all rough and finish carpentry necessary to complete the house, as shown on the plans and as specified. This includes layout, cutting and fitting framing, and other carpentry items. Any phase which is necessary for the completion of the house and not specifically covered in the plans or specifications shall be included as required.

Wood Framing

Dimension material for studs to be Standard (third grade); and for floor joists and framing, ceiling joists, rafters, beams, and trusses construction (second grade) in Douglas-fir, southern pine, or equivalent,[1] unless otherwise noted on the plans. All floor and ceiling joists, studs, and rafters shall be spaced 16 inches on center. Moisture content of framing lumber not to exceed 19 percent.

Subfloor

The subfloor shall be plywood to serve as a floor alone or as a base for resilient tile and shall consist of 3/4-inch C-C plugged Exterior grade, touch-sanded, and with matched edges in Douglas-fir, southern pine, or equivalent. When matched-edge plywood is not obtainable, square-edged plywood in the same grade and thickness can be substituted but 2- by 4-inch blocking shall be used for all longitudinal joints. Toenail 2- by 4-inch blocks flatwise in each joist space.

Roof Sheathing

Roof sheathing shall be 3/8-inch Douglas-fir or southern pine plywood or equal in Standard sheathing grade or nominal 1- by 6- or 1- by 8-inch boards in No. 3 Douglas-fir, southern pine, or equivalent. Boards shall be square edge, shiplap, or dressed and matched, and laid up tight at a moisture content of not more than 15 percent.

---

[1] See wall framing grades and span tables for allowable spans of other species (Federal Housing Administration tables) and American Lumber Standards for sizes and other information.

Insulation

Floors and walls of the first floor, walls and ceiling of the second floor, and the second floor area outside of the knee walls to be insulated with standard batt- or blanket-type flexible insulation with vapor barrier placed toward the inside of the building. Unless otherwise specified, minimum insulation thicknesses in the central and northern tiers of states shall be: Ceiling, 3 inches; wall and floor, 2 inches. Vapor barrier shall be placed toward the inside of the building. Vapor barrier to have a maximum perm value of 0.30.

Siding

Panel siding at gable ends shall be 3/8-inch thick and 4 foot wide exterior grade plywood in rough-sawn pattern with 1 by 2 inch batten at each stud. Remaining walls shall be panel siding of 5/8 inch by 4 by 9 foot exterior grade plywood in texture 1-11 (4-inch grooves) or equivalent. Edges of the sheets shall be dipped or brush coated with a water-repellent preservative before installation. A pigmented stain finish is recommended. Plywood shall be nailed at each stud and at ends of panels with galvanized or other rust-resistant nails spaced 7 to 8 inches apart. Use sixpenny nails for the 3/8-inch plywood and eightpenny for the 5/8-inch plywood.

Exterior Millwork

(a) Exterior finish. --Exterior trim and similar materials shall be No. 2 ponderosa pine or equivalent suitable for staining.

(b) Window frames and sash. --Complete double-hung windows shall be used with upper and lower sash cut to two horizontal lights, glazed with single-strength glass. Units to be treated with water-repellent preservative as outlined in Commercial Standard CS 190-64. Sash to be furnished fully balanced and fitted and with outside casing in place. Set in openings, plumb, and square. Screens shall be furnished, and storms when required.

(c) Exterior door frames and doors. --Exterior door frames shall have 1-3/8-inch rabbeted jambs and 1-5/8-inch oak sill or softwood sill with metal edge, all assembled. Set in openings, plumb, and square.

Exterior doors to be standard 1-3/4-inch with solid stiles and rails; panel type with glazed openings as shown on plans. Screen doors shall be furnished, or combinations when required.

(d) Screens. --Galvanized fly screen shall be used for gable end outlet ventilators and for inlet ventilators located in the plywood frieze board, as shown on plans.

Interior Millwork

(a) Interior door frames and doors. --Interior door frames and cased openings shall be nominal 1-inch ponderosa pine or equal in "D" Select. Stops shall be installed only where doors are specified.

Interior doors shall be 1-3/8 inches thick, five-cross-panel style with solid stiles and rails.

(b) Interior trim. --Interior trim shall be ponderosa pine or equal in "D" Select in ranch pattern in the following sizes:

Casings	--	11/16 by 2-1/4 inches
Stops	--	7/16 by 1-3/8 inches or wider
Base	--	7/16 by 2-1/4 inches
Base shoe	--	1/2 by 3/4 inch (when required)

Note: (1) Casing to be used at bottom of windows in place of stool and apron.
(2) Base shoe used along free-standing plywood wardrobes.

(c) Walls and ceilings. --All ceilings shall be finished with 3/8-inch gypsum board with recessed edges and with the length applied across the ceiling joists. End joints shall be staggered at least 16 inches. Walls shall be finished with 3/8-inch gypsum board with recessed edges and applied vertically. Application and joint treatment shall follow accepted practices. Install prefinished plywood in wall areas shown on plans.

Walls of tub recess shall be covered with plastic-finished hardboard panels over gypsum board. Install with mastic in accordance with manufacturer's directions. Inside corners, edges, and tub edges shall be finished with plastic moldings.

(d) Flooring. --Finish flooring throughout shall be 1/8-inch-thick asphalt tile in 9- by 9-inch size, "B" quality. Combination plywood subfloor shall be cleaned, nails driven flush, and joints sanded smooth where required. Tile shall be applied in accordance with manufacturer's recommendations. Rubber baseboard shall be furnished and installed in the bathroom, wood base in the remainder of the house.

(e) Hardware.--Furnish and install all rough and finish hardware complete as needed for perfect operation. Locks shall be furnished for all outside doors. Outside doors to be hung with three 4- by 4-inch loose-pin butt hinges and inside doors with two 3-1/2- by 3-1/2-inch loose-pin butt hinges. Bathroom five-cross-panel door shall be furnished with standard bathroom lock set. Standard screen door latches, hinges, and door closers shall be furnished and installed. Furnish and install semiconcealed cabinet hinges, pulls, and catches where required for cabinet or closet doors. All finish hardware to be finished in dull brass.

Sheet Metal Work and Roofing

Sheet Metal

Sheet metal flashing, when required for the prefabricated chimney and vent stack, shall be 28-gage galvanized iron or painted terneplate.

Roofing

Roofing shall be a minimum of 210-pound square-tab 12- by 36-inch asphalt shingles. A minimum of four 7/8-inch galvanized roofing nails shall be used for each 12- by 36-inch shingle strip. Any defects or leaks shall be corrected.

Electrical Work

The work shall include all materials and labor necessary to make the systems complete as shown on the plans. All work and materials shall comply with local requirements or those of the National Electrical Code. All wiring shall be concealed and carried in BX or other approved conduit to each outlet, switch, fixture, and appliance or electrical equipment such as furnace, hot water heater, and range when required, and as shown on the plan. Panel shall be 100 amp. capacity with overload cutout. Wall fixtures to consist of the following:
Two outside wall fixtures with crystal glass.
Two overhead (wall) fixtures, for kitchen and bath.

Heating

Heater and prefabricated chimney shall be installed as shown on the plans with supply ducts located in furred-down ceiling of hall. Heater shall be for LP or natural gas with a 100,000 minimum B.t.u. input or as required by design for each specific area. Cold air return at furnace base and from each corner of the house. Cold air duct shall consist of 1/8-inch transite-covered joist spaces along outside walls and connection to 10-inch-diameter or 6-inch by 12-inch rectangular galvanized or aluminum ducts to heater.

Plumbing

All plumbing shall be installed in accordance with local or National plumbing codes. Hot- and cold-water connections shall be furnished to all fixtures as required. Sewer and water and gas lines (when required) shall extend to building line with water shutoff valve. Framed and insulated box shall be used to protect water and sewer lines from freezing in crawl space where required. Cover with 1/8-inch transite or equal and insulate with 3 inches of fiberglass or styrofoam when required. Use a 16- by 16-inch vitrified tile or equal below groundline.

Furnish and install the following fixtures:
One kitchen sink--21 by 15 inches, self rim, steel, white, with fixtures.
One bathtub--5 foot, cast iron, white, left-hand drain, complete with shower rod and shower head, with fixtures.
One water closet--Reverse trap, white, with seat, fixtures, and shutoff valve.
One lavatory--19 by 17 inches, steel, white, and with fixtures and shutoff valves.
One hot water heater--50-gallon (minimum), gas or electric.
Washing machine connection with hot and cold water and drain.

Painting and Finishing

Exterior

Exterior plywood panel siding, facia, shutters, and soffit areas shall be stained with pigmented stain as required. Use light gray, yellow, or another light color stain for the trim and shutters and a darker stain (brown, olive, gray, etc.) for the panel siding or a reverse color selection as desired by owner. (Optional shutters to be stained on faces and edges.)

Window and door frames, window sash, screen doors, and similar millwork shall be painted a light color, or as owners request. Types of paint and procedures to comply with recommended practices and materials.

Interior

All woodwork shall be painted in semigloss. Walls and ceilings finished in latex flat, bathroom woodwork and ceiling shall be finished with semigloss.

Termite Protection

Termite protection shall be provided in termite areas by means of soil treatment or termite shields or both as required by local practices and regulations.

Concrete Blocks

Concrete blocks (used as an alternate to foundation of treated wood posts) shall comply with ASTM C-90, Grade U-II, for standard size and quality.

Concrete blocks shall be laid over concrete footings, as shown on the foundation plan. Footings shall be level and laid out to conform to the building line. Blocks shall be laid up with 3/8-inch-thick mortar joints, tooling the joints on all exposed exterior surfaces. Anchor straps, when used, shall be embedded to a depth of at least 12 inches.

BILL OF MATERIAL FOR RURAL HOME

Plan No. 4

The following material is required for construction of the rural home detailed in Plan No. 4; quality of material and treatments are given in the specifications.

Foundation

The foundation of treated posts set on concrete footings requires:

    1-1/4 cubic yards concrete
    15 treated foundation posts, 5 feet long or longer as required
        by slope, with 7-inch minimum top diameter

Floor Framing

Floor framing consisting of floor joists supported on ledgers nailed to the anchored floor beams requires:

4 --	2 x 12's	12 feet long
12 --	2 x 12's	16 feet long
46 --	2 x 8's	12 feet long
12 --	2 x 4's	12 feet long
40 lineal feet 22-gage x 2-inch galvanized anchor strap		

Floor

Requirements of floor tile and subfloor are:

    48 -- 4- x 8-foot sheets of 3/4-inch tongued-and-
        grooved plywood
    2,600 -- 9- x 9-inch asphalt tile (10 pct. waste) (with adhesive)

Wall and Partition Framing

Framing material for walls and partitions (studs and plates) includes:

133 --	2 x 4's	8 feet long
114 --	2 x 4's	12 feet long
16 --	2 x 6's	12 feet long

Ceiling and Roof Framing

Materials for rafters, joists, and a flush beam over the living area are:

25 --	2 x 4's	8 feet long
6 --	2 x 4's	12 feet long
54 --	2 x 6's	20 feet long
26 --	2 x 8's	12 feet long
25 --	2 x 8's	14 feet long
3 --	1 x 8's	12 feet long

Roof

Roofing and sheathing requirements are:

    45 -- 4- x 8-foot sheets of 3/8-inch plywood sheathing grade
        (Standard) (CD)
    14 squares -- 210-pound asphalt shingles

Siding

The following siding or equivalent alternates are required:

    10 -- 4- x 9-foot sheets 3/8-inch plywood, exterior grade
        (textured surface)
    16 -- 1 x 2 battens, 12 feet long
    28 -- 4- x 9-foot sheets rough-textured, 5/8-inch Texture 1-11
        or equal

Windows

All windows are double-hung and purchased treated and complete with screens, and storms when required. Quantity of each size is:

    1 -- 36/24
    7 -- 32/20
    5 -- 24/20
    1 -- 24/16

Exterior Doors

Doors are 1-3/4 inches thick, glazed; and frame, trim, and hardware are required for each. Screen doors shall be furnished, or combinations when required. Sizes are:

    Front -- 3 feet 0 inches wide and 6 feet 8 inches high
    Rear -- 2 feet 8 inches wide and 6 feet 8 inches high

Insulation

Blanket insulation with aluminum foil vapor barrier on one side is required for ceiling, walls, and floor.

    2,000 square feet -- 2 inches thick or as required, 16 inches
        wide
    1,200 square feet -- 3 inches thick or as required, 16 inches
        wide

Roof Ventilators

Requirements for ventilating the roof are:

    2 -- Peak-type outlet vents
    16 square feet -- Screen for inlet vent slots

Frieze Board

Material required for frieze board is:

    5 -- 4- x 8-foot sheets 3/8-inch plywood, exterior grade,
        textured surface

Interior Wall and Ceiling Finish

Gypsum board is used for all interior finish except two accent walls in living-dining area, second floor bedroom end walls, and bathroom, except for plastic-coated hardboard above the bathtub. Requirements are:

    74 -- 4- x 8-foot sheets of 3/8-inch gypsum board
    3 -- 4- x 8-foot sheets of plastic coated hardboard with
        corner and edge moldings (bath)
    22 -- 4- x 8-foot sheets of 1/4-inch prefinished plywood
        paneling
    3 -- 250-foot rolls of joint tape
    6 -- 25-pound bags of joint compound

Stairs

Material required for stairs is:

    2 -- 1 x 10's   14-foot-long stringers
    2 -- 2 x 4's   10 feet long
    2 -- 2 x 12's   14 feet long
    3 -- 1 x 8's   10 feet long
    11 -- Treads 5/4 x 10-1/2 x 2 feet 6 inches
    16 board feet of 1 x 4 fir flooring (platform)

Interior Doors

Interior door requirements are:

    1 set -- 2-foot 4-inch x 6-foot 8-inch hollow-core door
        with jambs, stops, and hardware
    2 sets -- Jambs for 2-foot 6-inch x 6-foot 8-inch doors
    2 sets -- Jambs for 3-foot by 6-foot 6-inch doors
    1 -- 4- x 8-foot sheet 1/2-inch plywood, interior AC

Interior Trim

Trim for windows, doors, and base includes:

330 feet -- 9/16- x 2-1/8-inch casing
340 feet -- 1/2- x 3-inch base

Cabinets

Material requirements for wood-frame and plywood cabinets are

3 -- 4- x 8-foot sheets 3/4-inch plywood, interior AC
1 -- 1 x 3   8 feet long
6 -- 1 x 4's   8 feet long

Wardrobes

Wardrobes consisting of closet poles with a shelf over require:

5 -- 4- x 8-foot sheets 3/4-inch plywood, interior AA
6 -- 4- x 8-foot sheets 1/2-inch plywood, interior AA
4 -- Closet poles, 1-5/16-inch diameter x 8 feet long
2 -- 1 x 3's, 8 feet long
7 pair -- Pole sockets for 1-5/16-inch poles

Front Stoop

The front stoop, consisting of planks laid across 2 x 4 framing
supported by treated posts, has the following material requirement

2 -- Treated posts, 5 feet long with 6-inch minimum top
     diameter
3 -- 2 x 4's   8 feet long
10 -- 2 x 6's   6 feet long
4 -- 1/2-inch galvanized carriage bolts, 8 inches long

Rear Stoop

Material requirements for the rear stoop are:

3 -- Treated posts, 5 feet long, with 6-inch minimum top
     diameter
4 -- 2 x 4's   8 feet long
9 -- 2 x 6's   8 feet long
6 -- 1/2-inch galvanized carriage bolts, 8 inches long

Nails

52 pounds -- Eightpenny common
30 pounds -- Sixteenpenny common
3 pounds -- Twentypenny common
4 pounds -- Tenpenny common, galvanized
2 pounds -- Sixteenpenny common, galvanized
3 pounds -- Fourpenny finish
20 pounds -- Eightpenny finish
18 pounds -- 3/4-inch galvanized roofing
30 pounds -- Fourpenny cooler

Paint and Finish

Quantities required for one coat of paint inside, two on exterior
(windows and doors), and one coat of stain outside are:

11 gallons -- Walls and ceiling (interior)
2 gallons -- Interior trim
7 gallons -- Exterior siding and trim (Use different body
             and trim color, as desired)
1 gallon -- Exterior paint (windows, doors, and frames)

Electrical

In addition to rough wiring and 100-amp. service, the following
items are required:

17 -- Duplex outlets
2 -- Wall-mounted interior lights
2 -- Wall-mounted exterior lights
3 -- Ceiling lights
5 -- Switches, single pole
2 -- Switches, 3-way

Heating

The heating system requires a 100,000 B.t.u. gas furnace with
10 registers, 6 cold-air returns, duct, a prefab chimney, controls,
and other items required for a complete system.

Plumbing

Complete plumbing must be provided for the following required
fixtures:

1 -- 5-foot bathtub
1 -- Water closet
1 -- Lavatory
1 -- Kitchen sink
1 -- 50-gallon water heater
1 -- 16- x 16- x 24-inch vitrified tile or equal (at sewer and
     water entrance)

ALTERNATES OR OPTIONS

Floor (Square-Edge Plywood)

When tongued-and-grooved plywood is not available, square-edge plywood with all edges blocked can be used. Material requirements for flooring and subfloor are:

    48 -- 4- x 8-foot sheets 3/4-inch plywood
    20 -- 2 x 4's, 12 feet long
  2,600 -- 9- x 9-inch asphalt tile (10 pct. waste) (with adhesive)

Shutters (Optional)

    2 -- 4- x 8-foot sheets 5/8-inch plywood, exterior grade, textured surface

Foundation (Concrete-Block)

The foundation of concrete blocks on poured concrete footings, plus masonry front and rear stoops, requires: (Note: Based on 4-ft. foundation depth.)

    7 cubic yards of concrete (footings)
  504 -- 8- x 8- x 16-inch concrete blocks
   85 -- 4- x 8- x 16-inch concrete solid-cap blocks
   72 -- 8- x 6- x 16-inch concrete blocks
   24 -- 8- x 6- x 8-inch concrete blocks (stoop)
   18 sacks prepared mortar
    2 cubic yards mason's sand
   60 square feet 6- x 6-inch mesh reinforcing (stoops)
    4 -- 1/2-inch reinforcing rods, 5 feet long (step)
    4 -- 1/2-inch reinforcing rods, 7 feet long (step)
  800 square feet 4-mil polyethylene film (soil cover)
    2 -- 8- x 16-inch foundation vents
    1 -- 16- x 16-inch (minimum) access door and frame

Floor Framing (For Concrete-Block Foundation)

    4 -- 2 x 12's   16 feet long
   58 -- 2 x 8's   12 feet long
    4 -- 2 x 4's   16 feet long
   45 lineal feet 22-gage x 2-inch anchor strap

Second-Floor Bathroom

A second bathroom can be added in a second-floor dormer. Materials required for constructing the dormer and providing bathroom fixtures are: (Note: As a less costly addition, a lavatory could be installed in each upstairs bedroom.)

   29 -- 2 x 4's   8 feet long
   14 -- 2 x 4's   16 feet long
   12 -- 2 x 6's   8 feet long
    4 -- 4- x 8-foot sheets of 5/8-inch plywood, exterior grade (rough-textured)
   16 -- 1 x 2 battens, 8 feet long
    7 -- 4- x 8-foot sheets of 1/4-inch prefinished plywood
    2 -- 4- x 8-foot sheets of 3/8-inch gypsum board
   40 -- 9- x 9-inch asphalt tile (with adhesive)
    1 -- 24/16 treated double-hung window (storm and screen)
    1 set -- 2-foot 4-inch x 6-foot 6-inch hollow-core door with jambs, stops, and hardware
    1 -- wall-mounted interior light
    1 -- switch
    1 -- hot-air register with duct
    1 -- 30- x 30-inch shower stall
    1 -- lavatory
    1 -- water closet

Bedroom Dormer

A bedroom dormer can be included with the second-floor bathroom addition. Materials required are:

   20 -- 2 x 4's   8 feet long
   12 -- 2 x 4's   16 feet long
    2 -- 4- x 8-foot sheets 5/8-inch plywood, exterior grade (textured surface)
    6 -- 1 x 2 battens, 8 feet long
    6 -- 4- x 8-foot sheets of 3/8-inch gypsum board
   56 -- 9- x 9-inch asphalt tile (with adhesive)
    1 -- 24/16 treated double-hung window (storm and screen)

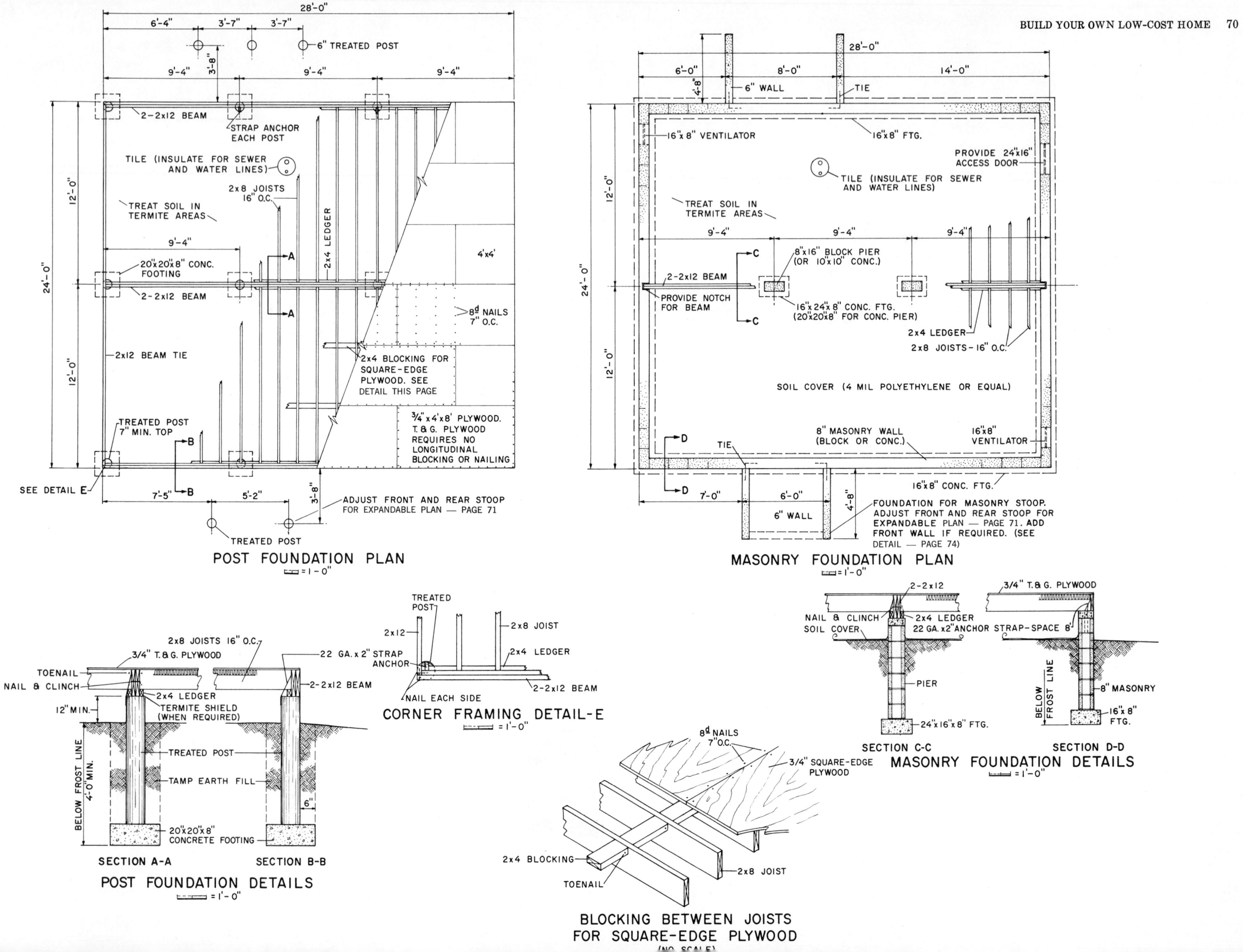

POST FOUNDATION PLAN
¼"=1'-0"

28'-0"
6'-4"   3'-7"   3'-7"
9'-4"   9'-4"   9'-4"
3'-8"
6" TREATED POST
2-2x12 BEAM
STRAP ANCHOR EACH POST
TILE (INSULATE FOR SEWER AND WATER LINES)
2x8 JOISTS 16" O.C.
2x4 LEDGER
TREAT SOIL IN TERMITE AREAS
9'-4"
20"x20"x8" CONC. FOOTING
2-2x12 BEAM
4'x4'
8ᵈ NAILS 7" O.C.
12'-0"
24'-0"
12'-0"
2x12 BEAM TIE
2x4 BLOCKING FOR SQUARE-EDGE PLYWOOD. SEE DETAIL THIS PAGE
TREATED POST 7" MIN. TOP
¾" x 4'x8' PLYWOOD. T. & G. PLYWOOD REQUIRES NO LONGITUDINAL BLOCKING OR NAILING
SEE DETAIL E
7'-5"   5'-2"
3'-8"
ADJUST FRONT AND REAR STOOP FOR EXPANDABLE PLAN — PAGE 71
TREATED POST

MASONRY FOUNDATION PLAN
¼"=1'-0"

28'-0"
6'-0"   8'-0"   14'-0"
4'-8"
6" WALL   TIE
16"x 8" VENTILATOR   16"x8" FTG.
PROVIDE 24"x16" ACCESS DOOR
TILE (INSULATE FOR SEWER AND WATER LINES)
TREAT SOIL IN TERMITE AREAS
9'-4"   9'-4"   9'-4"
2-2x12 BEAM
PROVIDE NOTCH FOR BEAM
8"x16" BLOCK PIER (OR 10"x10" CONC.)
16"x 24"x 8" CONC. FTG. (20"x20"x8" FOR CONC. PIER)
2x4 LEDGER
2x8 JOISTS - 16" O.C.
12'-0"
24'-0"
12'-0"
SOIL COVER (4 MIL POLYETHYLENE OR EQUAL)
8" MASONRY WALL (BLOCK OR CONC.)
16"x8" VENTILATOR
7'-0"   6'-0"
4'-8"
6" WALL
16"x8" CONC. FTG.
FOUNDATION FOR MASONRY STOOP. ADJUST FRONT AND REAR STOOP FOR EXPANDABLE PLAN — PAGE 71. ADD FRONT WALL IF REQUIRED. (SEE DETAIL — PAGE 74)

POST FOUNDATION DETAILS
¼" = 1'-0"

2x8 JOISTS 16" O.C.
¾" T. & G. PLYWOOD
22 GA. x 2" STRAP ANCHOR
TOENAIL
NAIL & CLINCH
2-2x12 BEAM
2x4 LEDGER
TERMITE SHIELD (WHEN REQUIRED)
12" MIN.
TREATED POST
TAMP EARTH FILL
BELOW FROST LINE 4'-0" MIN.
6"
20"x20"x8" CONCRETE FOOTING
SECTION A-A   **SECTION B-B**

CORNER FRAMING DETAIL-E
¼" = 1'-0"

TREATED POST
2x12
2x8 JOIST
2x4 LEDGER
22 GA. x 2" STRAP ANCHOR
2-2x12 BEAM
NAIL EACH SIDE

MASONRY FOUNDATION DETAILS
¼" = 1'-0"

2-2x12
¾" T.& G. PLYWOOD
2x4 LEDGER
22 GA. x2" ANCHOR STRAP-SPACE 8'
NAIL & CLINCH
SOIL COVER
PIER
24"x16"x8" FTG.
SECTION C-C
BELOW FROST LINE
8" MASONRY
16"x 8" FTG.
SECTION D-D

BLOCKING BETWEEN JOISTS FOR SQUARE-EDGE PLYWOOD
(NO SCALE)

8ᵈ NAILS 7" O.C.
¾" SQUARE-EDGE PLYWOOD
2x4 BLOCKING
TOENAIL
2x8 JOIST

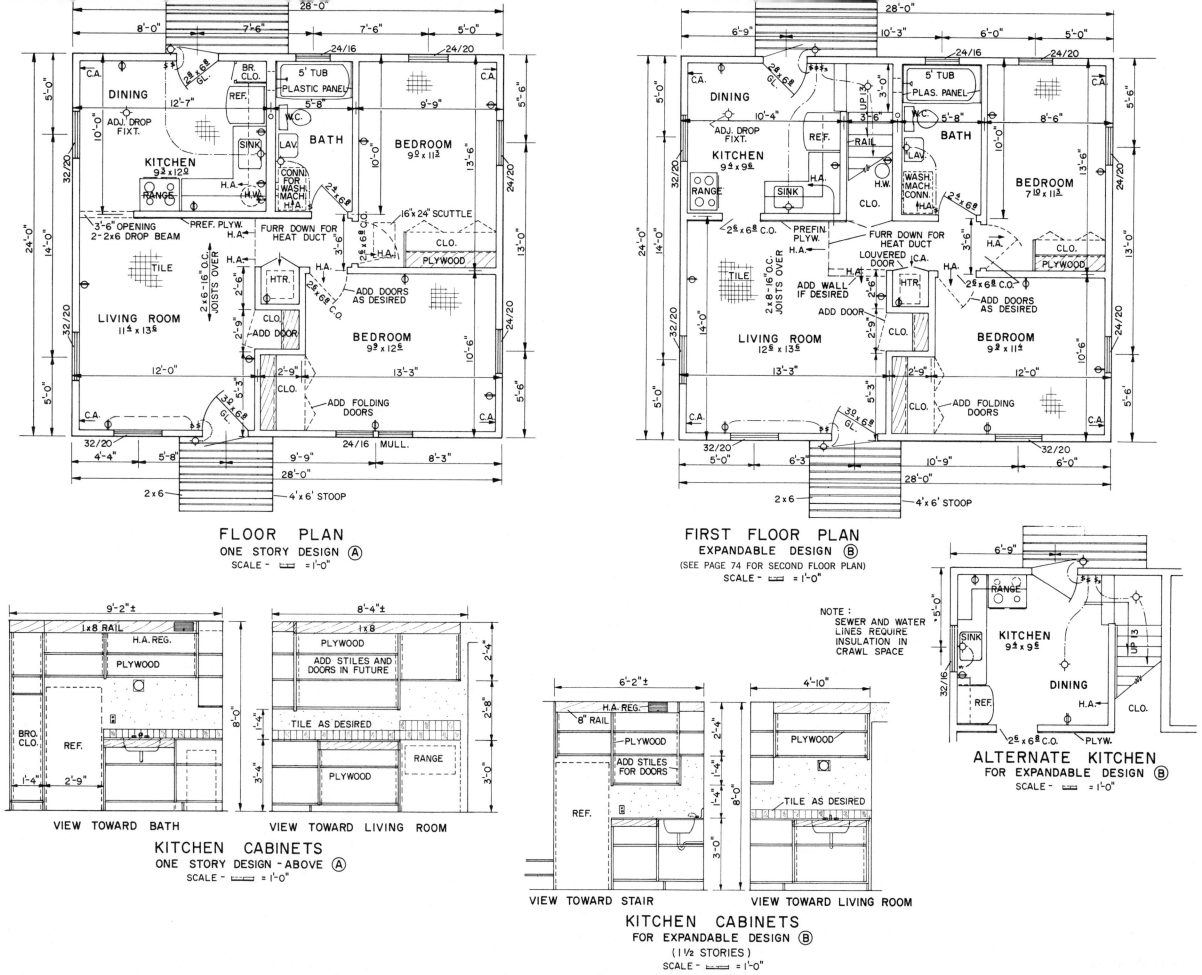

FLOOR PLAN
ONE STORY DESIGN Ⓐ
SCALE - ▭ = 1'-0"

FIRST FLOOR PLAN
EXPANDABLE DESIGN Ⓑ
(SEE PAGE 74 FOR SECOND FLOOR PLAN)
SCALE - ▭ = 1'-0"

NOTE:
SEWER AND WATER
LINES REQUIRE
INSULATION IN
CRAWL SPACE

KITCHEN CABINETS
ONE STORY DESIGN - ABOVE Ⓐ
SCALE - ▭ = 1'-0"

VIEW TOWARD BATH   VIEW TOWARD LIVING ROOM

VIEW TOWARD STAIR   VIEW TOWARD LIVING ROOM

KITCHEN CABINETS
FOR EXPANDABLE DESIGN Ⓑ
(1½ STORIES)
SCALE - ▭ = 1'-0"

ALTERNATE KITCHEN
FOR EXPANDABLE DESIGN Ⓑ
SCALE - ▭ = 1'-0"

HOUSE PLAN **5**   71

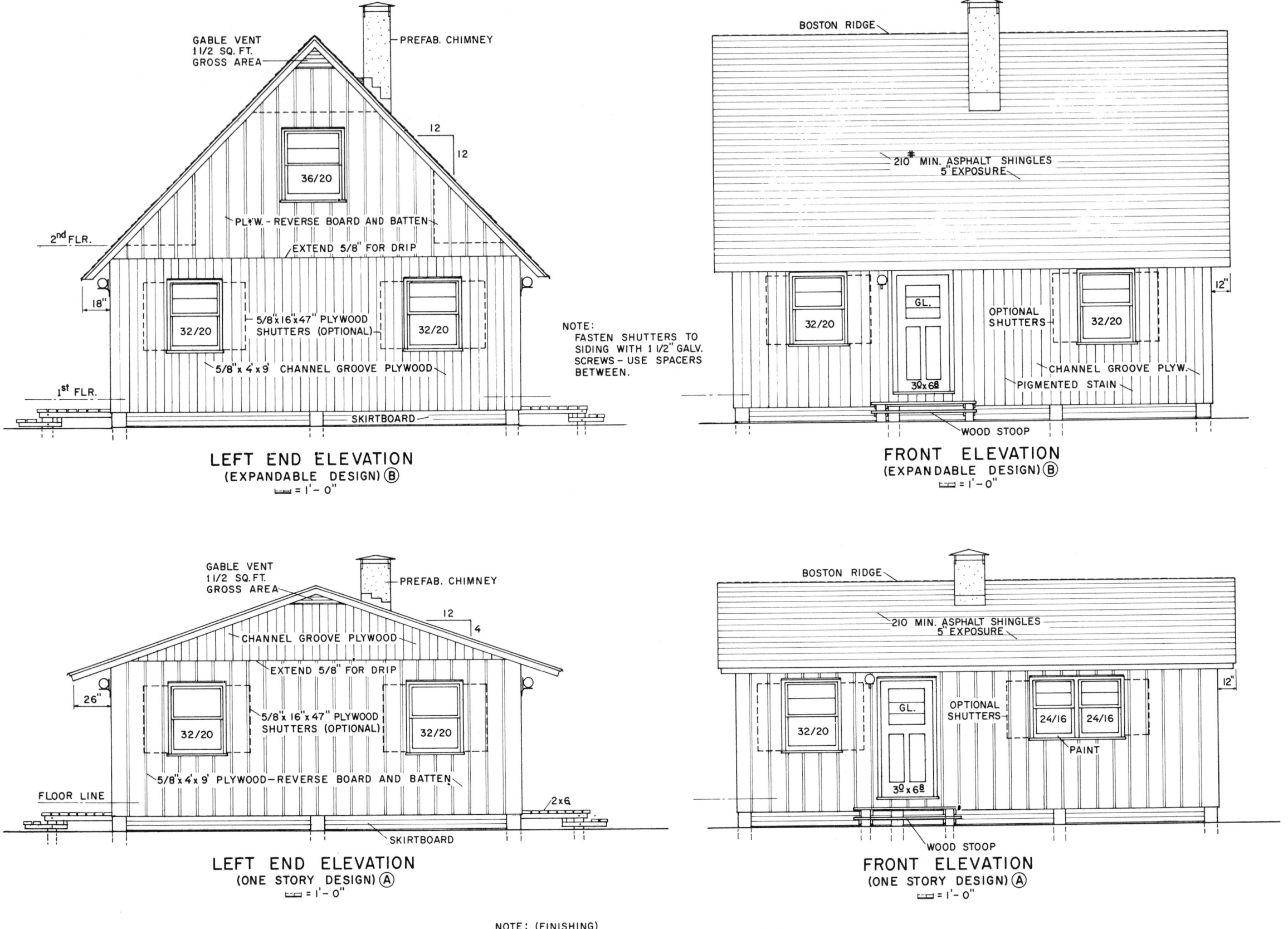

LEFT END ELEVATION
(EXPANDABLE DESIGN) Ⓑ
= 1'-0"

GABLE VENT
1 1/2 SQ. FT.
GROSS AREA

PREFAB. CHIMNEY

36/20

12
12

2nd FLR.

PLYW. - REVERSE BOARD AND BATTEN

EXTEND 5/8" FOR DRIP

18"

5/8" x 16" x 47" PLYWOOD
SHUTTERS (OPTIONAL)

32/20

32/20

1st FLR.

5/8" x 4 x 9' CHANNEL GROOVE PLYWOOD

SKIRTBOARD

NOTE:
FASTEN SHUTTERS TO
SIDING WITH 1 1/2" GALV.
SCREWS - USE SPACERS
BETWEEN.

FRONT ELEVATION
(EXPANDABLE DESIGN) Ⓑ
= 1'-0"

BOSTON RIDGE

210# MIN. ASPHALT SHINGLES
5' EXPOSURE

32/20

GL.

OPTIONAL
SHUTTERS

32/20

12"

30 x 68

CHANNEL GROOVE PLYW.

PIGMENTED STAIN

WOOD STOOP

LEFT END ELEVATION
(ONE STORY DESIGN) Ⓐ
= 1'-0"

GABLE VENT
1 1/2 SQ. FT.
GROSS AREA

PREFAB. CHIMNEY

CHANNEL GROOVE PLYWOOD

12
4

EXTEND 5/8" FOR DRIP

26"

5/8" x 16" x 47" PLYWOOD
SHUTTERS (OPTIONAL)

32/20

32/20

5/8" x 4 x 9' PLYWOOD - REVERSE BOARD AND BATTEN

FLOOR LINE

2 x 6

SKIRTBOARD

FRONT ELEVATION
(ONE STORY DESIGN) Ⓐ
= 1'-0"

BOSTON RIDGE

210# MIN. ASPHALT SHINGLES
5' EXPOSURE

32/20

GL.

OPTIONAL
SHUTTERS

24/16   24/16

PAINT

12"

3⁰ x 6⁸

WOOD STOOP

NOTE: (FINISHING)
SIDING - PIGMENTED STAIN - MEDIUM TO DARK COLOR
TRIM - PIGMENTED STAIN - LIGHT COLOR
WINDOWS - PAINT - WHITE OR LIGHT COLOR

NOTE: TRIM INCLUDES SHUTTERS, FACIA, FLY
RAFTERS, SOFFIT, MOLDINGS, ETC.

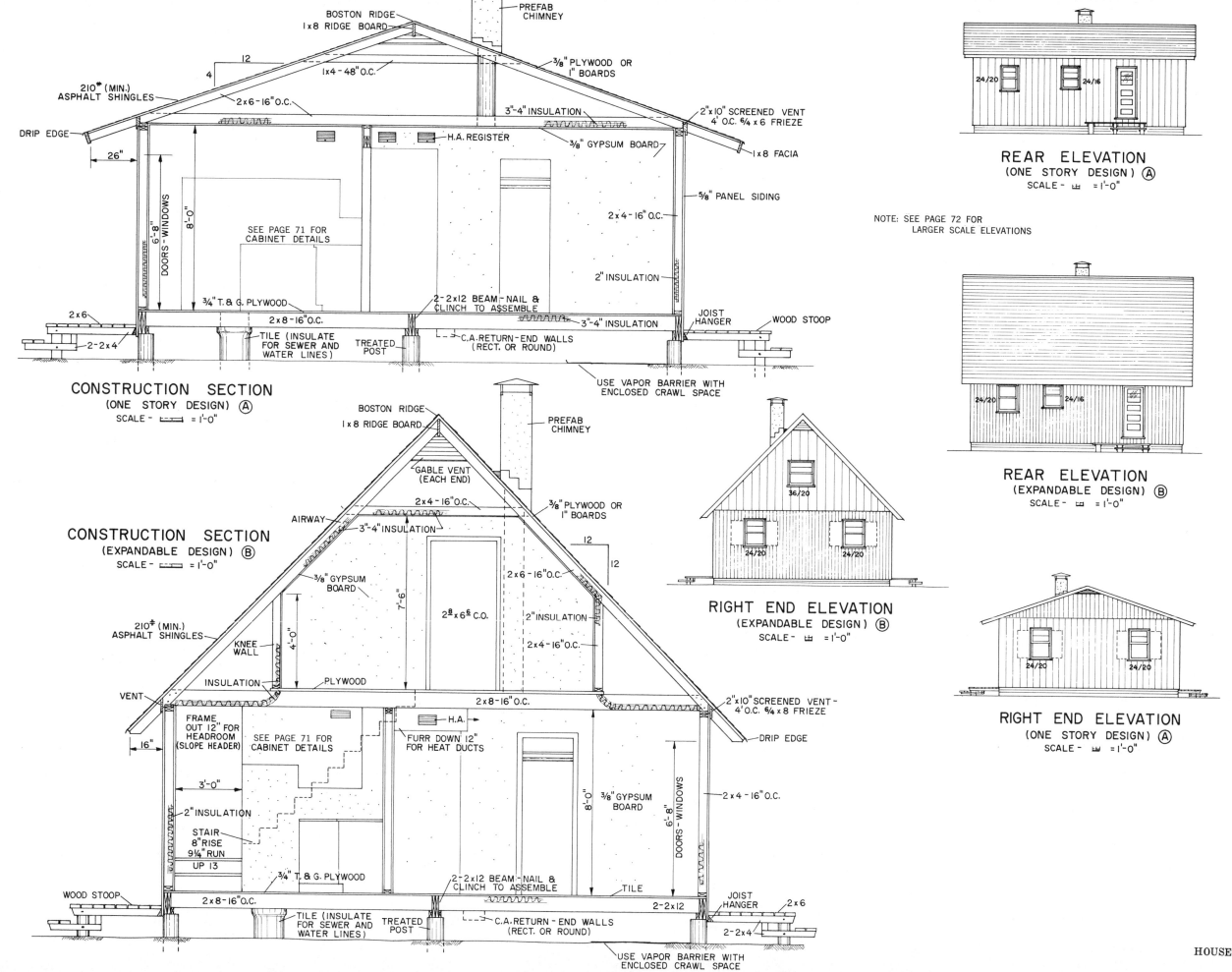

BOSTON RIDGE
1x8 RIDGE BOARD

PREFAB CHIMNEY

3/8" PLYWOOD OR 1" BOARDS

210# (MIN.) ASPHALT SHINGLES

1x4 - 48" O.C.

12
4

2x6 - 16" O.C.

3"-4" INSULATION

2"x10" SCREENED VENT 4' O.C. 6/4 x 6 FRIEZE

DRIP EDGE

H.A. REGISTER

3/8" GYPSUM BOARD

1x8 FACIA

26"

5/8" PANEL SIDING

DOORS - WINDOWS

8'-0"
6'-8"

2x4 - 16" O.C.

SEE PAGE 71 FOR CABINET DETAILS

2" INSULATION

3/4" T. & G. PLYWOOD

2-2x12 BEAM - NAIL & CLINCH TO ASSEMBLE

JOIST HANGER

WOOD STOOP

2x6

2x8 - 16" O.C.

3"-4" INSULATION

2-2x4

TILE (INSULATE FOR SEWER AND WATER LINES)

TREATED POST

C.A. RETURN - END WALLS (RECT. OR ROUND)

USE VAPOR BARRIER WITH ENCLOSED CRAWL SPACE

CONSTRUCTION SECTION
(ONE STORY DESIGN) A
SCALE - = 1'-0"

BOSTON RIDGE
1 x 8 RIDGE BOARD

PREFAB CHIMNEY

GABLE VENT (EACH END)

3/8" PLYWOOD OR 1" BOARDS

2x4 - 16" O.C.

AIRWAY

3"-4" INSULATION

12
12

CONSTRUCTION SECTION
(EXPANDABLE DESIGN) B
SCALE - = 1'-0"

3/8" GYPSUM BOARD

2x6 - 16" O.C.

210# (MIN.) ASPHALT SHINGLES

KNEE WALL

7'-6"
4'-0"

2 8/8 x 6 6/8 C.O.

2" INSULATION

2x4 - 16" O.C.

INSULATION

PLYWOOD

VENT

2x8 - 16" O.C.

2"x10" SCREENED VENT - 4' O.C. 6/4 x 8 FRIEZE

DRIP EDGE

FRAME OUT 12" FOR HEADROOM (SLOPE HEADER)

16"

SEE PAGE 71 FOR CABINET DETAILS

H.A.

FURR DOWN 12" FOR HEAT DUCTS

2" INSULATION

3'-0"

STAIR 8" RISE 9 1/4" RUN

UP 13

8'-0"
6'-8"

3/8" GYPSUM BOARD

DOORS - WINDOWS

2x4 - 16" O.C.

WOOD STOOP

3/4" T. & G. PLYWOOD

2x8 - 16" O.C.

2-2x12 BEAM - NAIL & CLINCH TO ASSEMBLE

TILE

JOIST HANGER

2x6

2-2x12

TILE (INSULATE FOR SEWER AND WATER LINES)

TREATED POST

C.A. RETURN - END WALLS (RECT. OR ROUND)

2-2x4

USE VAPOR BARRIER WITH ENCLOSED CRAWL SPACE

REAR ELEVATION
(ONE STORY DESIGN) A
SCALE - = 1'-0"

24/20   24/16

NOTE: SEE PAGE 72 FOR LARGER SCALE ELEVATIONS

REAR ELEVATION
(EXPANDABLE DESIGN) B
SCALE - = 1'-0"

24/20   24/16

RIGHT END ELEVATION
(EXPANDABLE DESIGN) B
SCALE - = 1'-0"

36/20

24/20   24/20

RIGHT END ELEVATION
(ONE STORY DESIGN) A
SCALE - = 1'-0"

24/20   24/20

HOUSE PLAN 5   73

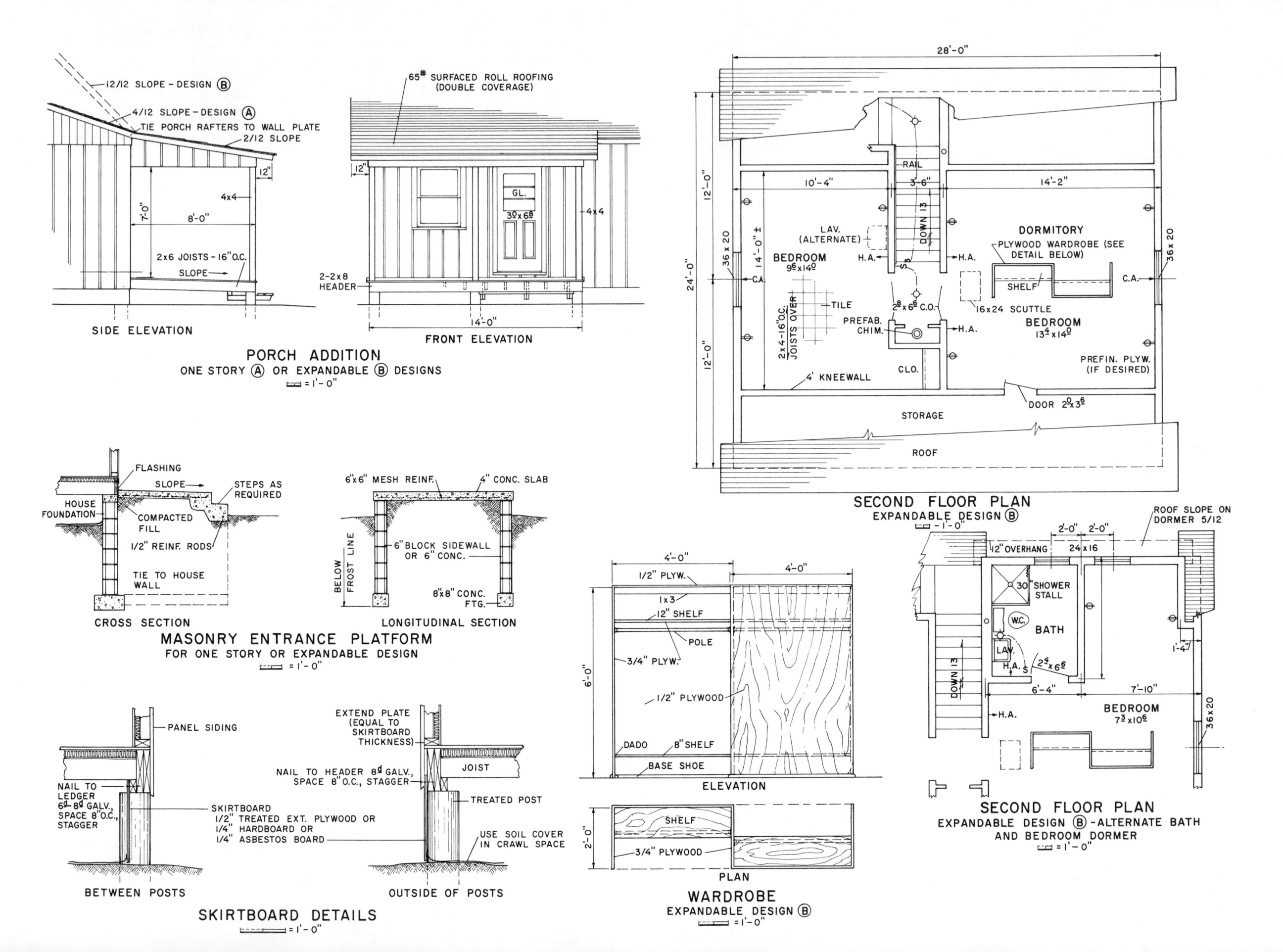

12/12 SLOPE – DESIGN Ⓑ
4/12 SLOPE – DESIGN Ⓐ
TIE PORCH RAFTERS TO WALL PLATE
2/12 SLOPE
12"
4x4
7'-0"
8'-0"
2 x 6 JOISTS – 16" O.C.
SLOPE

SIDE ELEVATION

65# SURFACED ROLL ROOFING
(DOUBLE COVERAGE)
12"
GL.
30 x 68
4x4
2-2 x 8
HEADER
14'-0"

FRONT ELEVATION

PORCH ADDITION
ONE STORY Ⓐ OR EXPANDABLE Ⓑ DESIGNS
= 1'- 0"

FLASHING
SLOPE
STEPS AS REQUIRED
HOUSE FOUNDATION
COMPACTED FILL
1/2" REINF. RODS
TIE TO HOUSE WALL

CROSS SECTION

6"x 6" MESH REINF.   4" CONC. SLAB
BELOW FROST LINE
6" BLOCK SIDEWALL OR 6" CONC.
8"x 8" CONC. FTG.

LONGITUDINAL SECTION

MASONRY ENTRANCE PLATFORM
FOR ONE STORY OR EXPANDABLE DESIGN
= 1'- 0"

PANEL SIDING
NAIL TO LEDGER 6ᵈ-8ᵈ GALV., SPACE 8" O.C., STAGGER
SKIRTBOARD 1/2" TREATED EXT. PLYWOOD OR 1/4" HARDBOARD OR 1/4" ASBESTOS BOARD

BETWEEN POSTS

EXTEND PLATE (EQUAL TO SKIRTBOARD THICKNESS)
JOIST
NAIL TO HEADER 8ᵈ GALV., SPACE 8" O.C., STAGGER
TREATED POST
USE SOIL COVER IN CRAWL SPACE

OUTSIDE OF POSTS

SKIRTBOARD DETAILS
= 1'- 0"

4'-0"   4'-0"
1/2" PLYW.
1x3
12" SHELF
POLE
3/4" PLYW.
1/2" PLYWOOD
6'-0"
DADO   8" SHELF
BASE SHOE

ELEVATION

SHELF
3/4" PLYWOOD
2'-0"

PLAN

WARDROBE
EXPANDABLE DESIGN Ⓑ
= 1'- 0"

28'-0"
RAIL
10'-4"   3'-6"   14'-2"
12'-0"
36 x 20
C.A.
14'-0" ±
LAV. (ALTERNATE)
H.A.
DOWN 13
DORMITORY
PLYWOOD WARDROBE (SEE DETAIL BELOW)
36 x 20
24'-0"
BEDROOM 9⁶ x14⁰
2 x 4–16" O.C. JOISTS OVER
TILE
PREFAB. CHIM.
8 x 6⁸ C.O.
H.A.
SHELF
C.A.
16 x 24 SCUTTLE
BEDROOM 13⁴ x14⁰
12'-0"
4' KNEEWALL
CLO.
STORAGE
PREFIN. PLYW. (IF DESIRED)
DOOR 2⁰ x3⁶
ROOF

SECOND FLOOR PLAN
EXPANDABLE DESIGN Ⓑ
= 1'- 0"

ROOF SLOPE ON DORMER 5/12
12" OVERHANG
2'-0" 2'-0"
24 x 16
30 SHOWER STALL
W.C.
BATH
DOWN 13
LAV.
H.A.
2⁴ x 6⁸
6'-4"
7'-10"
H.A.
BEDROOM 7³ x10⁶
1'-4"
36 x 20

SECOND FLOOR PLAN
EXPANDABLE DESIGN Ⓑ -ALTERNATE BATH AND BEDROOM DORMER
= 1'- 0"

SPECIFICATIONS

for

TWO OR FOUR BEDROOM WOOD-FRAME HOUSE

(One-story or one-and-one-half-story house, 24' -0" x 28' -0" in size, constructed over a crawl space)

All work related to construction of this house shall be done in a first-class manner. Details not included in specifications or plans shall comply with accepted practices for wood-frame construction.

Excavation - Grading

Sod, growing plants, shrubs, stumps, and trees shall be removed and ground smoothed in building area and 2 feet outside of building line. Excavate footings to required depth and size shown in plans. No forms are required if soil is stable. Locate excavated soil conveniently for backfilling around treated wood posts.

Concrete Work

Footings shall be poured over undisturbed soil in excavations to indicated thickness and size as shown on plan. Top surface to be level.

Mix concrete to a 1:2-1/2:3-1/2 mix. If premixed concrete is available, use 5-bag mix.

Treated Wood Posts

Pressure-treated wood posts with 7-inch minimum top diameter shall be treated to conform to Federal Specification TT-W-571.

Carpentry

General

This branch of the work comprises all rough and finish carpentry necessary to complete the house, as shown on the plans and as specified. This includes layout, cutting and fitting framing, and other carpentry items. Any phase which is necessary for the completion of the house and not specifically covered in the plans or specifications shall be included as required.

Wood Framing

Dimension material for studs to be Standard (third grade); and for floor joists and framing, ceiling joists, rafters, beams, and trusses construction (second grade) in Douglas-fir, southern pine, or equivalent,[1] unless otherwise noted on the plans. All floor and ceiling joists, studs, and rafters shall be spaced 16 inches on center. Moisture content of framing lumber not to exceed 19 percent.

Subfloor

The subfloor shall be plywood to serve as a floor alone or as a base for resilient tile and shall consist of 3/4-inch C-C plugged Exterior grade, touch-sanded, and with matched edges in Douglas-fir, southern pine, or equivalent. When matched-edge plywood is not obtainable, square-edged plywood in the same grade and thickness can be substituted but 2- by 4-inch blocking shall be used for all longitudinal joints. Toenail 2- by 4-inch blocks flatwise in each joist space.

Roof Sheathing

Roof sheathing shall be 3/8-inch Douglas-fir or southern pine plywood or equal in Standard sheathing grade or nominal 1- by 6- or 1- by 8-inch boards in No. 3 Douglas-fir, southern pine, or equivalent. Boards shall be square edge, shiplap, or dressed and matched, and laid up tight at a moisture content of not more than 15 percent.

---

[1] See wall framing grades and span tables for allowable spans of other species (Federal Housing Administration tables) and American Lumber Standards for sizes and other information.

Insulation

Floors and walls of the first floor, walls and ceiling of the second floor, and the second floor area outside of the knee walls to be insulated with standard batt- or blanket-type flexible insulation with vapor barrier placed toward the inside of the building. Unless otherwise specified, minimum insulation thicknesses in the central and northern tiers of states shall be: Ceiling, 3 inches; wall and floor, 2 inches. Vapor barrier shall be placed toward the inside of the building. Vapor barrier to have a maximum perm value of 0.30.

Siding

Panel siding shall be 5/8-inch thick and 4-foot wide exterior grade plywood in rough-sawn pattern. Remaining walls shall be panel siding of 5/8 inch by 4 by 9 foot exterior grade plywood in texture 1-11 (4-inch grooves). Pattern shall be reverse board and batten, channel groove, or equivalent. Edges of the sheets shall be dipped or brush coated with a water-repellent preservative before installation. A pigmented stain finish is recommended. Plywood shall be nailed at each stud and at ends of panels with galvanized or other rust-resistant nails spaced 7 to 8 inches apart. Use eightpenny nails for the 5/8-inch plywood.

Exterior Millwork

(a) Exterior finish. --Exterior trim and similar materials shall be No. 2 ponderosa pine or equivalent suitable for staining.

(b) Window frames and sash. --Complete double-hung windows shall be used with upper and lower sash cut to two horizontal lights, glazed with single-strength glass. Units to be treated with water-repellent preservative as outlined in Commercial Standard CS 190-64. Sash to be furnished fully balanced and fitted and with outside casing in place. Set in openings, plumb, and square. Screens shall be furnished, and storms when required.

(c) Exterior door frames and doors. --Exterior door frames shall have 1-3/8-inch rabbeted jambs and 1-5/8-inch oak sill or softwood sill with metal edge, all assembled. Set in openings, plumb, and square.

Exterior doors to be standard 1-3/4-inch with solid stiles and rails; panel type with glazed openings as shown on plans. Screen doors shall be furnished, or combinations when required.

(d) Screens. --Galvanized fly screen shall be used for gable end outlet ventilators and for inlet ventilators located in the plywood frieze board, as shown on plans.

Interior Millwork

(a) Interior door frames and doors. --Interior door frames and cased openings shall be nominal 1-inch ponderosa pine or equal in "D" Select. Stops shall be installed only where doors are specified.

Interior doors shall be 1-3/8 inches thick, five-cross-panel style with solid stiles and rails.

(b) Interior trim. --Interior trim shall be ponderosa pine or equal in "D" Select in ranch pattern in the following sizes:

Casings   -- 11/16 by 2-1/4 inches
Stops   -- 7/16 by 1-3/8 inches or wider
Base   -- 7/16 by 2-1/4 inches
Base shoe   -- 1/2 by 3/4 inch (when required)

Note: (1) Casing to be used at bottom of windows in place of stool and apron.
(2) Base shoe used along free-standing plywood wardrobes.

(c) Walls and ceilings. --All ceilings shall be finished with 3/8-inch gypsum board with recessed edges and with the length applied across the ceiling joists. End joints shall be staggered at least 16 inches. Walls shall be finished with 3/8-inch gypsum board with recessed edges and applied vertically. Application and joint treatment shall follow accepted practices. Install prefinished plywood in wall areas shown on plans.

Walls of tub recess shall be covered with plastic-finished hardboard panels over gypsum board. Install with mastic in accordance with manufacturer's directions. Inside corners, edges, and tub edges shall be finished with plastic moldings.

(d) Flooring. --Finish flooring throughout shall be 1/8-inch-thick asphalt tile in 9- by 9-inch size, "B" quality. Combination plywood subfloor shall be cleaned, nails driven flush, and joints sanded smooth where required. Tile shall be applied in accordance with manufacturer's recommendations. Rubber baseboard shall be furnished and installed in the bathroom, wood base in the remainder of the house.

(e) <u>Hardware</u>.--Furnish and install all rough and finish hardware complete as needed for perfect operation. Locks shall be furnished for all outside doors. Outside doors to be hung with three 4- by 4-inch loose-pin butt hinges and inside doors with two 3-1/2- by 3-1/2-inch loose-pin butt hinges. Bathroom five-cross-panel door shall be furnished with standard bathroom lock set. Standard screen door latches, hinges, and door closers shall be furnished and installed. Furnish and install semiconcealed cabinet hinges, pulls, and catches where required for cabinet or closet doors. All finish hardware to be finished in dull brass.

Sheet Metal Work and Roofing

Sheet Metal

Sheet metal flashing, when required for the prefabricated chimney and vent stack, shall be 28-gage galvanized iron or painted terneplate.

Roofing

Roofing shall be a minimum of 210-pound square-tab 12- by 36-inch asphalt shingles. A minimum of four 7/8-inch galvanized roofing nails shall be used for each 12- by 36-inch shingle strip. Any defects or leaks shall be corrected.

Electrical Work

The work shall include all materials and labor necessary to make the systems complete as shown on the plans. All work and materials shall comply with local requirements or those of the National Electrical Code. All wiring shall be concealed and carried in BX or other approved conduit to each outlet, switch, fixture, and appliance or electrical equipment such as furnace, hot water heater, and range when required, and as shown on the plan. Panel shall be 100 amp. capacity with overload cutout. Wall fixtures to consist of the following:
Two outside wall fixtures with crystal glass.
Two overhead (wall) fixtures, for kitchen and bath.

Heating

Heater and prefabricated chimney shall be installed as shown on the plans with supply ducts located in furred-down ceiling of hall. Heater shall be for LP or natural gas with a 100,000 minimum B.t.u. input or as required by design for each specific area. Cold air return at furnace base and from each corner of the house. Cold air duct shall consist of 1/8-inch transite-covered joist spaces along outside walls and connection to 10-inch-diameter or 6-inch by 12-inch rectangular galvanized or aluminum ducts to heater.

Plumbing

All plumbing shall be installed in accordance with local or National plumbing codes. Hot- and cold-water connections shall be furnished to all fixtures as required. Sewer and water and gas lines (when required) shall extend to building line with water shutoff valve. Framed and insulated box shall be used to protect water and sewer lines from freezing in crawl space where required. Cover with 1/8-inch transite or equal and insulate with 3 inches of fiberglass or styrofoam when required. Use a 16- by 16-inch vitrified tile or equal below groundline.

Furnish and install the following fixtures:
One kitchen sink--21 by 15 inches, self rim, steel, white, with fixtures.
One bathtub--5 foot, cast iron, white, left-hand drain, complete with shower rod and shower head, with fixtures.
One water closet--Reverse trap, white, with seat, fixtures, and shutoff valve.
One lavatory--19 by 17 inches, steel, white, and with fixtures and shutoff valves.
One hot water heater--50-gallon (minimum), gas or electric.
Washing machine connection with hot and cold water and drain.

Painting and Finishing

Exterior

Exterior plywood panel siding, facia, shutters, and soffit areas shall be stained with pigmented stain as required. Use light gray, yellow, or another light color stain for the trim and shutters and a darker stain (brown, olive, gray, etc.) for the panel siding or a reverse color selection as desired by owner. (Optional shutters to be stained on faces and edges.)

Window and door frames, window sash, screen doors, and similar millwork shall be painted a light color, or as owners request. Types of paint and procedures to comply with recommended practices and materials.

Interior

All woodwork shall be painted in semigloss. Walls and ceilings finished in latex flat, bathroom woodwork and ceiling shall be finished with semigloss.

Termite Protection

Termite protection shall be provided in termite areas by means of soil treatment or termite shields or both as required by local practices and regulations.

Concrete Blocks

Concrete blocks (used as an alternate to foundation of treated wood posts) shall comply with ASTM C-90, Grade U-II, for standard size and quality.

Concrete blocks shall be laid over concrete footings, as shown on the foundation plan. Footings shall be level and laid out to conform to the building line. Blocks shall be laid up with 3/8-inch-thick mortar joints, tooling the joints on all exposed exterior surfaces. Anchor straps, when used, shall be embedded to a depth of at least 12 inches.

BILL OF MATERIAL FOR RURAL HOME

The following material is required for construction of the rural home detailed in Plan No. 5; quality of material and treatments are given in the specifications. Materials for one-story house (Design A) are listed first; materials for one-and-a-half story house (Design B) follow; and materials for alternates or options are listed last.

ONE-STORY (DESIGN A)

Foundation

The foundation of treated posts set on concrete footings requires:

    1 cubic yard concrete
    12 treated foundation posts, 5 feet long or longer as required by
        slope, with 7-inch minimum top diameter

Floor Framing

Floor framing consisting of floor joists supported on ledgers nailed to the anchored floor beams requires:

    4 -- 2 x 12's   12 feet long
    9 -- 2 x 12's   20 feet long
    40 -- 2 x 8's   12 feet long
    12 -- 2 x 4's   10 feet long
    32 lineal feet 22-gage x 2-inch galvanized anchor strap

Floor

Requirements of floor tile and subfloor are:

    21 -- 4- x 8-foot sheets of 3/4-inch tongued-and-grooved
              plywood
    1,300 -- 9- x 9-inch asphalt tile (10 pct. waste) (with adhesive)

Wall and Partition Framing

Framing material for walls and partitions (studs and plates) includes:

    130 -- 2 x 4's   8 feet long
    59 -- 2 x 4's   12 feet long
    9 -- 2 x 6's   12 feet long

Ceiling and Roof Framing

Materials for rafters, joists, and a flush beam over the living area are:

    44 -- 2 x 6's   16 feet long
    21 -- 2 x 6's   12 feet long
    20 -- 2 x 6's   14 feet long
    3 -- 1 x 8's   10 feet long

Roof

Roofing and sheathing requirements are:

30 -- 4- x 8-foot sheets of 3/8-inch plywood sheathing grade
      (Standard) (CD)
10 squares -- 210-pound asphalt shingles

Siding

The following siding or equivalent alternates are required:

26 -- 4- x 9-foot sheets rough-textured, 5/8-inch reverse board
     and batten plywood siding
4 -- 4- x 8-foot sheets rough-textured, 5/8-inch channel groove
     plywood

Windows

All windows are double-hung and purchased treated and complete
with screens, and storms when required. Quantity of each size is:

3 -- 32/20
3 -- 24/20
3 -- 24/16

Exterior Doors

Doors are 1-3/4 inches thick, glazed; and frame, trim, and hardware are required for each. Screen doors shall be furnished, or combinations when required. Sizes are:

Front -- 3 feet 0 inches wide and 6 feet 8 inches high
Rear -- 2 feet 8 inches wide and 6 feet 8 inches high

Insulation

Blanket insulation with aluminum foil vapor barrier on one side is
required for ceiling, walls, and floor.

1,500 square feet -- 2 inches thick or as required, 16 inches
                         wide
700 square feet -- 3 inches thick or as required, 16 inches
                         wide

Roof Ventilators

Requirements for ventilating the roof are:

2 -- Peak-type outlet vents
14 square feet -- Screen for inlet vent slots

Trim

Material required for frieze board and facia is:

6 -- 6/4 x 6's   10 feet long
6 -- 1 x 8's   10 feet long

Interior Wall and Ceiling Finish

Gypsum board is used for all interior finish except one accent wall
in living area. The bathroom has plastic-coated hardboard above the
bathtub. Requirements are:

67 -- 4- x 8-foot sheets of 3/8-inch gypsum board
3 -- 4- x 8-foot sheets of plastic coated hardboard with corner
     and edge moldings (bath)
3 -- 4- x 8-foot sheets of 1/4-inch prefinished plywood paneling
3 -- 250-foot rolls of joint tape
6 -- 25-pound bags of joint compound

Interior Doors

Interior door requirements are:

1 set -- 2-foot 4-inch x 6-foot 8-inch hollow-core door with
        jambs, stops, and hardware
2 sets -- Jambs for 2-foot 6-inch x 6-foot 8-inch doors
1 -- 4- x 8-foot sheet 1/2-inch plywood, interior AC

Interior Trim

Trim for windows, doors, and base includes:

230 feet -- 9/16- x 2-1/8-inch casing
200 feet -- 1/2- x 3-inch base

Cabinets

Material requirements for wood-frame and plywood cabinets are:

```
4 -- 4- x 8-foot sheets 3/4-inch plywood, interior AC
1 -- 1 x 3          8 feet long
6 -- 1 x 4's        8 feet long
2 -- 1 x 8's        8 feet long
```

Wardrobes

Wardrobes consisting of closet poles with a shelf over require:

```
1 -- 4- x 8-foot sheet 3/4-inch plywood, interior AA
2 -- Closet poles, 1-5/16-inch diameter x 8 feet long
3 pair -- Pole sockets for 1-5/16-inch poles
```

Front Stoop

The front stoop, consisting of planks laid across 2 x 4 framing supported by treated posts, has the following material requirements:

```
 2 -- Treated posts, 5 feet long with 6-inch minimum top
         diameter
 3 -- 2 x 4's          8 feet long
10 -- 2 x 6's          6 feet long
 4 -- 1/2-inch galvanized carriage bolts, 8 inches long
```

Rear Stoop

Material requirements for the rear stoop are:

```
3 -- Treated posts, 5 feet long, with 6-inch minimum top
        diameter
4 -- 2 x 4's          8 feet long
9 -- 2 x 6's          8 feet long
6 -- 1/2-inch galvanized carriage bolts, 8 inches long
```

Nails

```
48 pounds -- Eightpenny common
26 pounds -- Sixteenpenny common
 2 pounds -- Twentypenny common
 3 pounds -- Tenpenny common, galvanized
 2 pounds -- Sixteenpenny common, galvanized
 2 pounds -- Fourpenny finish
12 pounds -- Eightpenny finish
14 pounds -- 3/4-inch galvanized roofing
25 pounds -- Fourpenny cooler
```

Paint and Finish

Quantities required for one coat of paint inside, two on exterior (windows and doors), and one coat of stain outside are:

```
7 gallons -- Walls and ceiling (interior)
2 gallons -- Interior trim
6 gallons -- Exterior siding and trim (Use different body and
                trim color, as desired)
1 gallon  -- Exterior paint (windows, doors, and frames)
```

Electrical

In addition to rough wiring and 100-amp. service, the following items are required:

```
11 -- Duplex outlets
 2 -- Wall-mounted interior lights
 2 -- Wall-mounted exterior lights
 1 -- Ceiling light
 4 -- Switches, single pole
```

Heating

The heating system requires a 75,000 B.t.u. gas furnace with 6 registers, 4 cold-air returns, duct, a prefab chimney, controls, and other items required for a complete system.

Plumbing

Complete plumbing must be provided for the following required fixtures:

1 -- 5-foot bathtub
1 -- Water closet
1 -- Lavatory
1 -- Kitchen sink
1 -- 30-gallon water heater (Under-counter type)
1 -- 16- x 16- x 24-inch vitrified tile or equal (at sewer and water entrance)

ONE-AND-A-HALF STORY (DESIGN B)

The following material is required for construction of the rural home detailed in Plan No. 5; quality of material and treatments are given in the specifications.

Foundation

The foundation of treated posts set on concrete footings requires:

1 cubic yard concrete
12 treated foundations posts, 5 feet long or longer as required by slope, with 7-inch minimum top diameter

Floor Framing

Floor framing consisting of floor joists supported on ledgers nailed to the anchored floor beams requires:

4 -- 2 x 12's	12 feet long
9 -- 2 x 12's	20 feet long
40 -- 2 x 8's	12 feet long
12 -- 2 x 4's	10 feet long

32 lineal feet 22-gage x 2-inch galvanized anchor strap

Floor

Requirements of floor tile and subfloor, including attic subfloor, are:

42 -- 4- x 8-foot sheets of 3/4-inch tongued-and-grooved plywood
2600 -- 9- x 9-inch asphalt tile (10 pct. waste) (with adhesive)

Wall and Partition Framing

Framing material for walls and partitions (studs and plates) includes:

182 -- 2 x 4's	8 feet long
80 -- 2 x 4's	12 feet long
10 -- 2 x 6's	12 feet long

Ceiling and Roof Framing

Materials for rafters and joists are:

20 -- 2 x 4's	8 feet long
44 -- 2 x 6's	20 feet long
20 -- 2 x 8's	12 feet long
20 -- 2 x 8's	14 feet long
3 -- 1 x 8's	10 feet long

Roof

Roofing and sheathing requirements are:

38 -- 4- x 8-foot sheets of 3/8-inch plywood, sheathing grade (Standard) (CD)
12 squares -- 210-pound asphalt shingles

Siding

The following siding or equivalent alternates are required:

26 -- 4- x 9-foot sheets rough-textured, 5/8-inch channel
        groove plywood
10 -- 4- x 9-foot sheets rough-textured, 5/8-inch reverse
        board and batten plywood siding

Windows

All windows are double-hung and purchased treated and complete
with screens, and storms when required. Quantity of each size is:

2 -- 36/20
4 -- 32/20
3 -- 24/20
1 -- 24/16

Exterior Doors

Doors are 1-3/4 inches thick, glazed; and frame, trim, and hardware are required for each. Screen doors shall be furnished, or
combinations when required. Sizes are:

Front -- 3 feet 0 inches wide and 6 feet 8 inches high
Rear -- 2 feet 8 inches wide and 6 feet 8 inches high

Insulation

Blanket insulation with aluminum foil vapor barrier on one side is
required for ceiling, walls, and floor.

1500 square feet -- 2 inches thick or as required,
                    16 inches wide
1000 square feet -- 3 inches thick or as required,
                    16 inches wide

Roof Ventilators

Requirements for ventilating the roof are:

2   -- Peak-type vents
14 square feet -- Screen for inlet vent slots

Frieze Board

Material required for frieze board is:

6 -- 6/4 x 6's   10 feet long

Interior Wall and Ceiling Finish

Gypsum board is used for all interior finish except one accent wall
in living area. The bathroom has plastic-coated hardboard above the
bathtub. Requirements are:

106 -- 4- x 8-foot sheets of 3/8-inch gypsum board
  3 -- 4- x 8-foot sheets of plastic-coated hardboard with corner
          and edge moldings (bath)
  6 -- 4- x 8-foot sheets of 1/4-inch prefinished plywood paneling
  5 -- 250-foot rolls of joint tape
 10 -- 25-pound bags of joint compound

Stairs

Materials for stairs are:

2 -- 1 x 10's   14-foot-long stringers
2 -- 2 x 4's   10 feet long
2 -- 2 x 12's   14 feet long
3 -- 1 x 8's   10 feet long
11 -- Treads 5/4 x 10-1/2 x 2 feet 6 inches
16 board feet of 1 x 4 fir flooring (platform)

Interior Doors

Interior door requirements are:

1 set -- 2-foot 4-inch x 6-foot 8-inch hollow-core door with
        jambs, stops, and hardware
3 sets -- Jambs for 2-foot 6-inch x 6-foot 8-inch doors
2 sets -- Jambs for 2-foot 6-inch x 6-foot 6-inch doors
2   -- 4- x 8-foot sheets of 1/2-inch plywood, interior AC

Interior Trim

Trim for windows, doors, and base includes:

295 feet -- 9/16- x 2-1/8-incl casing
285 feet -- 1/2- x 3-inch base

Cabinets

Material requirements for wood-frame and plywood cabinets are:

3 -- 4- x 8-foot sheets of 3/4-inch plywood, interior AC
1 -- 1 x 3   8 feet long
6 -- 1 x 4's   8 feet long
2 -- 1 x 8's   8 feet long

Wardrobes

Wardrobes consisting of closet poles with a shelf over require:

3 -- 4- x 8-foot sheets of 3/4-inch plywood, interior AA
2 -- 4- x 8-foot sheets of 1/2-inch plywood, interior AA
4 -- Closet poles, 1-5/16-inch diameter x 8 feet long
6 pair -- Pole sockets for 1-5/16-inch poles

Front Stoop

The front stoop, consisting of planks laid across 2 x 4 framing
supported by treated posts, has the following material requirements:

2 -- Treated posts, 5 feet long with 6-inch minimum top
        diameter

3 -- 2 x 4's   8 feet long
10 -- 2 x 6's   6 feet long
4 -- 1/2-inch galvanized carriage bolts, 8 inches long

Rear Stoop

Material requirements for the rear stoop are:

3 -- Treated posts, 5 feet long, with 6-inch minimum top
        diameter
4 -- 2 x 4's   8 feet long
9 -- 2 x 6's   8 feet long
6 -- 1/2-inch galvanized carriage bolts, 8 inches long

Nails

50 pounds -- Eightpenny common
26 pounds -- Sixteenpenny common
 2 pounds -- Twentypenny common
 3 pounds -- Tenpenny common, galvanized
 2 pounds -- Sixteenpenny common, galvanized
 2 pounds -- Fourpenny finish
12 pounds -- Eightpenny finish
16 pounds -- 3/4-inch galvanized roofing
25 pounds -- Fourpenny cooler

Paint and Finish

Quantities required for one coat of paint inside, two on exterior
(windows and doors), and one coat of stain outside are:

10 gallons -- Walls and ceiling (interior)
3 gallons -- Interior trim
7 gallons -- Exterior siding and trim (use different body and
                trim color, as desired)
1 gallon -- Exterior paint (windows, doors, and frames)

Electrical

In addition to rough wiring and 100-amp. service, the following items
are required:

17 -- Duplex outlets
 2 -- Wall-mounted interior lights
 2 -- Wall-mounted exterior lights
 3 -- Ceiling lights
 5 -- Switches, single pole
 2 -- Switches, 3-way

Heating

The heating system requires a 100,000 B.t.u. gas furnace with nine registers, six cold-air returns, duct, a prefab chimney, controls, and other items required for a complete system.

Plumbing

Complete plumbing must be provided for the following required fixtures:

    1 -- 5-foot bathtub
    1 -- Water closet
    1 -- Lavatory
    1 -- Kitchen sink
    1 -- 50-gallon water heater (undercounter type)
    1 -- 16- x 16- x 24-inch vitrified tile or equal (at sewer and
             water entrance)

Unfinished Second Floor

When the second floor is left unfinished, the following materials can be deducted from the bill of materials.

37	4- by 8-ft. sheets of 3/8-in. gypsum board
4	4- by 8-ft. sheets of 1/4-in. prefinished plywood paneling
2	250-ft. roll of joint tape
4	25-lb. bags of joint compound
65 ft.	9/16- by 2-1/8 in. casing
85 ft.	1/2- by 3-inch base
2 sets	jambs for 2-ft. 6-in. by 6-ft. 6-in. doors
2	4- by 8-ft. sheets of 3/4-inch plywood, interior AA
2	4- by 8-ft. sheets of 1/2-inch plywood, interior AA
2	closet poles, 1-5/8-in. diameter by 8 ft. long
3 pair	pole sockets for 1-5/16-inch poles
1300	9- by 9-in. asphalt tile (with adhesive)

ALTERNATES OR OPTIONS

Floor (Square-Edge Plywood)

When tongued-and-grooved plywood is not available, square-edge plywood with all edges blocked can be used. Material requirements for flooring and subfloor are:

Design A

    21 -- 4- x 8-foot sheets of 3/4-inch plywood
    10 -- 2 x 4's   12 feet long
    1300 -- 9- x 9-inch asphalt tile (10 pct. waste) (with adhesive)

Design B

    42 -- 4- x 8-foot sheets of 3/4-inch plywood
    20 -- 2 x 4's   12 feet long
    1300 -- 9- x 9-inch asphalt tile (10 pct. waste) (with adhesive)

Shutters (Optional)

    2 -- 4- x 8-foot sheets of 5/8-inch plywood, exterior grade,
             textured surface

Foundation (Concrete Block)

The foundation of concrete blocks on poured concrete footings, plus masonry front and rear stoops, requires: (Note: Based on 4-ft. foundation depth.)

      6 cubic yards of concrete (footings and stoops)
    462 -- 8- x 8- x 16-inch concrete blocks
     78 -- 4- x 8- x 16-inch concrete solid-cap blocks
     72 -- 8- x 6- x 16-inch concrete blocks
     24 -- 8- x 6- x 8-inch concrete blocks (stoops)
     18 sacks prepared mortar
      2 cubic yards mason's sand
     60 square feet 6- x 6-inch mesh reinforcing (stoops)
      4 -- 1/2-inch reinforcing rods, 5 feet long (step)
      4 -- 1/2-inch reinforcing rods, 7 feet long (step)
    700 square feet 4-mil polyethylene film (soil cover)
      2 -- 8- x 16-inch foundation vents
      1 -- 16- x 16-inch (minimum) access door and frame

Floor Framing (For Concrete-Block Foundation)

```
 3 -- 2 x 12's    20 feet long
46 -- 2 x 12's    12 feet long
 6 -- 2 x  4's    10 feet long
40 lineal feet of 22-gage x 2-inch anchor strap
```

Second-Floor Bathroom

A second bathroom could be added in a second-floor dormer. The dormitory-type bedroom is expanded into a portion of the dormer. Materials required for constructing the dormer and providing bathroom fixtures are: (Note: As a less costly addition, a lavatory could be installed in one or both upstairs bedrooms.)

```
49 -- 2 x 4's      8 feet long
26 -- 2 x 4's     16 feet long
12 -- 2 x 6's      8 feet long
 6 -- 4- x 8-foot sheets of rough-textured, 5/8-inch reverse
         board and batten plywood siding
15 -- 4- x 8-foot sheets of 3/8-inch gypsum board
96 -- 9- x 9-inch asphalt tile (with adhesive)
 2 -- 24/16 treated double-hung windows (storm and screen)
1 set -- 2-foot 4-inch x 6-foot 6-inch hollow-core door with jambs,
         stops, and hardware
 1 -- Wall-mounted interior light
 1 -- Switch
 1 -- Hot-air register with duct
 1 -- 30- x 30-inch shower stall
 1 -- Lavatory
 1 -- Water closet
```

Front Porch

Materials required for the front porch are:

```
 3          Treated posts, 5 ft. long, with 6-inch minimum
               top diameter
 1          2 by 4, 12 feet long
12          2 by 6's, 8 feet long
12          2 by 6's, 10 feet long
```

```
  1         2 by 6, 14 feet long
  4         2 by 8's, 14 feet long
  3         4 by 4's, 8 feet long
140 bd. ft. Fir flooring
  5         4- by 8-ft. sheets 3/8-inch plywood, sheathing
               grade (Standard) (CD)
300 sq. ft. 65-lb. roll roofing (surfaced)
```

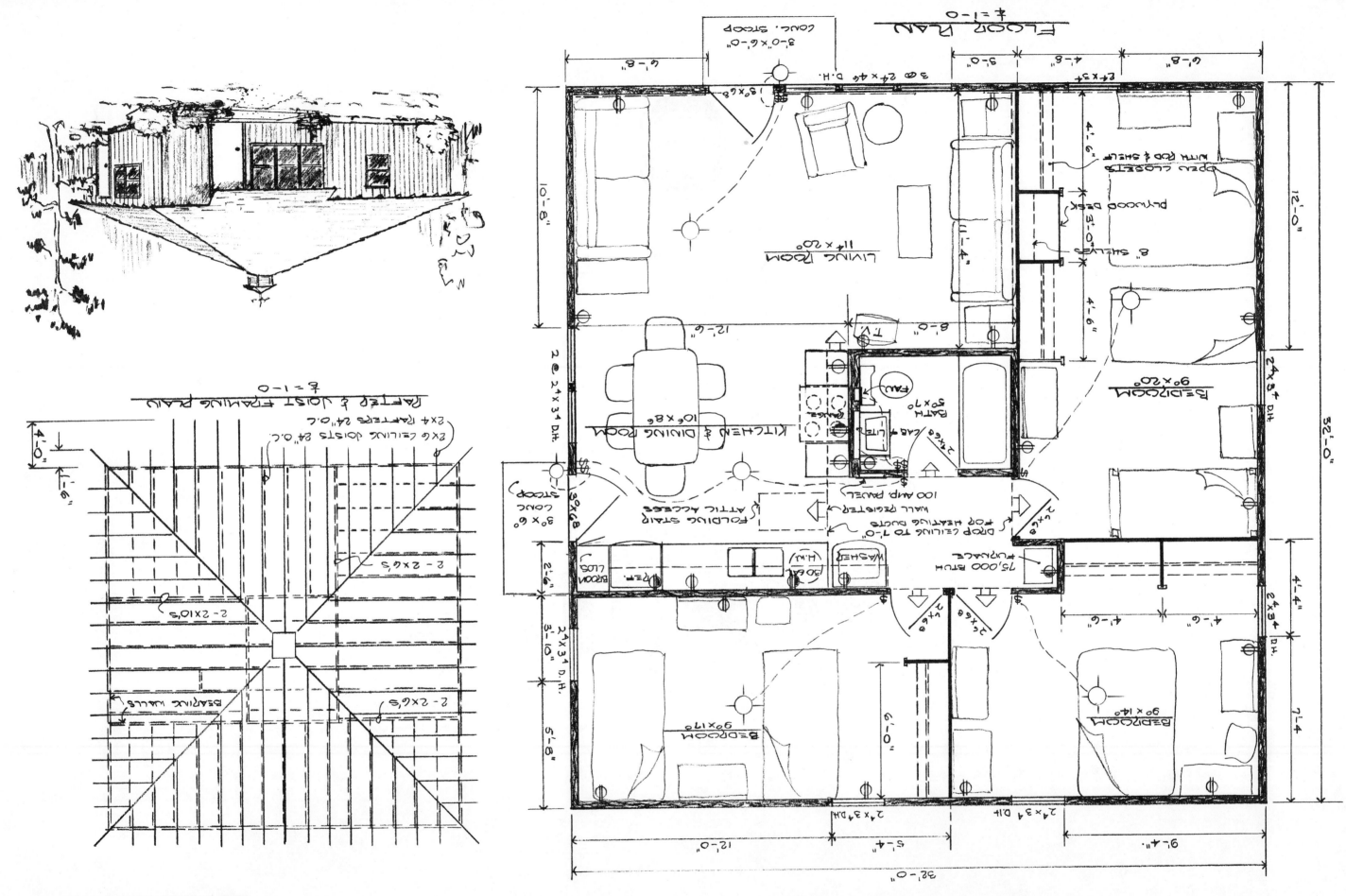

FLOOR PLAN
¼" = 1'-0"

LIVING ROOM
14' x 20'

KITCHEN & DINING ROOM
10' x 8'

BATH
5'0" x 7'0"

BEDROOM
9'0" x 20'

BEDROOM
9'0" x 17'0"

BEDROOM
9'0" x 14'0"

OPEN CLOSETS
WITH ROD & SHELF

PLYWOOD DESK

8' SHELVES

FAU

100 AMP PANEL

FOLDING STAIR
& ATTIC ACCESS

WALL REGISTER

DROP CEILING TO 7'-0"
FOR HEATING DUCTS

75,000 BTUH
FURNACE

WASHER

H.W.

BROOM CLOS.

T.V.

CONC. STOOP
3'-0" x 6'-0"

32'-0"

RAFTER & JOIST FRAMING PLAN
¼" = 1'-0"

2x4 RAFTERS 24" O.C.

2x6 CEILING JOISTS 24" O.C.

2 - 2x6's

2 - 2x10's

2 - 2x6's

BEARING WALLS

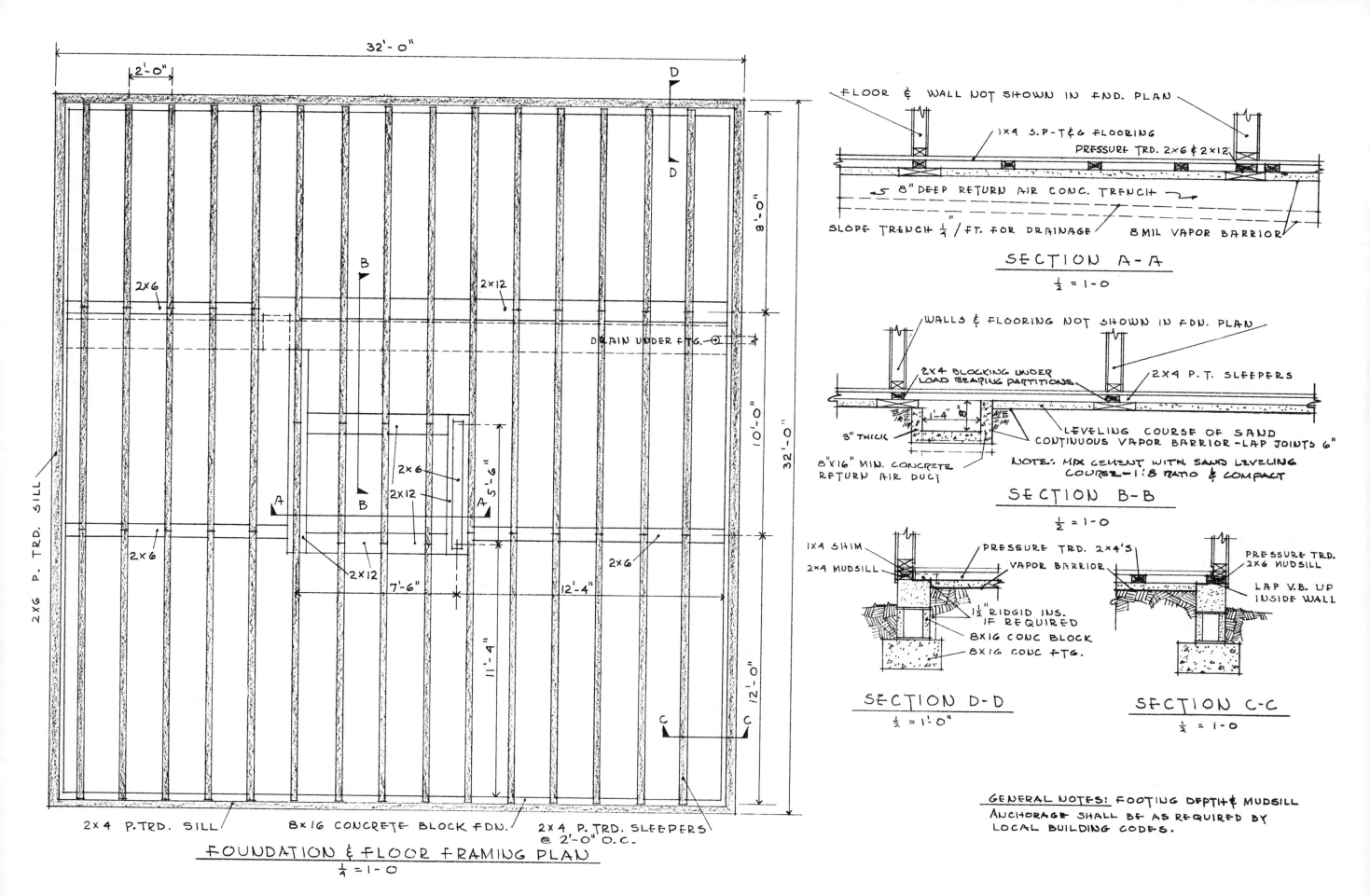

32'-0"

2'-0"

8'-0"

10'-0"

12'-0"

32'-0"

2×6

2×12

2×6

2×12

2×12

2×6

2×6

2×6

5'-6"

7'-6"

12'-4"

11'-4"

DRAIN UNDER FTG.

2×6 P. TRD. SILL

2×4 P. TRD. SILL

8×16 CONCRETE BLOCK FDN.

2×4 P. TRD. SLEEPERS @ 2'-0" O.C.

A — A

B — B

C — C

D — D

FOUNDATION & FLOOR FRAMING PLAN
$\frac{1}{4}$ = 1-0

FLOOR & WALL NOT SHOWN IN FND. PLAN

1×4 S.P-T&G FLOORING
PRESSURE TRD. 2×6 & 2×12

8" DEEP RETURN AIR CONC. TRENCH

SLOPE TRENCH $\frac{1}{4}$" / FT. FOR DRAINAGE

8 MIL VAPOR BARRIER

SECTION A-A
$\frac{1}{2}$ = 1-0

WALLS & FLOORING NOT SHOWN IN FDN. PLAN

2×4 BLOCKING UNDER LOAD BEARING PARTITIONS

2×4 P.T. SLEEPERS

1'-4"   8"

3" THICK

8"×16" MIN. CONCRETE RETURN AIR DUCT

LEVELING COURSE OF SAND
CONTINUOUS VAPOR BARRIER-LAP JOINTS 6"

NOTE: MIX CEMENT WITH SAND LEVELING COURSE -1:8 RATIO & COMPACT

SECTION B-B
$\frac{1}{2}$ = 1-0

1×4 SHIM

2×4 MUDSILL

PRESSURE TRD. 2×4'S
VAPOR BARRIER

1$\frac{1}{2}$" RIDGID INS. IF REQUIRED

8×16 CONC BLOCK

8×16 CONC FTG.

PRESSURE TRD. 2×6 MUDSILL

LAP V.B. UP INSIDE WALL

SECTION D-D
$\frac{1}{2}$ = 1'-0"

SECTION C-C
$\frac{1}{2}$ = 1-0

GENERAL NOTES: FOOTING DEPTH & MUDSILL ANCHORAGE SHALL BE AS REQUIRED BY LOCAL BUILDING CODES.

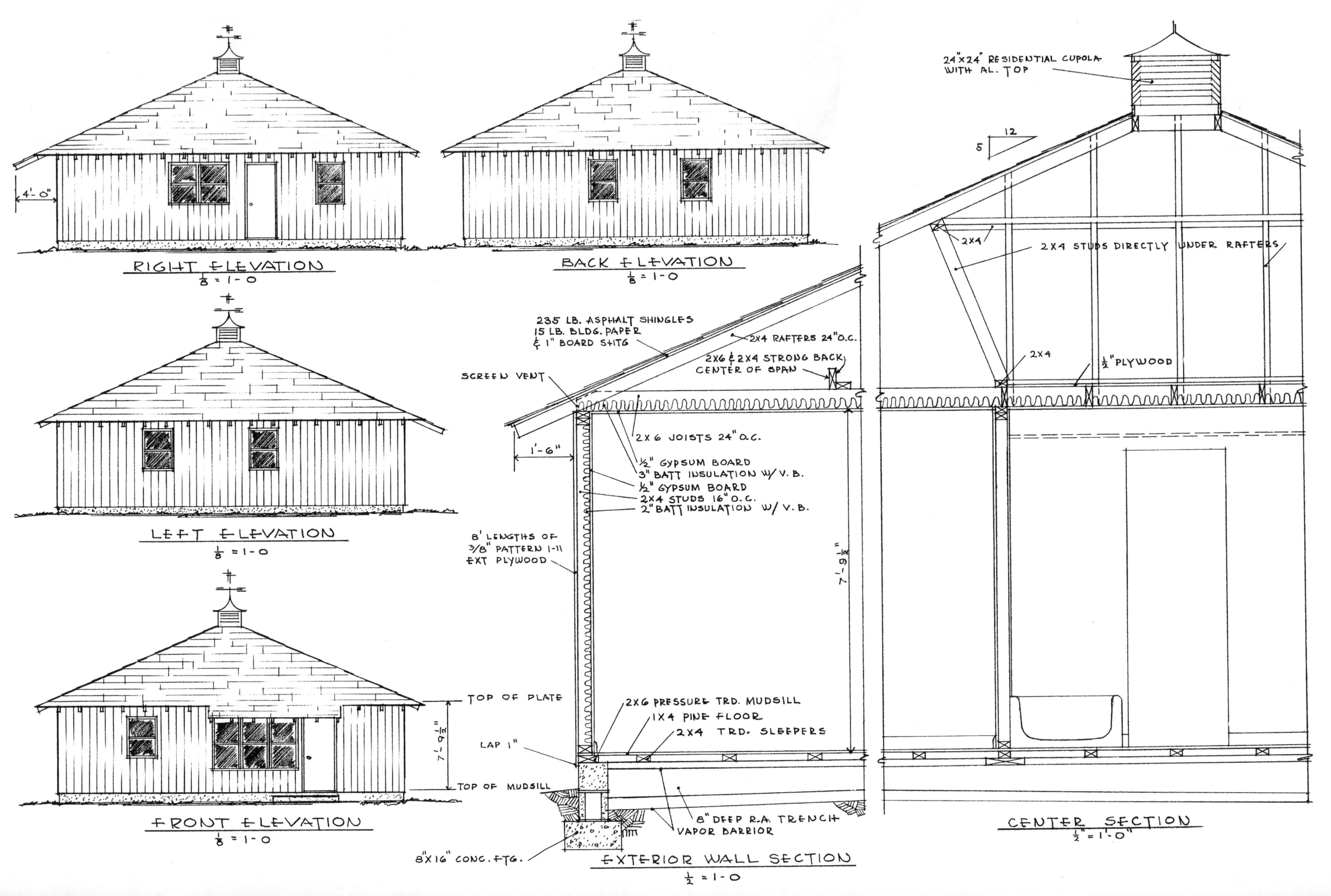

RIGHT ELEVATION
⅛ = 1-0

BACK ELEVATION
⅛ = 1-0

LEFT ELEVATION
⅛ = 1-0

FRONT ELEVATION
⅛ = 1-0

4'-0"

7'-9½"

TOP OF PLATE
LAP 1"
TOP OF MUDSILL

8"X16" CONC. FTG.

235 LB. ASPHALT SHINGLES
15 LB. BLDG. PAPER
& 1" BOARD SHTG.
2X4 RAFTERS 24" O.C.
2X6 & 2X4 STRONG BACK
CENTER OF SPAN

SCREEN VENT

1'-6"

2X6 JOISTS 24" O.C.
½" GYPSUM BOARD
3" BATT INSULATION W/ V.B.
½" GYPSUM BOARD
2X4 STUDS 16" O.C.
2" BATT INSULATION W/ V.B.

8' LENGTHS OF
3/8" PATTERN 1-11
EXT PLYWOOD

7'-9½"

2X6 PRESSURE TRD. MUDSILL
1X4 PINE FLOOR
2X4 TRD. SLEEPERS

8" DEEP R.A. TRENCH
VAPOR BARRIER

EXTERIOR WALL SECTION
½ = 1-0

24"X24" RESIDENTIAL CUPOLA
WITH AL. TOP

5 12

2X4
2X4 STUDS DIRECTLY UNDER RAFTERS
2X4
½" PLYWOOD

CENTER SECTION
½ = 1-0

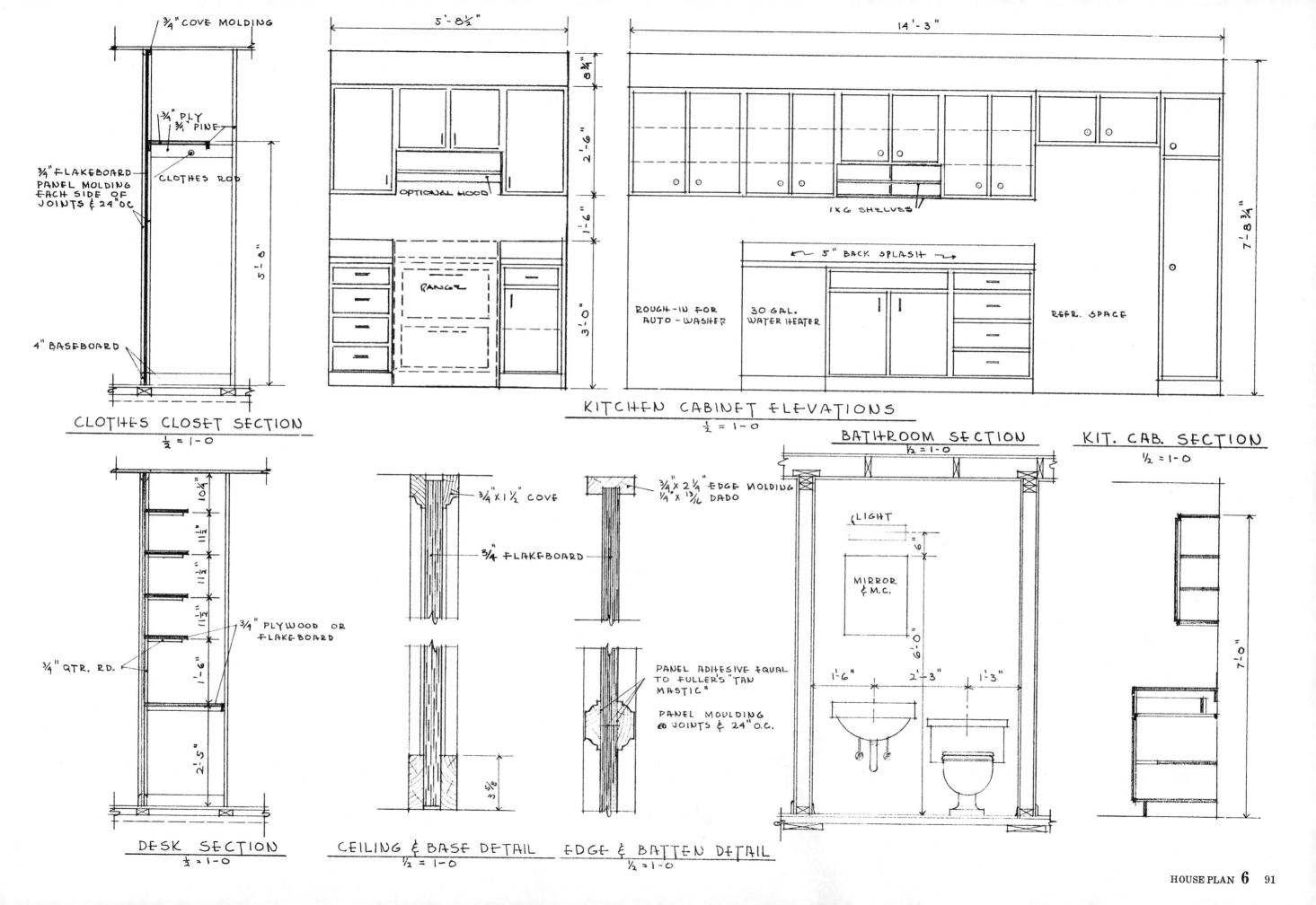

¾" COVE MOLDING

¾" PLY
¾" PINE

¾" FLAKEBOARD
PANEL MOLDING
EACH SIDE OF
JOINTS @ 24" OC

CLOTHES ROD

4" BASEBOARD

CLOTHES CLOSET SECTION
½ = 1-0

5'-8½"

OPTIONAL HOOD

RANGE

KITCHEN CABINET ELEVATIONS
½ = 1-0

14'-3"

1X6 SHELVES

5" BACK SPLASH

ROUGH-IN FOR
AUTO-WASHER

30 GAL.
WATER HEATER

REFR. SPACE

7'-8¾"

DESK SECTION
½ = 1-0

¾" PLYWOOD OR
FLAKEBOARD

¾" QTR. RD.

CEILING & BASE DETAIL
½ = 1-0

¾"X1½" COVE

¾" FLAKEBOARD

EDGE & BATTEN DETAIL
½ = 1-0

¾"X 2¼" EDGE MOLDING
¼"X 13/16 DADO

PANEL ADHESIVE EQUAL
TO FULLER'S "TAN
MASTIC"

PANEL MOULDING
@ JOINTS @ 24" O.C.

BATHROOM SECTION
½ = 1-0

LIGHT

MIRROR
& M.C.

6"

6'-0"

1'-6"   2'-3"   1'-3"

KIT. CAB. SECTION
½ = 1-0

7'-0"

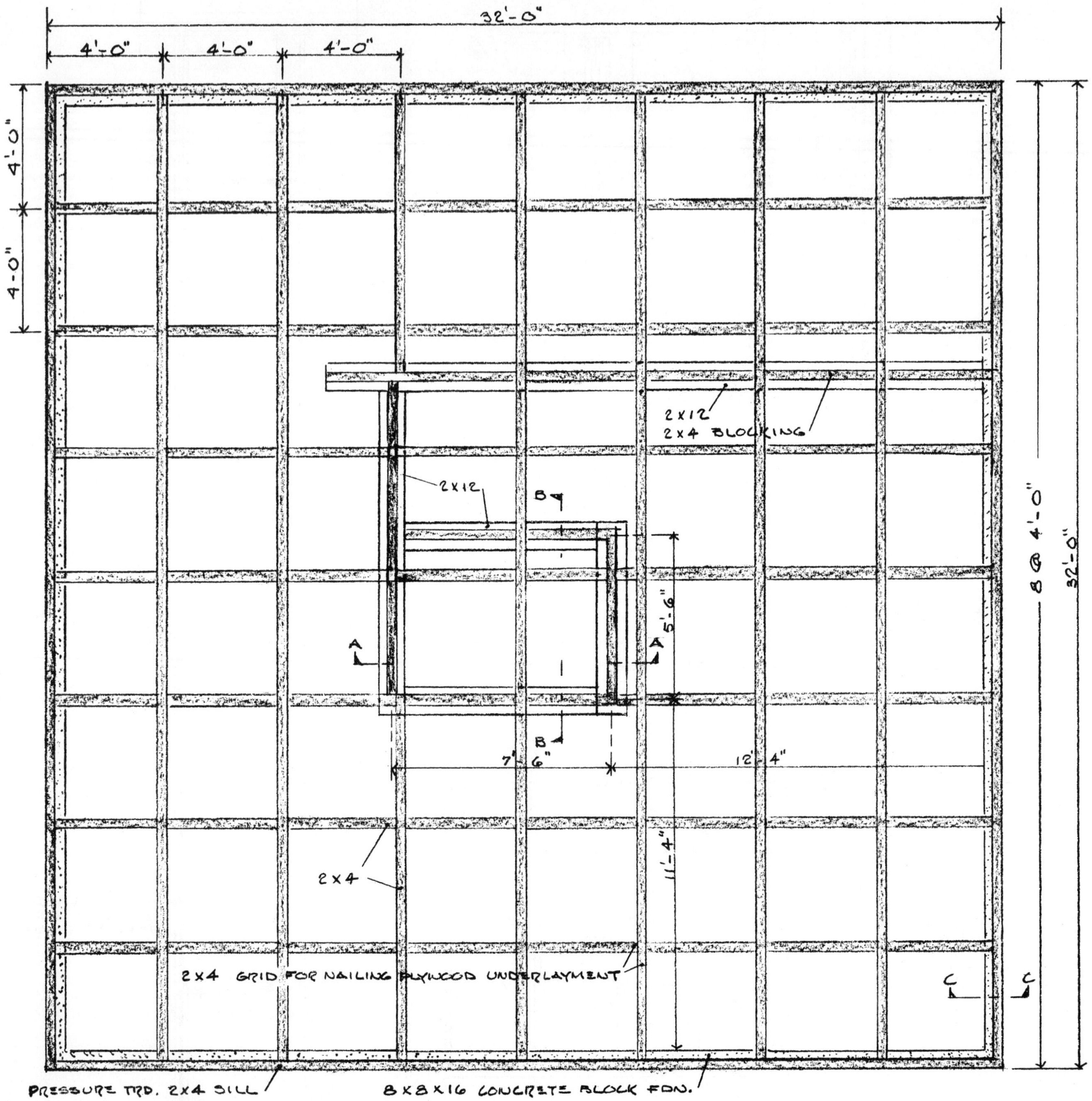

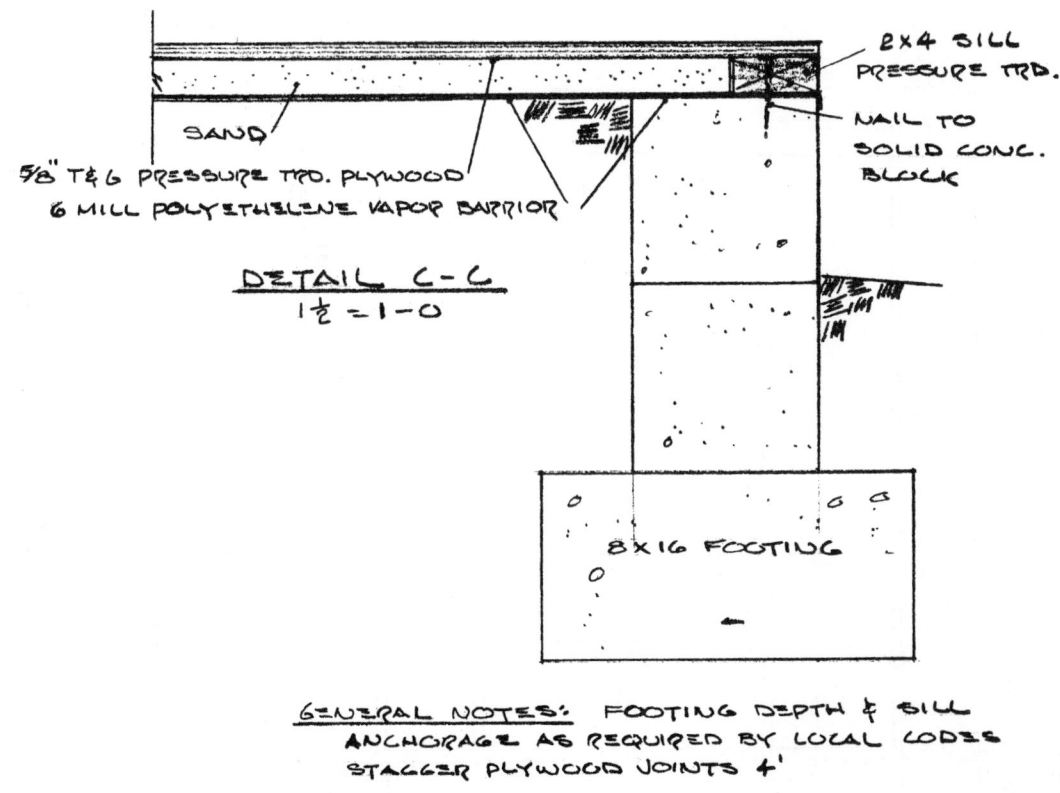

32'-0"

4'-0"   4'-0"   4'-0"

4'-0"

4'-0"

8 @ 4'-0"

32'-0"

2x12
2x4 BLOCKING

2x12

B

A   A

5'-6"

B

7' 6"   12' 4"

11' 4"

2x4

2x4 GRID FOR NAILING PLYWOOD UNDERLAYMENT

C   C

PRESSURE TRD. 2x4 SILL

8x8x16 CONCRETE BLOCK FDN.

ALTERNATE FOUNDATION AND FLOOR FRAMING
¼ = 1-0

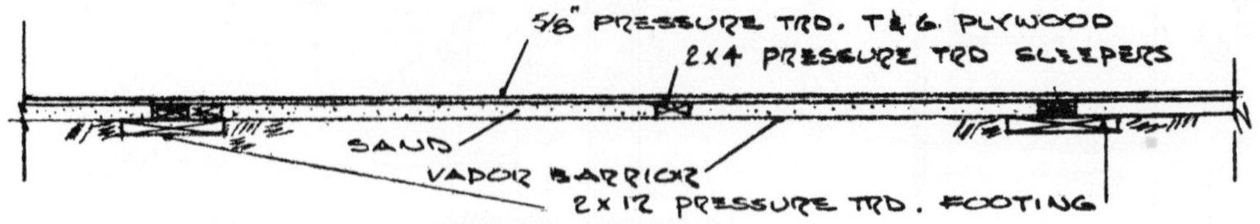

5/8" PRESSURE TRD. T&G PLYWOOD
2x4 PRESSURE TRD SLEEPERS

SAND
VAPOR BARRIER
2x12 PRESSURE TRD. FOOTING

DETAIL A-A
½ = 1-0

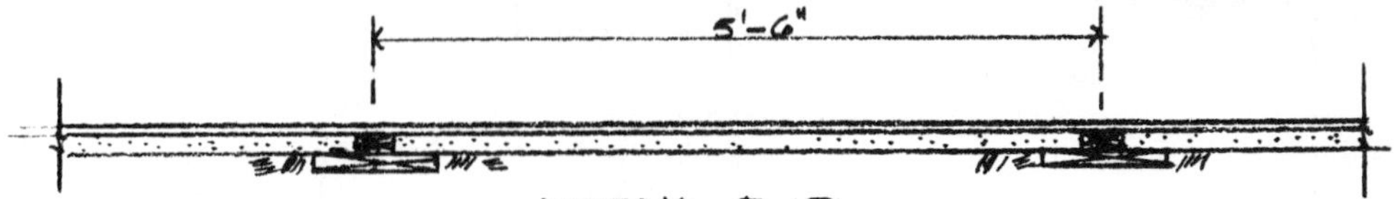

5'-6"

DETAIL B-B
½ = 1-0

2x4 SILL
PRESSURE TRD.

NAIL TO
SOLID CONC.
BLOCK

SAND

5/8" T&G PRESSURE TRD. PLYWOOD
6 MILL POLYETHELENE VAPOR BARRIER

DETAIL C-C
1½ = 1-0

8x16 FOOTING

GENERAL NOTES: FOOTING DEPTH & SILL
ANCHORAGE AS REQUIRED BY LOCAL CODES
STAGGER PLYWOOD JOINTS 4'

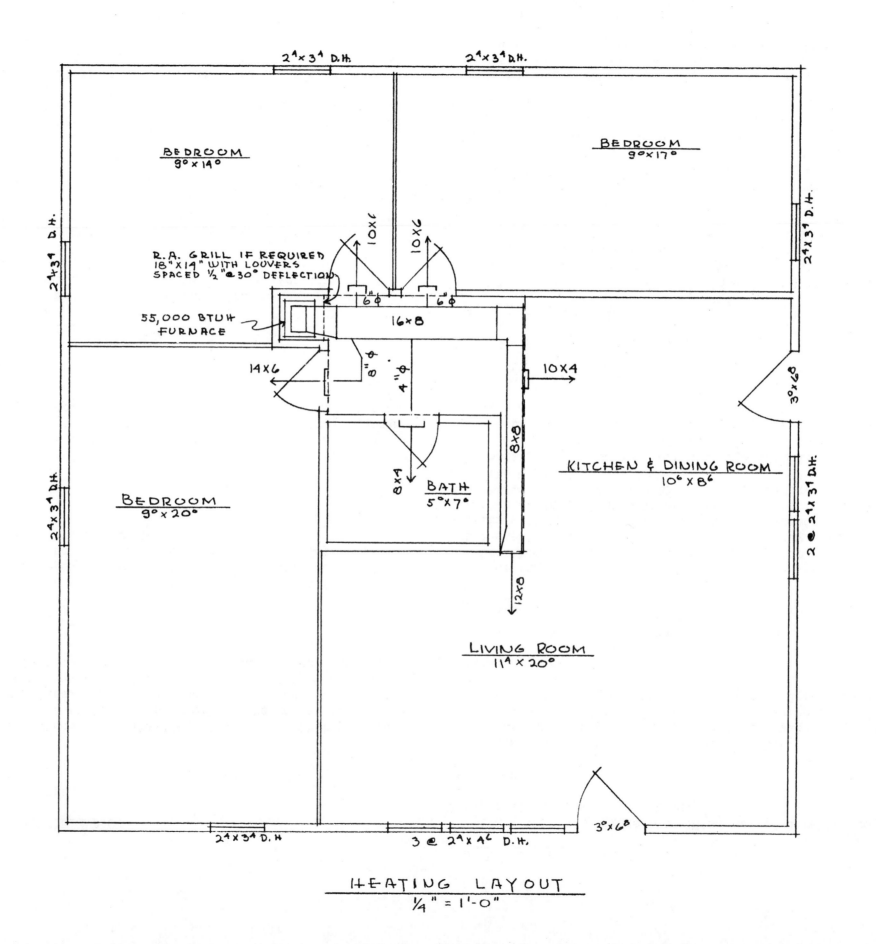

BEDROOM
9⁰ x 14⁰

BEDROOM
9⁰ x 17⁰

2⁴ x 3⁴ D.H.

2⁴ x 3⁴ D.H.

2⁴ x 3⁴ D.H.

2⁴ x 3⁴ D.H.

R.A. GRILL IF REQUIRED
18"x14" WITH LOUVERS
SPACED ½"@30° DEFLECTION

10x6

10x6

6"φ

6"φ

16x8

55,000 BTUH
FURNACE

14x6

8"φ

4"φ

10x4

3⁰ x 6⁸

8x8

KITCHEN & DINING ROOM
10⁶ x 8⁶

BEDROOM
9⁰ x 20⁰

8x4

BATH
5⁰ x 7⁰

2 @ 2⁴ x 3⁴ D.H.

12x8

LIVING ROOM
11⁴ x 20⁰

2⁴ x 3⁴ D.H.

3 @ 2⁴ x 4⁶ D.H.

3⁰ x 6⁸

HEATING LAYOUT
¼" = 1'-0"

SPECIFICATIONS

PLAN 6

General

Each item of material and equipment shall equal or exceed that described or indicated. All work shall be performed in a workmanlike manner and in accordance with the best practice. Mention of commercial products and sources does not constitute an endorsement of such products by the Forest Service or the Department of Agriculture to the exclusion of other equally acceptable products.

Excavation

Soil shall be scraped clean of all vegetation. If soil is difficult to level for the treated wood sleepers, cover with a leveling course of sand. Minimum excavation depth shall be 6 inches below finish grade. Backfill shall be compacted to the density of existing soil.

Foundations

Footings: 1:3:5 (2,000 PSI) concrete
Walls: 8 x 8 x 16 concrete block
Interior footings: Pressure treated wood in accordance with American Wood Preservers Association recommendations and AWPI quality control program LP-22. Each treated piece of wood shall bear the LP-22 AWPI quality control mark.

Exterior walls

Wood frame: No. 2 syp or fir studs 16" o.c.
Sheathing: None
Siding: Grade A-C plywood group 2; 3/8" thick; with channel grooves 4" or 8" o.c. or 1 x 2 inch battens 16" o.c. over siding. Applied directly to studs as described by the American Plywood Association for "sturd-i-wall" construction.
Exterior painting: Use a pigmented exterior penetrating stain as recommended by the manufacturer. Two coats of stain shall be applied so that all plywood edges are sealed. Color to be selected by owner from samples. The second coat of stain shall be applied before the first coat is dry.

Floor framing

Floating or Joist   No. 2 syp or fir sleepers shall be treated the same as the wood footings in item 2 and placed over 10 mil polyethylene vapor barrier.
Concrete slab: 1:2:3 mix of 3,000 psi concrete with 6 x 6 wire mesh reinforcing, poured over compacted 4" fill of crushed stone or aggregate and 6 mil polyethylene vapor barrier.

Finish flooring

1 x 4 inch syp, grade D or BTR., nailed directly to sleepers or joists. Sand, seal and wax in all rooms.

Partition Framing

Studs: No. 2 syp or fir 2 x 4's 16" o.c.
Flakeboard: High density, 3/4" thick, with "v" type or tongue-and-groove edges, similar to "Timblend" by Weyerhaeuser. Finish with one coat of oil-base primer (nonporous) and one coat latex enamel.

Ceiling framing

Joists: No. 2 syp or fir 2 x 6's 24" o.c.

Roof

(see pages 88 and 90)
Sheathing: Standard plywood with exterior glue, C-D, 3/8" thick, or syp board sheathing, grade no. 3. Board sheathing shall be used over exposed soffits with the 3/8" plywood sheathing shimmed up to align with the 1" board sheathing, or asphalt shingles shall be applied over 3/8" exterior plywood over the soffits with a roofing mastic. No nails shall penetrate into the exposed soffit.
Roofing: 15# roofing felt and 235# asphalt shingles applied with nails and cement: or selvage, grade C, double coverage.
Flashing: Asphalt roofing over ridges with galvanized or aluminum drip edges.

Gutters and Downspouts

None

Wall and Ceiling Finish

Walls: 3/8" factory painted gypsum board similar to "Blendtex" by U. S. Gypsum Company. Edges shall be tapered or rounded. Install with 6d grooved nails or an adhesive approved by U. S. Gypsum for this type of application. Touch-up paint shall be used to paint the nail heads. (Bathroom wall finish given in next item).
Ceilings: 1/2" factory painted gypsum board similar to "Blendtex" by U. S. Gypsum Company. As near as possible, board lengths should match room length or width to avoid end joints. Ceiling board shall be prescored with a square tile pattern. Application shall be the same as for wall panels, or as recommended by U. S. Gypsum Company.

Decorating

Colors and texture for factory applied paint shall be selected by the owner from samples, or a color chart.
Bathroom walls shall be painted with a primer and 2 coats enamel paint.

Bathroom ceiling finish shall be the same as in the rest of the house.

Interior Doors and Trim

Doors: 1-3/8", flush hollow core, lauan.
Door and window trim: 2-1/3" ranch, D select pine; paint with primer and two coats of enamel.
Base: 1 x 4 inch syp, D select: Prime and two coats of enamel, bevel top edge with sander.

Windows

Wood, double hung: Prime and two coats of paint. Windows shall be factory treated with wrp and complete with all hardware, exterior trim, weather-stripping, and screens. Caulk between trim and siding along the top edge of each window.

Entrance Doors

1-3/4" thickness, solid core lauan, with 5/4" pine or fir frames; provide a screen door for each entrance; caulk between trim and plywood siding along top edge of each door. Finish with (nonporous) oil-base primer and two coats exterior paint.

Cabinets and Equipment

Kitchen cabinets: Fir plywood with vinyl counter top and metal edging, stain, seal and wax. Back and end splash is the same.
Medicine cabinet: Allow $20.00
Other cabinets: 20" deep linen closet with fir door; painted to match trim. Shelves are 1 x 10 inch, grade 3 syp unpainted.

Stairs

Allow $50.00 for folding-type attic stair.

Plumbing

Provide four fixtures complete with all necessary fittings: 32" x 20" double or single kitchen sink, bath tub, 17" x 19" lavatory, water closet in white porcelain on steel.
Water heater: Minimum capacity 40 gallons; 10 year warranty; electric under-counter or drop-in counter top type.
Water piping: Galvanized steel, copper, or plastic as approved by local plumbing codes.
House drain: Provide sill cock in the lowest point of the water supply piping.
Hose bibb: Provide one exterior hose bibb.

Heating and Ventilating

Wall heater: 80,000 BTU gas-fired forced air furnace: Return air in the floor and discharge near the ceiling; 10 year warranty. Provide a baffle near the ceiling to direct the hot air into the living room and bedrooms. Provide heater flue as recommended by furnace manufacturer.
Bathroom exhaust: Allow $20.00.

Electric Wiring and Fixtures

Service: Overhead, 100 amperes.
Distribution panel: 100 amp. service panel with six branch circuits and three spare circuits.
All wiring in accordance with the National Electric Code.
Allow $35.00 for light fixtures.

Insulation

Roof: 3" mineral wool with integral vapor barrier.
Walls: 2" mineral wool with integral vapor barrier.

Finish Hardware

With prehung doors and windows.

Porches

4" concrete over 4" aggregate fill; steel trowel finish.

Landscaping

Planting, walks, drives, and finish grading: By owner.

Miscellaneous

All outside utilities, such as electricity, water, sewer, and gas to the house are provided by the owner or utility company. All utilities in the house shall be stubbed out of the house for convenient hookup to outside utilities.
Termite protection: 1 percent chlordane in water emulsion or equivalent treatment shall be applied to the soil around the footings and under the floor, and in the hollow cores of the concrete blocks. Apply 4 gallons of 1 percent chlordane per 10 linear feet to the soil along both sides of footings and around underground piping. Apply 1 gallon of 1 percent chlordane per 10 square feet as an overall treatment under the floor and under attached porches.

7

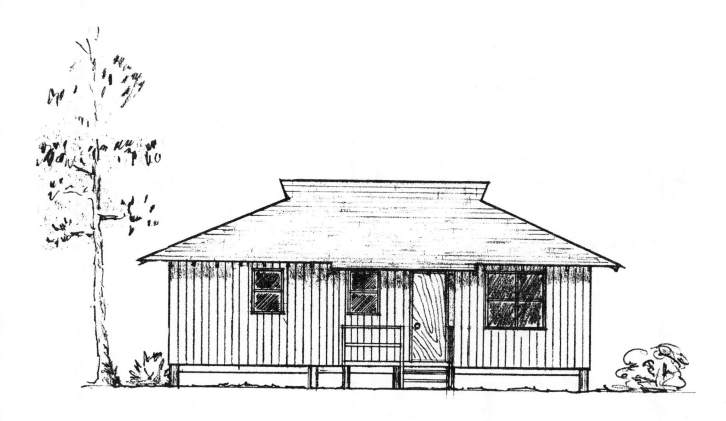

FRONT ELEVATION
$\frac{1}{8}=1-0$

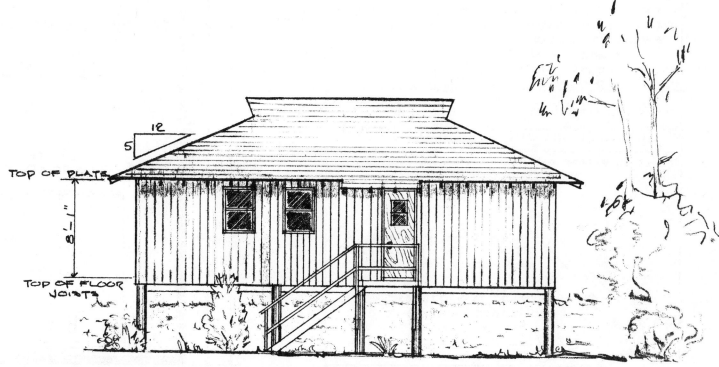

TOP OF PLATE

8'-1"

TOP OF FLOOR JOISTS

12
5

BACK ELEVATION
$\frac{1}{8}=1-0$

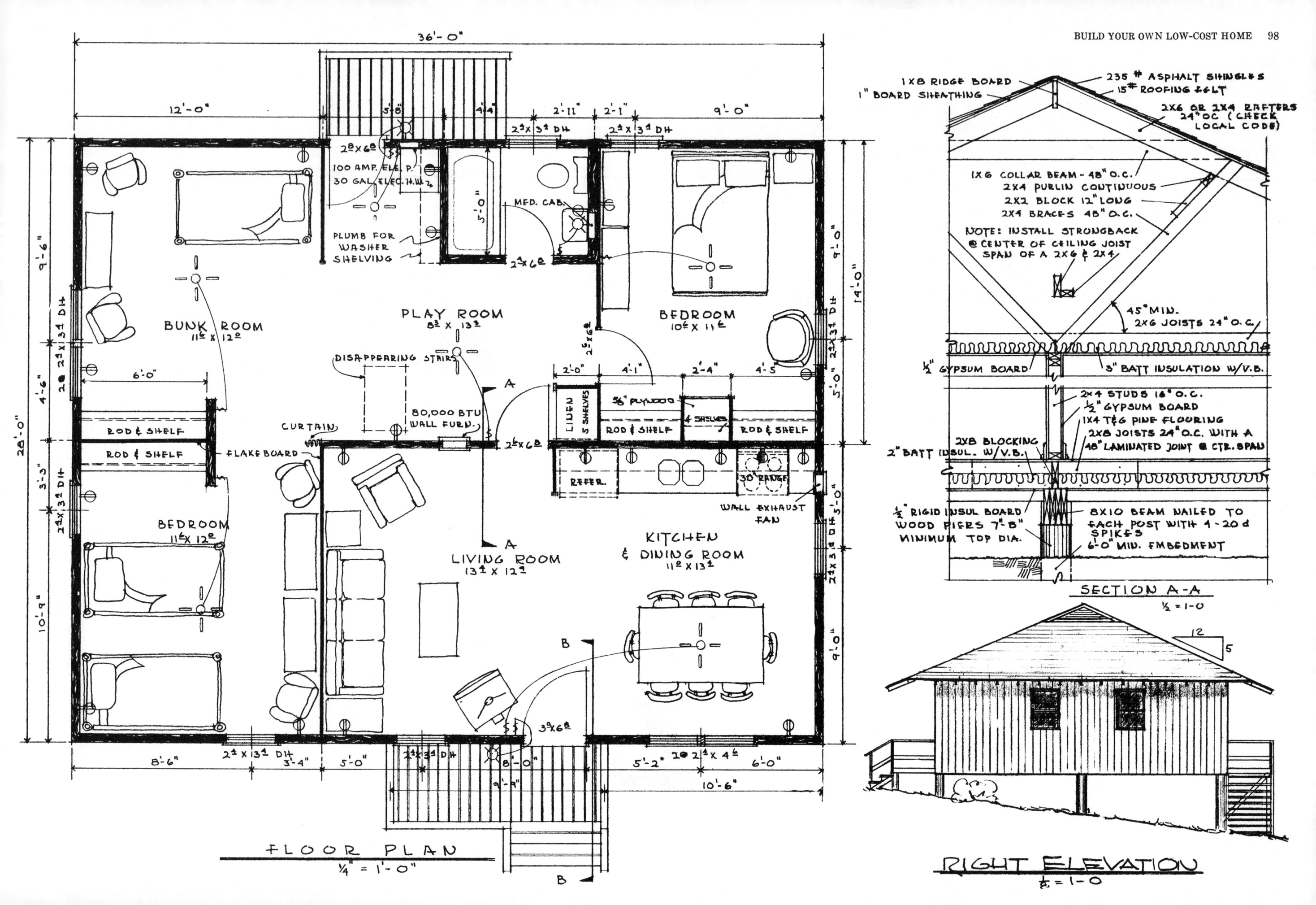

FLOOR PLAN
¼" = 1'-0"

RIGHT ELEVATION
¼" = 1'-0"

SECTION A-A
½ = 1'-0"

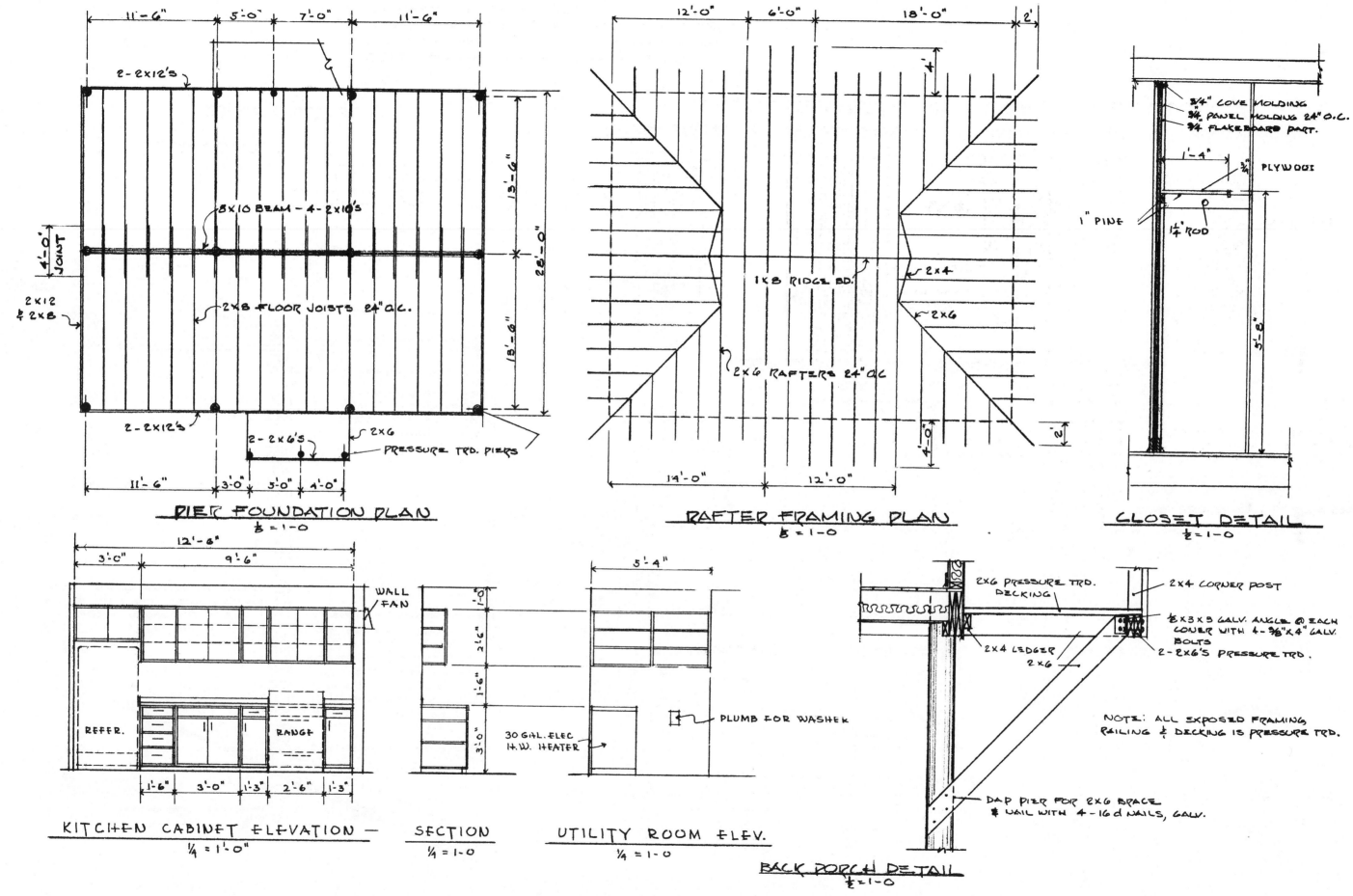

PIER FOUNDATION PLAN
⅛ = 1-0

2-2×12's

8×10 BEAM - 4-2×10's

2×12 & 2×8

2×8 FLOOR JOISTS 24" O.C.

2-2×12's

2-2×6's   2×6

PRESSURE TRD. PIERS

11'-6"   5'-0"   7'-0"   11'-6"

4'-0" JOIST

13'-6"   28'-0"   15'-6"

11'-6"   3'-0"   5'-0"   1'-0"

RAFTER FRAMING PLAN
⅛ = 1-0

12'-0"   6'-0"   18'-0"   2'

1×8 RIDGE BD.

2×4

2×6

2×6 RAFTERS 24" OC

14'-0"   12'-0"   4'-0"   2'

CLOSET DETAIL
½ = 1-0

¾" COVE MOLDING
¾ PANEL MOLDING 24" O.C.
¾ FLAKEBOARD PART.

1'-4"   ¾ PLYWOOD

1" PINE   1¼" ROD

5'-8"

KITCHEN CABINET ELEVATION —
¼ = 1-0"

WALL FAN

REFER.   RANGE

12'-6"

3'-0"   9'-6"

1'-6"   3'-0"   1'-3"   2'-6"   1'-3"

SECTION
¼ = 1-0

1'-0"   2'-6"   1'-6"   3'-0"

UTILITY ROOM ELEV.
¼ = 1-0

5'-4"

PLUMB FOR WASHER

30 GAL. ELEC. H.W. HEATER

BACK PORCH DETAIL
½ = 1-0

2×6 PRESSURE TRD. DECKING

2×4 CORNER POST

⅜×3×3 GALV. ANGLE @ EACH
CORNER WITH 4-⅜"×4" GALV.
BOLTS

2×4 LEDGER

2×6

2-2×6'S PRESSURE TRD.

NOTE: ALL EXPOSED FRAMING
RAILING & DECKING IS PRESSURE TRD.

DAP PIER FOR 2×6 BRACE
& NAIL WITH 4-16d NAILS, GALV.

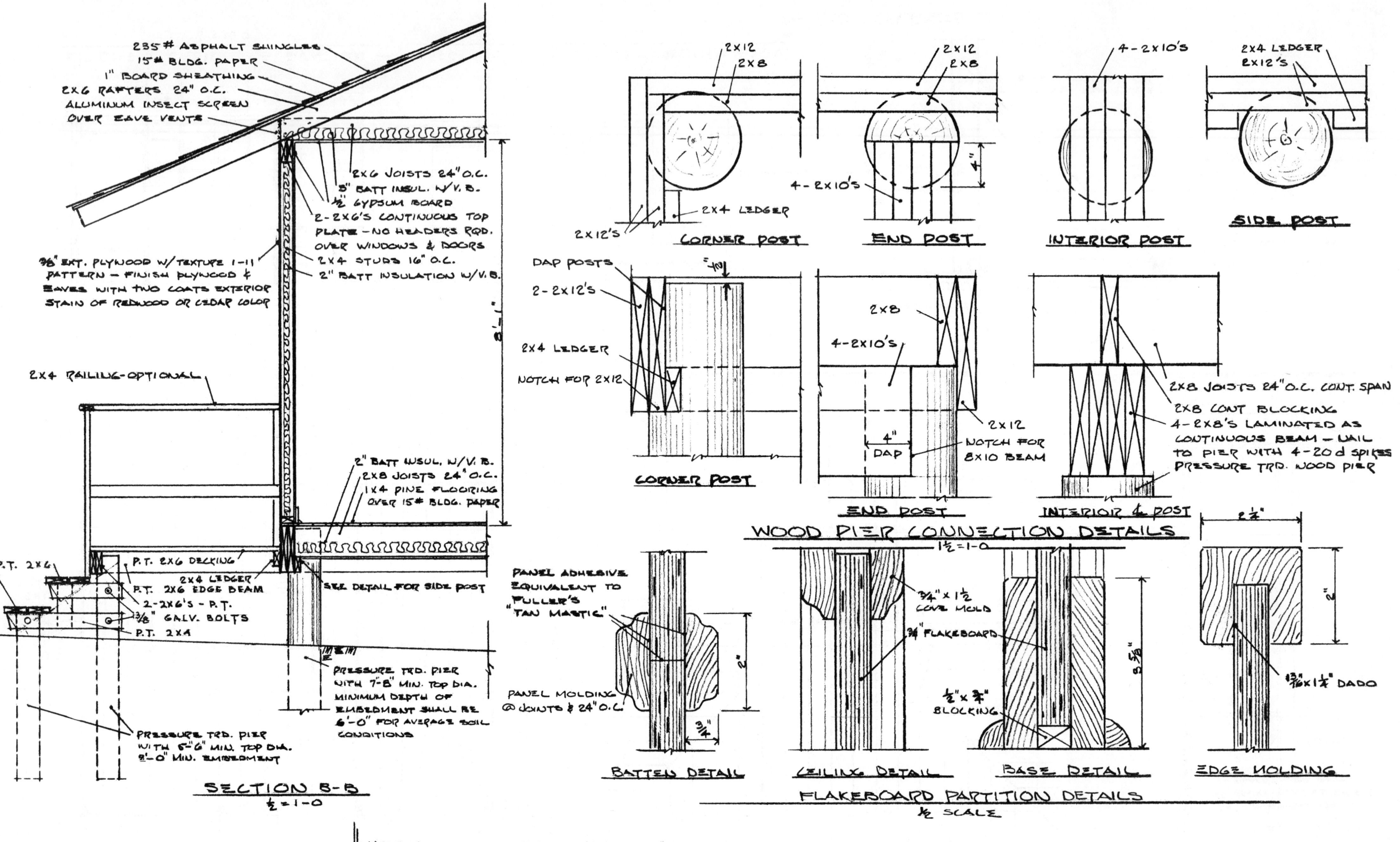

235# ASPHALT SHINGLES
15# BLDG. PAPER
1" BOARD SHEATHING
2X6 RAFTERS 24" O.C.
ALUMINUM INSECT SCREEN
OVER EAVE VENTS

2X6 JOISTS 24" O.C.
5" BATT INSUL. W/V.B.
½" GYPSUM BOARD
2-2X6'S CONTINUOUS TOP
PLATE – NO HEADERS RQD.
OVER WINDOWS & DOORS
2X4 STUDS 16" O.C.
2" BATT INSULATION W/V.B.

⅜" EXT. PLYWOOD W/ TEXTURE 1-11
PATTERN – FINISH PLYWOOD &
EAVES WITH TWO COATS EXTERIOR
STAIN OF REDWOOD OR CEDAR COLOR

2X4 RAILING-OPTIONAL

2" BATT INSUL. W/V.B.
2X8 JOISTS 24" O.C.
1X4 PINE FLOORING
OVER 15# BLDG. PAPER

SEE DETAIL FOR SIDE POST

P.T. 2X6
P.T. 2X6 DECKING
2X4 LEDGER
2X6 EDGE BEAM
2-2X6'S - P.T.
⅜" GALV. BOLTS
P.T. 2X4

PRESSURE TRD. PIER
WITH 7"-8" MIN. TOP DIA.
MINIMUM DEPTH OF
EMBEDMENT SHALL BE
6'-0" FOR AVERAGE SOIL
CONDITIONS

PRESSURE TRD. PIER
WITH 5"-6" MIN. TOP DIA.
8'-0" MIN. EMBEDMENT

SECTION B-B
½=1-0

2X12
2X8
2X4 LEDGER
2X12'S
CORNER POST

2X12
2X8
4 - 2X10'S
END POST

4 - 2X10'S
INTERIOR POST

2X4 LEDGER
2X12'S
SIDE POST

DAP POSTS
2 - 2X12'S
2X4 LEDGER
NOTCH FOR 2X12
CORNER POST

2X8
4-2X10'S
4"
DAP
2X12
NOTCH FOR
8X10 BEAM
END POST

2X8 JOISTS 24" O.C. CONT. SPAN
2X8 CONT BLOCKING
4-2X8'S LAMINATED AS
CONTINUOUS BEAM – NAIL
TO PIER WITH 4-20d SPIKES
PRESSURE TRD. WOOD PIER
INTERIOR ¢ POST

WOOD PIER CONNECTION DETAILS
1½=1-0

PANEL ADHESIVE
EQUIVALENT TO
"FULLER'S
"TAN MASTIC"

PANEL MOLDING
@ JOINTS & 24" O.C.

¾"

2"

BATTEN DETAIL

¾" X 1½
COVE MOLD
¾ FLAKEBOARD
½" X ¾"
BLOCKING
CEILING DETAIL

BASE DETAIL

2¼"
8 5/8"
1 3/16"X1½" DADO
EDGE MOLDING

FLAKEBOARD PARTITION DETAILS
½ SCALE

NOTE: PRESSURE TREATMENT OF PIERS
SHALL BE THAT WHICH IS KNOWN TO PROVIDE
A 30 YEAR AVERAGE SERVICE-LIFE FOR WOOD
EMBEDDED IN MOIST SOIL

SPECIFICATIONS

PLAN 7

General

Each item of material and equipment shall equal or exceed that described or indicated. All work shall be performed in a workmanlike manner and in accordance with the best practice. Mention of commercial products and sources does not contitute an endorsement of such products by the Forest Service or the Department of Agriculture to the exclusion of other equally acceptable products.

Site Grading

Grade as required to smooth out surface humps and valleys and to provide drainage away from the house. Minimum site disturbance is desired, therefore, grading should be done only where necessary to provide smooth surfaces and drainage.

Wood Piers and Porches

Piers and wood used in the porches shall be syp pressure treated in accordance with American Wood Preservers Association recommendations and the AWPI Quality Control Program LP-22. Each treated piece of wood shall bear the AWPI quality mark LP-22.

Exterior Walls

Wood frame: No. 2 syp or fir studs, 16" o.c.
Sheathing: None
Siding: Exterior 3/8" plywood, A-C, group 2; with channel grooves 4" or 8" o.c. or X-90 panel-groove masonite, applied directly to studs as described by the American Plywood Association for "sturd-i-wall" construction.
Finish: Pigmented exterior penetrating stain as recommended by the manufacturer. Apply two coats of stain so that all the plywood edges are sealed. The second coat of stain shall be applied before the first coat is dry. The X-90 masonite shall have a factory applied primer, cover with one coat of exterior paint.

Floor Framing

Joists: No. 2 syp or fir. Lap joists over the center beam so that bending stiffness is increased as detailed on page 98. Fasten 1/2" fiber insulation board to the underside of joists. Nail ends of joists to edge beams with four 16d box nails.

Finish Flooring

1 x 4 inch syp, grade D, tongue-and-groove, nailed directly to joists. Sand, seal and wax in all rooms.

Partition Framing

Studs: No. 2 syp or fir 2 x 4's 16" o.c.
Flakeboard: High density, 3/4" thick; similar to "Timblend" by Weyerhaeuser. Flakeboard shall be reinforced with battens and edge trim as described on page 100. Finish with one coat oil-base nonporous primer and one coat of latex enamel.

Ceiling Framing

Joists: No. 2 syp or fir 2 x 6's 24" o.c.

Roof

(See page 98 for framing details)
Sheathing: Standard plywood with exterior glue, C-D, 3/8" thick, or syp board sheathing, grade no. 2 or BTR. Board sheathing shall be used over exposed soffits with the 3/8" plywood sheathing shimmed up to align with the 1" board sheathing, or asphalt shingles shall be applied over 3/8" exterior plywood over the soffits with a roofing mastic. No nails shall penetrate the plywood into the exposed soffit.
Roofing: 15# roofing felt and 235# asphalt shingles applied with nails and cement, or selvage, grade C, double coverage.
Flashing: Asphalt roofing over ridges with galvanized or aluminum drip edges.

Gutters and Downspouts

None

Wall and Ceiling Finish

Walls: 3/8" factory painted gypsum board similar to "Blendtex" by U. S. Gypsum Company. Edges shall be tapered or rounded. Install with 6d grooved nails or an adhesive approved by U. S. Gypsum for this type of application. Touch-up paint shall be used to paint the nail heads. (Bathroom finish is given in next item).
Ceilings: 1/2" factory painted gypsum board similar to "Blendtex" by U. S. Gypsum Company. Ceiling board is scored with a square tile pattern. As near as possible, board lengths should match room length or width to avoid end joints. Application shall be the same as for wall panels, or as recommended by U. S. Gypsum.

Decorating

Colors and texture of factory applied paint shall be selected by the owner from samples or a color chart.
Bathroom walls shall be gypsum board covered with primer and 2 coats of enamel paint. Bathroom ceiling finish shall be the same as in the rest of the house.

Interior Doors and Trim

Doors: 1-3/8", flush hollow-core, lauan. Paint with two coats paint over an oil-base nonporous primer.

Door and window trim: 2-1/4" ranch, D and BTR. Pine painted with two coats of latex enamel over an oil-base nonporous primer.

Windows

Wood, double hung; prime and two coats of paint. Windows shall be factory treated with WRP and complete with all hardware, exterior trim, weather-stripping, and screens. Caulk between trim and siding along the top edge of each window.

Entrance Doors

1-3/4" thickness, solid core, lauan, with 5/4" pine or fir frames. Provide a screen door for each entrance. Caulk between trim and siding along the top edge of each door. Finish with an oil-base nonporous primer and two coats of exterior paint.

Cabinets and Equipment

Kitchen cabinets: Fir with vinyl counter top and metal edging. Finish with stain, seal and wax. Back and end splash is the same.

Medicine cabinet: Allow $20.00 for cabinet with side or top lights.

Shelving in the utility room shall be 1 x 12 inch syp, No. 2 painted same as the walls.

Attic Access

Provide a 3/8" x 20" x 36" bd plywood attic scuttle where shown on the plans. Insulate scuttle with 3" batt insulation stapled to plywood door.

Plumbing

Provide four fixtures complete with all necessary fittings: 32" x 20" double or single kitchen sink, bath tub, 17" x 19" lavatory, and water closet, in white porcelain on steel.

Water heater: Minimum capacity, 40 gallons; 10 year warranty; electric under-counter or counter top drop-in type.

Water piping: Galvanized steel, copper, or plastic as approved by local plumbing codes. Provide a sill cock in the lowest section of plumbing for a house drain. Also provide one exterior hose bibb.

Heating and Ventilation

Wall heater, 80,000 BTU gas-fired or oil forced-air furnace; return air shall be near the floor and discharge shall be near the ceiling in both the living room and play room. Provide a heater flue as recommended by the manufacturer.

Electric Wiring and Fixtures

Service: Overhead, 100 amperes.

Distribution panel: 100 amp. with six branch circuits and three spares.

All wiring in accordance with the National Electric Code.

Allow $30.00 for light fixtures.

Insulation

Roof: 3" mineral wool with integral vapor barrier.

Walls and floor: 2" mineral wool with integral vapor barrier.

Finish Hardware

With prehung doors and windows.

Landscaping

Planting, walks, drives, and finish grading by owner.

Miscellaneous

All outside utilities, such as electricity, water, sewer, and gas to the house are provided by the owner or utility company. All utilities in the house shall be stubbed out of the house for convenient hookup to outside utilities.

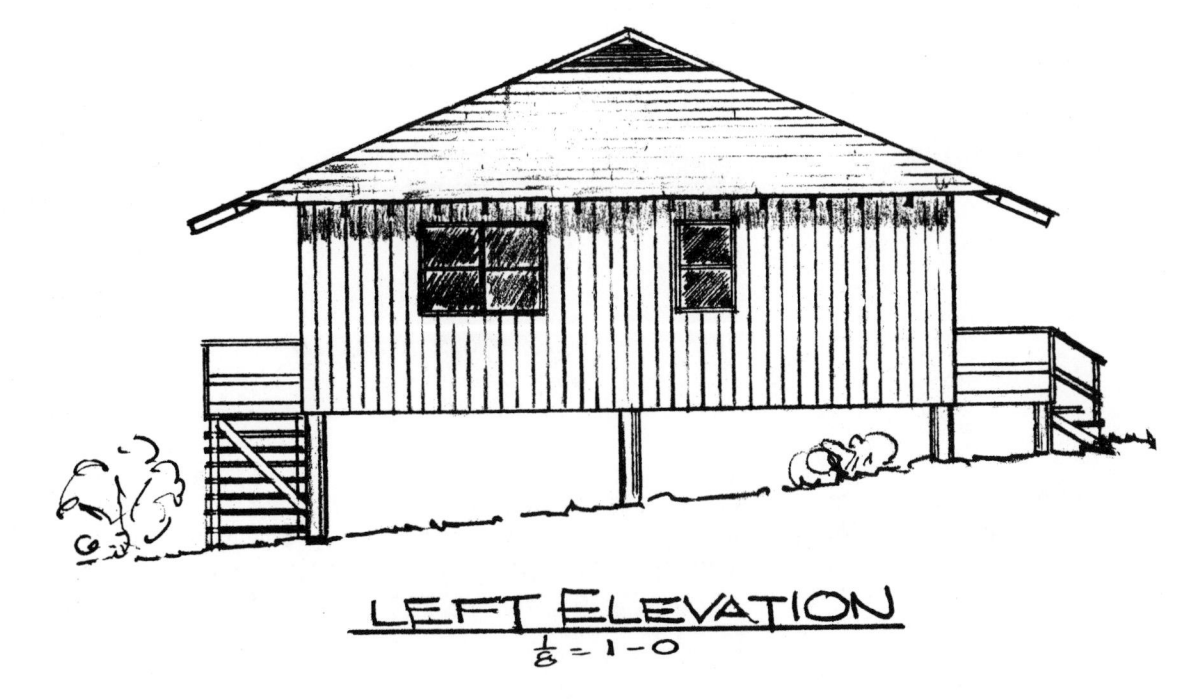

LEFT ELEVATION
1/8 = 1-0

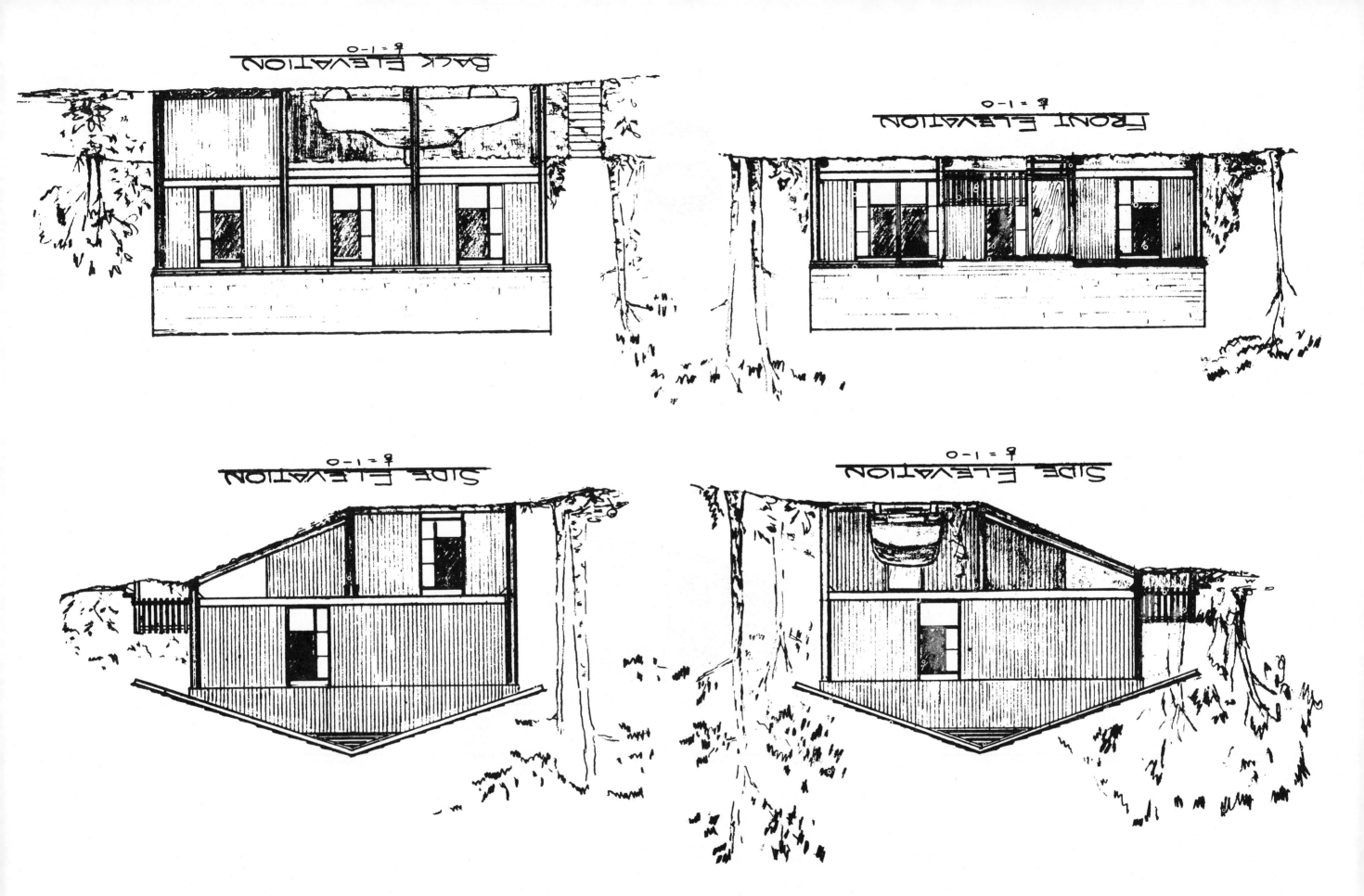

BACK ELEVATION
⅛" = 1'-0"

FRONT ELEVATION
⅛" = 1'-0"

SIDE ELEVATION
⅛" = 1'-0"

SIDE ELEVATION
⅛" = 1'-0"

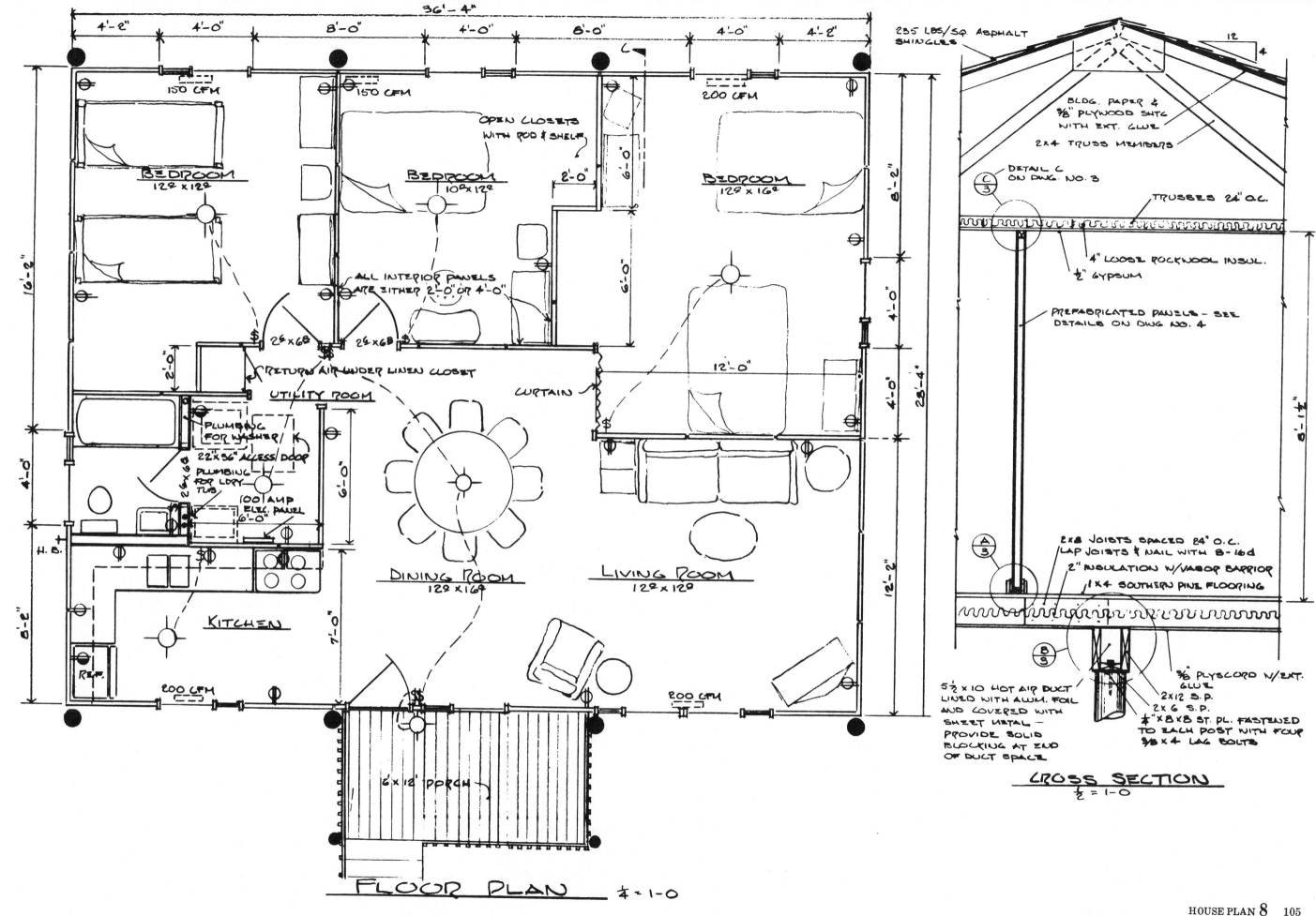

36'-4"

4'-2" | 4'-0" | 8'-0" | 4'-0" | 8'-0" | 4'-0" | 4'-2"

235 LBS/SQ. ASPHALT SHINGLES

150 CFM

150 CFM

200 CFM

12
4

OPEN CLOSETS WITH ROD & SHELF

BLDG. PAPER & 3/8" PLYWOOD SHTG. WITH EXT. GLUE

2x4 TRUSS MEMBERS

BEDROOM
12° x 12°

BEDROOM
10° x 12°

2'-0"

BEDROOM
12° x 16°

8'-2"

DETAIL C ON DWG. NO. 3

TRUSSES 24" O.C.

16'-2"

6'-0"

6'-0"

4" LOOSE ROCKWOOL INSUL.

1/2" GYPSUM

ALL INTERIOR PANELS ARE EITHER 2'-0" OR 4'-0"

25 x 68   24 x 68

PREFABRICATED PANELS — SEE DETAILS ON DWG NO. 4

RETURN AIR UNDER LINEN CLOSET

CURTAIN

12'-0"

4'-0"

4'-0"

28'-4"

UTILITY ROOM

2'-0"

PLUMBING FOR WASHER

22 x 36 ACCESS DOOR

26 x 68

PLUMBING FOR LDRY TUB

100 AMP ELEC. PANEL

6'-0"

4'-0"

6'-0"

H.B.

REF.

200 CFM

KITCHEN

7'-0"

DINING ROOM
12° x 16°

LIVING ROOM
12° x 12°

200 CFM

2x8 JOISTS SPACED 24" O.C. LAP JOISTS & NAIL WITH 8-16d

2" INSULATION W/VAPOR BARRIER

1x4 SOUTHERN PINE FLOORING

A
3

12'-2"

B
3

8'-2"

5 1/2 x 10 HOT AIR DUCT LINED WITH ALUM. FOIL AND COVERED WITH SHEET METAL — PROVIDE SOLID BLOCKING AT END OF DUCT SPACE

3/8 PLYSCORD W/EXT. GLUE

2x12 S.P.

2x6 S.P.

1/2" x 8 x 8 ST. PL. FASTENED TO EACH POST WITH FOUR 3/8 x 4 LAG BOLTS

6' x 12' PORCH

FLOOR PLAN   1/4 = 1-0

CROSS SECTION
1/2 = 1-0

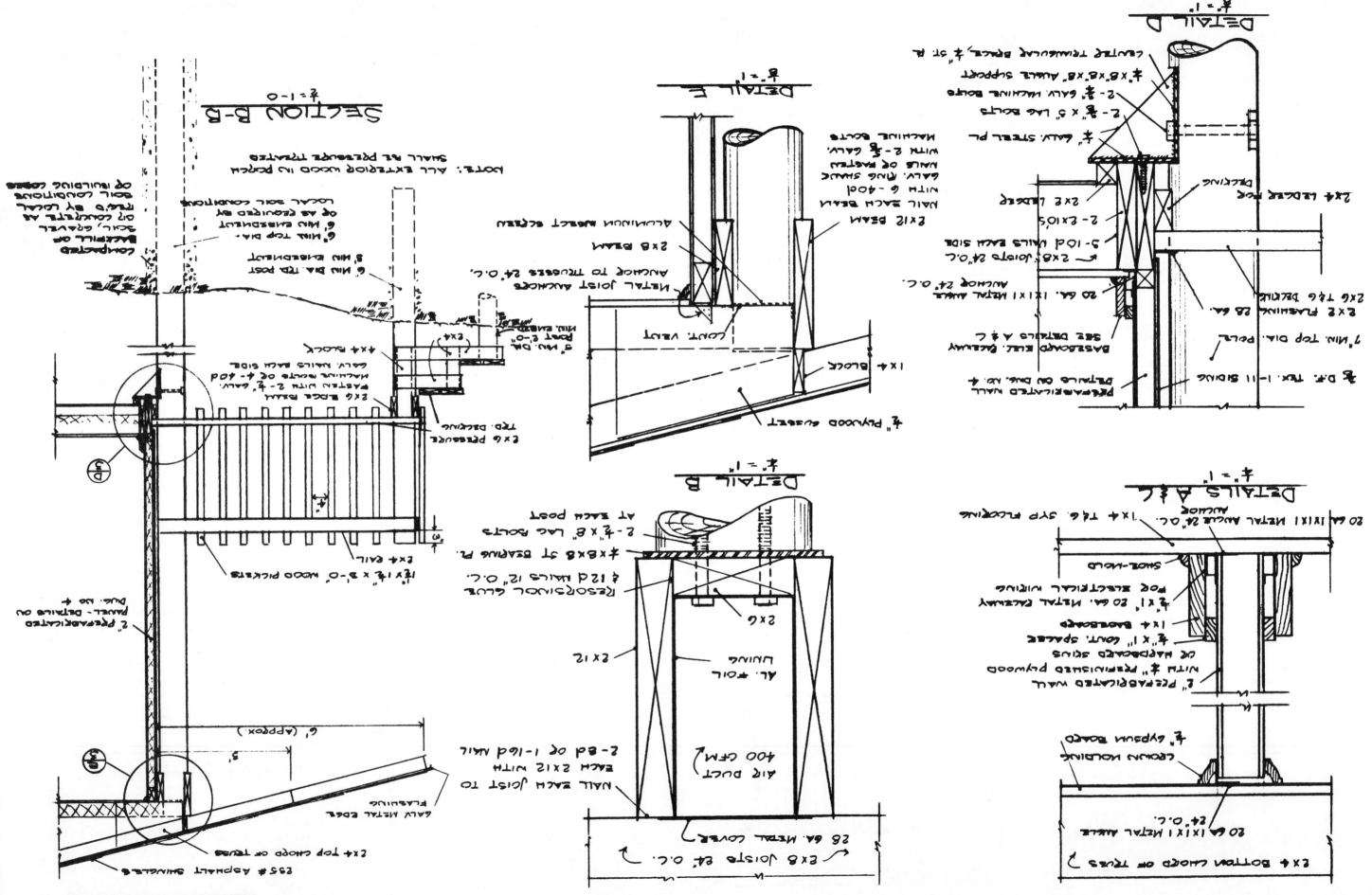

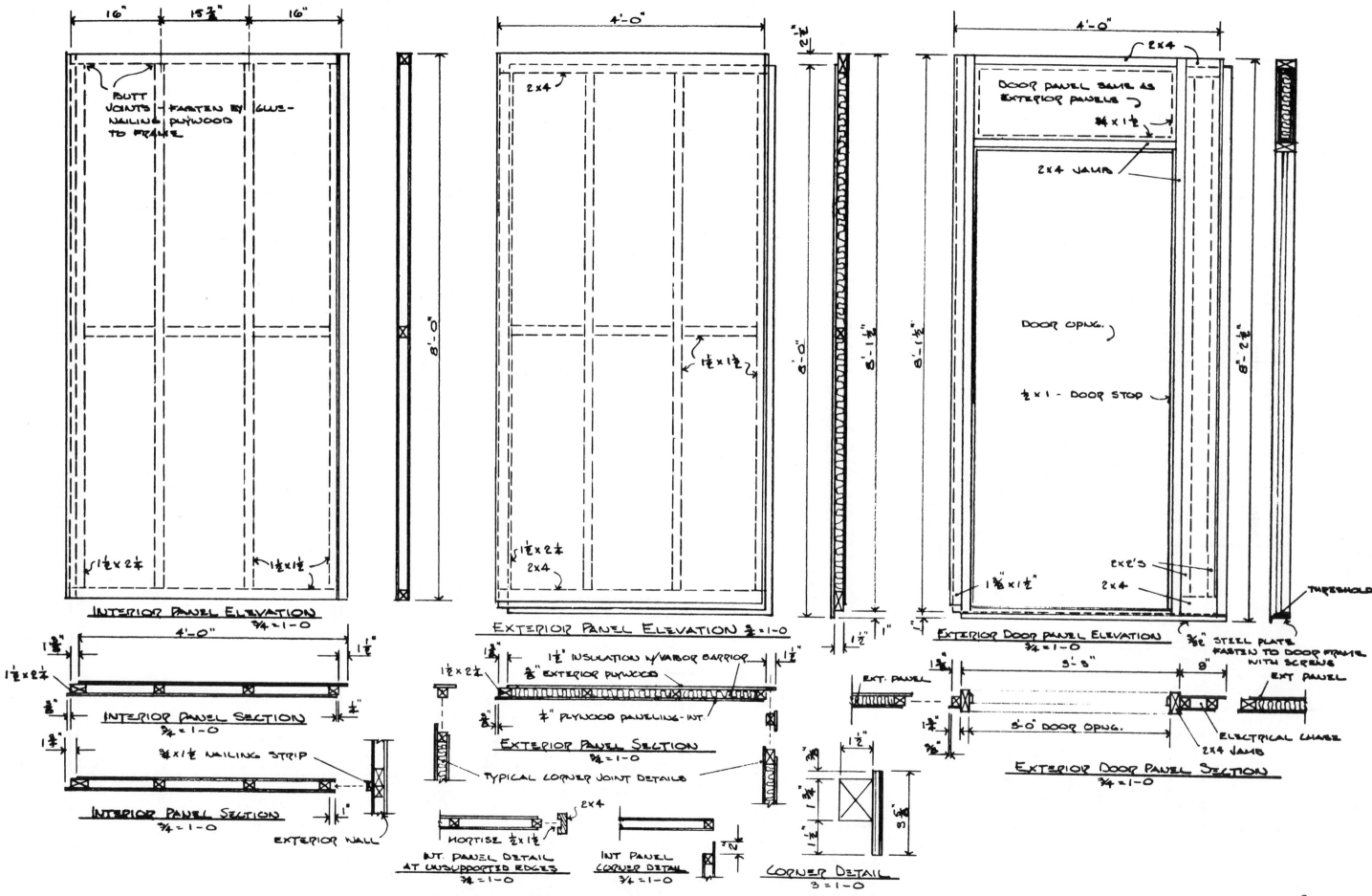

INTERIOR PANEL ELEVATION
3/4 = 1-0

16"   15 7/8"   16"

BUTT JOINTS - FASTEN BY GLUE-NAILING PLYWOOD TO FRAME

1 1/2 × 2 1/4

1 1/2 × 1 1/2

8'-0"

EXTERIOR PANEL ELEVATION 1/2 = 1-0

4'-0"

2×4

1 1/2 × 1 1/2

1 1/2 × 2 1/4
2×4

8'-0"

8'-1 1/2"

1 1/2"   1"   1 1/2"

EXTERIOR DOOR PANEL ELEVATION
3/4 = 1-0

4'-0"

2×4

DOOR PANEL SAME AS EXTERIOR PANELS

3/4 × 1 1/2

2×4 JAMB

DOOR OPNG.

1/2 × 1 - DOOR STOP

2×2'S

2×4

1 3/4 × 1 1/2

8'-1 1/2"

8'-2 3/4"

THRESHOLD

INTERIOR PANEL SECTION
3/4 = 1-0

4'-0"

1 1/2"   1 1/2"

1 1/2 × 2 1/4

3/4"

1/4"

INTERIOR PANEL SECTION
3/4 = 1-0

1 1/4"

3/4 × 1 1/2 NAILING STRIP

1"

EXTERIOR WALL

EXTERIOR PANEL SECTION
3/4 = 1-0

1 1/2" INSULATION W/ VAPOR BARRIER
3/8" EXTERIOR PLYWOOD

1 1/2 × 2 1/4

1 1/2"   1"

3/4"

1/4" PLYWOOD PANELING-INT.

TYPICAL CORNER JOINT DETAILS

MORTISE 1/2 × 1 1/2

2×4

INT. PANEL DETAIL AT UNSUPPORTED EDGES
3/4 = 1-0

INT PANEL CORNER DETAIL
3/4 = 1-0

1/2"

CORNER DETAIL
3 = 1-0

1 1/2"

1 3/4"

1 1/2"   1 3/4"

3 3/4"

EXT. PANEL

EXTERIOR DOOR PANEL SECTION
3/4 = 1-0

5'-3"

5'-0 DOOR OPNG.

1 3/4"

1 3/4"

3/8"

ELECTRICAL CHASE

2×4 JAMB

EXT PANEL

3/8" STEEL PLATE FASTEN TO DOOR FRAME WITH SCREWS

HOUSE PLAN 8   107

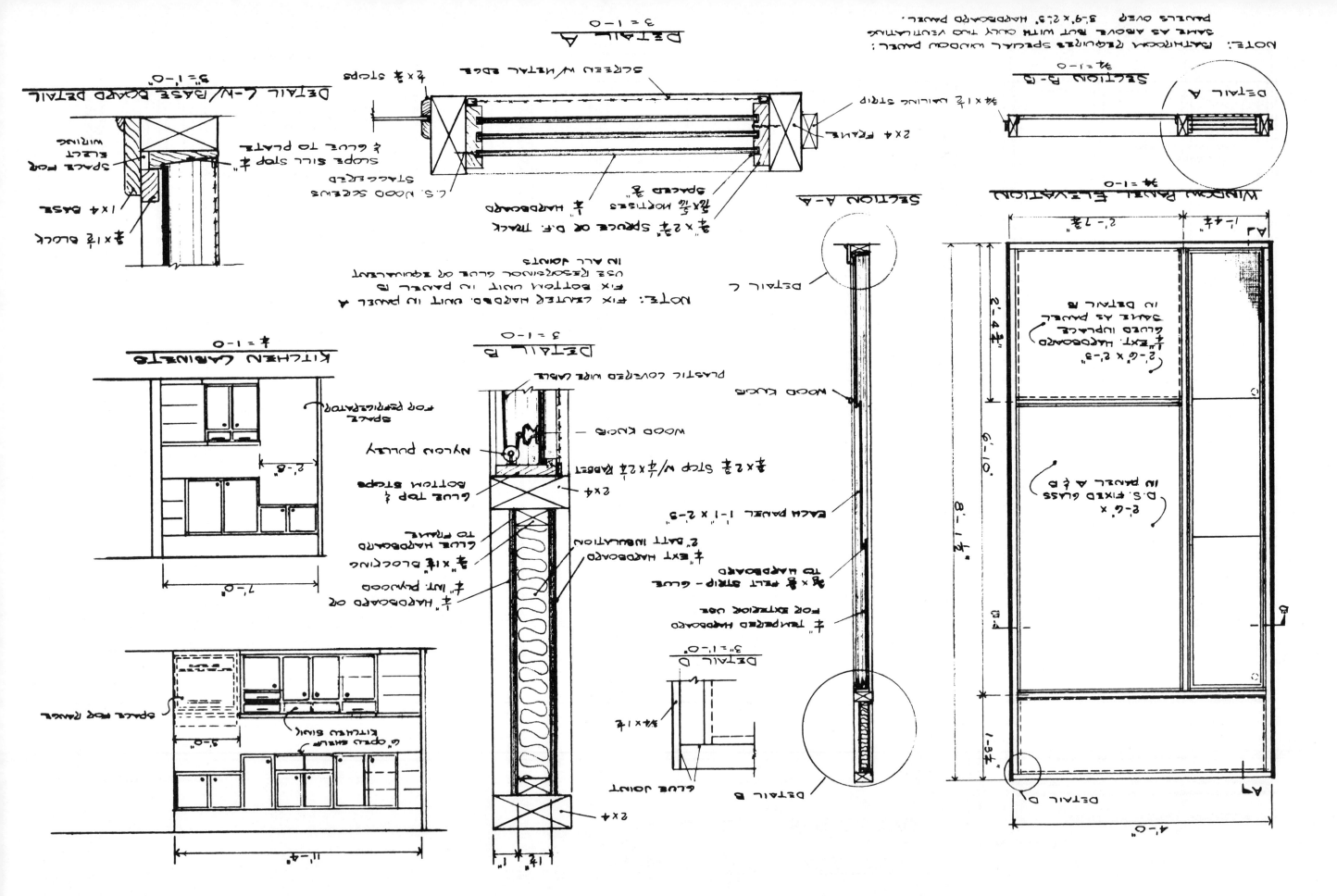

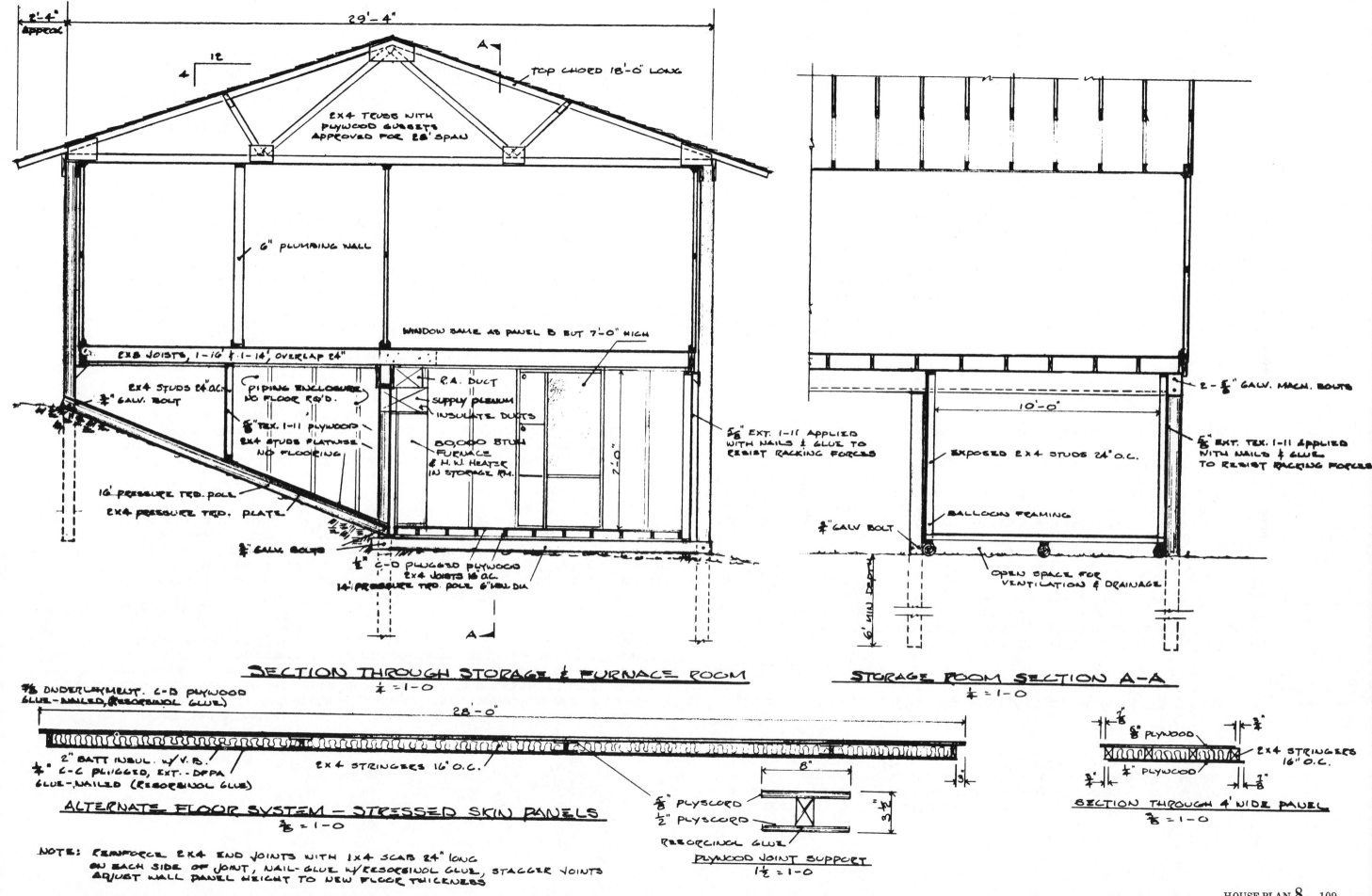

2'-4" APPROX.

29'-4"

12
4

TOP CHORD 18'-0" LONG

2x4 TRUSS WITH
PLYWOOD GUSSETS
APPROVED FOR 28' SPAN

6" PLUMBING WALL

WINDOW SAME AS PANEL B BUT 7'-0" HIGH

2x8 JOISTS, 1-16 & 1-14, OVERLAP 24"

2x4 STUDS 24" O.C.
¾" GALV. BOLT

PIPING ENCLOSURE
NO FLOOR RQ'D.

⅝"TEX. 1-11 PLYWOOD
2x4 STUDS FLATWISE
NO FLOORING

16' PRESSURE TRD. POLE
2x4 PRESSURE TRD. PLATE

¾" GALV. BOLTS

R.A. DUCT
SUPPLY PLENUM
INSULATE DUCTS

80,000 BTUH
FURNACE
& H.W. HEATER
IN STORAGE RM.

7'-0"

⅝" EXT. 1-11 APPLIED
WITH NAILS & GLUE TO
RESIST RACKING FORCES

½" C-D PLUGGED PLYWOOD
2x4 JOISTS 16" O.C.
14' PRESSURE TRD. POLE 6" MIN. DIA.

SECTION THROUGH STORAGE & FURNACE ROOM
¼" = 1'-0

2 - ⅝" GALV. MACH. BOLTS

10'-0"

⅝" EXT. TEX. 1-11 APPLIED
WITH NAILS & GLUE
TO RESIST RACKING FORCES

EXPOSED 2x4 STUDS 24" O.C.

BALLOON FRAMING

¾" GALV. BOLT

6' MIN. DEPTH

OPEN SPACE FOR
VENTILATION & DRAINAGE

STORAGE ROOM SECTION A-A
¼" = 1'-0

⅝ UNDERLAYMENT C-D PLYWOOD
GLUE-NAILED (RESORCINOL GLUE)

28'-0"

2" BATT INSUL. W/V.B.
½" C-C PLUGGED, EXT.-DFPA
GLUE-NAILED (RESORCINOL GLUE)

2x4 STRINGERS 16" O.C.

ALTERNATE FLOOR SYSTEM – STRESSED SKIN PANELS
⅜" = 1'-0

8"

⅝" PLYSCORD
½" PLYSCORD
RESORCINOL GLUE

PLYWOOD JOINT SUPPORT
1½" = 1'-0

⅝" PLYWOOD

2x4 STRINGERS
16" O.C.

½" PLYWOOD

SECTION THROUGH 4' WIDE PANEL
⅜" = 1'-0

NOTE: REINFORCE 2x4 END JOINTS WITH 1x4 SCAB 24" LONG
ON EACH SIDE OF JOINT, NAIL-GLUE W/RESORCINOL GLUE, STAGGER JOINTS
ADJUST WALL PANEL HEIGHT TO NEW FLOOR THICKNESS

HOUSE PLAN 8   109

SPECIFICATIONS

PLAN 8

General

Each item of material and equipment shall equal or exceed that described or indicated. All work shall be performed in a workmanlike manner and in accordance with the best practice. Mention of commercial products and sources does not constitute an endorsement of such products by the Forest Service or the Department of Agriculture to the exclusion of other equally acceptable products.

Site Grading

Grade as required to smooth out surface humps and valleys and to provide drainage away from the house. Minimum site disturbance is desired, therefore, grading should be done only where necessary to provide smooth surfaces and drainage and as needed to provide for the carport and storage area under the house when these items are included.

Wood Poles and Porch

Poles and wood used in the porch shall be syp, pressure treated in accordance with American Wood Preservers Association recommendations and the AWPI Quality Control Program LP-22. Each treated piece of wood shall bear the AWPI LP-22 quality control mark.

Exterior Walls

Framing members shall be syp, no. 1 dimension.
Sheathing: None
Siding: Ext. 3/8" fir or lauan plywood, A-C, group 2; with "V" or channel groove, 4" or 8" on center. Siding shall be applied to the framing members with a water resistant structural adhesive such as Fullers' "Tan Mastic". Framing members need not be fastened together if they are held in a jig while spreading the adhesive and placing the siding.
Finish: Apply two coats of pigmented exterior penetrating stain. Paint doors and trim with one coat of nonporous, oil-base primer and two coats of exterior paint. Place second coat of stain before first coat is dry.

Floor Framing

Joists: No. 2 dimension, syp or fir. See pages 105 and 109.

Finish Flooring

Wood flooring with joist system: 1 x 4 inch, syp, grade D, tongue-and-groove, nailed directly to joists. Sand, seal, and wax in all rooms. Finish flooring over the stressed skin panel floor system: Asphalt tile placed over 5/8" plywood, C-D underlayment grade with exterior glue.

Underlayment shall be glue-nailed to floor joists with 8d grooved nails, 6" o.c.; glue shall be a neoprene base adhesive for brush or roller application as recommended by the manufacturer, or resorcinol glue as described in Government Military specification MIL-A-22397.

Partition Framing

Studs: No. 1, syp, or fir. See details on page 107.

Roof and Ceiling Framing

Prefabricated trusses designed to span 28' with less than 1/2" deflection under a design load of 30 lbs/sq.ft. Either plywood or metal gusset plates may be used in accordance with the manufacturers design.

Roof and Ceiling Framing

Roof Sheathing: Standard plywood with exterior glue, C-D, 3/8" thick, or 1" board sheathing, Grade no. 2 or BTR. Board sheathing shall be placed over exposed soffits with the 3/8" plywood sheathing shimmed up to align with the board sheathing, or the asphalt shingles shall be applied over 3/8" plywood sheathing with a roofing mastic so that no nails penetrate through the plywood into the soffit.
Roofing: 15# roofing felt under 235# asphalt shingles or selvage, grade C, double coverage.
Flashing: Asphalt roofing over the ridge; galvanized or aluminum drip edges.

Gutters and Downspouts

None

Wall and Ceiling Finish

Walls: 3/8" factory painted gypsum board similar to "Blendtex" by U. S. Gypsum Company. Edges shall be tapered or rounded. Install with 6d grooved nails or an adhesive approved by U. S. Gypsum for this type of application. Touch-up paint shall be used to paint the nail heads. (Bathroom wall finish given in next item).
Ceilings: 1/2" factory painted gypsum board similar to "Blendtex" by U. S. Gypsum Company. As near as possible, board lengths should match room length or width to avoid end joints. Ceiling board shall be prescored with a square tile pattern. Application shall be same as for wall panels, or as recommended by U. S. Gypsum Company.

Decorating

Colors and texture for factory applied paint shall be selected by the owner from samples, or a color chart. Bathroom walls shall be painted with primer and two coats enamel paint. Bathroom ceiling finish shall be the same as in the rest of the house.

Interior Doors and Trim

Doors: 1-3/8", flush hollow core, lauan. Painted with one coat oil-base non-porous primer and two coats of enamel. Doors shall be prehung in a 2" x 4" frame so that the space above each door is open for air circulation. No trim shall be required except when required to widen the panel to a four foot width. Electrical wiring to wall switches and the switch boxes can be concealed in the narrow jamb extensions needed to widen the door panel.

Windows

Details on page 108. Prefabricate of No. 1 dimension lumber, syp or fir. Hardboard panels shall be medium density hardboard for exterior use. All joints shall be glued with phenol-resorcinol glue; apply glue joint pressure by nailing all joints. Felt weatherstripping between the sliding hardboard panels shall be fastened in place with a water resistant contact cement such as: Minnesota Mining and Manufacturing Company 3-M brand "Fastbond". Finish hardboard with a nonporous oil-base primer and two coats exterior paint.

Entrance Doors

1-3/4" thickness, solid core, lauan or fir, prehung in four foot wide panel according to details on page 107. Prefabrication of the door panel shall be similar to the window frames; use resorcinol-resin glue to fasten the frame together. Provide a wood screen door. Doors and trim shall be painted with an oil-base nonporous primer and two coats of exterior paint.

Cabinets and Equipment

Kitchen cabinets: Fir, beech, or birch with vinyl counter top and metal edging. Stain, seal and wax. Back and end splash is the same.
Linen closet: Shelving shall be 1 x 10 inch syp, grade no. 2, unpainted.
Medicine cabinet: Allow $20.00 for cabinet with side or top lights.

Attic Access

Provide a 3/8" x 20" x 36" bd plywood attic scuttle where shown on the plans. Insulate scuttle with 3" batt insulation stapled to the plywood door.

Plumbing

Provide five fixtures complete with all necessary fittings; 32" x 20" double or single kitchen sink, bath tub, 17" x 19" lavatory, and water closet in white porcelain on steel, and a low-cost fiber glass or cast iron laundry tub.
Water heater: Min. capacity, 40 gallons; 10 year warranty, gas or electric.
Water piping: Galvanized steel, copper, or plastic as approved by local plumbing codes. Provide a sill cock in the lowest section of plumbing for a house drain. Also provide one exterior hose bibb.

Heating and Ventilation

Furnace: 80,000 BTUH gas or oil forced air furnace; return air register installed below linen closet door; supply air registers shall be surface mounted type. Metal ducts from furnace to heated area shall be insulated. Supply ducts in the floor shall be either 6" round metal ducts or aluminum foil lined spaces between the floor joists. If foil is used it shall be placed over the 2" batt insulation. The main branch duct shall be as detailed on page 105. Foil shall be heavy gauge and stapled in place. Provide flue pipe as recommended by manufacturer.

Electric Wiring and Fixtures

Service: Overhead, 100 amperes
Distribution Panel: 100 amp. with at least six branch circuits and three spares.
Wiring: Installed in accordance with the National Electric code. Shallow outlet boxes shall be used for the duplex outlets in the wood baseboard raceway. Allow $30.00 for light fixtures.

Insulation

Roof: 3" mineral wool with integral vapor barrier.
Walls and floor: 2" mineral wool with integral vapor barrier.

Finish Hardware

With prehung, prefabricated, doors, windows and cabinets.

Landscaping

Planting, walks, drives, and finish grading by owner.

Miscellaneous

All outside utilities, such as, electricity, water, sewer, and gas to the house shall be provided by the owner or utility company. All utilities in the house shall be stubbed out of the house in the most convenient location for hookup to outside utilities.

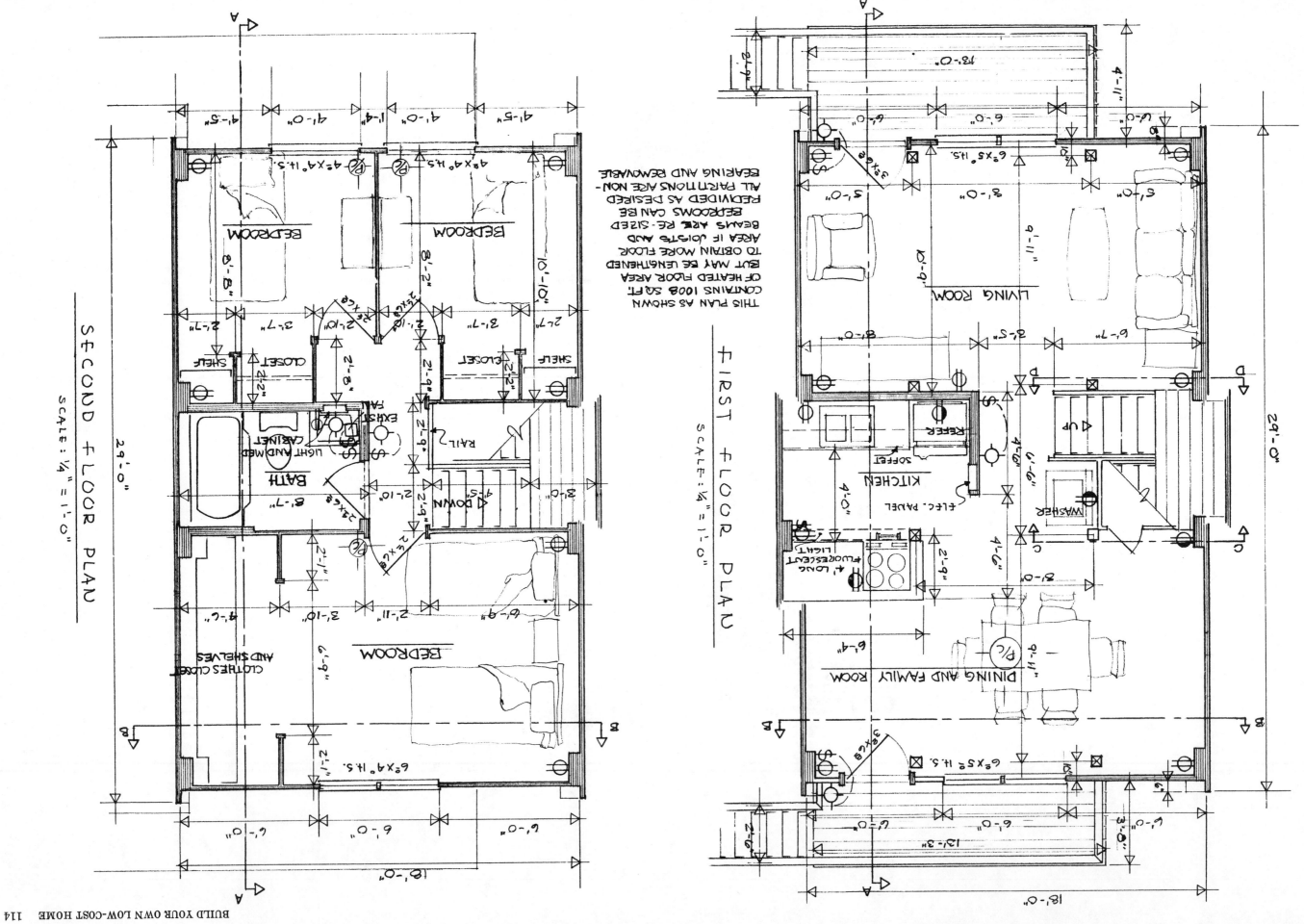

SECOND FLOOR PLAN
SCALE: ¼" = 1'-0"

FIRST FLOOR PLAN
SCALE: ¼" = 1'-0"

THIS PLAN AS SHOWN
CONTAINS 1008 SQ. FT.
OF HEATED FLOOR AREA
BUT MAY BE LENGTHENED
TO OBTAIN MORE FLOOR
AREA IF JOISTS AND
BEAMS ARE RE-SIZED.
BEDROOMS CAN BE
RE-DIVIDED AS DESIRED.
ALL PARTITIONS ARE NON-
BEARING AND REMOVABLE.

BEDROOM

BEDROOM

BEDROOM

BATH

CLOSET

CLOSET

SHELF

SHELF

CLOTHES CLOSET
AND SHELVES

LIGHT AND MED.
CABINET

EXHAUST FAN

DOWN

RAIL

LIVING ROOM

KITCHEN

DINING AND FAMILY ROOM

REFER

WASHER

ELEC. PANEL

UP

SOFFIT

4' LONG
FLUORESCENT
LIGHT

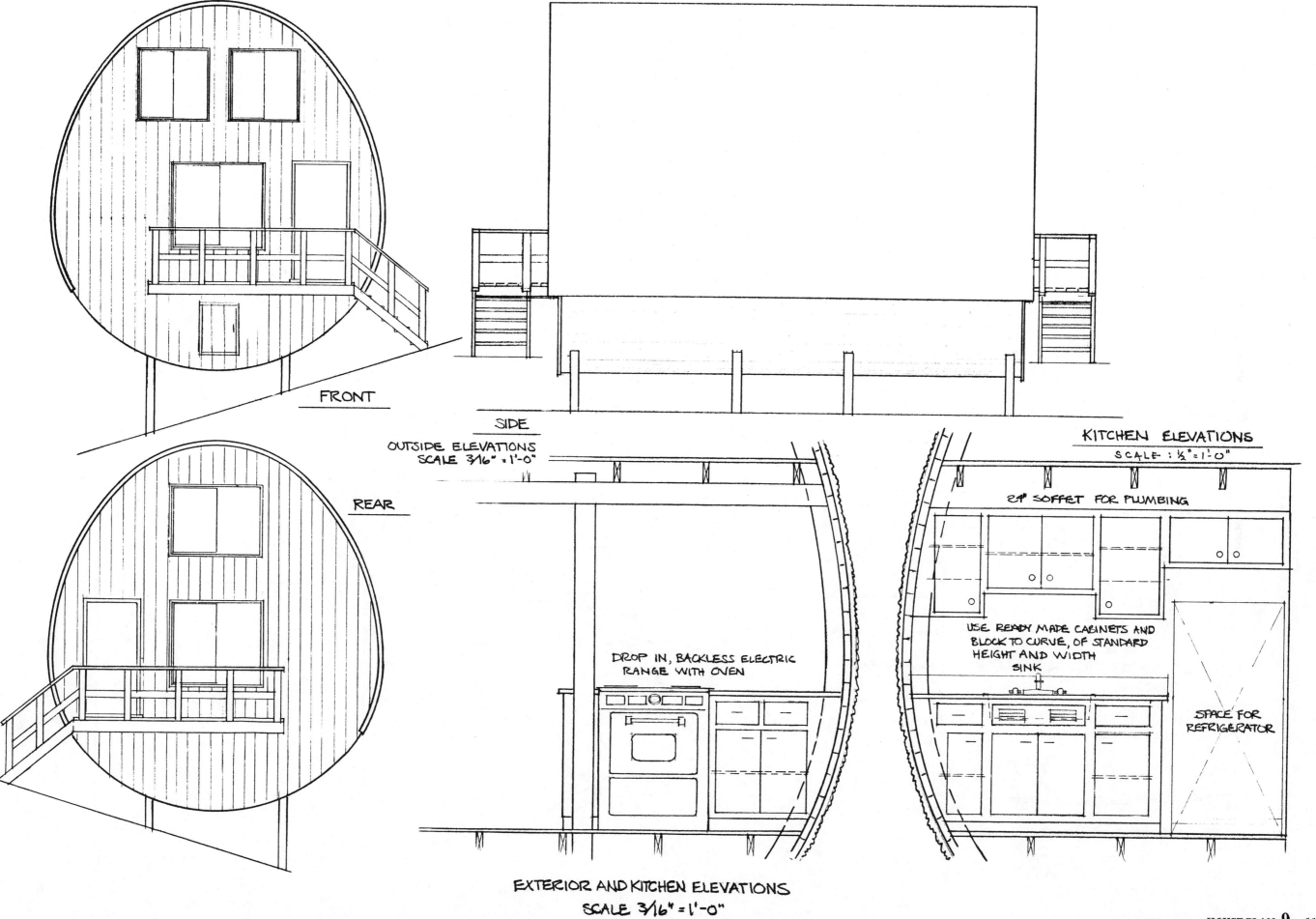

FRONT

SIDE

OUTSIDE ELEVATIONS
SCALE 3/16" = 1'-0"

REAR

KITCHEN ELEVATIONS
SCALE : 1/2" = 1'-0"

24" SOFFET FOR PLUMBING

DROP IN, BACKLESS ELECTRIC
RANGE WITH OVEN

USE READY MADE CABINETS AND
BLOCK TO CURVE, OF STANDARD
HEIGHT AND WIDTH
SINK

SPACE FOR
REFRIGERATOR

EXTERIOR AND KITCHEN ELEVATIONS
SCALE 3/16" = 1'-0"

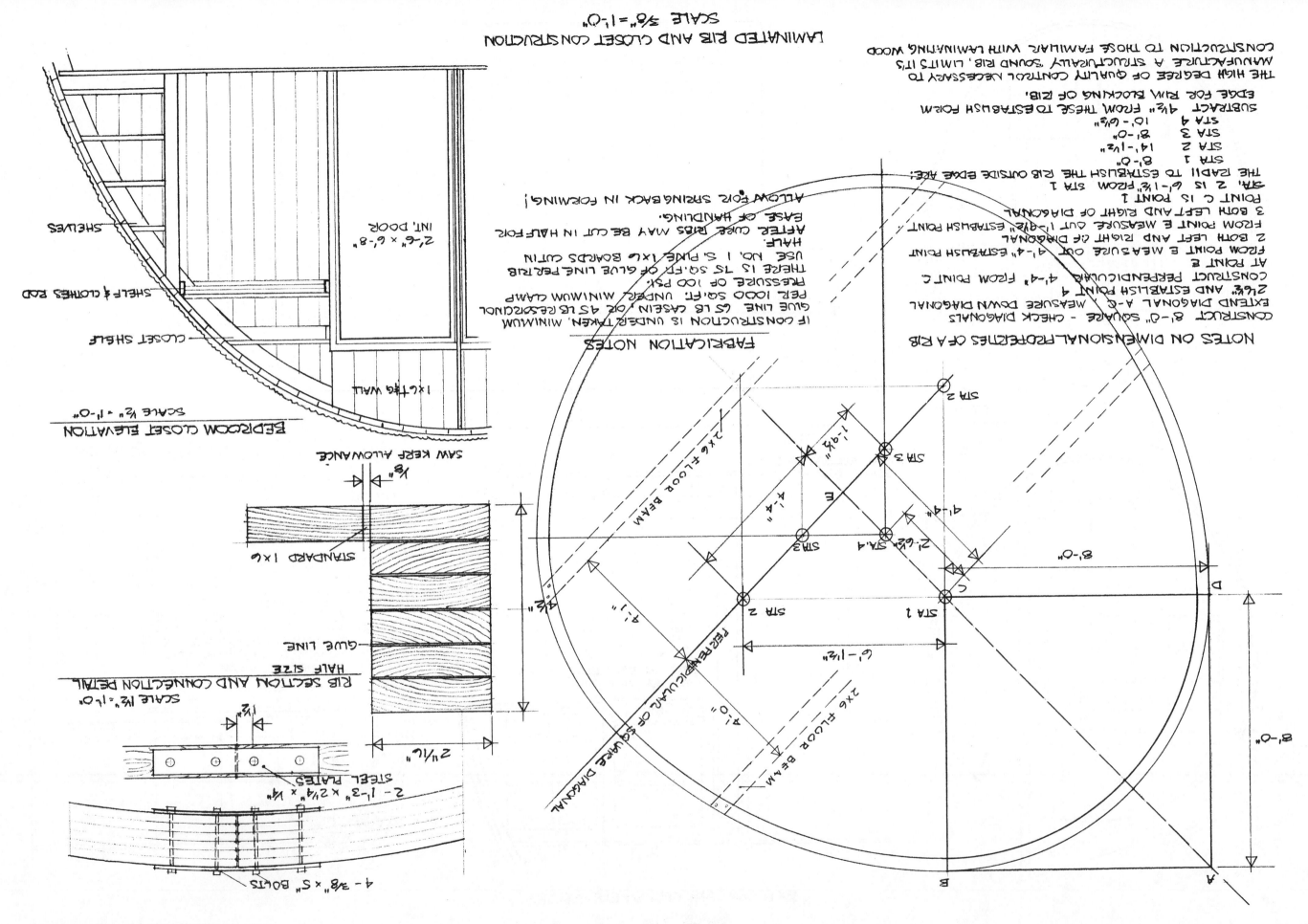

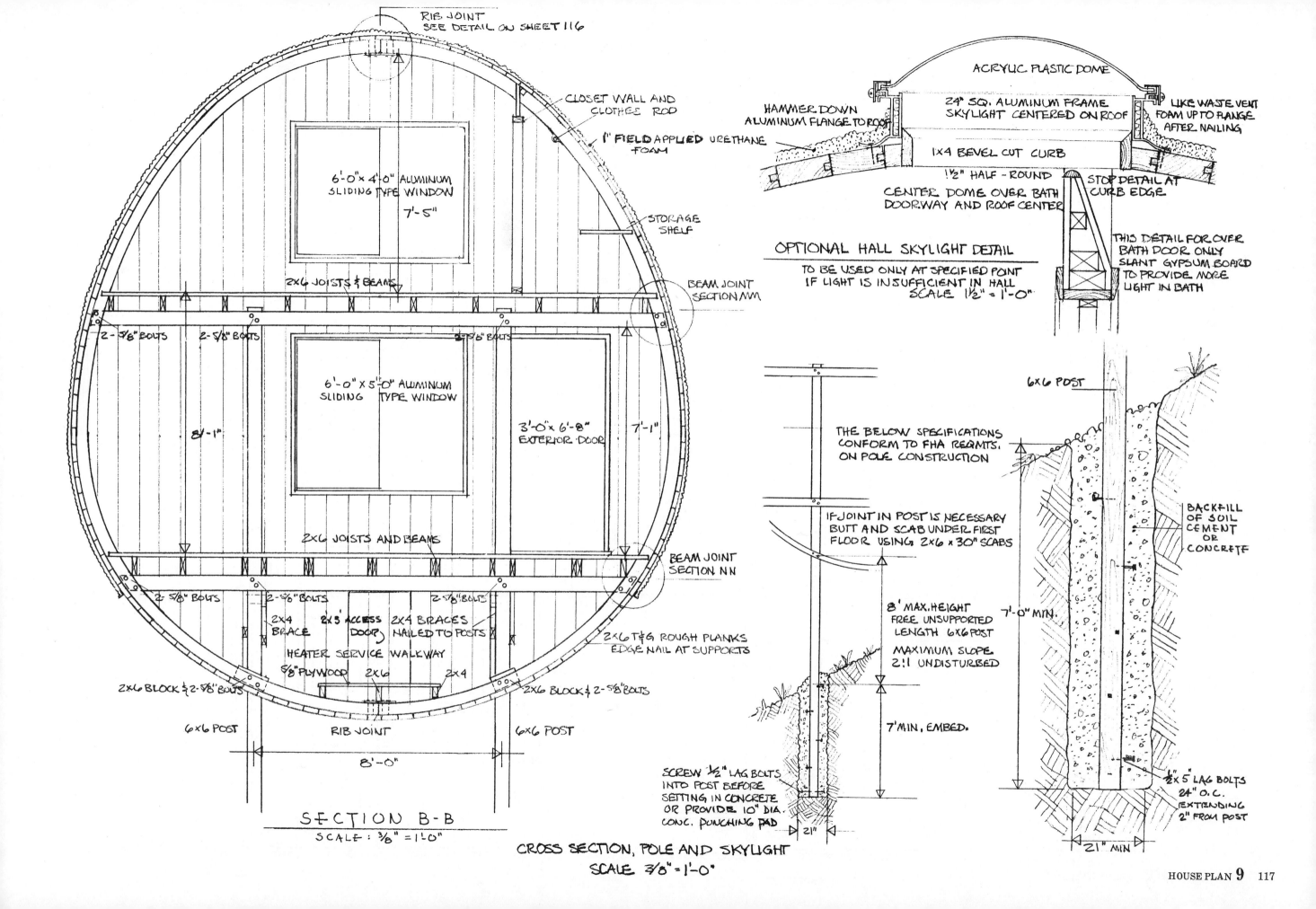

RIB JOINT
SEE DETAIL ON SHEET 116

CLOSET WALL AND
CLOTHES ROD

1" FIELD APPLIED URETHANE
FOAM

6'-0" x 4'-0" ALUMINUM
SLIDING TYPE WINDOW
7'-5"

STORAGE
SHELF

2x6 JOISTS & BEAMS

BEAM JOINT
SECTION MM

2-5/8" BOLTS   2-5/8" BOLTS   2-5/8" BOLTS

6'-0" x 5'-0" ALUMINUM
SLIDING TYPE WINDOW

8'-1"

3'-0" x 6'-8"
EXTERIOR DOOR   7'-1"

2x6 JOISTS AND BEAMS

BEAM JOINT
SECTION NN

2-5/8" BOLTS   2-5/8" BOLTS   2-5/8" BOLTS

2x4   2x5 ACCESS   2x4 BRACES
BRACE   DOOR   NAILED TO POSTS

HEATER SERVICE WALKWAY   2x6 T&G ROUGH PLANKS
                              EDGE NAIL AT SUPPORTS
5/8" PLYWOOD   2x6   2x4

2x6 BLOCK & 2-5/8" BOLTS   2x6 BLOCK & 2-5/8" BOLTS

6x6 POST   RIB JOINT   6x6 POST

8'-0"

SECTION B-B
SCALE: 3/8" = 1'-0"

ACRYLIC PLASTIC DOME

HAMMER DOWN
ALUMINUM FLANGE TO ROOF

24" SQ. ALUMINUM FRAME
SKYLIGHT CENTERED ON ROOF

LIKE WASTE VENT
FOAM UP TO FLANGE
AFTER NAILING

1x4 BEVEL CUT CURB

1½" HALF-ROUND

STOP DETAIL AT
CURB EDGE

CENTER DOME OVER BATH
DOORWAY AND ROOF CENTER

THIS DETAIL FOR OVER
BATH DOOR ONLY
SLANT GYPSUM BOARD
TO PROVIDE MORE
LIGHT IN BATH

OPTIONAL HALL SKYLIGHT DETAIL
TO BE USED ONLY AT SPECIFIED POINT
IF LIGHT IS INSUFFICIENT IN HALL
SCALE 1½" = 1'-0"

6x6 POST

THE BELOW SPECIFICATIONS
CONFORM TO FHA REQMTS.
ON POLE CONSTRUCTION

IF JOINT IN POST IS NECESSARY
BUTT AND SCAB UNDER FIRST
FLOOR USING 2x6 x 30" SCABS

BACKFILL
OF SOIL
CEMENT
OR
CONCRETE

8' MAX. HEIGHT
FREE UNSUPPORTED
LENGTH 6x6 POST

7'-0" MIN.

MAXIMUM SLOPE
2:1 UNDISTURBED

7' MIN. EMBED.

SCREW ½" LAG BOLTS
INTO POST BEFORE
SETTING IN CONCRETE
OR PROVIDE 10" DIA.
CONC. PUNCHING PAD

21"

½ x 5 LAG BOLTS
24" O.C.
EXTENDING
2" FROM POST

21" MIN.

CROSS SECTION, POLE AND SKYLIGHT
SCALE 3/8" = 1'-0"

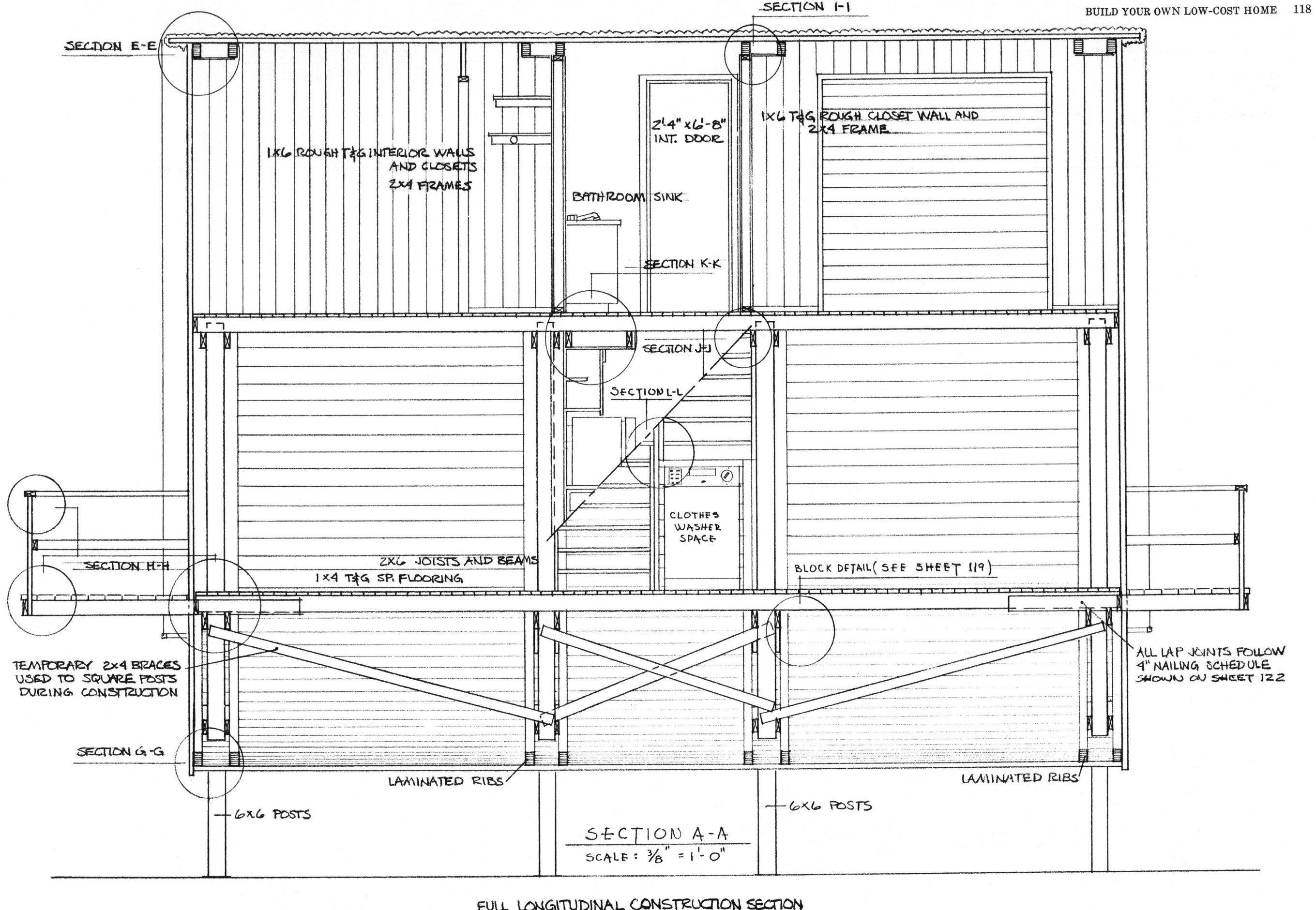

SECTION I-I

SECTION E-E

2'-4" X 6'-8"
INT. DOOR

1X6 T&G ROUGH CLOSET WALL AND
2X4 FRAME

1X6 ROUGH T&G INTERIOR WALLS
AND CLOSETS
2X4 FRAMES

BATHROOM SINK

SECTION K-K

SECTION J-J

SECTION L-L

CLOTHES
WASHER
SPACE

SECTION H-H

2X6 JOISTS AND BEAMS
1X4 T&G SP. FLOORING

BLOCK DETAIL (SEE SHEET 119)

TEMPORARY 2X4 BRACES
USED TO SQUARE POSTS
DURING CONSTRUCTION

ALL LAP JOINTS FOLLOW
4" NAILING SCHEDULE
SHOWN ON SHEET 122

SECTION G-G

LAMINATED RIBS

LAMINATED RIBS

6X6 POSTS

6X6 POSTS

SECTION A-A
SCALE: 3/8" = 1'-0"

FULL LONGITUDINAL CONSTRUCTION SECTION
SCALE 3/8" = 1'-0"

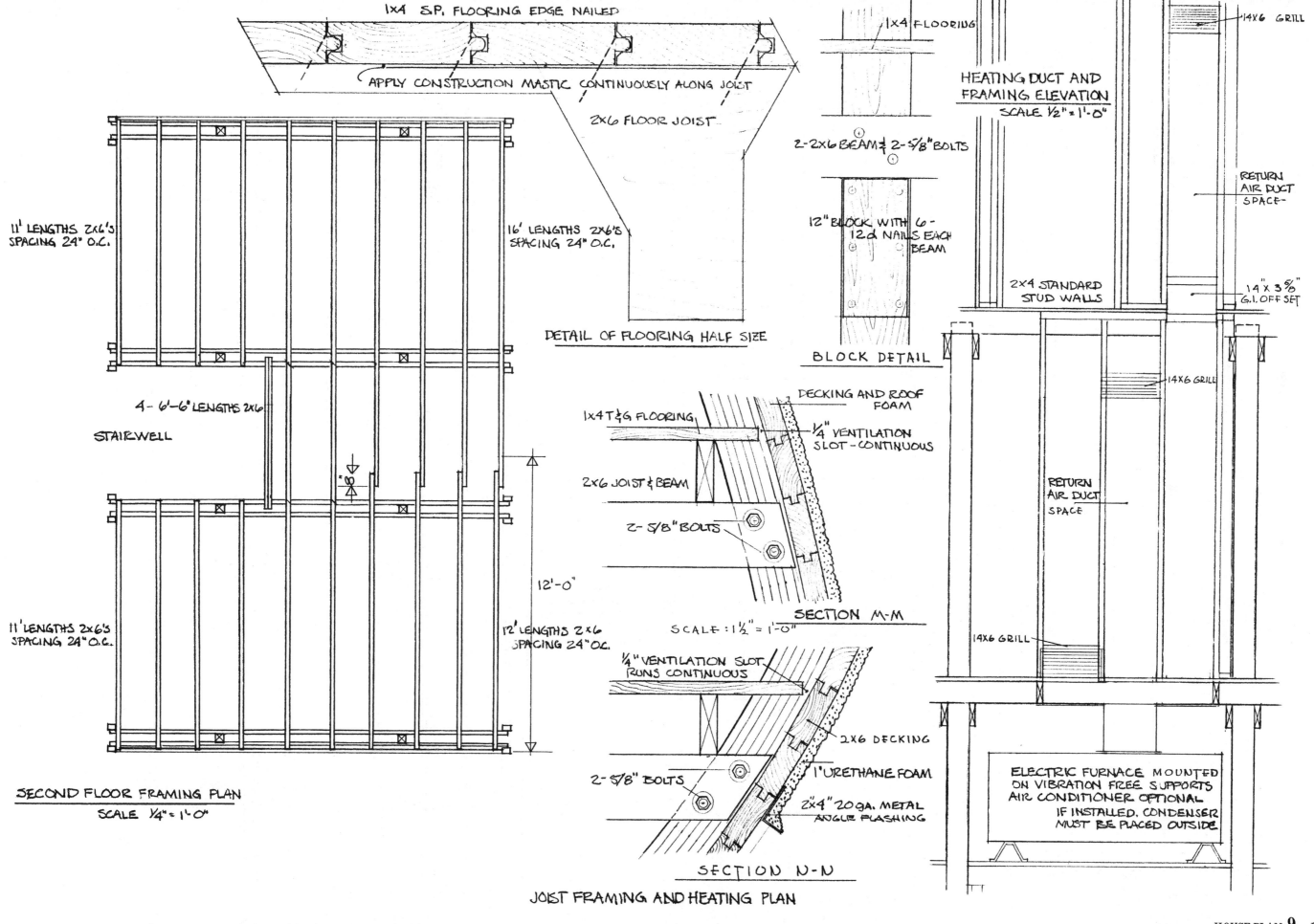

1x4 S.P. FLOORING EDGE NAILED

APPLY CONSTRUCTION MASTIC CONTINUOUSLY ALONG JOIST

2x6 FLOOR JOIST

DETAIL OF FLOORING HALF SIZE

1x4 FLOORING

2-2x6 BEAM & 2-5/8" BOLTS

12" BLOCK WITH 6 - 12d NAILS EACH BEAM

BLOCK DETAIL

14x6 GRILL

HEATING DUCT AND FRAMING ELEVATION
SCALE 1/2" = 1'-0"

RETURN AIR DUCT SPACE-

2x4 STANDARD STUD WALLS

14" x 3/8" G.I. OFF SET

14x6 GRILL

RETURN AIR DUCT SPACE

14x6 GRILL

11' LENGTHS 2x6'S SPACING 24" O.C.

16' LENGTHS 2x6'S SPACING 24" O.C.

4- 6'-6' LENGTHS 2x6

STAIRWELL

8"

12'-0"

11' LENGTHS 2x6'S SPACING 24" O.C.

12' LENGTHS 2x6 SPACING 24" O.C.

SECOND FLOOR FRAMING PLAN
SCALE 1/4" = 1'-0"

DECKING AND ROOF FOAM

1x4 T&G FLOORING

1/4" VENTILATION SLOT - CONTINUOUS

2x6 JOIST & BEAM

2- 5/8" BOLTS

SECTION M-M

SCALE : 1 1/2" = 1'-0"

1/4" VENTILATION SLOT RUNS CONTINUOUS

2x6 DECKING

1" URETHANE FOAM

2- 5/8" BOLTS

2"x4" 20 ga. METAL ANGLE FLASHING

SECTION N-N

JOIST FRAMING AND HEATING PLAN

ELECTRIC FURNACE MOUNTED ON VIBRATION FREE SUPPORTS AIR CONDITIONER OPTIONAL
IF INSTALLED, CONDENSER MUST BE PLACED OUTSIDE

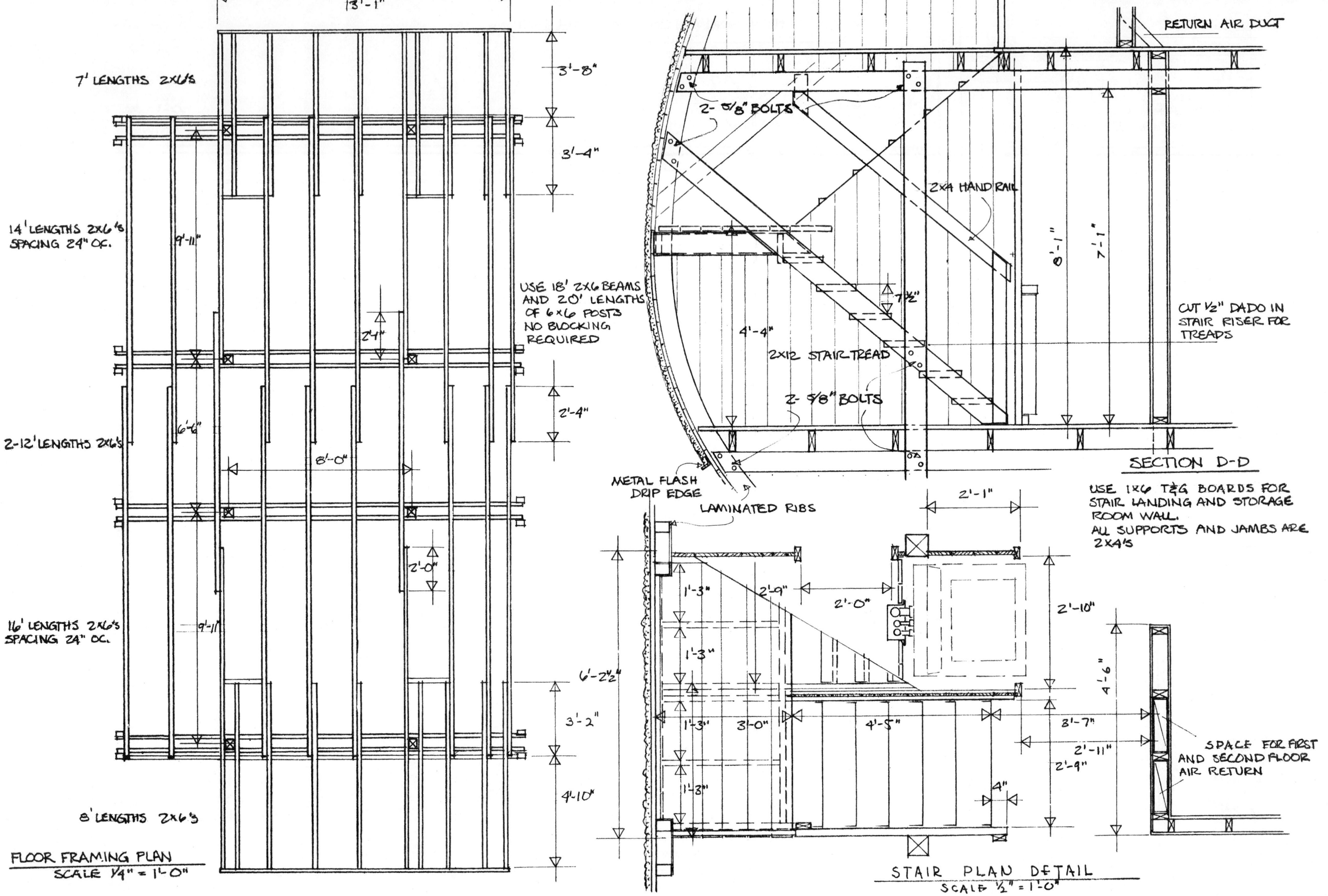

13'-1"

7' LENGTHS 2X6'S

3'-8"

3'-4"

14' LENGTHS 2X6'S
SPACING 24" O.C.

9'-11"

2'-4"

USE 18' 2X6 BEAMS
AND 20' LENGTHS
OF 6X6 POSTS
NO BLOCKING
REQUIRED

6'-6"

2-12' LENGTHS 2X6'S

8'-0"

2'-4"

16' LENGTHS 2X6'S
SPACING 24" O.C.

9'-11"

2'-0"

6'-2½"

3'-2"

8' LENGTHS 2X6'S

4'-10"

FLOOR FRAMING PLAN
SCALE ¼" = 1'-0"

RETURN AIR DUCT

2- 5/8" BOLTS

2X4 HAND RAIL

8'-1"

7'-1"

CUT ½" DADO IN
STAIR RISER FOR
TREADS

4'-4"

7½"

2X12 STAIR TREAD

2- 5/8" BOLTS

SECTION D-D

METAL FLASH
DRIP EDGE

LAMINATED RIBS

USE 1X6 T&G BOARDS FOR
STAIR LANDING AND STORAGE
ROOM WALL.
ALL SUPPORTS AND JAMBS ARE
2X4'S

2'-1"

2'-10"

1'-3"

2'-9"

2'-0"

1'-3"

4'-6"

1'-3"   3'-0"   4'-5"

3'-7"

2'-11"

1'-3"

2'-9"

4"

SPACE FOR FIRST
AND SECOND FLOOR
AIR RETURN

STAIR PLAN DETAIL
SCALE ½" = 1'-0"

JOIST FRAMING AND STAIR PLAN
SCALE ½" = 1'-0"

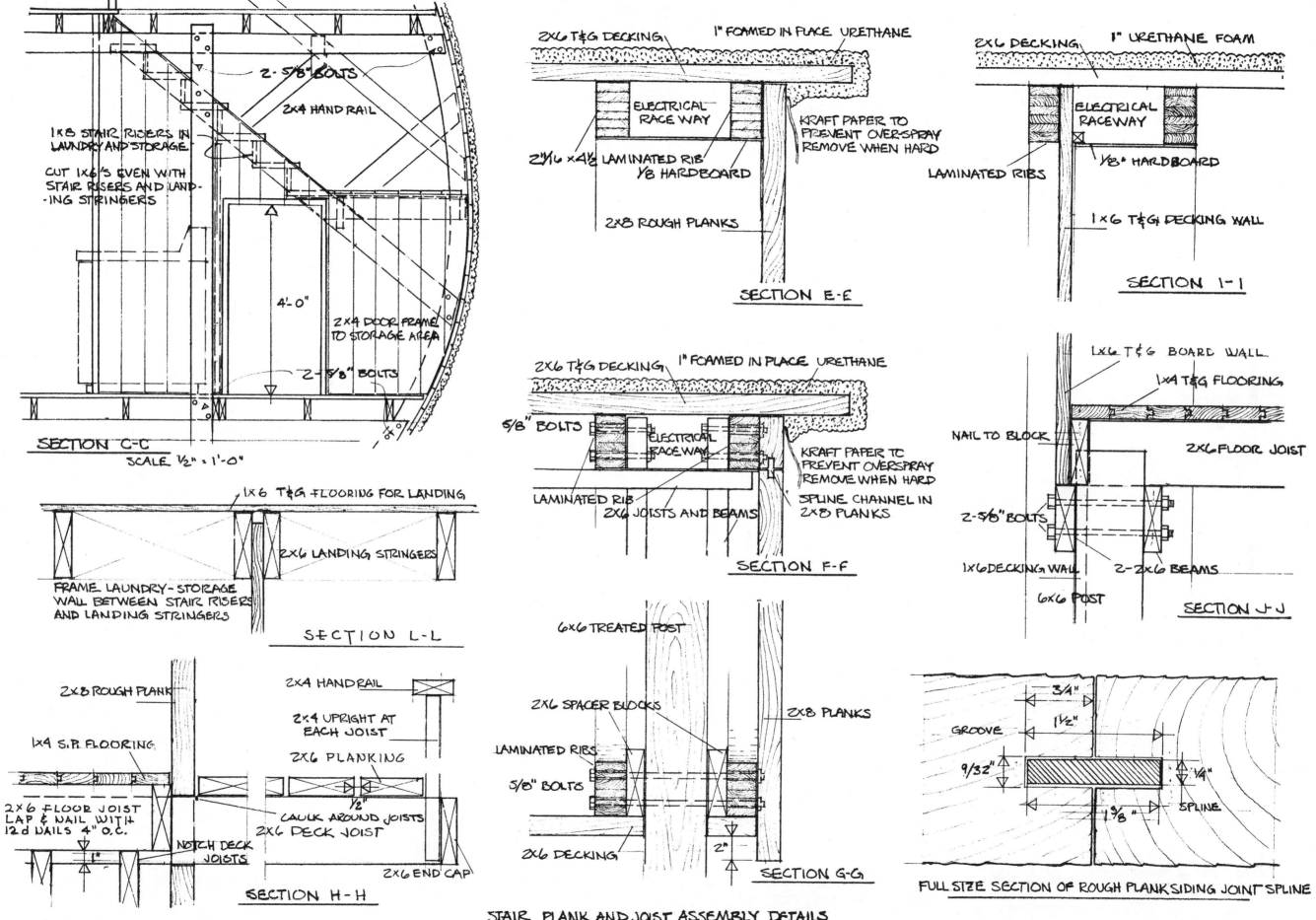

2-5/8" BOLTS

2x4 HAND RAIL

1x8 STAIR RISERS IN
LAUNDRY AND STORAGE

CUT 1x6'S EVEN WITH
STAIR RISERS AND LAND-
-ING STRINGERS

4'-0"

2x4 DOOR FRAME
TO STORAGE AREA

2-5/8" BOLTS

SECTION C-C
SCALE 1/2" = 1'-0"

1x6 T&G FLOORING FOR LANDING

2x6 LANDING STRINGERS

FRAME LAUNDRY-STORAGE
WALL BETWEEN STAIR RISERS
AND LANDING STRINGERS

SECTION L-L

2x8 ROUGH PLANK

1x4 S.P. FLOORING

2x6 FLOOR JOIST
LAP & NAIL WITH
12d NAILS 4" O.C.

NOTCH DECK
JOISTS

2x4 HANDRAIL

2x4 UPRIGHT AT
EACH JOIST

2x6 PLANKING

1/2"

CAULK AROUND JOISTS
2x6 DECK JOIST

2x6 END CAP

SECTION H-H

2x6 T&G DECKING   1" FOAMED IN PLACE URETHANE

ELECTRICAL
RACE WAY

2 11/16 x 4 1/2 LAMINATED RIB
1/8 HARDBOARD

2x8 ROUGH PLANKS

SECTION E-E

2x6 T&G DECKING   1" FOAMED IN PLACE URETHANE

5/8" BOLTS

ELECTRICAL
RACEWAY

LAMINATED RIB

2x6 JOISTS AND BEAMS

KRAFT PAPER TO
PREVENT OVERSPRAY
REMOVE WHEN HARD

SPLINE CHANNEL IN
2x8 PLANKS

SECTION F-F

6x6 TREATED POST

2x6 SPACER BLOCKS

LAMINATED RIBS

5/8" BOLTS

2x6 DECKING

2x8 PLANKS

2"

SECTION G-G

2x6 DECKING   1" URETHANE FOAM

ELECTRICAL
RACEWAY

1/8" HARDBOARD

LAMINATED RIBS

1x6 T&G DECKING WALL

SECTION I-I

1x6 T&G BOARD WALL

1x4 T&G FLOORING

NAIL TO BLOCK

2x6 FLOOR JOIST

2-5/8" BOLTS

1x6 DECKING WALL

2-2x6 BEAMS

6x6 POST

SECTION J-J

3/4"

1 1/2"

GROOVE

9/32"

1/4"

SPLINE

1 5/8"

FULL SIZE SECTION OF ROUGH PLANK SIDING JOINT SPLINE

STAIR, PLANK AND JOIST ASSEMBLY DETAILS
SCALE 1 1/2" = 1'-0"

SECTION K-K

STANDARD OVERHEAD CABINET
2'-0" SOFFIT
2x4 FURRING
WASTE OPENING
2x4 BLOCKING AROUND WASTE OPENING
2x4 BLOCK
1x4 T&G FLOORING
CUT OUT HOLE AS REQ'D FOR TOILET FLANGE

SHOWER WALL FINISH DETAIL

ALUMINUM CORNER
SHOWER ROD AND CURTAIN
½" GYP. BD. WALL
1x6 T&G WALL
ALUMINUM CORNER
WALL AND ROOFING SURFACE
LAMINATED RIB

DOOR HEAD, JAMB AND SILL
SCALE 1½"=1'-0"

2x6 PLANK WALL
CAULKING
CUT OUT JOIST AND PLANKS FOR THRESHOLD
2x6 JOIST
WEATHERSTRIP THRESHOLD
2x6 SILL
2x6 DECKING
1x4 FLOORING
EXT. DOOR

WINDOW SECTION SCALE 1½"=1'

SILL
2x8 ROUGH PLANK
CUT FLANGE OF WINDOW SECTION TO FIT NOTCH
MASTIC
USE ANY ALUM. SLIDING WINDOW

JAMB
USE ANY ALUM. SLIDING WINDOW
CUT FLANGE OF WINDOW SECTION TO FIT SPLINE NOTCH
2x8 ROUGH PLANK
MASTIC

HEAD
2x8 ROUGH PLANK
CUT FLANGE OF WINDOW SECTION TO FIT NOTCH
MASTIC
USE ANY TYPE OF ALUM. SLIDING WINDOW
FIT WINDOWS INTO NOTCHES IN PLANKS WHILE ASSEMBLING WALL SECTION, MASTIC JOINTS.

¼ ROUND ALUMINUM CORNER
½" GYPSUM BOARD AND ½" VINYL SURFACED HARD-BOARD AROUND TUB
2⅛"
1x6 T&G WALL
LAMINATED RIB AND ELECTRICAL RACEWAY
1" FOAM AND 2" DECKING

JOIST LAP NAILING SCHEDULE
2x6 JOISTS
LAP JOINT
2'-0" MINIMUM LAP
¾"
¾"
4"
4"

2x6 JAMB
1x1½ STOP
EXTERIOR DOOR
HINGE
MASTIC
SPLINE AND GROOVE 2x6 PLANK WALL

⅛" VINYL HARDBOARD
ALUMINUM STRIP SEAL
GYPSUM BOARD
2⅛"
TUB EDGE
1x6 T&G WALL
STANDARD STUD WALL

CONSTRUCTION SECTION FOR BEDROOM

BATH WALL CONNECTION

STANDARD FRAMED WALL & DOOR OPENING
2x4x⅝ STOP
2x6 FRAME
2'-4"x6'-8"x1⅜" INT. DOOR 2x6 FRAME
1x6 T&G WALL

3'-0"x6'-8"x1¾" SOLID CORE DOOR
2x6 HEAD
1x1½ STOP
MASTIC
FLASHING
2x8 ROUGH PLANKS

1x6 T&G WALL TOE NAIL TO 2x4
2x4 FRAME FOR CLOSET PARTITION SUPPORT

SPECIFICATIONS

PLAN 9

General

Each item of material and equipment shall equal or exceed that described or indicated. All work shall be performed in a workmanlike manner and in accordance with the best practice. Mention of commercial products and sources does not constitute an endorsement of such products by the Forest Service or the Department of Agriculture to the exclusion of other equally acceptable products.

Site Grading

Grade as required to smooth out surface humps and valleys and to provide drainage away from the house. Minimum site disturbance is desired, therefore, grading should be done only where necessary to provide smooth surfaces and drainage.

Post Foundation

Minimum depth for post embedment shall be 7 feet. Concrete footing requirements shall be determined by local soil conditions.

Wood Posts

Set as noted on page 117. Posts in contact with concrete or soil shall be pressure treated in accordance with American Wood Preservers Association recommendations and the AWPI Quality Control Program LP-22. Each piece of wood shall bear the AWPI quality mark LP-22.

Laminated Ribs

The layout for the eight ribs necessary is shown on page 116. Wood used shall be kiln dried southern pine or douglas fir (moisture content 12 to 17 percent) grade no. 1 or better and selected for straight grain.

Exterior Shell

2 x 6 T&G decking grade no. 2 or better kiln dried from 8 to 12 percent moisture content. Fasten to the ribs with 12d cement coated box nails and a bead of construction adhesive such as Fuller's "tan mastic" or equal.

Floor Framing

Floor beams shall be 2 x 6 no. 1 dimension. First and second floor joists shall be 2 x 6 no. 2 dimension 24" o.c. moisture content 14 to 17 percent.

Roof Covering and Insulation

Exterior decking shall be covered on the outside with 1" of foamed-in-place urethane on all the upper portions of the shell. Three-inch insulation, either fiberglass or rock wool, shall be installed between floor joists on the inside below the first floor to insulate living quarters from the crawl-space. Urethane foam shall be of at least 2 lbs. per cu.ft. density. It shall be applied only when the outside air temperature is 40° F or higher. Wood surface should be dry or it could be primed to expedite drying of the surface before placing the foam. Foam thickness shall be uniform and not less than 1". The foam shall be topcoated with a suitable, exterior, weather-resistant material recommended by the foam applicator which, in combination with the foam, will provide a minimum flammability performance of Class C rating in accordance with ASTM E-108 test procedure for built-up roof covering materials.

Exterior End Walls

2" thick rough sawn wood planks.
Thickness: 1-7/8" to 2-1/8"; width: 7-3/4" to 8-1/4".
Texture: Both faces sawn with a band saw.

Exterior End Walls

Grade: No. 1 boards except that holes and wane are not permitted. Pitch pockets or streaks shall be small. Warp, crook, and twist shall be limited to 1/4". Bow shall be limited to 1/2".
Moisture content: 12 to 17 percent.

Balcony and Exterior Stairs

Wood used shall be pressure treated or it shall be untreated redwood or cedar heartwood.
Decking, joists, and treads: 2 x 6 no. 2.
Railing: 2 x 4 no. 1.
Stringers: 2 x 10 no. 1.

Interior Partitions

Studs: No. 2 or better 16" o.c.
Boards: Single thickness 1 x 6 T&G no. 2 or better kiln dried from 8 to 12 percent moisture content. Surfaces may be patterned or smooth with one face rough-sawn.
Particleboard: (Optional) single thickness 5/8" or 3/4". Reinforce with wood moulding nailed and glued in place or use board with T&G edges.

Stud Wall Finish

Cover all stud walls with 1/2" thick gypsum wallboard and finish with perfatape joint system and 2 coats latex paint. Protect area around bathtub with 1/8" thick prefinished hardboard panels recommended for areas with high moisture content by the manufacturer. Install panels with a good grade of construction type adhesive as recommended by the manufacturer.

Finish Flooring

Wood flooring of 1 x 4 southern pine or fir grade D or better kiln dried from 8 percent to 12 percent moisture content shall be fastened with nails and a bead of construction adhesive directly to the floor joists. Sand and apply 2 coats of floor sealer and a coat of wax to all rooms except the kitchen and bathroom. These rooms shall be covered with a low cost vinyl sheet resilient flooring material installed in accordance with manufacturer's recommendations.

Doors

Entrance doors shall be flush 1-3/4" thick solid core lauan made with exterior glue. Interior doors shall be flush 1-3/8" thick hollow core lauan. Finish exterior doors with primer and 2 coats of paint. Interior doors shall be finished natural with filler and 2 coats of varnish. Provide 2 screen doors.

Windows

All horizontal sliding aluminum windows of the sizes shown on the drawings shall be manufactured to conform to all requirements for aluminum windows in the architectural aluminum manufacturers association master-specification which are USA standard specifications for aluminum windows: HS-B1 windows for residential-type buildings.
Acrylic-plastic dome skylight is optional.

Cabinets and Interior Detail

Kitchen cabinets and bathroom vanity: Job-made fir plywood or low cost prefinished factory or shop made without backs. Vinyl counter tops and backsplash with metal edging.

Cabinets and Interior Detail

Closet shelving: Pine or fir 1 x 12 grade no. 2 or better.
Medicine cabinet: Install recessed cabinet with mirror, light, and electrical outlet.

Decorating

All exterior exposed wood shall be given 2 coats of FPL water repellent preservative mixed as follows:

Pentachlorophenol conc. (10:1)	2 quarts
Boiled linseed oil	1-3/4 quarts
Paraffin wax	1/2 lb.
Thinner (mineral spirits)	4 gals.
Tinting colors--Add enough to give desired semi-transparent	
color. (approximately 1 pint)	

All interior unfinished wood shall be given 1 coat of natural sealer or 1 coat of pigmented stain.
1 x 6 T&G boards or flakeboard non-bearing walls shall be given 1 coat of pigmented stain.

Plumbing

Provide necessary piping and five fixtures with necessary fittings: Steel double basin kitchen sink, steel bathtub, lavatory, water closet, and 42 gal. electric water heater with 10-year warranty.
Water piping: Galv. steel, copper or plastic as approved by local plumbing codes. Provide sill cock in lowest point of water supply piping.
Hose bibb: Provide one exterior hose bibb.
Provide rough-in plumbing for automatic washer.

Heating

Forced-air furnace, 30,000 BTUH minimum capacity; return-air register near ceiling on each floor as shown on plans. Hot air to be supplied by floor registers in the first floor. Supply ducts are concealed in crawl space below the first floor. This heating system is sized for moderate climates. For cold climates, capacity of heating system should be increased according to local requirements.

Electric Wiring and Fixtures

Service shall be overhead with a 150 ampere panel located in the kitchen. Provide at least six branch circuits and three spare circuits.
Wiring shall be in accordance with the National Electric Code. Horizontal wiring shall be in the space below the first floor; run vertical wiring in the raceway formed by the ribs where necessary.
Light fixtures are as noted on the floor plan.
Provide a bathroom exhaust fan with a minimum capacity of 35 cu.ft. per minute.

10

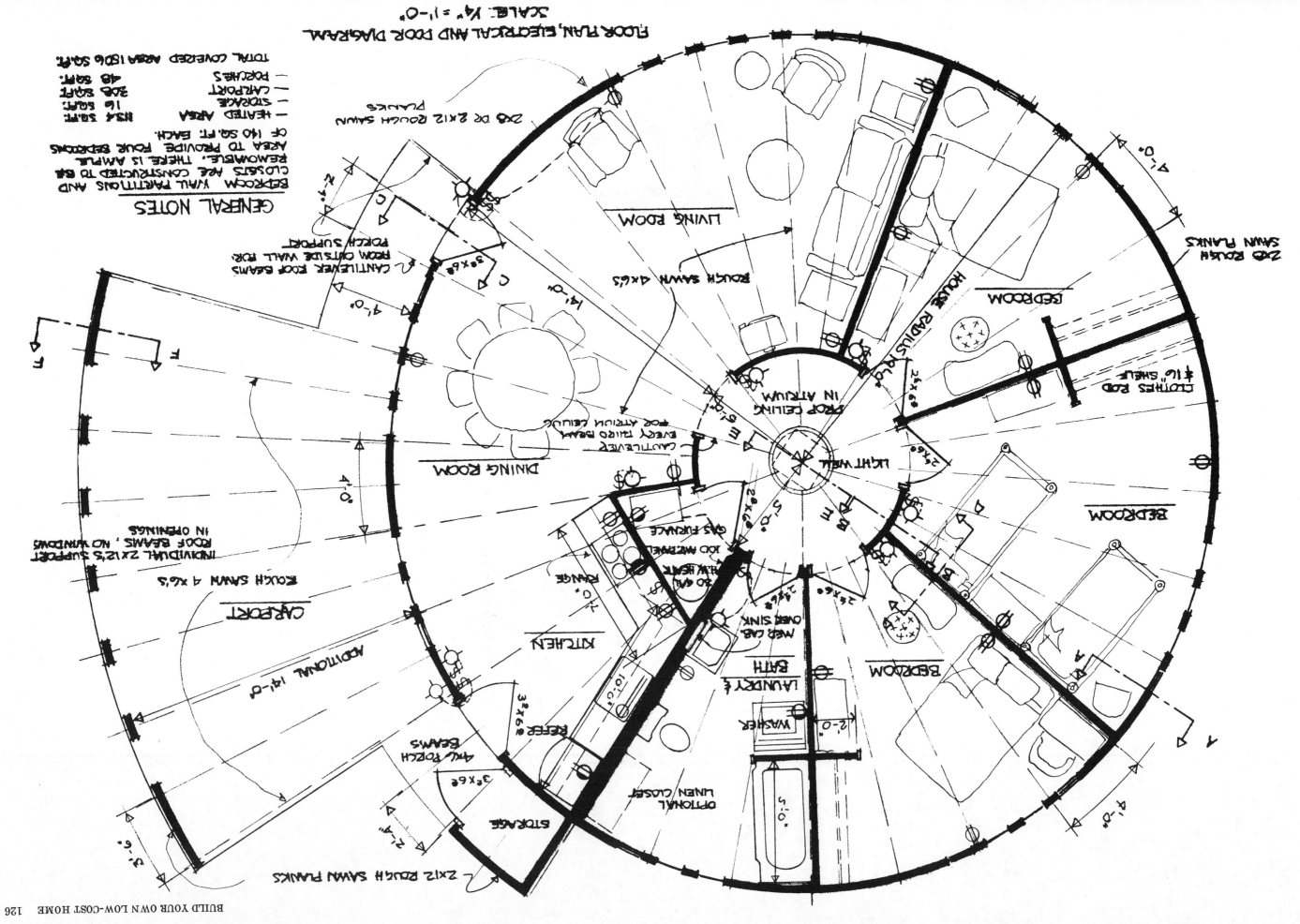

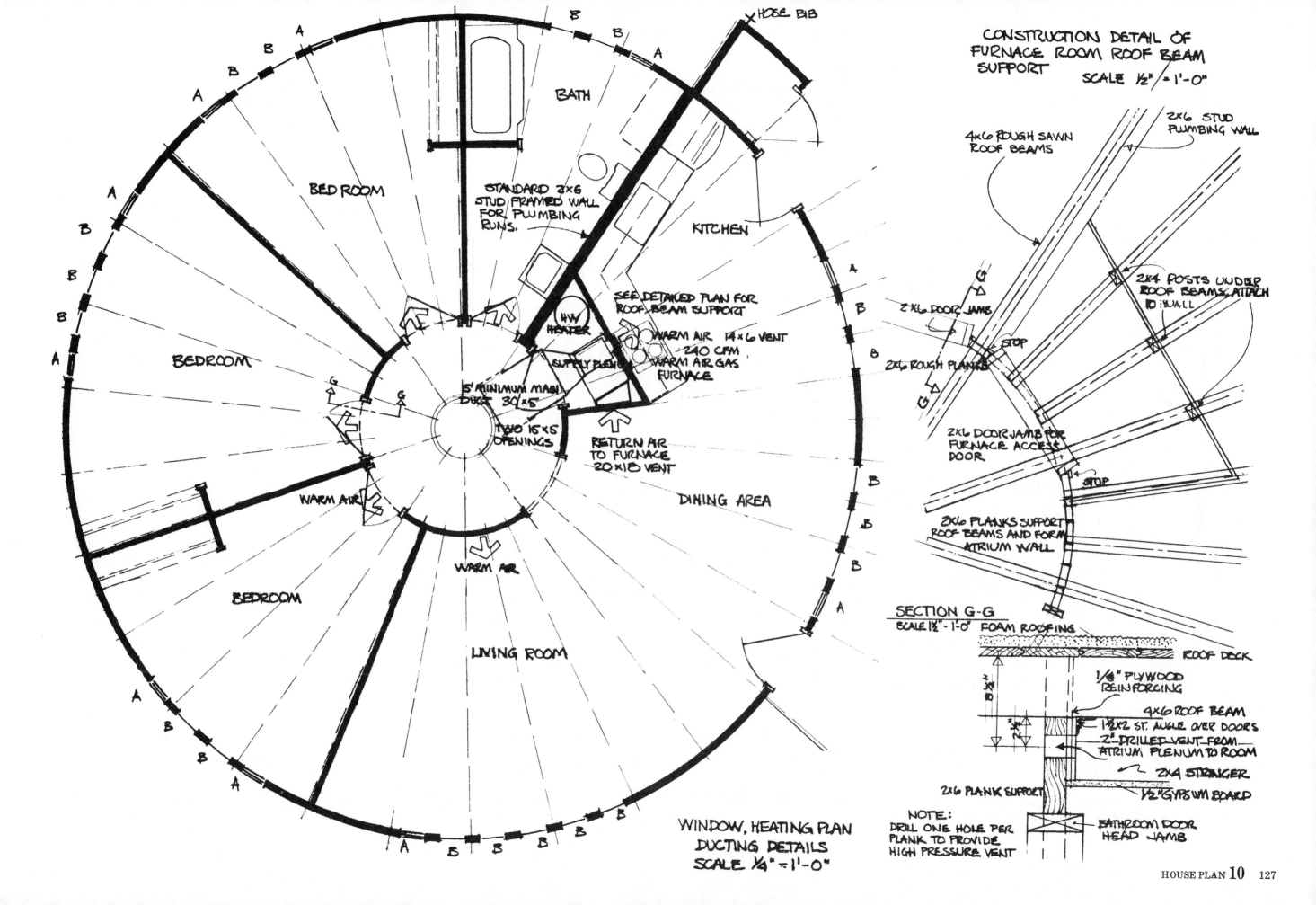

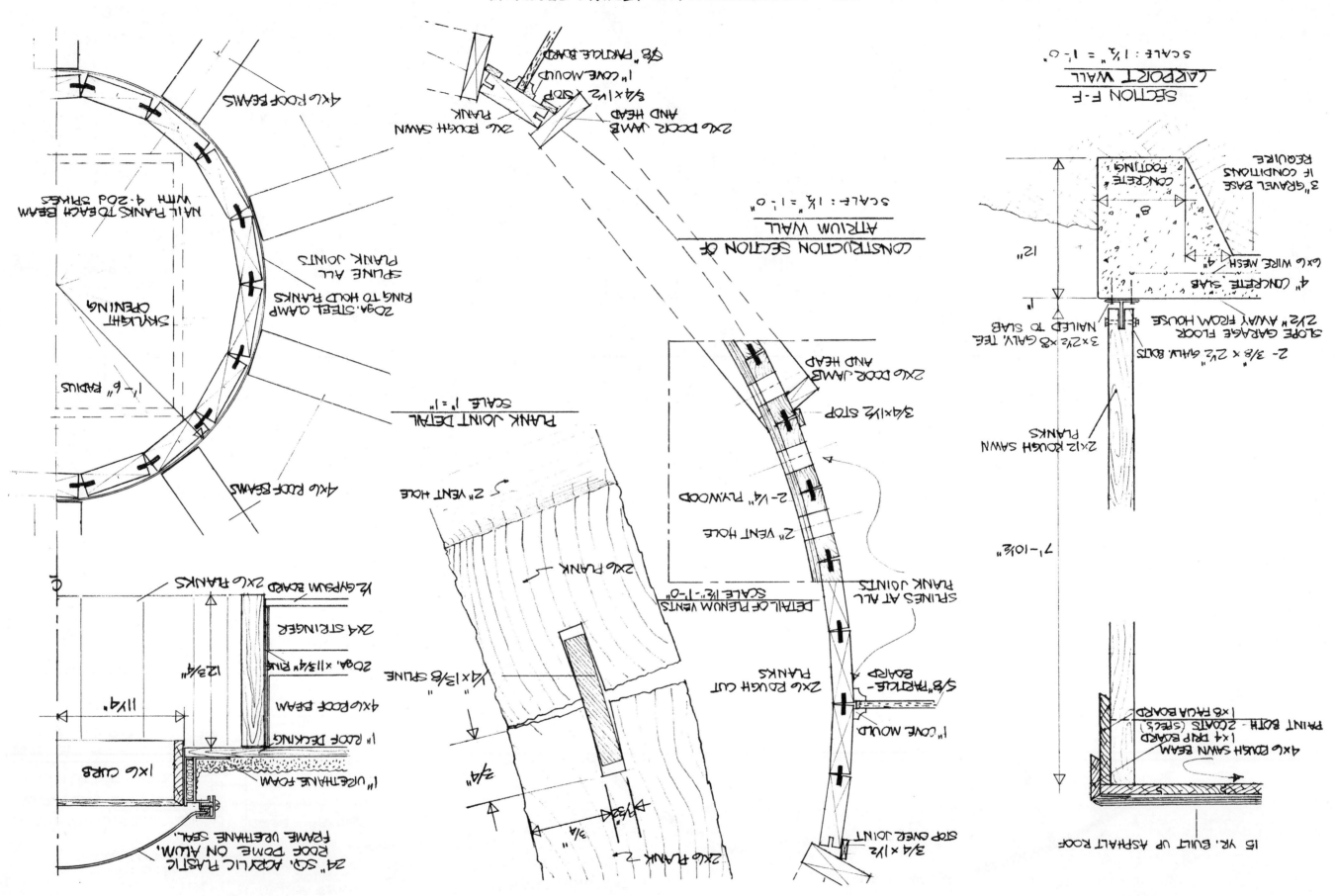

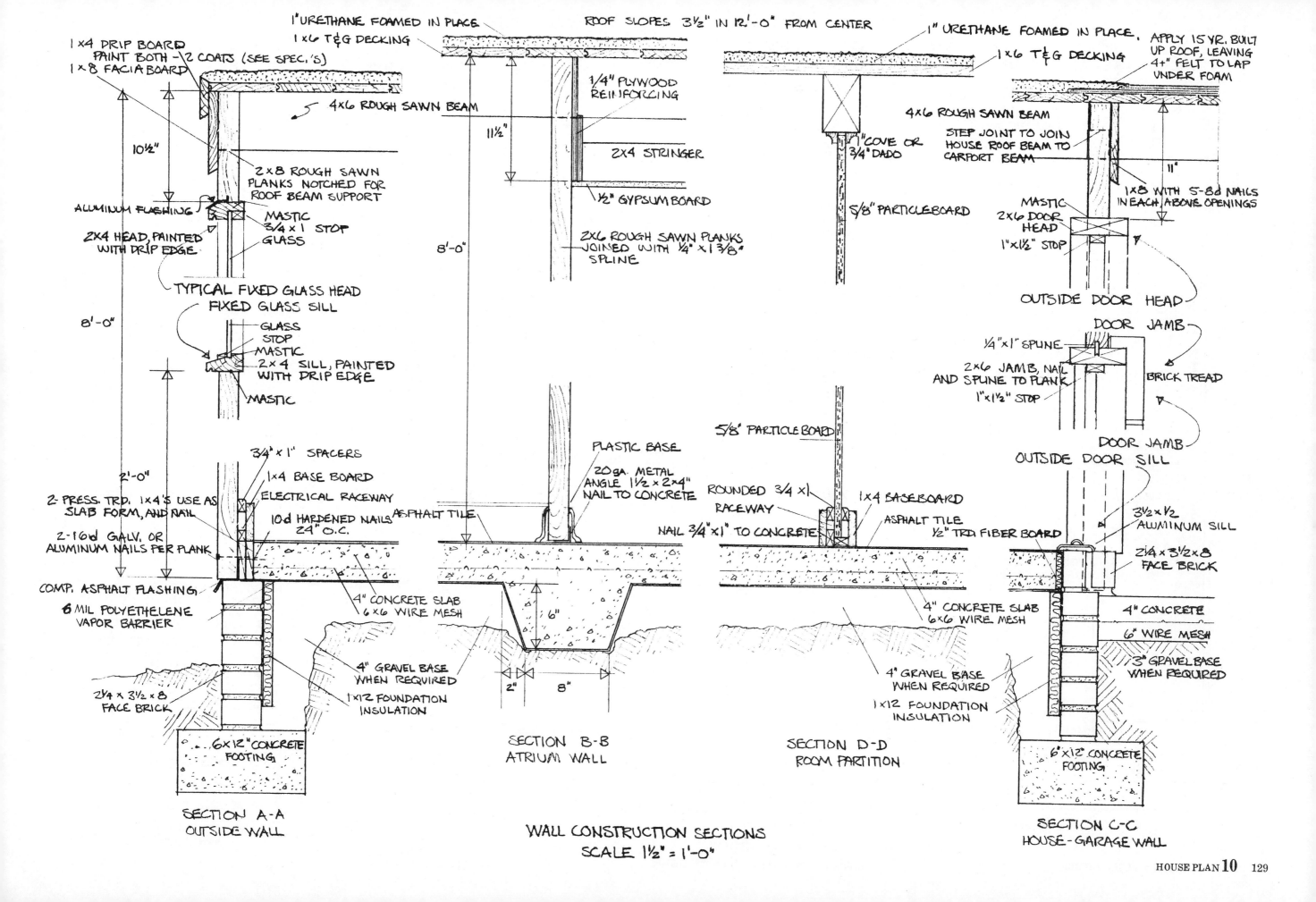

WALL CONSTRUCTION SECTIONS
SCALE 1½" = 1'-0"

SECTION A-A
OUTSIDE WALL

SECTION B-B
ATRIUM WALL

SECTION D-D
ROOM PARTITION

SECTION C-C
HOUSE-GARAGE WALL

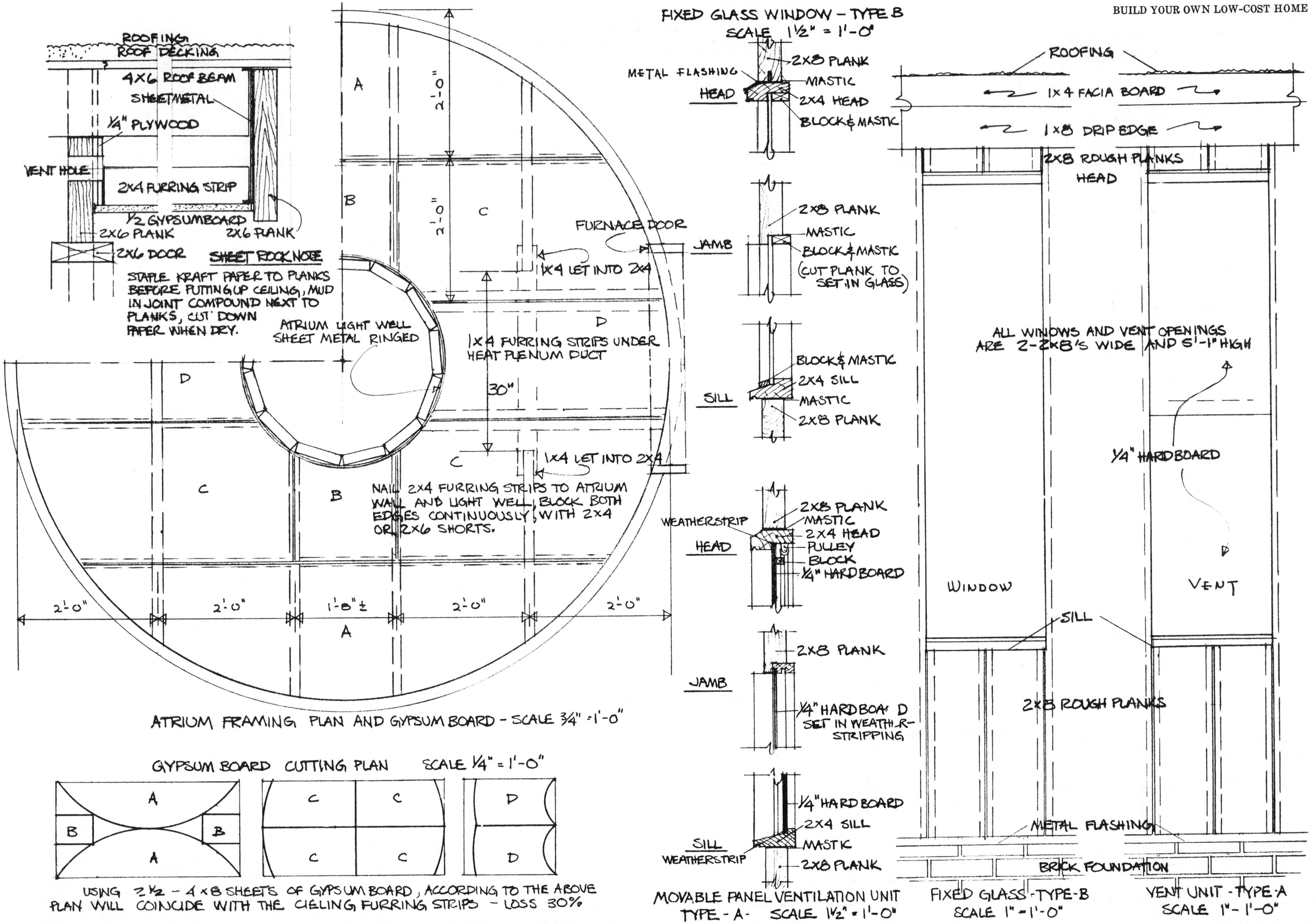

Detail (top left - roof/ceiling section):
- ROOFING
- ROOF DECKING
- 4×6 ROOF BEAM
- SHEET METAL
- ¼" PLYWOOD
- VENT HOLE
- 2×4 FURRING STRIP
- ½ GYPSUM BOARD
- 2×6 PLANK
- 2×6 PLANK
- 2×6 DOOR

SHEET ROCK NOTE
STAPLE KRAFT PAPER TO PLANKS BEFORE PUTTING UP CEILING, MUD IN JOINT COMPOUND NEXT TO PLANKS, CUT DOWN PAPER WHEN DRY.

FIXED GLASS WINDOW - TYPE B
SCALE 1½" = 1'-0"
- METAL FLASHING
- 2×8 PLANK
- MASTIC
- 2×4 HEAD
- BLOCK & MASTIC
- HEAD

- 2×8 PLANK
- MASTIC
- BLOCK & MASTIC (CUT PLANK TO SET IN GLASS)
- JAMB

- BLOCK & MASTIC
- 2×4 SILL
- MASTIC
- 2×8 PLANK
- SILL

Right detail (roof/facia):
- ROOFING
- 1×4 FACIA BOARD
- 1×8 DRIP EDGE
- 2×8 ROUGH PLANKS HEAD
- ALL WINDOWS AND VENT OPENINGS ARE 2-2×8'S WIDE AND 5'-1" HIGH
- ¼" HARDBOARD
- WINDOW
- VENT
- SILL
- 2×8 ROUGH PLANKS
- METAL FLASHING
- BRICK FOUNDATION

Atrium plan labels:
- A B C D
- FURNACE DOOR
- 1×4 LET INTO 2×4
- 1×4 FURRING STRIPS UNDER HEAT PLENUM DUCT
- 30"
- ATRIUM LIGHT WELL SHEET METAL RINGED
- 1×4 LET INTO 2×4
- NAIL 2×4 FURRING STRIPS TO ATRIUM WALL AND LIGHT WELL, BLOCK BOTH EDGES CONTINUOUSLY WITH 2×4 OR 2×6 SHORTS.
- D C B A
- 2'-0" 2'-0" 1'-8"± 2'-0" 2'-0"

ATRIUM FRAMING PLAN AND GYPSUM BOARD - SCALE ¾"=1'-0"

GYPSUM BOARD CUTTING PLAN   SCALE ¼" = 1'-0"
- A A
- B B
- C C C C
- D D

USING 2½ - 4×8 SHEETS OF GYPSUM BOARD, ACCORDING TO THE ABOVE PLAN WILL COINCIDE WITH THE CIELING FURRING STRIPS - LOSS 30%

MOVABLE PANEL VENTILATION UNIT TYPE-A (right middle):
- WEATHERSTRIP
- 2×8 PLANK
- MASTIC
- 2×4 HEAD
- PULLEY
- BLOCK
- ¼" HARDBOARD
- HEAD

- 2×8 PLANK
- ¼" HARDBOARD SET IN WEATHERSTRIPPING
- JAMB

- ¼" HARDBOARD
- 2×4 SILL
- MASTIC
- 2×8 PLANK
- SILL
- WEATHERSTRIP

MOVABLE PANEL VENTILATION UNIT TYPE-A-   SCALE 1½"-1'-0"

FIXED GLASS-TYPE-B SCALE 1"-1'-0"

VENT UNIT-TYPE-A SCALE 1"-1'-0"

ATRIUM FRAMING AND WINDOW SECTIONS

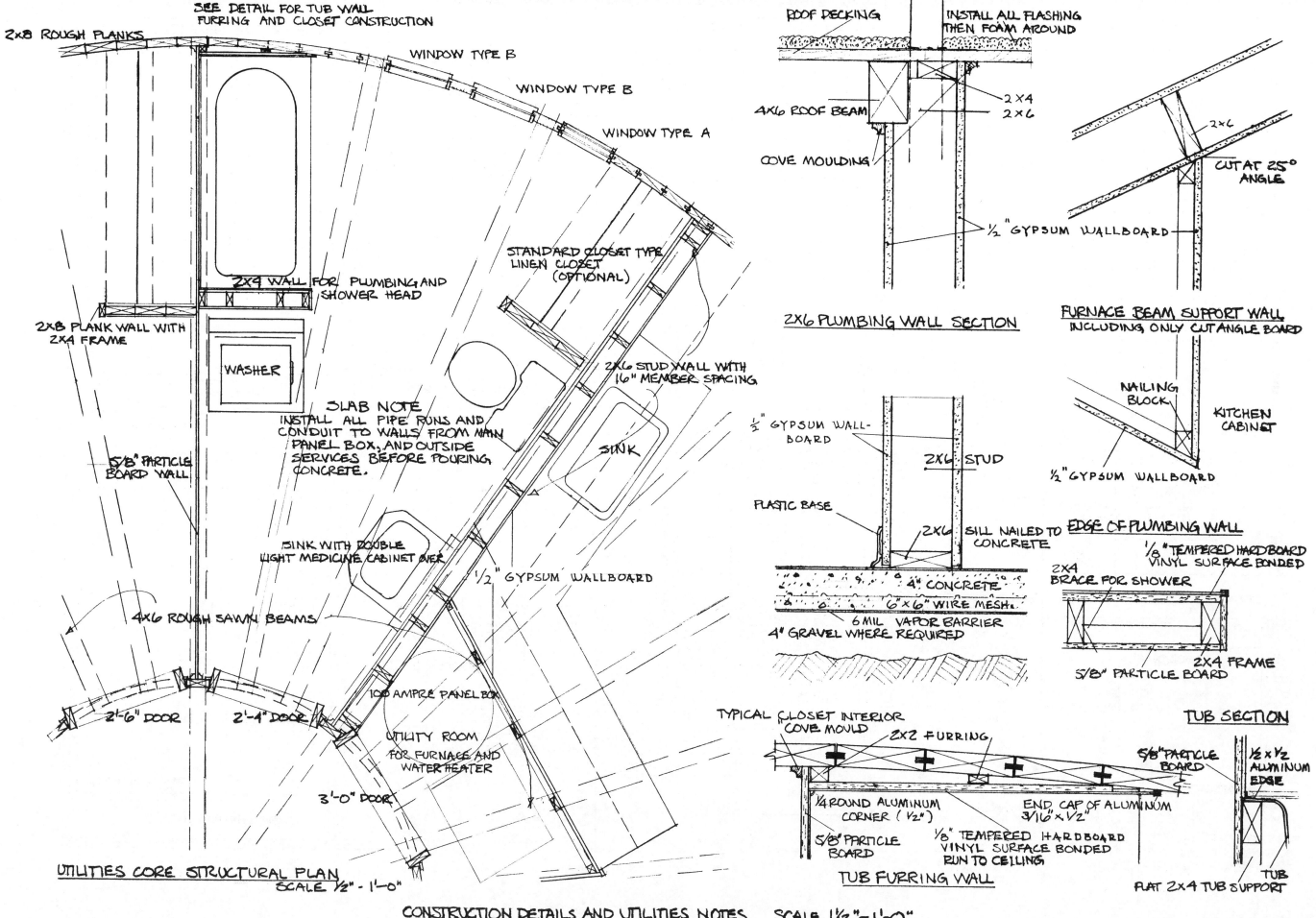

SEE DETAIL FOR TUB WALL FURRING AND CLOSET CONSTRUCTION

2×8 ROUGH PLANKS

WINDOW TYPE B

WINDOW TYPE B

WINDOW TYPE A

STANDARD CLOSET TYPE
LINEN CLOSET
(OPTIONAL)

2×4 WALL FOR PLUMBING AND SHOWER HEAD

2×8 PLANK WALL WITH 2×4 FRAME

WASHER

5/8" PARTICLE BOARD WALL

SLAB NOTE
INSTALL ALL PIPE RUNS AND CONDUIT TO WALLS FROM MAIN PANEL BOX, AND OUTSIDE SERVICES BEFORE POURING CONCRETE.

2×6 STUD WALL WITH 16" MEMBER SPACING

SINK

SINK WITH DOUBLE LIGHT MEDICINE CABINET OVER

1/2" GYPSUM WALLBOARD

4×6 ROUGH SAWN BEAMS

100 AMPRE PANEL BOX

2'-6" DOOR

2'-4" DOOR

UTILITY ROOM
FOR FURNACE AND WATER HEATER

3'-0" DOOR

UTILITIES CORE STRUCTURAL PLAN
SCALE 1/2" - 1'-0"

ROOF DECKING

INSTALL ALL FLASHING THEN FOAM AROUND

4×6 ROOF BEAM

2×4
2×6

COVE MOULDING

1/2" GYPSUM WALLBOARD

2×6 PLUMBING WALL SECTION

2×6
CUT AT 25° ANGLE

1/2" GYPSUM WALLBOARD

FURNACE BEAM SUPPORT WALL
INCLUDING ONLY CUT ANGLE BOARD

NAILING BLOCK

KITCHEN CABINET

1/2" GYPSUM WALLBOARD

1/2" GYPSUM WALLBOARD

2×6 STUD

PLASTIC BASE

2×6 SILL NAILED TO CONCRETE

4" CONCRETE

6×6" WIRE MESH

6 MIL VAPOR BARRIER

4" GRAVEL WHERE REQUIRED

EDGE OF PLUMBING WALL

1/8" TEMPERED HARDBOARD VINYL SURFACE BONDED

2×4 BRACE FOR SHOWER

2×4 FRAME

5/8" PARTICLE BOARD

TUB SECTION

TYPICAL CLOSET INTERIOR
COVE MOULD

2×2 FURRING

5/8" PARTICLE BOARD

1/2 × 1/2 ALUMINUM EDGE

1/4 ROUND ALUMINUM CORNER (1/2")

END CAP OF ALUMINUM 3/16" × 1/2"

5/8" PARTICLE BOARD

1/8" TEMPERED HARDBOARD VINYL SURFACE BONDED RUN TO CEILING

TUB FURRING WALL

FLAT 2×4 TUB SUPPORT

TUB

CONSTRUCTION DETAILS AND UTILITIES NOTES   SCALE 1 1/2"=1'-0"

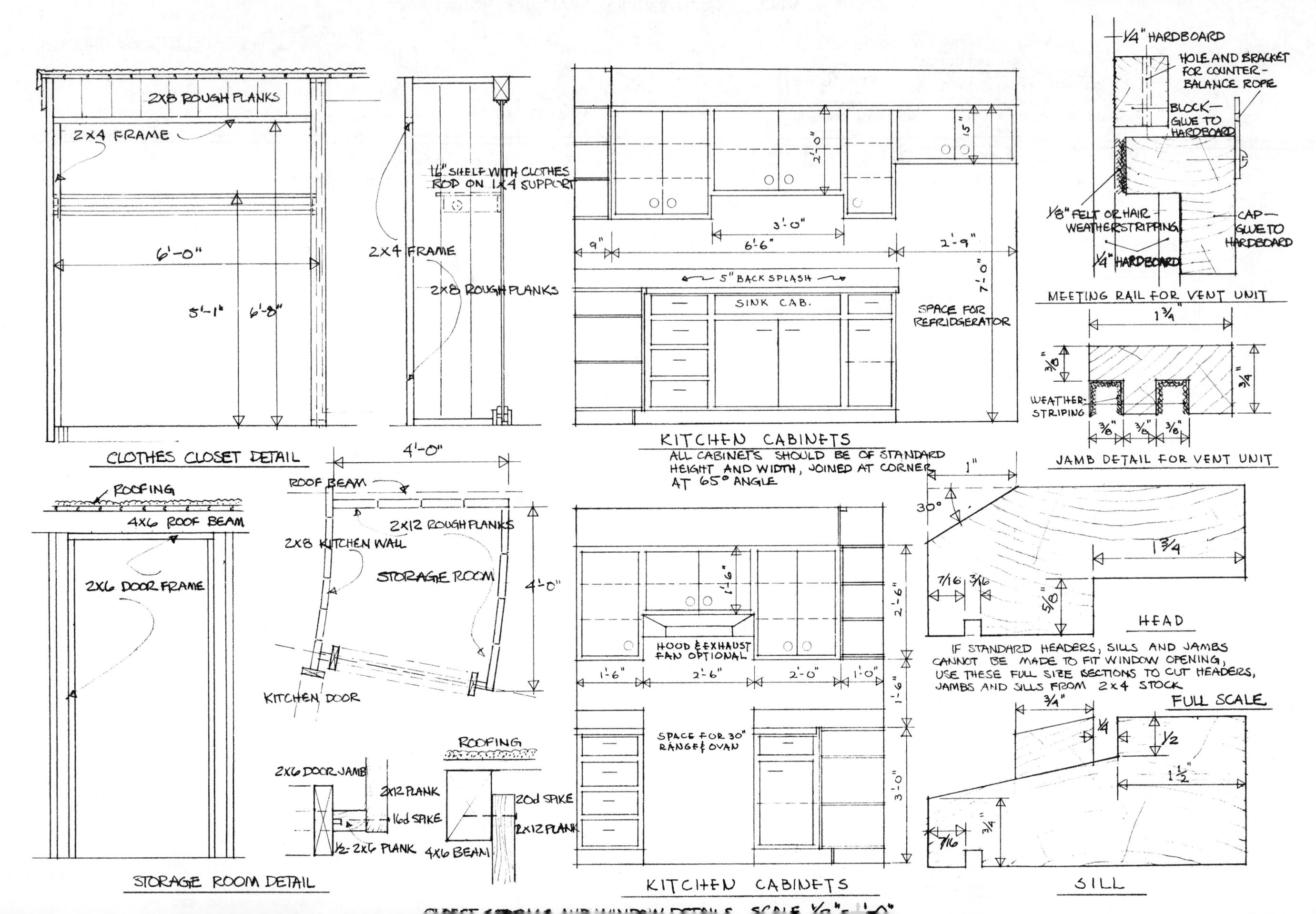

2X8 ROUGH PLANKS

2X4 FRAME

6'-0"

5'-1"   6'-8"

CLOTHES CLOSET DETAIL

16" SHELF WITH CLOTHES ROD ON 1X4 SUPPORT

2X4 FRAME

2X8 ROUGH PLANKS

ROOFING

4X6 ROOF BEAM

2X6 DOOR FRAME

STORAGE ROOM DETAIL

ROOF BEAM

2X12 ROUGH PLANKS

2X8 KITCHEN WALL

STORAGE ROOM

4'-0"

4'-0"

KITCHEN DOOR

2X6 DOOR JAMB

2X12 PLANK

16d SPIKE

½-2X6 PLANK   4X6 BEAM

ROOFING

20d SPIKE

2X12 PLANK

KITCHEN CABINETS

2'-0"

.5"

9"   6'-6"   2'-9"   7'-0"

5" BACK SPLASH

SINK CAB.

SPACE FOR REFRIDGERATOR

ALL CABINETS SHOULD BE OF STANDARD HEIGHT AND WIDTH, JOINED AT CORNER AT 65° ANGLE

KITCHEN CABINETS

1'-6"   2'-6"

HOOD & EXHAUST FAN OPTIONAL

1'-6"   2'-6"   2'-0"   1'-0"

SPACE FOR 30" RANGE & OVAN

3'-0"   1'-6"   2'-6"

¼" HARDBOARD

HOLE AND BRACKET FOR COUNTER-BALANCE ROPE

BLOCK—GLUE TO HARDBOARD

⅛" FELT OR HAIR WEATHERSTRIPPING

CAP—GLUE TO HARDBOARD

¼" HARDBOARD

MEETING RAIL FOR VENT UNIT

1¾"

⅜"   ¾"

WEATHER-STRIPING

⅜"   ⅜"   ⅜"

JAMB DETAIL FOR VENT UNIT

30°   1"

7/16   3/16

5/8

1¾

HEAD

IF STANDARD HEADERS, SILLS AND JAMBS CANNOT BE MADE TO FIT WINDOW OPENING, USE THESE FULL SIZE SECTIONS TO CUT HEADERS, JAMBS AND SILLS FROM 2X4 STOCK

FULL SCALE

¾"   ¼

½   1½"

7/16   ¾

SILL

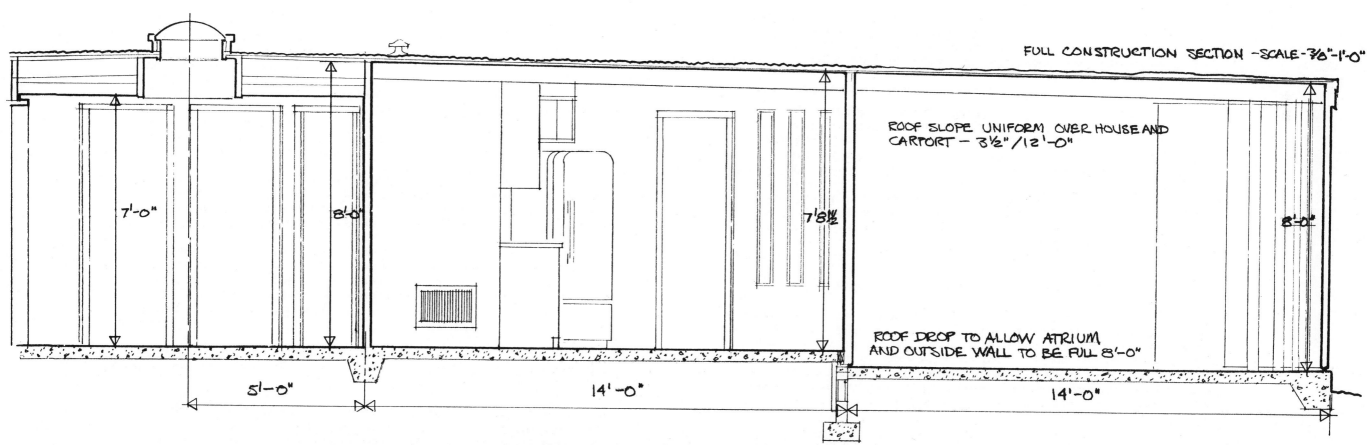

FULL CONSTRUCTION SECTION - SCALE - 3/8"=1'-0"

ROOF SLOPE UNIFORM OVER HOUSE AND CARPORT - 3½"/12'-0"

ROOF DROP TO ALLOW ATRIUM AND OUTSIDE WALL TO BE FULL 8'-0"

7'-0" 8'-0" 7'8½" 8'-0"

5'-0" 14'-0" 14'-0"

PERSPECTIVE AND FULL STRUCTURAL SECTION
SCALE 3/8" = 1'-0"

General: Each item of material and equipment shall equal or exceed that described or indicated. All work shall be performed in a workmanlike manner and in accordance with the best practice. Mention of commercial products and sources does not constitute an endorsement of such products by the Forest Service or the Department of Agriculture to the exclusion of other equally acceptable products.

Excavation: Scrape soil clean of all vegetation and remove roots larger than 2" diameter. Compact all backfill to density of undisturbed soil.

Foundations:
Footings: 1:3:5 (2000 psi) concrete.
Walls: Facing brick (ASTM C 216-64), grade SW, type FBS. Mortar shall be as described in ASTM C 476-63. Brick cores shall be filled with grout.
Insulation: Perimeter insulation shall be one-inch thick polystyrene or asphalt impregnated fiberboard manufactured for this type of application.

Floors: 1:2:3 (3,000 psi) concrete with 6x6 wire mesh reinforcing placed over a 6 mil polyethylene vapor barrier. When required by local codes, place 4" of compacted gravel or crushed stone under the slab. A smooth steel trowel finish is required as a base for asphalt or vinyl asbestos tile in the house. Steel trowel finish the porch and carport slabs.

Exterior Walls: 2" thick rough sawn wood planks.
Thickness: 1-7/8" to 2-1/8", width: 7-3/4" to 8-1/4".
Texture : Both faces sawn with a band saw.
Grade : No. 1 boards except that holes and wane are not permitted. Pitch pockets or streaks shall be small. Warp, crook and twist shall be limited to 1/4". Bow shall be limited to 1/2".
Moisture Content: 12 to 17 percent.
Treatment: Dip treat with FPL Water Repellent Preservative mixed as follows:

Pentachlorophenol conc. (10:1)	2 quarts
Boiled linseed oil	1-3/4 quarts
Paraffin wax	1/2 lb.
Thinner	4 gals.

Finish: Coat exterior with one coat of FPL pigmented Water-Repellent Preservative. Same formula as given above with one quart of tinting colors added. Coat interior face with one coat of pigmented stain similar to "Rez" stain by the Rez Company, Springdale, Pennsylvania.

Splines: 1/4" x 1-3/8" tempered hardboard for exterior use.
Fascia and trim: Two coats of paint over oil base primer or stain same as planks. Dip treat, as for the planks, before painting.
Nails: Use aluminum or galvanized steel nails.

If cedar, cypress, or redwood rough planks are used the dip treatment is not necessary.

Interior Non-Bearing Walls: 5/8" T&G particleboard prefinished or painted with primer and 1 coat of paint or heavy body stain.

Interior Stud Walls: Finish both sides with 1/2" gypsum wallboard, Perfatape joint system, and paint with 2 coats enamel.

Interior Plank Walls: 2" thick rough sawn planks. Same specifications as for exterior planks but planks are 6" wide. No treatment required. Finish with stain.

Beams: 4x6 - S4S or rough
Grade: No. 1 dimension
Moisture Content: 12 to 17 percent
Finish: One coat pigmented stain similar to "Rez"

Decking: 1x6 standard flooring, S4S, T&G
Actual dimension 25/32" x 5-3/16"

Grade: No. 2
Moisture Content: 8 to 12 percent
Finish: One coat of stain similar to "Rez"

Roofing: 1" Thick foamed-in-place polyurethane of at least 2 lbs. per cu. ft. density. Should only be applied when air temperature is 40°F or warmer. Wood surface shall be dry or it should be primed before placing the polyurethane. Foam thickness shall be uniform and no less than 1". The foam shall be topcoated with a suitable, exterior, weather-resistant material recommended by the foam applicator which, in combination with the foam, will provide a minimum flammability performance of Class C rating in accordance with ASTM E-108 test procedure for built-up roof covering materials.

Carport roofing shall be equivalent to bonded 15-year built-up asphalt.

Cabinets and Interior Detail:
Kitchen cabinets and bathroom vanity: Job-made fir plywood or low cost prefinished factory or shop-made without backs. Vinyl counter tops and backsplash with metal edging.
Closet Shelving: Pine or fir 1x12 grade No. 2 or better.
Medicine Cabinet: Install recessed cabinet with mirror, light and electrical outlet.

Plumbing: Provide necessary piping for four fixtures with necessary fittings: Steel double basin kitchen sink, steel bathtub, lavatory, and water closet.
Water Heater: 30 gal. min. capacity; 10 year warranty.
Water Piping: Galv. steel, copper, or plastic as approved by local plumbing codes. Provide sill cock in lowest point of water supply piping.

Provide rough-in plumbing for automatic washer.

Heating: Gas-fired forced-air furnace, 60,000 BTUH min. capacity; return air register near the floor and discharge through 2" round outlets near the ceiling. Provide drop ceiling space over central hall which will function as an air plenum. 2" round outlets shall be cut in the atrium walls between the radial beams.

This heating system is designed for moderate climates. For cold climates, capacity of heating system should be increased according to local heating requirements.

Electric Wiring and Fixtures:
Service: Overhead, 100 ampere panel in the furnace room with at least six branch circuits and three spare circuits.
Wiring: In accordance with the national electric code. Horizontal wiring shall be in the space provided by the wood baseboard; run a conduit under the aluminum threshold for wiring to bridge the exterior door openings. Vertical wiring can be installed in the plank edge groove next to door jambs by eliminating the spline, as necessary, or in the surface mold finished conduit. Switches should be a surface mount type.
Fixtures: Provide fixtures of the wall-mount type.

Miscellaneous: Outside utilities, such as, water, sewer, gas and electricity shall be provided by owner or utility company. Utilities in the house shall be stubbed out of house for convenient hookup.

Termite Protection: One percent chlordane in water emulsion or equivalent shall be applied to soil around footings and under the concrete slab. Apply 4 gallons of chlordane solution per 10 linear feet along each side of the perimeter footing. Apply one gallon of chlordane solution per 10 square feet as an overall treatment under all the concrete slab floors.
Windows: Single strength fixed glass.
Ventilating Units: 1/4-inch, medium density, exterior hardboard, primed and painted with 2 coats exterior paint. Cover with insect screen.
Doors: Exterior: Solid core lauan, complete with hardware and wood or aluminum screen door.
Interior: Hollow core lauan.
Finish exterior doors with primer and 2 coats of paint. Interior doors, finished natural with filler and 2 coats varnish.

11

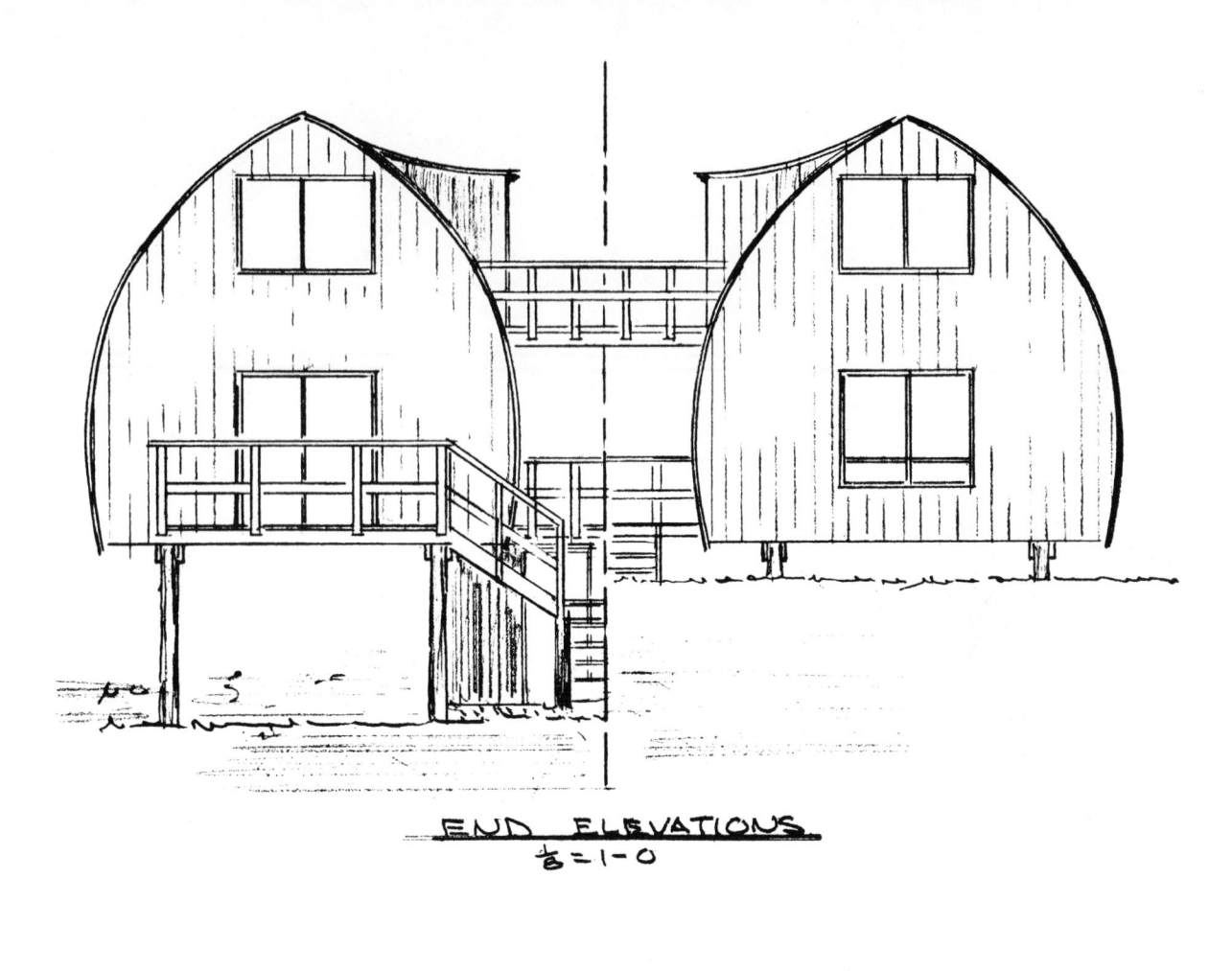

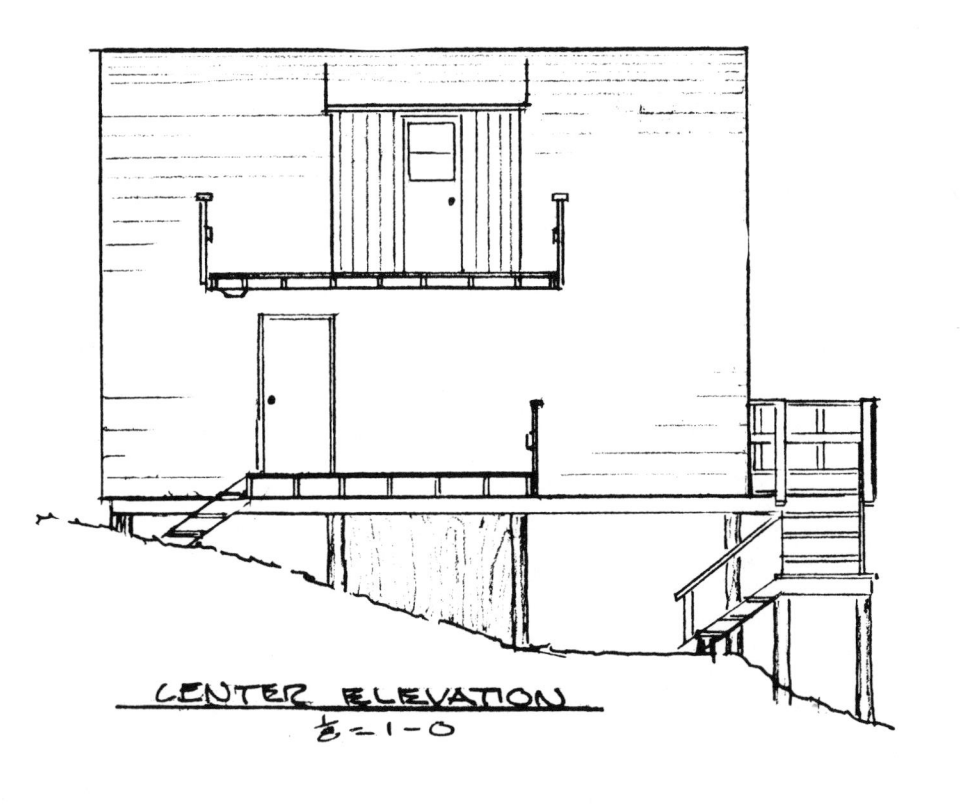

END ELEVATIONS
⅛=1-0

CENTER ELEVATION
⅛=1-0

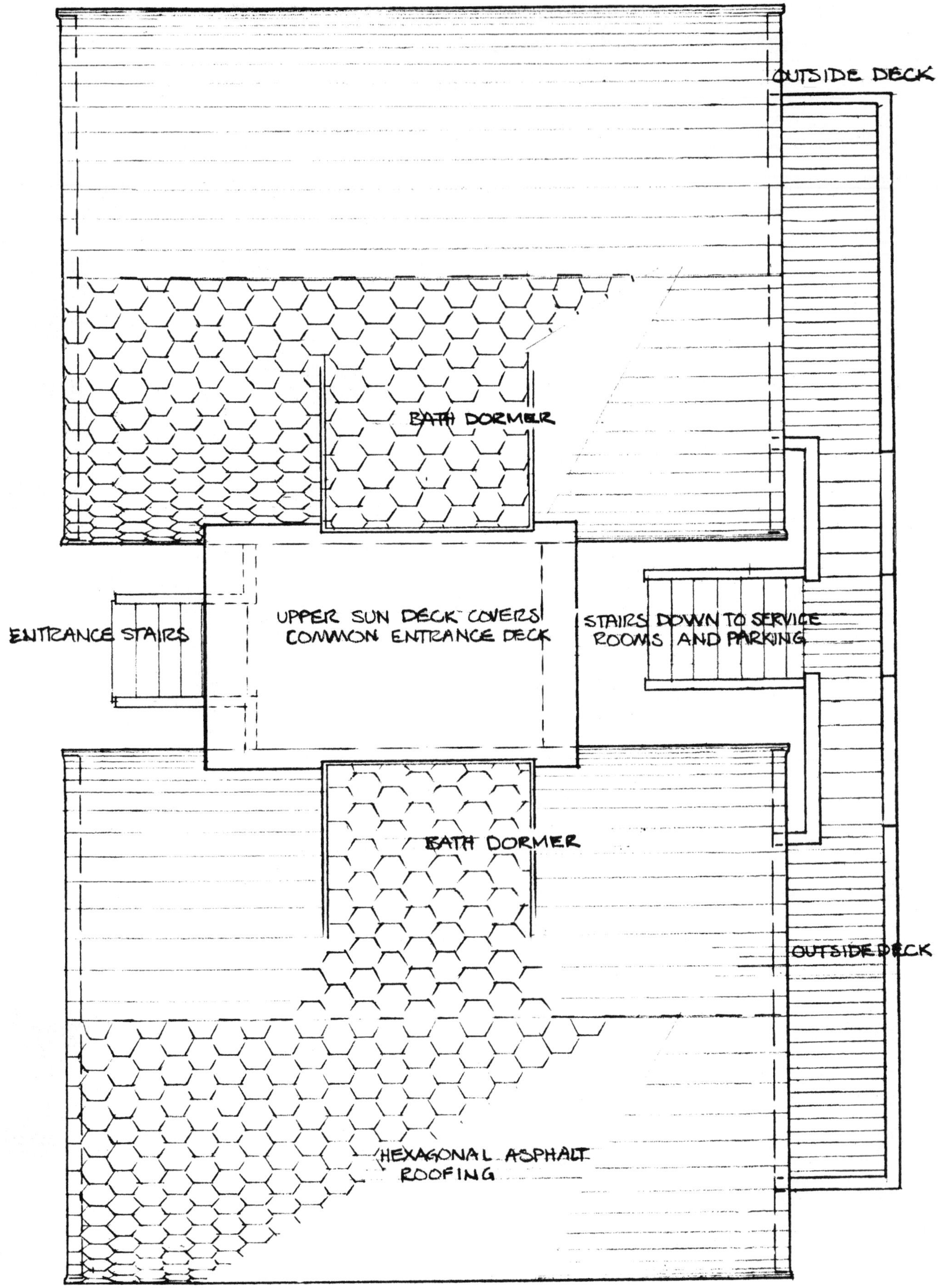

OUTSIDE DECK

BATH DORMER

ENTRANCE STAIRS

UPPER SUN DECK COVERS
COMMON ENTRANCE DECK

STAIRS DOWN TO SERVICE
ROOMS AND PARKING

BATH DORMER

OUTSIDE DECK

HEXAGONAL ASPHALT
ROOFING

ELEVATIONS & ROOF PLAN.   SCALE 3/16"=1'-0"

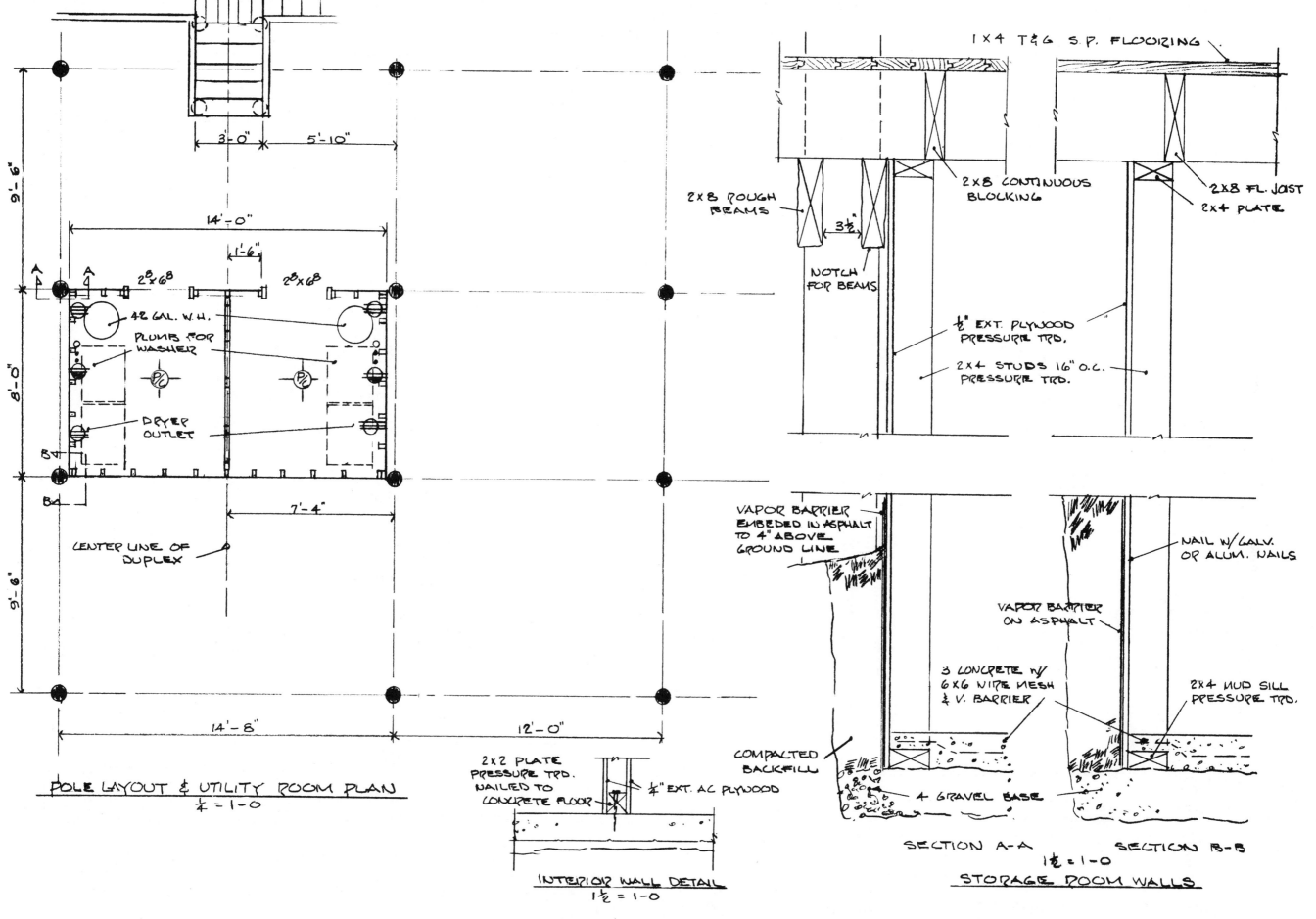

POLE LAYOUT & UTILITY ROOM PLAN
$\frac{1}{4} = 1-0$

INTERIOR WALL DETAIL
$1\frac{1}{2} = 1-0$

SECTION A-A   SECTION B-B
$1\frac{1}{2} = 1-0$
STORAGE ROOM WALLS

POLE LAYOUT & UTILITY ROOM PLAN

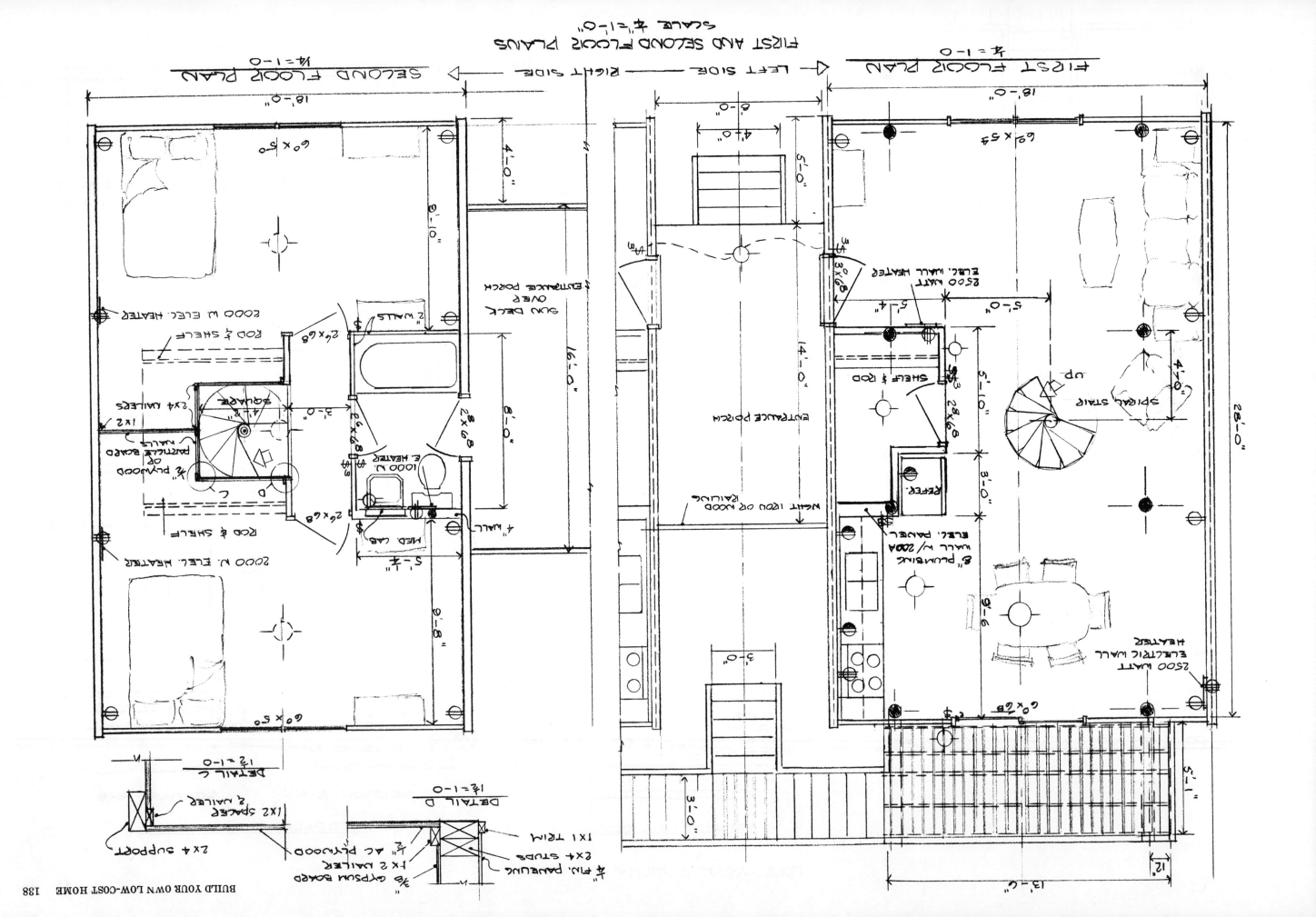

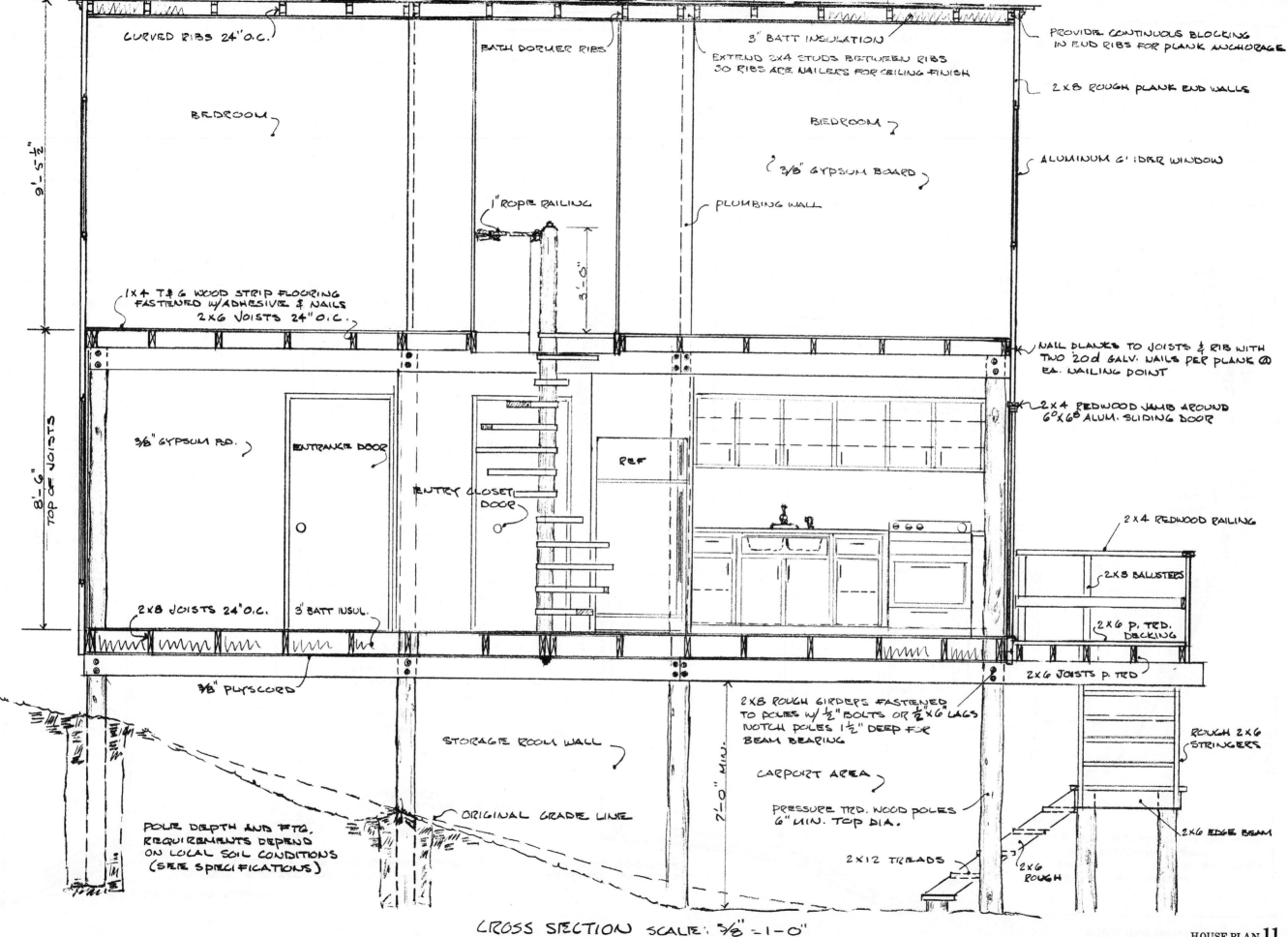

CURVED RIBS 24" O.C.

BATH DORMER RIBS

3" BATT INSULATION

EXTEND 2x4 STUDS BETWEEN RIBS
SO RIBS ARE NAILERS FOR CEILING FINISH

PROVIDE CONTINUOUS BLOCKING
IN END RIBS FOR PLANK ANCHORAGE

2x8 ROUGH PLANK END WALLS

BEDROOM

BEDROOM

3/8" GYPSUM BOARD

ALUMINUM GLIDER WINDOW

1" ROPE RAILING

PLUMBING WALL

3'-0"

9'-5½"

1x4 T&G WOOD STRIP FLOORING
FASTENED w/ADHESIVE & NAILS
2x6 JOISTS 24" O.C.

NAIL PLANKS TO JOISTS & RIB WITH
TWO 20d GALV. NAILS PER PLANK @
EA. NAILING POINT

2x4 REDWOOD JAMB AROUND
6'x6' ALUM. SLIDING DOOR

8'-6"
TOP OF JOISTS

3/8" GYPSUM BD.

ENTRANCE DOOR

REF

ENTRY CLOSET
DOOR

2x4 REDWOOD RAILING

2x3 BALLUSTERS

2x8 JOISTS 24" O.C.

3" BATT INSUL.

2x6 p. TRD.
DECKING

3/8" PLYSCORD

2x6 JOISTS p. TRD

2x8 ROUGH GIRDERS FASTENED
TO POLES w/ ½" BOLTS OR ½"x6" LAGS
NOTCH POLES 1½" DEEP FOR
BEAM BEARING

ROUGH 2x6
STRINGERS

STORAGE ROOM WALL

CARPORT AREA

7'-0" MIN.

POLE DEPTH AND FTG.
REQUIREMENTS DEPEND
ON LOCAL SOIL CONDITIONS
(SEE SPECIFICATIONS)

ORIGINAL GRADE LINE

PRESSURE TRD. WOOD POLES
6" MIN. TOP DIA.

2x6 EDGE BEAM

2x12 TREADS

2x6
ROUGH

CROSS SECTION SCALE: 3/8" = 1'-0"

2X6 CONT. RIDGE BOARD

CUTOUT FOR BATH DORMER & USE PIECES OF RIB FOR DORMER ROOF

2X6 HEADER

4' OF 5" GUTTER OVER DOORWAYS

ASPHALT SHINGLES OVER BUILTUP ROOFING

HEXAGONAL ASPHALT SHINGLES W/STAPLED TABS OVER BUILDING PAPER & 3/8" PLYSCORD W/ EXT. GLUE

2" BATHROOM WALL

1X8 CEDAR SIDING W/VERT. GROOVES
2X6 DOOR JAMB

PROVIDE 2X4 CURB UNDER DOOR THRESHOLD - EXTEND DECK FLASHING OVER CURB

1X3 PRESSURE TRD. GUTTER CURB OVER GUTTER FLASHING - EMBED IN ASPHALT MASTIC.
3/4 EXT. PLYWOOD - BUILTUP ROOFING & OUTDOOR CARPET

BATHROOM

1" ROPE RAILING

3/8" GYP. BD.

1" PINE FLOORING

NAIL JOISTS TO RIBS W/4-16d NAILS

2X6 JOISTS 24"O.C.   2X6 CONT. BLOCKING

2X6 FLOOR JOISTS 24" O.C.

2X8 AROUND STAIR WELL

2X4 STUDS 24" O.C. FASTENED TO RIBS IN KITCHEN AREA

SPACE 2X4 BLOCKS IN RIBS APPROX 16" O.C. AND WITH A BLOCK AT EACH HORIZONTAL PLYWOOD JOINT

NAIL JOISTS TO RIB BLOCK W/4-16d NAILS & PROVIDE 2" SLOPE FROM CENTER TO OUTSIDE EDGES.

3" THICK BATT INSULATION BETWEEN RIBS & 2X8 FLOOR JOISTS

14'-10" RADIUS TO OUTSIDE OF RIB

1/4" FINISHED PANELING

RADIUS POINT

SEE SHEET 141 FOR STAIRWAY DETAILS

1" PINE FLOORING

3/4" EXT. PLYWOOD FLOOR W/ DECK ENAMEL
2X6 CONT. BLOCKING

NAIL JOISTS TO RIBS W/4-16d NAILS

2X6 FLOOR JOISTS 24" O.C.

2X8 FLOOR JOISTS 24" O.C.

2X8 BLOCKING

3/8" PLYSCORD W/EXT. GLUE

3/8" PLYSCORD W/EXT. GLUE
2X8 BEAMS - ROUGH FASTENED TO EA. POLE W/ 2 - 1/2" X 5" LAG BOLTS

5'-1"

6'-0"

3'-0"

5 1/4"

2X4 BLOCK
1X2 EDGE STRIPS
7d GROOVED NAILS
3 NAILS EA. SIDE

DETAIL B-B
3=1-0

4 - 16d NAILS

1X4 SPACER
INSECT SCREEN
CONTINUOUS STRIP

DETAIL A
1 1/2=1-0

9'-5 1/2"

4'-6 3/4"

4'-6 3/4"

6'-1 1/2"

1'-6 MIN. TO 8'-0 MAX.

CROSS SECTIONAL & CONSTRUCTION DETAILS   SCALE 3/8"=1'-0"

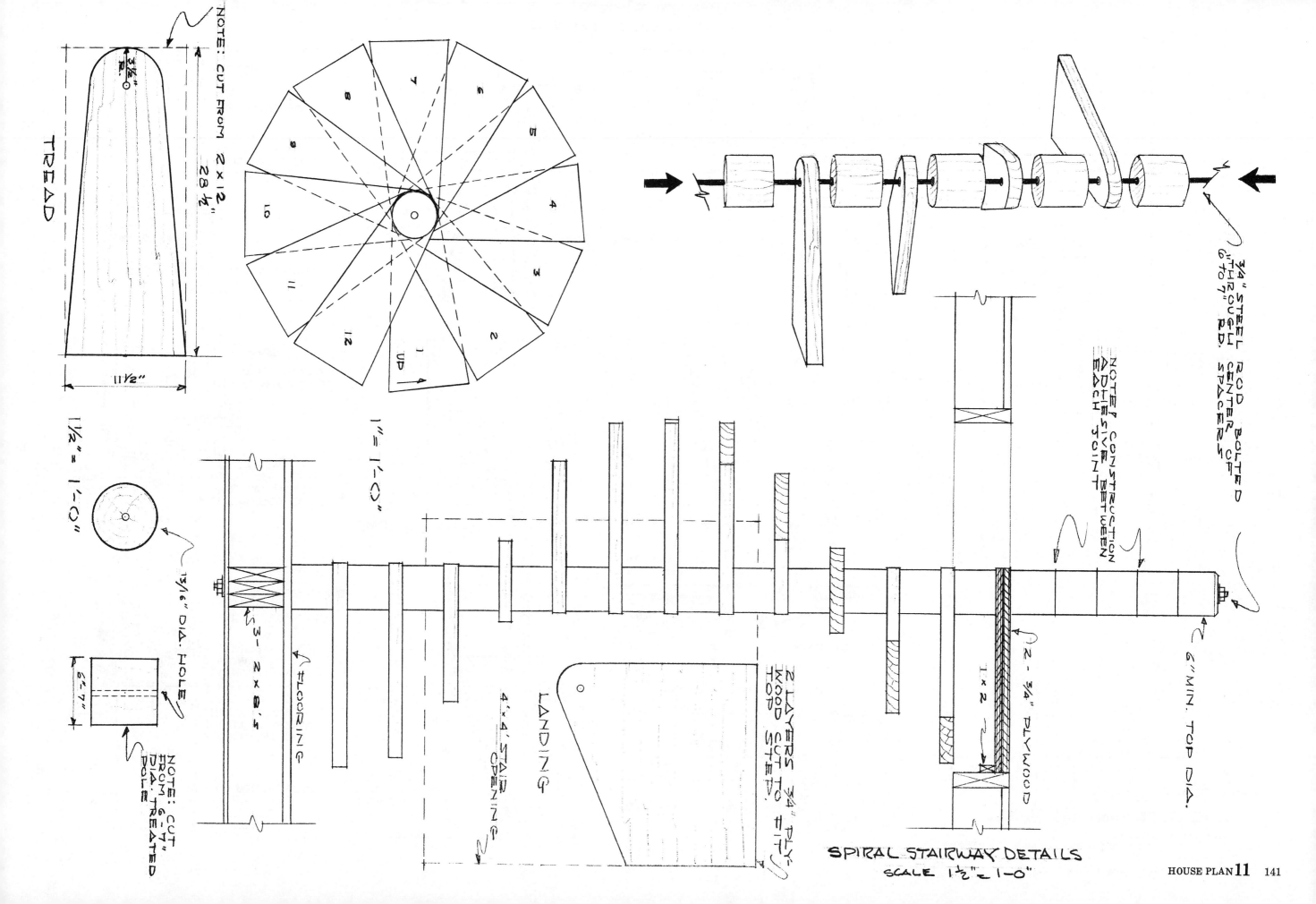

NOTE: CUT FROM 2×12

TREAD

3½" R.

28½"

11½"

1½" = 1'-0"

13/16" DIA. HOLE

NOTE: CUT FROM 6"-7" DIA. TREATED POLE.

6"-7"

1" = 1'-0"

7
8
6
9
5
10
4
11
3
12
2
UP 1

¾" STEEL ROD BOLTED 6" THROUGH CENTER OF 6" TO 7" R.D. SPACERS

NOTE: CONSTRUCTION ADHESIVE BETWEEN EACH JOINT

6" MIN. TOP DIA.

2 - ¾" PLYWOOD

1 × 2

3 - 2×8'S

FLOORING

4'×4' STAIR OPENING

LANDING

2 LAYERS ¾" PLY'S WOOD CUT TO FIT TOP STEP.

SPIRAL STAIRWAY DETAILS
SCALE 1½" = 1'-0"

HOUSE PLAN 11   141

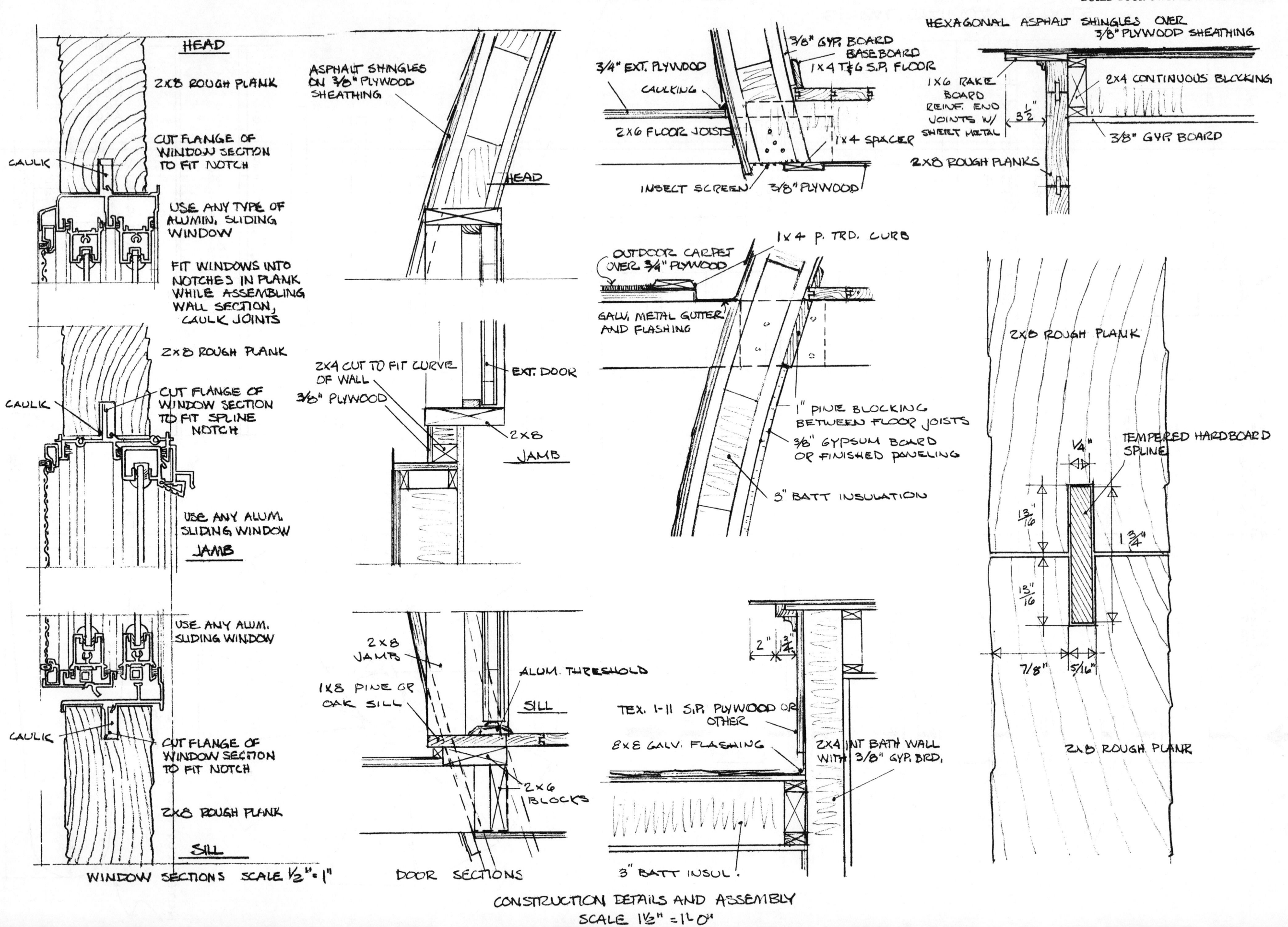

HEAD

2×8 ROUGH PLANK

CUT FLANGE OF WINDOW SECTION TO FIT NOTCH

CAULK

USE ANY TYPE OF ALUMIN. SLIDING WINDOW

FIT WINDOWS INTO NOTCHES IN PLANK WHILE ASSEMBLING WALL SECTION, CAULK JOINTS

2×8 ROUGH PLANK

CAULK

CUT FLANGE OF WINDOW SECTION TO FIT SPLINE NOTCH

USE ANY ALUM. SLIDING WINDOW

JAMB

USE ANY ALUM. SLIDING WINDOW

CAULK

CUT FLANGE OF WINDOW SECTION TO FIT NOTCH

2×8 ROUGH PLANK

SILL

WINDOW SECTIONS SCALE 1/2"=1"

ASPHALT SHINGLES ON 3/8" PLYWOOD SHEATHING

HEAD

2×4 CUT TO FIT CURVE OF WALL

3/8" PLYWOOD

EXT. DOOR

2×8

JAMB

2×8 JAMB

1×8 PINE OR OAK SILL

ALUM. THRESHOLD

SILL

2×6 BLOCKS

DOOR SECTIONS

3/4" EXT. PLYWOOD

CAULKING

2×6 FLOOR JOISTS

3/8" GYP. BOARD BASE BOARD

1×4 T&G S.P. FLOOR

1×4 SPACER

INSECT SCREEN   3/8" PLYWOOD

OUTDOOR CARPET OVER 3/4" PLYWOOD

1×4 P. TRD. CURB

GALV. METAL GUTTER AND FLASHING

1" PINE BLOCKING BETWEEN FLOOR JOISTS

3/8" GYPSUM BOARD OR FINISHED PANELING

3" BATT INSULATION

TEX. 1-11 S.P. PLYWOOD OR OTHER

8×8 GALV. FLASHING

2×4 INT. BATH WALL WITH 3/8" GYP. BRD.

2" 1/4"

3" BATT INSUL.

HEXAGONAL ASPHALT SHINGLES OVER 3/8" PLYWOOD SHEATHING

1×6 RAKE BOARD REINF. END JOINTS W/ SHEET METAL

3 1/2"

2×4 CONTINUOUS BLOCKING

3/8" GYP. BOARD

2×8 ROUGH PLANKS

2×8 ROUGH PLANK

TEMPERED HARDBOARD SPLINE

1/4"

13/16

1 3/4"

13/16

7/8"   5/16"

2×8 ROUGH PLANK

CONSTRUCTION DETAILS AND ASSEMBLY
SCALE 1 1/2"=1'-0"

SPECIFICATIONS

PLAN 11

General

Each item of material and equipment shall equal or exceed that described or indicated. All work shall be performed in a workmanlike manner and in accordance with best practices. Mention of commerical products and sources does not constitute an endorsement of such products by the Forest Service or Department of Agriculture to the exclusion of other equally acceptable products.

Site Grading

Grade as required to smooth out surface humps and valleys and to provide drainage away from the house. Minimum site disturbance is desired, however, on sites with enough slope the driveway can be extended under the duplex to provide carport area.

Pole Foundation

The Federal Housing Administration publication titled "Pole House Construction" should be used as a guide when pole foundation requirements need to be adjusted to local soil or site conditions. From this guide, pole foundation requirements in good soil (compact, well-graded sand and gravel, hard clay, or graded fine and coarse sand; 6000 PSF bearing value) are: 7 feet of embedment and a concrete punching pad 21 inches in diameter and 10 inches thick. Backfill with tamped earth, sand, gravel or crushed rock. Minimum pole tip diameter shall be 7 inches. In average soil (loose gravel, medium clay; bearing value, 3000 PSF). The hole shall be 30 inches in diameter, 6.5 feet deep, and backfilled with soil cement or concrete. Pole tip size shall be 7 inches.

Wood Poles

Pressure treated with a salt preservative in accordance with American Wood Preservers Association recommendations and the AWPI quality control program CP-22. Each pole shall bear the AWPI quality stamp CP-22.

Curved Ribs

A jig must be built to use in prefabricating the ribs. Page 140 shows the radius and dimensions to be used in laying out the jig. Each rib is constructed with 1" x 2" southern pine or fir, D grade, edge strips or chords, and 6"-long 2" x 4" spacer blocks as detailed on page 140. Twelve-inch 2" x 4" blocks are used where the floor joists are nailed to the ribs and eight-inch blocks should be used where joints occur in the 1" x 2" chords. Construction adhesive such as Fuller's "Tan Mastic" should be used to reinforce each chord joint. The 2" x 4" spacer blocks can be scrap material such as found in most wood truss manufacturing plants. These

blocks should be at least 6 inches long and spaced 16" o.c. so that the edge of each 4' wide sheet of plywood sheathing will be centered over a block for better anchorage. Each half rib shall be anchored to each floor joist with four 16d nails and to the 2" x 6" ridge board with four 12d nails.

Roof Sheathing

3/8" CC exterior plywood nailed to each rib with 6d annular grooved nails spaced 6" o.c. Aluminum ply-clips shall be used to support plywood edges between ribs.

Roofing

15 lbs. building paper and 16" x 16" hexagon, staple lock, asphalt shingles, 165 lbs/sq. Nail as recommended by shingle manufacturer. Provide galvanized metal flashing at sides of dormers and at each side of sundeck (see detail on page 140). Provide gutters at each end of sundeck.

Floor Framing

Floor beams shall be 2" x 8" rough sawn (mill run) southern pine or fir. Joints shall be centered on the poles and the poles shall be notched to receive the beams. Beams shall be fastened to each pole with two 1/2-inch diameter bolts or 1/2" x 6" lag bolts. Floor joists shall be no. 2 southern pine or construction grade Douglas fir. Nail floor joists to each beam with two 12d nails and to each half-rib with four 16d nails. Floor joists shall be full length 18' pieces and shall not be spliced. Install double joists adjacent to each end wall and under parallel partition walls. Floor joists with crook shall be placed so that the low point of crook is at center span. The weight of the exterior walls will then tend to straighten the joists. The lower side of the first-floor floor joists shall be covered with 3/8" CC exterior plywood or 1/2" fiberboard sheathing.

Insulation

Full thick batt insulation with integral vapor barrier shall be installed between the curved ribs and between first-floor joists, and in bathroom dormer walls.

Exterior Walls

2" x 8" rough sawn (mill run) redwood or cedar planks installed vertically and joined with a spline cut from 1/4" exterior tempered hardboard (see detail on page 142). Each plank shall be nailed to the double floor joists with two 20d galvanized spikes and to the rib blocking with two 16d galvanized nails. The plywood roof sheathing shall be nailed to the planks with two 8d nails per plank. Joints in the hardboard splines shall have a 45 degree bevel cut sloping down to the outside. Caulk the spline joints with latex exterior caulking. All exterior planks shall be full length boards. Planks shall be air-dried or kiln dried to 12 percent moisture content before installation. See page 142 for aluminum window details.

Sliding door installation shall be similar except that a redwood or cedar 2" x 4" frame shall first be installed in the rough door opening. Exterior latex caulking shall be used between the frame and the planks and between the aluminum sliding door frame and the 2" x 4" redwood or cedar frame.

Balcony and Exterior Stairs

Construction grade wood used shall be pressure treated or it shall be redwood or cedar heartwood.

Utility and Storage Room Walls

1/2" exterior plywood and all framing members shall be pressure treated with a salt preservative and shall bear the AWPI quality control mark LP-22. The outside of the plywood to a point about four inches above the ground shall be coated with a foundation asphalt seal coat. While the seal coat is wet it shall be covered with black polyethylene, 6 mils thick. Joints in the polyethlene shall be lapped 8" and sealed with asphalt mastic cement.

Utility and Storage Room Slab

1:3:5 (2000PSI) concrete about three inches thick. Concrete shall be placed over a vapor barrier which extends up 8" on the outside walls.

Interior Partitions

Studs shall be standard grade fir placed 16" o.c. Single thickness walls without framing shall be of 1" x 6" T&G "D" grade pine or fir paneling or 1/2" AC fir plywood, or 1/2" particleboard underlayment. See details on page 138.

Flooring

Single layer wood flooring shall be 1" x 4" southern pine or Douglas fir, "D" grade. Back side of flooring shall be flat and free of grade marks and saw cuts as this surface shall be the finish ceiling for the first floor. Flooring shall be fastened to each joist with nails and a 1/4" bead of mastic adhesive such as Fuller's "Tan Mastic" or Goodrich's "PL 400". Care should be taken in applying the adhesive so that it does not squeeze out at the sides of the joists. Flooring shall be kiln dried to less than 12 percent moisture content and it should be in place for at least one week before sanding. Sand with no. 1 grit sandpaper. If a heavy commercial sander is used, one sanding should be enough.

Cover wood flooring in the bathrooms with vinyl surfaced linoleum. Apply two coats of floor sealer and a coat of wax to all the wood floors except in the bathrooms.

Doors

Entrance doors shall be exterior flush, 1-3/4"-thick, solid core lauan, fir or birch. Interior doors shall be flush 1-3/8"-thick hollow core lauan, fir, or birch. Sliding aluminum doors shall have double insulating glass and screens. Finish the outside of the exterior doors with two coats of the same floor enamel used on the plywood deck. Interior door finish shall be two coats of flat varnish. Door jambs shall be of 2-inch construction grade fir dimension, and selected for straightness. Jambs shall be painted to match interior finish. No door trim is required.

Windows

Horizontal sliding aluminum windows with screens of the sizes shown on the drawings shall be manufactured to conform to requirements and specifications of the Architectural Aluminum Manufacturers Association: HS-B1 windows for residential-type buildings. An aluminum single-hung window with screen shall be in the exterior door to the bathroom. Aluminum flanges on the end wall windows shall be placed in plank grooves and caulked. No window trim is required.

Cabinets and Miscellaneous

Kitchen cabinets shall be job-made of fir plywood or they shall be low-cost prefinished factory or shop-made cabinets without backs. Provide formica counter tops with backsplash and molded edges. Closet shelving shall be no. 2 southern pine or construction-grade fir.

Provide and install a recessed medicine cabinet with mirror, light and electrical outlet.

Decorating

All exterior exposed wood except pressure-treated wood, shall be given one coat of FPL water repellent preservative mixed as follows:

Pentachlorophenol concentrate (10:1)	2 quarts
Boiled linseed oil	1-3/4 quarts
Paraffin wax	1/2 lb.
Mineral spirits	4 gals.
Colors-in-oil	1 pint

Interior exposed joists and beams shall be given one coat of pigmented stain. Interior end wall planks shall be given one spray coat of interior latex paint. All gypsum board walls except kitchen and bathrooms shall have one coat of heavy bodied latex paint applied with a roller. Bathroom and kitchen walls shall have two coats of latex enamel. Kitchen cabinets shall be painted or finished natural with two coats of enamel or varnish.

Finish the first floor ceiling (underside of second floor flooring) with one coat of floor sealer. Interior poles and the spiral stair column shall be cleaned and left unfinished. Spiral stair treads shall have a coat of stain and one coat of floor sealer.

Plumbing

Provide necessary piping and five fixtures with fittings in each unit: Steel double basin kitchen sink, steel bathtub, lavatory, water closet, and a 30 gal. gas water heater or 42 gal. electric water heater with a 10 year warranty. Water piping shall be galvanized steel, copper, or plastic as approved by local plumbing regulations. Provide one exterior hose bibb for each unit at a low point in the water supply piping so that it can be used to drain the system. Provide rough-in plumbing for one automatic washer for each unit in the utility rooms.

Heating

Provide five recessed electric wall heaters with fan and thermostat in each unit where shown on the floor plans, page 138, except that the bathroom heater can be without fan.

Heating system is designed for moderate climates. In cold climates the capacity of the heating system and insulation thickness should be increased according to local requirements.

Electric Wiring and Fixtures

200 ampere service and panel located in the entry closet. Wiring in accordance with the National Electrical code. Surface mounted metal wire-mold conduit shall enclose wiring to the dining room, kitchen, and balcony lights.

Light fixtures are as noted on the floor plans. Provide pull-chain light fixtures in the entry closets and in the utility rooms.

Construction Manual

by L. O. ANDERSON

Acknowledgment. This publication was prepared by the Forest Products Laboratory, Forest Service, U.S. Department of Agriculture. The author acknowledges valuable contributions to preparation of this manuscript from W. G. Youngquist, J. A. Liska, J. M. Black, G. E. Sherwood, and other members of the Laboratory staff.

The wood industry has also contributed to many sections of this manual through reviews prior to publication.

Contents

A MATTER OF COSTS

In the building of a low-cost home, the matter of cost must be considered at every step—in design, selection of materials, and in construction. Each square foot of area added to a plan increases the cost substantially. It is often wise to omit some features, even though desirable, and to add these at some opportune future time. Selection of satisfactory alternate materials can also account for substantial savings.

The unit cost of framing and enclosing a basic wood house does not vary a great deal and is generally determined by square footage. However, the type of foundation, materials used on the inside and outside of the basic wood frame, the type of windows and doors, number of kitchen cabinets and amount of other millwork materials, floor covering, and the caliber of the utilities included can vary a great deal and generally govern the overall cost of the house. For example, in an average single-story house, kitchen cabinets,

interior doors and trim, and hardwood floors account for about 15 percent of the total cost, and substitute materials or deletions in these areas result in substantial savings. The plumbing, electrical, and heating installations also account for about 15 percent of the total house cost, and savings can also be made by eliminating or delaying some of these phases of construction until later.

The cost of a basement in an average house can also amount to 15 percent of the total cost. It seems justified, therefore, in instances where cost is important, to eliminate a basement and have a crawl space consisting of a foundation of treated wood posts or masonry piers. In a small house, this could result in a saving of up to 50 percent of the cost of a conventional foundation.

With a good plan and adequate construction details, a small house can be constructed at a reasonable cost and yet provide for good family living and be as pleasing in appearance as higher cost houses.

MAJOR HOUSE PARTS

Figure 1 is an exploded view of a single-*story*,[3] wood-frame house showing the major parts. The floor system, interior and exterior walls, and the roof are the major components of such a house. Houses with flat or low-sloped roofs are usually variations of these systems. The A-frame, post and beam, and pole-frame are other systems used in house construction.

Floor System

Figure 1 shows a floor system constructed over a *crawl space* area. Supporting *beams* are fastened to treated posts embedded in the soil or to masonry *piers*. In the South, Central, and Coastal areas, provisions must be made for protection from termites. Construction of this type of support for the floor joists has a great advantage because grading is not required and thus it can be used on relatively steep or uneven slopes. Floor *joists* are fastened to these beams and the *subfloor* nailed to the joists. This results in a level, sturdy platform upon which the rest of the house is constructed.

Exterior Walls

Exterior walls, often assembled flat on the subfloor and raised in "tilt-up" fashion, are fastened to the perimeter of the floor platform. Exterior

---
[3] Key words in italics appear in the glossary

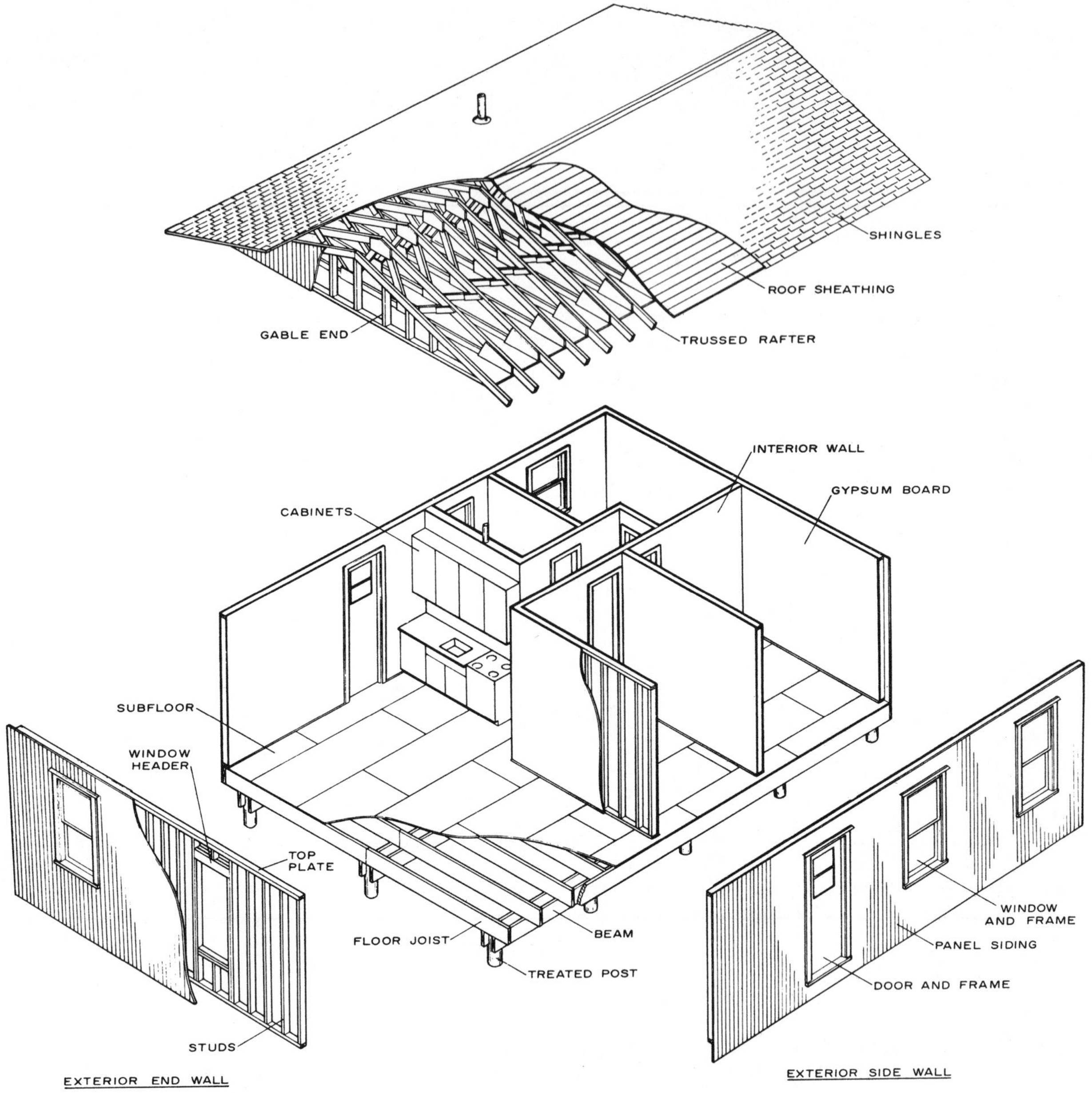

coverings and window and door units are included after walls are plumbed and braced.

Interior Walls

Interior walls are usually the next components to be erected unless *trussed* rafters (roof trusses) are used. Trussed rafters are designed to span from one exterior sidewall to the other and do not require support from interior *partitions*. This allows partitions to be placed as required for room dividers. When ceiling joists and rafters are used, a *bearing partition* near the center of the width is necessary.

Roof Trusses or Roof Framing

Several systems can be used to provide a roof over the house. One consists of normal ceiling joists and rafters which require some type of load-bearing wall between the sidewalls (fig. 2*A*). Another is the trussed rafter system (figs. 1 and 2*B*) (commonly called *trusses*). This design requires no load-bearing walls between the sidewalls. A third design consists of thick wood roof decking (fig. 2*C*). A fourth is open beams and decking which span between the exterior walls and a center wall or ridge beam (fig. 2*D*). The truss and the conventional joist-and-rafter construction require some type of finish for the ceiling. The decking (fig. 2*C*) or the beam and decking (fig. 2*D*) combinations can serve both as interior finish and as a surface to apply the roofing material.

FIGURE 1.—Exploded view of wood-frame house.

MATERIAL SELECTION

There are hundreds of materials on the market which can be used somewhere in the construction of a house. Many are costly and are meant primarily for use in the most expensive homes. Others may not be suitable for all of the intended uses. However, among these building materials are many that are reasonable in cost and perform efficiently. Most manufacturers recommend particular uses and application methods for each of their products, and few problems will occur if such recommendations are followed.

Wood

Wood in its various forms is perhaps the most common and well-known material used in house construction. It is used for framing of floors, walls, and roofs. It is sometimes used in board form as a covering material, but more often the covering materials take the form of plywood or other *panel* wood products. Wood is also used as *siding* or exterior covering, as interior covering, as interior and exterior trim, as flooring, in the many forms

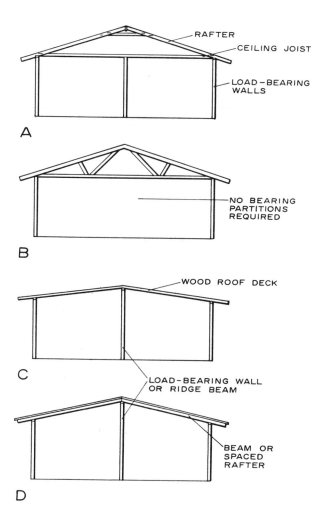

FIGURE 2.—Types of roof construction. *A*, Rafter and ceiling joists—sloped roofs; *B*, trussed rafter—sloped roofs; *C*, wood roof decking—low-sloped roofs; *D*, beam with wood or fiberboard decking.

and types of millwork, and also as shingles to cover roofs and sidewalls.

Wood is easy to form, saw, nail, and fit; even with simple handtools, and with proper use and protection will give excellent service. The *moisture content of wood* used in various parts of a house is important, and recommended moisture contents will be outlined in later sections of this handbook.

There are a number of basic standard wood and wood products used in the *construction* of wood-frame houses. The selection in the proper type and grade for each use is important.[4] The materials can be divided into groups by their use in the construction of a house: some require good strength, others workability, and still others necessitate good appearance.

[4] Anderson, L. O. Selection and Use of Wood Products for Home and Farm Building. U.S. Dept. Agr. Agr. Inform. Bul. 311. 1967.

Treated Posts

Wood posts or poles which are embedded in the soil and used for support of the house should be pressure treated. A number of species are used for these round members. The pressure treatment should conform to Federal Specification TT–W–571. Pressure treatments normally utilize the oil type of *preservatives* (empty-cell process) or leach-resistant waterborne salt preservatives (full-cell process.)

Dimension Material

Surfaced *dimension* material wood members 2 to 4 inches thick and other wood parts are not full size as they are received from the *lumber yard*. For example, a nominal 2 by 4 may have a finished thickness of 1½ to 1⁹⁄₁₆ inches and a width of 3½ to 3⁹⁄₁₆ inches, depending on the moisture content. These materials are sawn from green logs and must be surfaced as well as dried to a usable moisture content. These processes account for the difference in size between a finished dry member and a rough green member.

The following tabulation of sizes is being recommended to the American Lumber Standards Committee by the Southern Pine Inspection Bureau, West Coast Lumber Inspection Bureau, and Western Wood Products Association.

Nominal (inches)	Dry (inches)	Green (inches)
1	¾	25⁄32
2	1½	1⁹⁄₁₆
4	3½	3⁹⁄₁₆
6	5½	5⅝
8	7¼	7½
10	9¼	9½
12	11¼	11½
14	13¼	13½
16	15¼	15½

The green-dry size relationship should hold for dimension lumber up to 4 inches in nominal thickness.

The first materials to be used, after the foundation is in place, are the floor *joists* and *beams* upon which the joists rest. These require adequate strength in bending and moderate stiffness. The sizes used depend on a number of factors; the *span*, spacing, species, and grade. Recommended sizes are listed in most working plans. The second grade of a species, such as southern pine, western hemlock, or Douglas-fir, is commonly selected for these uses. In lower cost houses, the third grade is usually acceptable.

For best performance, the *moisture content* of most dimension materials should not exceed 19 percent.

Wall *studs* (the structural members making up the wall framing) are usually nominal 2 by 4 inches in size and spaced 16 or 24 inches apart. Their strength and stiffness are not as important as for the floor joists, and in low-cost houses the

third grade of a species such as Douglas-fir or southern pine is satisfactory. Slightly higher grades of other species, such as white fir, eastern white pine, spruce, the western white pines, and others, are normally used.

Members used for trusses, rafters, beams, and ceiling joists in the roof framing have about the same requirements as those listed for floor joists. For low-cost houses, the second grade can be used for trusses if the additional strength reduces the amount of material required.

Covering Materials

Floor *sheathing* (subfloor) consists of board *lumber* or *plywood*. Here, too, the spacing of the joists, the species of boards or plywood, and the intended use determine thickness of the subfloor. A single layer may serve both as subfloor and top surface material; for example, ⅝-inch or thicker tongued-and-groved plywood of Douglas-fir, southern pine, or other species in a slightly greater thickness can be used when joists are spaced no more than 20 inches on center. While Douglas-fir and southern pine plywoods are perhaps the most common, other species are equally adaptable for floor, wall, and roof coverings. The "Identification Index" system of marking each sheet of plywood provides the allowable rafter or roof truss and floor joist spacing for each thickness of a standard grade suitable for this purpose. A nominal 1-inch board subfloor normally requires a top covering of some type.

Roof sheathing, like the subfloor, most commonly consists of plywood or *board lumber*. Where exposed wood beams spaced 2 to 4 feet apart are used for low-pitched roofs, for example, wood decking, fiberboard roof deck, or composition materials in 1- to 3-inch thicknesses might be used. The thickness varies with the spacing of the supporting rafters or beams. These sheathing materials often serve as an interior finish as well as a base for roofing.

Wall sheathing, if used with a siding or secondary covering material, can consist of plywood, lumber, structural insulating board, or gypsum board. The type and method of sheathing application normally determine whether *corner bracing* is required in the wall. When 4- by 8-foot sheets of 25⁄32 regular or ½-inch-thick, medium-density, insulating fiberboard or 5⁄16-inch or thicker plywood are used vertically with proper nailing all around the edge, no bracing is required for the rigidity and strength needed to resist windstorms. There are plywood materials available with grooved or roughened surfaces which serve both as sheathing and finishing materials. Horizontal application of plywood, insulating fiberboard, lumber, and other materials usually requires some type of diagonal *brace* for rigidity and strength.

Exterior Trim

Some exterior trim, such as *facia* boards at cornices or gable-end overhangs, is placed before the roofing is applied. Using only those materials necessary to provide good utility and satisfactory appearance results in a cost saving. These trim materials are usually wood and, if relatively clear of *knots*, can be painted without problems. Lower grade boards with a rough-sawn surface can be stained.

Roofing

One of the lowest cost roofing materials which provides satisfactory service for sloped roofs is mineral-surfaced *asphalt roll roofing*. Asphalt shingles also give good service. Both are available in a number of colors. The material cost of asphalt *shingles* is about twice that of surfaced roll roofing. In a small, 24- by 32-foot house, use of surfaced roll roofing may mean a saving of $40 for material and about $20 for labor, which is less than 1 percent of the total cost of the house. However, an asphalt shingle would normally last longer and have a better apperance than the roll roofing.

Wood shingles have a pleasing appearance for sloped roofs. Although they are usually more costly than composition roofing, they could be used where availability, cost, and application conditions were favorable.

Window and Door Frames

Double-hung, casement, or awning wood windows normally consist of prefitted sash in assembled frames ready for installation. A double-hung window is one in which the upper and lower sash slide vertically past each other. A *casement sash* is hinged at the side and swings in or out. An awning window is hinged at the top and swings out. Separate sash in 1⅛- or 1⅜-inch thickness can be used, but some type of frame must be made that includes *jambs*, stops, *sill*, casing, and the necessary hardware. A low-cost, factory-built unit which requires only fastening in place may be the most economical. A fixed sash or a large window glass can be fastened by stops to a prepared frame and generally costs less than a movable-type window. It is normally more economical to use one larger window unit than two smaller ones. Screens should ordinarily be supplied for all operable windows and for doors. In the colder climates, storm windows and storm or *combination doors* are also desirable. Combination units, with screen and storm inserts, are commonly used.

Exterior Coverings

Exterior coverings such as horizontal wood *siding*, vertical boards, boards and *battens*, and similar forms of siding usually require some type of backing in the form of *sheathing* or nailers between studs. In mild climates, nominal 1-inch and thicker sidings are often used over a waterproof paper applied directly to the braced stud wall. There are many sidings of this type on the market in both wood and nonwood materials.

Combination sheathing-siding materials (panel siding) usually consist of 4-foot-wide sheets of plywood, exterior particleboard, or hardboard. Applied vertically before installation of window and door frames, such materials serve very well for exteriors. Plywood may be stained or painted, and the other materials should be painted. Paper-overlaid plywood also serves as a dual-purpose exterior covering material and takes paint well. Wood shingles and *shakes* and similar materials normally require a solid backing or spaced boards of some type.

Insulation

Most houses, even those of lowest cost, should have some type of *insulation* to resist the cold and to increase comfort during hot weather. There are various types of insulation, from insulating fiberboard to fill types, which can be used in the construction of a house. Perhaps the most common *thermal insulations* are the flexible (blanket and batt) and the fill types

A blanket insulation might be used between the floor joists or studs. Batt insulation of various types might be used between floor joists or in the ceiling areas. Most flexible insulations are supplied with a vapor barrier which resists movement of water vapor through the wall and minimizes *condensation* problems. A friction-type batt insulation is also available for use in floors, walls, or ceilings. Fill-type insulation is most commonly used in attic-ceiling areas.

The structural insulating board often serves as sheathing in the wall or as a fair insulating material under a plywood floor. Each material has its place, and selection should be based on climate as well as on cost and utility.

Interior Coverings

Many *dry-wall* (unplastered) interior coverings are available, from gypsum board to prefinished plywood. Perhaps the most economical are the gypsum board products. They are normally applied vertically in 4- by 8-foot sheets or horizontally in room-length sheets with the joint at midwall heights. They are also used for ceilings. Thicknesses range from 3/8 to 5/8 inch. *Butt joints* and corners require the use of tape and joint compound, or a *corner bead*, and add somewhat to labor costs over prefinished materials. Plastic-covered gypsum board is also available at additional cost, but must usually be installed with an adhesive. Hardboards, insulation board, plywood, and other sheet materials are available, as are wood and fiberboard paneling. The choice must be based on overall cost of material and labor as well as on ease of maintenance. Prefinished ceiling tile in 12- by 12-inch sizes and larger is also available.

Interior Finish and Millwork

Interior finish and *millwork* consist of doors and door frames, *base moldings*, window and door *trim*, kitchen and other *cabinets*, flooring, and similar items. The type and grade selected determine the cost to a great extent. Selection of simple *moldings*, lower cost species for jambs and other wood members, simple kitchen shelving, low-cost floor coverings, and the elimination of doors where practical will often make a difference of hundreds of dollars in the total cost of the house.

The most commonly used doors are the flush-type and the panel-type. The flush-type consists of thin plywood or similar facings with a solid or hollow core. The panel door consists of solid side stiles and cross*rails* with plywood or other panel fillers. For exterior types, both may be supplied with openings for glass. Exterior doors are usually 1¾ inches thick and interior doors 1⅜ inches thick.

Door jambs, casings, moldings, and similar millwork of a number of wood species can be obtained. Select the lower cost materials, yet those that will still give good service. Some species in this class are the pines, the spruces, and Douglas-fir.

Factory-built kitchen cabinets are expensive and can cost several hundred dollars in a moderate-size house. The use of open shelving which can be curtained and a good counter is almost a must in a low-cost house. Doors can be added at a later date.

Wood strip flooring or wood tile of hardwood species might be too costly to consider in the original construction, but could be installed at a future time. Softwood floorings or the lower cost hardwood floorings might be within the original budget. The use of lower cost asphalt tile or even a painted finish may be the best initial choice. However, when a woodboard subfloor is used, some type of underlayment is required under the tile. Particleboard, hardboard, and plywood are the most common materials for this use.

Nails and Nailing

In a wood-frame house, nailing is the most common method of fastening the various parts together. Nailing should be done correctly because even the highest grade member often does not serve its purpose without proper nailing. Thus, it is well to follow established rules in nailing the various wood members together. While most of the nailing will be described in future sections, table 1 lists recommended practices used for framing and application of covering materials. Figure 3 shows the sizes of common nails. Most finish and siding nails have the same equivalent lengths. For example, an eight*penny* common nail is the same length as an eightpenny galvanized siding nail, but not necessarily the same diameter.

TABLE 1.—*Recommended schedule for nailing the framing and sheathing of a well-constructed wood-frame house*

Joining	Nailing method	Nails: Number	Nails: Size	Nails: Placement
Header to joist	End-nail	3	16d	
Joist to sill or girder	Toenail	2–3	10d or 8d	
Header and stringer joist to sill	Toenail		10d	16 inches on center.
Bridging to joist	Toenail each end	2	8d	
Ledger strip to beam, 2 inches thick		3	16d	At each joist.
Subfloor, boards:				
1 by 6 inches and smaller		2	8d	To each joist.
1 by 8 inches		3	8d	To each joist.
Subfloor, plywood:				
At edges			8d	6 inches on center.
At intermediate joists			8d	8 inches on center.
Subfloor (2 by 6 inches, T&G) to joist or girder	*lind-nail* (casing) and face-nail.	2	16d	
Soleplate to stud, horizontal assembly	End-nail	2	16d	At each stud.
Top plate to stud	End-nail	2	16d	
Stud to soleplate	Toenail	4	8d	
Soleplate to joist or blocking	*Face-nail*		16d	16 inches on center.
Doubled studs	Face-nail, stagger		10d	16 inches on center.
End stud of intersecting wall to exterior wall stud	Face-nail		16d	16 inches on center.
Upper top plate to lower top plate	Face-nail		16d	16 inches on center.
Upper top plate, laps and intersections	Face-nail	2	16d	
Continous header, 2 pieces, each edge			12d	12 inches on center.
Ceiling joist to top wall plates	Toenail	3	8d	
Ceiling joist laps at partition	Face-nail	4	16d	
Rafter to top plate	Toenail	2	8d	
Rafter to ceiling joist	Face-nail	5	10d	
Rafter to valley or hip rafter	Toenail	3	10d	
Ridge board to rafter	End-nail	3	10d	
Rafter to rafter through ridge board	Toenail	4	8d	
	Edge-nail	1	10d	
Collar beam to rafter:				
2-inch member	Face-nail	2	12d	
1-inch member	Face-nail	3	8d	
1-inch diagonal let-in brace to each stud and plate (4 nails at top).		2	8d	
Built-up corner studs:				
Studs to blocking	Face-nail	2	10d	Each side.
Intersecting stud to corner studs	Face-nail		16d	12 inches on center.
Built-up girders and beams, 3 or more members	Face-nail		20d	32 inches on center, each side.
Wall sheathing:				
1 by 8 inches or less, horizontal	Face-nail	2	8d	At each stud.
1 by 6 inches or greater, diagonal	Face-nail	3	8d	At each stud.
Wall sheathing, vertically applied plywood:				
⅜ inch and less thick	Face-nail		6d	6-inch edge.
½ inch and over thick	Face-nail		8d	12-inch intermediate.
Wall sheathing, vertically applied fiberboard:				
½ inch thick	Face-nail			1½-inch roofing nail.[1]
25/32 inch thick	Face-nail			1¾-inch roofing nail.[1]
Roof sheathing, boards, 4-, 6-, 8-inch width	Face-nail	2	8d	At each rafter.
Roof sheathing plywood:				
⅜ inch and less thick	Face-nail		6d	6-inch edge and 12-
½ inch and over thick	Face-nail		8d	inch intermediate.

[1] 3-inch edge and 6-inch intermediate.

Painting and Finishing

There are many satisfactory *paints* and finishes for exterior use. *Pigmented stain* is one of the easiest types to apply and is also long lasting. It is available in many colors from light to dark and is generally one of the best finishes for rough or sawn wood surfaces. Exterior paints used on smooth-surfaced siding and trim or on the trim as an accent for stained walls should be applied in several coats for best service. The first may consist of a nonporous linseed oil *primer*. Following coats can consist of latex, alkyd, or oil-base exterior paints. A *water-repellent preservative* provides a natural clear finish for wood surfaces.

Many interior paints are suitable for walls and ceilings. Latex and alkyd types are perhaps the most common, but the oil types are also suitable.

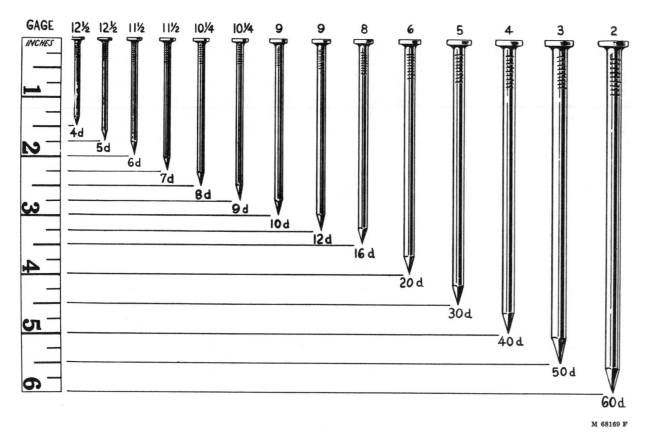

GAGE 12½ 12½ 11½ 11½ 10¼ 10¼ 9 9 8 6 5 4 3 2

4d
5d
6d
7d
8d
9d
10d
12d
16d
20d
30d
40d
50d
60d

M 68169 F

FIGURE 3.—Nail size table.

Floor and *deck paints* provide long wearing surfaces. One of the most common finishes for wood floors is the floor *sealer*, which provides a natural transparent surface.

Chimney

Some type of chimney will be required for the heating unit. A masonry chimney requires a rigid concrete base, bricks or other masonry, *flue lining*, plus labor to erect it. A manufactured chimney which is supported by the ceiling joists or rafters may be the best choice from the standpoint of overall cost.

Utilities

Cost of the heating, plumbing, and wiring phases of house construction is usually a high percentage of total cost. These costs can be reduced to a great extent by careful selection and planning. Electricity is readily available in many areas and should be included in most low-cost houses. A minimum number of circuits and few switched outlets will aid in reducing the overall installation cost.

Heating units might consist of a low-cost space heater for wood, oil, or gas, or a small, central forced-air system with a minimum amount of duct work. The difference between the two may amount to several hundred dollars. The space heater may be more than sufficient for houses constructed in the milder climates.

Water supply and sewage disposal systems are often the most costly and difficult to install of all the utilities. When municipal or other systems are available for water and sewer service, there are no problems except the cost of installation. When good water can be obtained from a shallow well, a pump and pressure tank will provide a water supply at a low cost. However, in areas where a deep well is needed, costs may be too great. In such cases, one well might be used to supply several houses when they are ideally grouped. Wells should ordinarily be located a minimum of 50 feet from a septic tank and 100 feet from an absorption field.

Disposal of sewage in areas where public systems are available presents no problem. Where public systems are not available, the use of a septic tank and absorption system is required. The satisfactory performance of such a system depends on drainage, soil types, and other factors. It is sometimes necessary, when costs are critical, to provide for future installation of a disposal system. Roughed-in connections for plumbing facilities can and should be made in the house during its construction when sewer connections are not immediately available or costs are too great. Long-term costs of sewer connection will be more reasonable if provisions are made during construction.

Water supply and sewage disposal systems are specialized phases of house construction when these facilities are not available from a municipal or central source. Advice and guidance of a local health officer and engineer from your county office should be requested.

FOUNDATION SYSTEMS

Site Selection and Layout

One of the first essentials in house construction is to select the most desirable property site for its location. A lot in a smaller city or community presents few problems. The front set-back of the house and side-yard distances are either controlled by local regulations or should be governed by other houses in the neighborhood. However, if the site is in a rural or outlying area, care should be taken in staking out the house location.

Good drainage is essential. Be certain that natural drainage is away from the house or that such drainage can easily be assured by modification of ground slope. Low areas should be avoided. Soil conditions should be favorable for excavation for the treated posts or masonry piers of the foundation. Large rocks or other obstructions may require changes in the type of footings or *foundation*.

After the site for the house has been selected, all plant growth and sod should be removed. The area can then be raked and leveled slightly for staking and location of the supporting posts or piers.

The foundation plan in the working drawings for the house shows all the measurements necessary for construction. The first step in locating the house is to establish a baseline along one side with heavy cord and solidly driven stakes located well outside the end building lines (stakes 1 and 2, fig. 4). This baseline should be at the outer faces of the posts, piers, or foundation walls. When a post foundation is used with an overhang, the post faces will be 13½ inches in from the building line when a 12-inch overhang is used (fig. 5). When masonry piers or wood posts are located at the edge of the foundation, the outer faces are the same as the building line. These details are normally included in the working drawings. A second set of stakes (3 and 4) should now be established parallel to stakes 1 and 2 at the opposite side according to the measurements shown in the foundation plan of the working drawing. When measuring across, be sure that the tape is at right angles to the first baseline. Just as the 1–2 baseline does, this line will locate the outer edge of posts or piers. A third set of stakes, 5 and 6, should then be established at one end of the building line (fig. 4).

A square 90° corner can be established by laying out a distance of 12 feet at line 1–2 and 9 feet along line 5–6. Short cords can be tied to the lines to mark these two locations. Now measure between the two marks and when the diagonal measurement is 15 feet, the two corners at stakes 1–5 and 3–6 are square (fig. 4). The length of the house is now established by the fourth set of stakes, 7 and 8. Finally, the centerline along the length of the house can be marked by stakes 9 and 10. A final check of the alinement for a true rectangular layout is made by measuring the diagonals from one corner to the opposite corner (fig. 4). Both diagonals should be the same length.

In some areas of the country, building regulations might restrict the use of treated wood foundation posts. A masonry foundation fully enclosing the crawl space may be necessary or preferred. For such houses, the details shown in the Appendix to this manual can be used. Details of skirtboard enclosures for post foundations are also included in the appendix.

Footings

The holes for the post or masonry pier *footings* can now be excavated to a depth of about 4 feet or as required by the depth of the *frostline*. They should be spaced as shown in the foundation plan of the working plans and in figure 5. The embedment depth should be enough so that the soil pressure keeps the posts in place.

Place the dirt a good distance away from the holes to prevent its falling back in. Size of the holes for the wood post and the masonry piers should be large enough for the footings. When posts or piers are spaced 8 feet apart in one direction and 12 feet in the other, a 20- by 20-inch or 24-inch-diameter footing is normally sufficient (fig. 5). In softer soils or if greater spacing is used, a 24- by 24-inch footing may be required.

Posts alone without footings of any type, but with good embedment, are being used for pole-type buildings. However, because the area of the bottom end of the pole against the soil determines its load capacity, this method is not normally recommended in the construction of a house where uneven settling could cause problems. A small amount of settling in a pole warehouse or barn would not be serious. Where soil capacities are very high and posts are spaced closely, it is likely that a footing support under the end of the post would not be required. However, because a good, stable foundation is important in any type of house, the use of adequate footings of some type must be considered.

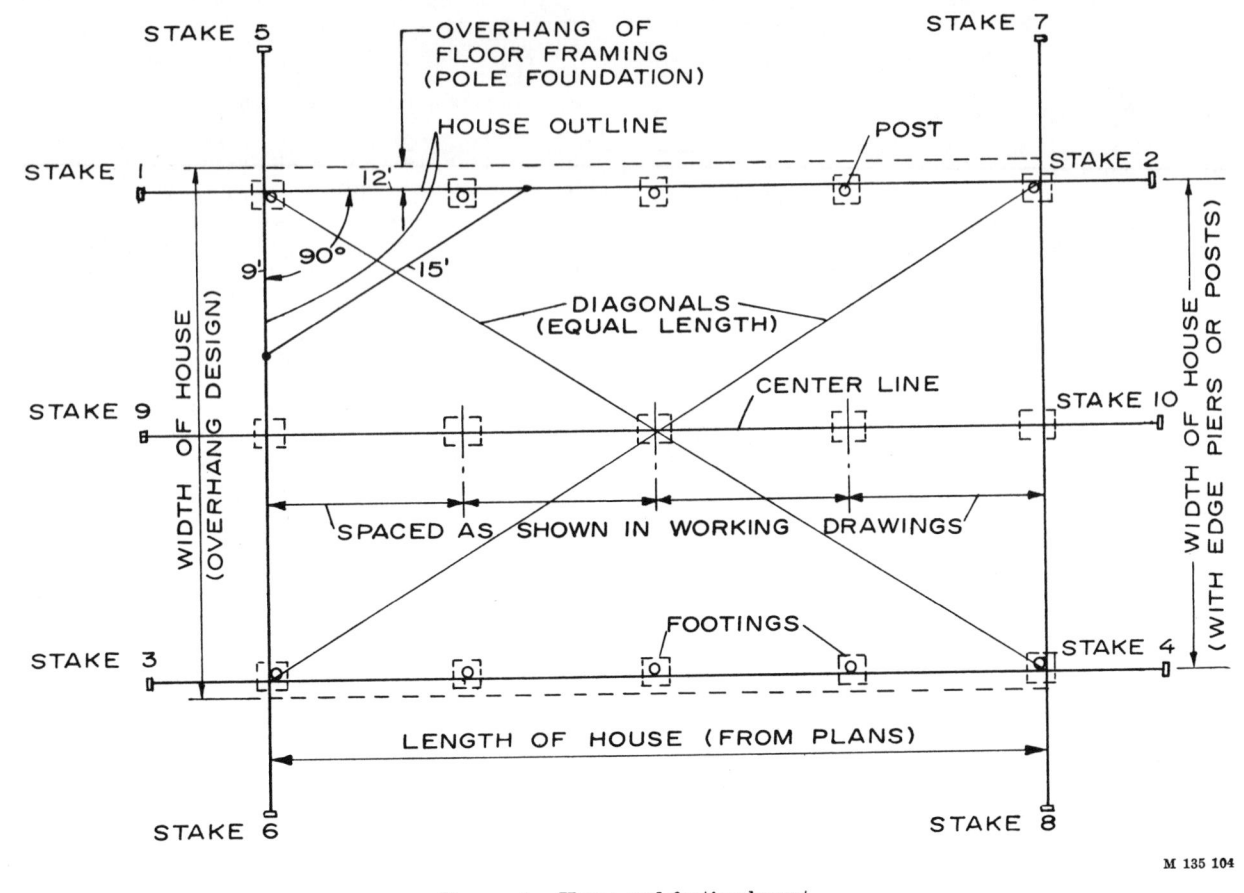

FIGURE 4.—House and footing layout.

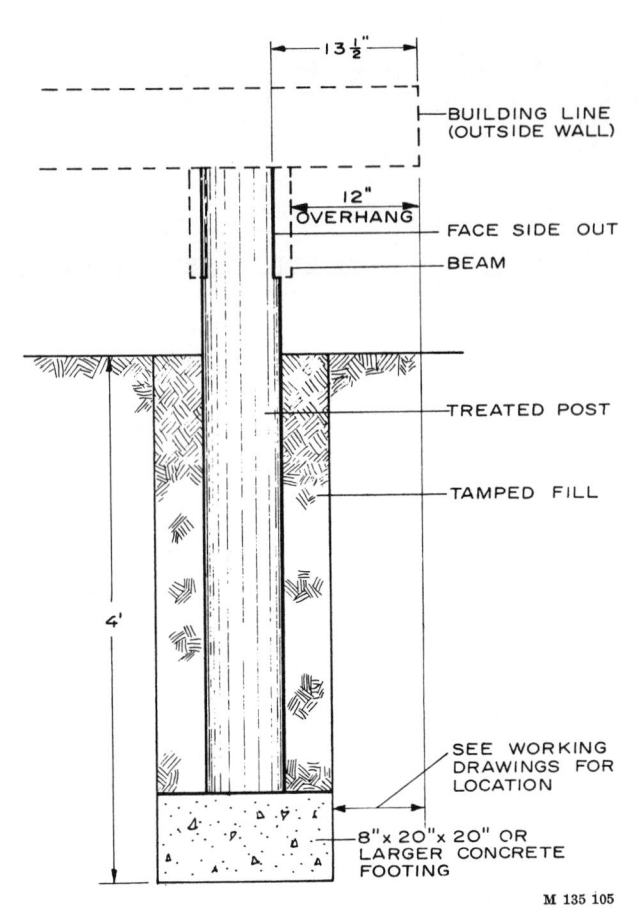

FIGURE 5.—Post embedment and footing alinement (overhang design.)

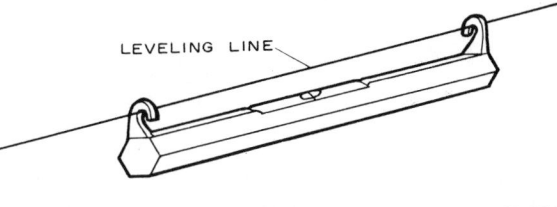

FIGURE 6.—Line level. Locate line level midway between building corners when leveling.

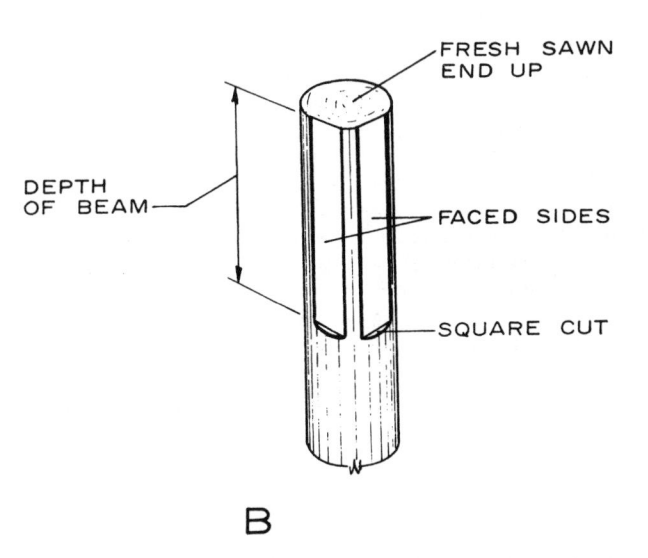

FIGURE 7.—Facing posts. A, Side or intermediate post; B, corner post (use largest).

After the holes have been dug to the recommended depth and cleared of loose dirt, an 8-inch-thick or thicker concrete footing should be poured (fig. 5). If premixed *concrete* is not available, it can be mixed by hand or by a small on-the-job mixer. Tops of the footings should be leveled by measuring down a constant distance from the level line. A 5- or 6-bag mix (premixed concrete) or a 1 to 2½ to 3½ (cement:sand:gravel) job-mixed concrete should be satisfactory. The footings for the post and pier foundations should be located as shown on the working drawings.

Post Foundations—With Side Overhang

Treatment of the foundation posts should conform to Federal Specification TT–W–571. Penetration of the preservative for foundation posts should be equal to one-half the radius and not less than 90 percent of the sapwood thickness. The selection of posts should be governed also by final finish and appearance. When cleanliness, freedom from odor, or paintability is essential, waterborne preservative-treated posts should be used. The important principle is not to use untreated posts in contact with the soil.

Treated posts having a top diameter as shown on the plans should be selected for each of the footing locations. The length can be determined by setting the layout strings to the level of the top of the beams and posts. Select the corner with the highest ground elevation and move the string on this stake to about 18 to 20 inches above the ground level at this point. The minimum clearance under joists or beams should be 12 inches. However, 18 to 24 inches or more is preferred when accessibility is desired. Then with the aid of a lightweight string or line level (fig. 6), adjust the cord on the other stakes so that the layout strings around the edge of the building and down the center are all truly level and horizontal. To insure accuracy, the line must be tight with no sag and the level located at the center. If available a surveyor's level will serve even better. Thus, the distance from the string to the top of concrete footings will now be the length of the posts needed at each location. A manometer-type level can also be used in establishing a constant elevation for the posts. This type of level consists of a long, clear plastic tube partly filled with water or other liquid. The water level at each end establishes the correct elevation.

Locate the notched and faced posts on the concrete footings using the cord on the stakes as a guide for the faced sides. Place and tamp 8 to 10 inches of dirt around them initially to hold them in place. Posts should be vertical and the faced side alined with the cord from the stakes along each side, the center, and the ends of the house outline. When posts are alined, fill in the remaining dirt. Fill and tamp no more than 6 inches in the hole at one time to insure good, solid embedment.

Select *beams* the size and length shown in the foundation plan of the working drawings. Moisture content should normally not exceed 19 per-

If pressure-treated posts are not available in the lengths just determined, use poles more than twice as long as required. Saw them in half and use *with the treated end down*. Now with a saw and a hand ax or drawknife, slightly *notch* and face one side for a distance equal to the depth of the beams (fig. 7A). The four largest diameter posts should be used for the corners and notched on two adjacent sides (fig. 7B). Facing should be about 1½ inches wide, except for corners or when beam joints might be made where 2½ inches is preferable.

Treated 6- by 6-inch or 8- by 8-inch posts can be used in place of the round posts when available. Although they may cost somewhat more and do *not* have the resistance of treated round posts, square posts will reduce on-site labor time.

cent. These beams are usually 2 by 10 or 2 by 12 inches in size and the lengths conform to the spacing of the posts. For example, posts spaced 8 feet apart will require 8- and 16-foot-long beams. The outside beam can now be nailed in place. Starting along one side at the corner, even with the leveling string, nail one beam to the corner post and each crossing post (fig. 8A). Initially, use only one twentypenny nail at the top of each beam, and don't drive it in fully. (The center should be left free to allow for a carriage bolt.) Side beam ends should project beyond the post about 1½ inches or the thickness of the end header (fig. 8B). When all outside beams and those along the center row of posts are erected, all final leveling adjustments should be made. In addition to the leveling cord from the layout stakes, use a carpenter's level and a straightedge to insure that each beam is level, horizontal, and in line with the cord. Final nailing can now be done on the first set of beams. Posts extending over the tops of the beams can now be trimmed flush.

The second set of beams on the opposite sides of the posts should now be installed. Because round posts vary in diameter, the facing on the second side has been delayed until this time. Use a strong cord or string and stretch along the length of the side of the foundation on the inside of the posts and parallel to the outside beams (fig. 9A). This will establish the amount of notching and facing to be done for each post. Use a saw to provide a square notch to support the second beam. All posts can be thus faced and the second beams nailed in place level with, and in the same way as, the outside beams. This facing is usually unnecessary when square posts are used (fig. 9B). However, additional bolts are required when the beam does not bear on a notch. Joints of the *headers* should be made over the center of the posts and staggered. For example, if an 8- and a 16-foot beam are used on the outside of the posts, stagger the joints by first using a 16-foot beam, then an 8-foot length, on the inside. Only one *joint* should be made at each support.

Drill ½-inch holes through the double beams and posts at the midheight of the beam, and install ½- by 8-, 10-, or 12-inch galvanized carriage bolts with the head on the outside and a large washer under the nut on the inside. Use two bolts for square posts without a notch (fig. 9B). At splices, use two bolts and stagger (fig. 10A). When available at the correct moisture content, single nominal 4-inch-thick beams might be used to replace the two 2-inch members (fig. 10B).

All poles and beams are now installed and the final earth tamping can be done around the poles where required. A final raking and leveling is now in order to insure a good base for the soil cover if required. There is now a solid level framework upon which to erect the floor joists.

Edge Piers—Masonry and Posts

When masonry piers or wood posts are used along the edge of the building line instead of for overhang floor framing as previously described, the 8-inch poured footings are usually the same size as shown in figure 11A. However, check the working drawings for the exact size. For masonry piers, the distance to the bottom of the footings should be governed by the depth of frost penetration. This may vary from 4 feet in the Northern States to less than 1 foot in the Southern areas. The wood posts normally require a 3- to 4-foot-deep hole. The masonry piers or posts should be alined so that the outside edges are flush with the outside of the building line (fig. 11A, B). The foundation plan in the working drawings covers these details further.

Concrete block, brick, or other masonry, or poured concrete piers can now be constructed over the footings. Concrete block piers should be 8 by 16 inches in size, brick or other masonry 12 by 12 inches, and poured concrete 10 by 10 inches. The tops of the piers should all be level and about 12 to 16 inches above the highest corner of the building area. Use any of the previously described leveling methods. Use a 22-gage by 2-inch-wide galvanized perforated or plain anchor strap for nailing into the beams. It should extend through at least two courses, filling the core when hollow masonry is used (fig. 11A). A prepared mortar mix with 3 or 3½ parts sand and ¼ part cement to each part of mortar or other approved mixes should be used in laying up the masonry units. The wood post installation details are shown in figure 11B. Anchor straps are nailed to each post and beam with twelvepenny galvanized nails.

Beams consisting of doubled 2 by 10 or 2 by 12 members (check the foundation plan of the working drawings) can now be assembled. Place them on the posts or piers and make the splices at this location. Make only one splice at each pier. Nominal 2-inch members can be nailed together with tenpenny nails spaced 16 inches apart in two rows. Fabrication details at the corner and intersection with the center beam and fastening of the beam tie (*stringer*) are shown in figure 11C.

Ledgers, used to support the floor joists, should be nailed to the inside of the nailed beams. The sizes are 2 by 2, 2 by 3, or 2 by 4 as indicated in the foundation plan of the working drawings. Ledgers should be spaced so that the top of the joists will be flush with the top of the edge and center beams when bearing on the ledgers (fig. 11A, B). Use sixteenpenny nails spaced 8 inches apart in a staggered row to fasten the ledger to the beam.

The foundation and beams are now in place ready for the assembly of the floor system.

An alternate method of providing footings for the treated wood foundation posts involves the use of temporary braces to position the posts while the

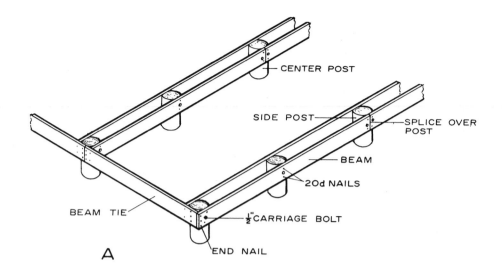

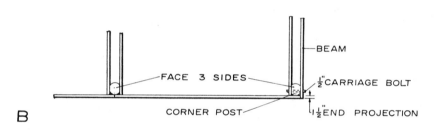

M 135 108

FIGURE 8.—Beam installation. A, Overall view; B, plan view.

concrete is poured (fig. 12). After the holes are dug, posts of the proper length are positioned and temporary braces nailed to them (fig. 12A). A minimum of 8 inches should be allowed for footing depth (fig. 12B). When posts are alined and set to the proper elevation, concrete is poured around them. After the concrete has set, holes are filled (*backfilled*) and earth tamped firmly around the posts. Construction of the floor framing can now begin.

This system of setting posts and pouring the concrete footings can also be used when a beam is located on each side of the posts (fig. 8). Posts are placed in the holes, the beams nailed in their proper position, and the beams alined and blocked to the correct elevation. After the concrete has set and the fill has been tamped in place, the beams can be bolted to the posts.

Termite Protection

In areas of the South and in many of the Central and Coastal States, *termite* protection must be considered in construction of crawl-space houses. Pressure-treated lumber or poles are not affected by termites, but these insects build passages to and can damage untreated wood. Perhaps the most common and effective present-day method of protection is by the use of soil poisons. Spraying soil with solutions of approved chemicals such as aldrin, chlordane, dieldrin, and heptachlor using recommended methods will proved protection for 10 or more years.

A physical method of preventing entry of termites to untreated wood is by the use of *termite shields*. These are made of galvanized iron, aluminum, copper, or other metal. They are located over continuous walls (fig. 13A) or over or around treated wood foundation posts (fig. 13 B and C). They are not effective if bent or punctured during or after construction.

Crawl spaces should have sufficient room so that an examination of poles and piers can be made easily each spring. These inspections normally provide safeguards against wood-destroying insects. Termite tubes or water-conducting fungus should be removed and destroyed and the soil treated with poison. Caution should be used in soil treatment, however, since the effective chemicals are often toxic to animal life and should not be used where individual water systems are present.

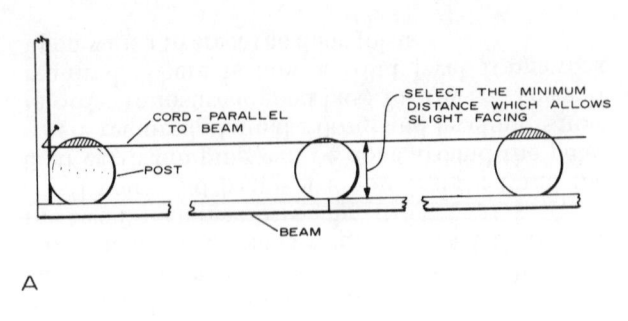

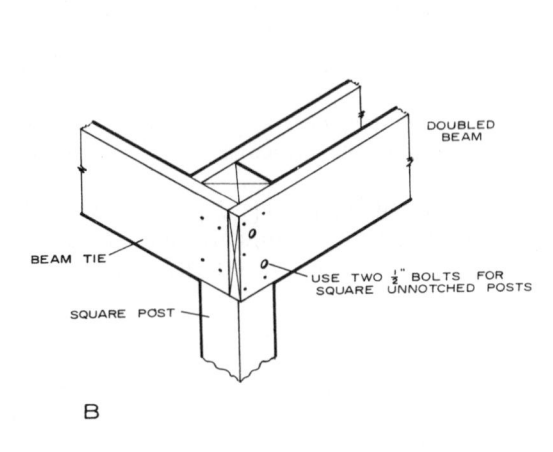

FIGURE 9.—Facing and fastening posts. A, Round posts; B, square post.

M 135 109

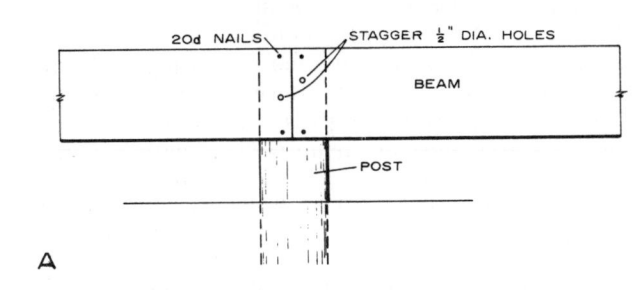

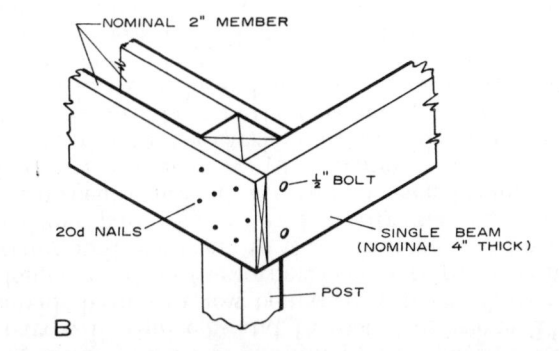

FIGURE 10.—Fastening beams to posts. A, Bolting; B, single beam.

M 135 110

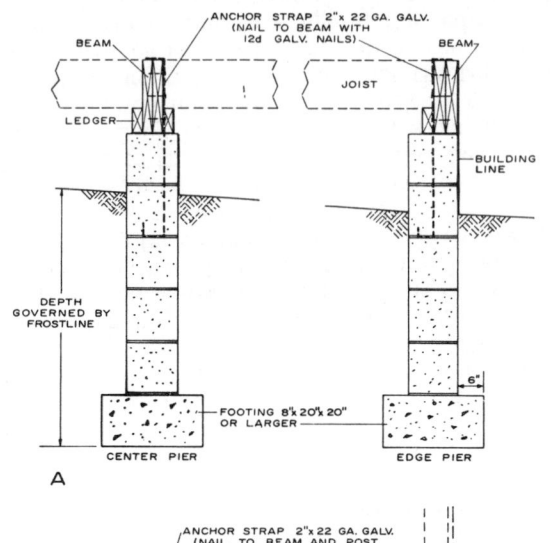

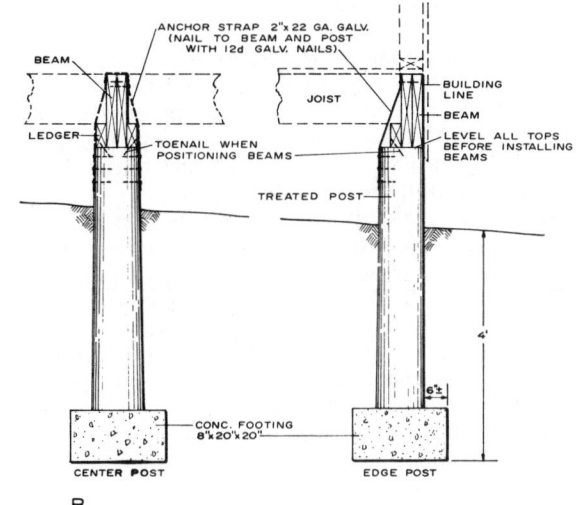

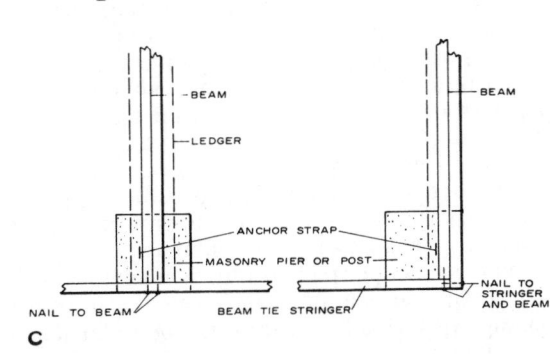

FIGURE 11.—Edge posts and masonry piers. A, Masonry edge piers; B, edge post foundation; C, corner and edge framing of beam.

M 135 923

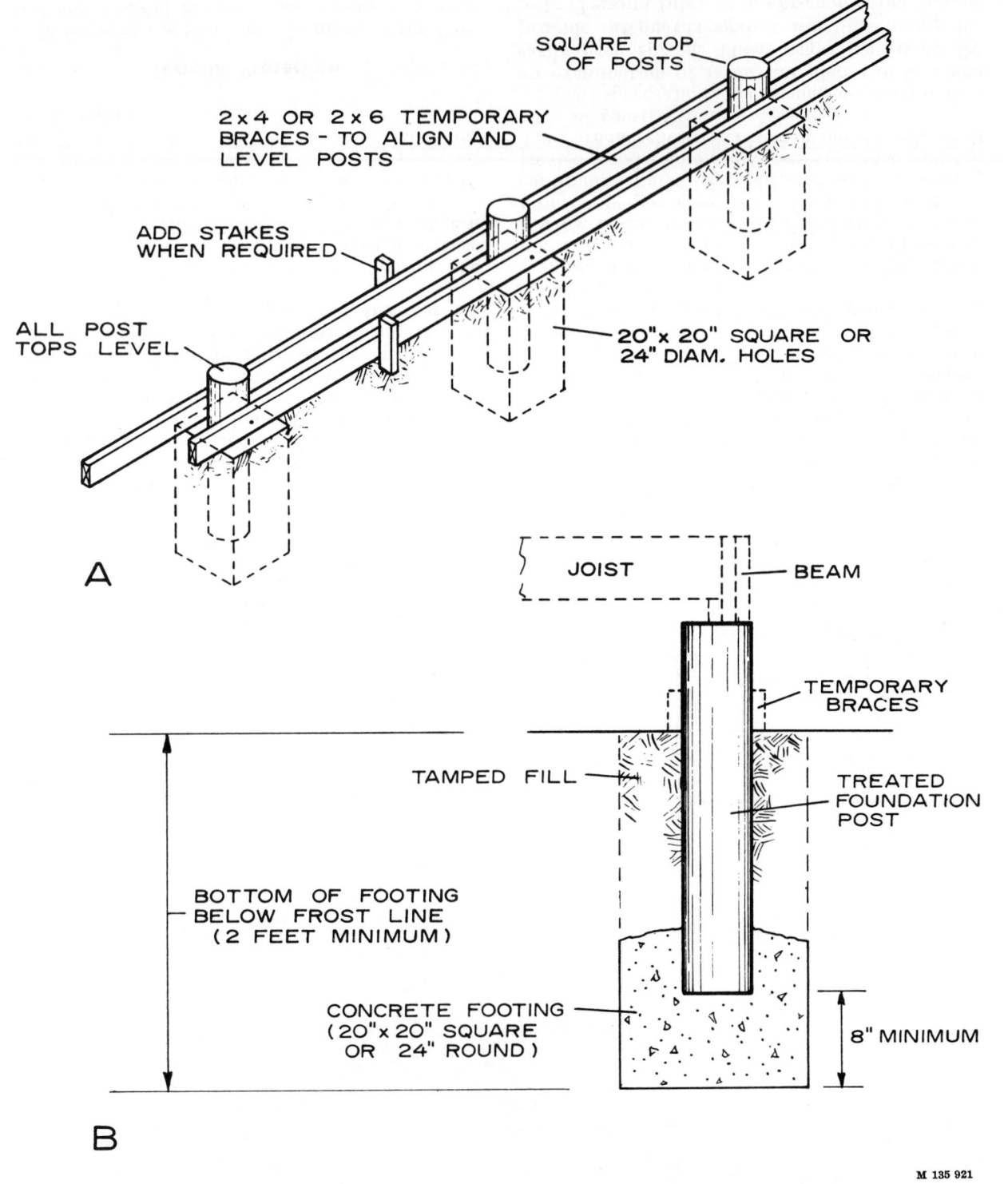

FIGURE 12.—Alternate method of setting edge foundation posts. A, Temporary bracing; B, footing position.

M 135 921

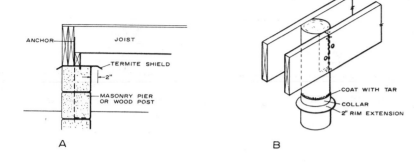

FIGURE 13.—Termite shields. *A*, On top of masonry or wood post; *B*, round posts; *C*, square posts

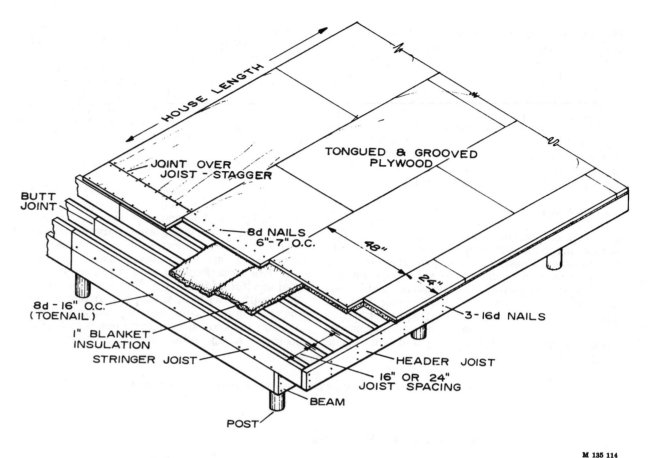

FIGURE 14.—Floor framing (post foundation with side overhang).

JOISTS FOR DIFFERENT FLOOR SYSTEMS

The beams, or beams and ledger strips, and the foundations are now in place and joists can be installed. Size and lengths of the floor joists, as well as the species and spacing, are shown in the floor framing layout in the working plans for the house being built. The joists may vary from nominal 2 by 8 inches in size to 2 by 10 inches or larger where spans are long. Moisture content of floor joists and other floor framing members should not exceed 19 percent when possible. Spacing of joists is normally 16 or 24 inches on center so that 8-foot lengths of plywood for subfloor will span six or four joist spaces.

In low-cost houses, savings can be made by using plywood for subfloor which also serves as a base for resilient tile or other covering. This can be done by specifying tongued-and-grooved edges in a plywood grade of C–C plugged Exterior Douglas-fir, southern pine, or similar species. Regular Interior Underlayment grade with exterior glue is also considered satisfactory. The *matched* edges provide a tight lengthwise joint, and end joints are made over the joists. If tongued-and-grooved plywood is not available, use square edged plywood and block between joists with 2 by 4's for edge nailing. Plywood subfloor also serves as a tie between joists over the center beam. Insulation should be used in the floor in some manner to provide comfort and reduce heat loss. It is generally used between or over the joists. These details are covered in the working drawings.

Single-floor systems can also include the use of nominal 1- by 4-inch matched finish flooring in species such as southern pine and Douglas-fir and the lower grades of oak, birch, and maple in 25/32-inch thickness. To prevent air and dust infiltration, joists should first be covered with 15-pound asphalt felt or similar materials. The flooring is then applied over the floor joists and the flood insula-

tion added when the house is enclosed. When this single-floor system is used, however, some surface protection from weather and mechanical damage is required. A full-width sheet of heavy plastic or similar covering can be used, and the walls erected directly over the film. When most of the exterior and interior work is done, the covering can be removed and the floor sanded and finished.

Post Foundation—With Side Overhang

The joists for a low-cost house are usually the third grade of such species as southern pine or Douglas-fir and are often 2 by 8 inches in size for spans of approximately 12 feet. If an overhang of about 12 inches is used for 12-foot lengths, the joist spacing normally can be 24 inches. Sizes, spacing, and other details are shown in the plans for each individual house.

The joists can now be cut to length, using a *butt joint* over the center beam. Thus, for a 24-foot-wide house, each pair of joists should be cut to a 12-foot length, less the thickness of the end header joist which is usually 1½ inches. The edge or stringer joists should be positioned on the beams with several other joists and the premarked headers nailed to them with one sixteenpenny nail (or just enough to keep them in position). The frame, including the edge (stringer) joists and the header joists, is now the exact outline of the house. Square up this framework by using the equal diagonal method (fig. 4). The overhang beyond the beams should be the same at each side of the house. Now, with eightpenny nails, *toenail* the joists to each beam they cross and the stringer joists to the beam beneath (fig. 14) to hold the framework exactly square. Add the remaining joists and nail the headers into the ends with three sixteenpenny nails. Toenail the remaining joists to the headers with eightpenny nails. When the center of a parallel

partition wall is more than 4 inches from the center of the joists, add solid blocking between the joists. The blocking should be the same size as the joists and spaced not more than 3 feet apart. Toenail blocking to the joists with two tenpenny nails at each side.

In moderate climates, 1-inch blanket insulation may be sufficient to insulate the floor of crawl-space houses. It is usually placed between the joists in the same way that thicker insulation is normally installed. Another method consists of rolling 24-inch-wide 1-inch insulation, across the joists, nailing or stapling it where necessary to keep it stretched with tight edge joints (fig. 14). Insulation of this type should have strong damage-resistant covers. Tenpenny ring-shank nails should be used to fasten the plywood to the joists rather than eightpenny common normally used. This will minimize nail movement or "nail pops' which could occur during moisture changes. The vapor barrier of the insulation should be on the upper side toward the subfloor. Two-inch and thicker blanket or batt insulation is placed between the joists and should be applied any time after the floor is in place, preferably when the house is near completion.

When the house is 20, 24, 28, or 32 feet wide,

the first row of tongued-and-grooved plywood sheets should be 24 inches wide, so that the butt-joints of the joists at the center beam are reinforced with a full 48-inch-wide piece (fig. 15). This plywood is usually ⅝- or ¾-inch thick when it serves both as subfloor and underlayment. Rip 4-foot-wide pieces in half and save the other halves for the opposite side. Place the square, sawed edges flush with the header and nail the plywood to each crossing joist and header with eightpenny common nails spaced 6 to 7 inches apart at edges and at intermediate joists (fig. 14). Joints in the next full 4-foot widths of plywood should be broken by starting at one end with a 4-foot-long piece. End joints will thus be staggered 48 inches. End joints should always be staggered at least one joist space, 16 or 24 inches. Be sure to draw up the tongued-and-grooved edges tightly. A chalked snap-string should be used to mark the position of the joists for nailing.

Edge Foundation—Masonry Pier or Wood Post

When edge piers or wood posts are used with edge support beams, the joists can be cut to length to fit snugly between the center and outside beams

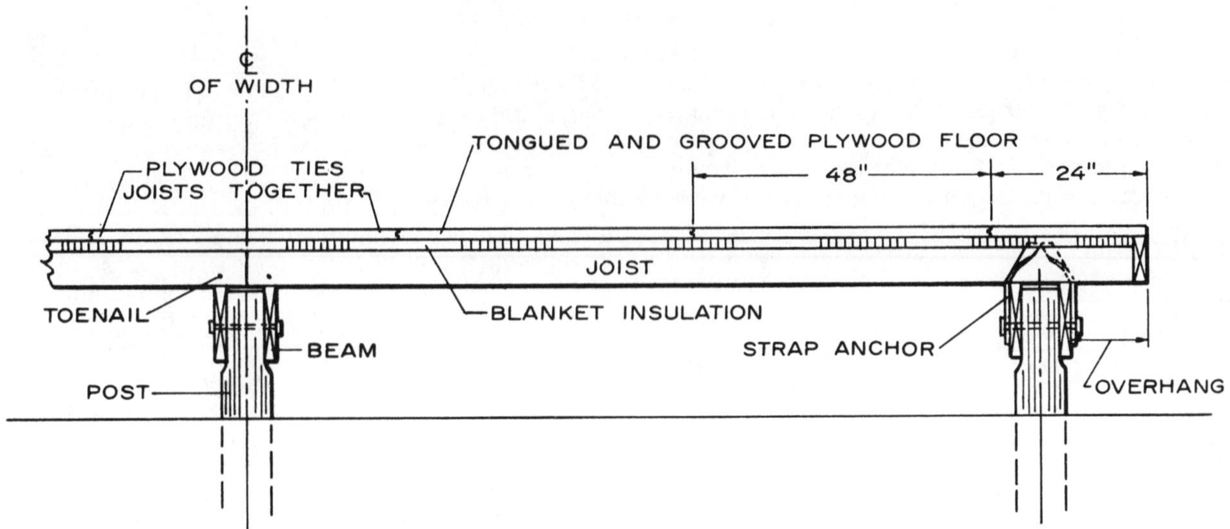

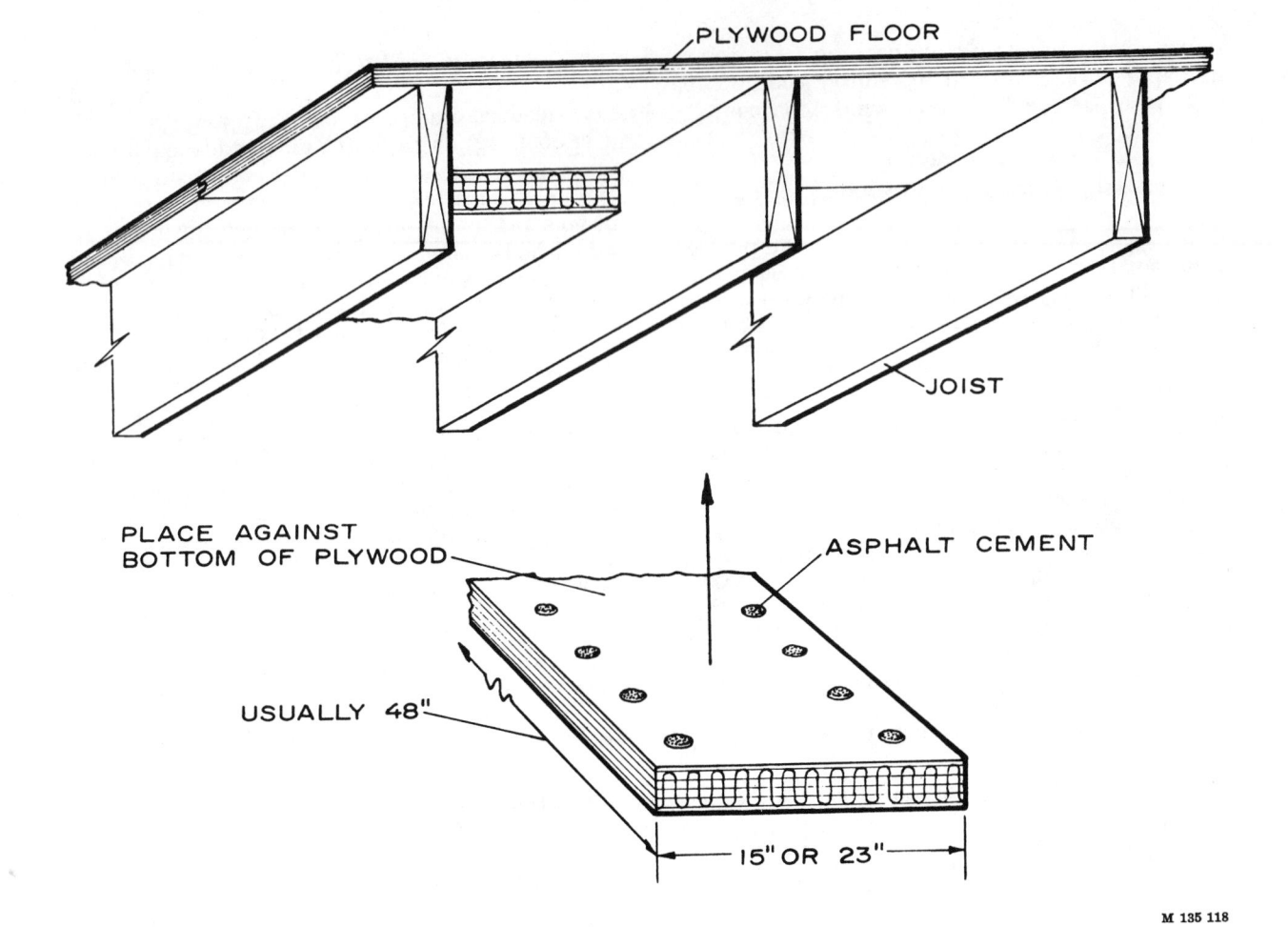

Ȼ
OF WIDTH

PLYWOOD TIES
JOISTS TOGETHER

TONGUED AND GROOVED PLYWOOD FLOOR

48" 24"

JOIST

TOENAIL

BLANKET INSULATION

BEAM

STRAP ANCHOR

POST

OVERHANG

M 135 117

FIGURE 15.—Floor framing details (post foundation).

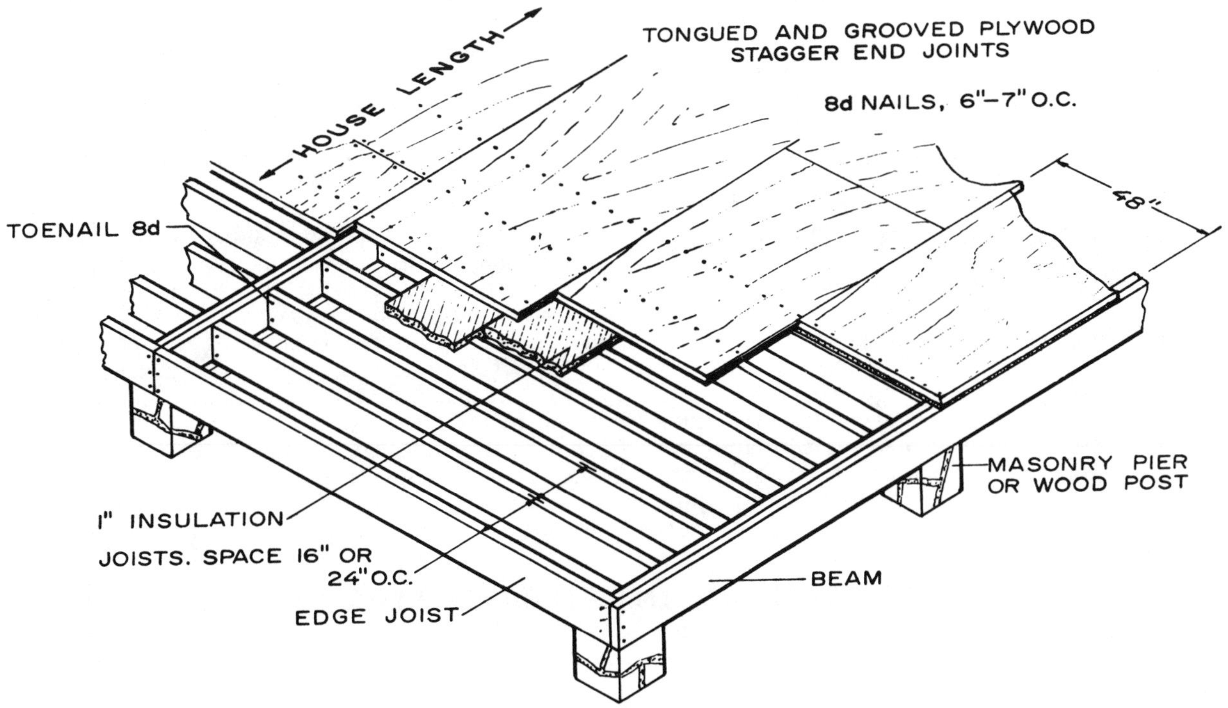

HOUSE LENGTH

TONGUED AND GROOVED PLYWOOD
STAGGER END JOINTS

8d NAILS, 6"-7" O.C.

TOENAIL 8d

48"

MASONRY PIER
OR WOOD POST

1" INSULATION
JOISTS. SPACE 16" OR
24" O.C.

EDGE JOIST

BEAM

M 135 115

FIGURE 16.—Floor framing for edge foundation (masonry piers or wood posts).

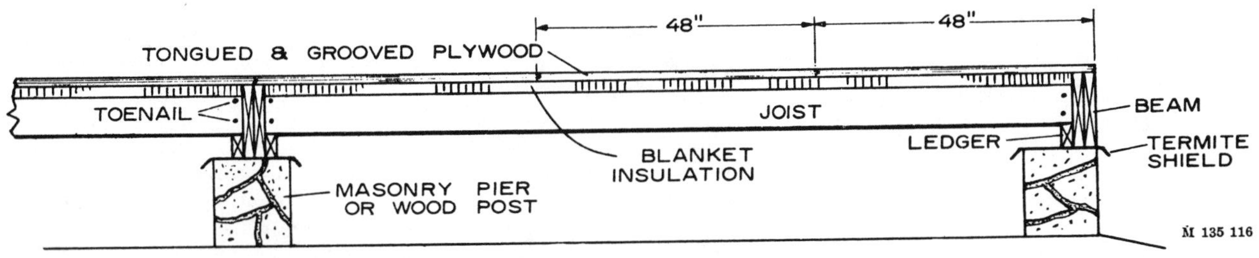

TONGUED & GROOVED PLYWOOD

48" 48"

TOENAIL

JOIST

BEAM

LEDGER

BLANKET
INSULATION

MASONRY PIER
OR WOOD POST

TERMITE
SHIELD

M 135 116

FIGURE 17.—Floor framing details (edge pier foundation).

PLYWOOD FLOOR

JOIST

PLACE AGAINST
BOTTOM OF PLYWOOD

ASPHALT CEMENT

USUALLY 48"

15" OR 23"

M 135 118

FIGURE 18.—Application of friction-fit batt insulation between floor joists.

so that they rest on the ledger strips. Sizes of headers, joists, and other details are shown on the working drawings for each individual house. Toenail each end to the beams with two eightpenny nails on each side (fig. 16). In applying the plywood subfloor to the floor framing, start with full 4-foot-wide sheets rather than the 2-foot-wide pieces used for the side overhang framing (fig. 17). The nail-laminated center beam provides sufficient reinforcing between the ends of joists. Apply the insulation and nail the plywood the same way as outlined in the previous section.

Insulation Between Joists

Thicker floor insulation than the 1-inch blanket is usually required for most houses. This will be indicated in the floor framing details of the working drawings or in the specifications. This type is normally used between the joists. Thus, the subfloor is nailed directly to the joists and the insulation placed between the joists after the subfloor is in place. Friction-fit (or similar insulating batts) 15 inches wide should be used for joists spaced 16 inches on center. Use 23-inch-wide batts for joists spaced 24 inches on center.

Friction-fit batts need little support to keep them in place. Small "dabs" of asphalt roof cement on the upper surfaces when installing against the bottom of the plywood will keep them in place (fig. 18). Standard batts can also be placed in this manner, but somewhat closer spacing of the cement might be required in addition to stapling along the edges. The use of a vapor barrier under the subfloor is important and is described in the section on "Thermal Insulation."

When other types of subfloor are specified, such as diagonal boards, some kind of overlay or finish is usually required. If tongued-and-grooved flooring is applied directly to and across the joists, a tie is normally required at the center butt joints of the floor joists. This is accomplished with a metal strap across the top of the joists or 1- by 4- by 20-inch wood strips (scabs) nailed across the faces of each set of joists at the joint with six eightpenny nails. When plywood subfloor is used, the sheets are centered over the center beam and joist ends to provide this tie for overhang floor framing.

Finally, if the plywood is likely to be exposed for any length of time before enclosing the house, a brush coat (or squeegee application) of water-repellent preservative should be used. This will not only repel moisture but will prevent or minimize any surface degradation.

FRAMED WALL SYSTEMS

Exterior sidewalls, and in some designs an interior wall, normally support most of the roof loads as well as serving as a framework for attaching interior and exterior coverings. When roof trusses spanning the entire width of the house are used, the exterior sidewalls carry both the roof and ceiling loads. Interior partitions then serve mainly as room dividers. When ceiling joists are used, interior partitions usually sustain some of the ceiling loads.

The exterior walls of a wood-frame house normally consist of *studs*, interior and exterior coverings, windows and doors, and insulation. Moisture content of framing members usually should not exceed 19 percent.

The framework for a conventional wall consists of nominal 2- by 4-inch members used as top and bottom *plates*, as studs, and as partial (cripple) studs around openings. Studs are generally cut to lengths for 8-foot walls when subfloor and finish floors are used. This length depends on the thickness and number of wall plates (normally single bottom and double top plates). Studs can often be obtained from lumber dealers in a precut length. Double headers over doors and windows are generally larger than 2 by 4's when the width of the opening is greater than 2½ feet. Two 2- by 6-inch members are used for spans up to 4½ feet and two 2- by 8-inch members for openings from 4½ to about 6½ feet. Headers are normally cut 3 inches (two 1½-inch stud thicknesses) longer than the rough opening width unless the edge of the opening is near a regular spaced stud.

Framing of Sidewalls

The exterior framed walls, when erected, should be flush with the outer edges of the plywood subfloor and floor framing. Thus, the floor can be used both as a layout area and for horizontal assembly of the wall framing. When completed, the entire wall can be raised in place in "tilt-up" fashion, the plates nailed to the floor system, and the wall *plumbed* and braced.

The two exterior sidewalls of the house can be framed first and the exterior end walls later. Cut two sets of plates for the entire length of the house, using 8-, 12-, or 16-foot lengths, staggering the joints. Joints should be made at the centerline of a stud (*on center*). Starting at one end, mark each 16 or 24 inches, depending on the spacing of the studs, and also mark the centerlines for windows, doors, and partitions. These measurements are given on the working drawings. These are cen-terline (*o.c.*) markings, except for the ends. With a small square, mark the location of each stud with a line about ¾ inch on each side of the centerline mark (fig. 19).

Studs can now be cut to the correct length. When a low-slope roof with wood decking (which also serves as a ceiling finish) is used, the stud length for an 8-foot wall height with single plywood flooring should be 95½ inches, less the thickness of three plates. Thus for plates 1½ inches thick, this will mean a stud length of 91 inches. When ceiling joists or trusses are used with the single plywood floor, this length can be about 92⅛ inches. These measurements are primarily to provide for the vertical use of 8-foot lengths of dry-wall sheet materials for the walls with the ceiling finish in place. Cornerposts can be made up beforehand by nailing two short 2- by 4-inch blocks between two studs (fig. 20). Use two twelvepenny nails at each side of each block.

Begin fabrication of the wall by fastening the bottom plate and the first top plate to the ends of each cornerpost and stud (with two sixteen-penny nails) into each member. As studs are nailed in place, provisions should be made for framing the openings for windows and doors (fig. 20). Studs should be located to form the rough openings, the sizes of which vary with the types of windows selected. The rough openings are framed by studs which support the window and door headers or *lintels*. A full-length stud should be located at each side of these framing studs (fig. 21).

The following allowances are usually made for rough opening widths and heights for doors and windows. Half of the given width should be marked on each side of the centerline of the opening, which has previously been marked on top and bottom plates.

A. *Double-hung window (single unit)*
   Rough opening width = glass width *plus* 6 inches
   Rough opening height = total glass height *plus* 10 inches
B. *Casement window (two sash)*
   Rough opening width = total glass width *plus* 11¼ inches
   Rough opening height = total glass height *plus* 6⅜ inches
C. *Exterior doors*
   Rough opening width = width of door *plus* 2½ inches
   Rough opening height = height of door *plus* 3 inches

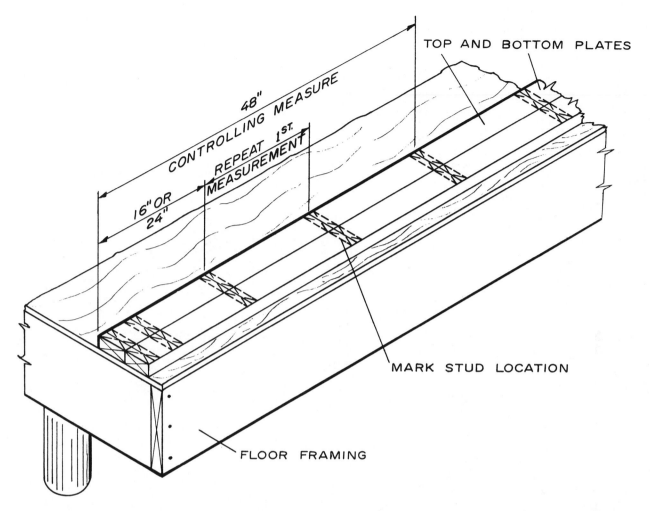

FIGURE 19.—Marking top and bottom plates.

M 135 119

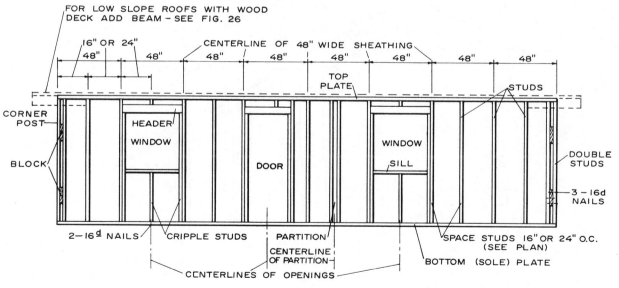

FIGURE 20.—Framing layout of typical wall.

M 135 120

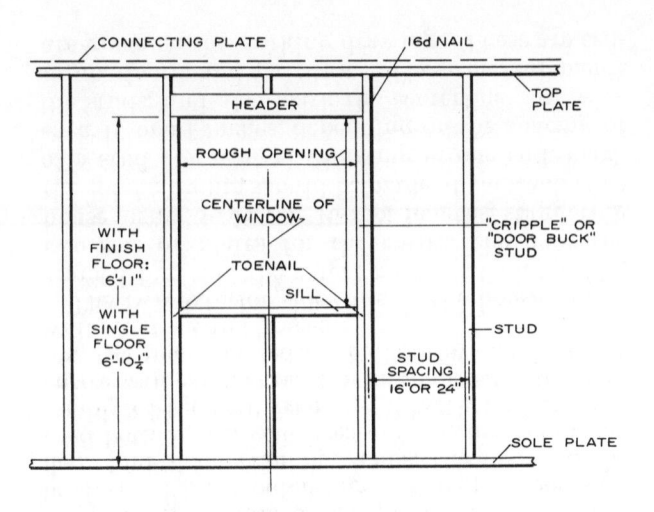

FIGURE 21.—Framing at window opening and height of window and door headers.

Clearances, or rough-opening sizes, for typical double-hung windows, for example, are shown in table 2.

TABLE 2.—*Frame opening sizes for double hung windows*

Window glass size (each sash)		Rough frame opening size	
Width *Inches*	Height *Inches*	Width *Inches*	Height *Inches*
24	16	30	42
28	20	34	50
32	24	38	58
36	24	42	58

The height of the window and door headers above the subfloor when doors are 6 feet 8 inches high and finish floor is used is shown in figure 21. When only resilient title is used over flooring made up of a single layer of material, the framing height for windows and doors should be 6 feet 10¼ inches for 6-foot 8-inch doors. The sizes of the headers should be the same as those previously outlined. Framing is arranged as shown in figure 21. Doubled headers can be fastened in place with two sixteenpenny nails through the stud into each member. Cripple (door *buck*) studs supporting the header on each side of the opening are nailed to the full stud with twelvepenny nails spaced about 16 inches apart and staggered. The sill and other short (cripple) studs are toenailed in place with two eightpenny nails at each side when end-nailing is not possible.

Doubled studs should normally be used on exterior walls where intersecting interior partitions are located. This is often accomplished with spaced studs, (fig. 22*A*) and provides nailing surfaces for interior covering materials. Blocking with 2-by-

4-inch members placed flatwise between studs spaced 4 to 6 inches apart in the exterior wall might also be used to fasten the first partition stud (fig. 22*B*). Blocks should be spaced about 32 inches apart. When a low-slope roof with gable overhang is used with wood decking, a beam extension is required at the top plates (figs. 20 and 26).

Erecting Sidewalls

When the sidewalls are completed, they can be raised in place. Nail several short 1- by 6-inch pieces to the outside of the beam to prevent the wall from sliding past the edge. The bottom plate is fastened to the floor framing with sixteenpenny nails spaced 16 inches apart and staggered when practical. The wall can now be plumbed and temporary bracing added to hold it in place in a true vertical position. Bracing may consist of 1- by 6-inch members nailed to one face of a stud and to a 2 by 4 block which has been nailed to the subfloor. Braces should be at about a 45° angle. If the wall framing is squared and braced, the panel siding or exterior covering can be fastened to the studs while the walls are still on the subfloor. In addition, window frames can be installed before erection of the wall. These processes are covered in following sections on "Exterior Wall Coverings" and "Exterior Frames."

End Walls—Moderate-Slope Roof

The exterior end walls for a gable-roofed house may be assembled on the floor in the same general manner as the sidewalls with a bottom plate and single top plate. However, the total length of the wall should be the exact distance between the inside of the exterior sidewalls already erected. Furthermore, only one end stud is used rather than the doubled cornerposts (fig. 23). Window and door openings are framed as outlined for the exterior sidewalls. When 48-inch-wide panel siding is used for the exterior, serving both as sheathing and siding, for example, the stud spacing should conform to the type of covering used. The center of the second stud in this wall should be 16 or 24 inches from the outside of the panel-siding material (fig. 24). This method of spacing should be used from each corner toward the center, and any adjustments required because of sheet-material width should be made at a center window or door.

End walls are erected in the same manner as the sidewalls with the bottom plate fastened to the floor framing. These walls also must be plumbed and braced. The end studs should be nailed at each side to the cornerposts with sixteenpenny nails spaced 16 inches apart. The upper top plate is added and extends across the sidewall plate (fig. 23).

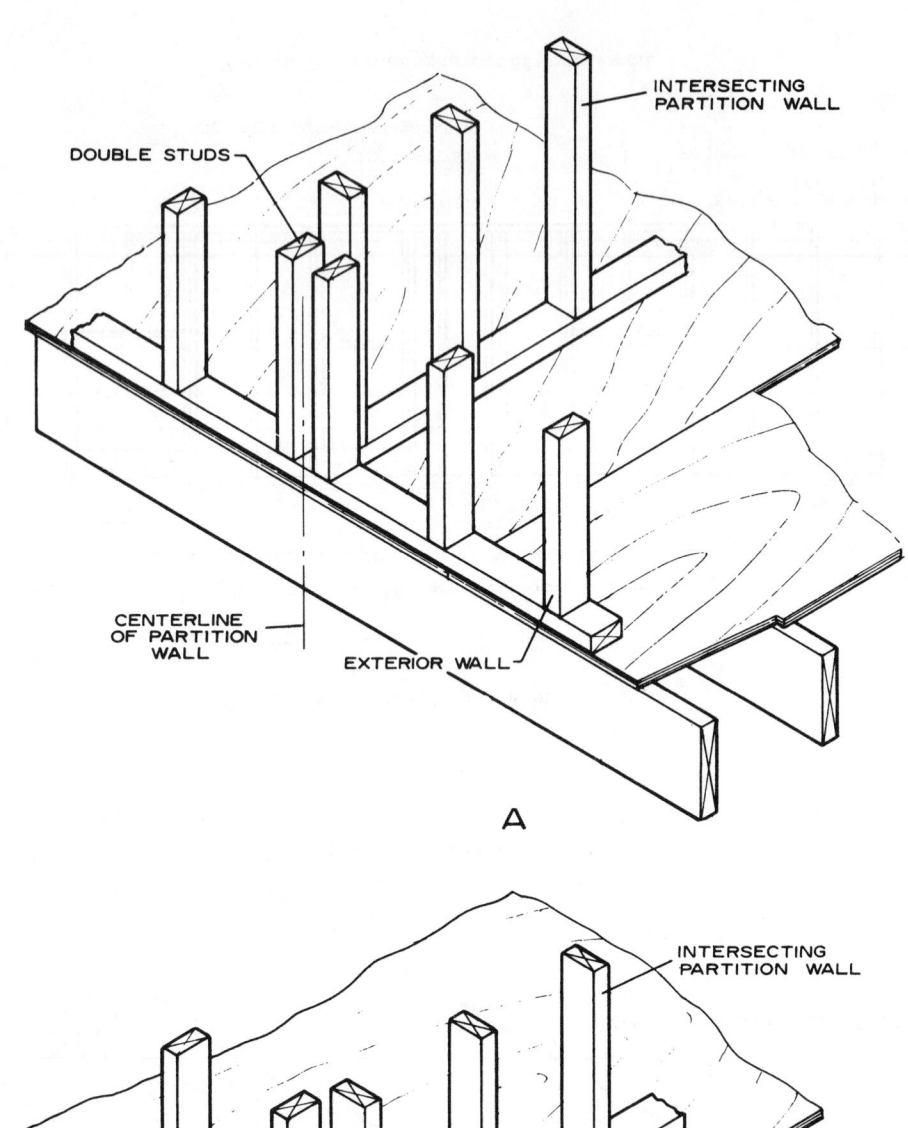

FIGURE 22.—Intersecting walls. *A*, Double studs; *B*, blocking between studs.

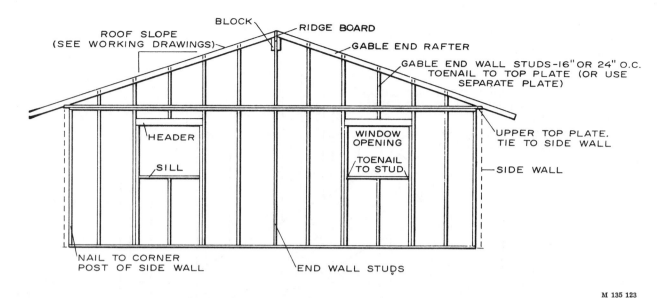

FIGURE 23.—End wall framing for regular slope roof (for trusses or rafter-type).

M 135 123

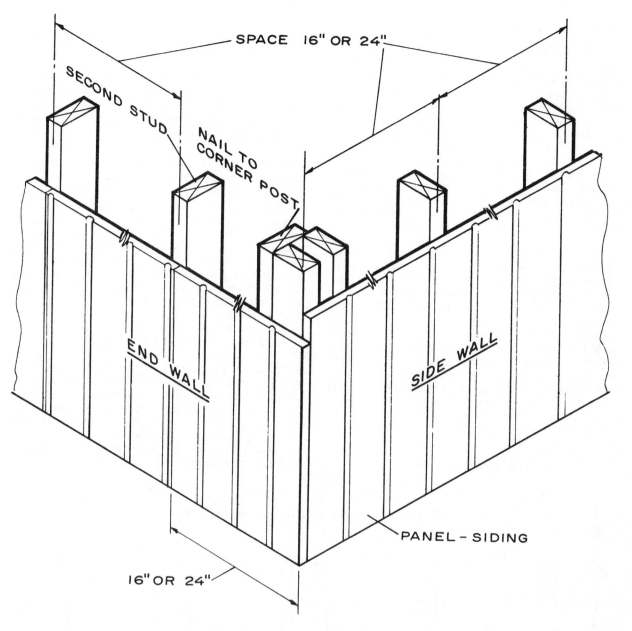

FIGURE 24.—Exterior side and end wall intersection.

M 135 124

The framing for the gable-end portion of the wall is often done separtely (fig. 23). Studs may be toenailed to the upper top wall plate, or an extra 2- by 6-inch bottom plate can be used, which provides a nailing surface for ceiling material in the rooms below. The top members of the gable wall are not plates; they are rafters which form the slope of the roof. Studs are notched to fit or may be used flatwise. Use the roof slope specified in the working drawings.

End Walls—Low-Slope Roof

End walls for a low-slope roof are normally constructed with *balloon framing*. In this design, the studs are full length from the bottom plate to the top or rafter plates which follow the roof slope (fig. 25). The stud spacing and framing for windows are the same as previously outlined. The top surface of the upper plate of the end wall should be in line with the outer edge of the upper top plate of the sidewall (fig. 26). Thus, when the roof decking is applied, bearing and nailing surfaces are provided at end and sidewalls. A beam extension beyond the end wall is provided to support the wood decking when a *gable*-end overhang is desired. This can be a 4- by 6-inch member which is fastened to the second sidewall stud (fig. 26).

The lower top plate of the end wall is nailed to the end of the studs before the upper top plate is fastened in place. For attaching the upper plate, use sixteenpenny nails spaced 16 inches apart and staggered. Two nails are used over the cornerposts of the sidewalls (fig. 26).

To provide for a center *ridge* beam which supports the wood decking inside the house, the area should be framed (fig. 27). After the beam is in place, twelvepenny nails are used through the stud on each side of the beam. The size of the ridge beam is shown on the working plans for each house which is constructed using this method. When decking is used for a gable overhang, the beam extends beyond the end walls.

Interior Walls

Interior walls in conventional construction (with ceiling joists and rafters) are erected in the same manner and at the same height as the outside walls. In general, assembly of interior stud walls is the same as outlined for exterior walls. The center load-bearing partition should be located so that ceiling joists require little or no wasteful cutting. Cross partitions are usually not load-bearing and can be spaced as required for room sizes. These spacings and other details are covered in the working drawing floor plan.

Studs should be spaced according to the type of interior covering material to be used. When studs are spaced 24 inches on center, the thickness of gypsum board, for example, must be ½ inch or greater. For 16-inch stud spacing, a thickness of ⅜ inch or greater can be used. Details of a typical intersection of interior walls are shown in figure 28. Load-bearing partitions should be constructed with nominal 2- by 4-inch studs, but 2- by 3-inch studs may be used for nonload-bearing walls. Doorway openings can also be framed with a single member on each side in nonload-bearing walls (fig. 28). Single top plates are commonly used on nonload-bearing interior partitions.

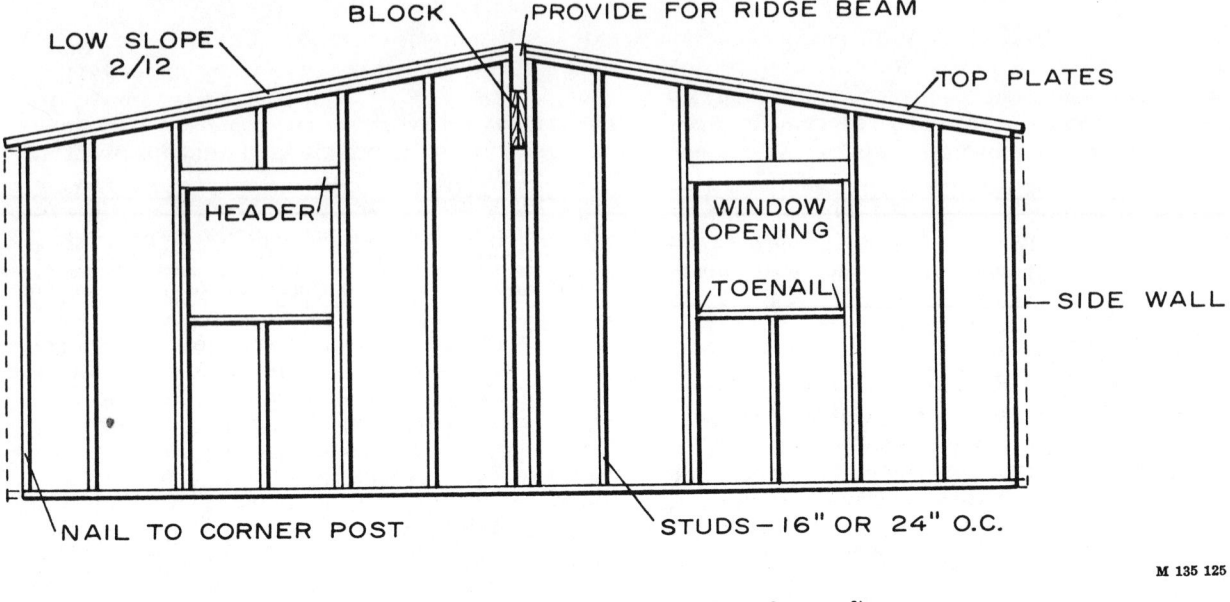

FIGURE 25.—Framing for end wall (low-slope roof).

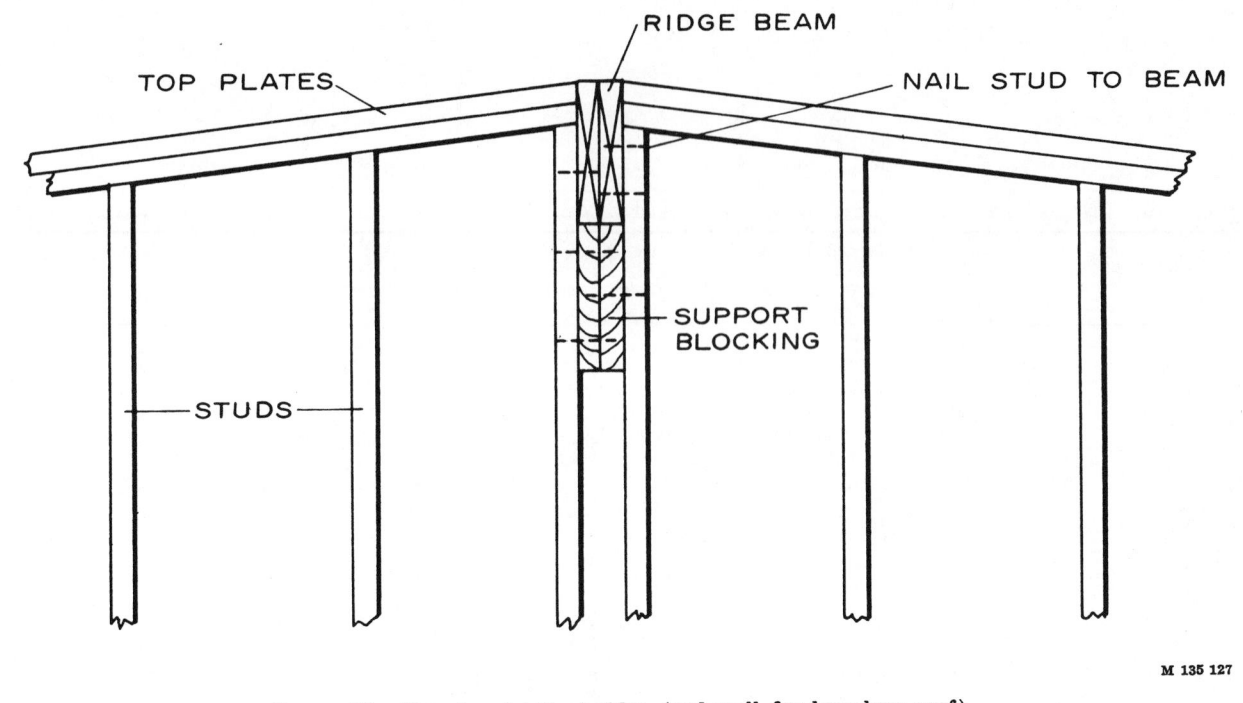

FIGURE 27.—Framing detail at ridge (end wall for low-slope roof).

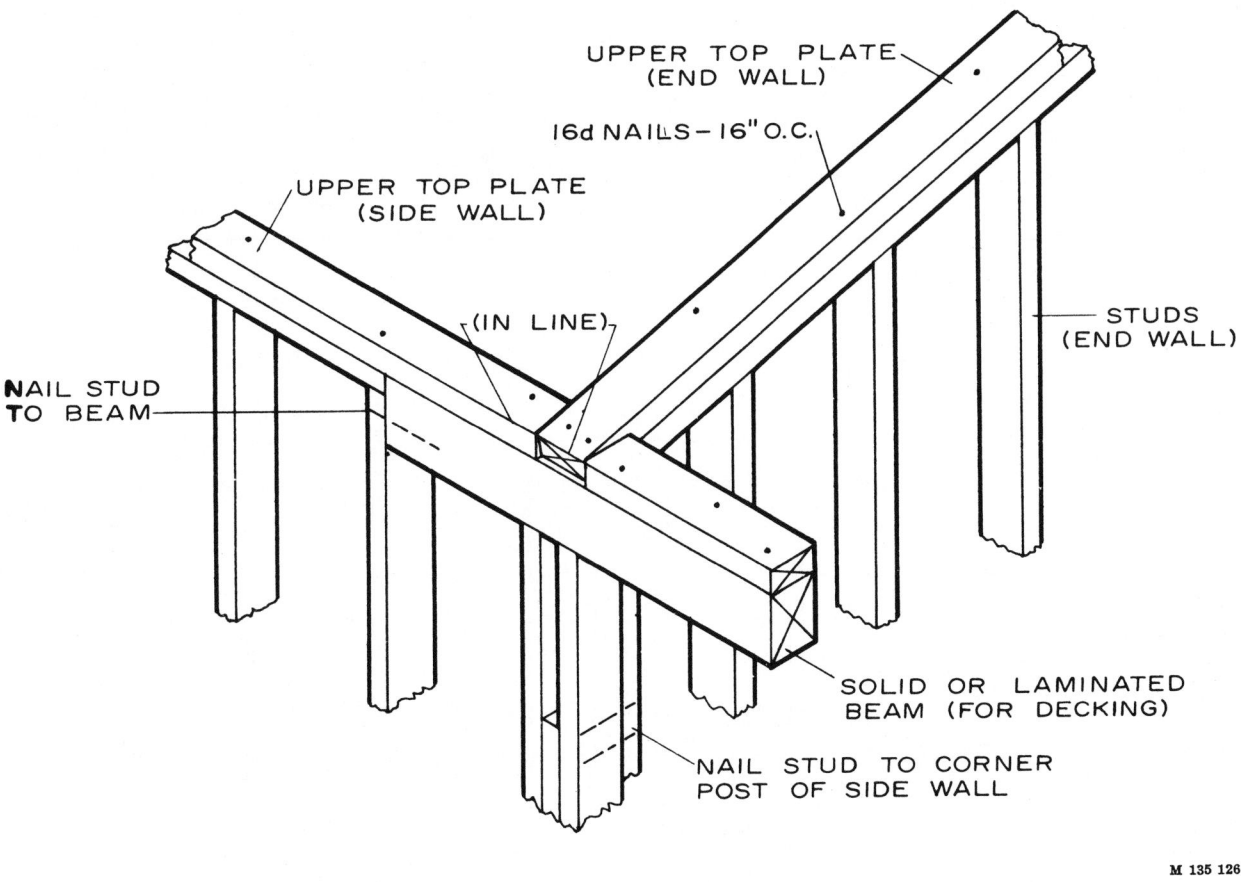

FIGURE 26.—Corner detail for low-slope roof with wood decking.

Roof trusses require no load-bearing interior partitions, so location of the walls and size and spacing of studs are determined by the house design and by the type of interior finish. The bottom chords of the trusses are often used to tie in with crossing partitions where required. Details of stud location at the intersection of an interior partition with an exterior wall are shown in figure 22 *A* and *B*.

When a low-slope roof is used with wood decking, a full-height wall or a ridge beam is required for support at the center (fig. 29). The ridge beam may span from an interior center partition to an outside wall, forming a clear open area beneath. Cross or intersecting walls are full height with a sloping top plate. In such designs, one method uses the following sequence: (a) Erect exterior walls, center wall, and ridge beam; (b) apply roof decking; and (c) install other partition walls. Size and spacing of the studs in the cross walls are usually based on the thickness of the covering material, as no roof load is imposed on them. These spacings and sizes are part of the working drawings.

The upper top plates (connecting plates) are used to tie the wall framing together at corners, at intersections, and at crossing walls. The upper plate crosses and is nailed to the plate below (figs. 26 and 28). Two sixteenpenny nails are used at each intersection. The remainder of the upper top plate is nailed to the lower top plate with sixteenpenny nails spaced 16 inches apart in a staggered pattern.

ROOF SYSTEMS

The primary function of a roof is to provide protection to the house in all types of weather with a minimum of maintenance. A second consideration is appearance; a roof should add to the attractiveness of the home, as well as being practical. Happily, a roof with a wide overhang at the cornice and the gable ends not only enhances appearance, but provides protection to side and end walls. Thus, even in lower cost houses, when the style and design permit, wide overhangs are desirable. Though they add slightly to the initial cost, savings in future maintenance usually merit this type of roof extension. Wood members used for roof framing should normally not exceed 19 percent moisture content.

As briefly described in the section on "Major House Parts," the two types of roofs commonly used for houses are (a) the low-slope and (b) the *pitched* roof. The flat or low-slope roof combines ceiling and roof elements as one system, which allows them to serve as interior finish, or as a fastening surface for finish, and as an outer surface for application of the roofing. The structural elements are arranged in several ways by the use of ceiling beams or thick roof decking, which spans from the exterior walls to a ridge beam or center bearing partition. Roof slope is usually designated as some ratio of 12. For example, a "4 in 12" roof slope has a 4-foot vertical rise for each 12 feet of horizontal distance.

The pitched roof, usually in slopes of 4 in 12 and

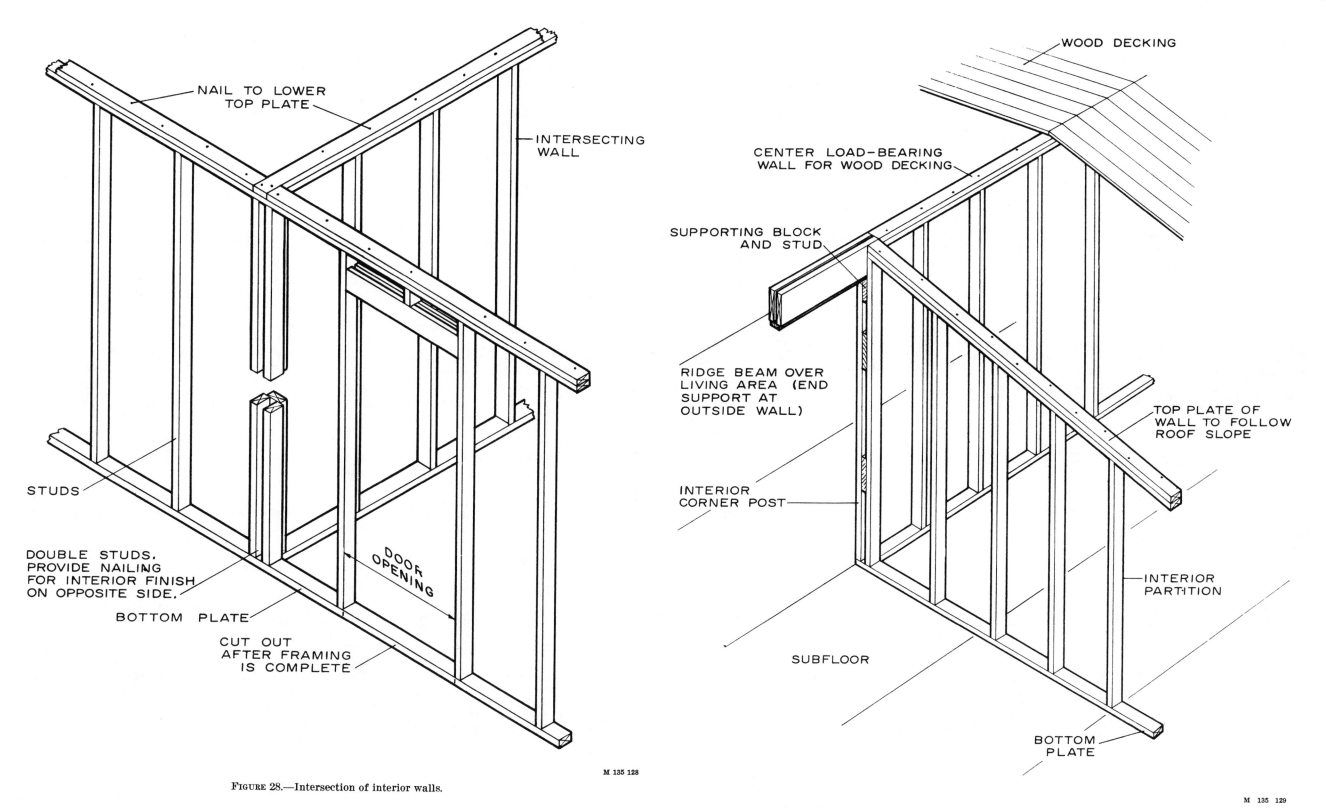

NAIL TO LOWER
TOP PLATE

INTERSECTING
WALL

STUDS

DOUBLE STUDS.
PROVIDE NAILING
FOR INTERIOR FINISH
ON OPPOSITE SIDE.

BOTTOM PLATE

DOOR OPENING

CUT OUT
AFTER FRAMING
IS COMPLETE

M 135 128

FIGURE 28.—Intersection of interior walls.

WOOD DECKING

CENTER LOAD-BEARING
WALL FOR WOOD DECKING

SUPPORTING BLOCK
AND STUD

RIDGE BEAM OVER
LIVING AREA (END
SUPPORT AT
OUTSIDE WALL)

INTERIOR
CORNER POST

TOP PLATE OF
WALL TO FOLLOW
ROOF SLOPE

INTERIOR
PARTITION

SUBFLOOR

BOTTOM
PLATE

M 135 129

FIGURE 29.—Ridge beam and center wall for low-slope roof.

greater, has structural elements in the form of (a) *rafters* and joists or (b) trusses (trussed rafters). Both systems require some type of interior ceiling finish, as well as roof sheathing. With slopes of 8 in 12 and greater, it is possible to include several bedrooms on the second floor when provisions are made for floor loads, a stairway, and windows.

Low-Slope Ceiling Beam Roof

One of the framing systems for a low-slope roof consists of spaced rafters (beams or *girders*) which span from the exterior sidewalls to a ridge beam or a center load-bearing wall. The rafter can be doubled, spaced 4 feet apart, and exposed in the room below providing a pleasing beamed ceiling effect. *Dressed and matched* V-groove boards can be used for roof sheathing and exposed to the room below. When plywood or other unfinished sheathing is used, a ceiling tile or other prefinished wallboard can be fastened to the undersurface. Such materials also serve as insulation. Thus, a very attractive ceiling can be provided using a light color for the ceiling and a contrasting stain on the beams. This type of framing can be varied by spacing single rafters on 16- or 24-inch centers. Separate covering materials would normally be used for the roof sheathing and for the ceiling, with flexible insulation between.

The size and spacing details for ceiling beams are shown on the working drawings for each house design. For example, when beams are doubled, spaced 48 inches apart, and the distance from outer wall to interior wall is about 11½ feet, two 2- by 8-inch members are satisfactory for most of the construction species such as Douglas-fir, southern pine, and hemlock. Use of some wood species, such as the soft pines, will require two 2- by 10-inch members for 48-inch spacing. When a spacing of 32 inches is desirable for appearance, two 2- by 6-inch members of the second grade of Douglas-fir or southern pine are satisfactory. In some of the species, such as southern pine and Douglas-fir, a solid 4- by 6-inch member provides sufficient strength for 48-inch spacing over an 11½-foot span.

The details of fastening and anchoring these structural members to the wall elements can vary somewhat. Variations from the details included in this manual are shown on the working drawings for each individual house.

Construction.—We will assume that the details in the working plans specify doubled 2- by 8-inch ceiling beams spaced 48 inches on center. When the beams do not extend beyond the wall, a lookout member is required for the *cornice* overhang. The center wall or ridge beam is in place, so the roof slope, which may vary between 1½ in 12 to

2½ in 12, has been established. As previously outlined in the section on wall systems, the ceiling beams should normally be erected before cross walls are established. Thus, the exterior sidewalls and the load-bearing center wall, all well braced and plumbed, are all that is required to erect the ceiling beams.

There are several methods in which the beams are supported at the center bearing wall or ridge beam: (a) By a 2- by 3-inch block fastened to the stud wall; (b) by a metal joist hanger; and (c) by notching the beam ends and fastening to the stud. The first two may be used for either a stud wall or a ridge beam. Fastening at the outside wall is generally the same for all three methods.

The first or sample beam can now be cut to serve as a pattern in cutting the remainder of the members. Figure 30*A* shows the location of the ceiling beam with respect to the exterior and load-bearing center walls. When beams themselves do not serve as roof extensions, they can be assembled by nailing a 2- by 6-inch *lookout* (roof extension) at the outer wall and a 2- by 4-inch spacer block at the interior center wall (fig. 30*B*). Use two twelvepenny nails on each side of the block and twelvepenny nails spaced 6 inches apart for the 2- by 6-inch lookout member. When a block nailed to the stud is used to support the interior beam end, the ends should be notched (fig. 30*C*).

Details at center wall or beam.—The first system of connecting the inside end of the ceiling beam is most adaptable to ridge-beam construction. It consists of fastening a nominal 2- by 3-inch block to the beam with 4½-inch lag screws (fig. 31*A*). The 2 by 3 should be the same depth as the ceiling beam. The beam ends are then bolted to the 2- by 3-inch block with ⅜- by 5-inch carriage bolts.

Using joist hangers (fig. 31*B*) to fasten the inside end of the ceiling beams is another method most adaptable to a ridge-beam system. Hangers are fastened to the ridge-beam face, the ceiling beams dropped in place, and the hangers nailed to the beams. Eight- or tenpenny nails are commonly used for nailing. Hangers will be exposed, but can be painted to match the color of the beams.

A third method which can be used at a center bearing wall includes notching the ends of the ceiling beams (figs. 30*C* and 31*C*). When the beam is in place, it is face-nailed to the stud at each side with two twelvepenny nails. Short 2- by 4-inch support blocks are then nailed at each side of the stud with twelvepenny nails (fig. 31*C*).

When solid 4- by 6-inch or larger members are used as ceiling beams in place of the doubled members, the joist hanger is probably the most suitable method of supporting the inside ends of the beams. If the solid or laminated beams are to be stained, care should be taken to prevent hammer marks.

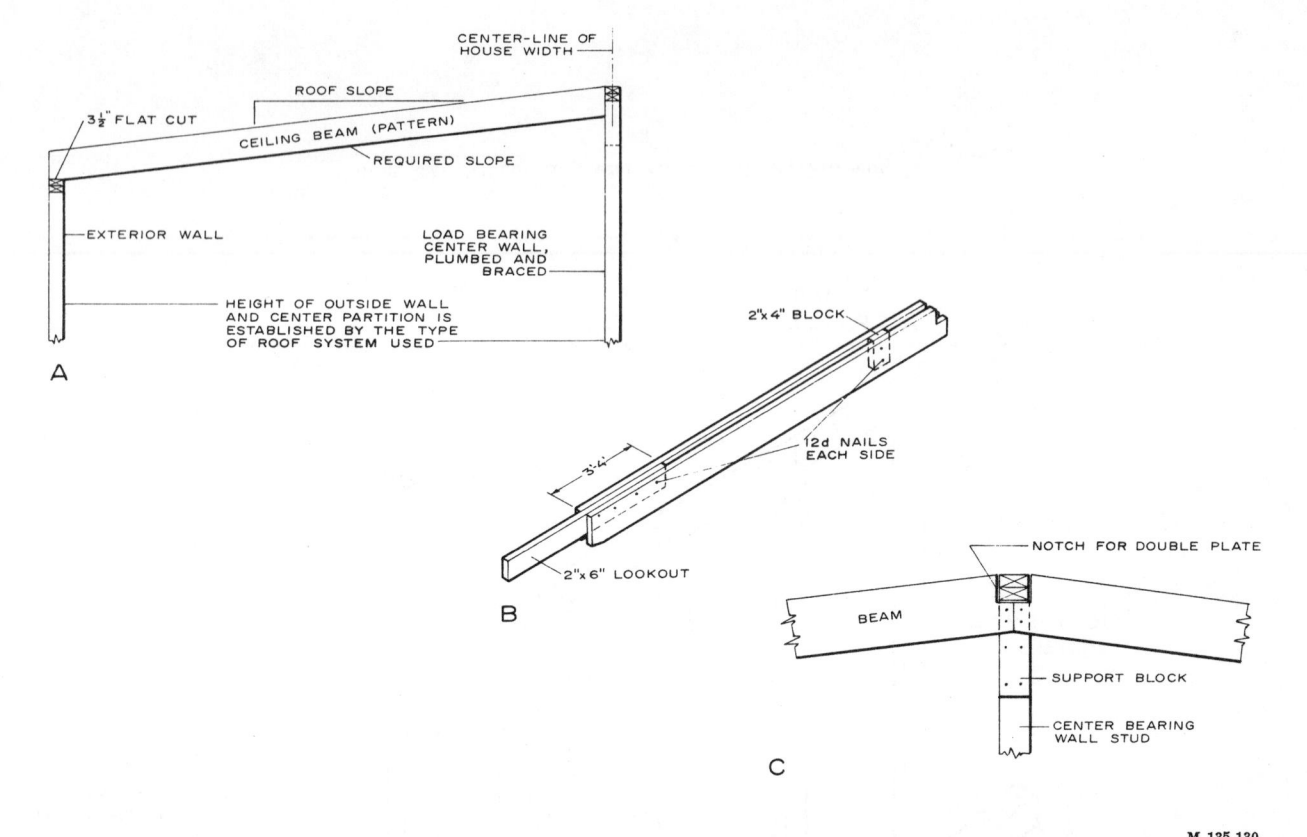

FIGURE 30.—Ceiling beam location and support methods. *A*, Lay out of typical beam; *B*, assembly of beam with roof extension (lookout); *C*, notch for stud support at center bearing wall.

Nailing ceiling beams at exterior walls.—The ceiling beams are normally fastened to the top plate of the outside walls by nailing. In windy areas, some type of strapping or metal bracket is often desirable (fig. 41*B*). The ceiling beams are toenailed to the top of the outside wall with two eightpenny nails at each side and a tenpenny nail at the ends (fig. 32). To provide nailing for panel siding and interior finish, 2- by 4-inch nailing blocks are fastened between the ceiling beams (fig. 32). Toenail with eightpenny nails at each edge and face.

Roof sheathing.—Ceiling beams and roof extensions are now in place and ready for installation of the roof sheathing. Roof sheathing can consist of 1- by 6-inch tongued-and-grooved V-groove) lumber with 25⁄32-inch fiberboard nailed over the top for insulation. Use two eightpenny nails for each board at each ceiling beam. The insulation fiberboard can be nailed in place with 1¼-inch roofing nails spaced 10 inches apart in rows 24 inches on center. Cross sections of the completed wall and roof framing are shown in figures 33 *A* and *B*. A nominal 1-inch member about 4¾ inches wide may be used to case the undersides of the beams.

A gable-end extension of 16 inches or less can

be supported by extending the dressed and matched V-edge roof boards (fig. 34*A*). A 2- by 2-inch or larger member (*fly rafter*) is nailed to the underside of the boards and serves to fasten the facia board and molding (fig. 34*B*). The V-groove of the underside of the 1 by 6 roof sheathing serves as a decorative surface.

Rafter-Joist Roof

Another type of construction for low-slope roofs similar to the ceiling beam framing is the rafter-joist roof, in which the members are spaced 16 or 24 inches apart and serve both as rafters and ceiling joists (fig. 35 *A* and *B*). Members may be 2 by 8 or 2 by 10 inches in size. Specific sizes are shown on the working drawings for each house plan. The space between joists is insulated, allowing space for a ventilating *airway*. Gypsum board or other types of interior finish can be nailed directly to the bottoms of the joists.

Rafter extensions can serve as nailing surfaces for the *soffit* of a closed cornice (fig. 35*A*). When an open cornice is used, a nailing block is required over the wallplates and between rafters for the siding or *frieze* board.

The inside ends of the rafter-joists bear on an

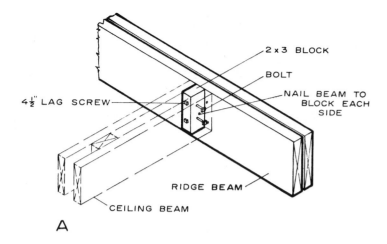

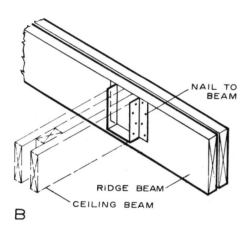

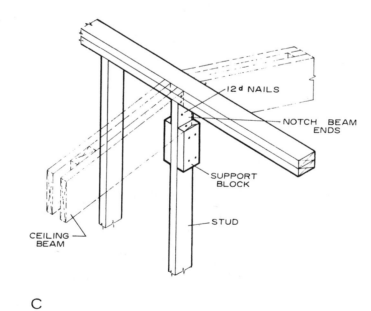

FIGURE 31.—Beam connection to ridge-beam or load-bearing wall. *A*, Block support; *B*, joist hanger; *C*, stud support block.

M 135 131

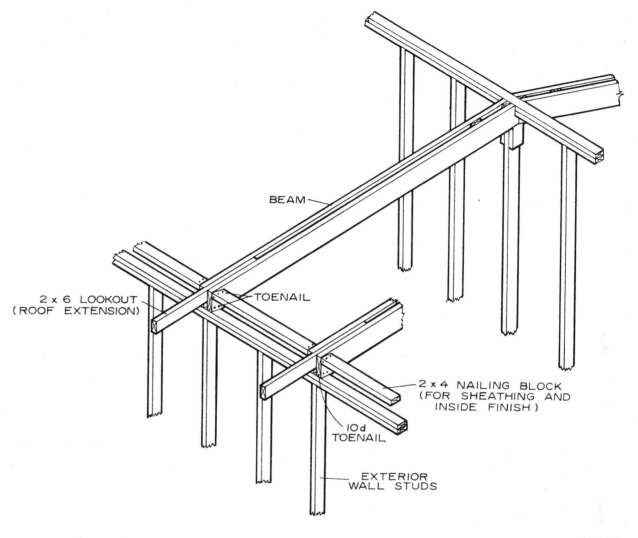

M 135 132

FIGURE 32.—Fastening ceiling beams at exterior walls.

interior load-bearing wall (fig. 35*B*). Beams are toenailed to the plate with eightpenny nails on each side. A 1- by 4-inch wood or ⅜-inch plywood *scab* is used to connect opposite rafter-joists. This fastens the joists together and serves as a positive tie between the exterior sidewalls.

Low-Slope Wood-Deck Roof

A simple method of covering low-slope roofs is with wood decking. Decking should be strong enough to span from the interior center wall or beam to the exterior wall. Decking can also extend beyond the wall to form an overhang at the *eave* line (fig. 36*A*). This system requires dressed and matched nominal 2- by 6-inch southern pine or Douglas-fir decking or 3- by 6-inch solid or laminated decking (cedar or similar species) for spans

of about 12 feet. The proper sizes are shown in the working drawings. While this system requires more material than the beam and sheathing system, the labor involved at the building site is usually much less.

When gable-end extension is desired, some type of support is required beyond the end wall line at plate and ridge. This is usually accomplished by the projection of a small beam at the top plate of each sidewall (figs. 20 and 26) and at the ridge. Often the extension of the double top plate of the sidewall is sufficient. Depending on the type and thickness, the decking must sometimes be in one full-length piece without joints unless there are intermediate supports in the form of an interior partition. When such an interior wall is present, a butt joint can be made over its center. The working drawings cover these various details.

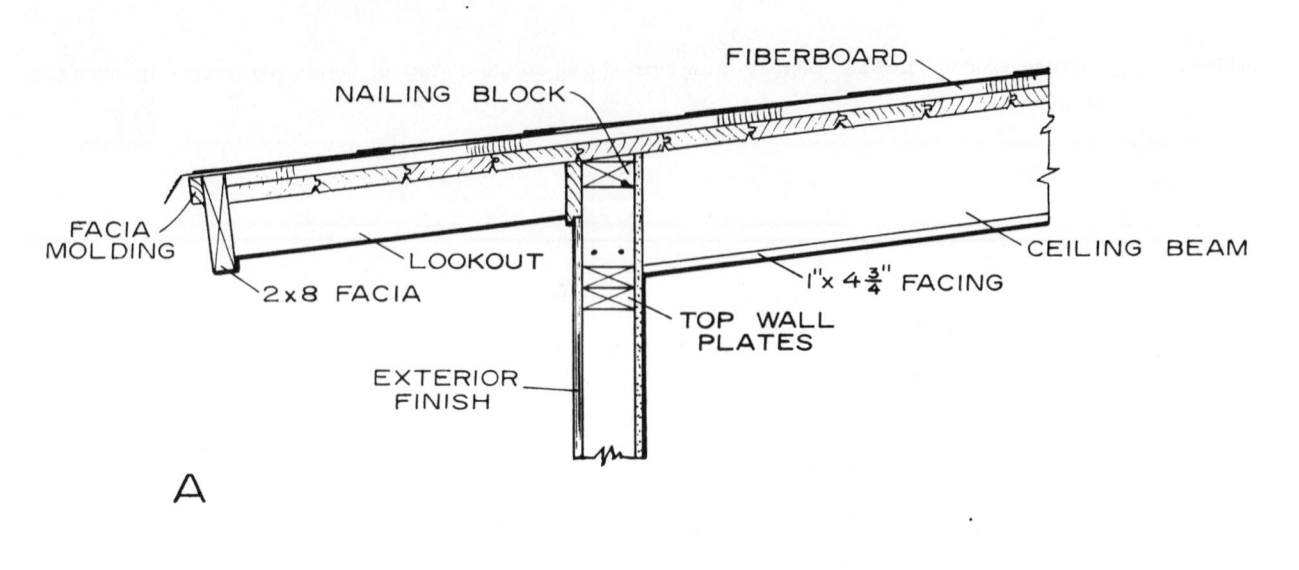

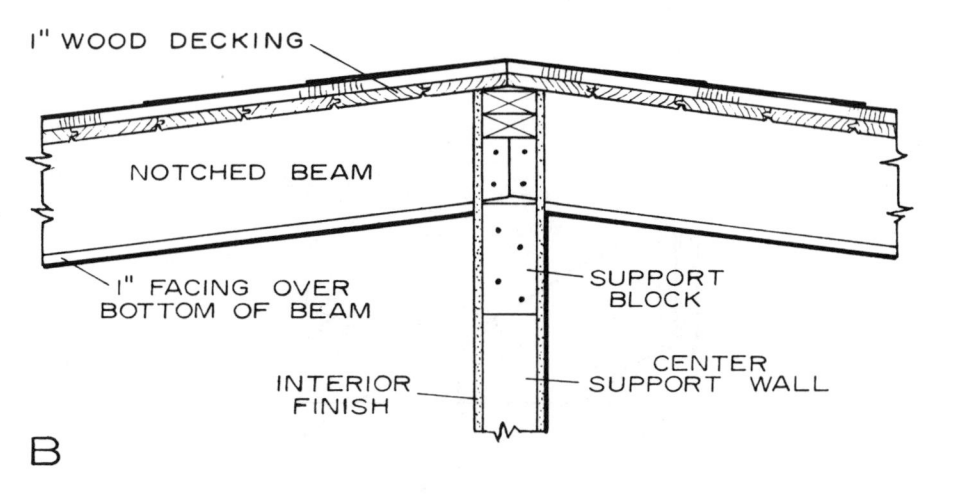

FIGURE 33.—Cross sections of completed walls and roof framing. A, Section through exterior wall; B, section through center wall.

M 135 133

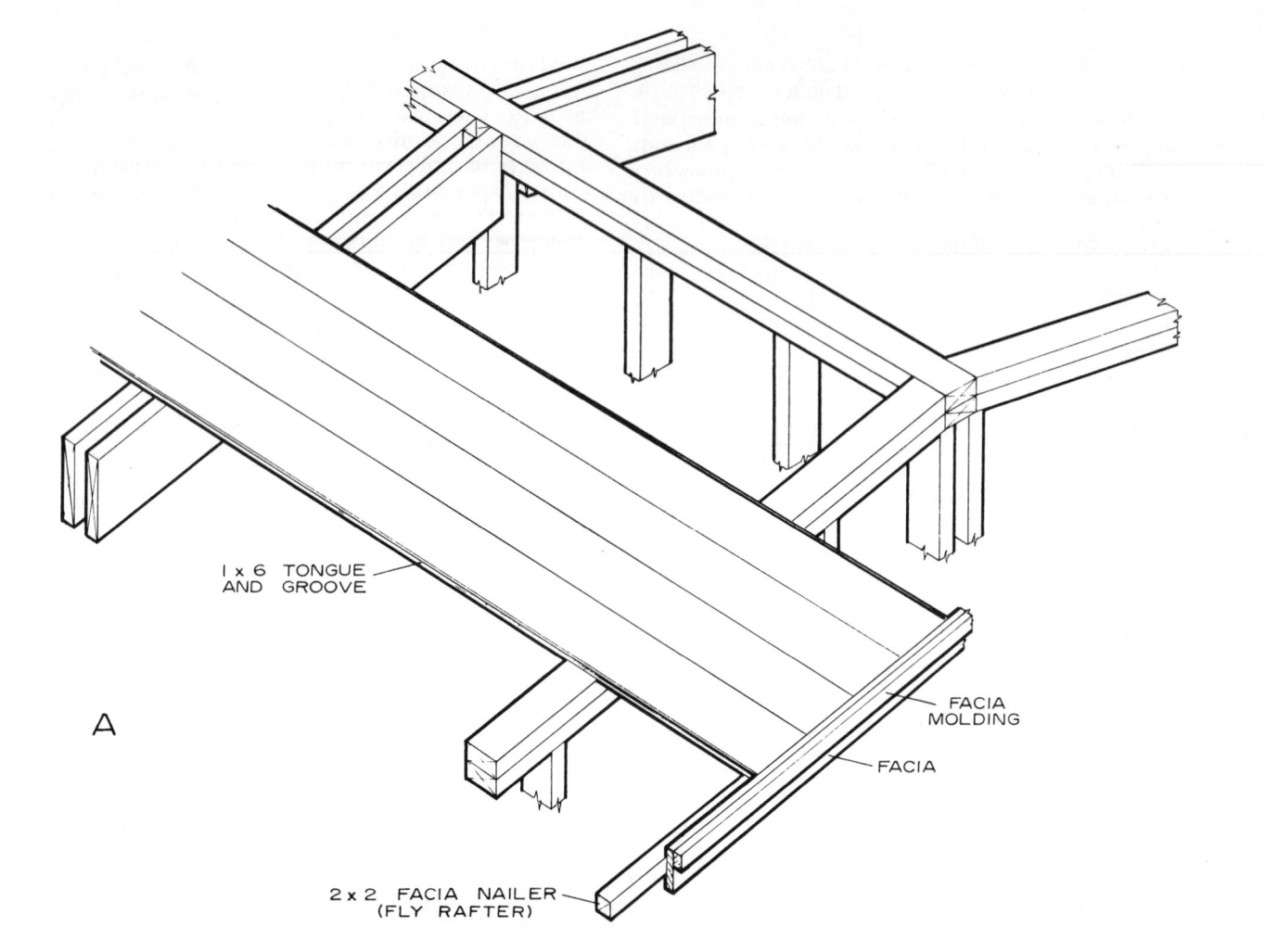

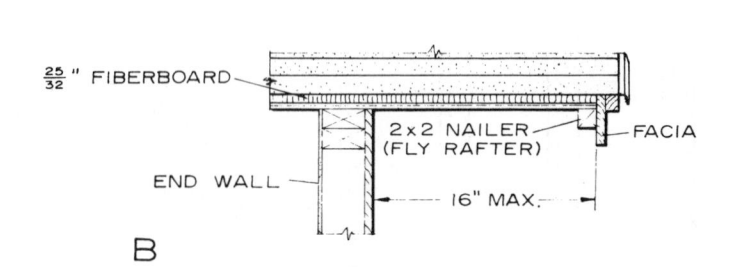

FIGURE 34.—Gable-end extension detail. A, Gable extension; B, fly rafter.

M 135 134

Figure 36 shows the method of applying wood decking. This type of wood decking usually has a decorative V-edge face which should be placed down. Often a light-colored stain or other finish is applied to the wood decking before it is installed. Prefinished members can also be obtained. Each 2- by 6-inch decking member is face-nailed to the ridge beam or center wall and to the top plates of the exterior wall with two sixteenpenny ring-shank nails (fig. 36A). In addition, sixpenny finish nails should be toenailed along each joint on 2- to 3-foot centers (fig. 36B). A 40° angle or less should be used so that the nail point does not penetrate the underside. Nailheads should be driven flush with the surface.

When nominal 3- by 6-inch decking in solid or laminated form is required, it is face-nailed with two twentypenny ring-shank nails at center and outside wall supports. Solid 3- by 6-inch decking usually has a double tongue and groove and is provided with holes between the tongues for horizontal edge nailing (fig. 36C). This edge nailing is done with 7- or 8-inch-long ring-shank nails, often furnished by manufacturers of the decking. Laminated decking can be nailed along the lengthwise joints with sixpenny nails through the groove and tongue. Space nails about 24 inches apart.

Decking support at the load-bearing center wall and at the ends of the sidewalls may also be provided by an extension of the top plates (fig. 37).

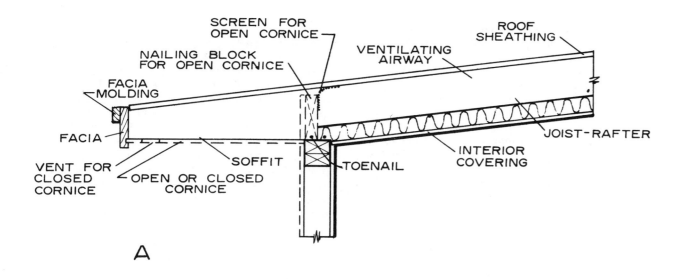

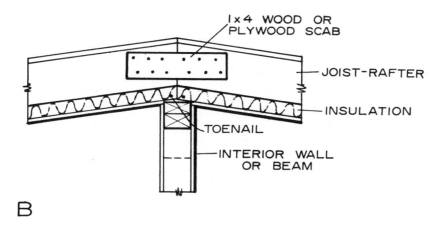

FIGURE 35.—Rafter-joist construction. *A*, Detail at exterior wall; *B*, detail at interior wall.

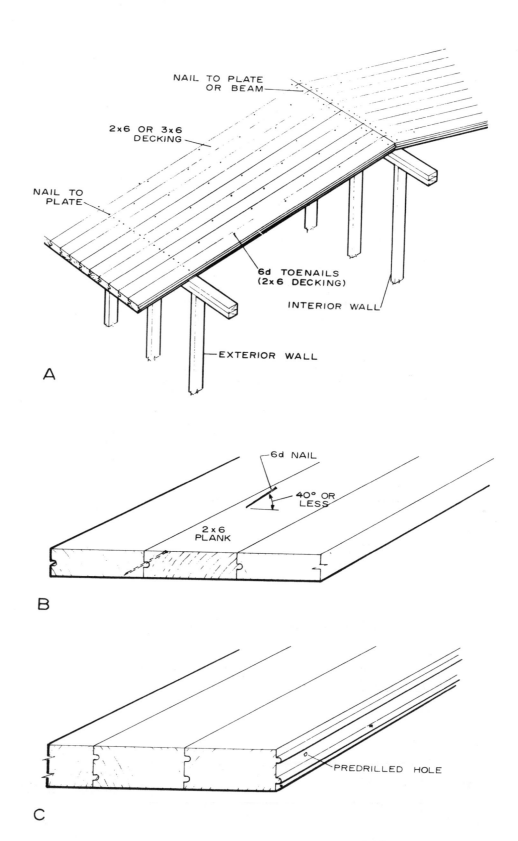

FIGURE 36.—Wood-deck construction. *A*, Installing wood decking; *B*, toenailing horizontal joint; *C*, edge nailing 3- by 6-inch solid decking.

The sides of the members can be faced later, if desired, with the same material used for siding or with 1- by 6- and 1- by 8-inch members.

Insulation for Low-Slope Roofs

It is somewhat more difficult and costly to provide the low-slope roof with a great amount of insulation, except when the rafter-joist system is used with both interior and exterior covering. However, in the colder northern areas of the country and even in the Central States, some type of insulation is required over the roof in addition to the 2- or 3-inch-thick wood decking. This is usually accomplished at a low cost by the use of (a) 25/32-inch insulating board sheathing placed over the wood decking, (b) ½-inch insulation board or tile used on the underside, or (c) a combination of both materials. The use of an expanded foam insulation, such as polystyrene, in sheet form as a base for the ½-inch insulation board or tile on the underside of the decking will provide increased resistance to heat loss.

The "U" [5] value of a wall or roof is a measure

[5] "U" is the amount of heat, expressed in British thermal units, transmitted in 1 hour through 1 square foot of surface per 1° F. difference in temperature between the inside and outside air.

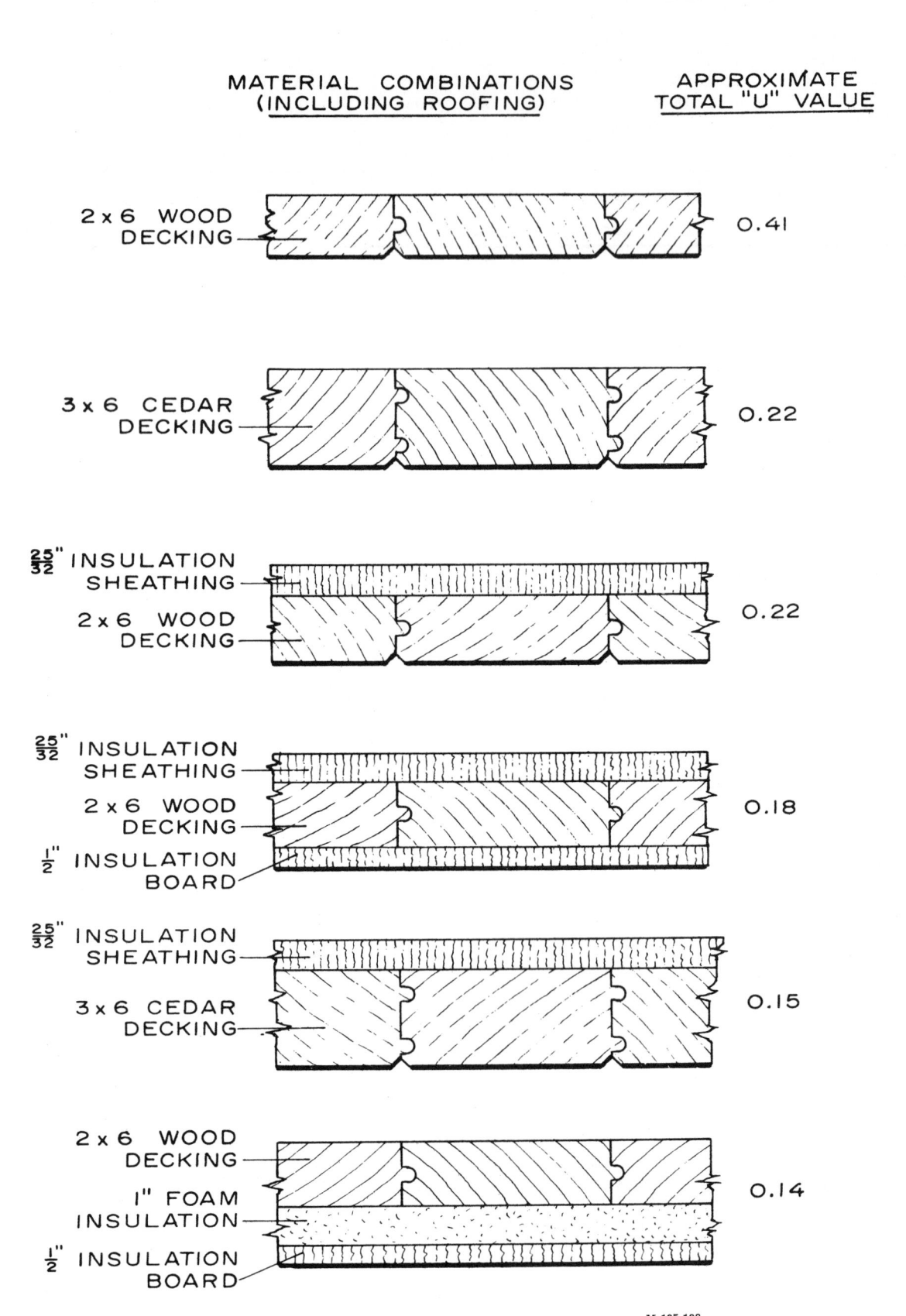

FIGURE 37.—Extension of wallplate for decking support.

of heat loss or gain, and the lower the figure is, the better the insulating value. In areas with mild winters, the use of the 2- by 6- or 3- by 6-inch decking alone should be sufficient. In moderate temperature areas, the use of the 3- by 6-inch cedar or similar decking alone, or the 2- by 6-inch decking with a cover of 25/32-inch insulating board sheathing, is probably sufficient. In the northern tier of Central and Eastern States, however, it is desirable to have a roof with even better insulating properties. This is done by the use of 3- by 6-inch decking with a cover of 25/32-inch insulating board sheathing, or by the use of an expanded foam plastic covered with 1/2-inch insulating board or tile on the underside of 2- by 6-inch decking. Figure 38 shows the various materials and combinations of materials and their approximate "U" values.

The method of installing the 25/32-inch insulating sheathing over the wood decking is relatively simple. The 4- by 8-foot sheets should be laid horizontally across the decking. Use 1¼- or 1½-inch roofing nails spaced 10 inches apart in rows 24 inches apart along the length.

Insulating board or tile in 1/2-inch thickness and the expanded foam insulation are installed with wallboard adhesive designed for these materials. Manufacturers normally recommend the type and method of application. With 1/2- by 12- by 12-inch tile, for example, a small amount of adhesive in each corner and the use of hand pressure as the tile is placed is one system which is often used. When tile is tongued and grooved, stapling is the usual method of installation. Larger sheets of 1/2-inch insulating board may require a combination of glue and some nailing. Expanded foam insulation is ordinarily installed with approved adhesives.

When 1-inch wood decking is used over the joist-beam system (fig. 33 A and B), the use of at least 25/32-inch insulating sheathing over the boards and 1/2-inch insulating board or tile on the inside is normally recommended. A 1-inch thickness of expanded foam insulation under the 1/2-inch tile would provide even better insulation. When the inner face of the decking is to be covered, lower grade 2- by 6-inch decking is commonly used.

Trim For Low-Slope Roofs

Simple trim in the form of facia boards can be used at roof overhangs and at side and end walls. When 2- by 6-inch lookouts are used in the ceiling-beam roof, a 2- by 8-inch *facia* member is usually required to span the 48-inch spacing of the beams (fig. 33 A). In addition, a 1- by 2-inch facia molding may be added. Use two sixteenpenny galvanized nails in the ends of each lookout member. The facia molding may be nailed with six- or sevenpenny galvanized nails on 16-inch centers.

Trim for roofs with nominal 2- or 3-inch-thick wood decking can consist of a 1- by 4- or 1- by 6-inch member with a 1- by 2-inch facia molding at the side and end-wall overhangs (fig. 39 A and B). A 1- by 4-inch member can be used for 2-inch roof decking with or without the 25/32-inch insulating fiberboard. When 3-inch roof decking is used with the fiberboard, a 1- by 6-inch piece is generally required. Nail the facia and molding to the decking with eightpenny galvanized nails spaced about 16 inches apart. The roof deck is now ready for the roofing material.

Pitched Roof

A pitched-roof house is commonly framed by one of two methods: (a) With trussed rafters or (b) with conventional rafter and ceiling joist members. These framing methods are used most often for roof slopes of 4 in 12 and greater. The common W-truss (fig. 40A) for moderate spans requires less material than the joist and rafter system, as the members in the upper and lower chords are usually only 2 by 4 inches in size for spans of 24 to 32 feet. The king-post truss (fig. 40B) for spans of 20 to 24 feet uses even less material than the W-truss, but is perhaps more suitable for light to moderate roof loads. Low-slope roof trusses usually require larger members. In addition to lowering material costs, the truss has the advantage of permitting freedom in location of interior partitions because only the sidewalls carry the ceiling and roof loads.

The roof sheathing, trim, roofing, interior ceiling finish, and type of ceiling insulation used do not vary a great deal between the truss and the conventional roof systems. For plywood or lumber sheathing, 24-inch spacing of trusses and rafters and joists is considered a normal maximum.

FIGURE 38.—Insulating values of various materials and material combinations.

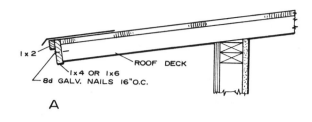

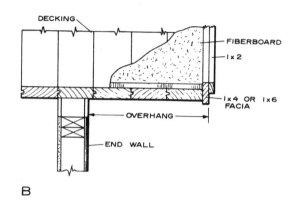

FIGURE 39.—Facia for wood-deck roof. A, Sidewall overhang; B, end-wall overhang.

Greater spacing can be used, but it usually requires a thicker roof sheathing and application of wood stripping on the undersides of the ceiling joists and trusses to furnish a support for ceiling finish. Thus, most W-trusses are designed for 24-inch spacing and joist-rafter construction for 24- or 16-inch spacing. Trusses generally require a higher grade dimension material than the joist and rafter

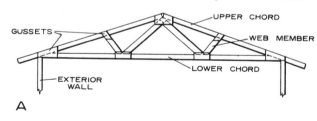

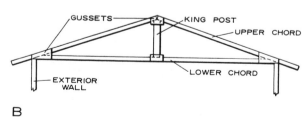

FIGURE 40.—Trussed rafters. A, W-type truss; B, king-post truss.

roof. However, specific details of the roof construction are covered in the working drawings for each house.

Trussed Roof

The common truss or trussed rafter is most often fabricated in a central shop. While some are constructed at the job side, an enclosed building provides better control for their assembly. These trusses are fabricated in several ways. The three most common methods of fastening members together are with (a) metal truss plates, (b) plywood gussets, and (c) ring connectors.

The metal truss plates, with or without prongs, are fastened in place on each side of member intersections. Some plates are nailed and others have supplemental nail fastening. Metal-plate trusses are usually purchased through a large lumber dealer or manufacturer and are not easily adapted to on-site fabrication. The trusses using fully nailed metal plates can usually be assembled at a small central shop.

The plywood-gusset truss may be a nailed or nailed-glued combination. The nailed-glued combination, with nails supplying the pressure, allows the use of smaller gussets than does the nailed system. However, if on-site fabrication is necessary, the nailed gusset truss and the ring connector truss are probably the best choices. Many adhesives suitable for trusses generally require good temperature control and weather protection not usually available on site. The size of the gussets, the number of nails or other connectors, and other details for this type of roof are included in the working drawings for each house.

Completed trusses can be raised in place with a small mechanical lift on the top plates of exterior sidewalls. They can also be placed by hand over the exterior walls in an inverted position, and then rotated into an upright position. The top plates of the two sidewalls should be marked for the location of each set of trusses. Trusses are fastened to the outside walls and to 1- by 4- or 1- by 6-inch temporary horizontal braces used to space and aline them until the roof sheathing has been applied. Locate these braces near the ridge line.

Trusses can be fastened to the top wallplates by toenailing, but this is not always the most satisfactory method. The heel gusset in a plywood-gusset or metal truss is located at the wallplate and makes toenailing difficult. However, two tenpenny nails at each side of the truss can be used in nailing the lower chord to the plate (fig. 41 A). Predrilling may be necessary to prevent splitting. A better system involves the use of a simple metal connector or bracket obtained from local lumber dealers. Brackets should be nailed to the wallplates at sides and top with eightpenny nails and to the lower chords of the truss with sixpenny or 1½-inch roofing nails (fig. 41 B) or as recommended by the manufacturer.

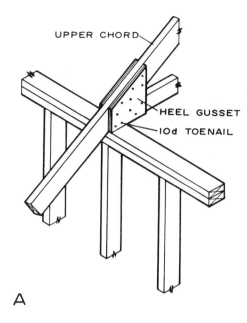

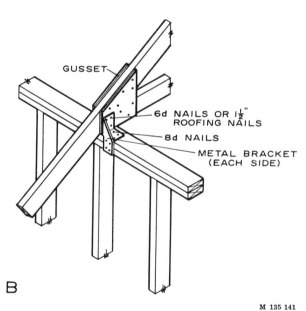

FIGURE 41.—Fastening trusses to wallplate. A, Toenailing; B, metal bracket connector.

The gable-end walls for a pitched roof utilizing trusses are usually made the same way as those described in the section on "Wall Systems" and shown in figure 23.

Rafter and Ceiling Joist Roof

Conventional roof construction with ceiling joists and rafters (fig. 42) can begin after all load-bearing and other partition walls are in place. The upper top plate of the exterior wall and the load-bearing interior wall serve as a fastening area for ceiling joists and rafters. Ceiling joists are installed along premarket exterior top wallplates and are toenailed to the plate with three eightpenny nails. The first joist is usually located next to the top plate of the end wall (fig. 43). This provides edge-nailing for the ceiling finish. Ceiling joists crossing a center loadbearing wall are face-nailed to each other with three or four sixteenpenny nails. In addition, they are each toenailed to the plate with two eightpenny nails.

Angle cuts for the rafters at the *ridge* and at the exterior walls can be marked with a carpenter's square using a reference table showing the overall rafter lengths for various spans, roof slopes, and joist sizes. These tables can usually be obtained from your lumber dealer. However, if a rafter table is not available, a baseline can be laid out on the subfloor across the width of the house, marking an exact outline of the roof slope, ridge, board and exterior walls. Thus, a rafter pattern can be made, including cuts at the ridge, wall, and the overhang at the eaves.

Rafters are erected in pairs. The *ridge board* is first nailed to one rafter end with three tenpenny nails (fig. 44). The opposing rafter is then nailed to the first with a tenpenny nail at the top and two eightpenny nails toenailed at each side. The outside rafter is located flush with and a part of the gable-end walls (fig. 43).

While the ridge nailing is being done, the rafters should be toenailed to the top plates of the exterior wall with two eightpenny nails (fig. 43). In addition, each rafter is face-nailed to the ceiling joist with three tenpenny nails. The remaining rafters are installed the same way. When the ridge board must be spliced, it should be done at a rafter with nailing at each side.

If gable-end walls have not been erected with the end walls, the gable-end studs can now be cut and nailed in place (fig. 43). Toenail the studs to the plate with eightpenny nails and face-nail to the end rafter from the inside with two tenpenny nails. In addition, the first or edge ceiling joist can be nailed to each gable-end stud with two tenpenny nails. Gable-end studs can also be used flatwise between the end rafter and top plate of the wall.

When the roof has a moderately low slope and the width of the house is 26 feet or greater, it is often desirable to nail a 1- by 6-inch *collar beam* to every second or third rafter (fig. 42) using four eightpenny nails at each end.

Framing for Flush Living-Dining Area Ceiling

A living-dining-kitchen group is often designed as one open area with a flush ceiling throughout. This makes the rooms appear much larger than they actually are. When trusses are used, there

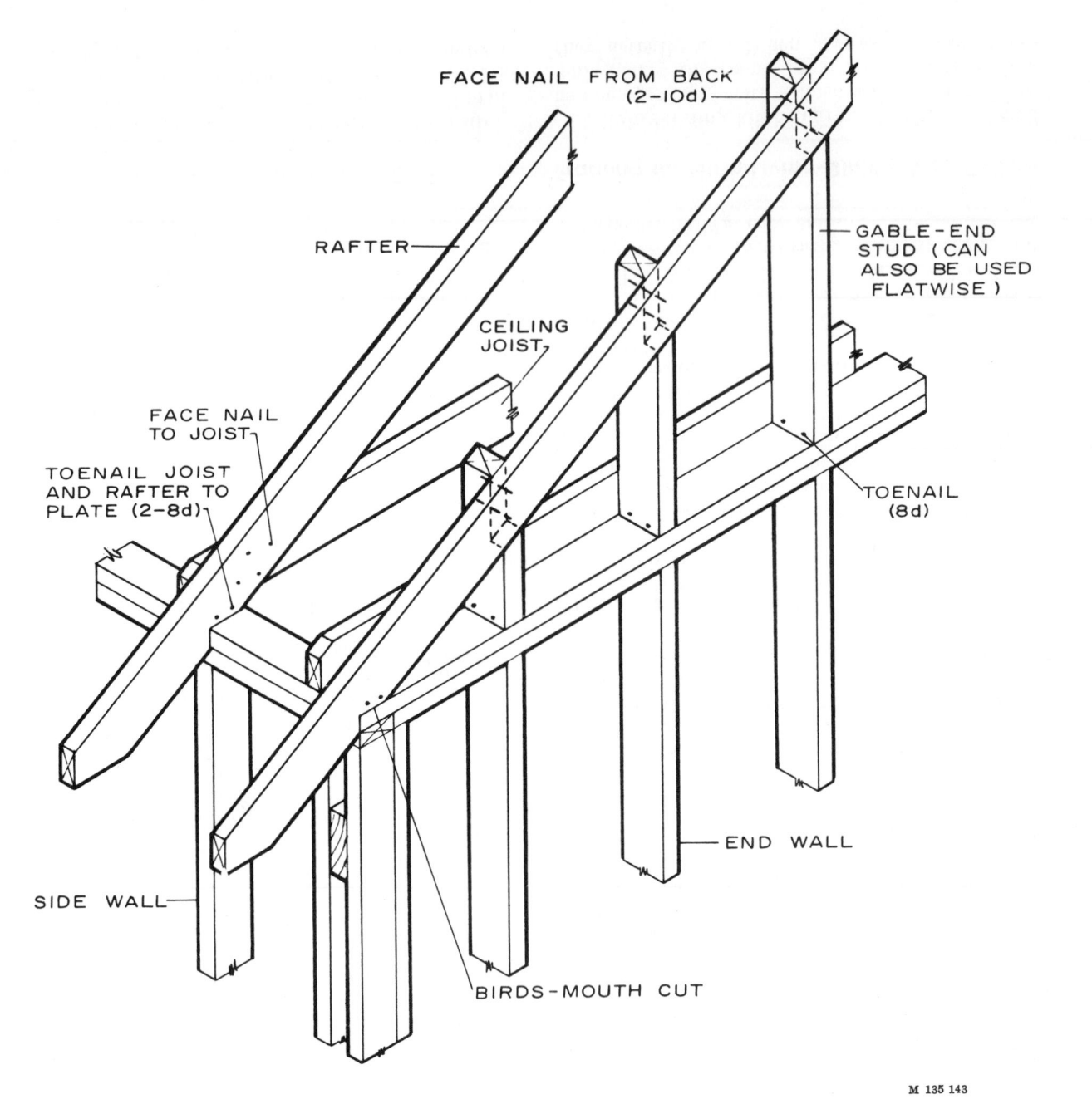

FIGURE 42.—Rafter and ceiling joist roof framing.

M 135 142

FIGURE 43.—Fastening rafters and ceiling joists to plate and gable-end studs.

M 135 143

is no problem, because they span from one exterior wall to the other. However, if ceiling joists and rafters are used, some type of *beam* is needed to support the interior ends of the ceiling joists. This can be done by using a flush beam, which spans from an interior cross wall to an exterior end wall. Joists are fastened to the beams by means of joist hangers (fig. 45). These hangers are nailed to the beam with eightpenny nails and to the joist with sixpenny nails or 1½-inch roofing nails. Hangers are perhaps most easily fastened by first nailing to the end of the joist before the joist is raised in place.

An alternate method of framing utilizes a wood bracket at each pair of ceiling joists tieing them to a beam which spans the open living-dining area (fig. 46). This beam is blocked up and fastened at each end at a height equal to the depth of the ceiling joists.

Roof Sheathing

Plywood or lumber roof sheathing is most commonly used for pitched roofs. Nominal 1-inch boards no wider than 8 inches can be used for trusses or rafters spaced not more than 24 inches on center. Sheathing (standard) and other grades of plywood are marked for the allowable spacing of the rafters and trusses for each species and thickness used. For example, a "24/0" mark indicates it is satisfactory as roof sheathing for 24-inch spacing of roof members, but not satisfactory for subfloor.

Nominal 1-inch boards should be laid up without spacing and nailed to each rafter with two eightpenny nails. Plywood sheets should be laid

across the roof members with staggered end joints. Use sixpenny nails for ⅜-inch and thinner plywood and eightpenny nails for ½-inch and thicker plywood. Space the nails 6 inches apart at the edges and 12 inches at intermediate fastening points.

When gable-end overhangs are used, extend the trim to the plywood or roofing boards when necessary before the 2- by 2- or 2- by 4-inch fly rafter (facia nailer) is nailed in place.

Roof Trim

Roof trim is installed before the roofing or shingles are applied. The cornice and gable (*rake*) trim for a pitched roof can be the same whether trusses or rafter-ceiling joist framing are used. In its simplest form, the trim consists of a facia board, sometimes with molding added. The facia is nailed to the ends of the rafter extensions or to the fly rafters at the gable overhang. With more complete trim, a soffit is usually included at the cornice and gables.

Cornice

The facia board at rafter ends or at the extension of the truss is often a 1- by 4- or 1- by 6-inch member (fig. 47A). The facia should be nailed to the end of each rafter with two eightpenny galvanized nails. Trim rafter ends when necessary for a straight line. Nail 1- by 2-inch facia molding with one eightpenny galvanized nail at rafter locations. In an open cornice, a frieze board is often used between the rafters, serving to terminate siding or siding-sheathing combinations at the rafter line (fig. 47A).

A simple closed cornice is shown in figure 47B. The soffit of plywood, hardboard, or other material is nailed directly to the underside of the rafter extensions. Blocking may be required between rafters at the wall line to serve as a nailing surface for the soffit. Use small galvanized nails in nailing the soffit to the rafters. When inlet attic ventilation is specified in the plans, it can be provided by a screened slot (fig. 47B), or by small separate ventilators.

When a horizontal closed cornice is used, *look-outs* are fastened to the ends of the rafter and to the wall (fig. 47C). They are face-nailed to the rafters and face- or toenailed to the studs at the wall. Use twelvepenny nails for the face-nailing and eightpenny nails for the toenailing.

Gable End

The gable-end trim may consist of a fly rafter, a facia board, and facia molding (fig. 48A). The 2- by 2- or 2- by 4-inch fly rafter is fastened by

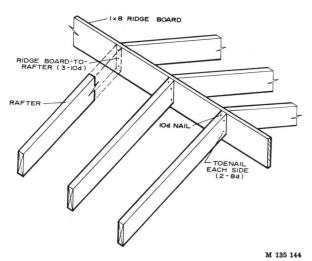

FIGURE 44.—Fastening rafters at the ridge.

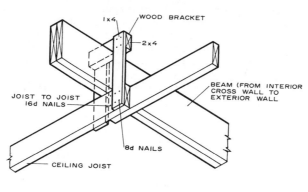

FIGURE 46.—Framing for flush ceiling with wood brackets.

nailing through the roof sheathing. Depending on the thickness of the sheathing, use sixpenny or eightpenny nails spaced 12 inches apart. In this type of gable end, the amount of extension should be governed by the thickness of the roof sheathing. When nominal 1-inch boards or plywood thicker than ½ inch is used, the extension should generally be no more than 16 inches. For thinner sheathings, limit the extensions to 12 inches.

A closed gable-end overhang requires nailing surfaces for the soffit. These are furnished by the fly rafter and a nailer or nailing blocks located against the end wall (fig. 48B). An extension of 20 inches might be considered a limit for this type of overhang.

Framing for Chimneys

An inside chimney, whether of masonry or prefabricated, often requires that some type of fram-

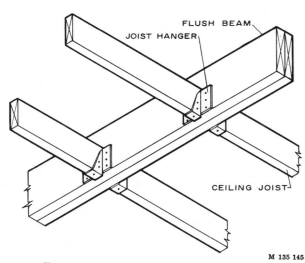

FIGURE 45.—Flush beam with joist hangers.

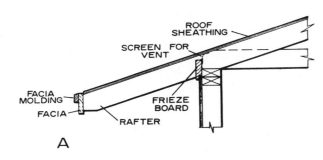

A

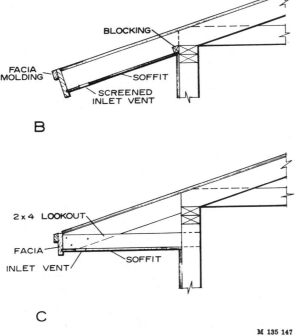

B

C

FIGURE 47.—Cornice trim. A, Open cornice; B, sloped closed cornice; C, horizontal closed cornice.

ing be provided, where it extends through the roof. This may consist of simple headers between rafters below and above the chimney location, or require two additional rafter spaces (fig. 49). The chimney should have a 2-inch clearance from the framing members and 1 inch from roof sheathing. When nominal 2- or 3-inch wood decking is used, a small header can be used at each end of the decking at the chimney location for support.

CHIMNEYS

Some type of chimney will be required for the heating unit, whether the home is heated by oil, gas, or solid fuel. It is normally erected before the roofing is laid but also can be installed after. Chimneys, either of masonry or prefabricated, should be structurally safe and provide sufficient draft for the heating unit and other utilities. Local building regulations often dictate the type to be used. A masonry chimney requires a stable foundation below the frostline and construction with acceptable brick or other masonry units. Some type of *flue lining* is included, together with a cleanout door at the base.

The prefabricated chimney may cost less than the full masonry chimney, considering both materials and labor, as well as providing a small saving in space. These chimneys are normally fastened to and supported by the ceiling joists and should be Underwriter Laboratory tested and approved. They are normally adapted to any type of fuel and come complete with roof flashing, cap assembly, mounting panel, piping, and chimney housing.

ROOF COVERINGS

Roof coverings should be installed soon after the cornice and rake trim are in place to provide protection for the remaining interior and exterior work. For the low-cost house, perhaps the most practical roof coverings are roll roofing or asphalt shingles for pitched roofs and roll roofing in double coverage or *built-up roof* for flat or very low-slope roofs. A good maintenance-free roof is important from the standpoints of protection and the additional cost involved in replacing a cheaper roof after only a few years.

Asphalt Shingles

Asphalt *shingles* may be used for roofs with slopes of 2 in 12 to 7 in 12 and steeper under certain conditions of installation. The most common shingle is perhaps the 3 in 1, which is a 3-tab strip, 12 by 36 inches in size. The basic weight may vary somewhat, but the 235-pound (per square of 3 bundles) is now considered minimum. However,

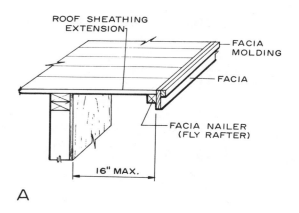

A

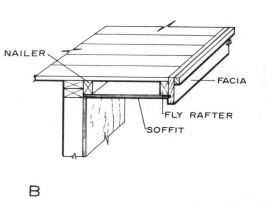

B

FIGURE 48.—Gable-end trim. A, Open gable overhang; B, closed gable overhang.

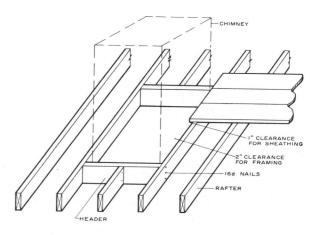

FIGURE 49.—Roof framing at chimney.

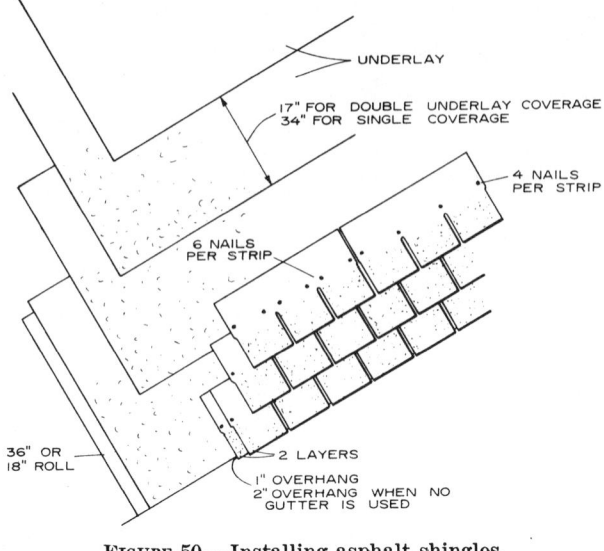

FIGURE 50.—Installing asphalt shingles.

many roofs with 210-pound shingles are giving satisfactory service. A small gable roof house uses about 10 squares of shingles, so use of a better shingle would mean about $10 to $20 more per house. Cost of application would be the same.

Installation

Underlay.—A single underlay of 15-pound, saturated felt is used under the shingles for roof slopes of 4 in 12 to 7 in 12. A double underlay (double coverage) is required for slopes of 2 in 12 to 4 in 12. Roof slopes over 7 in 12 usually require no underlay. For single underlay, start at the eave line with the 15-pound felt, roll across the roof, and nail or staple the felt in place as required. Allow a 2-inch head lap and install the second strip. This leaves a 34-inch exposure for the standard 36-inch-width rolls. Continue in this manner.

A double underlay can be started with two layers at the eave line, flush with the facia board or molding. The second and remaining strips have 19-inch head laps with 17-inch exposures (fig. 50). Cover the entire roof in this manner, making sure that all surfaces have double coverage. Use only enough staples or roofing nails to hold the underlay in place. Underlay is normally not required for wood shingles.

Shingles.—Asphalt tab shingles are fastened in place with ¾- or ⅞-inch galvanized roofing nails or with staples, using at least four on each strip (fig. 50). Some roofers use six for each strip for greater wind resistance; one at each end and one at each side of each notch. Locate them above the notches so the next course covers them.

A starter strip and one or two layers of shingles are used at the eave line with a 1-inch overhang beyond the facia trim and ½- to ¾-inch extension at the gable end. When no gutters are used, the overhang should be about 2 inches. This will form

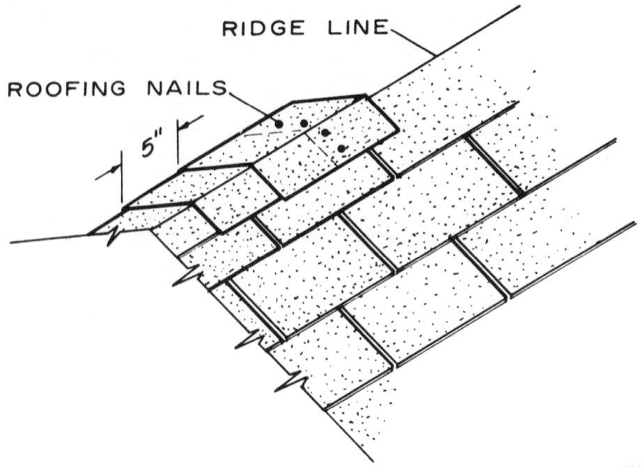

a curve during warm weather for a natural drip. Metal edging or flashing is sometimes used at these areas. For slopes of 2 in 12 to 4 in 12, a 5-inch exposure can be used with the double underlay (fig. 50). For slopes of 4 in 12 and over, a 5-inch exposure may also be used with a single underlay.

Ridge

A *Boston ridge* is perhaps the most common method of treating the ridge portion of the roof. This consists of 12- by 12-inch sections cut from the 12- by 36-inch shingle strips. They are bent slightly and used in lap fashion over the ridge with a 5-inch exposure distance (fig. 51). In cold weather, be careful that the sections do not crack in bending. The nails used at each side are covered by the lap of the next section. For a positive seal, use a small spot of asphalt cement under each exposed edge.

Roll Roofing

When cost is a factor in construction of a house, the use of mineral-surfaced roll roofing might be considered. While this type of roofing will not be as attractive as an asphalt shingle roof and perhaps not as durable, it may cost up to 15 percent less for a small house than standard asphalt shingles.

Roll roofing (65 pounds minimum weight in one-half lap rolls with a mineral surface) should be used over a double underlay coverage. Use a starter strip or a half-roll at the eave line with a 1-inch overhang and nail in place 3 to 4 inches above the edge of the facia (fig. 52). When *gutters* are not included initially, use a 2-inch extension to form a drip edge. Space roofing nails about 6 inches apart. Surface nailing can be used when roof slopes are 4 in 12 and greater.

The second (full) roll is now placed along the eave line over a ribbon of asphalt roofing cement or lap-joint material. In low slopes, nailing is done above the lap, cement applied, and the next roll

positioned so that the nails are covered. Edge overhang should be about ½ to ¾ inch at the gable ends. When vertical lap joints are required, nail the first edge, then use asphalt adhesive under a minimum 6-inch overlap. Use a sufficient amount of adhesive or lap-joint material to insure a tight joint. On steep slopes, surface nailing along the vertical edge is acceptable. The ridge can be finished with a Boston-type covering or by 12-inch-wide strips of the roll roofing, using at least 6 inches on each side.

Chimney Flashing

Flashing around the chimney at the junction with the roof is perhaps the most important flashed area in a simple gable roof. The Boston ridge over the shingles must be well installed to prevent wind-driven rain from entering, and the flashing around the chimney must also be well done. Prefabricated chimneys are supplied with built-in flashing which slides under the shingles above and over those below. A good calking or asphalt sealing compound around the perimeter completes the installation.

A masonry chimney requires flashing around the perimeter, which is placed as shingle flashing under the shingles at sides and top and extends at right angles up the sides (fig. 53). In addition, counterflashing is used on the base of the chimney over the shingle flashing. This is turned in a masonry joint, wedged in place with lead plugs, and sealed with a calking material. Galvanized sheet metal, aluminum, and terneplate (coated sheet iron or steel) are the most common types used for flashing around the chimney. If they are not rust-resistant, they should be given a coat or two of good metal paint.

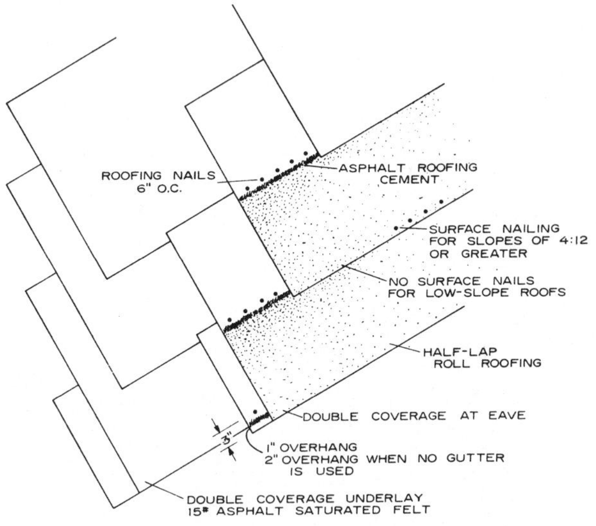

FIGURE 52.—Installing roll roofing.

EXTERIOR WALL COVERINGS

Exterior coverings used over the wall framing commonly consist of a sheathing material followed by some type of finish siding. However, sheathing-siding materials (panel siding) serve as both sheathing and finish material. These materials are most often plywoods or hardboards. While they are somewhat higher in price than conventional sheathing alone, they make it possible to use only a single exterior covering material. Low-cost sheathing materials can be covered with various types of siding—from spaced vertical boards over plywood sheathing to horizontal bevel siding over fiberboard, plywood, or other types of sheathing. All combinations should be studied so that cost, utility, and appearance are considered in the selection. The working drawings of the house indicate the most suitable siding materials.

Sheathing

In a low-cost house, it is advisable to use a sheathing or a panel-siding material which will provide resistance to racking and thus eliminate the need for diagonal corner bracing on the stud wall. Notching studs and installing bracing can add substantially to labor cost. When siding material does not provide this rigidity and strength, some type of sheathing should be used. Materials which provide resistance to racking are: (a) Diagonal board sheathing, (b) structural insulation board (fiberboard) sheathing in ²⁵⁄₃₂-inch regular density or ½-inch intermediate fiberboard or nail-base fiberboard sheathing for direct application of shingles, and (c) plywood. The fiberboard and plywood sheathing must be applied vertically in 4- by 8-foot or longer sheets with edge and center nailing to provide the needed racking resistance. Horizontal wood boards may also be used for sheathing but require some type of corner bracing.

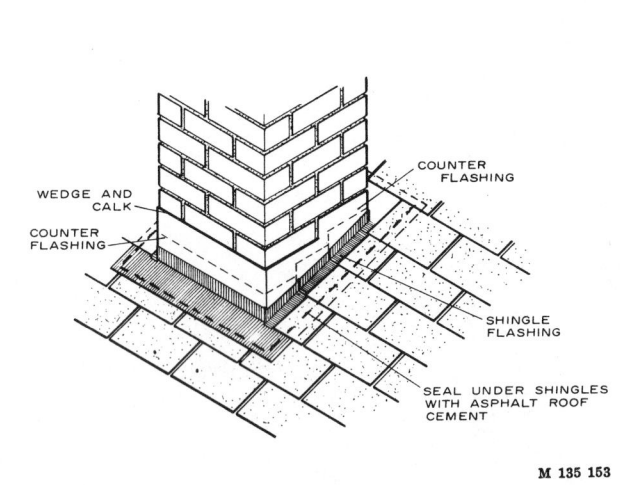

FIGURE 53.—Chimney flashing.

FIGURE 51.—Boston ridge.

Diagonal Boards

Diagonal wood sheathing should have a nominal thickness of ⅝ inch (resawn). Edges can be square, *shiplapped*, or tongued-and-grooved. Widths up to 10 inches are satisfactory. Sheathing should be applied at as near a 45° angle as possible as shown in figure 54. Use three eightpenny nails for 6- and 8-inch-wide boards and four eightpenny nails for the 10-inch widths. Also provide nailing along the floor framing or beam faces. Butt joints should be made over a stud unless the sheathing is end and side matched. Depending on the type of siding used, sheathing should normally be carried down over the outside floor framing members. This provides an excellent tie between wall and floor framing.

Structural Insulating Board

Structural *insulating board* sheathing (fiberboard type) in 4-foot-wide sheets and in $^{25}/_{32}$-inch regular-density or ½-inch intermediate fiberboard grades provides the required rigidity without bracing. It must be applied vertically in 8-foot and longer sheets with edge and center nailing (fig. 55). Nails should be spaced 3 inches apart along the edges and 6 inches apart at intermediate supports. Use 1¾-inch roofing nails for the $^{25}/_{32}$-inch sheathing and 1½-inch nails for the ½-inch

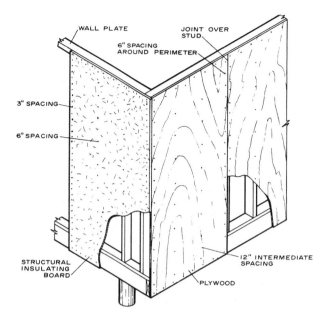

M 135 155

FIGURE 55.—Sheathing with insulating board or plywood (vertical application).

sheathing. Vertical joints should be made over studs. Siding is normally required over this type of sheathing.

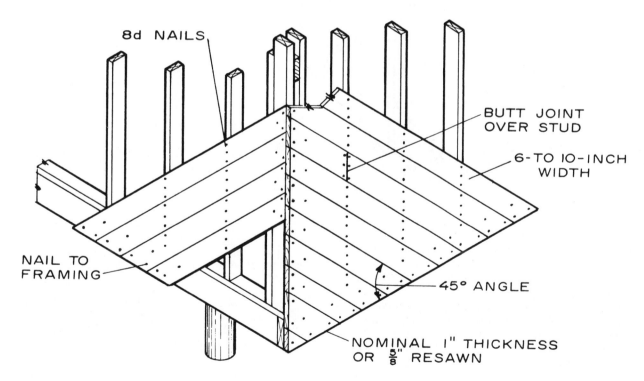

FIGURE 54.—Diagonal board sheathing.

M 135 154

Plywood

Plywood sheathing also requires vertical application of 4-foot-wide by 8-foot or longer sheets (fig. 55). Standard (sheathing) grade plywood is normally used for this purpose. Use $^{5}/_{16}$ inch minimum thickness for 16-inch stud spacing and ⅜ inch for 24-inch stud spacing. Nails are spaced 6 inches apart at the edges and 12 inches apart at intermediate studs. Use sixpenny nails for $^{5}/_{16}$-inch ⅜-inch-thick plywood. Because the plywood sheathing in $^{5}/_{16}$- or ⅜-inch sheets provides the necessary strength and rigidity, almost any type of siding can be applied over it.

Plywood and hardboard are also used as a single covering material without sheathing, but grades, thickness, and types vary from normal sheathing requirements. This phase of wall construction will be covered in the following section.

Sheathing-Siding Materials—Panel Siding

Large sheet materials for exterior coverage (*panel siding*) can be used alone and serve both as sheathing and siding. Plywood, hardboard, and exterior particleboard in their various forms are perhaps the most popular materials used for this purpose. The proper type and size of plywood and hardboard sheets with adequate nailing eliminate the need for bracing. Particleboard requires corner bracing.

These materials are quite reasonable in price, and plywood, for example, can be obtained in grooved, rough-sawn, embossed, and other surface variations as well as in a paper-overlay form. Hardboard can also be obtained in a number of surface variations. The plywood surfaces are most suitable for pigmented stain finishes in various colors. The medium-density, paper-overlay plywoods are an excellent base for exterior paints. Plywoods used for panel siding are normally exterior grades.

The thickness of plywood used for siding varies with the stud spacing. Grooved plywood, such as the "1–11" type, is normally ⅝ inch thick with ⅜- by ¼-inch-deep grooves spaced 4 or 6 inches apart. This plywood is used when studs are spaced a maximum of 16 inches on center. Ungrooved plywoods should be at least ⅜ inch for 16-inch stud spacing and ½ inch thick for 24-inch stud spacing. Plywood panel siding should be nailed around the perimeter and at each intermediate stud. Use sixpenny galvanized siding or other rust-resistant nails for the ⅜-inch plywood and eightpenny for ½-inch and thicker plywood and space 7 to 8 inches apart. Hardboard must be ¼ inch thick and used over 16-inch stud spacing. Exterior particleboard with corner bracing should be ⅝ inch thick for 16-inch stud spacing and ¾ inch thick for 24-inch stud spacing. Space nails 6 inches apart

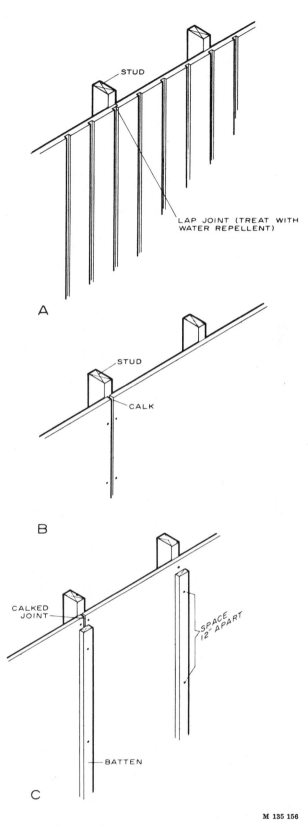

M 135 156

FIGURE 56.—Joint treatment for panel siding. *A*, Lap joint; *B*; calked butt joint; *C*, butt joint with batten.

around the edges and 8 inches apart at intermediate studs.[6]

The vertical joint treatment over the stud may consist of a shiplap joint as in the "1–11" paneling (fig. 56A). This joint is nailed at each side after treating with a water-repellent preservative. When a square-edge butt joint is used, a sealant calk should be used at the joint (fig. 56B).

_____

[6] Federal Housing Administration. Use of Materials Bull. UM–32. Architectural Standards Division. 1961.

A square-edge butt joint may be covered with battens, which can also be placed over each stud as a decorative variation (fig. 56C). Joints should be calked and the batten nailed over the joint with eightpenny galvanized nails spaced 12 inches apart. Nominal 1- by 2-inch battens are commonly used.

A good detail for this type of siding at gable ends consists of extending the bottom plate of the gable ⅝ to ¾ inch beyond the top of the wall below (fig. 57). This allows a termination of the panel at the lower wall and a good drip section for the gable-end panel.

Siding—With and Without Sheathing

There are a number of sidings, mainly for horizontal application, which might be suitable for walls with or without sheathing. The types most suitable for use over sheathing are: (a) The lower cost lap sidings of wood or hardboard, (b) wood or other type shingles with single or double coursing, (c) vertical boards, and (d) several nonwood materials. Initial cost and maintenance should be the criteria in the selection. _Drop siding_ and nominal 1-inch paneling materials can be used

without sheathing under certain conditions. However, such sidings require (a) a rigidly braced wall at each corner and (b) a waterproof paper over the studs before application of the siding.

Application

Bevel siding.—When siding is used over sheathing, window and door frames are normally installed first. This process will be discussed in the next section, "Exterior Frames." The exposed face of sidings such as _bevel siding_ in ½- by 6-inch, ½- by 8-inch, or other sizes should be adjusted so that

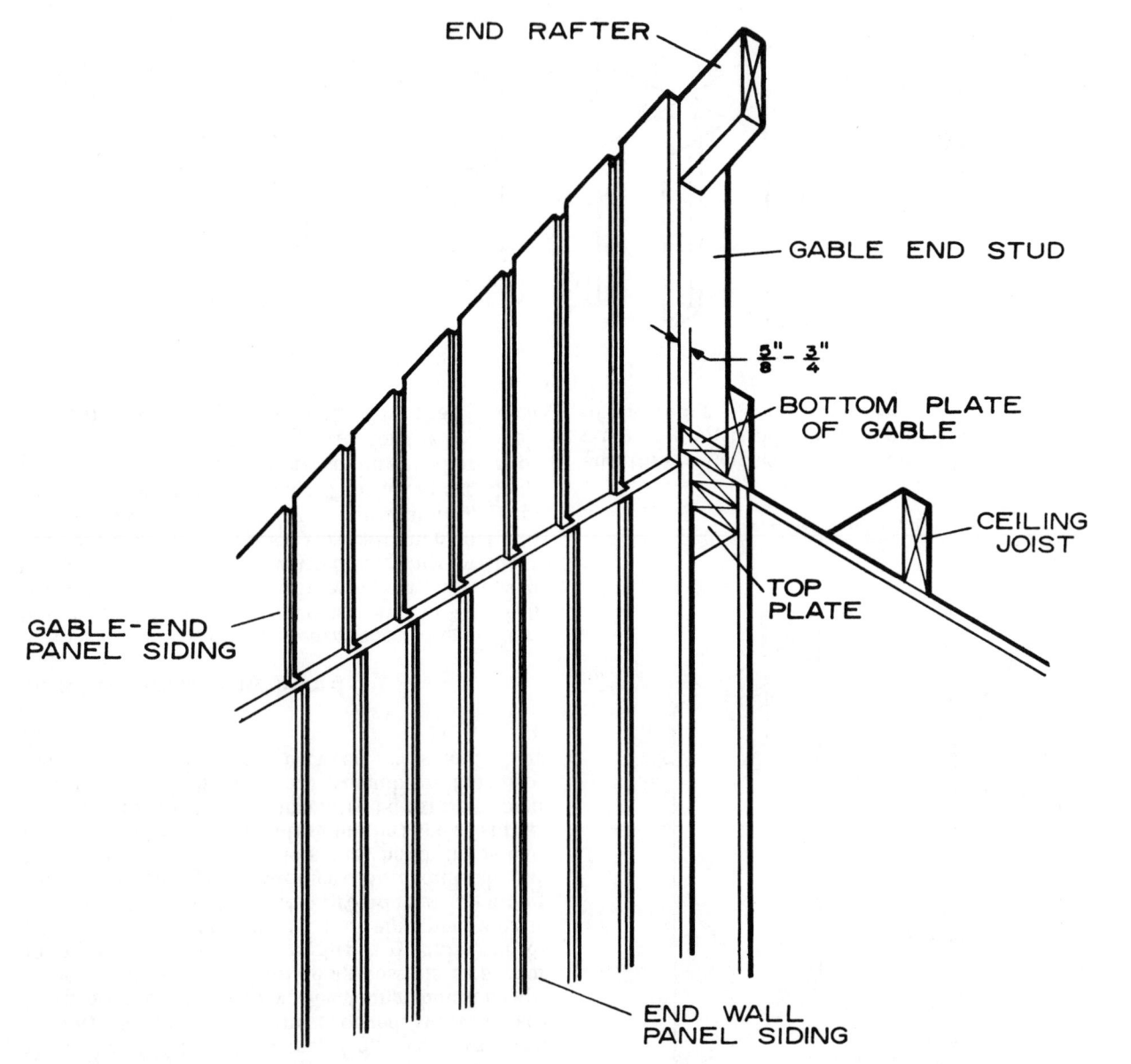

FIGURE 57.—Panel siding at gable end.

M 135 157

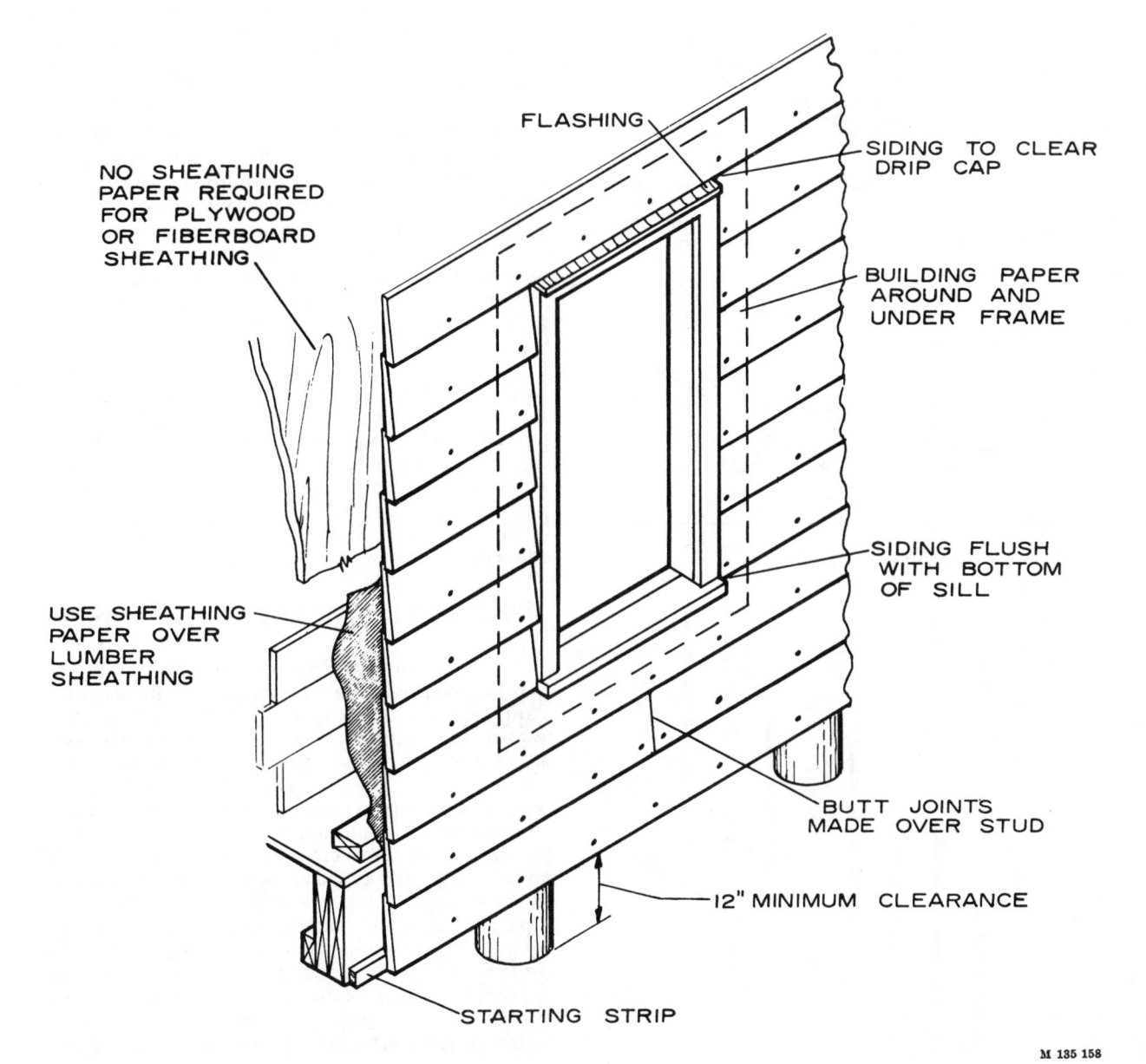

FIGURE 58.—Installing bevel siding.

M 135 158

the butt edges coincide with the bottom of the sill and the top of the *drip cap* of window frames (fig. 58). Use a sevenpenny galvanized siding nail or other corrosion-resistant nail at each stud crossing for the ½-in.-thick siding. The nail should be located so as to clear the top edge of the siding course below. Butt joints should be made over a stud. Other horizontal sidings over sheathing should be installed in a similar manner. Nonwood sheathings require nailing into each stud.

Interior corners should butt against a 1½- by 1½-inch corner strip. This wood strip is nailed at interior corners before siding is installed. Exterior corners can be mitered, butted against *corner boards*, or covered with metal corners. Perhaps the corner board and metal corner are the most satisfactory for bevel siding.

Vertical siding.—In low-cost house construction, some vertical sidings can be used over stud walls without sheathings; others require some type of sheathing as a backer or nailing base. Matched (tongued-and-grooved) paneling boards can be used directly over the studs under certain conditions. First, some type of corner bracing is required for the stud wall. Second, nailers (blocking) between the studs are required for nailing points, and third, a waterproof paper should be placed over the studs (fig. 59). Galvanized sevenpenny finish nails, which should be spaced no more than 24 inches apart vertically, are blind-nailed through the tongue at each cross nailing block. When boards are nominal 6 inches and wider, an additional eightpenny galvanized nail should be face-nailed (fig. 59). Boards should extend over and be nailed to the headers or stringers of the floor framing.

Rough-sawn vertical boards over a plywood backing provide a very acceptable finish. The plywood should be an exterior grade or sheathing grade (standard) with exterior glue. It should be ½ inch thick or 5/16 inch thick with nailing blocks between studs (fig. 60). Rough-sawn boards 4 to 8 inches wide surfaced on one side can be spaced and nailed to the top and bottom wallplates and the floor framing members and to the nailing blocks (fig. 60). Use the surfaced side toward the plywood. A choice in the widths and spacings of boards allows an interesting variation between houses.

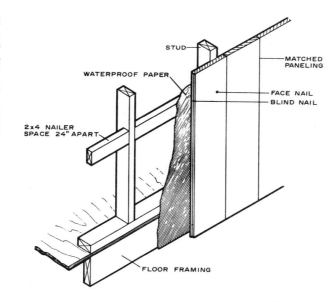

M 135 159

FIGURE 59.—Vertical paneling boards over studs.

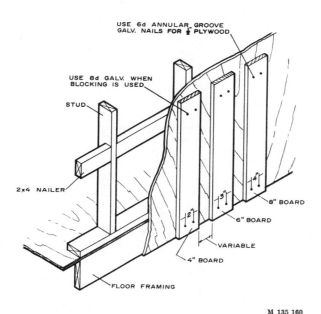

M 135 160

FIGURE 60.—Vertical boards over plywood.

EXTERIOR FRAMES

Windows and Doors

Window and exterior door units, which include the frames as well as the *sash* or doors, are generally assembled in a manufacturing plant and arrive at the building site ready for installation. Doors may require fitting, however. Simple jambs and sill units for awning or hopper window sash can be made in a small shop with the proper equipment, the wood treated with a water-repellent preservative, and sash fitted and prehung. Only the sash would need to be purchased. However, this system of fabrication is practical only for the simplest units and only when a large number of the same type are required. Thus, for double-hung and sill units for awning or hopper window sash

desirable to select the lower cost standard-size units and use a smaller number of windows. A substantial saving can be made, for example, by using one large double-hung window rather than two smaller ones.

Window frames are generally made with nominal 1-inch jambs and 2-inch sills. Sash for the most part are 1⅜ inches thick. Exterior door frames are made from 1½- to 1¾-inch stock. Exterior doors are 1¾ inches thick and the most common are the flush and the panel types.

As a general rule, the amount of natural light provided by the glass area in all rooms (except the kitchen) should be about 10 percent of the floor area. The kitchen can have natural or artificial light, but when an operating window is not available, ventilation should be provided. A bathroom usually is subject to the same requirements. From the standpoint of safety, houses should have two exterior doors. Local regulations often specify any variations of these requirements. The main exterior door should be 3 feet wide and at least 6 feet 6 inches high; 6 feet 8 inches is a normal standard height for exterior doors. The service or rear door should be at least 2 feet 6 inches wide; 2 feet 8 inches is the usual width. These details are covered in the working drawings for each house.

Types of Windows and Doors

Perhaps the most common type of window used in houses is the double-hung unit (fig. 61). It can be obtained in a number of sizes, is easily *weatherstripped*, and can be supplied with storms or screens. Frames are usually supplied with prefitted sash and the exterior casing and drip cap in place.

Another type of window, which is quite reasonable in cost and perhaps the one most adaptable to small shop fabrication in a simple form, is the "awning" or "hopper" type (fig. 62).

Other windows, such as the *casement sash* and sliding units, are also available but generally their cost is somewhat greater than the two types described. The fixed or stationary sash may consist of a simple frame with the sash permanently fastened in place. The frame for the awning window would be suitable for this type of sash (fig. 62).

Door frames are also supplied with exterior side and head casing and a hardwood sill or a softwood sill with a reinforced edge (fig. 63). Perhaps the most practical exterior door, considering cost and performance, is the panel type. A number of styles and patterns are available, most of them featuring some type of glazed opening (fig. 64). The solid-core flush door, usually more costly than the panel type, should be used for exteriors in most central and northern areas of the country in preference to the hollow-core type. A hollow-core door is ordinarily for interior use, because it warps

excessively during the heating season when used on the outside. However, it would probably be satisfactory for exterior use in the southern areas.

Installation

Window Frames

Preassembled window frames are easily installed. They are made to be placed in the rough wall openings from the outside and are fastened in place with nails. When a panel siding is used in place of a sheathing and siding combination, the frames are usually installed after the siding is in place. When horizontal siding is used with sheathing, the frames are fastened over the sheathing and the siding applied later.

To insure a water- and windproof installation for a panel-siding exterior, a ribbon of calking sealant (rubber or similar base) is placed over the siding at the location of side and head casing (fig. 65). When a siding material is used over the sheathing, strips of 15-pound felt should be used around the opening (fig. 58).

The frame is placed in the opening over the calking sealant (preferably with the sash in place to keep it square), and the sill leveled with a carpenter's level. Shims can be used on the inside if necessary. After leveling the sill, check the side casing and jamb with the level and square. Now nail the frame in place using tenpenny galvanized nails through the casing and into the side studs and the header over the window (fig. 66). While nailing, slide the sash up and down to see that they work freely. The nails should be spaced about 12 inches apart and both side and head casing fastened in the same manner. Other types of window units are installed similarly. When a panel siding is used, place a ribbon of calking sealer at the junction of the siding and the sill. Follow this by installing a small molding such as quarter-round.

Door Frames

Door frames are also fastened over panel siding by nailing through the side and head casing. The header and the joists must first be cut and trimmed (fig. 67). Use a ribbon of calking sealer under the casing. The top of the sill should be the same height as the finish floor so that the *threshold* can be installed over the joint. The sill should be shimmed when necessary to have full bearing on the floor framing. A *quarter-round* molding in combination with calking when necessary for a tight windproof joint should be used under the door sill when a panel siding or other single exterior covering is used. When joists are parallel to the plane of the door, headers and a short support member are necessary at the edge of the sill (fig. 67). The threshold is installed after the finish floor has been laid.

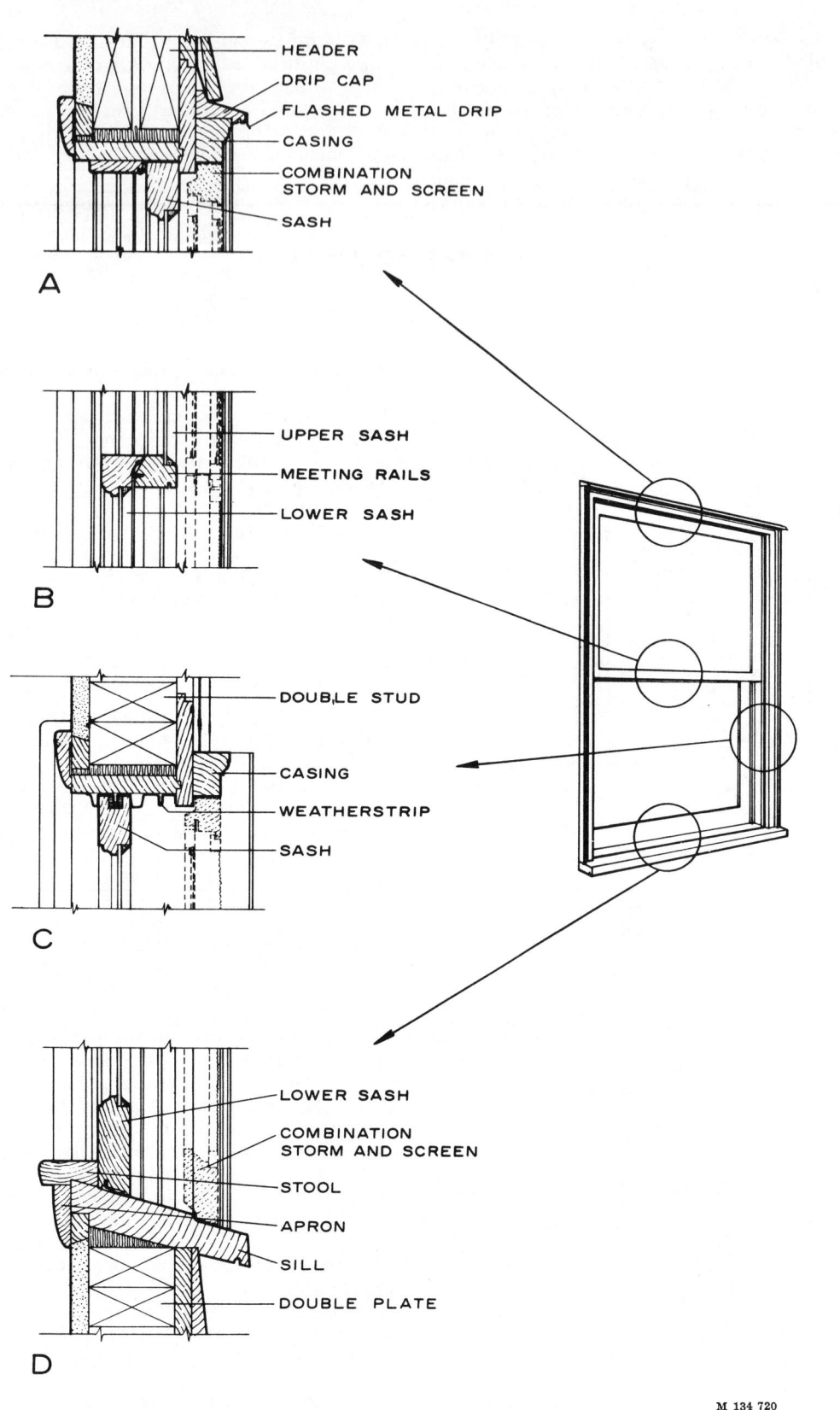

HEADER
DRIP CAP
FLASHED METAL DRIP
CASING
COMBINATION
STORM AND SCREEN
SASH

A

UPPER SASH
MEETING RAILS
LOWER SASH

B

DOUBLE STUD
CASING
WEATHERSTRIP
SASH

C

LOWER SASH
COMBINATION
STORM AND SCREEN
STOOL
APRON
SILL
DOUBLE PLATE

D

M 134 720

FIGURE 61.—Double-hung window unit. Cross sections: *A*, Head jamb; *B, meeting rails; C*, side jamb; *D*, sill.

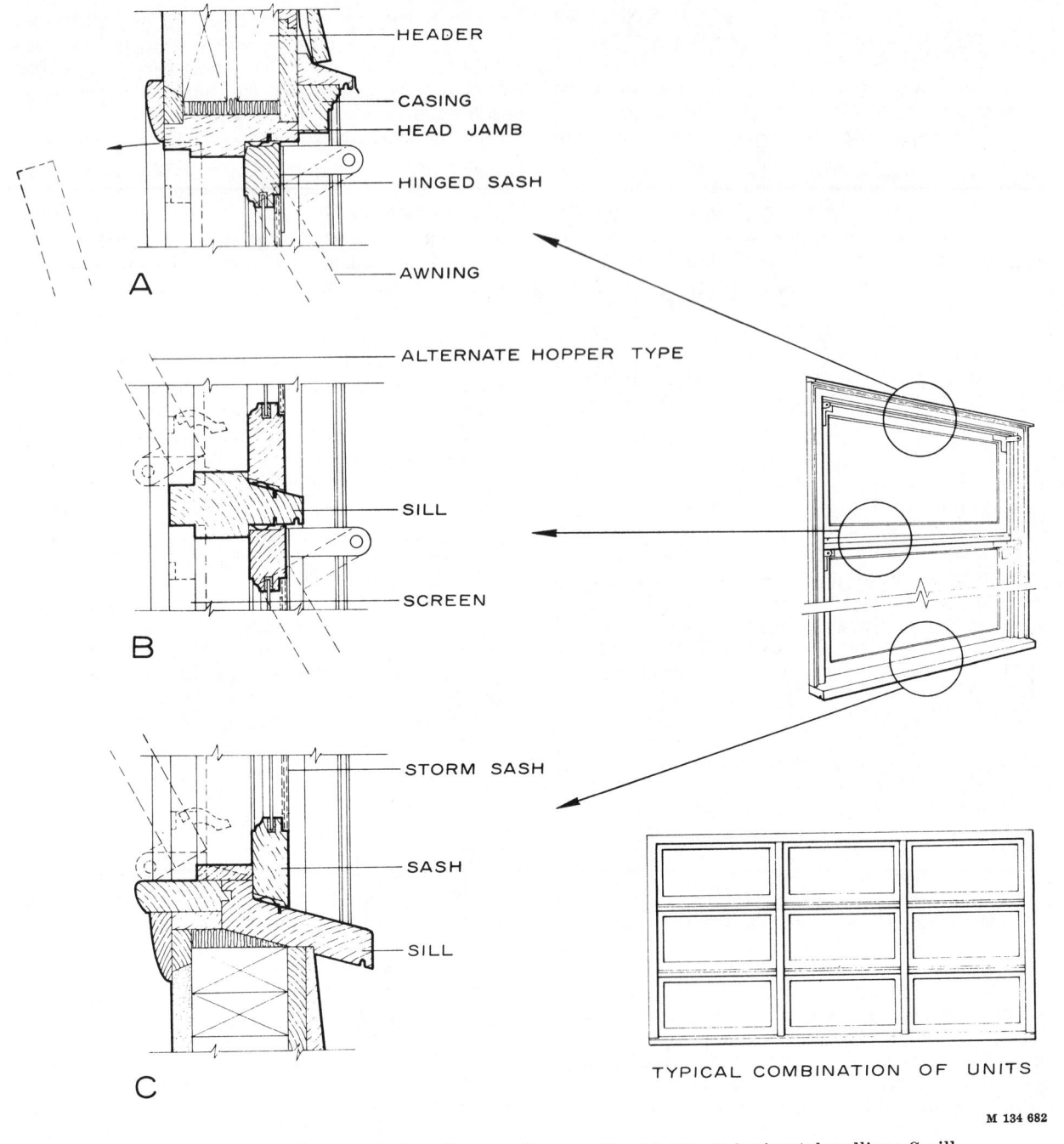

HEADER
CASING
HEAD JAMB
HINGED SASH
AWNING

A

ALTERNATE HOPPER TYPE

SILL
SCREEN

B

STORM SASH
SASH
SILL

C

TYPICAL COMBINATION OF UNITS

M 134 682

FIGURE 62.—Awning or hopper window. Cross sections: *A*, Head jamb; *B*, horizontal mullion; *C*, sill.

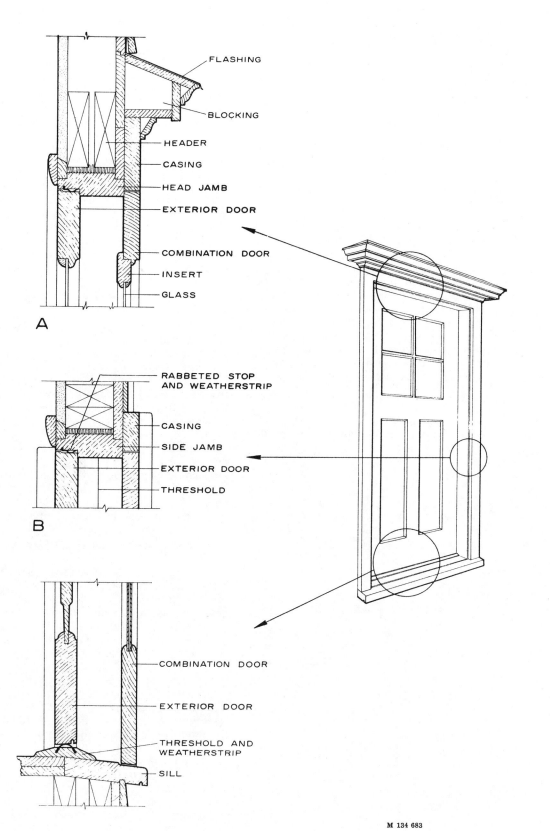

FLASHING

BLOCKING

HEADER

CASING

HEAD JAMB

EXTERIOR DOOR

COMBINATION DOOR

INSERT

GLASS

A

RABBETED STOP
AND WEATHERSTRIP

CASING

SIDE JAMB

EXTERIOR DOOR

THRESHOLD

B

COMBINATION DOOR

EXTERIOR DOOR

THRESHOLD AND
WEATHERSTRIP

SILL

M 134 683

FIGURE 63.—Exterior door and frame. Exterior door and combination-door (screen and storm) cross sections: A, Head jamb; B, side jamb; C, sill.

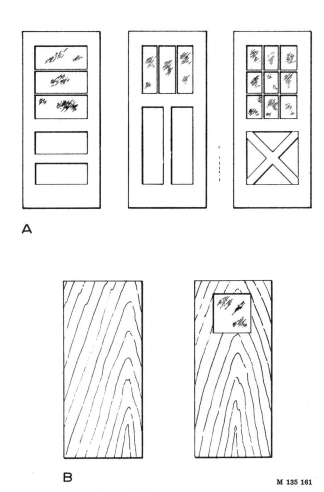

A

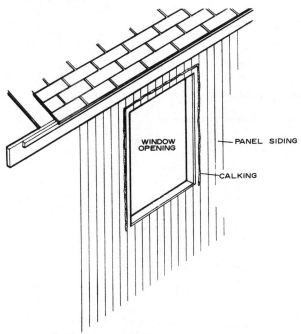

B   M 135 161

FIGURE 64.—Exterior doors. A, Panel type; B, flush type.

WINDOW
OPENING

PANEL SIDING

CALKING

M 135 162

FIGURE 65.—Calking around window opening before installing frame.

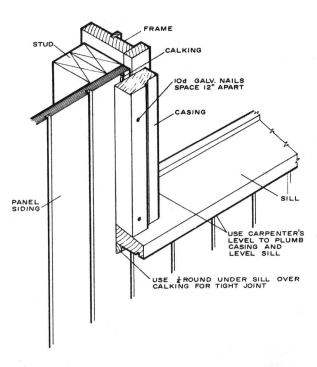

FRAME

CALKING

STUD

10d GALV. NAILS
SPACE 12" APART

CASING

PANEL
SIDING

SILL

USE CARPENTER'S
LEVEL TO PLUMB
CASING AND
LEVEL SILL

USE ¼ ROUND UNDER SILL OVER
CALKING FOR TIGHT JOINT

M 135 163

FIGURE 66.—Installation of double-hung window frame.

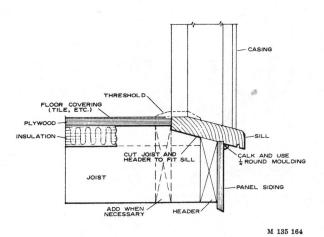

CASING

THRESHOLD

FLOOR COVERING
(TILE, ETC.)

PLYWOOD

INSULATION

SILL

CUT JOIST AND
HEADER TO FIT SILL

CALK AND USE
¼ ROUND MOULDING

JOIST

PANEL SIDING

ADD WHEN
NECESSARY

HEADER

M 135 164

FIGURE 67.—Door installation at sill.

FRAMING DETAILS FOR PLUMBING AND OTHER UTILITIES

In cold northern areas, installing plumbing in a basementless house requires a little more care than in a house with a basement. Some protection for the drain and supply piping in the form of an insulated box from subfloor to the ground is required. Thus, supply and drain lines should be located so as to eliminate long runs. Most plans for low-cost houses will back the kitchen and bath against a common utility wall so that all plumbing lines can be concentrated there for lower cost installation. In those houses which do not include all the facilities initially, plumbing lines should be roughed in so that connections can be made at a later date with little trouble.

Floor framing should be arranged so that little or no cutting of joists is required to install closet bends and other drainage and supply lines. This may require the use of a small header, for example, to frame out for the connections.

Plumbing Stack Vents

The utility wall between the kitchen and bath should be constructed so that connections can be made easily. This is usually done by using a nominal 2- by 6-inch plate and placing the studs flatwise at each side (fig. 68A). This will provide the needed wall thickness for the bell of a 4-inch cast-iron soil pipe, which is larger than the thickness of a 2- by 4-inch stud wall. It is also possible to furr out several studs to a 6-inch width at the *soil stack*, rather than thickening the entire wall. In areas where building regulations permit the use of a 3-inch vent pipe, a 2- by 4-inch stud wall may be used, but it requires reinforcing scabs at the top plate (fig. 68B). Use twelvepenny nails to fasten the scabs.

Bathtub Framing

The floor joists in the bathroom which support the tub or shower should be arranged so that no cutting is necessary in connecting the drainpipe. This usually requires only a small adjustment in spacing of joists (fig. 69). When joists are parallel to the length of the tub, they are usually doubled under the outer edge (fig. 69). Tubs are supported at the enclosing walls by hangers or by woodblocks. The wall at the fixtures should also be framed to allow for a small access panel.

Cutting Floor Joists

Floor joists should be cut, notched, or drilled only where there is little effect on their strength. While it is desirable to prevent cutting whenever possible, alterations are sometimes required. Joists should then be reinforced by nailing a 2- by 6-inch scab with twelvepenny nails to each side of

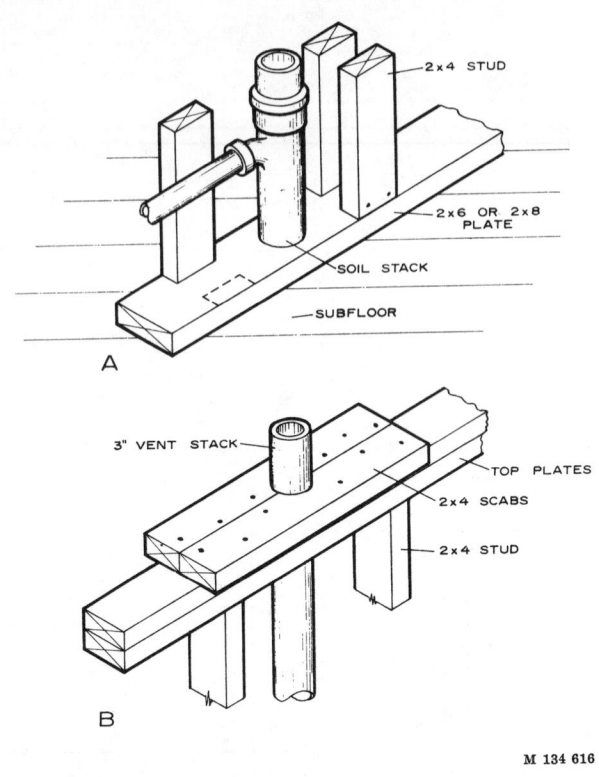

FIGURE 68.—Framing for vent stack. *A*, 4-inch soil pipe; *B*, 3-inch stack vent.

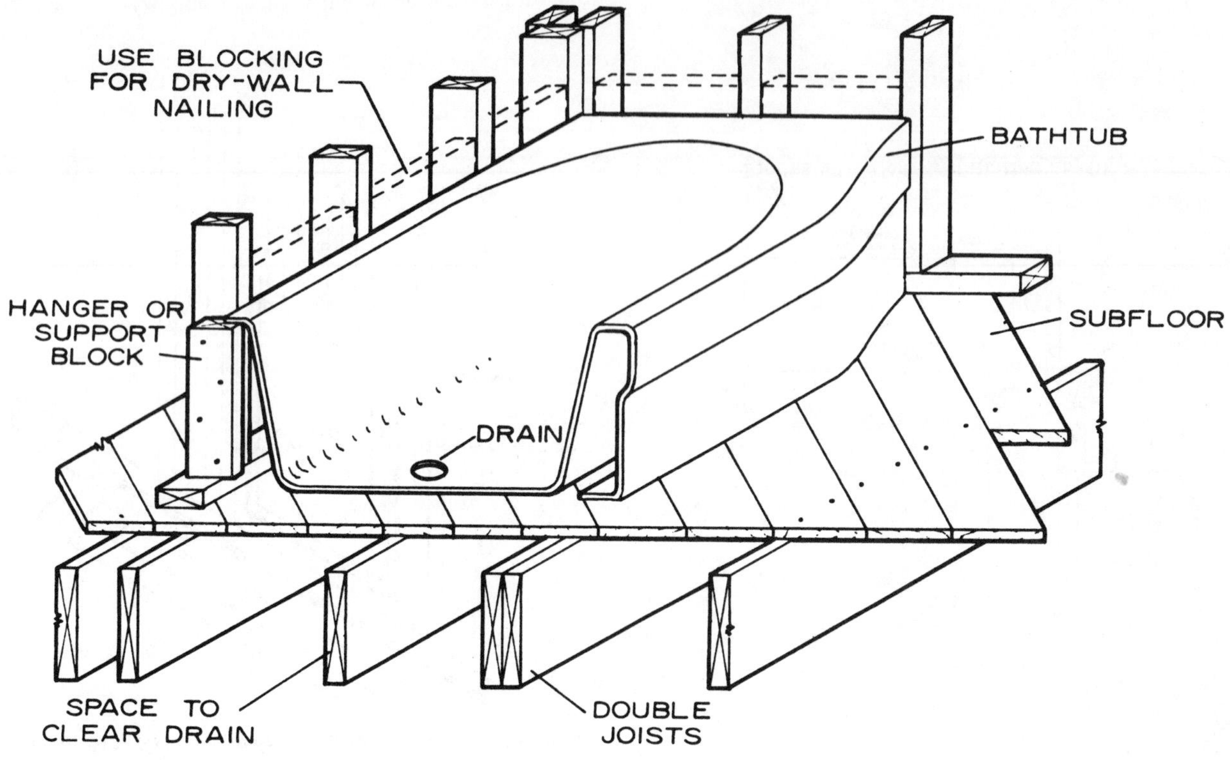

the altered member. An additional joist adjacent to the cut joist can also be used.

Notching the top or bottom of the joist should only be done in the end quarter of the span and to not more than one-sixth of the depth. Thus, for a nominal 2- by 8-inch joist 12 feet long, the notch should be not more than 3 feet from the end support and no more than about 1¾ inches deep. When a joist requires more severe alteration, headers and tail beams can be used to eliminate the need for cutting (fig. 70). Proper planning will minimize the need for altering joists.

When necessary, holes may be bored in joists if the diameters are no greater than 2 inches and the edges of the holes are not less than 2½ inches from the top or bottom edges (fig. 71). This usually limits a 2-inch-diameter hole to joists of nominal 2- by 8-inch size and larger.

Wiring

Wiring should be installed to comply with the National Electric Code or local building requirements. House wiring for electrical services is usually started sometime after the house has been enclosed. The initial phase of wiring is termed "roughing in" and includes installing outlet and switch boxes and the connecting cable, with wire in the boxes ready for connecting. This work is done before the insulation is placed in the wall and before application of the dry-wall finish.

Framing changes for wiring are usually minor and consist only of holes drilled in the studs for the flexible *conduit*. Wall switches at doors should be located at the side of the doubled studs so that no cutting is necessary. They should be 48 to 54 inches above the floor.

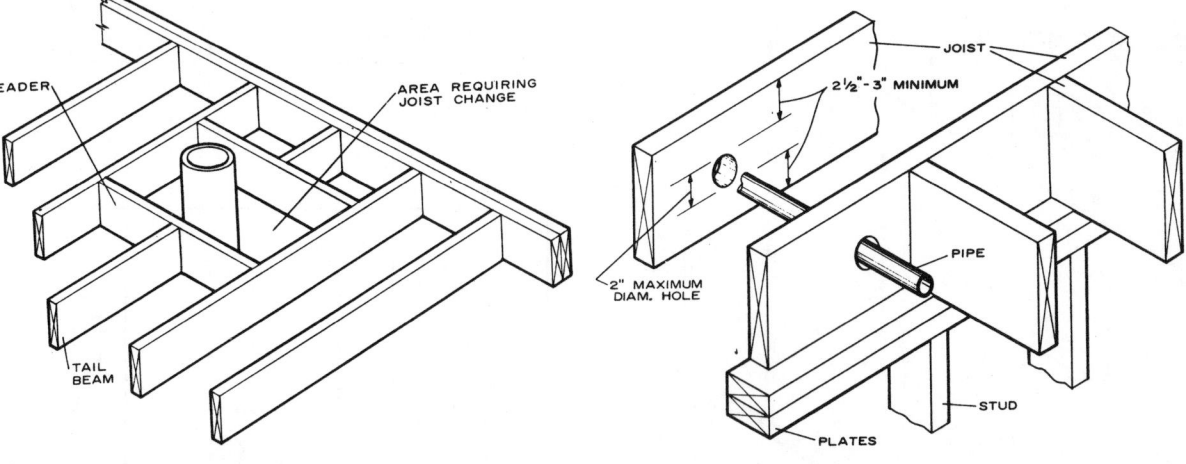

FIGURE 69.—Framing for bathtub.

FIGURE 70.—Headers for joists to eliminate cutting.

FIGURE 71.—Boring holes in joists.

THERMAL INSULATION

Thermal insulation is used in a house to minimize heat loss during the heating season and to reduce the inflow of heat during hot weather. Resistance to the passage of warm air is provided by materials used in wall, ceiling, and floor construction.

In constructing a crawl-space house, other factors must be considered in addition to providing insulation, such as: (a) Use of a *vapor barrier* with the insulation; (b) protection from ground moisture by the use of a vapor barrier ground cover (especially true if the crawl space is enclosed with a full foundation or skirt boards); and (c) use of both attic and crawl-space ventilation when required. Insulation and vapor barriers are discussed here. Ventilation is covered in the next section.

The amount of insulation used in the walls, floor, and ceiling usually depends on what section of the country the house is located in. Low-cost houses constructed in the northern tier of States where winters are quite severe should have, when possible, at least a 2-inch blanket insulation or equivalent in the walls and 4 inches of fill or batt insulation above the ceiling. In a crawl-space house, a 4-inch friction-type batt or other type of insulation would normally be satisfactory for the floor.

For houses in the Central States with moderate winters, 1 inch in the walls, 4 inches in the ceilings, and 1 or 2 inches of insulation in the floor should be satisfactory. In the South, for economy, floor and wall insulation could be eliminated and the ceiling insulation reduced to a 2-inch blanket or batt. However, a 1-inch blanket in the walls and floors would help to provide desirable comfort during the hot summer months.

Types of Insulation

Commercial insulating materials which are most practical in the construction of low-cost houses are: (a) Flexible types in blanket and batt forms, (b) loose-fill types, and (c) *rigid insulation* such as building boards or insulation boards. Others include reflective insulations, expanded plastic foams, and the like.

The common types of blanket and batt insulation, as well as loose-fill types, are made from wood and cotton fiber and mineral wool processed from rock, slag, or glass. Insulating or building board may be made of wood or cane fibers, of glass fibers, and of expanded foam.

In comparing the relative insulating values of various materials, a 1-inch thickness of typical blanket insulation is about equivalent to (a) 1½ inches of insulating board, (b) 3 inches of wood, or (c) 18 inches of common brick. Thus, when practical, the use of even a small amount of thermal insulation is good practice.

The insulating values of several types of flexible insulation do not vary a great deal. Most loose-fill insulations have slightly lower insulating values than the same material in flexible form. However, fill insulations, such as *vermiculite*, have less than 60 percent the value of common flexible insulations. Most lower density sheathing or structural insulating boards have better insulating properties than vermiculite.

Vapor Barriers

Vapor barriers are often a part of blanket or batt insulation, but they may also be a separate material which resists the movement of water vapor to cold or exterior surfaces. They should be placed as close as possible to the warm side of all exposed walls, floors, and ceiling. When used as ground covers in crawl spaces, they resist the movement of soil moisture to exposed wood members. In walls, they eliminate or minimize condensation problems which can cause paint peeling. In ceilings they can, with good *attic ventilation,* prevent moisture problems in attic spaces.

Vapor barriers commonly consist of: (a) Papers with a coating or lamination of an asphalt material; (b) plastic films; (c) aluminum or other metal foils; and (d) various paint coatings. Most blanket and batt insulations are supplied with a laminated paper or an aluminum foil vapor barrier. Friction-type batts usually have no vapor barriers. For such insulation, the vapor barrier should be added after the insulation is in place. Vapor barriers should generally be a part of all insulating processes.

Vapor barriers are usually classed by their *"perm"* value, which is a rate of water-vapor movement through a material. The lower this value, the greater the resistance of the barrier. A perm rating of 0.50 or less is considered satisfactory for vapor barriers. Two-mil (0.002-inch-thick) polyethylene film, for example, has a perm rating of about 0.25.

When the crawl space is enclosed during or after construction of the house, or the soil under the house is quite damp, a *soil cover* should be used. This vapor barrier should have a perm value of 1.0 or less and should be laid over the ground, using about a 4-inch lap along edges and ends. Stones or half-sections of brick can be used at the laps and around the perimeter to hold the material in place. The ground should be leveled before placing the cover. Materials such as polyethylene, roll roofing, and asphalt laminated barriers are satisfactory for ground covers.

Where and How to Insulate

Insulation in some form should be used at all exterior walls, floors, and at the ceiling as a sep-

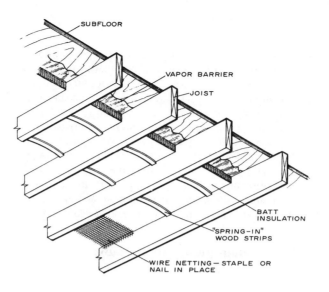

M 135 166

FIGURE 72.—Installing insulating batts in floor.

arate material or as a part of the house structure in most climates. The recommended thicknesses for various locations, given at the beginning of this chapter, can be used as a guide in insulating the house.

Floors

Blanket insulation in 1-inch thickness can be installed under a tongued-and-grooved plywood subfloor as previously described and illustrated in figure 14. However, this type is most commonly applied between the joists. In applying insulation, be sure that the vapor barrier faces up, against the bottom of the plywood.

The use of friction or other types of insulating batts between joists has been shown in figure 18. This insulation can be installed any time after the house has been enclosed and roofing installed. When friction-type insulation without a vapor barrier is used, a separate vapor barrier should be placed over the joists before the subfloor is nailed in place. Laminated or foil-backed kraft paper barriers or plastic films can be used. They should be lapped 4 to 6 inches and stapled only enough to hold the barriers in place until the subfloor is installed.

When batts are not the friction type, they usually require some support in addition to the adhesive shown in figure 18. This support can be supplied simply by the use of small, 3/16- by 3/4-inch or similar size, wood strips cut slightly longer than the joist space so that they spring into place (fig. 72). They can be spaced 24 to 36 inches apart or as needed. Wire netting nailed between joists may also be used to hold the batt insulation (fig. 72). The 1-inch-thick or thicker blanket insulation can also be installed in this way if desired.

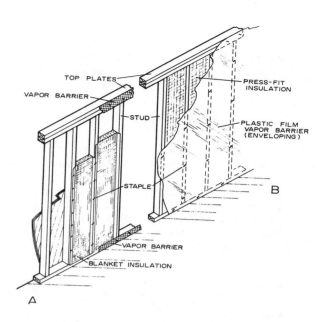

M 135 167

FIGURE 73.—Wall insulation. *A*, Blanket insulation with vapor barrier; *B*, plastic film vapor barrier.

Wall Insulation

When blanket or batt insulation for the walls contains a vapor barrier, the barrier should be placed toward the room side and the insulation stapled in place (fig. 73*A*). An additional small strip of vapor barrier at the bottom and top plates and around openings will insure good resistance to vapor movements in these critical areas.

When friction or other insulation without a vapor barrier is used in the walls, the entire interior surface should be covered with a vapor barrier. This is often accomplished by the use of wall-height rolls of 2-or 4-mil plastic film (fig. 73*B*). Other types of vapor barriers extending from bottom plate to top plate are also satisfactory. The studs, the window and door headers, and plates should also be covered with the vapor barrier for full protection. The full-height plastic film is usually carried over the entire window opening and cut out only after the dry wall has been installed. Staple or tack just enough to hold the vapor barrier in place until the interior wall finish is installed.

Ceiling Insulation

Loose-fill or batt-type ceiling insulation is often placed during or after the dry-wall ceiling finish is applied, depending on the roof design. In ceilings having no attic or joist space, such as those with wood roof decking, the insulation is normally a part of the roof construction and may include ceiling tile, thick wood decking, and structural insulating board in various combinations. This type of construction has been covered in the section on framing of low-slope roofs and figure 38.

Loose-fill insulation, blown or hand placed, can be used where there is an attic space high enough for easy access. It can be poured in place and leveled off (fig. 74A). A vapor barrier should be used under the insulation.

Batt insulation with attached vapor barrier can be used in most types of roof and ceiling constructions with or without an attic space. The batt insulation is made to fit between ceiling or roof members spaced 16 or 24 inches on center. After

the first row of gypsum board sheets has been applied in a level ceiling, the batts (normally 48 inches long) are placed between ceiling joists with the vapor barrier facing down. The next row of gypsum board is applied and the batts added. At the opposite side of the room, the batts should be stapled lightly in place before the final dry-wall sheets are applied. When one set of members serves as both ceiling joists and rafters, an airway should be allowed for ventilation (fig. 74B).

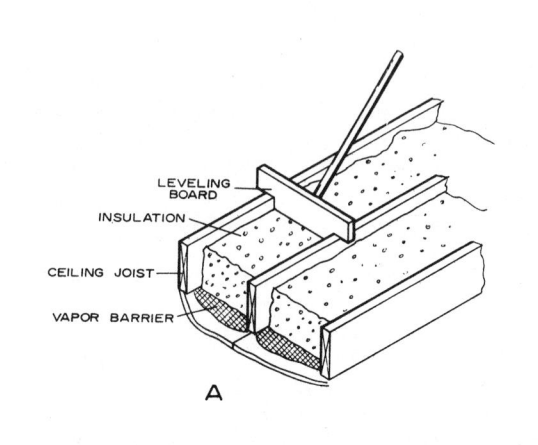
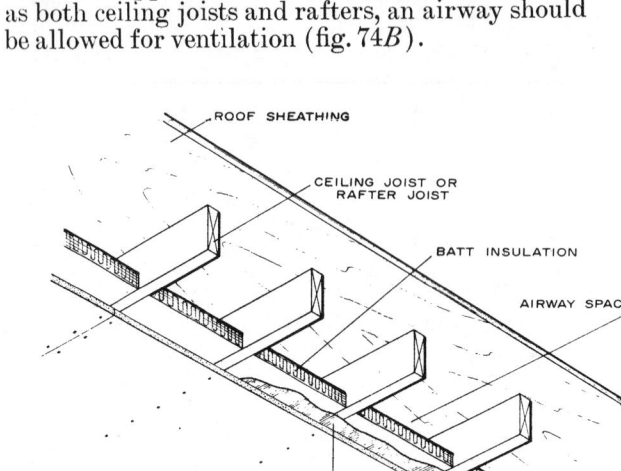

M 135 168

FIGURE 74.—Ceiling insulation. A, Fill type; B, batt type.

VENTILATION

Providing ventilation is an important phase of construction for all houses regardless of their cost. This includes ventilation of attic areas, the spaces between combination joist-rafters, and the crawl space. Only a small amount of crawl-space ventilation is normally required when the crawl space is entirely enclosed and a soil cover is used. Good *attic ventilation* is important to prevent condensation of moisture which can enter from the heated rooms below. Furthermore, good attic ventilation means a cooler attic in the summertime and greater comfort in the living areas below.

Attic Ventilation

The two types of attic ventilators used are the inlet and the outlet ventilator. Inlet ventilators are normally located in the soffit area of the cornice or at the junction of the wall and roof. They may be single ventilators or a continuous *vent*.

In some houses, it is practical to use only the outlet ventilators usually in the gable end of a house that has no room for inlet ventilators.

Both inlet ventilators and outlet ventilators

should be used whenever possible. In a house with an open cornice, inlet ventilators are usually most effective when installed in the frieze board which fits between the open rafters. Two saw cuts can be made in the top of the frieze board, the wood between removed, and screen installed on the back face (fig. 75). These openings are distributed along the sidewall to insure good ventilation. These details are ordinarily indicated in the working drawings for each house.

Outlet Ventilators

Outlet ventilators should be located as near the ridge of a pitched roof as possible. In a gable-roofed house, the outlet ventilators are located near the top of the gable end (fig. 76 A and B.) Many types are available with wood or metal *louvers*. Some of the additional forms are shown in figure 76 C, D, and E. When ladder framing is used on a wide gable overhang, ventilators are often used along the soffit area (fig. 76F). Ladder framing is formed by lookout members which bear on an interior truss or rafter and on the end wall and

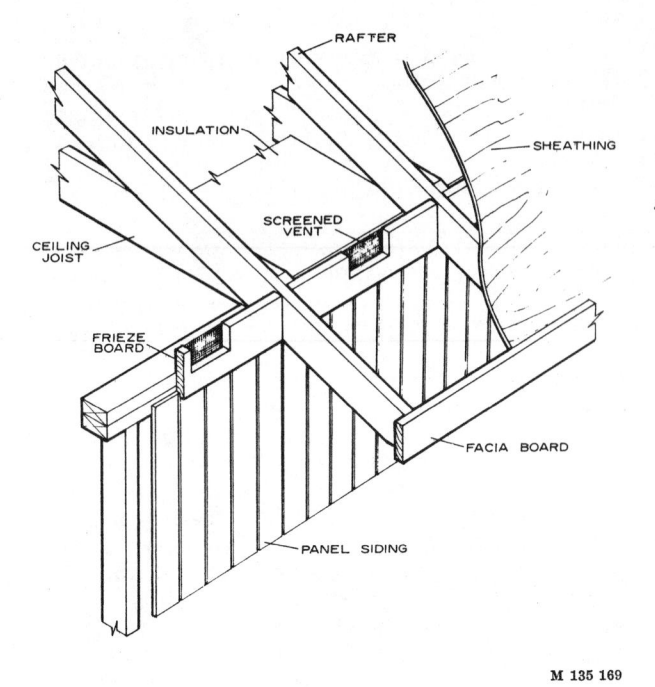

M 135 169

FIGURE 75.—Inlet ventilators for open cornice.

extend beyond to a fly rafter. Roof ventilators are available in various forms. They consist of covered and screened metal units designed to fit most roof slopes. They are adapted to gable- or *hip-roof* houses and should be located on the rear slope of the roof as near the ridge as possible.

Inlet Ventilators

Inlet ventilators installed in the soffit area of a closed cornice can consist of individual units spaced as required (fig. 77A). Another system of inlet ventilation consists of a narrow slot cut in the soffit (fig. 77B). All ventilators should be screened.

Amount of Ventilation

The net or face area of the ventilators required for a house is normally based on some ratio of the ceiling area. The net area is the total area of the ventilator with deductions made for the screening and louvers. When insect screen is used, the total area is reduced by half. In other words, a 1-square-foot ventilator would have a ½-square-foot net area. When louvers are present in addition to the screen, the total net area is only about 40 percent of the total.

The following tabulation shows the total recommended net inlet and outlet areas for various roofs

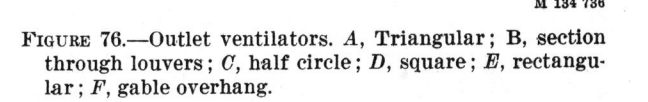

M 134 736

FIGURE 76.—Outlet ventilators. A, Triangular; B, section through louvers; C, half circle; D, square; E, rectangular; F, gable overhang.

in the form of ratios of total minimum net ventilating area to ceiling area:

Type of roof	Inlet	Outlet
Gable roof with outlet ventilators only		1/300
Gable roof with both inlet and outlet ventilators	1/900	1/900
Hip roof with inlet and outlet ventilators (distributed)	1/900	1/900
Flat or low-slope roofs with ventilators in soffit or eave area only (located at each side of house)		1/250

As an example, assume a house has 900 square feet of ceiling area and a gable roof with a soffit, so both inlet and outlet ventilators can be used. Screen reduces the area by half, so areas required are 1/450 of the ceiling. Thus 900 x 1/450=2 square feet. So use two outlet ventilators, each with 1 square foot. The total inlet area (well distributed) should also total 2 square feet.

Crawl-Space Ventilation

As previously mentioned, crawl-space ventilation is not required unless the space is entirely closed. When required, small ventilators can be

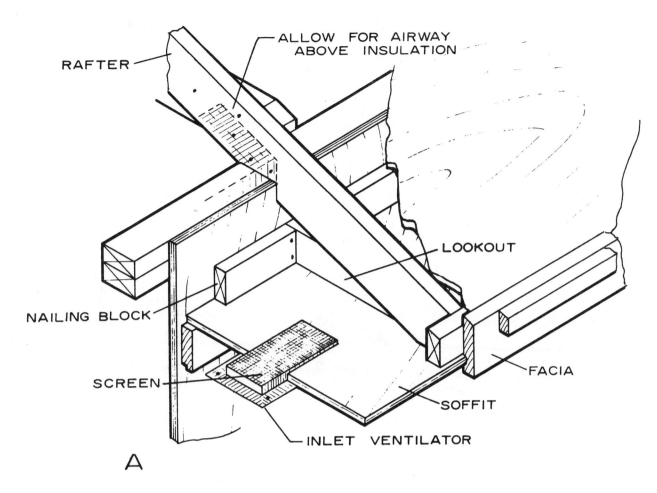

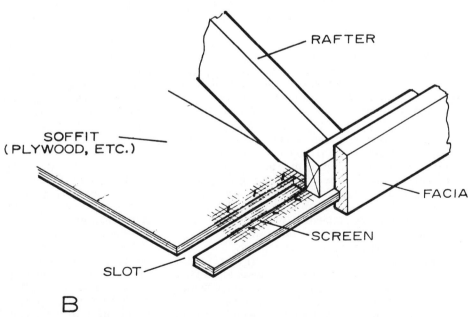

M 134 737

FIGURE 77.—Soffit inlet ventilators. *A*, Spaced units; *B*, slot type.

located in the foundation walls on at least two opposite sides. The amount of ventilation depends on the presence of a ground cover or vapor barrier. When a vapor barrier is used, the total recommended net area of the ventilators is 1/1,500 of the floor area. Use at least two screened vents located on opposite ends of the house. When no vapor barrier is present, the total net area should be 1/150 of the floor area with the ventilators well distributed.

INTERIOR WALL AND CEILING FINISH

Some of the most practical low-cost materials for interior finish are the gypsum boards, the hardboards, the fiberboards, and plywood. Hardboard, fiberboard, gypsum board, and plywood are often prefinished and require only fastening to the studs and ceiling joists. The gypsum boards can also be obtained prefinished, but in their most common and lowest cost form, they have a paper facing which requires painting or wallpapering. A plaster finish is usually more costly than the dry-wall materials and perhaps should not be considered for low-cost houses. Furthermore, a plaster finish must be applied by a specialist. Dry-wall finishes can be installed by the semiskilled workman after a minimum of training.

In addition to the four types of sheet materials, an insulating board or ceiling tile can be used for the ceiling. Prefinished tile in 12- by 12-inch and larger sizes usually requires nailing strips fastened to the underside of the ceiling joists or truss members. Tile can also be applied to the underside of roof boards in a beam-type ceiling or on the inner face of the wood decking on a wood-deck roof.

Wood and fiberboard paneling in tongued-and-grooved V-edge pattern in various widths can also be used as an interior finish, especially as an accent wall, for example. When applied vertically, nailers are used between or over the studs.

The type of interior finish materials selected for a low-cost house should primarily be based on cost. These materials may vary from a low of 5 to 6 cents per square foot for ⅜-inch unfinished gypsum board to as much as three times this amount for some of the lower cost prefinished materials. However, consideration should be made of the labor involved in joint treatment and painting of unfinished materials. As a result, in some instances, the use of prefinished materials might be justified. These details and material requirements are included in the working drawings or the accompanying specifications for each house. Before interior wall and ceiling finish is applied, insulation should be in place and wiring, heating *ducts*, and other utilities should be roughed in.

Material Requirements

The thickness of interior covering materials depends on the spacing of the studs or joists and the type of material. These requirements are usually a part of the working drawings or the specifications. However, for convenience, the recommended thicknesses for the various materials are listed in the following tabulation based on their use and on the spacing of the fastening members:

Interior Material Finish Thickness

Finish	Minimum material thickness (inches) when framing is spaced	
	16 inches	24 inches
Gypsum board	⅜	½
Plywood	¼	⅜
Hardboard	¼	
Fiberboard	½	¾
Wood paneling	⅜	½

For ceilings, when the long direction of the gypsum board sheet is at right angles to the ceiling joists, use ⅜-inch thickness for 16-inch spacing and ½-inch for 24-inch joist spacing. When sheets are parallel, spacing should not exceed 16 inches for ½-inch gypsum board. Fiberboard ceiling tile in ½-inch thickness requires 12-inch spacing of nailing strips.

Gypsum Board

Application

Gypsum board used for dry-wall finish is a sheet material composed of a gypsum filler faced with paper. Sheets are 4 feet wide and 8 feet long or longer. The edges are usually recessed to accommodate taped joints. The ceiling is usually covered before the wall sheets are applied. Start at one wall and proceed across the room. When batt-type ceiling insulation is used, it can be placed as each row of sheets is applied. Use fivepenny (1⅝-inch-long) cooler-type nails for ½-inch gypsum and fourpenny (1⅜-inch) nails for ⅜-inch gypsum board. Ring-shank nails ⅛ inch shorter than these can also be used. Nailheads should be large enough so that they do not penetrate the surface.

Adjoining sheets should have only a light contact with each other. End joints should be staggered and centered on a ceiling joist or bottom chord of a truss. One or two braces slightly longer than the height of the ceiling can be used to aid in installing the gypsum sheets (fig. 78). Nails are spaced 6 to 8 inches apart and should be very lightly dimpled with the hammerhead. Do not break the surface of the paper. Edge or end joints should be double-nailed. Minimum edge nailing distance is ⅜ inch.

Vertical or horizontal application can be used on the walls. Horizontal application of gypsum board is often used when wall-length sheets eliminate vertical joints. The horizontal joint thus requires only taping and treating. For normal application, horizontal joint reinforcing is not required. However, nailing blocks may be used between studs for a damage-resistant joint for the thinner gypsum sheets (fig. 79A). Horizontal application is also suitable for the laminated system in which ⅜-inch gypsum sheets are nailed vertically and room-length sheets are applied horizontally with a wallboard or contact adhesive. While this results in an excellent wall, it is much more costly than the single application.

Gypsum board applied vertically should be nailed around the perimeter and at intermediate studs with 1⅜- or 1⅝-inch nails, depending on the thickness. Nails should be spaced 6 to 8 inches apart. Joints should be made over the center of a stud with only light contact between adjoining sheets (fig. 79B). Another method of fastening the sheets is called the "floating top." In this system, the top horizontal row of nails is eliminated and the top 6 or 8 inches of the sheet are free. This is said to prevent fracture of the gypsum board when there is movement of the framing members.

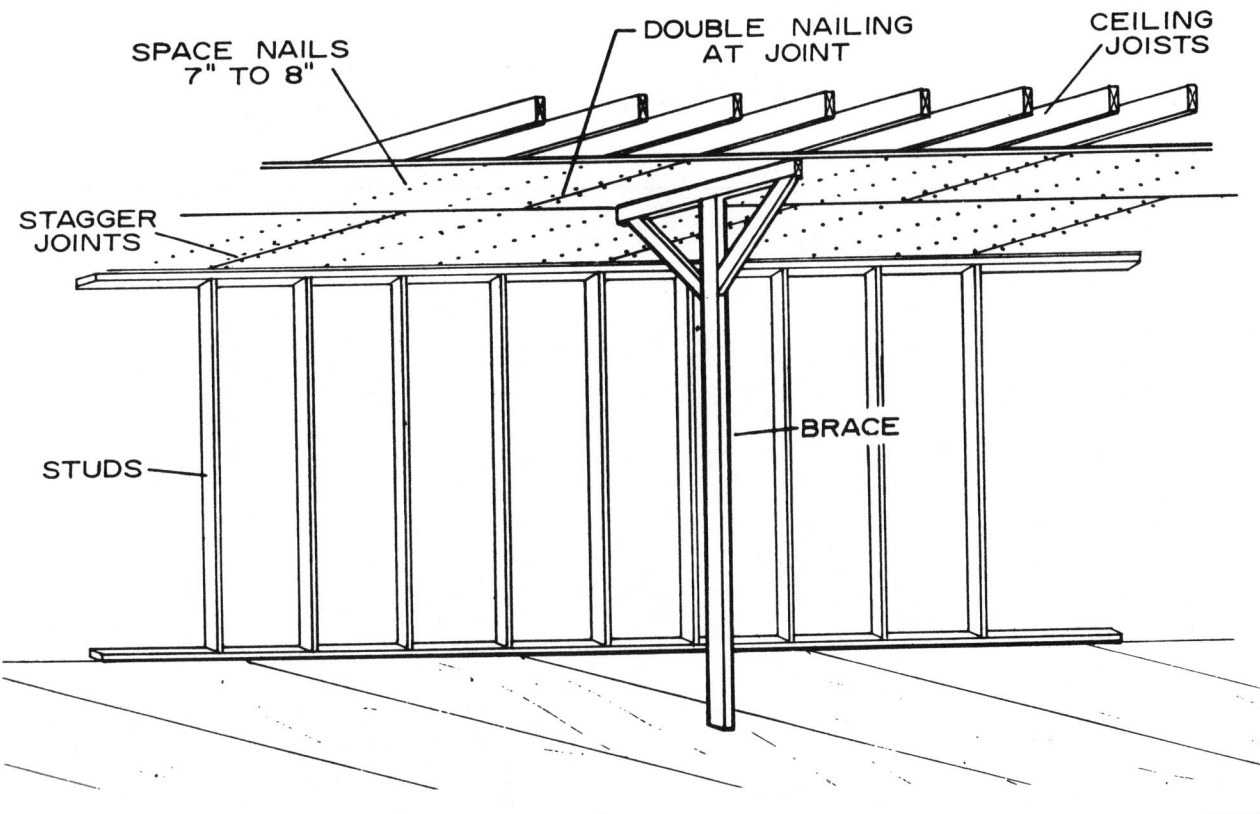

FIGURE 78.—Installing gypsum board on ceiling.

Joint Treatment

The conventional method of preparing gypsum dry-wall sheets for painting includes the use of a *joint cement* and perforated joint tape. Some gypsum board is supplied with a strip of joint paper along one edge, which is used in place of the tape. After the gypsum board has been installed and each nail driven in a "dimple" fashion (fig. 80A), the walls and ceiling are ready for treatment. Joint cement ("spackle" compound), which comes in powder or ready-mixed form, should have a soft putty consistency so that it can be easily spread with a trowel or wide putty knife. Some manufacturers provide a joint cement and a finish joint compound which is more durable and less subject to shrinkage than standard fillers. The procedure for taping (fig. 80B) is as follows:

1. Use a wide spackling knife (5-inch) to spread the cement over the tapered and other butt edges, starting at the top of the wall.

2. Press the tape into the recess with the knife until the joint cement is forced through the small perforations.

3. Cover the tape with additional cement to a level surface, feathering the outer edges. When edges are not recessed, apply tape in the normal manner, but feather out the cement farther so that the joint is level.

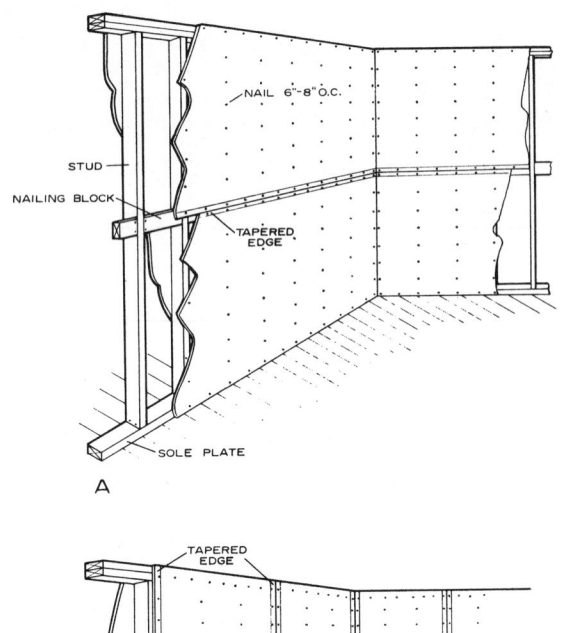

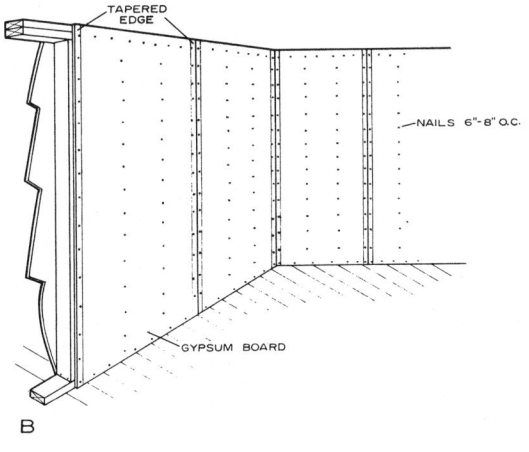

M 135 171

FIGURE 79.—Installing gypsum board on walls. A, Horizontal application; B, vertical application.

4. When dry, sand lightly and apply a thin second coat, feathering the edges again. A third coat may be required after the second has dried.

5. After cement is dry, sand smooth.

6. For hiding nail indentations at members between edges, fill with joint cement. A second coat is usually required.

Interior and exterior corners may be treated with perforated tape. Fold the tape down the center to a right angle (fig. 80C). Now, (a) apply cement on each side of the corner, (b) press tape in place with the spackle or *putty* knife, and (c) finish with joint cement and sand when dry. Wallboard corner beads of metal or plastic also can be used to serve as a corner guide and provide added strength. They are nailed to outside corners and treated with joint cement. The junction of the wall and ceiling can also be finished with a wood molding in any desired shape, which will eliminate

the need for joint treatment (fig. 80D). Use eight-penny finish nails spaced about 12 to 16 inches apart and nail into the wallplate behind.

Treatment around window and door openings depends on the type of casing used. When a casing bead and trim are used instead of a wood casing, the jambs and the beads may be installed before or during application of the gypsum wall finish. These details will be covered in the section on "Interior Doors, Frames, and Trim."

Plywood and Hardboard

The application of prefinished 4-foot-wide hardboard and plywood sheets is relatively simple. They are normally used vertically and can be fastened with small finish nails (brads). Use nails 1½ inches long for ¼- or ⅜-inch-thick materials and space about 8 to 10 inches apart at all edges and intermediate studs. Edge spacing should be about ⅜ inch. Set the nails slightly with a nail set. Many prefinished materials are furnished with small nails that require no setting because their heads match the color of the finish.

The use of panel and contact adhesives in applying prefinished sheet materials is becoming more popular and usually eliminates nails, except those used to aline the sheets. Manufacturer's directions should be followed in this method of application.

In applying sheet materials such as hardboard or plywood paneling, it is good practice to insure dry, warm conditions before installing. Furthermore, place the sheets in an upright position against the wall, lined up about as they will be installed, and allow them to take on the condition of the room for at least 24 hours. This is also true for wood or fiberboard paneling covered in the following paragraphs.

Wood or Fiberboard Paneling

Tongued-and-grooved wood or fiberboard (insulating board) paneling in various widths may be applied to walls in full lengths or above the wainscot. Wood paneling should not be too wide (nominal 8-inch) and should be installed at a moisture content of about 8 percent in most areas of the country. However, the moisture content should be about 6 percent in the dry Southwest and about 11 percent in the Southern and Coastal areas of the country. In this type of application, wood strips should be used over the studs or nailing blocks placed between them (fig. 81). Space the nailers not more than 24 inches apart.

For wood paneling, use a 1½- to 2-inch finishing or casing nail and blind-nail through the tongue. For nominal 8-inch widths, a face nail may be used near the opposite edge. Fiberboard paneling (planking) is often supplied in 12- and 16-inch widths and is applied in the same manner as the

M 135 170

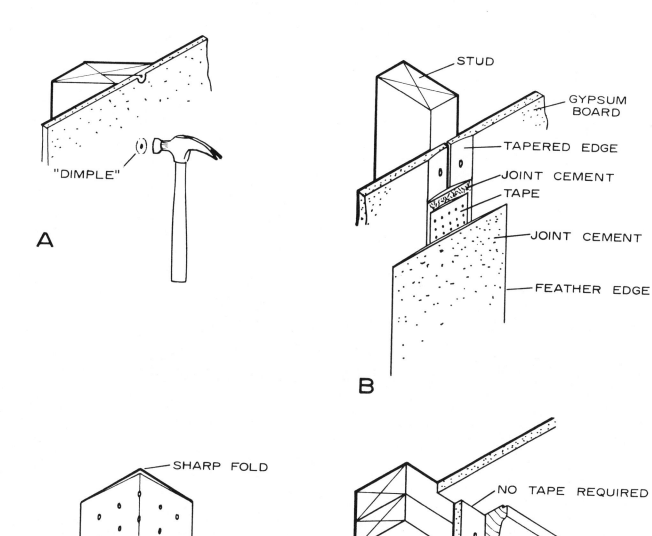

FIGURE 80.—Preparing gypsum dry-wall sheets for painting. *A*, Drive nails in "dimple" fashion; *B*, detail of joint treatment; *C*, corner tape; *D*, ceiling molding.

M 134 760

When tile is edge-matched, stapling is also satisfactory.

A suspended ceiling with small metal or wood hangers, which form supports for 24- by 48-inch or smaller drop-in panels, is another system of applying this type of ceiling finish. It is probably more applicable to the remodeling of older homes with high ceilings, however.

A third, and perhaps the most common, method of installing ceiling tile, is with the use of wood strips nailed across the ceiling joists or roof trusses. These are spaced 12 inches on center. A nominal 1- by 3- or 1- by 4-inch wood member can be used for roof or ceiling members spaced not more than 24 inches on center (fig. 82*A*). A nominal 2- by 2- or 2- by 3-inch member should be satisfactory for truss or ceiling joist spacing of up to 48 inches. Use two sevenpenny or eight-

penny nails at each joist for the nominal 1-inch strips and two tenpenny nails for the nominal 2-inch strips. Use a low-density wood, such as the softer pines, as most tile installation is done with staples.

In locating the strips, first measure the width of the room (the distance parallel to the direction of the ceiling joists). If, for example, this is 11 feet 6 inches, use 10 full 12-inch- square tiles and a 9-inch-wide tile at each side edge. Thus, the second wood strips from each side are located so that they center the first row of tiles, which can now be ripped to a width of 9 inches. The last row will also be 9 inches, but do not rip these tiles until the last row is reached so that they fit tightly. The tile can be fitted and arranged the same way for the ends of the room.

Ceiling tiles normally have a tongue on two

wood paneling. In addition to the blind nail or staple at the tongue, two face nails may be required. These are usually set slightly unless they are color-matched. A 2-inch finish nail is usually satisfactory, depending on the thickness. Panel and contact adhesives may also be used for this type of interior finish, eliminating the majority of the nails except those at the tongue. On outside walls, use a vapor barrier under the paneling (fig. 81).

Ceiling Tile

Ceiling tile may be installed in several ways, depending on the type of ceiling or roof construction. When a flat-surfaced backing is present, such as between beams of a beamed ceiling in a low-slope roof, the tiles are fastened with adhesive as recommended by the manufacturer. A small spot of a mastic type of construction adhesive at each corner of a 12- by 12-inch tile is usually sufficient.

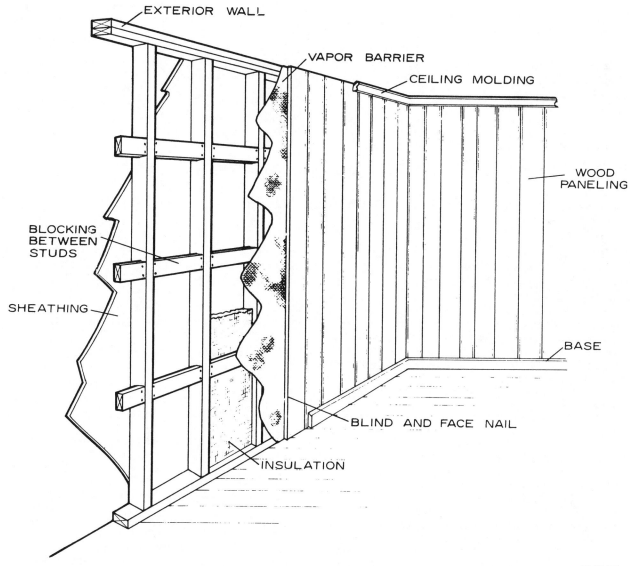

FIGURE 81.—Application of vertical paneling.

M 135 172

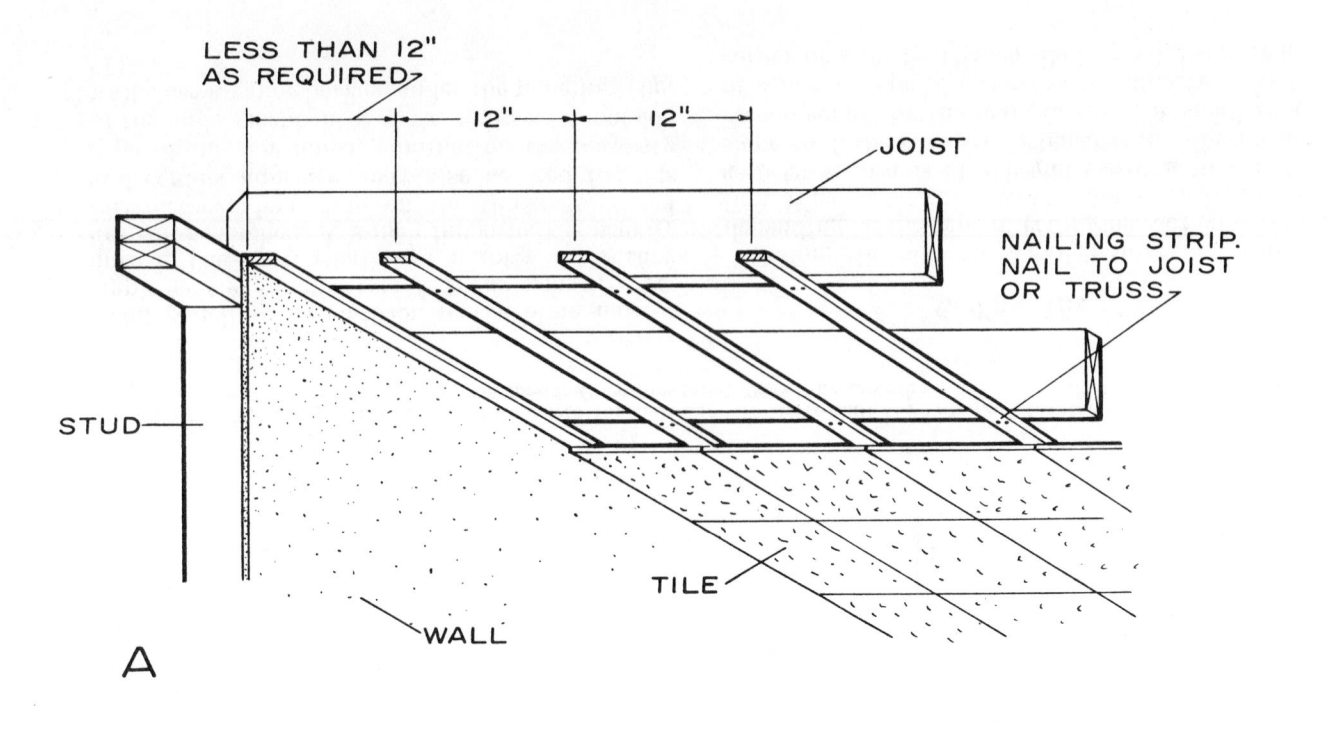

adjacent sides and a groove on the opposite adjacent sides. Start with the leading edge ahead and to the open side so that they can be stapled to the nailing strips. A small finish nail or adhesive should be used at the edge of the tiles in the first row against the wall. Stapling is done at the leading edge and the side edge of each tile (fig. 82B). Use one staple at each wood strip at the leading edge and two at the open side edge. At the opposite wall, a small finish nail or adhesive must again be used to hold the tile in place.

Most ceiling tile of this type has a factory finish, and painting or finishing is not required after it is in place. Because of this, do not soil the surface as it is installed.

Bathroom Wall Covering

When a complete prefabricated shower stall is used in the bathroom instead of a tub, no special wall finish is required. However, if a tub is used, some type of waterproof wall covering is normally required around it to protect the wall. This may consist of several types of finish from a coated hardboard paneling to various ceramic, plastic, and similar tiles.

In the interest of economy, one of the special plastic-surfaced hardboard materials is perhaps a good choice. These are applied in sheet form and fastened with an adhesive ordinarily supplied by the manufacturer of the prefinished board. Plastic or other type moldings are used at the inside corners, at tub edges, at the joints, and as end caps. Several types of calking sealants also provide satisfactory joints.

Other finishes such as ceramic, plastic, and metal tile are installed over a special water-resistant type of gypsum board. Adhesive is spread with a serrated trowel and the 4¼- by 4¼-inch or other size tile pressed in place. A joint cement is used in the joints of ceramic tile after the adhesive has set. The plastic, metal, or ceramic type of wall covering around the tub area would usually cost somewhat more than plastic-surfaced hardboard. However, almost any type of wall finish can be added at the convenience of the homeowner at any time after the house is constructed.

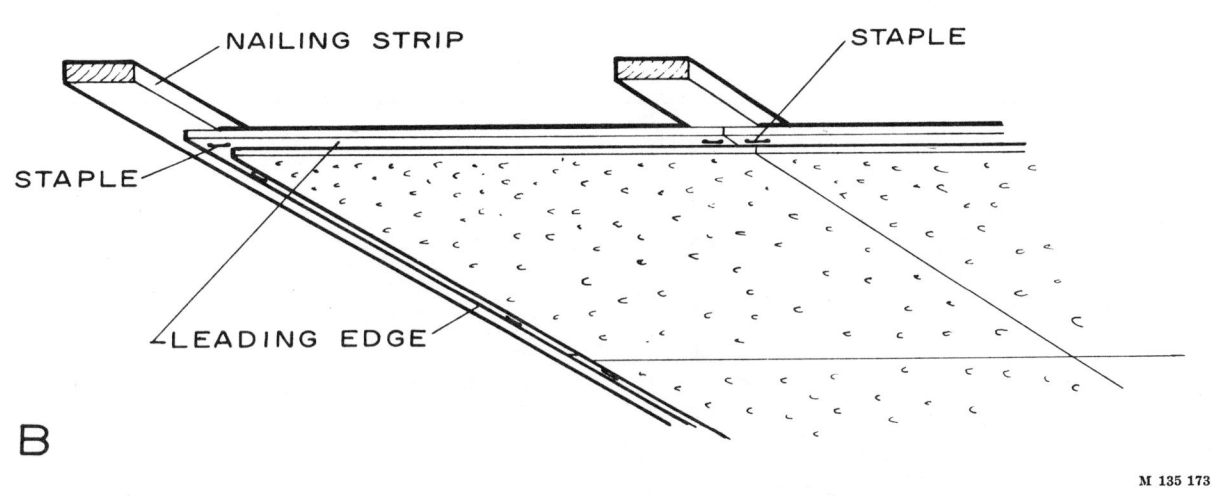

FIGURE 82.—Ceiling tile installation. A, Nailing strip location; B, stapling.

FLOOR COVERINGS

It is common practice to install wood flooring after the wall finish is applied. This is generally followed by installation of interior trim such as door jambs, casing, base, and other moldings. Wood floors would then be sanded and finished *after* the interior work is completed. Some variation of this is necessary when casing bead and trim are used in dry-wall construction to eliminate the need for standard wood casing around windows and doors. In this instance, the door jambs are installed before the wall finish is applied. Adjustment for the flooring thickness is then made by raising the bottom of the door jambs. Details of the casing bead and trim for dry-wall finishes are included in the next section—"Interior Doors, Frames, and Millwork."

However, for finish floors such as resilient tile and prefinished wood block flooring, it is usually necessary to have most, if not all, the interior work completed before installation. This is especially true of resilient flooring. Manufacturers' recommendations usually state that all tradesmen will have completed their work, even the painters, before the resilient tile is installed. In such cases, a resilient cove base might be a part of the finish, rather than the conventional wood base.

Types of Flooring

The term "finish flooring" usually applies to the material used as the final wearing surface. In its simplest form, it may be merely a *sealer* or a paint finish applied to a tongued-and-grooved plywood subfloor. Perhaps one of the most practical floor coverings for low-cost houses is some type of resilient tile such as asphalt, rubber, vinyl asbestos, etc. These materials may vary a great deal in cost. Because they are applied with an adhesive, the installation costs are usually quite low when compared to other finish flooring. However, when prices are competitive with other materials, wood finish floors in the various patterns might be selected.

Hardwood strip flooring in the best grades is used in many higher cost houses (fig. 83A). Thinner tongued-and-grooved strip flooring (fig. 83B) and thin square-edged flooring (fig. 83C) are lower in cost than 25/32-inch strip flooring and might be considered for use initially or at a later date. The use of low-grade softwood strip flooring with a natural or painted finish can also be considered. However, the installation costs of these materials are usually higher than those for resilient coverings. Many types require sanding and finishing after they are nailed in place. Another wood flooring, the parquet or wood block floor (fig. 84), is usually prefinished, is supplied in 6- by 6- or 9- by 9-inch squares, and is installed by nailing or with an adhesive. These materials, while costing more than strip flooring, require no finishing.

Thus, the cost of a finish flooring for a small house may vary from a few dollars for a floor sealer or paint on the plywood to an installed cost of $350 or more for finish floors. When a complete floor covering is required, some type of resilient tile is perhaps the best initial choice for a low-cost house. Later on, the more desirable wood floors can be easily applied over existing tile floors.

Installation of Flooring

Strip Flooring

Before laying strip flooring, be sure that the subfloor is clean and covered with a *building paper* when a board subfloor is used. This will aid in preventing air infiltration and help maintain a comfortable temperature at the floor level when a crawl space is used. The building paper should be chalklined at the joists as a guide in nailing the strip flooring. Before laying the flooring, the bundles should be opened and the flooring spread out and exposed to a warm, dry condition for at least 24 hours, and preferably 48 hours. Moisture content of the flooring should be 6 percent for the dry Southwest area, 10 percent for Southern and Coastal areas, and 7 percent for the remainder of the country.

Strip flooring should be laid at right angles to the joists, (fig. 85A). Start at one wall, placing the first board ½ to ⅝ inch away from the wall and face-nail so that the base and shoe will cover the space and nails (fig. 85B). Next, blind-nail the first strip of flooring and each subsequent piece with eightpenny flooring nails (for $^{25}\!/_{32}$-inch thickness) at each joist crossing. Nail through the tongue and into the joist below with a nail angle of 45° to 50°. Set each nail to the surface of the

tongue. Each piece should be driven up lightly for full contact. Use a hammer and a short piece of scrap flooring to protect the edge. The last flooring strip must be face-nailed at the wall line, again allowing ½- to ⅝-inch space for expansion of the flooring.

Other thinner types of strip flooring are nailed in the same way, except that sixpenny flooring nails may be sufficient. Square-edge flooring must be face-nailed using two 1½-inch finish nails (brads) on about 12-inch centers.

Wood Block Flooring

Wood block flooring with matching tongued-and-grooved edges is often fastened by nailing, but may be installed with an adhesive. Other block floorings made from wood-base materials are also available. Manufacturers of these specialty floors can supply the correct adhesive as well as instructions for laying. Their recommended methods are based on years of experience, and when followed, should provide maintenance-free service.

Resilient Tile

Most producers of resilient tile provide detailed instructions regarding installation. This covers the underlayment, adhesives, and other requirements. However, most resilient tiles are applied in much the same way.

The underlayment may be plywood which serves both as a subfloor and an underlayment for the tile. A subfloor of wood boards requires an underlayment of plywood, hardboard, or particleboard. Nails should be driven flush with the surface, cracks and joints filled and sanded smooth, and the surface thoroughly cleaned.

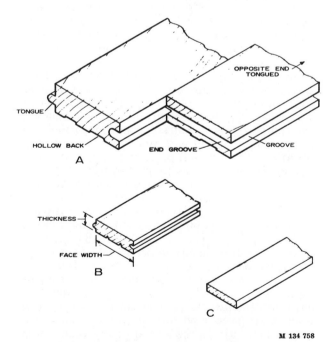

M 134 758

FIGURE 83.—Strip flooring. *A,* Side and end matched; *B,* side matched; *C,* square edged.

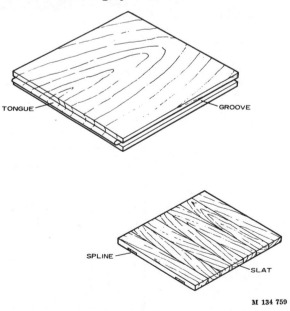

M 134 759

FIGURE 84.—Wood block flooring.

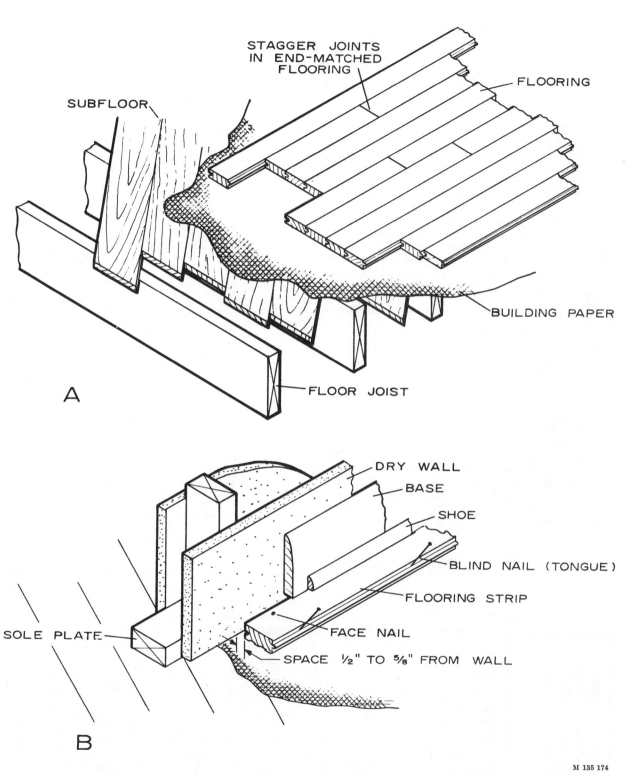

A

B

M 135 174

FIGURE 85.—Installing strip flooring. *A,* General application; *B,* laying first strip.

Next, a center baseline should be marked on the subfloor in each direction of the room (fig. 86A). Centerlines should be exactly 90° (a right angle) with each other. This can be assured by using a 3:4:5-foot measurement along two sides and the diagonal (fig. 86A). In a large room, a 6:8:10-foot measuring combination can be used.

Now, spread the adhesive with a serrated trowel (both as recommended by the manufacturer) over one of the quarter-sections outlined by the centerlines. Waiting (drying) time should conform to the directions for the adhesive.

Starting at one inside corner, lay the first tile exactly in line with the marked centerlines. The second tile can be laid adjacent to the first on one side (fig. 86B). The third tile laid adjacent to the first at the other centerline on the other side of the quarter section. Thus, in checkerboard fashion, the entire section can be covered. The remaining three sections can be covered in the same way. Some tile requires only pressing in place; others should be rolled after installing for better adherence.

The edge tiles around the perimeter of the room must be trimmed to fit to the edge of the wall. A clearance of ⅛ to ¼ inch should be allowed at all sides for expansion. This edge is covered with a cove base of the same resilient material or with a standard wood base. Wood base is usually lower in cost than the resilient cove base, but installation costs are somewhat greater.

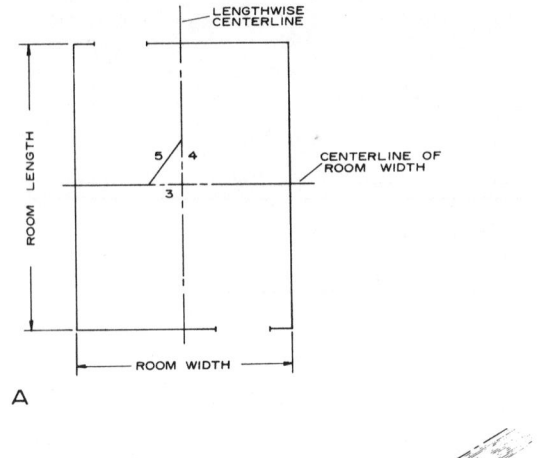

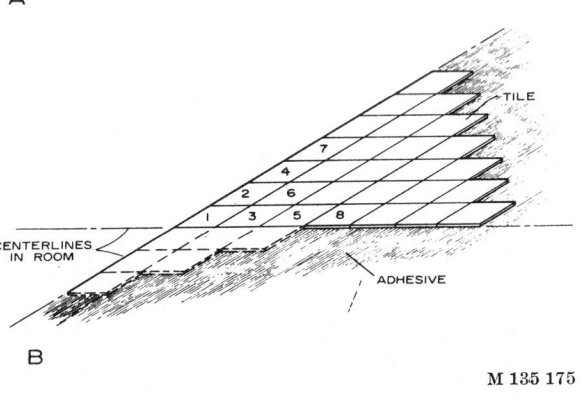

B

M 135 175

Figure 86.—Installing resilient tile. A, Center baseline; B, order of laying tile.

INTERIOR DOORS, FRAMES, AND MILLWORK

The cost of interior finish such as cabinets, door frames, doors, and moldings varies a great deal with wood species and styles. For example, pine casing used as trim for door and window frames may cost only half as much as some hardwood trim. However, some types of interior panel doors made of pine may cost twice as much as a mahogany flush door. Choice of materials should be based both on cost and utility. Such details are covered in the building plans and specifications.

The number and types of cabinets used in a house can make a substantial difference in the overall cost. Prefinished base cabinets with counter and wall cabinets for kitchens may range in price from $30 to $35 and more per lineal foot. This should be compared to the lower cost of simple shelving with provisions for installation of the doors at a later date; this may mean a saving of several hundred dollars. When a cost reduction is needed to keep within the limits of available funds, some such substitution may be necessary.

The moisture content of all interior wood finish when installed is important in the overall perform-

ance. The recommended moisture content for interior finish varies between 6 and 11 percent, depending on climatic conditions. Recommended moisture content is the same as outlined for wood and fiberboard paneling in the section on "Interior Wall and Ceiling Finish."

Interior Doors and Trim

Parts

Door frames.—The rough door openings provided for during framing of the interior walls should accommodate the assembled frames. The allowance was 2½ inches plus the door width and 3 inches plus the door height. When thin resilient tile is used over the subfloor, the allowance is 2¼ inches for door height. Frames consist of a head *jamb* with two side jambs and the stops. When a wood casing is used around the door frame as trim, the width of the jambs is the same as the overall wall thickness. When a metal casing is used with the dry wall, eliminating the need for the wood

casing, the jamb width is the same as the stud depth width. The side and head jambs and the stop are assembled as shown in figure 87A. Jambs may be purchased in sets or can be easily made in a small shop with a table or radial-arm saw.

Casing.—Casing is the trim around the door opening. It is nailed to the edge of the jamb and to the door buck (edge stud). A number of shapes are available, such as colonial (fig. 87B), ranch (fig. 87C), and plain (fig. 87D). Casing widths vary from 2¼ to 3½ inches, depending on the style. Thicknesses vary from ½ to ¾ inch. A casing bead or metal casing used to trim the edges of the gypsum board at the door and window jambs (fig. 87A) eliminates the need for the wood casing.

Doors.—Two general styles of interior doors are the panel and the flush door. The interior flush door is normally the hollow-core type (fig. 88A),

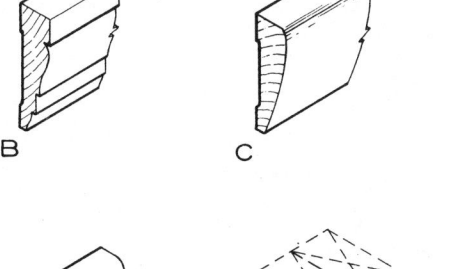

A   B   C

M 135 177

Figure 88.—Interior doors. A, Flush; B, five-cross-panel; C, colonial, panel type.

which costs much less than the solid core. The five-cross-panel door (fig. 88B) is usually lower in cost than the colonial type (fig. 88C).

Standard widths for interior doors are: (a) Bedroom and other rooms, 2 feet 6 inches; (b) bathroom, 2 feet 4 inches; (c) small closet and linen closet, 2 feet. Interior door heights should be the same as for exterior doors; standard height is 6 feet 8 inches. Doors of these sizes can be obtained from most lumber dealers.

Doors should be hinged so that they open in the direction of natural entry. They should also swing against a blank wall whenever possible, never into a hallway. Door swing directions and sizes are shown on the working drawings.

Installation of Doors

Frames.—When jambs are not preassembled, side jambs are nailed to the head jamb with three eightpenny coated nails (fig. 87A). Cut the side jambs to the correct length before nailing. A temporary brace can then be nailed across the bottom of the side jambs so the width is the same throughout the full height of the door.

The frame is now placed in the opening and fastened to the wall studs with the aid of shingle wedges used between the side jamb and the rough door buck (side stud) (fig. 89A). Plumb and fasten one side first, using four or five sets of wedges along the height, and nail the jamb with pairs of eightpenny finish nails at each wedged area. Square the top corners of the opening and fasten the opposite jamb in the same manner. Use a straightedge along the face of the jambs when lining them up with the wedges.

Casings.—Casings are nailed to the edges of the jamb and to the door buck. First, cut off the shingle wedges flush with the wall. Position the casing with about a ³⁄₁₆-inch edge distance from the face of the jamb (fig. 89A). Depending on the

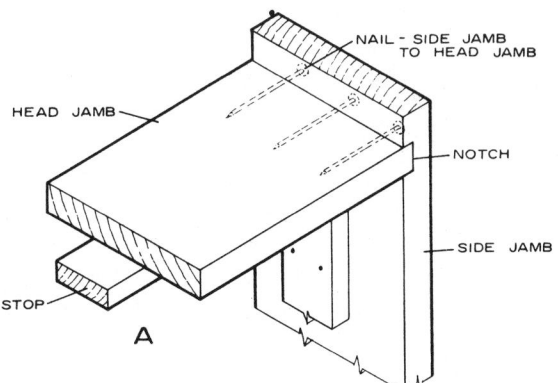
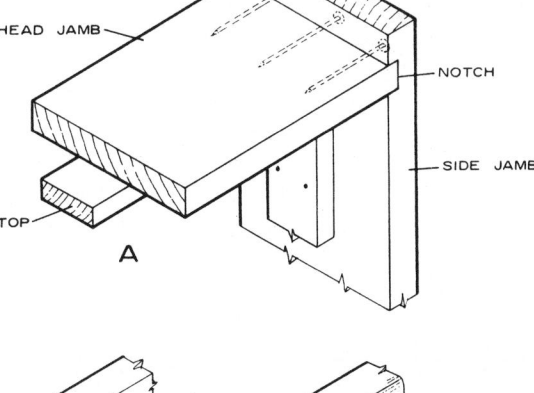

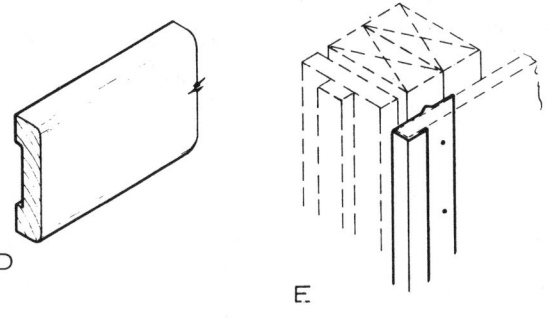

M 135 176

Figure 87.—Door frame and trim. A, Frame components and assembly; B, colonial casing; C, ranch casing; D, plain casing; E, metal casing.

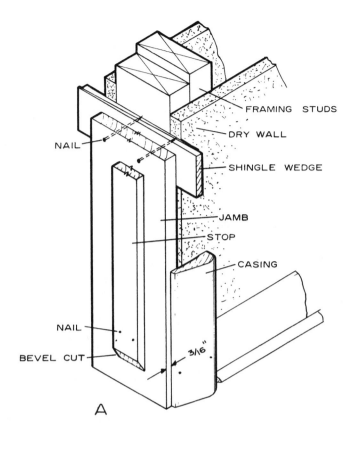

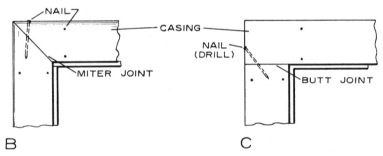

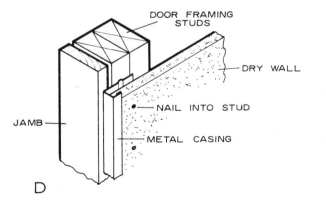

FIGURE 89.—Installing door frames and trim. *A*, Side jamb; *B*, molded casing; *C*, rectangular casing; *D*, metal casing

M 135 178

thickness of the casing, sixpenny or sevenpenny casing or finish nails should be used. When the casing has one thin edge, use a 1½-inch brad or finish nail along this edge. Space the nails in pairs about 16 inches apart.

Casings with molded forms (fig. 87 *B* and *C*) must have a *mitered joint* where head and side casings join (fig. 89*B*). Rectangular casing can be butt-joined (fig. 89*C*). Casing for the interior side of exterior door frames is installed in the same way.

Metal casing used instead of wood casing can be nailed in place in two ways. After the jambs have been installed and before the gypsum board is placed, the metal casing can be nailed to the door buck around the opening (fig. 87*E*). The gypsum board is then inserted into the groove and nailed to the studs in normal fashion. The second method consists of placing the metal casing over the edge of the gypsum board, positioning the sheet properly with respect to the jamb and nailing through both the gypsum board and the casing into the stud behind (fig. 89*D*). Use the same type nails and nail spacing as described in the section on "Interior Wall and Ceiling Finish" for gypsum board.

Doors and stops.—The door opening is now complete. Without the door in place, it is often referred to as a "cased opening." When cost is a major factor, the use of this opening with a curtain rod and curtain will insure some privacy. Door stops can be fitted and doors hung later.

The door is fitted between the jambs by planing the sides to the correct width. This requires a careful measurement of the width before planing. When the correct width is obtained, the top is squared and trimmed to fit the opening. The bottom of the door is now sawed off with the proper floor clearance. The side, top, and bottom clearances and the location of the hinges are shown in figure 90. Remember that paint or finish takes up some of the space, so allow for this.

The narrow wood strips used as stops for the door are usually 7/16 inch thick and may be 1½ to 2¼ inches wide. They are installed on the jambs with a mitered joint at the junction of the head and side jambs. A 45° bevel cut at the bottom of stops 1 to 1½ inches above the finish floor will eliminate a dirt pocket and make cleaning or refinishing of the floor much easier (fig. 89*A*).

Before fitting the exterior doors, install a threshold between side jambs to cover the junction of the sill and the flooring (or allow for the threshold). Nail to the floor and sill with finish nails.

Installation of Door Hardware

Four types of hardware sets available in a number of finishes are commonly used for doors. They are classed as: (a) Entry lock for exterior doors, (b) bathroom set (inside lock control with a safety slot for opening from the outside), (c) bedroom lock set (keyed lock), and (d) passage

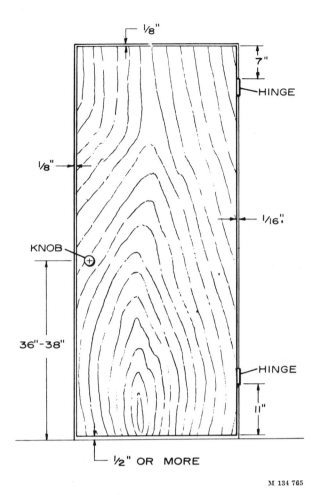

M 134 765

FIGURE 90.—Door clearances.

set (without lock). Two hinges are normally used for 1⅜-inch interior doors. To minimize warping of exterior doors in cold climates, use three hinges. Exterior doors, 1¾ inches thick, require 4- by 4-inch loose-pin hinges and the 1⅜-inch interior doors 3½- by 3½-inch loose-pin hinges.

Hinges.—Hinges are *routed* or *mortised* into the edge of the door with about a 3/16- or ¼-inch back spacing (fig. 91*A*). This may vary slightly, however. Adjustments should be made, if necessary, to provide sufficient edge distance so that screws have good penetration in the wood. Locate the hinges as shown in figure 90 and use one hinge half to mark the outline of the cut. If a router is not available, mark the hinge outline and the depth of the cut and remove the wood with a wood chisel. The depth of the routing should be such that the surface of the hinge is flush with the wood surface. Screws are included with each hinge set and should be used to fasten the hinge halves in place.

The door is now placed in the opening and blocked for the proper clearances. Stops should be tacked in place temporarily so that the door surface is flush with the edge of the jamb. Mark the location of the door hinges on the jambs, re-

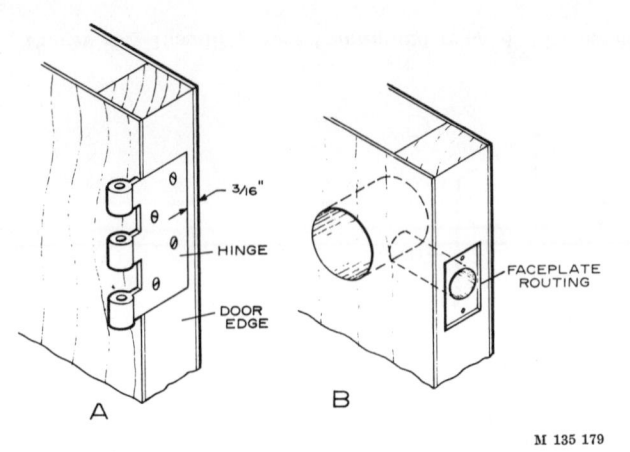

FIGURE 91.—Installing door hardware. *A*, Hinge; *B*, lock.

move the door, and with the remaining hinge halves and a small square mark the outline. The depth of the routed area should be the same as that on the door (the thickness of the hinge half). After fastening the hinge halves, place the door in the opening and insert the pins. If marking and routing were done correctly, the door should fit perfectly and swing freely.

Locks.—Door lock and latch sets are supplied with paper templates which provide the exact location of holes for the lock and latch. Follow the printed directions, locating the door knob 36 to 38 inches above the floor (fig. 90). Most lock sets require only one hole through the face of the door and one at the edge (fig. 91*B*). Latches are used with or without a face plate, depending on the type of lock set.

Strike plate.—The strike plate is used to hold the door closed by means of the latch. It is routed into the jamb (fig. 92*A*). Mark the location of the latch on the jamb when the door is in a near-closed position and outline the strike plate to this position. Rout enough to bring the strike plate flush with the face of the jamb.

Stops.—The stops which have been temporarily nailed in place while fitting the door and door hardware can now be permanently nailed. Exterior door frames with thicker jambs have the stop rabbeted in place as a part of the jamb. Finish nails or brads 1½ inches long are satisfactory for nailing. The stop at the lock side should be nailed first, setting it against the door face when the door is latched. Use nails in pairs spaced about 16 inches apart. The clearances and stop locations shown in figure 92*B* should be generally followed.

Window Trim

The casing used around the window frames on the interior of the house is usually the same pattern as that used for the interior door frames.

There are two common methods of installing wood trim at window areas: (a) With a *stool* and *apron* (fig. 93*A*) and (b) with complete casing trim (fig. 93*B*). Metal casing is also used around the entire window opening.

In a prefitted double-hung window, the stool is normally the first piece of trim to be installed. It is notched out between the jambs so that the forward edge contacts the lower sash rail (fig. 93*A*). Of course, in windows that are not preassembled, the sash must be fitted before the trim is installed. The stool is now blind-nailed at the ends with eightpenny finish nails so that the casing at the side will cover the nailheads. With hardwood, predrilling is usually required to prevent splitting. The stool should also be nailed at midpoint to the sill, and later to the apron when it is installed. Toenailing may be substituted for face-nailing to the sill (fig. 93*A*).

The casing is now applied and nailed as described for the door frames, except that the inner edge is flush with the inner face of the jambs so that the *stop* covers the joint (fig. 93*A*). The stops are now fitted similarly to the interior door stops and placed against the lower sash so that it can slide freely. A 1½-inch casing nail or brad should be used. Use nails in pairs spaced about 12 inches apart. When full-length weatherstrips are included with the window unit, locate the stops against them to provide a small amount of pressure. Cut the apron to a length equal to the outer width of the casing line (fig. 93*A*) and nail to the framing sill below with eightpenny finish nails.

When casing is used to finish the bottom of the window frame instead of the stool and apron, a narrow stool or stop is substituted (fig. 93*B*). Casing along the bottom of the window is then applied in the same way as at the side and head of the window.

When metal casing is used as trim around window openings, it is applied to the sill as well as at the side and head of the frame. Consequently, the jambs and sill of the frame are not as deep as when wood casing is used. The stops are also narrower by the thickness of the dry-wall finish. The metal casing is used flush with the inside edge of the window jamb (fig. 93*C*). This type of trim is installed at the same time as the dry wall and in the same way described for the interior door frames.

Other types of windows, such as the awning or hopper types or the casement, are trimmed about the same as the double-hung window. Casing of the same types shown in figure 87 *B*, *C*, *D*, and *E* can also be used for these units.

Base Moldings

Types

Some type of trim or finish is normally used at the junction of the wall and the floor. This can

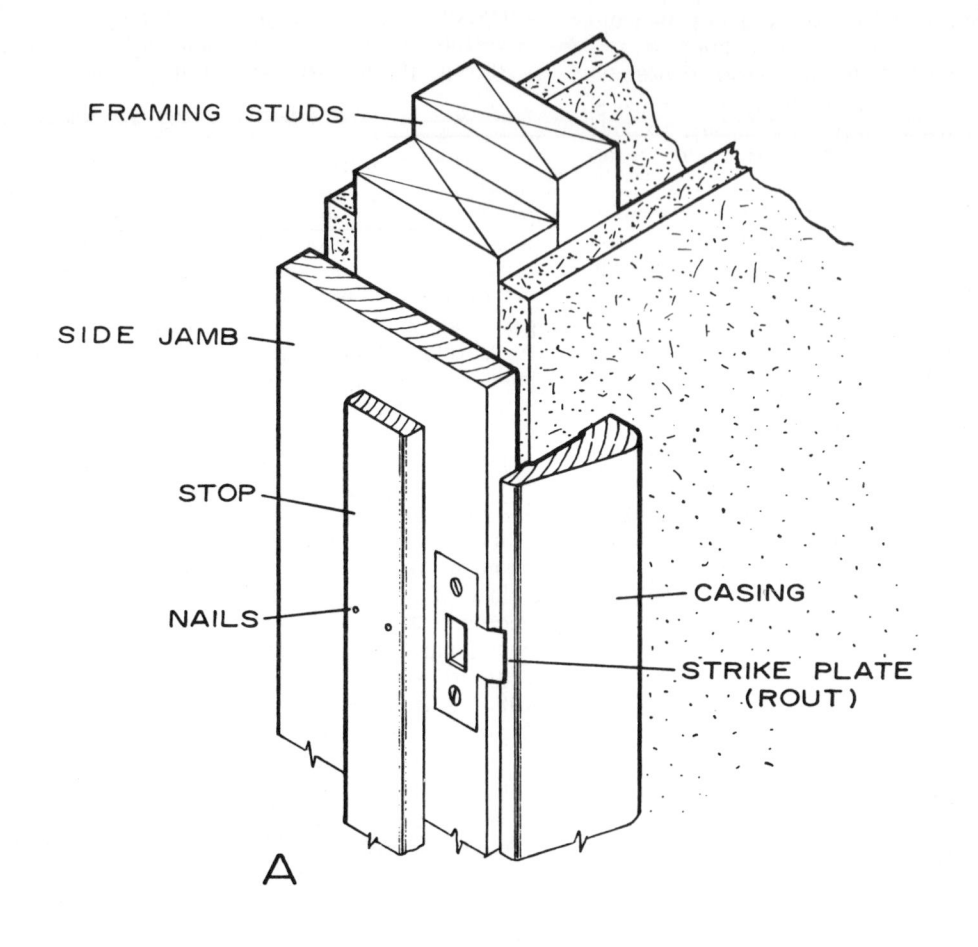

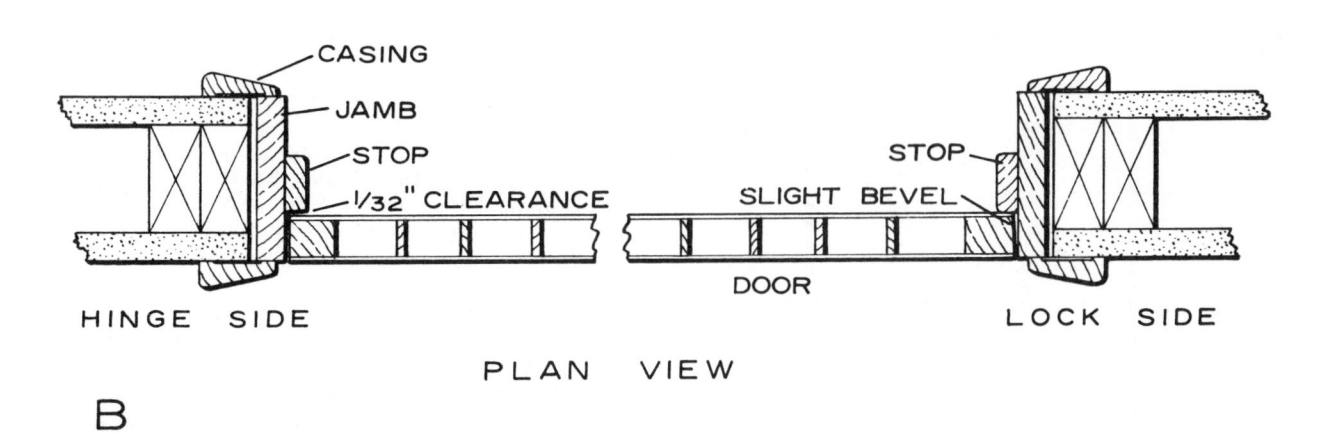

FIGURE 92.—Door installation. *A*, Strike plate; *B*, stop clearances.

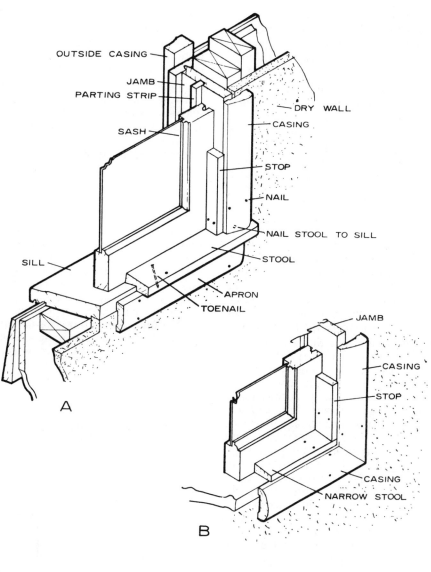

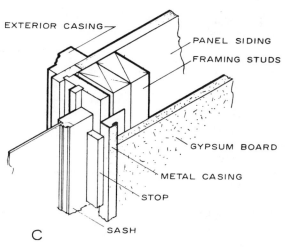

FIGURE 93.—Window trim. *A*, With stool and apron; *B*, wood casing at window; *C*, metal casing at window.

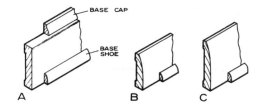

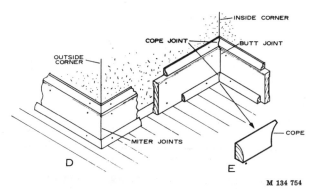

FIGURE 94.—Base moldings. *A*, Two-piece; *B*, narrow; *C*, medium width; *C*, installation; *E*, coped joint.

Cabinets

As discussed in the first part of this section, kitchen and other cabinets can increase the cost of a house substantially. Thus, in many cases, it may be necessary to use the most simple forms of storage areas to remain within a limited budget. However, even when the cabinets must be quite simple, it is good practice to provide for additions which can be made later such as the installation of the doors and door hardware.

Kitchen Arrangements

A kitchen, no matter how small, should be laid out so that there is a good relationship between the

consist of a simple wood member which serves as both the *base* and *base shoe* or a more elaborate two-piece unit with a square-edge base and base cap (fig. 94*A*). One-piece standard base may be obtained in a 2¼-inch width (fig. 94*B*) or 3¼-inch medium width (fig. 94*C*). The true base shoe, sometimes called *quarter-round*, is not actually quarter-round as it is ½ by ¾ inch in size. In the interest of economy, the base shoe can be eliminated, using only a single-piece base. Resilient floors may be finished with a simple narrow wood base or with a resilient *cove* base which is installed with adhesives.

Installation

Wide square-edge *baseboard* should be installed with a butt joint at inside corners and mitered joint at outside corners (fig. 94*D*). It should be nailed to each stud with two eightpenny finishing nails. Molded single-piece base, *base molding*, and *base shoe* should have a coped joint at inside corners and a mitered joint at outside corners. A *coped joint* is one in which the first piece has a square-cut end against the wall and the second member at the inside corner has a coped joint. This is accomplished by sawing a 45° miter cut and, with a coping saw, trimming along the mitered edge to fit the adjoining molding (fig. 94*E*). This results in a tight inside joint. The base shoe should be nailed to the subfloor with long slender nails, and not to the baseboard itself. This will prevent openings between the shoe and the floor if floor joists dry out and shrink.

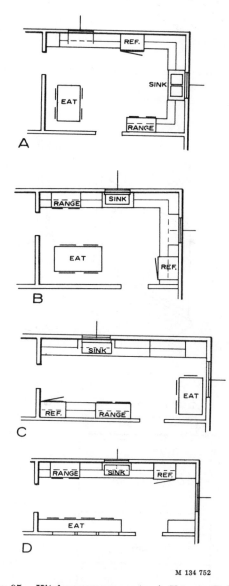

FIGURE 95.—Kitchen arrangements. *A*, U-type; *B*, L-type; *C*, parallel wall; *D*, sidewall.

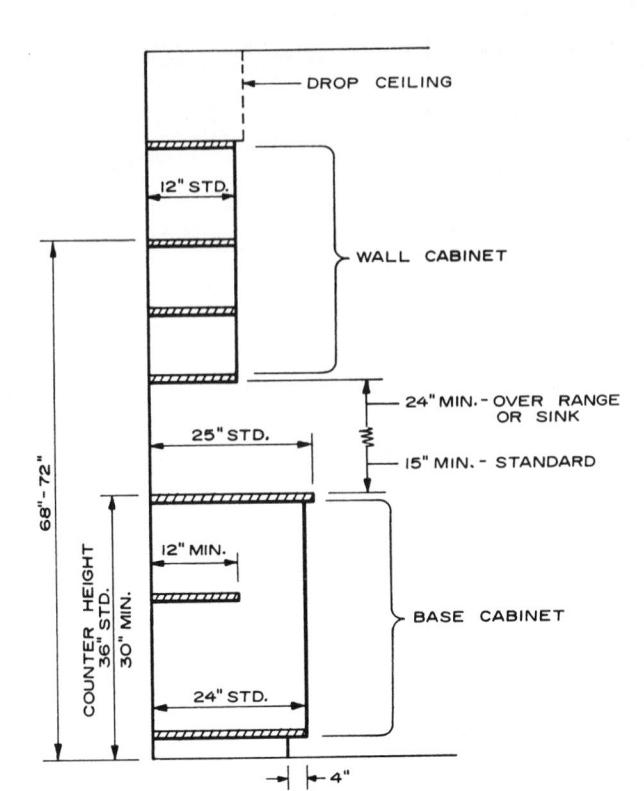

FIGURE 96.—Kitchen cabinet proportions.

refrigerator, the sink, and the stove. This is desirable in order to save steps and time in the preparation of meals. Kitchen sizes and shapes vary a great deal and usually control the arrangement of the utilities and the cabinets. Figure 95 shows the four common types of kitchen layouts: (a) U-type, (b) L-type, (c) parallel wall, and (d) sidewall type. The L-type and the sidewall type (fig. 95 B or D) are perhaps those most adaptable to a small kitchen. Kitchen layouts are shown on the working drawings for each house.

Kitchen Cabinet Units

Kitchen cabinets are normally classed as (a) base cabinets and (b) wall cabinets. The base or floor unit, which contains a counter, may include both drawers and doors and shelves in various combinations. The wall units are normally a series of shelves with hinged or sliding doors located above the base cabinets. The proportions and sizes of these cabinets are shown in figure 96. A standard height for the base unit is 36 inches, with a top width of 25 inches. A low-cost counter top may consist simply of plywood with a resilient surface

covering. The more elaborate tops usually have a plastic laminated surface with a molded edge and backsplash.

Construction of Low-Cost Kitchen Cabinets

Low-cost kitchen cabinets can consist of a series of shelves enclosed with vertical dividers and ends. They can be designed so that flush doors can be added later at little cost and with no alterations. Curtains across the top of the opening can be temporarily used.

Base units.—Figure 97 shows the details of a simple base unit. Any combination of opening widths and shelf spacing can be used. Ripping 4-foot-wide sheets of plywood or particleboard in half provides material for ends, dividers, and shelves. Use ⅝ or ¾-inch thickness in an AC grade when only one side is exposed. When shelf layout is decided, saw slots across the width of the ends and dividers so that shelves will fit them. These *dados* are usually ¼ inch deep. Provide for about a 3½-by-3½-inch toe space at the bottom. When assembling, nail the ends and dividers to the shelves with eightpenny nails spaced 5 to 6 inches apart. Use finish nails where ends are exposed. A 1- by 3-inch rail is used at the top in front to aid in fastening the top to the cabinet (fig. 97A). This will later serve to frame the doors. A 1- by 4-inch cleat is used across the back at the top, serving to fasten the cabinet to the wall studs, as well as for fastening the top (fig. 97B). The ends and dividers are notched to receive this cleat (fig. 97C). On finished ends, this notch is cut only halfway through. Fasten the cabinet to the wall by nailing or screwing through the back cleat into each stud with eightpenny nails or 2-inch screws.

The top of plywood or particleboard is nailed in place onto the ends, back cleat, and top rail with eightpenny finish nails. When the top has a plastic finish, use small metal angles around the interior and fasten them to the cabinet and top with small screws. When side stiles and doors are added later, a pleasant, utilitarian cabinet will result (fig. 97D). Until then, however, curtains can be used across the openings.

Any combination of base cabinets can be constructed. The sink cabinet usually consists only of a pair of doors and a bottom shelf. Vent slots are usually cut in the top cross rail. A cutout is necessary in the top to provide for a self-rimming or rimmed sink.

Wall units.—Wall units are about 30 inches high when installed below a drop ceiling. When carried to the ceiling line, they may be 44 or 45 inches in height. The depth is usually about 12 inches. A 4-foot-wide sheet of plywood or particleboard can be ripped in four pieces if this depth is used. As in base unit construction, the wall cabinet can consist of dadoed ends and one or more vertical dividers

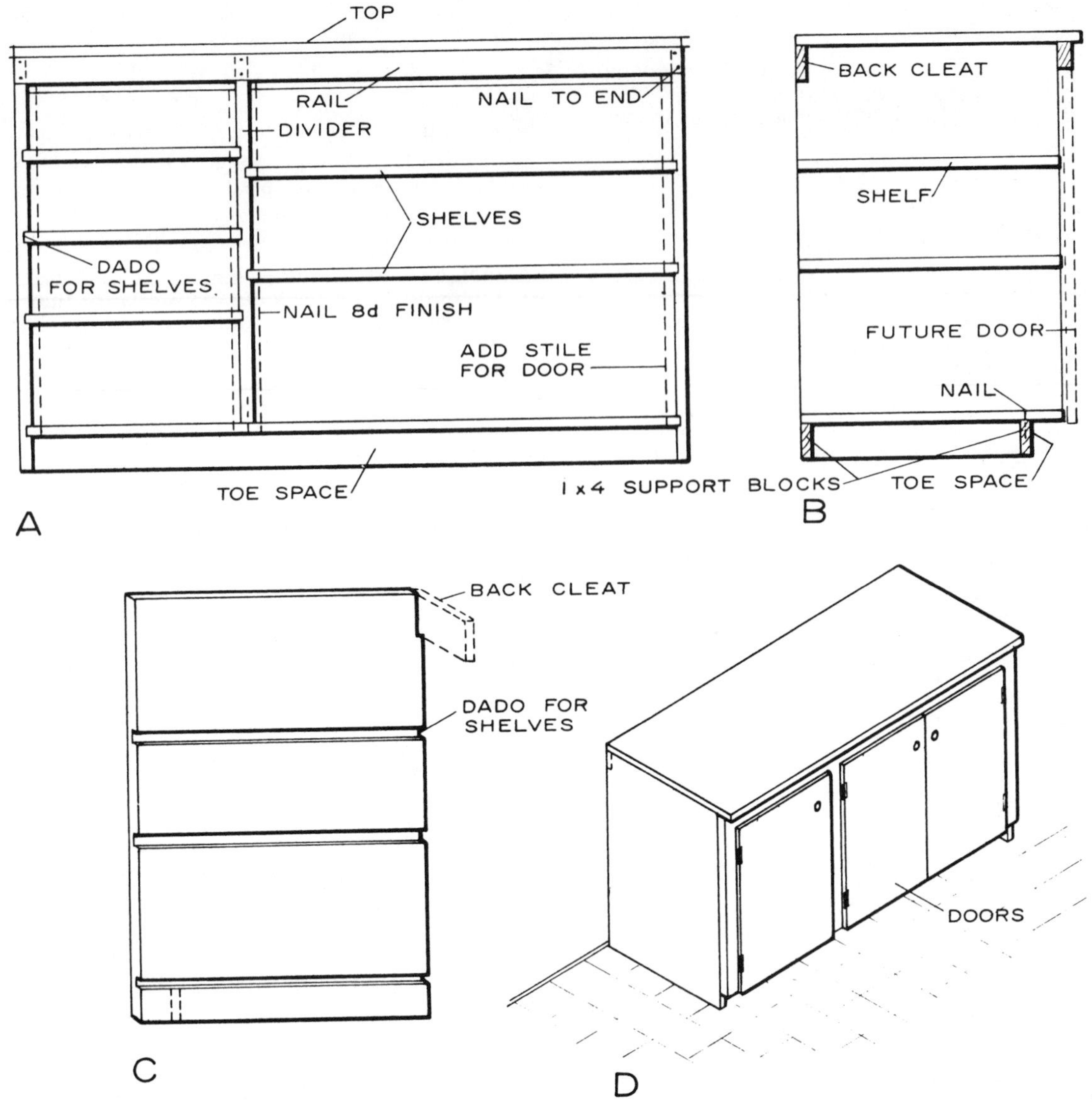

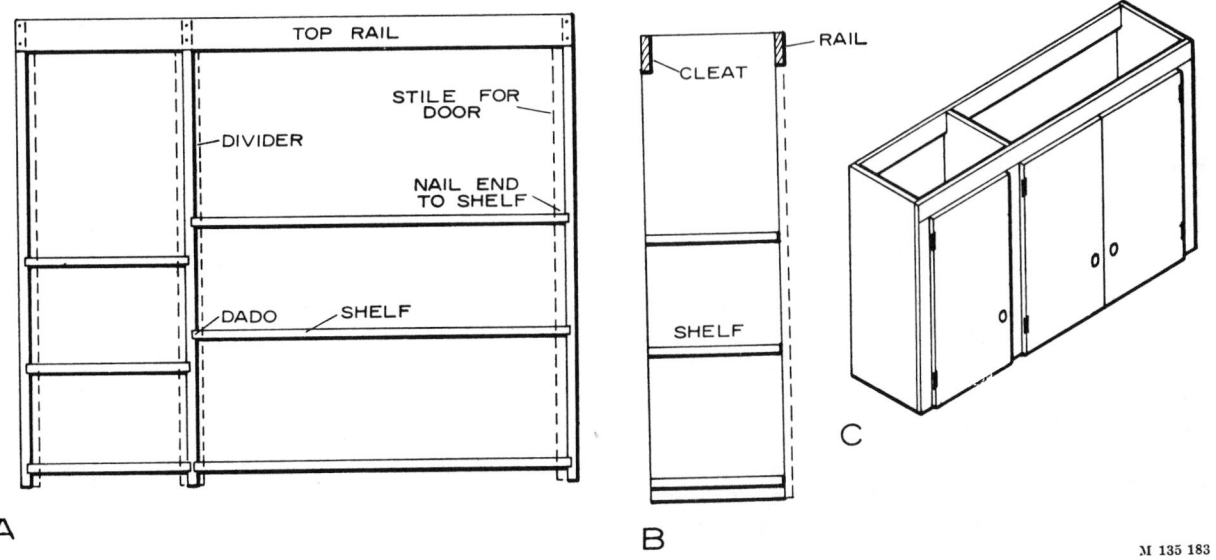

FIGURE 97.—Kitchen cabinet base unit. A, Front view; B, section; C, end from interior; D, overall view.

FIGURE 98.—Kitchen cabinet wall unit. A, Front view; B, section; C, overall view.

nailed to the shelves (fig. 98A). Use eightpenny finish nails when the end is exposed. The cleat is used to fasten the cabinet to the wall (fig. 98B). A top rail ties the sides and dividers together and, when the vertical stiles are added, provides framing for doors (fig. 98C).

Wardrobe-Closet Combinations

Closets are often eliminated in a low-cost house for economic reasons. A closet requires wall framing, interior and exterior covering, a door frame and door, and trim. However, some type of storage area should be included which will be pleasant in appearance, yet low in cost. Practical storage areas, often called wardrobe-closets, consist of wood or plywood sides, shelves, and some type of door or curtain. Figure 99 shows a simple built-in wardrobe that can be initially curtained. A folding door unit can be added later.

Wardrobe-closets are normally built of 5⁄8- or 3⁄4-inch plywood or particleboard. Provide dados for the shelf or shelves, as used on the kitchen cabinets. A back cleat at the top provides a member for fastening the unit to the wall. The sides can be trimmed at the floor with a base shoe molding which, with toenailing, keeps the sides in place. Add a simple closet pole. Fasten the unit to the wall at the top cleat and, when in a corner, also to the side wall (fig. 99). Any size or combination of wardrobes of this type can be built in during construction of the house or added later. Shelves or partial shelves can be provided in the bottom section for shoe storage.

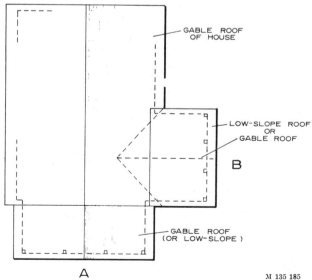

FIGURE 99.—Wardrobe-closet.

PORCHES

Additions such as a *porch* or an attached garage improve the appearance of a small house. Furthermore, in some areas of the country, the porch serves as a gathering place for family and neighbors and becomes almost a necessity.

While it is probably more practical to build a porch at the same time as the house proper, the porch can also be constructed quite readily after the house is completed. The cost of porches can vary a great deal, depending on design. A fully enclosed porch with windows and interior finish would add substantially to the cost of a house. On the other hand, the cost of an open porch with roof, floor, and simple supporting posts and footings might be well within the reach of many home builders. If desired, an open porch could be improved in the future by enclosing all or part of it.

Types of Open Porches

Two locations for porches might be considered for a low-cost house. One is on the end of a house (fig. 100A). Another is at the side of a house (fig. 100B). The porch at the end of a gable-roofed house may have a gable roof similar to the house

itself. The slope of the roof should usually be the same as the main roof. When the size of the porch

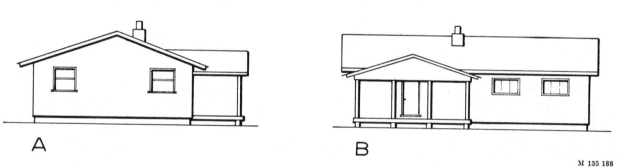

FIGURE 100.—Porch locations. A, End of house; B, side of house.

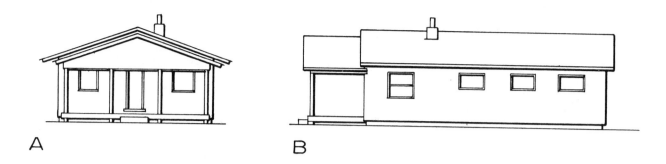

FIGURE 101.—End porch. A, End view; B, side view.

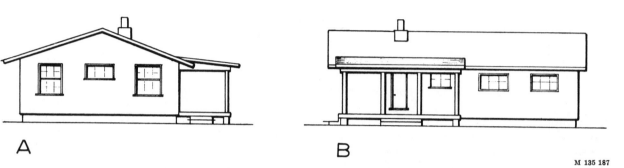

FIGURE 102.—Side porch with low-slope roof. A, End view; B, side view.

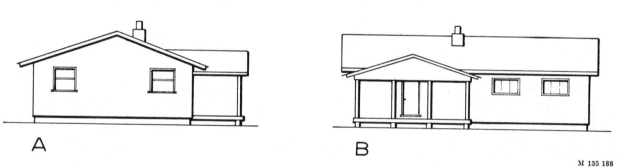

FIGURE 103.—Side porch with gable roof. A, End view; B, side view.

is somewhat less than the width of the house, the roofline will be slightly lower (fig. 101). When the porch is the same width, the roofline of the house is usually carried over the porch itself. A low-pitch roof in a shed or hip style can also be used for a porch located at the end of a house.

A low-slope roof can also be used for a porch at the side of a gable-roofed house (fig. 102). This system of room construction is usually less expensive than other methods, as the rafters also serve as ceiling joists.

Another method of roofing a porch at the side of the house is with the gable roof (fig. 103). While somewhat more costly than a flat or low-pitch roof, it is probably more pleasing in appearance. Both rafters and ceiling joists are normally used in this system. Thus, if a porch is to be a part of the original house or constructed later, select the style most suited to the design of the house and to the available funds.

Construction of Porches

While many types of foundations might be used for a porch as well as for the house, we will consider only the post or pier type because of its lower cost. A full-masonry foundation wall with proper footings will increase the cost substantially over the post or pier type. With a proper soil cover and a skirtboard of some type, the performance and appearance of such a post or pier foundation will not vary greatly from that of a full-masonry wall.

Floor System

The floor system for the open porch should consist of treated wood posts or masonry piers constructed in the same way as those outlined in the section on foundation systems for the house proper. These posts or piers should bear on footings and support nail-laminated floor beams which are anchored to the posts. These beams, of doubled

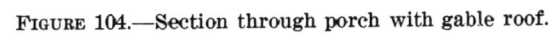

FIGURE 104.—Section through porch with gable roof.

M 135 189

and nailed 2- by 8- or 2- by 10-inch members, serve to support the floor joists by means of *ledgers* (fig. 104). The beams span between the wall line of the house and the posts at the .outside edge of the porch. Nail 2- by 3- or 2- by 4-inch ledger members to both sides of the intermediate beams and to one side of single edge beams at the ends of the porch with sixteenpenny nails spaced 8 to 10 inches apart. The beams should be located so that the floor surface of an 8-foot-wide porch slopes outward a total of at least 1½ inches for drainage. Beams are spaced about 10 feet or less apart across the width of the porch, but this depends on the size of joists and the beams. These details are ordinarily shown on the plans.

Joist and beam tables can also be used to determine the correct span-spacing-size relationship. Use a metal joist hanger or angle iron when fastening the beam ends to the floor framing of the house (fig. 104), or allow the ends to bear on a post or

pier. A single header (with ledger) the same size as the beam is used at the ouside edge of the porch.

Now, cut the floor joists to fit between the laminated beams so that they rest on the ledgers. Space them properly according to the details in the working drawings, and toenail the ends to the beam with two eightpenny nails on each side.

Dressed and matched porch flooring, in nominal 1- by 4-inch size, can be applied to the floor joists or installed after the roof framing and roofing are in place. To protect the floor from damage, it is perhaps best to delay this phase of construction. This requires the use of temporary braces for the roof until the flooring and porch posts are installed.

Framing for Gable Porch Roof

A doubled member or nail-laminated beam is required to carry the roof load whether a gable or

low-slope roof is used. These beams are made up by using spacers of *lath* or plywood between 2-inch members so that the beam is the same size (3½ inches) as the nominal 4- by 4-inch solid posts used for final support of the roof. End beams made up of doubled 2-inch members are fastened to the outside beam and to the house (fig. 104). Thus, the outline of the porch is now formed by the front and end beams. One method of assembling this roof framing is by nailing it together over the floor framing and raising it in place. Temporary 2- by 4-inch or larger braces are used to support this beam framing while the roof is being constructed. Use enough braces to prevent movement. Use joist hangers or a length of angle iron to fasten one end of the beam to the house framing. The beam ends can also be carried through the wall and supported by auxiliary studs when possible. It is often desirable to provide a 6-foot 8-inch or a 7-foot clearance from the porch floor to the bottom of the beams so that standard units can be used if screening or enclosing is planned in the future.

Ceiling joists are now fastened to the beam at one end and to the studs of the house at the other. They should be spaced 16 or 24 inches on center to provide nailing for a ceiling material.

Rafters, either 2- by 4- or 2- by 6-inch in size depending on the span, are now measured and cut at the ridge and wall line as described in the section on pitched roofs. A 1- by 6-inch ridgepole is used to tie each pair of rafters together. Gable end studs are now cut to fit between the end rafters and the outside beam (fig. 104). Space them to accommodate the panel siding or other finish. Toenail the studs to the outside beam and to the end rafters.

The roof sheathing, the fly rafters, and the roofing are applied as described in the sections on roof systems and coverings. Use flashing at the junction of the roof and the end wall of the house when applying the roofing.

The matched flooring may now be applied to the floor across the joists. Extend it beyond the outer

edge (fig. 104). Use sevenpenny or eightpenny flooring nails and blind-nail to each joist. It is good practice to apply a saturating coat of water-repellent preservative on the surface and edges. This will provide protection until the floor is painted. Some decay-resistant wood species require little protection other than this treatment.

The nominal 4- by 4-inch posts can now be installed. When they are cut to length, drill and drive a small ⅜- or ½-inch-diameter pin into the center of one end. A matching hole is drilled into the floor, a mastic calk applied to the area, and the post positioned (fig. 104). Use a large galvanized washer between the post and the floor. This will allow moisture to evaporate and prevent decay. Use toenailing and metal strapping to tie the post to the roof framing. In areas of high winds, use a *bolt* or lag screw instead of the pin from the post to some part of the floor framing.

Matched boards, plywood, or similar covering materials can be used to finish the ceiling surface. The exterior and interior of the laminated beams are normally cased with nominal 1-inch boards except where siding at the gable end can be carried over the exposed face of the beam. A 1- by 4-inch member is normally used under the beam and between the posts. All exposed nailing should be done with galvanized or other rust-resistant nails.

Framing for Low-Slope Porch Roof

Framing a flat or low-slope roof for a porch is relatively simple. A nailed beam, similar to the type used for the gable roof, is required to support the ends of rafter-joists (fig. 105). Single end members, however, are used to tie the beam to wall framing of the house rather than a doubled end beam. Temporary posts or braces are used to hold the beam framing after it is in place. A minimum roof slope of 1 inch in a foot is desirable for drainage.

Cut the rafters and toenail them to the beam with eightpenny nails and face-nail the opposite ends

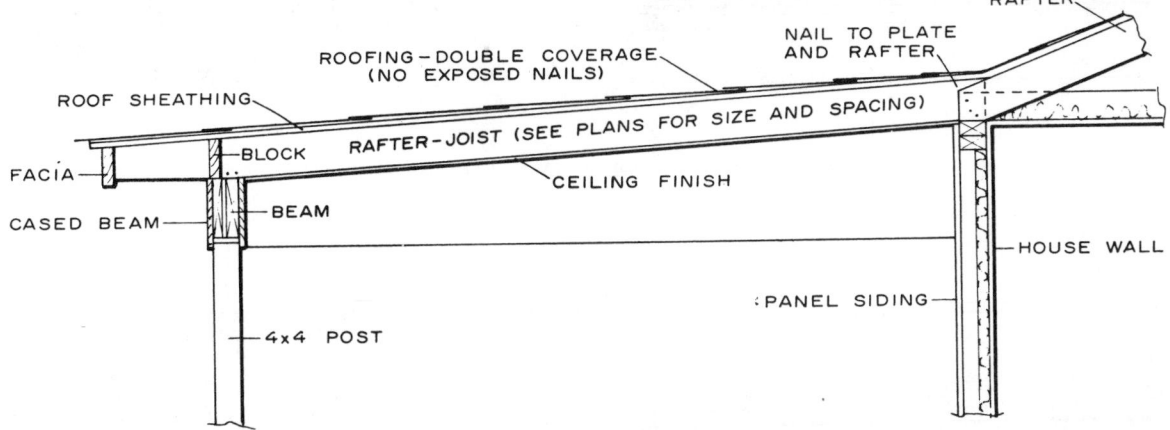

FIGURE 105.—Section through side porch with low-slope roof.

M 135 190

to the rafter or the ceiling joists of the house (fig. 105). When spacing is not the same and members do not join the rafters or ceiling joists of the house, toenail the ends of the porch rafters to the wall plate. Plywood or board sheathing is applied, and when end overhang is desired, a fly rafter is added. When desired, 1- by 6-inch facia boards are applied to the ends of the rafters and to the fly rafter with sevenpenny or eightpenny galvanized siding nails. Roofing is applied as has been recommended for low-slope roofs; underlayment followed by double-coverage surfaced roll roofing. On low slopes, no exposed nails are used. A ribbon of asphalt roof cement or lap seal material is used under the lapped edge. Extend the roofing beyond the facia enough to form a natural drip edge. Ceiling covering and other trim are used in the same manner as for the gable roof.

STEPS AND STAIRS

Outside entry platforms and steps are required for most types of wood-frame houses. Houses constructed over a full basement or crawl space normally require a platform with steps at outside doors. In houses with masonry foundations, these outside entry stoops consist of a concrete perimeter wall with poured concrete steps. However, a well-constructed wood porch will serve as well and normally cost less.

Inside stairs leading to an attic or second-floor bedrooms in a house with a steep roof slope, or to the basement, must be provided for during construction of the house. This includes framing of the floor joists to accommodate the stairway and providing walls and *carriages* for the *treads* and *risers*. Even though the second floor might not be completed immediately, a stairway should be included during construction of such houses.

Outside Stoops

Outside wood stoops, platforms, and open plank stairs should give satisfactory service if these simple rules are followed: (a) All wood in contact with or embedded in soil should be pressure-treated, as outlined in the early section on "Post Foundations"; (b) all untreated wood parts should have a 2-inch minimum clearance above the ground; (c) avoid pockets or areas in the construction where water cannot drain away; (d) if possible, use wood having moderate to good decay resistance;[7] (e) use initial and regular applications of water-repellent preservative to exposed untreated wood surfaces; and (f) use vertical grain members.

Wood Stoop—Low Height

A simple all-wood stoop consists of treated posts embedded in the ground, cross or bearing members, and spaced treads. One such design is shown in figure 106A. Because this type of stoop is low, it can serve as an entry for exterior doors where the floor level of the house is no more than 24 inches above the ground. Railings are not usually required. The platform should be large enough so that the storm door can swing outward freely. An average size is about 3½ feet deep by 5 feet wide.

Use treated posts of 5- to 7-inch diameter and embed them in the soil at least 3 feet. Nail and bolt (with galvanized fasteners) a crossmember (usually a nominal 2- by 4-inch member) to each side of the posts (fig. 106B). The posts should be faced slightly at these areas. For a small, 3½- by 5-foot stoop, four posts are usually sufficient. Posts are spaced about 4 feet apart across the front.

Supports for the tread of the first step are supplied by pairs of 2- by 4-inch members bolted to the forward posts (fig. 106A). The inner ends are blocked with short pieces of 2- by 4-inch members to the upper crosspieces (fig. 106A). Treads consist of 2- by 4- or 2- by 6-inch members, spaced about ¼ inch apart. Use two sixteenpenny galvanized plain or ring-shank nails for each piece at each supporting member.

Some species of wood have natural decay resistance and others are benefited by the application of a water-repellent preservative followed by a good deck paint. If desired, a railing can be added by bolting short upright members to the 2- by 4-inch crossmembers. Horizontal railings can be fastened to the uprights.

Wood Stoop—Medium Height

A wood entry platform requiring more than one or two steps is usually designed with a railing and stair stringers. If the platform is about 3½ by 5 feet, two 2- by 12-inch carriages can be used to support the treads (fig. 107A). In most cases, the bottoms of the carriages are supported by treated posts embedded in the ground or by an embedded treated timber. The upper ends of the carriages are supported by a 2- by 4-inch ledger fastened to posts and are face-nailed to the platform framing with twelvepenny galvanized nails. The carriage at the house side can be supported in the same way when interior posts are used.

When the platform is narrow, a nominal 3- by 4-inch ledger is fastened to the floor framing of the house with fortypenny galvanized spikes or 5-inch lag screws. The 2- by 6-inch floor planks are nailed to the ledger and to the double 2- by 4-inch beam bolted to the post (fig. 107B). Use two sixteenpenny galvanized plain or ring-shank nails for each tread. When a wide platform is desired, an inside set of posts and doubled 2 by 4 or larger beams should be used.

Railings can be made of 2- by 4-inch uprights bolted or lagscrewed to the outside beams. These members are best fastened with galvanized bolts or lag screws. Horizontal railing in 1- by 4- or 1- by 6-inch size can then be fastened to the uprights. When an enclosed skirting is desired, 1- by 4-inch slats can be nailed to the outside of the beam and an added lower nailing member (fig. 107A). Treat all exposed untreated wood with a heavy application of water-repellent preservative. When a paint finish is desired, use a good deck paint. See section on "Painting and Finishing" for details.

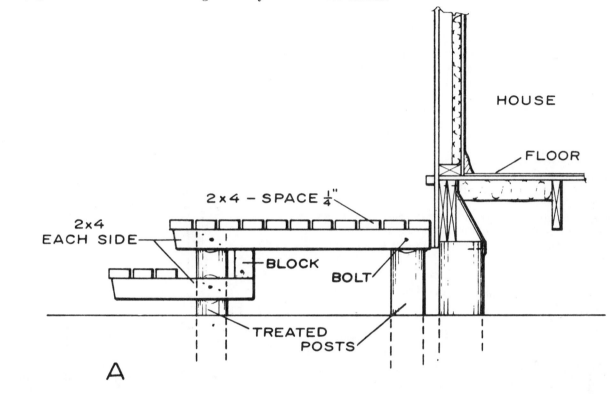

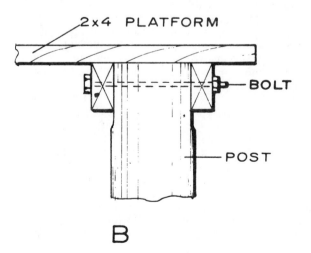

FIGURE 106.—Low-height wood stoop. A, Side elevation; B, connection to post.

M 135 191

[7] Anderson, *ibid.*

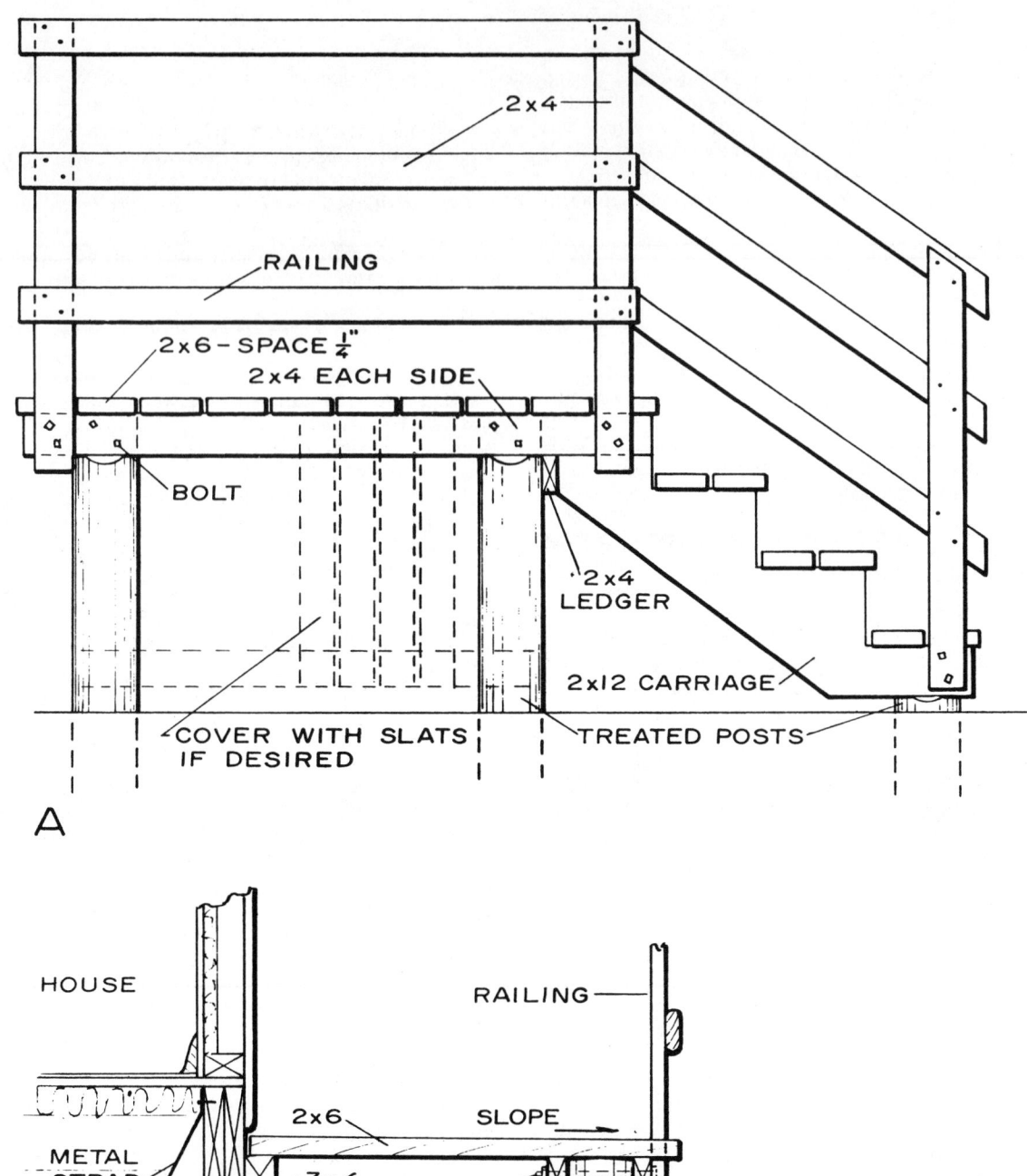

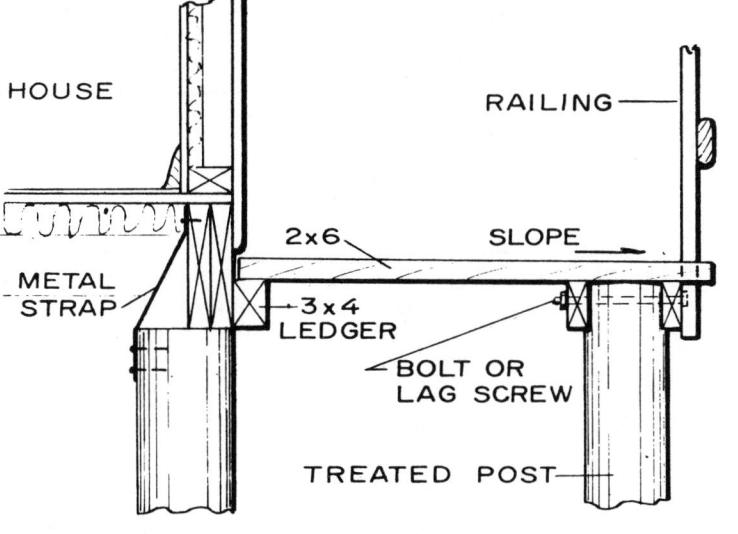

FIGURE 107.—Medium-height wood stoop. *A,* Side elevation; *B,* connection to post.

M 135 192

Inside Stairs

When stairs to a second-floor area are required, the first-floor ceiling joists are framed to accommodate the stairway. When basement stairs are used, the first-floor joists must also be framed for the stairway. Two types of simple stair *runs* are commonly used in a small house, the straight run (fig. 108*A*) and the long L (fig. 108*B*). An open length of 10 feet is normally sufficient for adequate headroom with a width of 2½ to 3 feet. A clear width of 2 feet 8 inches is considered minimum for a main stair.

Two of the most important considerations in the design of inside stairways are headroom and the relation of the riser height to the length of the tread. The minimum headroom for stairs should be 6 feet 4 inches for basements or secondary stairs and 6 feet 8 inches for main stairs (fig. 190*A*). The relation of the riser to the run is shown in figure 109*B*. A good rule of thumb to apply is: The riser times the tread in inches should equal about 75.

When the length of the stairway is parallel to the joists the opening is framed (fig. 110). When the stairway is arranged so that the opening is perpendicular to the length of the joists, the fram-

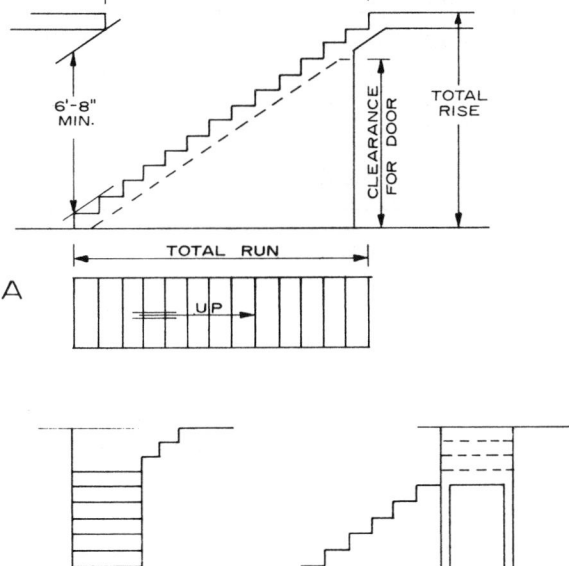

FIGURE 108.—Stair types. *A,* Straight run; *B,* long L.

M 134 727

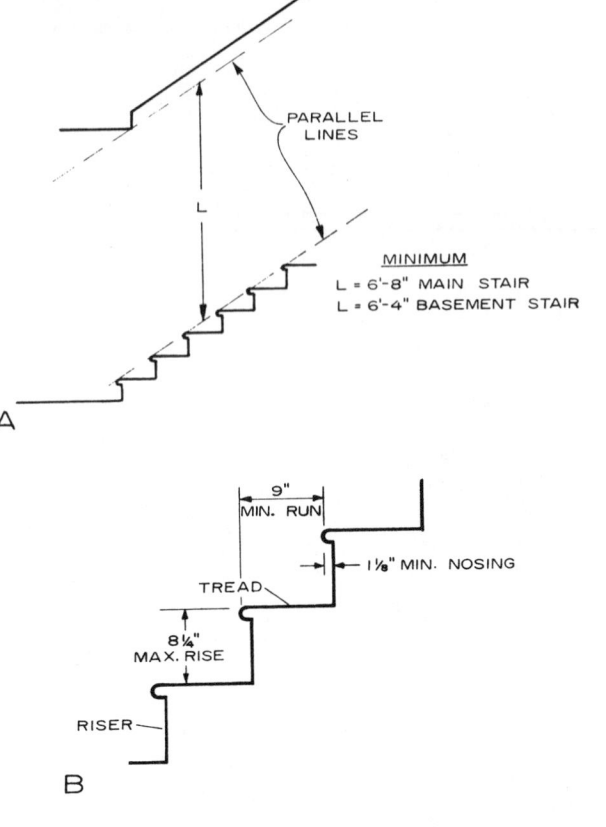

FIGURE 109.—Stair measurements. *A,* Head room; *B,* riser-tread sizes.

M 134 701

ing should follow the details shown in figure 111. Nailing and framing should comply with table 1 and the descriptions in the section on "Floor Systems."

The stair carriages are normally made from 2-by 12-inch members. They provide support for the stairs and nailing surfaces for the treads and risers. The carriages can be nailed to a finish stringer and the wall studs behind with a sixteenpenny nail at each stud (fig. 112*A*). The carriages can also be mounted directly to the wall studs or over the drywall finish and the finish stringer notched to them (fig. 112*B*). When no wall is present to fasten the tops of the carriages in place, use a ledger similar to that shown in figure 107*A* for an outside stair. The tops of the carriages are notched to fit this ledger. Two carriages are sufficient when treads are at least 1 1/16 inches thick and the stair is less than 2 feet 6 inches wide. Use three carriages when the stair is wider than this. When plank treads 1⅝ inches thick are used, two carriages are normally sufficient for stair widths up to 3 feet.

After the carriages are mounted to the wall and treads and risers cut to length, nail the bottom riser to each carriage with two eighteenpenny finish

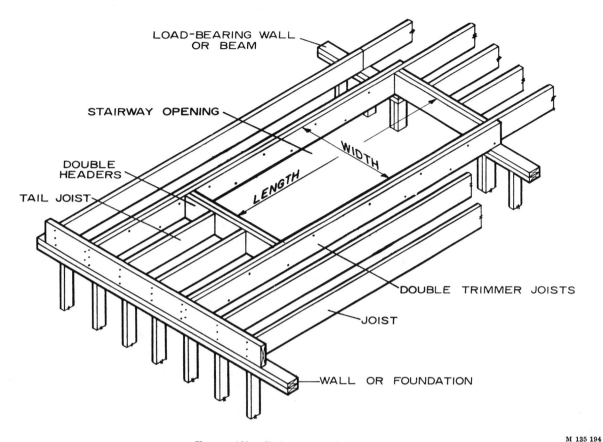

FIGURE 110.—Stairway parallel to joists.

M 135 194

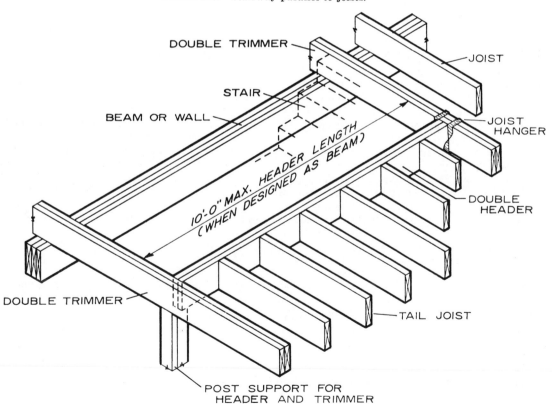

FIGURE 111.—Stairway perpendicular to joists.

M 135 195

nails. The first tread, if $1\frac{1}{16}$ inches thick, is then nailed to each carriage with two tenpenny finish nails and to the riser below with at least two tenpenny finish nails. Proceed up the stair in this same manner. If $1\frac{5}{8}$-inch-thick treads are used, a twelvepenny finish nail may be required. Use three nails at each carriage, but eliminate nailing to the riser below. All finish nails should be set.

Finished stairs with stringers routed to fit the ends of the treads and risers, and with railing and *balusters* or a handrail, are generally used in main stairs to second-floor rooms in moderate-cost houses, but probably should not be considered for low-cost homes.

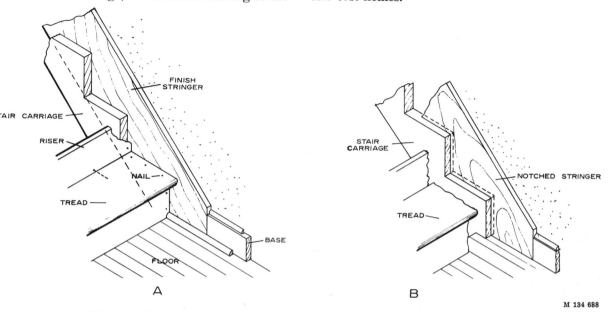

FIGURE 112.—Stair construction details. *A*, Full stringer; *B*, notched stringer.

M 134 688

PAINTING AND FINISHING

Exterior Wood Finishing

Wood Properties and Finish Durability

The durability of an exterior finish is materially affected by the wood characteristics. Woods that are high in *density* (heavy), such as dense hardwoods, will be more difficult to finish effectively than lightweight woods.

The amount and distribution of summerwood (darker *grained* portions) on the surface of softwood lumber also influence the success of the finishing procedure. Finishes, particularly paints, will last longer on surfaces with a low proportion of summerwood.

The manner in which lumber is sawn from the log influences its finishing characteristics. Paint-type and film-forming finishes always perform best on *vertical-grain* lumber because the summerwood is better distributed on the surface and because vertical-grain lumber is low in swelling.

All woods shrink or swell as they lose or absorb water. Species which shrink and swell the least are best for painting.[8] Checking, warping of wood, and paint peeling are more likely to be critical on woods which are hard, dense, and high in swelling.

Wood that is free of knots, pitch pockets, and other defects is the preferred base for paints, but these defects have little adverse effect on penetrating-type finishes. Smoothly planed surfaces are best for paint finishes, while rougher or sawn surfaces are preferred for penetrating (non-film-forming) finishes.

Types of Exterior Finishes

Unfinished wood.—Permitting the wood to weather naturally without protection of any kind is, of course, very simple and economical. Wood fully exposed to all elements of the weather, rain and sun being the most important, will wear away at the approximate rate of only a quarter of an inch in a century. The time required for wood to weather to the final gray color will depend on the severity of exposure. Wood in protected areas will be much slower to gray than wood fully exposed

[8] *Ibid.*

to the sun on the south side of a building. Early in the graying process, the wood may take on a blotchy appearance because of the growth of micro-organisms on the surface. Migration of wood extractives to the surface also will produce an uneven and unsightly discoloration, particularly in areas that are not washed by rain.

Unfinished lumber will warp more than lumber protected by paint. Warping varies with the density, width, and thickness of the board, basic wood structure, and species. Warp increases with density and the width of the board. To reduce warping to a minimum, best results are obtained when the width of boards does not exceed eight times the thickness. Flat-grain boards warp more than vertical-grain lumber. Baldcypress, the cedars, and redwood are species which have only a slight tendency to warp.

Water-repellent-preservative finishes.—A simple treatment of an exterior wood surface with a water-repellent preservative markedly alters the natural weathering process. Most pronounced is the retention of a uniform natural tan color in the early stages of weathering and a retardation of the uneven graying process which is produced by the growth of mildew on the surface. The water-repellency imparted by the treatment greatly reduces the tendency toward warping, excessive shrinking, and swelling which lead to splitting, and retards the leaching of extractives from the wood and water stain at ends of boards.

This type of finish is quite inexpensive, easily applied, and very easily refinished. Estimated costs for material would be approximately $0.50 to $2 per 100 square feet (spreading rate of 100 to 200 square feet per gallon). Water-repellent preservatives can be applied by brushing, rolling, dipping, and spraying. It is important to thoroughly treat all lap and butt joints and ends of boards. Many brands of effective water-repellent preservatives are on the market. A saving could be made by making a solution from the following components:

Penta concentrate (10:1)	2 quarts.
Boiled linseed oil	1.75 quarts.
Paraffin wax	0.25 to 0.50 pound.
Mineral spirits, turpentine, No. 1 or No. 2 fuel oil.	4 gallons.

Color pigments can also be added to this type of finish. Mix 2 to 6 fluid ounces of colors to each gallon of water-repellent preservative.

The initial applications may be short-lived (1 year), especially in humid climates and on species that are susceptible to mildew, such as sapwood and certain hardwoods. Under more favorable conditions, such as on rough cedar surfaces which will absorb large quantities of the solution, the finish will last more than 2 years.

When blotchy discolorations of mildew start to appear on the wood, re-treat the surface with water-repellent-preservative solution. If extractives have accumulated on the surface in protected areas, clean these areas by mild scrubbing with a detergent or trisodium-phosphate solution.

The continued use of these water-repellent-preservative solutions will effectively prevent serious decay in wood in above-ground installation. This finishing method is recommended for all wood species and surfaces exposed to the weather.

Only aluminum or stainless steel nails will prevent discoloration on the siding. Galvanized nails will show light stains after several years. Steel nails without rust-resistance treatment should not be used.

Penetrating pigmented stain finishes.—The penetrating stains also are effective and economical finishes for all kinds of lumber and plywood surfaces, especially those that are rough-sawn, weathered, and textured. Knotty wood boards and other lower quality grades of wood which would be difficult to paint also can be finished successfully with penetrating stains.

These stains penetrate into the wood without forming a continuous film on the surface. Because there is no film or coating, there can be no failure by cracking, peeling, and blistering. Stain finishes are easily prepared for refinishing and easily maintained.

The penetrating pigmented stains form a flat and semitransparent finish. They permit only part of the wood-grain pattern to show through. A variety of colors can be achieved with finish. Shades of brown, green, red, and gray are possible. The only color which is not available is white. This color can be provided only through the use of white paint.

Stains are quite inexpensive and easy to apply. To avoid the formation of lap marks, the entire length of a course of siding should be finished without stopping. Only one coat is recommended on smoothly planed surfaces, where it will last 2 to 3 years. After refinishing, however, the second coat will last 6 to 7 years because the weathered surface has adsorbed more of the stain than the smoothly planed surface.

Two-coat staining is possible on rough-sawn or weathered surfaces, but both coats should be applied within a few hours of each other. When using a two-coat system, the first coat should never be allowed to dry before the second is applied, because this will seal the surface and prevent the second coat from penetrating. A finish life of up to 10 years can be achieved when two coats are applied to a rough or weathered surface.

Very satisfactory penetrating stains can be prepared by home-mixing the following ingredients:

Boiled linseed oil	3 gallons.
Penta concentrate	½ gallon.
Paraffin wax	½ pound.
Colors-in-oil (tinting colors)	1 quart.
Paint thinner	1 gallon.

Boiled linseed oil is available in most paint stores and mail-order houses. Penta concentrate is a common name for a solution of pentachloro-phenol which is about a 40 percent concentration and is also known as a 10 to 1 concentrate. It is available from several manufacturers by mail order. Paraffin wax, used to seal jelly glasses, can be bought from local grocery stores. Colors-in-oil or tinting colors are available from paint stores and artists' supply stores. Paint thinners which can be used are mineral spirits or *turpentine*. In areas where available, No. 1 or No. 2 fuel oil also can be used. In warm moist areas which enhance fungal growth, the penta content should be doubled.

All ingredients will go into solution quite easily if temperatures are 70° F. or above. Dissolving the wax, which is the most difficult step in the process, can be aided by cutting it into fine chips or by melting in a double boiler before adding to other ingredients. Allow the solution to stand overnight and occasionally stir vigorously during use to keep pigments uniformly suspended.

***CAUTION:* Turpentine, mineral spirits, and other paint thinners are volatile flammable solvents. Their concentrated vapors should not be breathed or exposed to sparks or flames that can ignite them. It is safer to mix ingredients outdoors or in an open garage than in a closed room in a house.**

Stained surface should be refinished only when the colors fade and bare wood is beginning to show. A light steel-wooling and hosing with water to remove surface dirt and mildew are all that are needed to prepare the surface. Restain after the surfaces have thoroughly dried.

Clear film finishes.—Clear finishes based on *varnish,* which form a coating or film on the surface, should not be used on wood exposed fully to the weather. These finishes are quite expensive and often begin to deteriorate within 1 year. Refinishing is a frequent, difficult, and time-consuming process.

Exterior paints.—Of all the finishes, paints provide the widest selection of color. When properly selected and applied, it will also provide the most protection to wood against weathering. The durability of paint coatings on exterior wood, however, is affected by many variables, and much care is needed in the selection of the wood surface material, type of paint, and method of application to achieve success in painting. The original and maintenance costs are higher for a paint finish than for either the water-repellent-preservative treatment or penetrating-stain finish.

Paint performance is affected by species, density, wood structure, extractives, and defects such as knots and pitch pockets.

Best paint durability will be achieved on the select high grades of vertical-grain western redcedar, redwood, and low-density pines such as the white pines, sugar pine, and ponderosa pine. Exterior-grade plywood which has been overlaid with medium-density resin-treated paper is another wood-base material on which paint will perform very well.

Follow these three simple steps when painting wood:

(1) Apply water-repellent preservative to all joints by brushing or spraying. Treat all lap and butt joints, ends, and edges of lumber, and window sash and trim. Allow 2 warm days of drying before painting.

(2) Prime the treated wood surface with an oil-base paint free of zinc-oxide pigment. Do *not* use a porous blister-resistant paint as primer on wood surfaces. Apply sufficient primer so the grain of the wood cannot be seen. Open joints should be calked after priming.

(3) Apply two topcoats of high-quality oil, alkyd, or latex paint over the primer. Two topcoats, especially, should be used on the south side, which has the most severe exposure.

Interior Finishes

Interior finishes for wood and dry-wall or plaster surfaces are usually intended to serve one or more of the following purposes:

(1) Make the surface easy to clean.
(2) Enhance the natural beauty of wood.
(3) Achieve a desired color decor.
(4) Impart wear resistance.

The type of finish depends largely upon type of area and the use to which the area will be put. The various interior areas and finish systems employed in each are summarized in table 3. Wood surfaces can be finished either with a clear finish or a paint. Plaster-base materials are painted.

Wood Floors

Hardwood floors of oak, birch, beech, and maple are usually finished by applying two coats of wood seal, also called floor seal, with light sanding between coats. A final coat of paste wax is then applied and buffed. This finish is easily maintained by rewaxing. The final coat can also be a varnish instead of a sealer. The varnish finishes are used when a high gloss is desired.

When floors are to be painted, an *undercoater* is used, and then at least one topcoat of floor and deck enamel is applied.

Wood Paneling and Trim

Wood trim and paneling are most commonly finished with a clear wood sealer or a stain-sealer combination and then topcoated after sanding with at least one additional coat of sealer or varnish. The final coat of sealer or varnish can also be covered with a heavy coat of paste wax to produce a surface which is easily maintained by rewaxing. Good depth in a clear finish can be achieved by finishing first with one coat of a high-gloss varnish followed with a final coat of semigloss varnish.

Wood trim of nonporous species such as pine can also be painted by first applying a coat of primer or undercoater, followed with a coat of latex, flat, or *semigloss oil-base paint*. Semigloss and *gloss paints* are more resistant to soiling and more easily cleaned by washing than the flat oil and latex paints. Trim of porous wood species such as oak and mahogany requires filling before painting.

Kitchen and Bathroom Walls

Kitchen and bathroom walls, which normally are plaster or dry-wall construction, are finished best with a coat of undercoater and two coats of *semigloss enamel*. This type of finish wears well, is easy to clean, and is quite resistant to moisture.

Dry Wall and Plaster

Plaster and dry-wall surfaces, which account for the major portion of the interior area, are finished with two coats of either *flat oil* or latex paint. An initial treatment with size or sealer will improve holdout (reduce penetration of succeeding coats) and thus reduce the quantity of paint required for good coverage.

TABLE 3.—*What interior finish to use—and where*

	Primer or undercoater	Rubber latex	Flat oil paint	Semigloss paint	Floor (wood) seal[1]	Varnish[1]	Floor or deck enamel
Wood floors	X				X	X	X
Wood paneling and trim	X	X	X	X	X	X	
Kitchen and bathroom walls	X			X			
Dry wall and plaster	X	X	X				

[1] Paste wax can be applied over floor seal and varnish base.

GLOSSARY OF HOUSING TERMS

Airway. A space between roof insulation and roof boards for movement of air.

Apron. The flat member of the inside trim of a window placed against the wall immediately beneath the stool.

Asphalt. Most native asphalt is a residue from evaporated petroleum. It is insoluble in water but soluble in gasoline and melts when heated. Used widely in building for such items as waterproof roof coverings of many types, exterior wall coverings, and flooring tile.

Attic ventilators. In houses, screened openings provided to ventilate an attic space. They are located in the soffit area as inlet ventilators and in the gable end or along the ridge as outlet ventilators. They can also consist of powerdriven fans used as an exhaust system. See also *Louver*.

Backfill. The replacement of excavated earth into a trench or pier excavation around and against a basement foundation.

Balusters. Usually small vertical members in a railing used between a top rail and the stair treads or a bottom rail.

Base or baseboard. A board placed around a room against the wall next to the floor to finish properly between floor and plaster or dry wall.

Base molding. Molding used to trim the upper edge of interior baseboard.

Base shoe. Molding used next to the floor on interior baseboard. Sometimes called a carpet strip.

Batten. Narrow strips of wood used to cover joints or as decorative vertical members over plywood or wide boards.

Beam. A structural member transversely supporting a load.

Bearing partition. A partition that supports any vertical load in addition to its own weight.

Bearing wall. A wall that supports any vertical load in addition to its own weight.

Bed molding. A molding in an angle, as between the overhanging cornice, or eaves, of a building and the sidewalls.

Blind-nailing. Nailing in such a way that the nailheads are not visible on the face of the work. Usually at the tongue of matched boards.

Blind stop. A rectangular molding, usually ¾ by 1⅜ inches or more in width, used in the assembly of a window frame. Serves as a stop for storm and screen or combination windows and to resist air infiltration.

Boiled linseed oil. Linseed oil in which enough lead, manganese, or cobalt salts have been incorporated to make the oil harden more rapidly when spread in thin coatings.

Bolts, anchor. Bolts to secure a wooden sill plate to concrete or masonry floor or wall or pier.

Boston ridge. A method of applying asphalt or wood shingles at the ridge or at the hips of a roof as a finish.

Brace. An inclined piece of framing lumber applied to wall or floor to stiffen the structure. Often used on walls as temporary bracing until framing has been completed.

Buck. Often used in reference to rough frame opening members. Door bucks used in reference to metal door frame.

Built-up roof. A roofing composed of three to five layers of asphalt felt laminated with coal tar, pitch, or asphalt. The top is finished with crushed slag or gravel. Generally used on flat or low-pitched roofs.

Butt joint. The junction where the ends of two timbers or other members meet in a square-cut joint.

Cabinet. A shop- or job-built unit for kitchens or other rooms. Often includes combinations of drawers, doors, and the like.

Casing. Molding of various widths and thicknesses used to trim door and window openings at the jambs.

Casement frames and sash. Frames of wood or metal enclosing part or all of the sash, which may be opened by means of hinges affixed to the vertical edges.

Collar beam. Nominal 1- or 2-inch-thick members connecting opposite roof rafters. They serve to stiffen the roof structure.

Combination doors or windows. Combination doors or windows used over regular openings. They provide winter insulation and summer protection. They often have self-storing or removable glass and screen inserts. This eliminates the need for handling a different unit each season.

Concrete, plain. Concrete without reinforcement, or reinforced only for shrinkage or termperature changes.

Condensation. Beads or drops of water, and frequently frost in extremely cold weather, that accumulate on the inside of the exterior covering of a building when warm, moisture-laden air from the interior reaches a point where the temperature no longer permits the air to sustain the moisture it holds. Use of louvers or attic ventilators will reduce moisture condensation in attics. A vapor barrier under the gypsum lath or dry wall on exposed walls will reduce condensation in walls.

Conduit, electrical. A pipe, usually metal, in which wire is installed.

Construction, dry-wall. A type of construction in which the interior wall finish is applied in a dry condition, generally in the form of sheet materials or wood paneling, as contrasted to plaster.

Construction, frame. A type of construction in which the structural parts are of wood or depend upon a wood frame for support. In building codes, if masonry veneer is applied to the exterior walls, the classification of this type of construction is usually unchanged.

Coped joint. Fitting woodwork to an irregular surface. In moldings, cutting the end of one piece to fit the molded face of the other at an interior angle to replace a miter joint.

Corner bead. A strip of formed sheet metal, sometimes combined with a strip of metal lath, placed on corners before plastering to reinforce them. Also, a strip of wood finish three-quarters round or angular placed over a plastered corner for protection.

Corner boards. Used as trim for the external corners of a house or other frame structure against which the ends of the siding are finished.

Corner braces. Diagonal braces at the corners of frame structure to stiffen and strengthen the wall.

Cornice. Overhang of a pitched roof at the eave line, usually consisting of a facia board, a soffit for a closed cornice, and appropriate moldings.

Counterflashing. A flashing usually used on chimneys at the roofline to cover shingle flashing and to prevent moisture entry.

Cove molding. A molding with a concave face used as trim or to finish interior corners.

Crawl space. A shallow space below the living quarters of a basementless house, sometimes enclosed.

d. See *Penny.*

Dado. A rectangular groove across the width of a board or plank. In interior decoration, a special type of wall treatment.

Deck paint. An enamel with a high degree of resistance to mechanical wear, designed for use on such surfaces as porch floors.

Density. The mass of substance in a unit volume. When expressed in the metric system (in g. per cc.), it is numerically equal to the specific gravity of the same substance.

Dimension. See *Lumber, dimension.*

Doorjamb, interior. The surrounding case into and out of which a door closes and opens. It consists of two upright pieces, called side jambs, and a horizontal head jamb.

Dormer. A projection in a sloping roof, the framing of which forms a vertical wall suitable for windows or other openings.

Downspout. A pipe, usually metal, for carrying rainwater from roof gutters.

Dressed and matched (tongued and grooved). Boards or planks machined in such a manner that there is a groove on one edge and a corresponding tongue on the other.

Drier, paint. Usually oil-soluble soaps of such metals as lead, manganese, or cobalt, which, in small proportions, hasten the oxidation and hardening (drying) of the drying oils in paints.

Drip cap. A molding placed on the exterior top side of a door or window frame to cause water to drip beyond the outside of the frame.

Dry-wall. see *Construction, dry wall.*

Ducts. In a house, usually round or rectangular metal pipes for distributing warm air from the heating plant to rooms, or air from a conditioning device, or as cold air returns. Ducts are also made of asbestos and composition materials.

Eaves. The overhang of a roof projecting over the walls.

Face nailing. To nail perpendicular to the initial surface or to the junction of the pieces joined.

Facia or fascia. A flat board, band, or face, used sometimes by itself but usually in combination with moldings, often located at the outer face of the cornice.

Flashing. Sheet metal or other material used in roof and wall construction to protect a building from seepage of water.

Flat paint. An interior paint that contains a high proportion of pigment, and dries to a flat or lusterless finish.

Flue. The space or passage in a chimney through which smoke, gas, or fumes ascend. Each passage is called a flue, which, together with any others and the surrounding masonry, make up the chimney.

Flue lining. Fire clay or terra-cotta pipe, round or square, usually made in all of the ordinary flue sizes and in 2-foot lengths, used for the inner lining of chimneys with a brick or masonry work around the outside. Flue lining in chimneys runs from about a foot below the flue connection to the top of the chimney.

Fly rafter. End rafters of the gable overhang supported by roof sheathing and lookouts.

Footing. A masonry section, usually concrete in a rectangular form wider than the bottom of the foundation wall or pier it supports.

Foundation. The supporting portion of a structure below the first-floor construction, or below grade, including the footings.

Framing, balloon. A system of framing a building in which all vertical structural elements of the bearing walls and partitions consist of single pieces extending from the top of the foundation sill plate to the roofplate and to which all floor joists are fastened.

Framing, platform. A system of framing a building in which floor joists of each story rest on the top plates of the story below or on the foundation sill for the first story, and the bearing walls and partitions rest on the subfloor of each story.

Frieze. In house construction, a horizontal member connecting the top of the siding with the soffit of the cornice or roof sheathing.

Frostline. The depth of frost penetration in soil. This depth varies in different parts of the country. Footings should be placed below this depth to prevent movement.

Furring. Strips of wood or metal applied to a wall or other surface to even it and usually to serve as a fastening base for finish material.

Gable. The triangular vertical end of a building formed by the eaves and ridge of a sloped roof.

Gloss (paint or enamel). A paint or enamel that contains a relatively low proportion of pigment and dries to a sheen or luster.

Girder. A large or principal beam of wood or steel used to support concentrated loads at isolated points along its length.

Grain. The direction, size, arrangement, appearance, or quality of the fibers in wood.

Grain, edge (vertical). Edge-grain lumber has been sawed parallel to the pith of the log and approximately at right angles to the growth rings; i.e., the rings form an angle of 45° or more with the surface of the piece.

Gusset. A flat wood, plywood, or similar type member used to provide a connection at the intersection of wood members. Most commonly used at joints of wood trusses. They are fastened by nails, screws, bolts, or adhesives.

Gutter or eave trough. A shallow channel or conduit of metal or wood set below and along the eaves of a house to catch and carry off rainwater from the roof.

Header. (a) A beam placed perpendicular to joists and to which joists are nailed in framing for chimney, stairway, or other opening. (b) A wood lintel.

Heartwood. The wood extending from the pith to the sapwood, the cells of which no longer participate in the life processes of the tree.

Hip. The external angle formed by the meeting of two sloping sides of a roof.

Hip roof. A roof that rises by inclined planes from all four sides of a building.

Insulation board, rigid. A structural building board made of wood or cane fiber in ½- and 25⁄32-inch thicknesses. It can be obtained in various size sheets, in various densities, and with several treatments.

Insulation, thermal. Any material high in resistance to heat transmission that, when placed in the walls, ceilings, or floors of a structure, will reduce the rate of heat flow.

Jack rafter. A rafter that spans the distance from the wallplate to a hip, or from a valley to a ridge.

Jamb. The side and head lining of a doorway, window, or other opening.

Joint. The space between the adjacent surfaces of two members or components joined and held together by nails, glue, cement, mortar, or other means.

Joint cement. A powder that is usually mixed with water and used for joint treatment in gypsum-wallboard finish. Often called "spackle."

Joist. One of a series of parallel beams, usually 2 inches thick, used to support floor and ceiling loads, and supported in turn by larger beams, girders, or bearing walls.

Knot. In lumber, the portion of a branch or limb of a tree that appears on the edge or face of the piece.

Landing. A platform between flights of stairs or at the termination of a flight of stairs.

Lath. A building material of wood, metal, gypsum, or insulating board that is fastened to the frame of a building to act as a plaster base.

Ledger strip. A strip of lumber nailed along the bottom of the side of a girder on which joists rest .

Light. Space in a window sash for a single pane of glass. Also, a pane of glass.

Lintel. A horizontal structural member that supports the load over an opening such as a door or window.

Lookout. A short wood bracket or cantilever to support an overhanging portion of a roof or the like, usually concealed from view.

Louver. An opening with a series of horizontal slats so arranged as to permit ventilation but to exclude rain, sunlight, or vision. See also *Attic ventilators.*

Lumber. Lumber is the product of the sawmill and planing mill not further manufactured other than by sawing, resawing, and passing lengthwise through a standard planing machine, cross cutting to length, and matching.

Lumber, boards. Yard lumber less than 2 inches thick and 2 or more inches wide.

Lumber, dimension. Yard lumber from 2 inches to, but not including, 5 inches thick, and 2 or more inches wide. Includes joists, rafters, studs, plank, and small timbers. The actual size dimension of such lumber after shrinking from green dimension and after machining to size or pattern is called the dress size.

Lumber, matched. Lumber that is dressed and shaped on one edge in a grooved pattern and on the other in a tongued pattern.

Lumber, shiplap. Lumber that is edge-dressed to make a close rabbeted or lapped joint.

Lumber, yard. Lumber of those grades, sizes, and patterns which are generally intended for ordinary construction, such as framework and rough coverage of houses.

Masonry. Stone, brick, concrete, hollow-tile, concrete-block, gypsum-block, or other similar building units or materials or a combination of the same, bonded together with mortar to form a wall, pier, buttress, or similar mass.

Meeting rails. Rails sufficiently thicker than a window to fill the opening between the top and bottom sash made by the parting stop in the frame of double-hung windows. They are usually beveled.

Millwork. Generally all building materials made of finished wood and manufactured in millwork plants and planing mills are included under the term "millwork." It includes such items as inside and outside doors, window and doorframes,

blinds, porchwork, mantels, panelwork, stairways, moldings, and interior trim. It normally does not include flooring, ceiling, or siding.

Miter joint. The joint of two pieces at an angle that bisects the joining angle. For example, the miter joint at the side and head casing at a door opening is made at a 45° angle.

Moisture content of wood. Weight of the water contained in the wood, usually expressed as a percentage of the weight of the ovendry wood.

Mortise. A slot cut into a board, plank, or timber, usually edgewise, to receive tenon of another board, plank, or timber to form a joint.

Molding. A wood strip having a curved or projecting surface used for decorative purposes.

Natural finish. A transparent finish which does not seriously alter the original color or grain of the natural wood. Natural finishes are usually provided by sealers, oils, varnishes, water-repellent preservatives, and other similar materials.

Nonloadbearing wall. A wall supporting no load other than its own weight.

Notch. A crosswise rabbet at the end of a board.

O.C., on center. The measurement of spacing for studs, rafters, joists, and the like in a building from center of one member to the center of the next.

Paint. A combination of pigments with suitable thinners or oils to provide decorative and protective coatings.

Panel. In house construction, a thin flat piece of wood, plywood, or similar material, framed by stiles and rails as in a door or fitted into grooves of thicker material with molded edges for decorative wall treatment.

Paper, sheathing or building. A building material, generally paper or felt used in wall and roof construction as a protection against the passage of air and sometimes moisture.

Parting stop or strip. A small wood piece used in the side and head jambs of double-hung windows to separate upper and lower sash.

Partition. A wall that subdivides spaces within any story of a building.

Penny. As applied to nails, it originally indicated the price per hundred. The term now serves as a measure of nail length and is abbreviated by the letter d.

Perm. A measure of water vapor movement through a material (grains per square foot per hour per inch of mercury difference in vapor pressure).

Pier. A column of masonry, usually rectangular in horizontal cross section, used to support other structural members.

Pigment. A powdered solid in suitable degree of subdivision for use in paint or enamel.

Pitch. The incline slope of a roof, or the ratio of the total rise to the total width of a house; i.e., an 8-foot rise and a 24-foot width are a ⅓ pitch roof. *Roof slope* is expressed in inches of rise per 12 inches of run.

Plate. Sill plate: a horizontal member anchored to a masonry wall. Sole plate: bottom horizontal member of a frame wall. Top plate: top horizontal member of a frame wall supporting ceiling joists, rafters, or other members.

Plumb. Exactly perpendicular; vertical.

Plywood. A piece of wood made of three or more layers of veneer joined with glue and usually laid with the grain of adjoining plies at right angles. Almost always an odd number of plies are used to provide balanced construction.

Porch. A roofed area extending beyond the main house. May be open or enclosed and with concrete or wood frame floor system.

Preservative. Any substance that, for a reasonable length of time, will prevent the action of wood-destroying fungi, borers of various kinds, and similar destructive life when the wood has been properly coated or impregnated with it.

Primer. The first coat of paint in a paint job that consists of two or more coats; also the paint used for such a first coat.

Putty. A type of cement usually made of whiting and boiled linseed oil, beaten or kneaded to the consistency of dough, and used in sealing glass in sash, filling small holes and crevices in wood, and for similar purposes.

Quarter round. A small molding that has the cross section of a quarter circle.

Rafter. One of a series of structural members of a roof designed to support roof loads. The rafters of a flat roof are sometimes called roof joists.

Rafter, hip. A rafter that forms the intersection of an external roof angle.

Rafter, valley. A rafter that forms the intersection of an internal roof angle. The valley rafter is normally made of doubled 2-inch-thick members.

Rail. Cross members of panel doors or of a sash. Also the upper and lower members of a balustrade or staircase extending from one vertical support, such as a post, to another.

Rake. The inclined edge of a gable roof (the trim member is a rake molding).

Ridge. The horizontal line at the junction of the top edges of two sloping roof surfaces.

Ridge board. The board placed on edge at the ridge of the roof into which the upper ends of the rafters are fastened.

Rise. In stairs, the vertical height of a step or flight of stairs.

Riser. Each of the vertical boards closing the spaces between the treads of stairways.

Roll roofing. Roofing material, composed of fiber and saturated with asphalt, that is supplied in rolls containing 108 square feet in 36-inch widths. It is generally furnished in weights of 45 to 90 pounds per roll.

Roof sheathing. The boards or sheet material fastened to the roof rafters on which the shingle or other roof covering is laid.

Routed. See *Mortised.*

Run. In stairs, the net width of a step or the horizontal distance covered by a flight of stairs.

Sash. A single light frame containing one or more lights of glass.

Saturated felt. A felt which is impregnated with tar or asphalt.

Scab. A short piece of wood or plywood fastened to two abutting timbers to splice them together.

Sealer. A finishing material, either clear or pigmented, that is usually applied directly over uncoated wood for the purpose of sealing the surface.

Semigloss paint or enamel. A paint or enamel made with a slight insufficiency of nonvolatile vehicle so that its coating, when dry, has some luster but is not very glossy.

Shake. A thick handsplit shingle, resawed to form two shakes; usually edge grained.

Sheathing. The structural covering, usually wood boards or plywood, used over studs or rafters of a structure. Structural building board is normally used only as wall sheathing.

Sheathing paper. See *Paper, sheathing.*

Shingles. Roof covering of asphalt, asbestos, wood, tile, slate, or other material cut to stock lengths, widths, and thicknesses.

Shingles, siding. Various kinds of shingles, such as wood shingles or shakes and nonwood shingles, that are used over sheathing for exterior sidewall covering of a structure.

Shiplap. See *Lumber, shiplap.*

Siding. The finish covering of the outside wall of a frame building, whether made of horizontal weatherboards, vertical boards with battens, shingles, or other material.

Siding, bevel (lap siding). Wedge-shaped boards used as horizontal siding in a lapped pattern. This siding varies in butt thickness from ½ to ¾ inch and in widths up to 12 inches. Normally used over some type of sheathing.

Siding, drop. Usually ¾ inch thick and 6 and 8 inches in width with tongued-and-grooved or shiplap edges. Often used as siding without sheathing in secondary buildings.

Siding, panel. Large sheets of plywood or hardboard which serve as both sheathing and siding.

Sill. The lowest member of the frame of a structure, resting on the foundation and supporting the floor joists or the uprights of the wall. The member forming the lower side of an opening, as a door sill, window sill, etc.

Soffit. Usually the underside covering of an overhanging cornice.

Soil cover (ground cover). A light covering of plastic film, roll roofing, or similar material used over the soil in crawl spaces of buildings to minimize moisture permeation of the area.

Soil stack. A general term for the vertical main of a system of soil, waste, or vent piping.

Sole or sole plate. See *Plate.*

Span. The distance between structural supports such as walls, columns, piers, beams, girders, and trusses.

Square. A unit of measure—100 square feet—usually applied to roofing material. Sidewall coverings are sometimes packed to cover 100 square feet and are sold on that basis.

Stain, shingle. A form of oil paint, very thin in consistency, intended for coloring wood with rough surfaces, like shingles, without forming a coating of significant thickness or gloss.

Stair carriage. Supporting member for stair treads. Usually a 2-inch plank notched to receive the treads; sometimes termed a "rough horse."

Stool. A flat molding fitted over the window sill between jambs and contacting the bottom rail of the lower sash.

Storm sash or storm window. An extra window usually placed on the outside of an existing window as additional protection against cold weather.

Story. That part of a building between any floor and the floor or roof next above.

String, stringer. A timber or other support for cross members in floors or ceilings. In stairs, the support on which the stair treads rest; also stringboard.

Stud. One of a series of slender wood or metal vertical structural members placed as supporting elements in walls and partitions. (Plural: studs or studding.)

Subfloor. Boards or plywood laid on joists over which a finish floor is to be laid.

Tail beam. A relatively short beam or joist supported in a wall on one end and by a header at the other.

Termites. Insects that superficially resemble ants in size, general appearance, and habit of living in colonies; hence, frequently called "white ants." Subterranean termites *do not* establish themselves in buildings by being carried in with lumber, but by entering from ground nests after the building has been constructed. If unmolested, they eat out the woodwork, leaving a shell of sound wood to conceal their activities, and damage may proceed so far so to cause collapse of parts of a structure before discovery. There are about 56 species of termites known in the United States; but the two main species, classified from the manner in which they attack wood, subterranean (ground-inhabiting) termites, the most common, and dry-wood termites, found almost exclusively along the extreme southern border and the Gulf of Mexico in the United States.

Termite shield. A shield, usually of noncorrodible metal, placed in or on a foundation wall or other mass of masonry or around pipes to prevent passage of termites.

Threshold. A strip of wood or metal with beveled edges used over the finished floor and the sill of exterior doors.

Toenailing. To drive a nail at a slant with the initial surface in order to permit it to penetrate into a second member.

Tread. The horizontal board in a stairway on which the foot is placed.

Trim. The finish materials in a building, such as moldings, applied around openings (window trims, door trim) or at the floor and ceiling of rooms (baseboard, cornice, picture molding).

Trimmer. A beam or joist to which a header is nailed in framing for a chimney, stairway, or other opening.

Truss. A frame or jointed structure designed to act as a beam of long span, while each member is usually subjected to longitudinal stress only, either tension or compression.

Turpentine. A volatile oil used as a thinner in paints and as a solvent in varnishes. Chemically, it is a mixture of terpenes.

Undercoat. A coating applied prior to the finishing or top coats of a paint job. It may be the first of two or the second of three coats. In some usage of the word, it may become synonymous with priming coat.

Vapor barrier. Material used to retard the movement of water vapor into walls and prevent condensation in them. Usually considered as having a perm value of less than 1.0. Applied separately over the warm side of exposed walls or as a part of batt or blanket insulation.

Varnish. A thickened preparation of drying oil or drying oil and resin suitable for spreading on surfaces to form continuous, transparent coatings, or for mixing with pigments to make enamels.

Vent. A pipe or duct which allows flow of air as an inlet or outlet.

Vermiculite. A mineral closely related to mica, with the faculty of expanding on heating to form lightweight material with insulation quality. Used as bulk insulation and also as aggregate in insulating and acoustical plaster and in insulating concrete floors.

Water-repellent preservative. A liquid designed to penetrate into wood and impart water repellency and a moderate preservative protection. It is used for millwork, such as sash and frames, and is usually applied by dipping.

Weatherstrip. Narrow or jamb-width sections of thin metal or other material to prevent infiltration of air and moisture around windows and doors.

APPENDIX—FOUNDATION ENCLOSURES

A treated wood post foundation is normally constructed with a crawl space having 18- to 24-inch clearance. This access space may be used for placing floor insulation, for installing a vapor barrier soil cover, for examining and treating soil in termite areas, and for other needs. In colder climates, it is often desirable to enclose a crawl space by some low-cost means, even though the floor is insulated. This is commonly done by fastening skirt boards of a long-lasting sheet material to the outside beams or floor framing. Enclosed crawl spaces should have a soil cover and a small amount of ventilation to assure satisfactory performance.

When a treated post foundation is not used, a masonry wall of concrete or concrete block construction will provide a satisfactory enclosure. Unlike the skirtboard enclosure, the masonry wall normally acts as a support for the floor framing system. Ventilation and the use of a soil cover are also required for a masonry foundation. The soil cover can consist of a 4-mil polyethylene or similar material placed over the soil under the house. Its use reduces ground moisture movement to wood members, which could result in excessive moisture and condensation. Ventilation can consist of standard foundation vents made for this purpose.

Masonry House Foundations

Although a treated wood post foundation will reduce the cost of a crawl-space house substantially, local conditions or a personal choice may indicate the use of a full masonry wall. This type of foundation, like the treated post type, will often require only a minimum amount of grading. Concrete block or poured concrete walls and piers with appropriate footings are accepted methods of providing supporting walls for the floor framing. Their use normally eliminates the need for outer beams as the joists are supported by the walls. Only a center flush or drop beam is required. However, the concrete block wall introduces the need for masonry work, which in some areas may be difficult to obtain.

The perimeter layout for the masonry foundation can be made in the same manner as has been outlined for the wood post foundation system (fig. 4). The outside line of the masonry walls will be the same as the outside line of the floor framing. The centerline of the interior load-bearing masonry piers is normally the same as for the posts of the wood foundation. Figure 113 is the plan of a typical masonry foundation for a crawl-space house. Footings are required for the outside walls as well as for the masonry piers which support the center beam. A soil cover of polyethylene or similar vapor barrier material should be used in all enclosed crawl-space houses. This prevents ground moisture from moving into the crawl-space area. Uncovered ground can result in high moisture content of floor framing, insulation, and other materials in the crawl space. A poured concrete wall requires some type of formwork while concrete block wall and piers are laid up directly on the footings. The information on concrete and the proper mortar mix for the concrete block is outlined in the chapter on "Foundation Systems" in this manual.

The spacing of the center piers will depend on the size of the center beams. Longer distances between piers will require larger or deeper beams than moderate spans of 8 to 10 feet. These details are shown on the working drawings for each house.

Footings

Footing size is determined by the thickness of the foundation wall. A rule of thumb which is often used for small wood-frame houses under normal soil conditions is: The footing depth should equal the wall thickness and the footing width should be twice the wall thickness. Thus, an 8-inch masonry wall will require a 16- by 8-inch footing (fig. 114). The foundation plan will show the footing size for each house. Unusual soil conditions will often require special footing design.

The bottom of the footings should be located below frost line. This may be 4 feet or more in the Northern States. Local regulations or the footing details of neighboring well-constructed houses will indicate this depth. If the soil is stable, no forms are required for the sides of the footing trench.

One of the important factors in footing construction is to have the top level all around, especially when concrete block construction is to be used. Drive elevation stakes around the perimeter of the footing so that they can be used as guides when pouring the concrete. These elevations can be established by measuring down from the leveling line described in the chapter on "Foundation Systems." Concrete for footings should be poured over undisturbed soil.

A concrete block wall should normally be finished with a 4-inch solid cap block at the top to provide a good bearing surface for the joists, headers, and stringers (fig. 114). Anchor straps for the perimeter joists or headers are desirable in areas where high winds occur. They often consist of perforated or plain 22-gage or heavier galvanized metal straps about 2 inches wide. They are used with a bent "L" shaped base which is placed one or more courses below the cap block. They extend above the top of the wall so that they can be fastened to the edge headers, stringers, or joists. Space them about 8 feet apart and fasten by nailing (fig. 114).

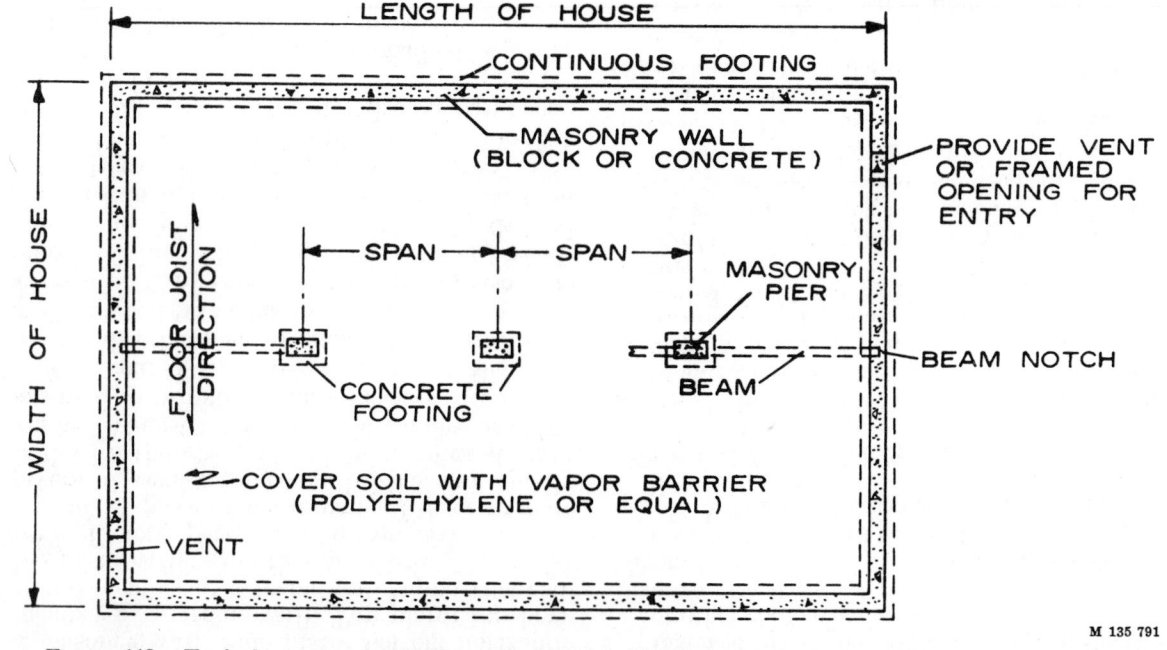

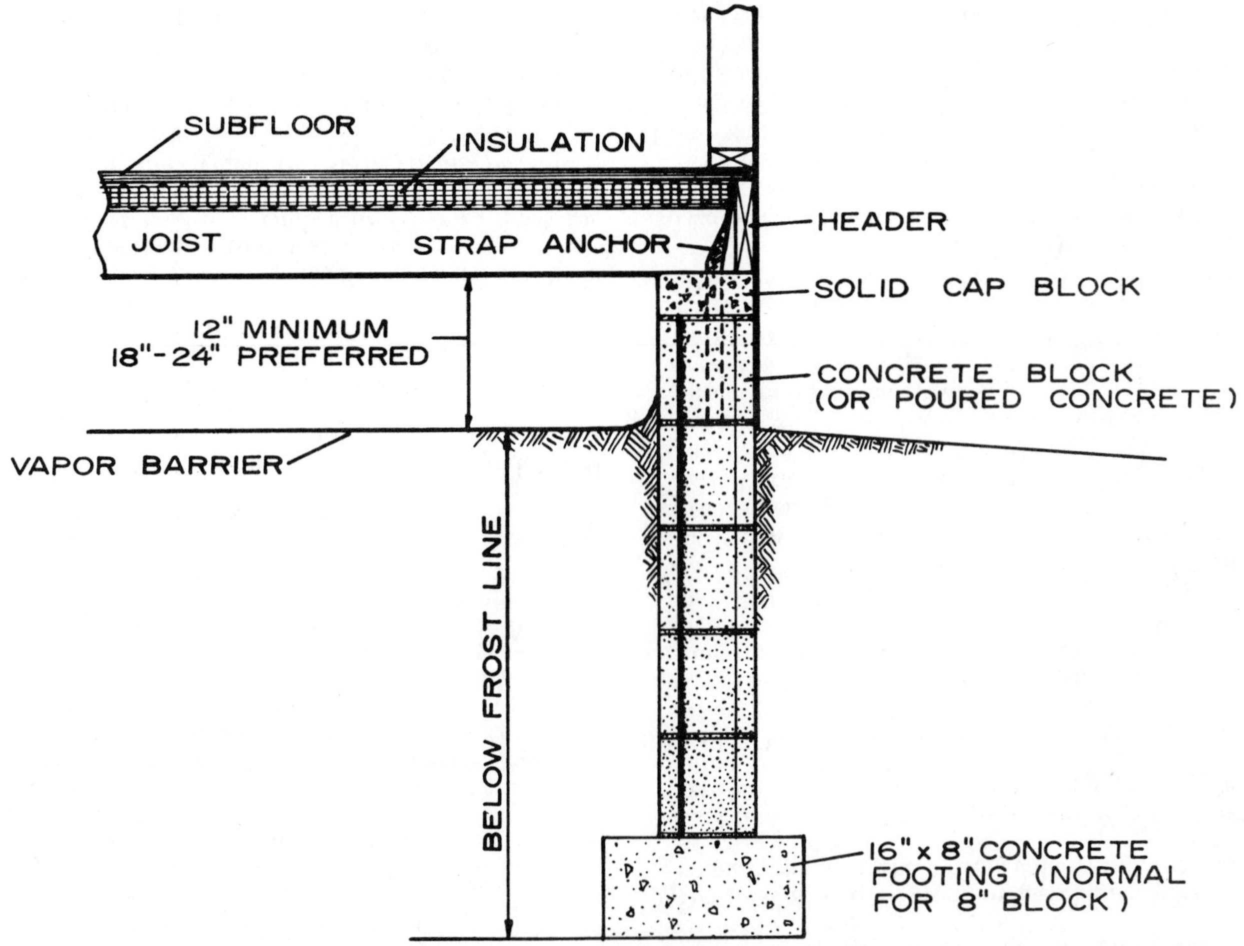

M 135 791

FIGURE 113.—Typical masonry foundation wall (concrete block or poured concrete for crawl-space house).

M 135 790

FIGURE 114.—Section through exterior masonry wall (for crawl-space house).

Center Beams

The height of the center masonry piers with relation to the wall height is determined by the type of center beam used. The flush beam uses ledgers to support the joists, but when a drop beam is used the joists bear directly on the top surface. Each system requires a different depth notch for the masonry end walls. This is to assure that the top of all joists, headers, stringers, and the flush beam, when used, have the same elevation.

Flush beam.—The flush beam allows for more clearance in the crawl space as only the amount equal to the depth of the ledgers extends below the bottom of the joists (fig. 115A). The joists rest on the ledger and are toenailed to the beam. A strap anchor or a bolt should be used to anchor the beam in high wind areas.

A notch must be provided in the end walls for beam support (fig. 115B). The depth of this notch is equal to the depth of the ledgers. Bearing on the wall should be at least 4 inches. A clearance of about ½ inch should be allowed at the sides and ends of the beam. This will provide an airway to prevent the beam from retaining moisture. The size of the notch or beam opening in the wall (when 2- by 4-inch ledgers are used and the beam consists of two nominal 2-inch-thick members) would be approximately:

Length (along length of wall).	7 inches
Width _____	4½ inches (4-inch bearing area, plus clearance)
Height (or depth) _____	3½ inches (or width of ledgers)

The top of the beam should be flush with the top of the joists (fig. 115B).

In a 6-inch concrete block wall, the mason provides the beam notch. When a poured concrete wall is used, a small wood box the size of the notch is fastened to the forms before pouring.

Drop beam.—The drop beam is supported by the masonry piers and the end walls of the foundation. Joists rest directly on the beam (fig. 116A). A lap or butt joint can be used for the joists over the beam. In areas of high winds, it is advisable to use a strap anchor or a long bolt to fasten the beam to the piers. One disadvantage of this type of beam is the difference in the amount of wood at the center piers and at the outer walls which can shrink or swell. It is desirable to equalize the amount of wood at both the center and outside walls whenever possible. The flush beam closely approaches this desirable construction feature. The end foundation walls have a notch to provide bearings areas for the ends of the beams (fig. 116B). This notch should have the same depth as the beam height. Allow clearance at the sides and end for air circulation. Assembly of the beams, the joist arrangement, and other general details are discussed in the chapter on "Floor Systems" in this manual. Specific details on the size, spacing, and location of the beams and joists are included in the floor framing plan of the working drawings for each house.

Masonry Foundation for Entry Steps

The construction of wood entry steps has been discussed in the chapter on "Steps and Stairs." This type of wood stoop provides a satisfactory entry platform and steps at a reasonable cost. However, when masonry walls are used in the foundation of the main house, it may be desirable to also provide a masonry foundation for the entry steps.

Figure 117A shows the foundation plan for a typical masonry entry platform and step. The walls are normally of 6-inch concrete blocks or poured concrete. Block units 4 inches thick or a 4-inch poured wall have also been used for the supporting front and sidewalls. The size of the top platform for a main entry step should be a minimum of 5 feet wide and 3½ feet deep. The foundation in figure 117A would result in a 6-foot by 3½-foot top with two steps or 6 by about 5 feet when one step is used.

The outer wall and footings are sometimes eliminated in providing support for the concrete steps. Then only the two wing walls are constructed. In such cases, the concrete steps are reinforced with rods to prevent cracking when the soil settles. Use at least two ½-inch diameter rods located about 1 inch above the bottom of the step.

It is important in constructing a masonry entry stoop to tie the wall into the house foundation walls and to have the bottom of the step footings below frost level. A concrete footing should be used for the concrete block wall to establish a level base as well as a bearing for the wall (fig. 117B). The footing should be at least 6 inches wide even though the wall may be less than this. Footings are normally not required for the 6-inch poured wall as the bearing area of the poured wall is usually sufficient. Ties or anchors to the house wall can consist of ½-inch reinforcing rods for the poured wall or standard masonry wall reinforcing for the block wall. These are placed as the house wall is erected. In block construction, both the house foundation wall and the wall for the entry stoop can be erected at the same time and tied together with interlocking blocks.

The finish concrete slab should be reinforced with a wire mesh when fill is used. Concrete is poured over the block wall forming the steps and platform (fig. 117B). Boards at each side of the step and platform and one at each riser provide the desired formwork for the concrete.

Skirtboard Materials for Wood Post Foundation

Sheet materials such as exterior grade plywood, hardboard, or asbestos board are most suitable for enclosing a wood post foundation. They need little

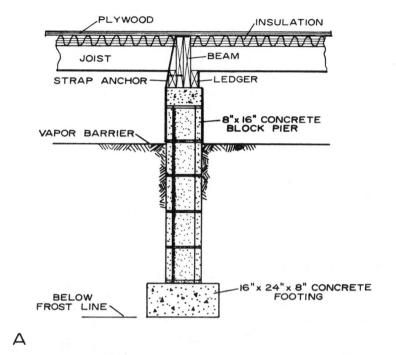

A

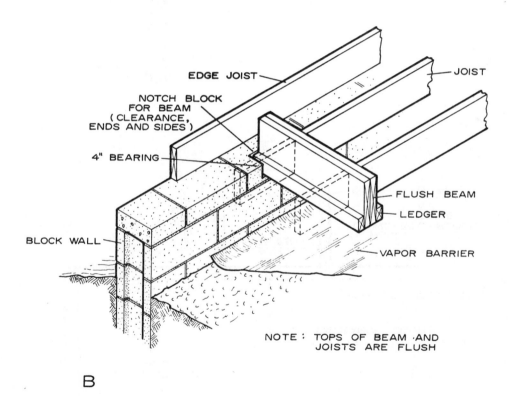

B

M 135 787

FIGURE 115.—Details of concrete block pier for center flush beam. A, cross section; B, detail at exterior end wall.

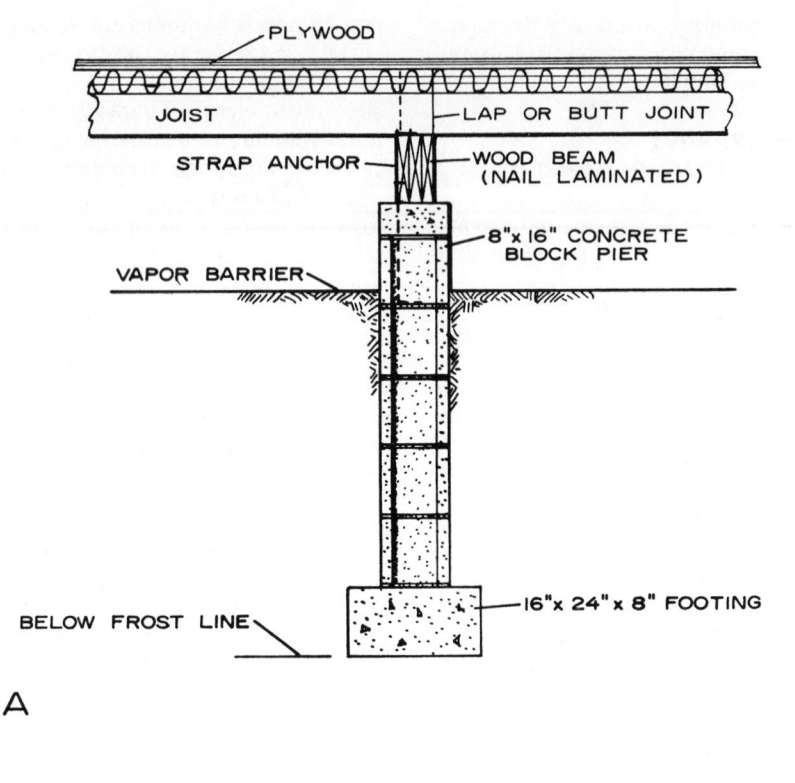

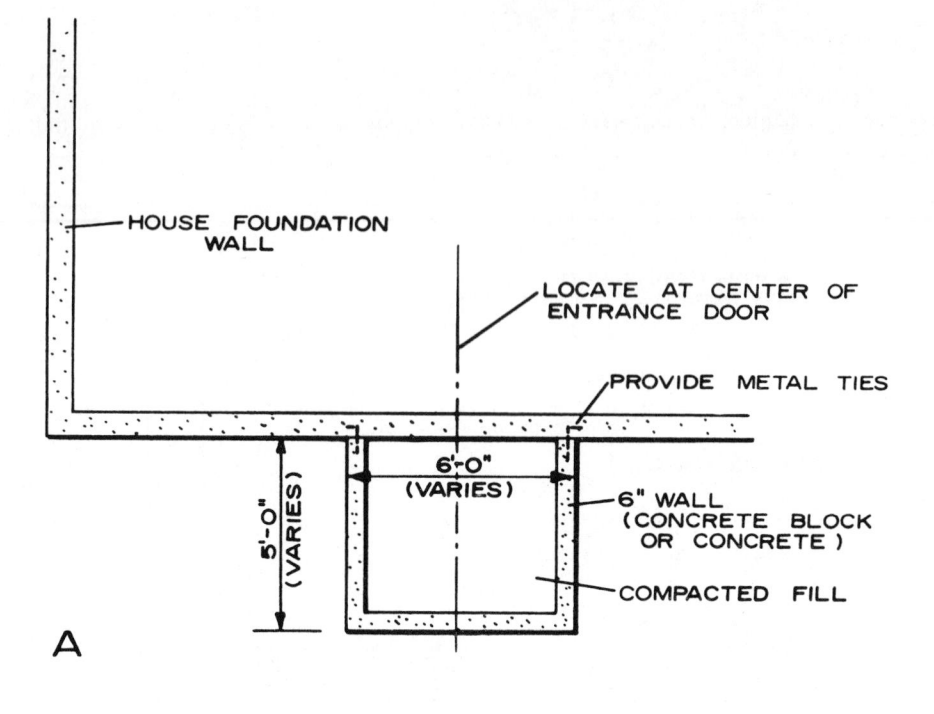

A

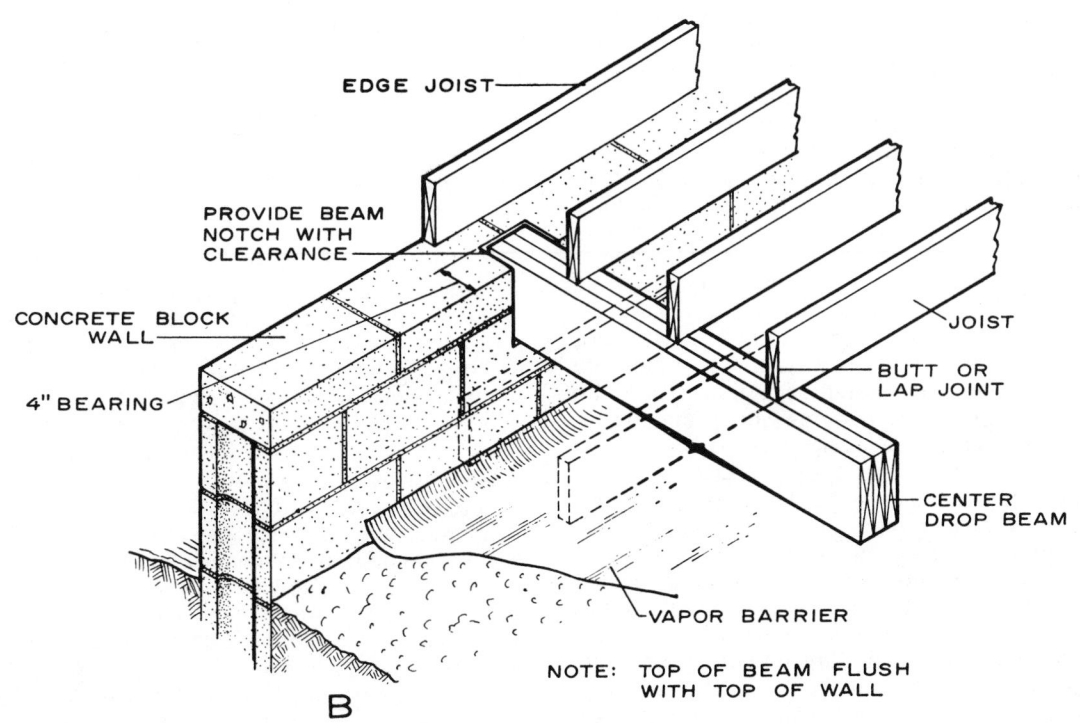

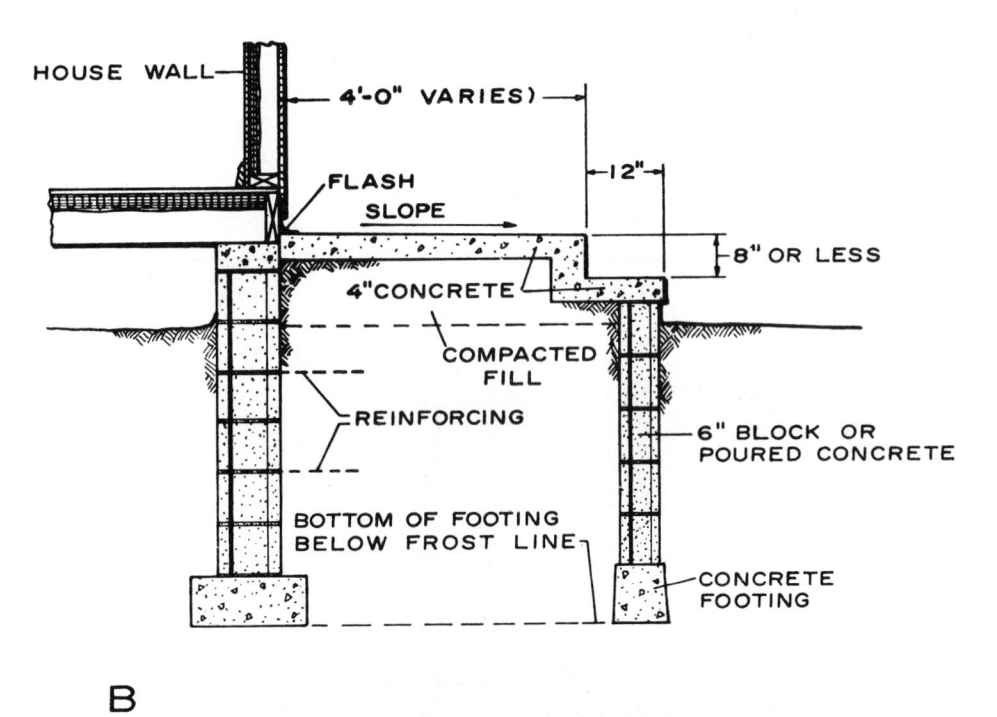

B

M 135 789

M 135 788

FIGURE 116.—Details of block pier for center drop beam. *A*, cross section; *B*, detail at exterior end wall.

FIGURE 117.—Details of typical masonry entrance steps. *A*, plan view; *B*, section view.

if any framing and can be installed during or after construction of the house. When the skirtboard will be in contact with or located near the ground, it is most desirable to use a treated plywood when available. However, a 3-minute dip coat of a penta preservative or a water-repellent preservative along the exposed edges will provide some desirable protection for untreated material. It is also desirable to treat the exposed edges of hardboard with water-repellent preservative. Although asbestos board and metal skirtboards do *not* require preservative treatment, they are not as resistant to impacts as plywood and hardboard. Plywood and hardboard can be easily painted or stained to match the color of the house.

Plywood for skirtboards should be an exterior grade to resist weathering. A standard or sheathing grade with exterior glue is the most economical and can be readily stained. Plywood with rough-sawn or grooved surfaces commonly used for panel siding is also satisfactory.

Tempered hardboard probably provides somewhat better performance than regular-density (Standard) hardboard. However, with paint or similar protective coatings, the lower cost regular-density hardboard should give satisfactory performance. Asbestos board normally requires predrilling to prevent cracking when nailing near the edges.

Skirtboard for House With Edge Beams

Two relatively simple means of fastening the skirtboards to the floor framing can be used. The first method must be employed during construction of the floors and walls. The second can be used either during construction or after the house has been completed.

First method.—Figure 118 illustrates the first method of providing a nailing surface for the skirtboard material. The subfloor and the bottom plate of the walls are extended beyond the edge beam a distance equal to the thickness of the skirtboard (fig. 118*A*). The skirtboard is then nailed to the beam and to the foundation posts. Splices should be made at the post when possible. When splices must be made between the posts, use a 2-by 4-inch vertical nailing cleat on the inside. Fourpenny or fivepenny galvanized siding or similar nails can be used for the ¼-inch hardboard or asbestos board. Space them about 8 inches apart in a staggered pattern. Use sixpenny nails for ⅜-inch plywood and sevenpeny or eightpenny nails for ½-inch plywood skirtboards with the same 8-inch spacing. The panel siding is nailed directly over the top portion of the skirtboard. Nailing recommendations for the siding are given in the chapter on "Exterior Wall Coverings."

The detail for the end wall in this type of installation is shown in figure 118*B*. A 2- by 4-inch cleat should also be used for the skirtboard joints when they occur between the foundation posts.

Some support or a backing may be required for

the bottoms of the skirtboard to provide stability and resistance to impacts from the outside especially with thinner materials. Treated posts, treated 2- by 4-inch stakes, or embedded concrete blocks can be used for this purpose. Treated posts or stakes can be driven behind the skirtboard and the concrete blocks can be embedded slightly for added resistance (fig. 118 *A* and *B*). Space these supports about 4 feet apart or closer if required.

Second method.—A second method of installing the skirtboard can be used either after the house has been completed or during its construction. This system consists of nailing the skirtboard to the inner face of the ledger (fig. 119). The skirtboard must be fitted between the posts which are partly exposed. Use the same method of nailing and blocking at the bottom of the boards as previously described. In addition, toenail the ends of the boards into the posts which they abut. Figure 119*A* shows the details of installation at a sidewall and figure 119*B* shows the details at an end wall. Use treated posts or stakes or concrete blocks as backers at the bottom of the skirtboard as previously described.

Skirtboard for House With Interior Beam

In those crawl-space houses with interior supporting beams and posts and with side overhang, the application of skirtboards is much the same as when the beams are located under the outside walls. The skirtboard may be nailed to the outside of the joist header or to the inner face (fig. 120*A*). When it is fastened to the exterior face, the subfloor and the bottom wall plate are extended beyond the header a distance equal to the thickness of the skirtboard material. The skirtboard can also be fastened to the inside face of the header, but then it must be notched at each joist (fig. 120*A*). Use the same type of nails and nailing patterns described for the details shown in figures 118 and 119.

Details at the end walls of the house are much the same as those at the sidewalls (fig. 120*B*). When the skirtboard is nailed to the inner surface of the edge joist, no notching is required except at the center and edge beams. Use backers for the bottom of the skirtboard as previously described.

Soil Cover, Ventilation, and Access Door

An enclosed crawl space should not only be protected with a soil cover but should also have a small amount of ventilation. A soil cover of 4-mil polyethylene or similar vapor barrier material placed over the earth in the crawl space will minimize soil moisture movement to floor members and floor insulation. Lap the material 4 to 6 inches at the seams, and carry it up the walls or skirtboards a short distance. Use sections of concrete block or small field stones to keep the material in place.

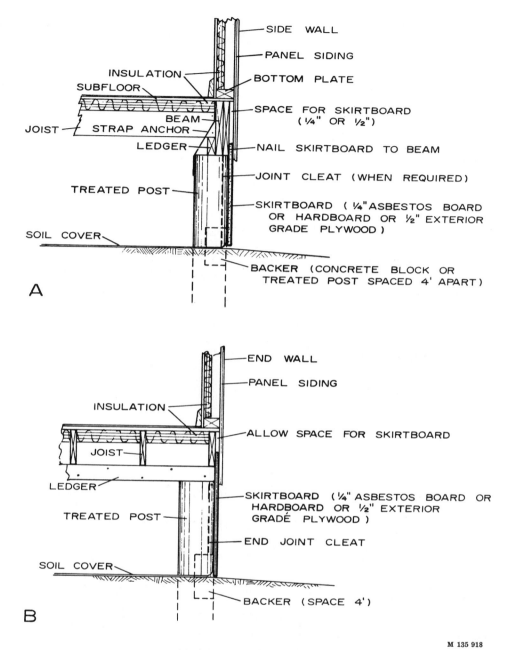

A

B

FIGURE 118.—Skirtboard for house with edge beams (to be applied during construction). *A*, Section through sidewall; *B*, section through end wall.

When the use of a soil poison is required in termite areas, do not install the soil cover for several days after poisoning or until the soil becomes dry again.

Ventilators should be installed on two opposite walls when practical. Standard 16- by 8-inch foundation vents can be used in concrete block foundations. Usually, in small houses, two screened ventilators, each with a net opening of 30 to 40 square inches, are sufficient when a soil cover is used. Crawl spaces with skirtboard enclosures should

also be ventilated with small screened vents.

Access doors should be provided in crawl spaces. With a masonry foundation, they can consist of a 16- by 24-inch or larger frame with a plywood or other removable or hinged panel. Install the frame as the wall is constructed. With skirtboard enclosures, provide a simple removable section. When practical, the access doors should be located at the rear or side of the foundation and at the lowest elevation when a slope is present.

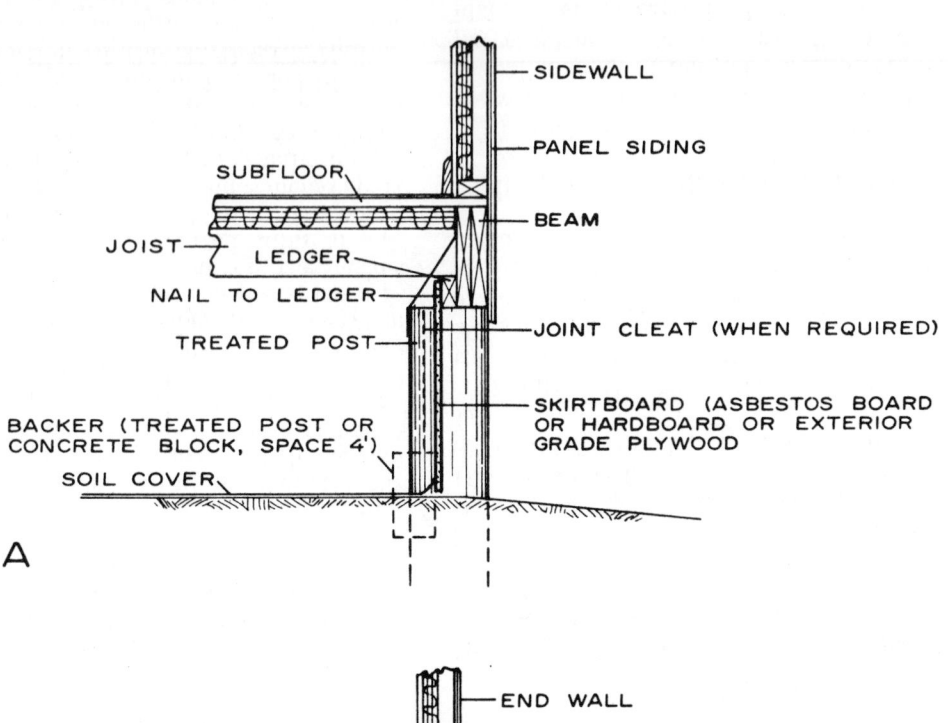

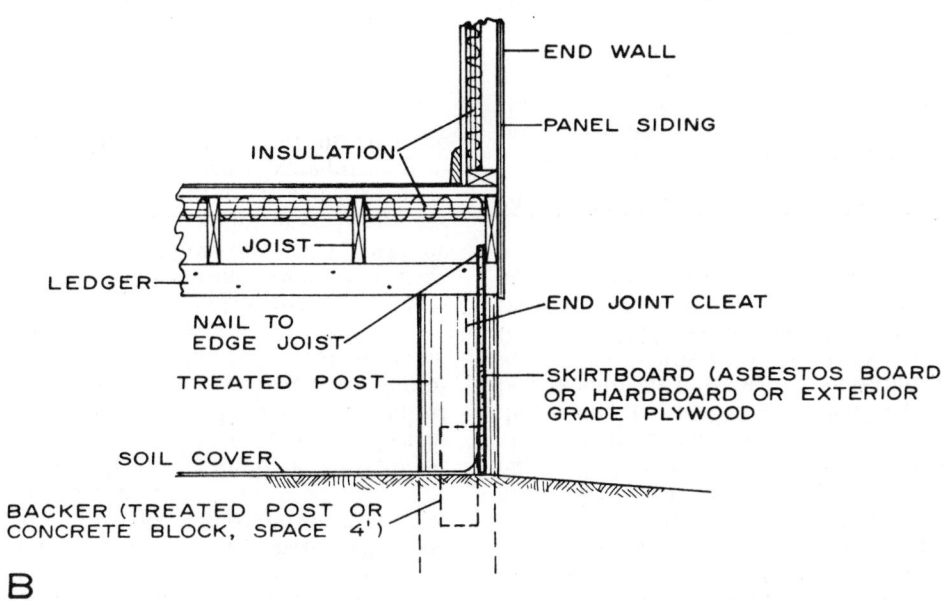

M 135 919

FIGURE 119.—Skirtboard for house with edge beams (can be applied after house is constructed). *A*, Section through sidewall; *B*, section through end wall.

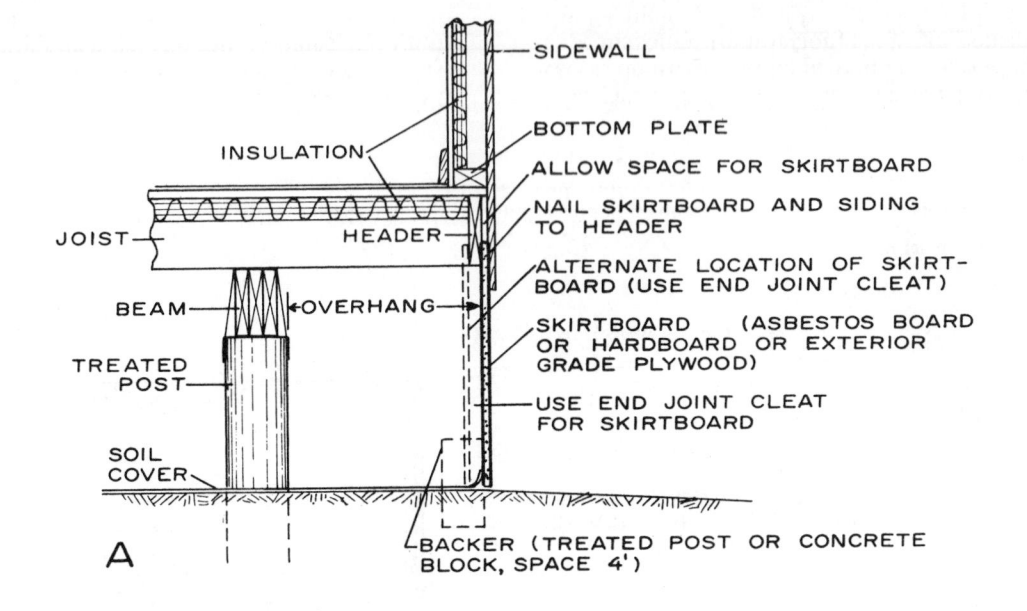

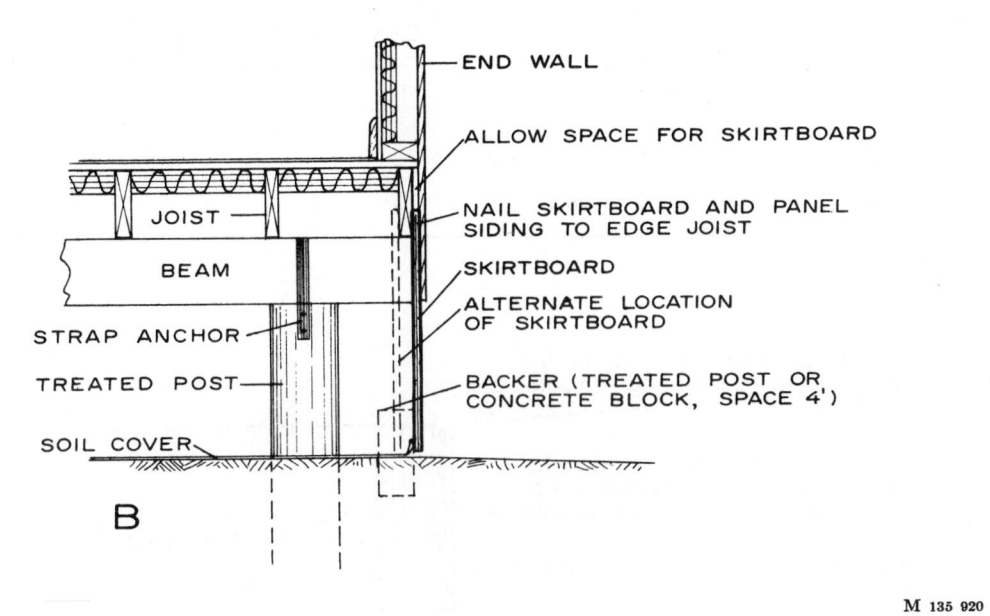

M 135 920

FIGURE 120.—Skirtboard for house with interior beam (with overhang). *A*, Section through sidewall; *B*, section through end wall.